The Hitler state

The Hitler state

*The foundation and development of the
internal structure of the Third Reich*

Martin Broszat
Translated by John W. Hiden

Longman
London and New York

Longman Group Limited
Longman House
Burnt Mill, Harlow, Essex, UK

Published in the United States of America
by Longman Inc., New York

English translation © John W. Hiden 1981

The German edition, *Der Staat Hitlers*, by Martin
Broszat, was first published by Deutscher Taschenbuch
Verlag in 1969.

First published 1981

British Library Cataloguing in Publication Data

Broszat, Martin
  The Hitler state.
  1. Germany—Politics and government—
  1933–1945
  I. Title
  320.9′43′086   JN3952   80-40302

  ISBN 0-582-49200-9
  ISBN 0-582-48997-0 Pbk

Printed in Singapore by Kyodo Shing Loong Printing Industries Pte Ltd

Contents

JN
3952
B768

Glossary and abbreviations	vi
Foreword to the English edition	ix
1. The political and constitutional preconditions of the Third Reich	1
2. *Modus-operandi* and structure of the Hitler movement before 1933	17
3. The monopoly of political power (1933)	57
4. The coordination of the Länder outside Prussia and the new problem of centralism and particularism	96
5. The foundation and alteration of the social system	133
6. Party and state in the early stages of the Third Reich	193
7. The civil service and the administration	241
8. The Reich government and the Führer's authority in the first years after 1933	262
9. Departmental polyocracy and the forms of Führer absolutism	294
10. Law and justice	328
11. Conclusion	346
Bibliography	362
Index	370

Glossary and abbreviations

ADGB	Allgemeiner Deutscher Gewerkschaftsbund — General Federation of German Trade Unions.
Amtsbezirk	An administrative unit and the Oldenburg equivalent of the Prussian Regierungsbezirk
Amtshauptmann	The senior administrative official of an Amtsbezirk
Amtsleiter	Official appointed for special duties in the central Reich directorate of the NSDAP (e.g. Amtsleiter for Propaganda 1925–8, Gregor Strasser). Became Reichsleiter after 1933.
BA	Bundesarchiv (Koblenz)
Auswärtiges Amt	German Foreign Office
BVP	Bayerische Volkspartei — Bavarian People's Party
DAF	Deutsche Arbeitsfront — German Labour Front (headed by Dr Robert Ley)
DDP	Deutsche Demokratische Partei — German Democratic Party
DGFP	*Documents on German Foreign Policy*
DNVP	Deutschnationale Volkspartei — German National People's Party
DVP	Deutsche Volkspartei — German People's Party
DZA	Deutsches Zentralarchiv (Potsdam)
Geheimrat	Equivalent to a privy councillor
Gau	The main regional unit for administration of the NSDAP party organization
Gauleiter	Regional leader of the NSDAP
Gestapa	Geheimes Staatspolizeiamt — Secret State Police Office

Gestapo	Geheime Staatspolizei — Secret State Police
Gruppenführer (S.A.)	Rank corresponding to that of a Major-General in the British Army
GS	*Preussische Gesetzsammlung*
IfZ	Institut für Zeitgeschichte (Munich)
JMBl	*Justiz-Ministerial-Blatt für die preussische Gesetzgebung und Rechtspflege*
KPD	Kommunistische Partei Deutschlands — German Communist Party
Kreis	Can denote an electoral district but was an administrative unit of the NSDAP (the main sub-division of a Gau)
Kreisbeuftragte	District delegate of the Party
Kreisleiter	District leader of the NSDAP in charge of the Kreis administration
Kreistag	District assembly
Land (Länder in plural)	One of the territorial divisions of Republican Germany each having their own governments. Controlled after 1933 by the central government through the Reich Governors
Landkreis	Rural sub-division of a Regierungsbezirk in Prussia
Landesinspekteur	Provincial Inspector — the administrative post set up by Gregor Strasser in 1932
Landrat	Chief authority in the administration of a Landkreis
Landtag	State legislature
MBliV	*Ministerialblatt für die Preussische innere Verwaltung*
Ministerialdirektor	Head of a department in a ministry. Literally, Ministerial Director
Ministerialdirigent	Assistant director in a ministry
Ministerialrat	Senior counsellor in the civil service usually head of a section in a ministry
NSBO	Nationalsozialistische Betriebszellenorganisation — National Socialist Factory Cell Organization
NSDAP	Nationalsozialistische Deutsche Arbeiterpartei — National Socialist German Workers' Party (Nazi Party)
Oberpräsident	Senior administrative official in Prussian provinces

Oberregierungsrat	Senior government counsellor
Obergruppenführer (S.S.)	Equivalent to Lieutenant-General in British Army
Obersturmbannführer (S.S.)	Equivalent to Lieutenant-Colonel in British Army
OKH	Oberkommando des Heeres — Army High Command
OKW	Oberkommando der Wehrmacht — High Command of the Armed Forces
Old Reich	Germany before the incorporation of Austria
PVG	Preussisches Polizeiverwaltungsgesetz
Regierungsbezirk	Administrative sub-division of a Prussian Province (roughly the size of an average English County)
Regierungspräsident	Senior administrative official in a Regierungsbezirk
Reichsleiter	See Amtsleiter
Reichsorganisationsleiter	National Organization Leader of the NSDAP
RGBl	*Reichsgesetzblatt* — Reich Law Gazette
RMBliV	*Ministerialblatt des Reichs und Preussischen Ministerium des Innern*
S.A.	Sturmabteilungen — Storm troopers
SD	Sicherheitsdienst — The Security Service of the S.S., under Heydrich
SPD	Sozialdemokratische Partei Deutschlands — German Social Democratic Party
S.S.	Schutzstaffeln — Protection squads, or guard detachments, literally. The Third Reich's 'elite' formations
Stahlhelm	Nationalist ex-servicemen's organization founded by Franz Seldte in 1918
Stadtkreis	Urban district
Uschla	Untersuchungs- und Schlichtungs-Ausschuss — The NSDAP's Investigation and Arbitration Committee, forerunner of the later NSDAP Party Court (after 1 Jan. 1934)
VDA	Volksbund für das Deutschtum im Ausland — Union of Germans Abroad
VJHZ	*Vierteljahrshefte für Zeitgeschichte*
Wehrkreis	Military region. The main military territorial organization in Germany.

Foreword to the English edition

When this book first appeared over ten years ago in a paperback version which has since been reprinted several times, there was already a wealth of historical literature on Nazi Germany. The release for historical investigation of German documents from the Hitler period captured by victorious Allied Powers had increasingly made it possible from the 1950s to reconstruct and to explain different aspects of National Socialist foreign, domestic, war and occupation policies. At the same time the growth of detailed research embodied the danger of historians retreating into specialization. There appeared to be little inclination to synthesize the new findings into a more general study of the National Socialist regime.

It was against such a background that this book was conceived in the mid-1960s, as an attempt not primarily to recount yet again what had happened in the Third Reich, but to analyze the internal set-up and changing power structure of this system. The main preoccupation concerned the 'how' rather than the 'what'. I was also determined to stick closely to the findings of empirical research and to authentic sources, to avoid speculation and only cautiously to venture into the realm of general interpretation. My examination of the internal power structure of the Nazi regime while writing this book has not therefore yielded a general theory of the Third Reich; but it does perhaps offer the elements of an improved understanding of how this historically novel form of government functioned. The components of this structural history also hopefully make more intelligible many of those apparent contradictions of National Socialist rule which also baffled contemporaries.

In various ways my work offers a corrective to the oversimplified picture of a monolithic system and of a well-oiled super state, which derived from the concept of totalitarianism, and which also understandably arose because so many contemporaries were influenced by the final phase of the war, by the full extent of the criminality of the National Socialist regime, first revealed after 1945, and by the enormous effort which had been required to bring down Hitler's Germany. But the Third Reich cannot only be assessed from the vantage of totalitarian extremism in its final phase. Its internal com-

position did not remain the same from beginning to end but under-
went essential changes. What presented itself as the new government of National Socialist Germany in 1933/4, after the seizure of
power was completed, was in effect a form of power sharing between the new National Socialist mass movement and the old conservative forces in state and society. The NSDAP had admittedly
achieved a party political monopoly and destroyed the possibility of
activity for all other political forces, but it had not, unlike the Soviet
Union, gained full control of the state institutions and armed forces.
Instead, until about 1936/7, there existed a conflict-ridden balance
between state and Party, between authoritarian forces of order and
the impulses coming from the Party, with its political and ideological pretensions as yet unappeased. This balance was regulated from
time to time through decisions made by Hitler, who as the popularly
acclaimed Führer stood above both state and Party. Until 1936/7
the National Socialist regime could be described as a semi-
authoritarian, semi-fascist form of government, tending both to
strengthen the central power of the state and authoritarian dictatorship, and yet containing dynamic elements generated by the
popular appeal to the masses.

Such a balance had at least ensured the relative stability and
rationality of the regime, but was overturned eventually after the
territorial expansion of the Third Reich, and particularly after the
onset of war. As the National Socialist leadership pursued a more
aggressive course at home and abroad and as tasks were frequently
re-allocated, the conservative allies and office holders in the state
administration, armed forces and the diplomatic world were progressively displaced by Hitler's partisans. The great victories of
National Socialist foreign policy during this phase, which brought
Hitler to a peak of popularity and popular acclaim, ensured that his
position as leader became more absolute. At the same time this
process increasingly exposed the fatal effect on institutions of the
principle of personal leadership which had already been developed
in the NSDAP prior to 1933. Hitler's special authority as Führer
was not founded like Stalin's on the control of the central organizational apparatus of the Party and state, but in the last resort on his
charismatic appeal, and the ability this gave to integrate the nation
as a whole. It was typical of Hitler's style of leadership that he chose
not to exercise careful and continuous control at the centre of the
system, but instead intervened from outside – often abruptly and
arbitrarily – as the supreme Führer, equally 'removed' from the
Party and state organizations. The absolute supremacy of the
Führer in the Third Reich did not entail strict allegiance to any fixed
hierarchical order, or even to orderly channels of command and dictatorship. Instead it increasingly involved the sporadic carrying out
of the Führer's will in an unpredictable manner, through the efforts
of different dignitaries of the state or of the Party, or even some-

times via subordinate adjutants or contacts Hitler practised no direct and systematic leadership but from time to time jolted the government or the Party into action, supported one or the other initiative of Party functionaries or departmental heads and thwarted others, ignored them or left them to carry on without a decision. Even his direct involvement in foreign policy and war was in keeping with this approach. It concentrated on the often hastily improvized preparation and execution of spectacular and risky moves, and was a constant bid to change the situation and never to consolidate it. Thus in all those areas of policy with which Hitler never or seldom bothered, the absolute supremacy of the Führer spawned a growing system of rival power centres, all trying to put forward schemes in the name of Hitler, all trying to get access to him and to get 'Führer commands' to back them up.

The institutional form of this 'Führer absolutism' did not portend as is often mistakenly assumed, a strengthening of the hierarchical solidarity and uniformity of the state and Party as a whole, but implied a growing antagonism between the individual rival office holders, as well as an end to legal and administrative regularity, and in the last resort a 'denationalization' of the system. The title chosen for my book – 'The Hitler State' – reflects these findings and points to this inconsistency; to the fact that National Socialist control under Hitler's absolute leadership could not be reconciled with the normal practice and organization of government, and indeed more and more undermined the essentials not only of the constitution but of the state as such.

There was a link then, between this structural development and the action taken by the regime, and this is a central thesis of my investigation. The 'polyocracy' of individual office holders, each seeking to recommend himself to Hitler through a particular ability to get things done, ultimately led to a proliferation of arbitrary decisions and acts of violence. It put an end to collective and regularized forms of rational policy discussion, and of the control of information and power. And below Hitler there was no overall political responsibility. Such a development atomized offices and responsibilities and reduced the state administration to the agent of despotism, where it only succeeded with difficulty in checking the destructive effects of this fragmentation of government.

The constitutional development briefly outlined above first made it possible to translate into institutional terms, through special organs of the S.S. and police, those secret, frequently unwritten directives or expressions of Hitler's will, for example for the liquidation of Jews. And it was possible to allocate the necessary measures in such a way that their full extent and meaning were no longer recognizable, even to the individual branches of the state administration involved in carrying them out. The ultimately suicidal extension of its military commitment by the Nazi regime, beginning with the campaign against Russia, must also be seen in conjunction with the extension of the Führer's absolutism to the military sphere from late autumn 1941. This produced a situation where the overall exercise of military responsibility through the General Staff or the Supreme Command of the Armed Forces was no longer possible, and where a rivalry developed between the different service branches of the armed forces as well as within the Army Command, in a way similar to that in the state administration and in the Party. National Socialist rule, as manifested under Hitler's leadership and in the way it finally developed, was indeed always capable of generating enormous energy, but not of retaining lasting power or of systematic construction. It was an expression of a dynamic force, dependent on crisis, with monumental and ultimately destructive consequences, but it did not provide a model for stable government.

These and other central themes in my account derive to some extent from the insights formulated and developed by prominent political scientists who emigrated from Hitlerian Germany during the Second World War, although they could hardly consult internal German sources; Ernst Fraenkel on the 'Dual State', Franz Neumann with his designation of the governmental system in the Third Reich by the mythical symbol 'Behemoth', or Hannah Arendt and her dictum about the disruptive dynamic force of National Socialism. The wealth of new literature published on the Third Reich during the past decade has brought out more clearly many elements of my structural analysis. In his study of the complex of ideological and cultural policy under Alfred Rosenberg's direction, where the chaos of leadership and responsibility played a prominent role from the outset, Reinhard Bollmus applied the concept of the 'conqueror state' to domestic as well as foreign policy. In his large two-volume history of the NSDAP Dietrich Orlow came to the conclusion that the pattern of power sharing and authority within the Party could only be analyzed in the last resort in the form of a changing history of personal relations between individual office holders. Recent works on the armaments policy of the National Socialist regime during the Second World War demonstrate the role which conflicts of interest and leadership disputes also played in this realm. The British historian Tim Mason was able to illustrate through his extensive study of the Third Reich's labour policy, that the popular basis of the 'Führer absolutism' functioned not only to mobilize support; he shows that Hitler's critical dependence on popular backing, not least within the labour force, frequently forced concessions even at the cost of the efficiency of the war economy. The most important of these new research findings are listed in the bibliography to the English edition.

Occasionally there has also been a general reaction against the application of structural history to the Nazi regime as part of the reaction against the recent leftist interpretations of fascism appearing in the last decade. This is particularly true of many of the new products of the Hitler literature, which give the impression that the personal will of Adolf Hitler himself solely or primarily determined the history of the Third Reich. However hard it may seems at present, in view of such controversies, to arrive at a definitive interpretation of the system of National Socialist dominion, that is all the more reason (in the light of the new books on Hitler) to react critically to the growing tendency of historians to resort to the history of personalities.

Even the excessive Führer cult in Nazi Germany, that persuasive belief in the Leader which had a meaning and real importance far beyond determining ideology, for the integration and mobilization of the German people in the Nazi era, cannot be understood simply in terms of personality, as a result of the superior strength of will and leadership of Adolf Hitler. Albrecht Tyrell has already been able to demonstrate for the period when the Hitler myth was developing in the NSDAP in the early 1920s, that Hitler was hesitant about assuming a role which was emphatically made for the psychological and political needs of someone of his background. The recently concluded study by the British historian Ian Kershaw also shows strikingly the degree to which the Führer myth was not only fostered by Hitler himself and promoted by propaganda, but was shaped by the national and social expectations of large sectors of German society. Moreover during the Third Reich the pseudo-religious aura of the Führer, which was the chief basis for his elevated position and which gave him superiority over his conservative allies too, was not simply the result of personal political ability, but was anchored in the social, political and institutional needs of the Third Reich. It was precisely because of the lack of any logical ideology suitable for totalitarian indoctrination, and because of the collapse of all efforts after 1933 to achieve a solid reform of the social and political system and to fix it constitutionally, that the myth of the Führer remained the only viable social and political ideal of the Third Reich. And in view of the absence of, or collapse of any regularized institutional mechanism for reaching compromise or settling conflicts within the Nazi regime, the 'Leader' was repeatedly called on as a source of appeal and as the arbiter of exponents of conflicting interests and power groups in the Third Reich; he was increasingly needed and therefore again confirmed as indispensable. At the same time the continuing need to prolong the Führer cult inevitably also meant the progressive development of Hitler's absolute position. It was not Hitler alone who enforced absolute control; despotism was also the outcome of the regime's internal law of motion, which from the outset was geared to the Führer cult.

Our study and many more recent accounts also show that the characteristic conflict between rival forces in the Third Reich can by no means be understood merely in terms of a Machiavellian policy of 'divide and rule', deliberately instituted by Hitler to make himself indispensable. On the contrary, it was a largely unavoidable corollary of the Führer's absolutism, and in practice was not conducive to the long-term survival of the regime. The Third Reich was only able to conduct systematic and successful policies as long as its radical ideological momentum and the antagonism deriving from this were restrained and contained by the conservative, authoritarian elements of the administration, armed forces and business, who were bent on preserving their state and power, and as long as the regime's foreign policy kept within the framework of traditional nationalist aims. The progressive escape of the Führer's authority and of the totalitarian forces directly under the Führer from the constraints of such a compromise, which had also entailed observing reasons of state to some extent, steered the regime towards self-destruction. It was not by chance that as Hitler overstepped the bounds of traditional nationalist foreign policy in 1939 and began to pursue the ideological goal of the 'final solution', he increasingly gambled with and ultimately lost through his own decisions, all that had been gained earlier.

Even in the final war years, when totalitarian extremism had long since reached a climax, the Hitler regime was certainly capable of generating astonishing energy, but it had long been incapable of the rational exercise of power. In the face of such changes and inconsistencies any explanation of the Third Reich centring on Hitler's person would have to assume that a fundamental change had occurred in this man, who from the outset was both a fanatic and a skilled political tactician. Yet there is nothing in Hitler's own pronouncements to support the idea of such a fundamental change. We can only explain why the Hitler regime ultimately fell prey to a policy of irrational self-destruction after years of astonishingly impressive success, against the background of ever changing structural and institutional circumstances.

Martin Broszat
Munich
August 1980

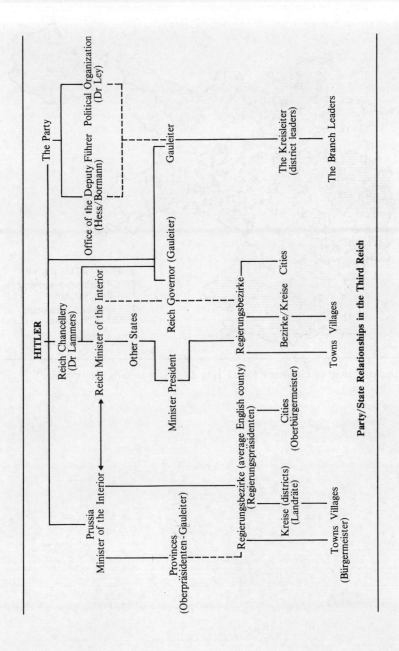

Party/State Relationships in the Third Reich

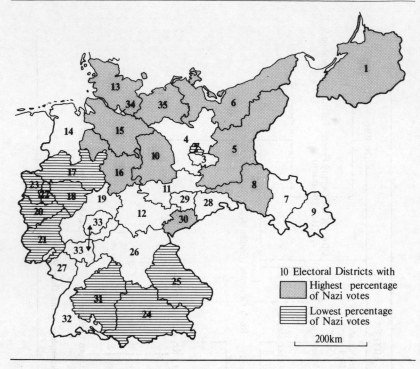

Electoral map of Germany for 31 July 1932 (for details see opposite)

Votes cast in favour of the NSDAP

Reichstag elections:	4 May 1924	7 Dec. 1924	20 May. 1928	14 Sept. 1930	31 July 1932	6 Nov. 1932	5 Mar. 1933
Number of seats:	32	14	12	107	230	196	288
National vote (%):	6·5	3·0	2·6	18.3	37·3	33·1	43·9
District vote (%)							
1 East Prussia	8·6	6·2	0·8	22·5	47·1	39·7	56·5
2 Berlin	3·6	1·6	1·4	12·8	24·6	22·5	31·3
3 Potsdam II	6·5	2·9	1·8	16·7	33·0	29·1	38·2
4 Potsdam I	5·8	2·8	1·6	18·8	38·2	34·1	44·4
5 Frankfurt a.d. Oder	5·0	3·2	1·0	22·7	48·1	42·6	55·2
6 Pomerania	7·3	4·2	1·5	24·3	48·0	43·1	56·3
7 Breslau	4·0	1·4	1·0	24·2	43·5	40·4	50·2
8 Liegnitz	1·5	1·5	1·2	20·9	48·0	42·1	54·0
9 Oppeln	2·6	1·5	1·0	9·5	29·2	26·8	43·2
10 Magdeburg	4·9	3·0	1·7	19·5	43·8	39·0	47·3
11 Merseburg	8·7	4·3	2·7	20·5	42·6	34·5	46·4
12 Thuringia	9·9	5·4	3·7	19·3	43·4	37·1	47·2
13 Schleswig-Holstein	7·4	2·7	4·0	27·0	51·0	45·7	53·2
14 Weser-Ems	7·4	4·8	5·2	20·5	38·4	31·9	41·4
15 East Hanover	8·6	4·4	2·6	20·6	49·5	42·9	54·3
16 South-Hanover-Brunswick	7·6	3·4	4·4	24·3	46·1	40·6	48·7
17 Westphalia-North	3·5	1·3	1·0	12·2	25·7	22·3	34·9
18 Westphalia-South	1·5	1·1	1·6	13·9	27·2	24·8	33·8
19 Hesse-Nassau	5·6	2·5	3·6	20·8	43·6	41·2	49·4
20 Cologne-Aachen	1·5	0·6	1·1	14·5	20·2	17·4	30·1
21 Koblenz-Trier	1·3	—	2·1	14·9	28·8	26·1	38·4
22 Düsseldorf-East	3·9	1·6	1·8	17·0	31·6	27·0	37·4
23 Düsseldorf-West	2·6	0·9	1·2	16·8	27·0	24·2	35·2
24 Upper Bavaria-Swabia	17·0	4·8	6·2	16·3	27·1	24·6	40·9
25 Lower Bavaria	10·2	3·0	3·5	12·0	20·4	18·5	39·2
26 Franconia	20·7	7·5	8·1	20·5	39·9	36·4	45·7
27 Palatinate	5·7	1·9	5·6	22·8	43·7	42·6	46·5
28 Dresden-Bautzen	4·5	1·5	1·8	16·1	39·3	34·0	43·6
29 Leipzig	7·9	1·8	1·9	14·0	36·1	31·0	40·0
30 Chemnitz-Zwickau	7·7	4·2	4·3	23·8	47·0	43·4	50·0
31 Württemberg	4·1	2·1	1·9	9·4	30·3	26·2	42·0
32 Baden	4·8	1·9	2·9	19·2	36·9	34·1	45·4
33 Hesse-Darmstadt	2·9	1·3	1·9	18·5	43·1	40·2	47·4
34 Hamburg	6·0	2·3	2·6	19·2	33·7	27·2	38·9
35 Mecklenburg	20·8	11·9	2·0	20·1	44·8	37·0	48·0

From G. Pridham and J. Noakes (ed.) *Documents on Nazism*, Jonathan Cape, 1974, pp. 115–16.

Chapter One

The political and constitutional preconditions of the Third Reich

The National Socialist coalition with the national conservative right and the political exclusion of the democratic left

The crisis-ridden years of the Weimar Republic, from the Treaty of Versailles to the occupation of the Ruhr and the inflation, were the background to the early history of the NSDAP; the years of the Party's first political successes, still confined to Bavaria and South Germany, which ended with the abortive Hitler putsch of 9 November 1923. The ensuing phase of relative stability for the Republic coincided with the decline of the NSDAP which was re-founded at the beginning of 1925. The spread of its organization during this period to West, North and East Germany cannot conceal the fact that between 1925 and 1928 the Hitler movement was politically almost wholly unsuccessful. Its membership fluctuated markedly and support was largely stagnant, and the aim after 1925 of a legal takeover of power through the elections yielded only meagre results in the Länder and in the Reich (Reichstag elections 1928: 2.6 per cent of the vote for the NSDAP). The third, crucial phase did not begin until the combined economic and national crisis of 1929/30. The National Socialist Party, which for ten years had been a small radical rightist minority, suddenly became a nationwide gathering mass movement which had absorbed 75 per cent of former voters of the parties of the middle and right within

Table 1.1 The decline of the middle-class parties 1928–1932

Reichstag elections	Socialist parties (SPD, KPD) (%)	NSDAP (%)	Centre Party (%)	Other middle-class parties (%)
20.5.1928	40.5	2.6	15.1	41.8
14.9.1930	37.6	18.3	14.8	29.3
31.7.1932	36.2	37.4	15.7	10.7

three years and was able to capture 37.4 per cent of all votes by July 1932.

The success story of the NSDAP mirrored the tragedy of the Republic and vice versa. No other party – not even the KPD – was so dependent for its success on the crisis. More precisely, success or failure was determined by the extent to which the socio-political forces of the 'bourgeois middle' and conservative right were prepared to treat with the NSDAP, to join it or to make arrangements with it. The sudden mass swing to the NSDAP after 1929/30 far exceeded any other movements between the parties during the Weimar Republic's history. It was due almost exclusively to the mobilization of hitherto non-voters and of the bulk of those middle-class voters who had been far less firmly attached to their loosely-grouped liberal interest parties than the ideologically-committed supporters of the Centre Party or of the Socialist parties. This was less a matter of a shift within the democratic party system than its destruction through the activation and rallying of those who had so far avoided the democratic process of decision-making or who had participated in this unwillingly. The NSDAP could not accomplish such a revolution by itself. It required the protection, or at least the goodwill, of middle-class and conservative forces in the government, armed forces, the Church, commerce and politics, which had also been the case in Munich before 1923. The NSDAP thrived on the sort of desire for more decisive measures so easily aroused during crises, and on the demand for a more effective and, if need be, enforced cure for Germany's ills. In that respect the Nazi Party was not so much a revolutionary as a parasitic force; the most effective power agitating for the restoration of authoritarian notions of order in state and society and at the same time a militant popular enemy of Socialism and Communism. The circumstances permitting the rise of the NSDAP in Bavaria before 1923 were as appropriate for it as the situation in the Reich from 1929/30.

The reactionary regime which gained power in Munich after the overthrow of the Soviet Republic there provided the ideal breeding ground for the early NSDAP. The active encouragement which the Bavarian Reichswehr, imbued as it was with the counter-revolutionary spirit of the Freikorps, bestowed on the *völkisch*-patriotic organizations from the summer of 1919, and on the anti-Socialist Home Guards and their later substitute organization the patriotic Defence Leagues, was of crucial importance for the development of the NSDAP and the S.A. Influential patrons gave official protection and provided the essential material and personal preconditions for political and militant action; patrons like the ambitious staff officer and later S.A. Chief, Ernst Röhm, or the Police Chiefs Ernst Pöhner and Hans von Seisser, who gained office through the Bavarian 'Law and Order Bloc' under Gustav

Kahr in 1920/1. Without such top-level backing a social nonentity like Hitler would hardly have been so willingly 'passed round' the bohemian circles, salons and associations of patriotic Munich society (Dietrich Eckhart, the publisher Bruckmann, the piano manufacturer Bechstein, Professor Karl Haushofer, etc.) like some sort of super political-agitator, nor would he have been given the contacts and assistance which were so vital to the NSDAP at that stage.

Although its followers were then still few, the Hitler movement's involvement with an influential sector of the local notables and with the state executive helped to ensure that in Bavaria in 1922/3, it became the vanguard of those anti-democratic forces aiming for an authoritarian national dictatorship. Chief State Commissioner von Kahr and the Commander of the Bavarian Reichswehr division, von Lossow, were already in breach of the constitution when Hitler tried to get them openly to oppose the central government, but the putschist style of the attempted *coup d'état* of 9 November 1923 cannot disguise the fact that Hitler was then even less able than in 1932/3 to seize power with National Socialist forces alone. Without the crucial support of respected and established forces in state and society nothing could be achieved in either situation. To that extent there was no difference between the 'government' of Hitler, Kahr, Ludendorff, Pöhner, and Seisser, which was proclaimed under false pretences on the evening of 8 November 1923, and the government of Hitler, Hindenburg, Papen, Hugenberg, and Seldte, which actually came into being on 30 January 1933.

This sort of protection from the anti-Republican, National Conservative camp, similar to that in Bavaria before 1923, also enabled the NSDAP to come in from the political wilderness of radical sectarianism for the first time after 1929/30 on the national stage and to become the focal point for the discontented whose numbers rose rapidly with the economic crisis. The agreement between the 'National Opposition' which the new leader of the German Nationalist People's Party (DNVP), Alfred Hugenberg, had called into being during the summer of 1929, before the real depression set in, to campaign for a referendum against the Young Plan, was of particular significance. As a result of this arrangement – the forerunner of the Harzburg Front of October 1931 – Hitler could play an active role for the first time in a central issue of German politics, this time as a partner of Hugenberg, of Stahlhelm leader Seldte, and other worthy members of the national right. The campaign against the Young Plan lasted several months and it was not only free publicity in the Hugenberg press which the NSDAP got out of it. It also gradually made the Hitler movement respectable and credit-worthy once more – for after 1925 it had been tainted with failure, a near illegal putschist party. It also brought the movement new, powerful patronage, including that of the former President of the Reichsbank, Schacht, who resigned over the negotiations for the Young Plan and joined the National Opposition. The campaign was not always opposed with conviction and skill by the government but above all it gave the NSDAP the chance to play its trump card in the contest with its reactionary and conservative partners; namely its superior powers of agitation. Thus, after years of political stagnation, the NSDAP gained its first striking electoral successes during the second half of 1929, in individual Länder and municipalities and in the student bodies at the universities. This political overture to the economic crisis (a sharp rise in unemployment was first evident in the winter of 1929/30) allowed the NSDAP to present itself as a new, active force of opposition and gave it the prestige and attraction from which it then benefited during the crisis and which automatically continued after further successes, as long as the crisis lasted and intensified.

Yet the final stage of the Republic also showed what could be done to counter the ominous growth of the Hitler movement if it was resolutely opposed, as when Brüning's emergency government and the Prussian government, controlled by the Social Democrats, adopted combined political and executive measures because of their alarm at the growth of the NSDAP and its disruptive agitation.[1] And in fact the Republic was not really breached by the weight of ballot papers, for the NSDAP fell far short of gaining an absolute majority even during its greatest successes. The growing readiness of government circles to bargain with Hitler was more important, a trend which was also noticeable in the agrarian and business interest groups. One crucial trial of strength, which the NSDAP won, concerned the ban on the S.A. by Brüning's government on 13 April 1932. The ban was lifted in the summer of that year, thanks to the deciding influence of the Reichswehr (Schleicher), which notwithstanding its suspicions of Hitler was keen to exploit the military potential of the S.A. and in any event wanted to avoid a direct conflict with it. As a result, first the Reich Minister of the Interior, Groener, then the whole Brüning government resigned. Papen's reactionary interim government knocked away a few more important props of democracy, especially by its coup against the acting Social Democratic government of Prussia and the disposal of the Social Democratic representatives and heads of the Prussian administration. This in itself paved the way for the later 'co-ordination' (*Gleichschaltung*) in the Third Reich. The final political engagement was lost when Schleicher, the last Chancellor of the Republic, was not empowered by the Reich President to continue with an emergency government backed by force of arms, which alone could have prevented Papen meanwhile from preparing the ground for Hitler to become Chancellor in coalition with members of the National Opposition. The intervention of agrarian and business interest groups was a key factor here. Influential protection from above was more important than any direct financial support of the NSDAP and helped to hoist Hitler into the Chancellor's saddle.

By contrast the real hardship of the NSDAP in the years 1924 to 1928 was due to the almost complete loss of their earlier protection because of Hitler's prison sentence and the ban against his speaking in certain Länder. Really it was only in this phase, when its ideology and propaganda moved farther to the left and it temporarily assumed national-revolutionary rather than nationalist, anti-semitic traits, that the NSDAP was outside political society and swimming against the current. Indeed, these crisis-free years revealed that left to its own devices the NSDAP could do little to throw off the stigma of being a political outsider.

The functioning and stability of the Weimar Republic depended largely on the ability and readiness for coalition between the liberal parties of the middle and the Social Democrats, who had assumed the leadership of the young democracy in 1918/19 and who remained the strongest party in the Reich until the summer of 1932 and the most important and reliable supporters of the Republic. The decline of the Republic was thus to a considerable extent identical with the inability of the Weimar Coalition to govern, and more specifically with the loss of power by the Social Democrats. The fact that the severe crises between 1919 and 1923 *were* ultimately overcome, particularly the attempted subversion by the right (the Kapp Putsch, the Küstrin Putsch of the 'Black' Reichswehr, the Hitler Putsch), was due above all to the co-operation between the liberal 'middle' parties and the Social Democrats, with their shared determination to defend the parliamentary Republic. This was expressed among other things by the Law for the Defence of the Republic of 1922. It was surely significant that in 1923 the Chief of the Army Command, General von Seeckt, did not risk using the powers which were given him by the state of emergency to deal with leftist and rightist enemies of the Republic in order to set up a military dictatorship, as both left and right alike had feared.

At that time the conservative and German Nationalist right shrank from a direct challenge to the forces of democracy, not least because there was still a real danger of revolution by the radical left, in the struggle against which the Social Democrats were hardly dispensable. True, the anti-Communist marriage of convenience between Ebert and Groener, which in socio-political terms also functioned as a joint defence of the Socialist revolution, indeed benefited the Reichswehr and the conservative forces in state and society, but it also bound these to the Social Democrats as long as revolution threatened from the left.

This constellation changed after 1923, when Moscow called off the revolutionary tactics of the German Communists. The KPD, with an average of between 9 and 13 per cent of the vote, remained a strong but nonetheless calculable political constant, still causing unrest but hardly an acute threat to the state. The end of this direct threat from the left and the economic consolidation did indeed temporarily relieve the Republic but did not favour its long-term stabilization. On the contrary, prosperity and the end of anxiety about revolution rather weakened the attachment to democracy of the liberal middle classes and upper classes whilst the economic improvement brought a restoration of their traditional political and social attitudes. These were also strongly encouraged in the industrial sector by the marked concentrations of big businesses and corporations.

The changed situation expressed itself both in the more bitter socio-political conflicts between trade unions and employers (Ruhr iron strike at the end of 1928) and above all in the fact that in 1924 the conciliation nurtured between the liberal middle parties and the Socialists between 1919 and 1923 began to disappear. The SPD was no longer represented in Reich governments between November 1923 and June 1928. There was a clear shift of political opinion towards the right and this was also marked by the election of Hindenburg as Reich President in 1925.

The period of economic prosperity also exposed more clearly the defects and negative qualities of the parliamentary system: the rapid change of governments, the dependence of Ministers on their parties, with a consequent weakening of any coalition cabinet, the interference in government by party leaders and parliamentary parties, the dominating influence of interest groups and thus the diminished authority of governments. As a result even before the world economic crisis had made itself felt in Germany, opinion was widespread among the middle classes that the party system was finished. The former governing parties – Democrats, German People's Party (DVP), Centre Party, German Nationalist People's Party (DNVP) – forfeited 10 per cent of their votes in the Reichstag election of May 1928. The electors of the DNVP in particular reproached their strongly monarchical and anti-democratic party for some of its leading personalities giving up their policy of obstruction in principle and participating in government (decline of the DNVP from 20 to 14 per cent of the vote).

After this election, which greatly intensified the splintering of parties, the only way for governmental policies to be continued, especially Stresemann's foreign policy, was to renew the co-operation between the parties of the middle and the SPD. But such co-operation, demanded by the election results and reasons of state, conflicted far more than had been the case before 1924 with the self-confidence and power of the parties and interest groups to the right of the SPD, not least the Reichswehr and bureaucracy. The fact that the SPD won an electoral victory in 1928 in spite of this development burdened the 'Great Coalition' intolerably from the outset. Under their new leader, Hugenberg, the DNVP moved sharply into opposition after the election results. As a result the parties of the middle and right still represented in the government were all the more compelled to work with the SPD, even to allow it to have the dominating position. In turn, discomfort with this coalition grew in the parties to the right of the SPD and was fanned by numerous disputes and conflicting interests. And parallel with this, efforts increased to change this state of affairs in non-democratic ways, since things could not be put right by parliamentary governments. During the year 1928/9 the Centre Party also moved farther to the right under its new chairman (Prelate Kaas). The spokesmen both of the agrarian 'Green Front' and of heavy industry openly expressed their displeasure with the Great Coalition, which also lost its most important unifying force with Stresemann's death in 1929. In the winter of 1929/30, when it was obvious that compromise over certain social policy issues was no longer possible between the employers' wing of the DVP and the trade union wing of the SPD, the political leaders of the Reichswehr (Schleicher, Groener) urged the creation of an authoritarian 'Hindenburg Cabinet' of the right-middle without the SPD. And because at the crucial moment stubborn vested interests triumphed over a readiness for compromise within the SPD this also contributed decisively to the collapse of the last parliamentary government under the Social Democrat Hermann Müller and to the SPD's withdrawal from the responsibilities of government.

But the transition to Brüning's emergency government was by no means the result of the pressure of reasons of state. On the contrary, the makers of Brüning's minority government agreed that the Reich President's authorization to issue emergency decrees (Article 48 of the Constitution) should only be granted to a cabinet based on the right-middle and not to a Social Democratic Chancellor. And the order to govern without the Social Democrats also finally made it impossible for Brüning in the summer of 1930 to agree to a Socialist proposal to balance the budget, which might have been passed by parliament against the wishes of the DVP. As a result the way was open for the Reichstag to be dissolved. This gave the NSDAP its spectacular success in the elections of September 1930 and with the growing resort to emergency decrees increased Brüning's dependence on the Reich President and the right-wing forces behind him. The further shift to the right by Brüning's government in the autumn of 1931 (departure of the 'leftist' Centre Party Ministers Wirth and Stegerwald, the take-over of the Ministry of the Interior by Reichswehr Minister Groener) discredited still more the 'above party' character of Brüning's stabilization policy. And when Groener and Brüning finally fell in spring 1932 the agreement on toleration between the emergency government and the SPD ended too, an agreement which had at least left the Socialists with an indirect influence and which had kept in check the destructive policies of the extremists of the right and left in the Reichstag.

It was significant that the NSDAP's policy, like that of the other forces of the National Opposition during the years 1930–2, was above all directed at destroying the remaining governing coalitions or understandings between the liberal parties or between the Centre Party and the SPD. This did not succeed in the Reichstag until spring 1932 and the referendum staged by the Stahlhelm, the NSDAP and the DNVP in spring 1931 to bring down the SPD-controlled Prussian government (SPD, DDP, Centre), also failed. Admittedly the NSDAP scored a series of victories with these tactics in the smaller *Länder* and municipalities, first in Thuringia in January 1930, in Braunschweig in autumn 1930, and in Anhalt, Oldenburg and Mecklenburg in 1932.

Governments which were set up in these states before 1933 under the controlling influence of the NSDAP were really based on the alliance of the German Nationalist and liberal parties with the NSDAP. Their motives were similar to those that had been displayed when the Great Coalition collapsed in the Reich in March 1930. An alliance with Hitler's Party was infinitely more preferable to the parties to the right of centre than any government led by the SPD. This trend, which ultimately led to the surrender of the middle-class parties to the NSDAP and their desertion by the voters, was in reality the first act of the Third Reich. The NSDAP's incessant condemnation not only of the Communist but also of the Social Democratic left which was popular with the middle classes increasingly isolated the SPD.

Papen's coup against Prussia (20 July 1932), which destroyed the most important basis of what was still the most reliable Republican administration and executive, was of crucial importance. Here, too, the SPD leadership was not entirely blameless since it made formal protests and lodged complaints before the Supreme Court but shunned meeting force with force. Whatever the prospects were for active resistance one thing is certain, giving up the Prussian stronghold without a struggle dealt a fatal blow to the Socialists' will to power and to resist which until then had been relatively intact. In the last resort it had been the defence organized by the SPD, particularly in the shape of the Reichsbanner Black–Red–Gold and the 'Iron Front' – called into being by the General Association of German Trade Unions–which had put the SPD in a position to counter the S.A. and the Hitler Youth effectively on the streets and in public meetings (unlike the middle-class parties), and also to maintain their position in the eyes of the electorate as a continuing factor for social stability. It was not by chance that the S.A. detested the Reichsbanner as much as it did the Communist Red Front Combat League. Since politics and elections in 1932 were largely decided in the streets, the significance of the passive surrender by the militant socialist forces in the face of Papen's coup against Prussia can hardly be overestimated. Yet the Socialist leaders were probably correct in rating very low the chances of active resistance. Developments since 1930 had already isolated the SPD too much for them to expect support from others. The actual removal from power had been long prepared and this intensive preparation also finally enabled Hitler to arrange for a government which was unanimous in its desire for the more or less enforced exclusion of the left. The coalition between the NSDAP and the most reactionary forces of the National Conservative camp and the determination to cut out the democratic left (and naturally the Communists) were interdependent.

The effects of the emergency system of government during the final years of the Republic

From the outset elements of an authoritarian system were part of the all too hastily improvised Weimar Republic. Above all the democratization of the bureaucracy and of the Reichswehr was at best partial.

The subordination in accordance with the constitution of the military, and especially the Chief of the Army High Command to the Minister of Defence, which was not contested before the Kapp Putsch, was subsequently abandoned in practice in conjunction with Seeckt's reform of the Defence Ministry. Seeckt knew how to contrive matters so that alongside the supreme command, which the constitution accorded to the Reich President, the supreme 'command authority' was recognized as his and the military leadership's prerogative. In practice this resulted in a direct relationship between President and the Chief of the Army High Command (and of the Chief of the Naval Command) and confined the Defence Ministry's civilian authority to the concerns of the military budget and administration. After Seeckt's resignation (1926) and General Groener's appointment as Minister of Defence (1928), the military then also controlled the political summit of the Ministry of Defence, and from there acquired a decisive influence on more general political matters through the newly created Ministeramt under General von Schleicher, with his connections with 'old comrades' in the Reich Chancellory (Planck) and the Presidential Palace (Oscar von Hindenburg). Although the 'political Generals' Groener and Schleicher were looked on askance as '*Vernunftsrepublikaner*' by a large part of the Officer Corps, and although they were more critical of the NSDAP than other officers, both of them deliberately tried to strengthen the position of the Reichswehr and of the Reich President within the framework of the Republic. The transition to an emergency system of government (March 1930), when Schleicher was first active as a maker of governments, was bound to benefit the Reichswehr too, as long as the Field Marshal of Imperial Germany was President of the Republic.

Groener's claim before Reichswehr officers in autumn 1930 was symptomatic of the changed situation: 'Not a single move can be made in German politics without the Reichswehr having a decisive say in it.'[2] How strong was the special position of the Reichswehr was also shown by the fact that the Reichswehr budget was completely excluded from the rigorous economy measures of the Brüning government. As the State Secretary in the Reich Ministry of Finance, Paul Schäffer, confirmed in November 1931, in budgetary affairs there was 'already a military dictatorship'.[3]

In 1930 the Reichswehr leaders were still predominantly distrustful and averse to the growing Hitler movement and the S.A. The arrest of three National Socialist Reichswehr officers in Ulm and the ensuing trial for high treason revealed the deep concern about the Reichswehr being undermined, which was probably well founded in respect of the younger officers and the contacts with former officers who had been S.A. leaders. But a more indulgent and benevolent attitude of the Reichswehr leadership towards the S.A. was very soon evident after Hitler had denied having any revolutionary aims at the Leipzig trial on 25 September 1930 (oath of legality). In the spring of 1931 initial contact had been made between Schleicher and Röhm. The stronger the S.A. became the more its potential for the Reichswehr was considered. Above all it offered positive help in strengthening the border defence in the East, especially in East Prussia, where in 1931/2 the Army Command considered it had to reckon once more with a possible Polish attack. Beyond this, and in conjunction with the Geneva disarmament negotiations which were expected to end Germany's existing inferiority of arms, the S.A. was also viewed as a reserve for the future general strengthening of the Army. Above all, the determination to strengthen the Army and armaments, which grew in proportion to the increase of Reichswehr influence in the state, created great goodwill for Hitler, who tirelessly demanded the rearming of the German people.

The changed attitude was seen among other things in a Reichswehr edict of 29 January 1932, which lifted the ban on the entry of NSDAP members to the Army. When Groener in his other capacity as Reich Minister of the Interior none the less allowed himself to be talked into banning the S.A., especially under pressure from Prussia and other *Lands*, it cost him the support of his close friend Schleicher, who in agreement with the Chief of the Army Command (von Hammerstein) criticized the ban to Hindenburg. This finally brought about Groener's fall and, after the formation of the Papen–Schleicher cabinet, the lifting of the ban on the S.A. Schleicher's aim of taming the Hitler movement by involving it with the responsibilities of office failed, however, because Hitler was adamant in demanding the leadership of a National government, refusing the proffered post of Vice-Chancellor; and because when Schleicher himself became Chancellor he could not split the NSDAP and persuade the more complaisant section of the Party under Gregor Strasser to enter the government.

It was through this policy that Schleicher finally became Hitler's detested enemy and even on 30 January 1933 the NSDAP leaders seriously feared that Schleicher might use the Reichswehr to make a last-minute coup to prevent a Hitler government. But Hitler had no difficulty in finding officers in the persons of General Blomberg and Colonel Reichenau who were willing to take over the Defence Ministry instead of Schleicher and also to guarantee the Reichswehr's loyalty to Hitler as Chancellor.

Even so, when Hitler took over the government he had to reckon with the strong position which the Reichswehr had made for itself in the previous years. Even in the Third Reich the Army remained a 'state within a state', which managed to stave off the influence of the NSDAP more effectively than all the other branches of the executive.

The other pillar of authoritarian tradition was the professional civil service, especially in inner government circles and in the ministerial bureaucracy, whose standing and influence had been strengthened during the authoritarian emergency government.

Already mostly bound by origins and education to the monarchical-authoritarian tradition, the greater part of the bureaucracy in the Reich and in the Länder had been unable to reconcile with the party state of the Weimar Republic their traditional conception of the 'servant of the state' as the guardian and representative of a disciplined society. Party politics, with its vested interests, and parliamentary democracy, as the forum of pluralistic political and social forces, earned the barely concealed contempt of the old civil servants, who saw in the state a higher point of power and order. The formal constitutional oath, which required no specific acknowledgement of the Republic, had been generally taken with the reservation that it entailed serving 'the state' (in the higher sense) but not defending the Republican state form. In keeping with the predominantly liberal doctrines of constitutional law, the true higher purpose of the state after the end of the monarchy was identified with the eternal and supra-individual Nation, the sovereign power and the above-party national community as a whole, which could be endangered by the parties.

In fact the resulting party and political neutrality of the bureaucracy entailed a strong resentment against democracy and a clear affinity to authoritarian and élitist political ideals. But in addition there was a particular receptiveness to the ideology and propaganda of the National right, which proclaimed the aim of destroying the parliamentary system. Admittedly such an attachment to an abstract conception of state, to the bureaucrat's impartial devotion to duty and the special position of the civil service – a relic of the German and particularly Prussian tradition – also often made older civil servants immune to that brand of radical National Socialist demagogy which mobilized the 'street' against the government and which opposed the state's authority with its private party authority by means of its own combat leagues. Even in the latter phase of the Weimar Republic, when the conservative right-wing parties had lost a great many votes, most of the higher civil servants, especially the ministerial bureaucracy in Berlin, stood nearer to the conservative right as epitomized by the DNVP or the Conservative People's Union (Treviranus) than to the NSDAP.

It is true that a growing doubt was also apparent chiefly among the younger civil servants about the old conception of the 'state servant', whose feudal, authoritarian origins and traditional social prestige could be reconciled neither with the modest economic standing of the civil servant nor with the world view of the younger generation. Besides, the material worries of the bureaucrats were ominously increased by Brüning's policy of economizing and running down the civil service. If Brüning's above-party, authoritarian attempts to balance the budget relied above all on the bureaucracy and in fact significantly increased the influence of the ministerial bureaucracy, then the financial sacrifice simultaneously inflicted on officialdom ensured that political radicalization increasingly affected the civil service in turn. The NSDAP also won over numerous supporters among the professional civil servants from 1930/1. And even in Länder controlled by Social Democrats for years the receptiveness to the National Socialist slogans was noticeable in the administrations and executives, not least in the police forces where the specific police duty to keep the peace engendered a distinct politico-social notion of order.

In constitutional terms, the transition to the emergency system of government by emergency decree naturally tipped the balance towards the state authority. The Reich ministerial bureaucracy, which now replaced the Reichstag as the real law-giver, increased its influence and power. The Republic developed into an authoritarian state run by civil servants parallel to its decline as a parliamentary democracy under Brüning. The Reichstag met only at long intervals after the autumn of 1930 and generally merely to pass a series of emergency decrees. This practice, which led to a protest withdrawal by the National Opposition (NSDAP and DNVP) as early as February 1931, inevitably further discredited the parliamentary system and contributed to a widespread disregard of the separation of legislature and executive provided for by the constitution. Finally it also meant that the hierarchical authoritarian attitudes of the bureaucracy to the state and the authoritarian emergency government iself (together with the uncontrollable forces involved in this) became more influential.

The growing resort to emergency decrees, which were by no means always necessary, decisively altered the sense of paragraph 48 of the constitution. What was envisaged here as a temporary exception became habitual and new governmental and state practice. Thus the emergency governments institutionalized a practice which was exceptionally useful to Hitler. Of all the essential means of taking over the state and established order in the spring of 1933, Hitler's government made use of the presidential power to issue decrees, and it is difficult to imagine how there could have been a seizure of power without this device.

The emergency government also inevitably increased the importance and influence of the Reich President far beyond what the constitution envisaged and at the same time it also increased the influence of those groups in the ante-chamber of the Presidential Palace. The policy of '*Osthilfe*' which Brüning intensified provided millions for the debts of east German landowners, although of course it could never meet all the needs of east German agriculture which was disadvantaged by its locale and structure; nor did it prevent those same east Elbian landowners who dominated the Reich Land League from opposing Brüning in 1931 and gaining the ear of Hindenburg, who as Lord of the Manor of Neudeck in East Prussia was particularly exposed to the influence of his peers.

Yet a growing discomfort with Brüning, and later with the short-lived Schleicher cabinet, was also noticeable amongst industrialists. Many of these had hoped that the government's economy and emergency measures would lead to a still greater reduction of wages and social welfare payments. More depressing, however, was the fact that with the economic crisis there was a wave of new concentrations and mergers of large concerns and banks. At the same time there was increased state interference in the economy because of government stabilization policies and this increasingly violated the principle of the liberal-capitalist private economy. Although themselves increasingly compelled to amalgamate, numerous industrialists showed their perplexity by levelling charges of state socialism and state capitalism at Brüning and Schleicher. Papen had a more favourable press with industry in spite of the more active programme of state-created employment which he introduced in September 1932 under the growing pressure of public opinion. This was supposed to be made palatable to industry, however, not only by means of special credits (in the form of tax vouchers) for employing additional manpower, but by the provision that in cases where more employment was created wage norms could be undercut by up to 50 percent. Thus the trade unions spoke, not without justice, of the economy being revived 'at the expense of the workers'.[4]

Unlike the 'Green Front' which was already being influenced more and more by National Socialist agrarian propaganda after 1931/32, the industrialists were still largely sceptical about the NSDAP at the beginning of 1932, in spite of Hitler's concern with big business, even though Schacht, Thyssen and a number of influential representatives of the industrial and banking world had meanwhile demonstratively ranged themselves alongside Hitler. But as a circular of the Reich Association of German Industry of January 1932 shows,[5] their vote was dead against Brüning's economic policy and contributed to his downfall, as did that of the farmers and the Reichswehr. And a year later, when Schleicher's work-creation scheme annulled Papen's decree lowering wages and looked for more support from the trade unions, leading industrialists did not hesitate to intercede openly against Schleicher in favour of a Hitler cabinet in their address to the Reich President.

The emergency system of government concealed such influences more successfully than a parliamentary system but made them none the less more effective. The prompt dismissal of Brüning and Schleicher, who had at first enjoyed Hindenburg's special trust, was indicative of the real state of affairs whereby the Republic suffered from the accumulating and uncontrollable influences on the Reich President. It was not the Reichstag that had given Brüning a confidence vote in April 1932, but the senile Reich President acting like a monarch, and the interest groups and advisers of a court faction who decided the fate of the government and of the state. The emergency system, which at the outset of the Brüning government could still count as a credible above-party attempt to heal the Republic, hardly served the public good but on the contrary the cause of powerful vested interests.

Brüning's effort to get at least the republican state of law if not the parliamentary system and party democracy through the crisis, and the attempt to push through what measures seemed necessary through an efficient, functional, bureaucratic emergency government, was not doomed from the start. It foundered, however, not least because quick results were not forthcoming or fell below the impatient expectations of the masses, and the radical extremist parties systematically did everything to undermine trust in the government. Brüning's deflationary financial policy contributed to this process; it relied too much on the economy's capacity to heal itself and was a fatal error which exaggerated the main weakness of his attempt to stabilize, namely the absence of any anchorage in responsible social groups. The emergency governments of Brüning, Papen and Schleicher looked all the more like closed governments remote from the people because these cabinets of 'experts' were largely incapable of publicizing their aims effectively or of making them popularly intelligible, whereas the movement led by Hitler effected an unexampled mobilization of emotions and resentments. Further, at the end of 1932, after the collapse of the Papen government, which had only had the support of the rump of the Nationalist parliamentary party in the Reichstag, Hindenburg's growing reluctance to continue giving presidential powers or even a long-term mandate to rule by decree to any Chancellor who could not get the support of the parties to the right of centre (which now meant above all, however, the NSDAP) was a response to the growing isolation from public opinion into which the emergency government had manoeuvred itself.

From then on the pressures coming from the restorative and reactionary forces for the inclusion of the NSDAP in the government became stronger and more unscrupulous, because only Hitler's mass movement could give them the necessary popular backing, which could hardly be achieved with the Centre Party let alone with the Social Democrats with whom they could not and would not make deals. The moment seemed favourable for such an arrangement in January 1933, when the elections of November 1932 brought a drop in the NSDAP votes for the first time, from 37 to 32 per cent, which was partly due to the slight slackening of the crisis and partly due to Hitler's all-or-nothing tactics (these had created considerable disquiet in the NSDAP in conjunction with the Schleicher–Strasser contacts and the exhausted Party funds). A cabinet where Hitler was flanked by Papen as well as the representatives of the Nationalist right and the conservative Ministers of the previous cabinets, now also seemed more acceptable to Hindenburg, who until then had been obstinately opposed to the Chancellorship of the 'bohemian corporal'.

Notes and references

1. The measures taken at that time included among others the ban issued by the Prussian Minister of the Interior Severing against Prussian officials taking part in National Socialist organizations on 5 July 1930; the steps taken by the Social Democratic Berlin Police President Grzesinski to close S.A. premises in Berlin in February 1931, and an emergency decree issued by the Reich government on 28 March 1931, for dealing with political demonstrations. Public statements by the Centre Party leader Kaas and the Catholic bishops against National Socialism in January/February 1931 as well as the reactivation at this time of the Reichsbanner Black-Red-Gold must be included among the efforts made by the Prussian and Reich governments and the forces supporting them to defend against National Socialism.

2. Cited in Thilo Vogelsang, *Reichswehr, Staat und NSDAP* (Stuttgart, 1963), p. 95.

3. Cited in Erich Eyck, *Geschichte der Weimarer Republik* (Zurich, Stuttgart, 1956), vol. 2, p. 394.
4. Quoted from Dieter Petzina, 'Hauptprobleme der deutschen Wirtschaftspolitik 1932–1933', in *Vierteljahrshefte für Zeitgeschichte (VJHZ)*, 15, 1967, Heft 4, p. 24.
5. Cf. Wilhelm Treue, 'Die deutschen Unternehmer in der Weltwirtschafts-krise 1928–1933', in *Staats- und Wirtschaftskrise des Deutschen Reiches*, ed. W. Conze and H. Raupach (Stuttgart, 1966), p. 109.

Chapter Two

Modus-operandi and structure of the Hitler movement before 1933

Ideology, propaganda and charismatic leadership

The outer organizational form and leadership technique of the National Socialist movement was largely determined by its inner structure, which showed itself in the relationship between ideology, propaganda and leadership.

Nationalistic, pan-German, racist and anti-semitic, anti-Marxist and anti-Liberal ideas formed the basis of the National Socialist ideology; ideas which had already appeared in Germany in this or that connection before 1914 but which had grown markedly more virulent only after the experience of First World War, surrender and revolution. In the first phase of its existence (until 1923) the NSDAP was one of the numerous *völkisch* groups which had sprung up and multiplied pretty well all over Germany at the end of the War as the expression of an individual patriotic protest and defiance.

The usual, utopian formula of the *völkisch* groups was the regeneration of Germandom as the pre-condition of a future re-birth and greatness. This aim lent itself to various interpretations and as a result the *völkisch* movement splintered into numerous sectarian groups and associations, notwithstanding the fact that their general ideas influenced a broad sector of the nation. Adolf Hitler had already nourished himself in Vienna before 1914 on the German racist and anti-semitic ideological tracts which were more readily available there owing to the mixture of nationalities in the Habsburg monarchy. He returned from the war and after the overthrow of the Soviet Republic he found in Munich a mood which seemed to confirm completely the truth of the *völkisch*, anti-semitic 'world view' and the necessity of drawing political conclusions from this. However, as the motor and leader of the NSDAP, which he joined in September 1919, he deliberately avoided and prevented an all too dogmatic definition of ideological positions. The ideological utterances and output of leading National Socialists continued to be thereafter more or less personal opinions or specific ideological variations, which could be represented alongside other, often opposing opinions without the NSDAP being committed to them. The more the NSDAP became the Hitler movement, however, the more binding became those elements of the *völkisch* ideology and programme to which Hitler had personally committed himself as the absolute leader of the NSDAP. They can be reduced to the few fixed points of a nationalism founded on biological and race theory. Early on a stereotyped, popular-scientific styled, fanatical anti-semitism appeared in Hitler's speeches and writings, wherein 'Jewry' figured as a universal, actual and metaphysical world enemy, a bacillus sapping the strength and individuality of the nations. There was also the belief in the 'natural law' of the eternal 'struggle of the species' and thus the 'right of the stronger'.

With the sureness of instinct of the practised demagogue, Hitler realized that the *völkisch* ideology was based not on intellectual reasoning but on passionate emotions, fears and longings, and by its very nature defied theoretical systematization and could be most attractive by being less specific, so long as the basic aim was clear: the desire and will for a complete revitalization of the nation. Anti-Marxism, anti-semitism and the proclaiming of and struggle against other enemies functioned above all to strengthen the will to fight and to harden against humanitarian scruples. The race theory served to heighten national self-awareness, attributing social hardships to Jews and other enemies of the people. And the great future living space in the East was the ultimate goal, the vision of a completely new power base for the nation and a heroic existence for the master race, which promised the German people delivery from all their economic and material constraints. The more the fundamental purpose of this ideology was preached and taken up, the more it created a conviction which was finally determined to bring into existence what had at the beginning only been affirmed. Where the ideological basis was so lacking success was all the more important for confirming the rightness of its ideas and aims. From the beginning a far-reaching interplay and interchange between ideology and propaganda, belief and action was inherent in the NSDAP, which in Hitler had its pivotal point and this made the need to succeed the driving force of the movement. National Socialism was the extreme attempt to change the world by transforming the subjective consciousness (not the objective realities) and to offset the missing objective pre-conditions of German world power and greatness by vitalizing and unleashing German national self-awareness and national energies.

From the beginning Hitler aimed to raise the NSDAP above the *völkisch* organizations, which were all more or less mere talking shops, and to make it a dynamic and active new-style combat movement. Admittedly, the Party continued to remain, true to its ideological base, a *völkisch* party. But as it succumbed to the spell of Hitler's powers as an agitator, it was concerned less with ideological and programmatic discussion in the first instance than with attempting to release the potential emotions and energy which underlay the *volkisch* conception. Thus Hitler also welcomed the aggressive name of 'workers' party' and the label of 'National Socialism'. Essential elements of style which the Party incorporated also originated from the opposed Marxist pattern: the Socialist Party address 'comrade' was taken over and the colour red for flags, swastika arm bands, and election posters: National Socialist words were put to Socialist fighting songs and (especially under Goebbels's direction in Berlin) the Communist organization was copied (street and factory cells etc.).

But what was especially characteristic of the NSDAP as of other fascist movements was the link between the *völkisch* agitationist Party and the para-military fighting organization, here in the shape of the 'Storm Detachments' (*Sturmabteilungen* — S.A.), formed in the spring of 1920 and organized with the active help of officers from the national Freikorps and Defence Leagues. The S.A., with some 3,000 men in 1923, grew to be the most active and powerful combat group amongst the radical rightist Defence Leagues in Bavaria and it was through the S.A. above all that the use of physical force or the threat of it became an established instrument in the Nazi struggle for power. It was thanks to the S.A. that it had already been possible in the autumn of 1922 for the Hitler movement to put on those provocative demonstrations (first example the 'German Day' in Coburg on 14–15 October 1922) along the lines of the punitive forays of the fascist action squads in Italy, during which it frequently came to fisticuffs with the Communists. The S.A. in particular enabled the NSDAP to carry into politics the 'spirit of the front' and it was the chief instrument for the deliberate use of political terror, which also demonstrated the Party's own strength where demagogy and ideology alone could not convince. But, with its parades and deployments, the S.A. also helped the NSDAP in to the wings of 'authority', and with its consecration of the standards and its bands it helped to give the Party that military pomp which was attuned to the mentality of a population ever receptive to shooting matches and martial music.

Although former officers predominated as leaders in the S.A. as in other Defence Leagues and although considerable importance was attached to military training and organization, the S.A. stemmed from the early organized Party hecklers and always played an important propaganda role at Party meetings and demonstrations. It was precisely this combination of Defence League and Party troop which distinguished the S.A. from the other para-military associations of the right, which either disbanded after 1923 or became more or less non-political veteran organizations (like the Stahlhelm.)

Thanks to this combination and to the resulting method of agitating (the local S.A. groups often played a more important role than the Party organization after the re-founding of the NSDAP after 1925, for example in Berlin), the NSDAP was able to 'hibernate' even during the relative stability of the Weimar Republic between 1924 and 1928 and to attract the supporters of rival *volkisch* parties, especially the German People's Freedom Party, and other radical rightist Defence Leagues. Although the NSDAP's political significance was slight during this phase, an important centre of activity continued during this period in that the Party in effect became the sole heir of the radical-rightist *völkisch* groups. It was therefore in an unchallenged position in the camp of right-wing extremism when the radicalization of the masses set in with the economic crisis.

Moreover, the more marked social revolutionary and at times even national bolshevist traits of the NSDAP in these years resulted less from ideological conviction than from the dynamic element of the NSDAP and S.A., from the high proportion of young people, pupils and students alike, unemployed ex-soldiers and Freikorps fighters, who made up the most active part of the movement and represented a social and political factor of dynamic mobility. In comparison with the NSDAP between 1922 and 1925, its part allies, part rivals from the German People's Freedom Party (and later the Nationalists and Stahlhelm partners of the 'Harzburg Front') were far more representative of the older generation and of the middle-class or aristocratic establishment. The relationship was in many respects that of old man and impetuous youth. NSDAP members saw themselves as national revolutionaries and Socialists (even if they were only anarchists) and regarded the *völkisch* or Nationalist leaders as reactionaries. The NSDAP's particular combat style attracted a section of the *völkisch*-nationalistic youth just as much as it appeared repulsive, as 'proletarian' as a 'demon of the streets' and of the 'masses' to most of the older men, fixated on their clubs and societies and their 'concept' of *völkisch*, or to the élitist Nationalists.

What contributed to the more pronounced social revolutionary tendencies within the NSDAP in this period was the fact that, in spreading to the urban-industrial centres of North-West Germany, the Party was confronted more by the Socialist-organized working class (the Party was barely represented in the countryside until 1929/30). The NSDAP's 'Study Group North West', which was set up in the autumn of 1925 under Gregor Strasser's direction, with the support of his younger brother Otto Strasser, the young Goebbels and other activists (including the later Gauleiter Karl Kaufmann, Erich Koch, Josef Terboven, Franz von Pfeiffer), represented at that time a more serious and ingenious variant of National Socialism than that contained in the provincial Party Programme of the Munich NSDAP of 24 January 1920, under the slogan

'Break the slavery of invested capital', which was coined above all by the early Party ideologist, Gottfried Feder.

The key phrases contained in this original Programme (25 points): 'Abolition of unearned income', of 'ground rent' and of 'land speculation', including the demand for the 'death penalty' for 'common criminals, usurers and profiteers', came from the arsenal of naive petit-bourgeois protests against 'finance capital'. And in spite of the communal and anti-capitalist wrapping, the demands for communalizing or leasing big department stores, the aim of nationalising 'all businesses already formed into corporations' (point 12), profit-sharing in large industrial enterprises (point 13), and the desire for land reform suitable to 'national requirements' (point 17), all amounted to middle-class reform rather than to a Socialist programme. Although on the other hand the NSDAP Gauleiter of North-West Germany supported the Communist proposal for the expropriation of the Royal Princes during the winter of 1925/6, or even, like Strasser and Goebbels, put in a passionate plea for an anti-capitalist alliance with the Soviet Union, such a leftist tendency could hardly be reconciled with the liberal and conservative ideas of the National right.

It was, however, equally typical that this left wing eventually capitulated virtually without protest, when Hitler resolutely opposed the Strasser group's attempt to get a formal revision of the original Party Programme at the NSDAP's party leader's Conference in Bamberg (14 Feb. 1926) and categorically forbade any further discussion of the Programme. This passive submission demonstrated what little binding force the NSDAP's formal political Programme had in the last resort. True, social revolutionary efforts were not finished after Bamberg; Goebbels for example continued to make skilful use of social revolutionary fervour even as Gauleiter in Berlin, but it had been proved that in any choice between Hitler and particular points in the Programme, most of the Gauleiter opted for the Führer, not for the Programme. In fact the Strasser programme offered no clear alternative. In spite of a different emphasis (more anti-capitalism, less anti-semitism) it adhered to the basic aim of the *völkisch* ideology. Hitler's reaffirmation of National Socialism was more consistent than the *völkisch*, corporate-statist mixture of Strasser's ideas in so far as it was unequivocally concerned with propaganda rather than with a programme; namely, it was primarily geared to transforming social discontent into a national dynamic force and directing it against the enemies of the people at home and towards expansion abroad.

Like National Socialism, most of the other ideological-propagandist leitmotivs of Nazism had a peculiar hybrid, half-reactionary, half-revolutionary relationship to established society, to the political system and tradition. What we termed the parasitic character of the Nazi movement is again evident here: this ideology was almost like a backward-looking Utopia. It derived from romantic pictures and clichés of the past, from warlike-heroic, patriarchal or absolutist ages, social and political systems, which, however, were translated into the popular and avant-garde, into the fighting slogans of a totalitarian nationalism. The élitist notion of aristocratic nobility became the *völkisch* 'nobility of blood' of the 'master race', the princely 'theory of divine right' gave way to the popular national Führer; the obedient submission to the active national 'following'.

The new formulae seemed both to end the old conflict of the Imperial-Wilhelmine age between the authoritarian state and industrial society and also to be a return to the 'healthy' ideals of the pre-democratic order. This Janus-like quality characterized the whole arsenal of National Socialist phraseology. The affirmation as it were of a pre-societal naturalness and a 'more intimate' community, determined by the mystical forces of nationality, of 'blood and soil' and 'ancestral inheritance', is directly transformed through the manipulatory techniques of the biological-scientific *Homo faber*, to 'purification' by sterilization, euthanasia and liquidation of the Jews, to 'Germanization' through resettlement, racial selection etc.

The same applies to the question of continuity or discontinuity of the foreign policy programme. Hitler and the NSDAP took up most of the radical aims which had arisen in Wilhelmine Germany from the combination of expansionist industrial capitalism, the power-dynamic of the Hohenzollern military monarchy, and the absolutist ideas of a still largely caste-ridden authoritarian state bureaucracy and élitist leadership in an age of nationalism. Yet the fanatical nationalism of the masses, which found expression in the NSDAP and was to be organized and activated by them more strongly than ever, signified at the same time the destruction of the élitist and authoritarian presuppositions of the old order. The National Socialist reversion to the imperialist pan-German positions of the Wilhelmine era was – after world war and revolution – only possible at the price of a popular change and dynamism, and of the conversion of patriotism to a racist totalitarianism, which had no more time for the old authoritarian state than it had for the aristocratic and upper middle-class establishment and its values.

The First World War had shown for the first time to what extent national energies could be raised in the name of the 'civil truce', and that the total mobilization of nationalism could blunt the awareness of social differences. This was to be an epoch-making experience for National Socialism. Hitler's real programme was to turn the wheel of history back to 1914 but in so doing to create the mentality of war and total mobilization in peace time, and here the charismatic leader and drummer could achieve more than the attraction of ideology.

Charismatic leadership, as the 'revolutionary force in an epoch bound by tradition' (Max Weber), was bound to meet with a sympathetic response in the German middle classes, with their strongly traditionalist political ideas, the more the fragile foundations of the existing political order disintegrated through the revolutionary events of the War and its aftermath. Years before 1914 the National right opposition of the pan-Germans had already longed for and prophesied the displacement of the feeble imperial rule of Wilhelm II by a charismatic national leader. The nation's psychological readiness for such a leader and 'renewer' of the nation proffered the role which Hitler merely needed to assume. However, he could only play it convincingly and successfully because of his unusual abilities as a propagandist. Hitler's influence, his aura as Führer and his charisma depended to an exceptional extent on his talent as a speaker, which literally formed the foundation of his political career.

There is evidence that even from the early beginnings of the NSDAP speeches by Hitler were 'enjoyed' as a sort of popular entertainment, which aroused the willing enthusiasts beforehand like a sporting event. Here there was 'something afoot', here accounts would be 'settled' ruthlessly! But demagogic aggression alone could not have achieved this unique effect if Hitler had not at the same time had a masterly understanding of how to convey the impression of 'holy seriousness'. It was precisely the combination of popular oratory, which also knew how to make very good use of sarcasm, with the solemn stance of the political missionary that separated Hitler both from coarser agitators like Hermann Esser or Julius Streicher, and from such effective (but less credible) intellectual orators as Joseph Goebbels, and gave him (Hitler) a far-reaching effect (on ordinary as well as more pretentious listeners) which was unmatched in the Party.

The extent to which he deliberately deployed his rhetorical armoury, change of speed and volume, transition from 'pianissimo' to 'fortissimo', the studied technique of creating the proper atmosphere (the use of flags and music, intentionally late arrival of the long-awaited speaker in the crowded hall, etc.) cannot conceal, however, that Hitler not only knew how to create a mood but that, conversely, his effectiveness as a speaker was also dependent to a great extent on the readiness of his audience to approve. The slow testing of the mood of a gathering as he spoke, the time which Hitler always needed to 'warm up' both himself and the meeting, and the way in which he then let himself be roused and carried on by the applause, testify to his dependence on the public response. Notably, in the politically calmer (and thus for him more difficult) years between 1925 and 1928, Hitler often refused or hesitated for a long time before making a speech if he was not sure of a success.

Given the impression of resoluteness which he offered, Hitler knew how to articulate and at the same time to celebrate what his listeners half consciously desired and felt. He voiced what they secretly thought and wanted, reinforced their still unsure longings and prejudices, and thereby created for them a deeply satisfying self-awareness and the feeling of being privy to a new truth and certainty. Such leadership and oratory did not require a refined intellectual discrimination or a calm, mature individuality and personality, but – as with the leaders of other fascist or equally irrational mass and revivalist movements – a psychological and emotional disposition which was itself so infected by the mood of crisis and panic of the time that it instinctively sounded the correct note; a person who with the growing self-awareness of the successful agitator increasingly discovered his own mission in life and that meaning to his existence for which he had so long searched in vain.

Such a leader was not predestined to be a great force in history simply because of his own extraordinary individual talents. Hitler's uniqueness can hardly be grasped or explained biographically either. His sudden rise from intellectual and personal mediocrity to the political arena seems, rather, to confirm that such a leadership could only develop in the context of a specific crisis atmosphere and collective psychology. The unusual passion with which Hitler embraced the general pathology of German nationalism and concentrated his entire energies on expressing it and converting it to action, enabled him to become the 'Führer'. It was the crisis which transformed the eccentric and crank into the unerring demagogue. Hitler was far less a political teacher than Lenin; he was more a catalyst, the fuel and accelerator of real tensions and crises of conscience, which could set in motion monstrous processes and effects without contributing anything new. His historical role consisted essentially in transforming the individual political neurosis into a collective neurosis, in making the widespread general unrest the sounding-board for his own obsession and dynamic force, and translating this into action. Hitler's leadership therefore also points to the paradox that, on the one hand, he was merely an anonymous exponent of an actual crisis atmosphere, but that on the other, this unrest could only break through politically through him as the suggestive integrating figure.

Our description began with Hitler the orator but it also explains a great deal of his effect as head of the Party and later of the government. Talking also played its part here. Hitler's exceptional ability to impress and to convince his listeners (Party functionary, Minister, foreign diplomat, etc.), his virtuoso acting and dramatic ability, unanimously attested by various contemporary observers, his capacity to adjust completely to the listener of the moment, was to some extent merely a variation of the demagogue's art, which sensed the outlook of his listener and knew how to appeal to it.

That Hitler's superior power as an orator and agitator was the crucial reason for his leading position in the Party is evident from the early history of the NSDAP. Only with Hitler as an attraction could the small NSDAP take the risk in the spring of 1920 of holding mass public meetings in Munich, whereby the Party quickly left its obscurity, enjoyed a notable increase in membership, and also gained access to politically and socially influential persons and supporters. In the forty-six meetings staged by the NSDAP between November 1919 and November 1920, Hitler appeared thirty-one times as the main speaker.[1] The fact that Hitler was indispensable as the propagandist and driving force of the Party also made it easy for him at the end of 1921 to demand and to obtain the appointment of chairman with far-reaching powers in the face of an opposing fraction of the Party. Thereafter the period of collective leadership was definitely over. The first chairman soon became the 'Führer', the NSDAP more and more the Hitler movement.

The later development of the NSDAP into a widespread movement of the National Opposition, which also resulted in a considerable growth of the S.A. (NSDAP members grew by the end of 1932 to about 800,000, those of the S.A. to about 500,000), left the basic feature of the fanatical fighting organization unchanged. Indeed it was only with the expansion of the NSDAP and the rapid successes of the electoral battles after 1929/1930, which were now affected by the general process of political radicalization, that the growing spread of political terror and violence developed, above all in the conflict with the Communists and the Reichsbanner.

The number of opponents murdered by the National Socialists and conversely the number of National Socialist 'martyrs' inscribed on a 'roll of honour' ran into hundreds.[2] Hitler himself openly acknowledged the political criminality of his Party when in a published telegram on 22 August 1932 he expressed his 'unbounded devotion' towards five S.A. members who were condemned to death on the same day for their bestial murder of a Communist worker in Potempa (Upper Silesia) in accordance with an emergency decree of 9 August 1932 against political terror. (The men were pardoned in 1933.) The leader of the National Socialists was well aware that the murder of Communists hardly horrified broad sections of the aroused middle classes. On the contrary they were received by them with secret enjoyment. A disastrous rise in political crimes in the struggle between the radical extremist parties was due above all to the frequency of new elections and election campaigns (in 1932 alone there were five big election dates: two ballots for the Reich Presidential elections in March/April 1932; the Landtag elections in Prussia and other Länder on 24 April; and the Reichstag elections of 31 July and 6 November). The virtually ceaseless electoral conflicts of 1932 really enabled the NSDAP to play their trump card for the first time. 'With incomparable zeal the National Socialists joined the election campaigns and surpassed anything previous in the way of agitation in Germany.'[3]

In technical respects, too, the NSDAP put the past in the shade. The first use of aircraft for the quick propaganda sortie enabled Hitler to speak in forty-six towns during two one-week 'flights over Germany' in the election campaign of April 1932, and in fifty urban mass meetings during the fourteen-day-long third 'flight over Germany' in July 1932. The sensational aspect of this propaganda, duly registered by the critical or foreign press, was already driving hundreds of thousands to Hitler meetings and made the Führer of the NSDAP seem the most dynamic figure in German politics. Under these conditions those suggestive displays at Hitler's meetings which had already been tried out in the previous years reached their climax. Everywhere the local Party organizations with their uniformed units made a striking picture of a determined retinue, and with decorative flags, music and introductory speakers this ensured the ideal limelight for Hitler to appear as the prominent Führer and provided the perfect setting for his skills as a demmagogue.

The development of the NSDAP into a mass movement, providing Hitler with the opportunity to make himself known to the wider public in one election campaign after the other, putting him in direct contact with large audiences as the superior propagandist of the movement, first brought the Hitler myth to its full bloom. It was only now that Hitler achieved a popular mass acclaim far beyond the Party and this in turn directly affected his standing in the Party. Here too it strengthened the Hitler aura, the Führer Byzantinism and absolutism in place of the political *camaraderie*. Indicative of this was the fact that from 1929/30 the greeting and battle formula 'Heil Hitler!', first introduced by Goebbels in Berlin, established itself within the Party.

Such a development to a national party and the electoral tactics, which were deliberately aimed at the mass of middle-class rural voters as well as the army of industrial workers particularly hit by the crisis (especially the unemployed and white-collar workers), entailed a certain change of propaganda. Thus, as is often overlooked, the essential *völkisch*, anti-semitic elements of the ideology were clearly underplayed in comparison with the early life of the NSDAP's, even in Hitler's big election speeches, as well as in the NSDAP's, main organ, the *Völkischer Beobachter*. What was much more prominent after 1929/30 was the massive defamation of the government as a fraudulent and bankrupt jobbing system in the pay of the Western Powers who were intent on milking Germany and enslaving it, and in addition the hate-filled character assassination of the Marxist parties. The main work of the *völkisch* and racial theorist, National Socialist philosopher Alfred Rosenberg first published in 1930, *The Myth of the Twentieth Century*, really appeared at an inconvenient time and was all the less welcome to Hitler in that it gave the Church and the Centre Party a renewed opportunity to point to the fundamental anti-Christian attitudes of National Socialism. In fact the NSDAP was particularly at pains during the Republic's final years to prove its positive attitude towards Christianity, and by criticizing the atheism of the Marxist parties to win Christian Conservative votes and to commend itself as a coalition party against the Social Democrats to the Centre Party, the DNVP and the liberal middle parties in Land politics (where it was often a matter of school and cultural policy questions). This was also connected with another, hitherto neglected area of National Socialist propaganda: the deliberate spread of agitation to the countryside, especially in Protestant North and East Germany where, as the agitation against the Young Plan had already shown, the unpolitical rural population proved to be a particularly favourable sounding-board.

At the beginning of March 1930, the NSDAP's Reich directorate published a generally pro-farmer programme for agriculture which was directed against 'Jewish economic liberalism'. And the leader of the agrarian policy section of the Party who was appointed at the same time – the *völkisch* agrarian ideologist Richard Walter Darré – energetically went about building up his own 'Agrarian Policy Apparatus' parallel to the Party organization with the help of a network of NSDAP rural agents. After the agricultural crisis, which in Germany preceded the world economic crisis proper, had weakened the traditional electoral attitudes among small farmers, labourers and tenants, the NSDAP was able to break through in the agricultural provinces of North and East Germany with exceptional speed and to become the keenest rival of the hitherto dominant DNVP and the Country People's Party. The development in Schleswig-Holstein was most dramatic, the centre of the first farmers' revolts, where between 1928 and 1930 the DNVP vote fell from 23 to 6.1 per cent, whilst in the same period the NSDAP climbed from 4 to 27 per cent of the electorate. However, the radicalization of the rural population in the NSDAP's favour meant at the same time that there was no radicalization favouring the left. In that respect at least the NSDAP's success in the countryside also served the interests of the conservative and Nationalist estate holders as the 'lesser evil', particularly since the NSDAP hardly pressed in earnest for the idea of land reform contained in the Party Programme of 1920. Here, as in other respects, a deliberately conservative stylization of the NSDAP was more marked after 1929/30, which admittedly did not prevent the Party from also expounding the National Socialism of the Hitler movement in the big towns most affected by mass unemployment.

For the millions of new Hitler voters, who (more for psycholo-

gical reasons than material ones) wanted nothing to do with the
Marxist parties and who overwhelmingly adopted an apolitical,
ultra-nationalist stance, voting for the NSDAP meant not so much
a deliberate acknowledgement of National Socialist ideology as a
rejection of the existing circumstances and the approval of the Hitler movement as probably the strongest force for change. The
NSDAP's typical lack of rational analysis of social and political relations, the lack of clarity and the ambiguity in its Programme,
were thus hardly found to be a disadvantage. On the contrary this
seemed to many to be evidence of flexibility and frankness and
reinforced the hope of individuals and specific groups that the Hitler movement would help precisely to achieve *his* aims, would be
influential in *their* cause. Adapted as it was to given regional and
politico-social relationships with remarkable skill, National Socialist
propaganda knew to an astonishing degree how to appeal to all.
The fact that it was able to demonstrate with the financier Alfred
Hugenberg in Bad Harzburg at the same time as that self-same
Hugenberg was being reviled by the NSDAP's factory cell organization as the most detested figure of reaction, that Hitler's Party preached legality and revolution at the same time, that for one
and the same Party votes came not only from leading members of
the Reich Association of German Industry, the Chairman of the
great Reich Land League, Count Kalckreuth, from Hohenzollern
princes and generals, as well as from workers, students and intellectuals who were anti-capitalist and inclined towards anarchy, was
already being diagnosed by critical contemporaries as an almost inconceivable phenomenon of universal camouflage.

The assumption that those whose economic existence was especially affected by the crisis automatically went over to the NSDAP
(or KPD) must also be qualified. Often the economic depression
was not converted directly into political radicalization but took
astonishing psychological detours. The extent of the economic
damage to the middle classes and petit-bourgeoisie did not just
simply correspond to the degree of susceptibility to the NSDAP.
The NSDAP did not have its greatest successes in the large industrial cities, where most of the unemployed workers and white-collar
groups lived, but in the country and the small towns. Here, in a
setting still governed by traditions, the isolated bankrupt of whom
everybody heard caused more panic than the mass misery in the
big cities, where people were used to different things and in any
case could not share very much in the numerous and anonymous
individual cases. Moreover, it was often not the hardship which
was or was not suffered, but the particularly uncomfortable visible
evidence of grief in the closer milieu of the small towns and villages which provoked the call for drastic solutions. The 'hanging
about' by the unemployed, the rise in crime resulting from this and
other obviously visible manifestations threatening cleanliness, de-

cency and order, were tantamount to a 'Bolshevist state of affairs' in the eyes of not a few self-righteous citizens and made them particularly receptive to National Socialist appeals. These promised the restoration of strict order and in contrast to the 'decay of culture and morals', offered the prospect of a true culture and a healthy body politic.

Given the extreme variety of National Socialist propaganda and political programming, it seems at first striking that there were no noteworthy splits during the *Kampfzeit* (time of struggle); indeed not even the formation of effective internal Party opposition groups. In the last resort, however, the inability to create ideological or political interest fronts within the NSDAP simply confirms that National Socialism was not primarily an ideological and programmatic, but a charismatic movement, whose ideology was incorporated in the Führer, Hitler, and which would have lost all its power to integrate without him. Hitler was never merely the spokesman for an idea that would have had an equivalent importance and existence without him. On the contrary, the abstract, utopian and vague National Socialist ideology only achieved what reality and certainty it had through the medium of Hitler. Thus there could be no effective opposition against Hitler in the name of the National Socialist ideology. Where this was none the less attempted, as for example by Otto Strasser and his mainly intellectual following, the features of the National Socialist ideology, which were composed of emotions, resentments and dreams, were exchanged for an ideology directed towards concrete material action (which was consistent in that respect and naturally permitted no omnipotent Führer) and failed to appreciate the charismatic foundation of the National Socialist movement. It had been far more typical of the general attitude of Party functionaries from the various ancillary organizations of the NSDAP before and after 1933 that however much they thrashed out bitter quarrels amongst themselves they did not as a rule turn against Hitler, but tried to win him over to their respective interpretations of the National Socialist ideology and programme. That is they basically recognized him as the interpreter of the correct 'idea' and did not question his supreme authority to rule on ideological matters too.

The sociology, organization and personnel of the NSDAP; its auxiliary organizations and associations

From the official Party statistics of the NSDAP published in 1935, it appears that between 14 September 1930 and 30 January 1933, the Party had grown from 129,000 to 849,000 members and the number of NSDAP local branches had increased from 1,378 to 11,845 between 1928 and 1932.[4] Women, who played an important role among NSDAP voters, were notably weakly represented in the Party membership with only 5 per cent, which undoubtedly stemmed from the all-male character of the combat party. The share of young men in the NSDAP was much higher. No less than 43 per cent of the total of 720,000 new members joining the Party between 1930 and 1933 were in the 18- to 30-year-old age group, 27 per cent being between 30 and 40. Compared with the middle-class parties, and even with the SPD, the NSDAP was a markedly 'young party'. For the Saxon district of Oschatz-Grimma it was reckoned in the spring of 1931 that Party members in the 18- to 30-year-old age group made up only 19.3 per cent of the SPD, compared with 61.3 per cent for the NSDAP. Similarly, young deputies were also preponderant among the National Socialists in the parliaments (like the Communists). In the Reichstag elected on 14 September 1930, deputies under the age of 40 accounted for only 10 per cent for the SPD, whereas for the NSDAP and KPD parliamentary groups the figures were roughly comparable at around 60 per cent.[5]

Sociologically, the Party's development after 1930 confirmed with relatively slight deviations the composition already characteristic of the NSDAP earlier on. This becomes clear if comparison is made between the social or occupational categories of employed Party members (almost 90 per cent of the total membership)[6] for the period before and after 1930, with the figures or quotas for the corresponding groups of the total employed in Germany.[7] The varied representation of social and occupational groups in the NSDAP is still clearer if the respective quotas are compared with the Party members falling within them (see column 4, Table 2.1).

At first glance the diversified sociological stratification of the NSDAP – its structure as a people's party as it were – is striking. The relatively high share of the middle-class or 'petit bourgeois' social and occupational groups is, however, undeniable. White-collar workers, craftsmen, tradesmen, officials, and those from free professions were, on a percentage basis, about twice as strongly represented in the NSDAP as in the employed total as a whole. The high proportion of farmers in the NSDAP is more remarkable in that the farming population was normally less inclined towards active politics than town dwellers. Compared with its share of the total employed in Germany, the working class was obviously under-represented in the NSDAP, although before 1930 they made up 28 per cent, and between 1930 and 1933 even 33.5 per cent of employed Party members. A more exact analysis of the proportion of workers is not possible because of the lack of statistical data. What is certain, however, is that of the almost 270,000 workers who joined the Party before 1933, between 120,000 to 150,000 were out of work.[8] The regional variations in the proportion of NSDAP membership from the working class are also worth noting. In the

Table 2.1 The sociological structure of the NSDAP prior to 1933 (Figures for employment within the Reich and in the NSDAP according to social and occupational categories)

Those employed	In the Reich (census of 1925)	%	In the NSDAP prior to 14 Sept. 1930	%	Among new NSDAP members (between 14 Sept. 1930 and 30 Jan. 1933)	%	NSDAP members among those employed (prior to 30 Jan. 1933) %
Workers	14 443 000	45.1	34 000	28.1	233 000	33.5	1.9
Self-employed							
(a) Agriculture and forestry (farmers)	2 203 000	6.7	17 100	14.1	90 000	13.4	4.9
(b) Industry and handicraft (artisans and employed in manufacturing)	1 785 000	5.5	11 000	9.1	56 000	8.4	3.9
(c) Trade and commerce (tradesmen)	1 193 000	3.7	9 900	8.2	49 000	7.5	4.9
(d) Free professions	477 000	1.5	3 600	3.0	20 000	3.0	4.9
Public servants							
(a) Teachers	334 000	1.0	2 000	1.7	11 000	1.7	4.0
(b) Others	1 050 000	3.3	8 000	6.6	36 000	5.5	
White collar workers	5 087 000	15.9	31 000	25.6	148 000	22.1	3.4
Domestic employees (mostly female)	5 437 000	17.3	4 400	3.6	27 000	4.9	0.6
Total	32 009 000	100	121 000	100	670 000	100	2.5

industrial, overcrowded areas (for example, in the Rhineland and Westphalia, in Berlin and Upper Silesia) with a high proportion of big concerns and correspondingly a more strongly unionized labour force, the figure was well below average (about 1.5 per cent), whereas in areas with numerous small industries (Saxony, Thuringia and Baden) it was well above average with 2 to 3 per cent.[9]

The sociological picture of the NSDAP would undoubtedly shift still more clearly towards the lower middle class if it were possible to measure the electorate exactly, in terms of social and occupational groups. But what can be taken for granted is that the overwhelming majority of small farmers and cottagers voted NSDAP in 1932.[10] (Agricultural holdings with less than 5 hectares made up about 75 per cent of the over-all total in Germany in 1925, but only one-sixth of the total area!) The same is probably also true of the millions of white-collar workers, annuitants, pensioners, small shopkeepers, and craftsmen who, from an economic viewpoint, often existed at the level of the proletariat but saw themselves as belonging to the middle classes and were therefore psychologically particularly hard hit by the economic crisis.

A sociological analysis of the Party's leaders and functionaries would be just as revealing as that of the membership. Evidence for this can be found only to a very limited extent, but there are some pointers. For the first decade of the NSDAP's history, when the small struggling movement hardly promised the prospect of power and political sinecures, the influx of opportunists, who played an overwhelming role after 1930 and above all in the first months of 1933, was as yet quite insignificant. The then activists, S.A. leaders, local branch leaders and Gau leaders, and Party speakers, joined the Party as believers ready for action. Only rarely were the belief in the ideology and the need for action sharply separated. In any event, given the conditions of the extremist fighting, agitationist Party, which often had to operate illegally, only those who were exceptionally active could establish themselves and endure as leaders and functionaries before 1928/9. In this process, to be sure, different talents and thus different leadership selection processes were demanded of the S.A. and the Political Organization (P.O.) of the Party. In the S.A. the dare-devil, organizer type of group 'commander' was preponderant, recruited from young wartime volunteers (partly former students), officers and Freikorps fighters. Ideological conviction generally played a minor role: the spirit of the combat league and conspirator prevailed. The arrogant self-confidence of many S.A. leaders – exemplified by such men as Walter Stennes, Edmund Heines, Count Helldorf, Manfred von Killinger, August Schneidhuber, and Baron von Eberstein – immunized the S.A. troopers to some extent – as did the often cynical, nihilistic ethos of the all-male association – against Hitler's almost 'feminine' demagogy and suggestivity. Leaders of noble origin were not rare in the S.A. but were virtually absent among the Party's Gauführer.

In the Party Organization, where the chief concern was with the spoken and written word, the officer and mercenary leader type was generally not suitable. Most of the NSDAP Gauführer before 1933 were not quite so young as the S.A. and S.S. leaders. Nearly all of them belonged to the generation of 1890–1900, and therefore had mostly grown up before 1914. Apart from elementary schooling, they generally had had some further education (secondary school, commercial college, teacher-training college, university), but most had little or no professional experience behind them before they fought in the First World War as soldiers or officers. Officers demobilized after 1918, who played a significant role in the S.A., were only exceptionally Gauführer of the NSDAP (Friedrich Wilhelm Loeper, Alfred Meyer, Otto Telschow). By comparison, two categories of vocational training or activity predominated amongst the old Gauführer: former teachers or trainee teachers (Josef Bürckel, Artur Dinter, Paul Hinkler, Rudolf Jordan, Franz Maierhofer, Bernhard Rust, Hans Schemm, Gustav Simon, Julius Streicher, Josef Wagner, Robert Wagner), and commercial clerks, or those engaged in commerce who had had more than just an elementary education (Albert Forster, Josef Grohe, Theo Habicht, Heinrich Lohse, Martin Mutschmann, Fritz Reinhardt, Carl Röver, Josef Terboven). None of the Gauführer was familiar by training or education with the proletarian milieu. Further schooling was much more usual (frequently final examination too) and generally a further vocational or university training which was interrupted by the war. A completed higher education, as with Joseph Goebbels and Robert Ley, was the exception – indeed, an interrupted education was typical. The majority of Gauführer had not returned to the university or to their career after the war but had been active in some or other Freikorps or border defence unit, or had been frustrated in trying to resume their careers. In most cases the wrench from the normal middle-class vocational existence caused by the war and post-war formed the background of those who were active as organizers and leaders in the NSDAP.

The spread of the Party and S.A. organization was essentially achieved from below through the initiative of local and regional Party and S.A. leaders, even in Bavaria and South Germany before 1923 and still more so in West, North, Central and East Germany after 1925. Whoever founded a new local branch of the NSDAP and organized or won through as leader in a larger area before subsequently seeking confirmation from Munich, was generally also recognized as local branch leader or Gauführer. Confirmation by the Party headquarters or by Hitler was indeed obligatory, but in most cases it was a mere formality. The decentralized and in many respects centrifugal build-up of the Party was conditioned among other things after 1925 by the fact that Hitler could not appear publicly in various Länder until 1927, as a result of the ban on his speaking. In any case, as with the later organization of the government of the state, Hitler was basically of the opinion that the best man for the movement was the one who could succeed through his own activity, as well as in any conflict with his rivals. In this respect Hitler also showed virtually unlimited patience over shady practices, denunciations, cases of corruption, etc. Before 1928 it was not rare for local branch leaders to be elected by members of the Party. Hitler did not formally veto this democratic procedure until 1929.

The aggressive agitationist and combative style of the NSDAP, which alone helped it to win certain local victories before 1928/9, the tireless oratory of individual Party activists, as shown in Goebbels's diary of 1925/6, the perennial readiness of the S.A. for demonstrations and marches etc., demanded and favoured a wealth of invention and spontaneity among local National Socialist leaders and branches. The fate of the Hitler movement in the first decade of its existence depended to a considerable degree on the local Party and S.A. matadors, on their abilities or shortcomings. The growing success of the NSDAP in Berlin under Goebbels's lead from 1926/7 was an example of this. It also often happened, however, that a local branch leader failed or a local group was paralysed by personal feuding and discord, which not infrequently led to the members leaving the Party and the collapse of the entire local branch. Party enrolments and resignations, foundations and dissolutions of small local branches were extraordinarily frequent and typical of the NSDAP in this decade.

During this less brilliant period of the *Kampfzeit* the leadership stock of 'old fighters' emerged; those who also later held the top Party posts, above all the positions of Gauleiter. This original stock of local NSDAP worthies, notwithstanding their dependence on Hitler and the Munich party headquarters, enjoyed a relatively strong popular and organizational power base (also in the shape of local leadership cliques and sponsors) and thus considerable freedom of movement. The leadership principle did not entail a strictly hierarchical dependence on above for this old guard. They had pronounced self-confidence, like the S.A. leaders. Here, too, the Hitler cult was kept within limits before 1933. Individual initiative and their own claim to lead played an essential part among the tough, long-serving Party leaders. Therefore it proved extremely difficult, indeed often impossible, to organize the Party more systematically and hierarchically when the mass growth after 1930 demanded such a tighter organization. This also remained a burdensome problem after 1933. At the Gauleiter level in particular, the NSDAP was also represented in later years by leaders who basically stemmed from the fighting years before 1930. They were often hardly pleased by the requirements of the mass Party between 1930 and 1933, let alone with the problems of totalitarian government after 1933. Even in the later phase of the Third Reich, the Hitler state was burdened with these 'old fighters' from the early years of the National Socialist movement in key positions, and Hitler avoided attacking their position. In the Second World War moreover, especially in the occupied territories where Hitler considered that the best method of government was to put in distinguished and energetic satraps, a number of old Gauleiter often wielded even more power in the end (Bürckel, Terboven, Koch, Lohse, Forster). The high-handed exercise of power which thus occurred and which could not be curbed even by Himmler's S.S. and Security Police (most extreme example, the rule of Erich Koch in the Reich Commissionership in the Ukraine from 1941) was almost a return to the practice of the *Kampfzeit* at the beginning of the NSDAP, with the struggle now diverted abroad against the enemies of the race.

The S.A. and its corps of leaders proved to be still more self-willed. After the re-foundation of the NSDAP Hitler was at first determined not to permit the S.A. to function any longer as a relatively independent armed force under its own leadership. There was a break with Röhm over this (1925). When the former National Socialist Gauleiter Franz Pfeffer von Salomon began the new build-up at the end of 1925 as Supreme S.A. leader (*Obersten S.A.-Führer* – OSAF), the aim was to subordinate the S.A. clearly to the Political Organization of the Party (among other things through the now obligatory Party membership for S.A. men). In a series of key S.A. orders, von Pfeffer impressed on the S.A. that in future it was to be the fighting organization of the Party in the first instance, and was to conduct a political 'struggle without weapons', above all through disciplined public demonstrations. In fact this discipline, which was demanded and practised by the Hitler movement's style of demonstration, clashed with the permanent revolutionary tendency of the S.A.

The structural counterpart of this was the conflict between the necessary hierarchical arrangement of the over-all S.A. organization and the continuing cliquish, gang-like character of the lower S.A. units. Here, as from the Freikorps days, the loyalty of the all-male society to the leader was paramount. The criminal jargon and bruiser mentality which is still evident in many of the memoirs of the S.A.'s *Kampfzeit* appearing after 1933,[11] the knuckledusters and other substitute S.A. weapons, the S.A. dives and beer halls in the big towns, all show how much the S.A. bordered on the criminal and developed a gang-like morality.

In spite of the Pfeffer reforms, the latent state of tension between the S.A. and the Political Organization of the Party was not ended. The primacy claimed by the dignitaries of the Political Organization conflicted with the S.A.'s just feeling that they were the real 'fighting troops' of the movement and its most effective part. The maxim that the S.A. man was to fight not to speak, reflected this difference in mentality.

With the movement's growth in numbers and the much changed tactical approach of the Party after 1930, this difference became more pronounced as did the S.A.'s tendency towards autonomous organization. Whilst Hitler's 'legal road' and the collaboration practised with the middle classes and German Nationalists in the various Land and town governments created the illusion of a swing to the right, the S.A. moved to the left after the mass rise in unemployment, and its proletarian element was greatly strengthened, especially in the towns. The charge of bossdom levelled by the S.A. against the Party high-ups was rooted among other things in the opinion of the S.A. leaders that an insufficient share had been allotted to them of the deputies' posts and allowances which had fallen to the NSDAP in the Reich, Länder and municipalities, and that the S.A. was generally accorded shabby financial treatment by the Party Organization. Hitler was only able to resolve severe quarrels between the Berlin S.A., under its leader Captain (retired) Walter Stennes, and the Berlin Party organization under Goebbels in September 1930, through his personal intervention. After the simultaneous resignation of OSAF von Pfeffer, Hitler himself assumed the post of Supreme S.A. Leader in order to bring his personal leadership to bear more on the S.A. too. And from October 1930 an unconditional oath of loyalty was demanded of each S.A. leader to the person of Hitler, the Party Leader and Supreme S.A. Leader. But since the actual exercise of leadership and power of command none the less remained with the S.A. Chief of Staff (Ernst Röhm once more from the beginning of 1931), little was gained, particularly since it was only now that the organizational independence and spread of the S.A. entered its decisive phase.

Whereas in accordance with the all-important electoral propaganda the Party Organization was structured regionally according to *Gaue* which (from 1928) roughly coincided with the thirty-five Reichstag constituencies and alongside each of which were placed S.A. *Gau* detachments, in 1931 Röhm installed ten S.A. Gruppenführer (including Austria) above this level who had no counterpart in the Party's territorial structure. The S.A. Gruppenführer, who invariably commanded in several Gaue, were subordinate only to the S.A. Chief of Staff and to Hitler. At the same time – and this was conditioned to some extent by the enormous growth in membership – the S.A.'s military principle of organization was again reinforced. By setting up in 1929 a special S.A. reserve force (for S.A. members over 40) the S.A. leadership had already ensured that the active cadres were reserved for young men. Apart from this a series of special units had already been set up in 1930: the Motorized S.A., Mounted S.A., Airforce S.A., and Naval S.A. as well as information, pioneer and medical units and in addition the National Socialist Automobile Corps (NSAK). This was renamed the National Socialist Motor Transport Corps (NS-*Kraftfahrer Korps* – NSKK) and at first functioned as a reserve for the motorized S.A. until later (after the Röhm affair) it was combined with the motorized shock units, separated from the S.A. and made autonomous as an 'affiliated task force' of the NSDAP. The setting up of schools for S.A. leaders (S.A.-*Führerschulen*) for example the opening of the S.A.'s Reichsfuhrer school in Munich in 1931, or the S.A. Masterships of the Ordinance, S.A. Kitchens, a series of S.A. Homes and S.A. Relief Organizations (a sort of appeal organization) was also typical of the far-reaching autonomy of the S.A. These establishments became of considerable importance, particularly for the large number of unemployed S.A. members in the big cities. In order to absorb – to some extent at least – the risks of S.A. actions, an S.A. insurance scheme was also set up in 1929, and this was expanded into a general 'NSDAP Relief Fund' in 1930. Against regular insurance contributions (30 pfennigs per month, which was obligatory for S.A. members) the 'Relief Fund' paid out in the event of any death, disablement or damages caused at the Party's instance; it also made solitary benefits payments or regular aid. The 'Relief Fund' quickly became an important Party venture and provided its leader, Martin Bormann, with an influential position in the Party's central financial administration.

In April 1931, after Stennes's dismissal at Röhm's instigation the Berlin S.A. again rebelled. As a result the S.S. appeared for the first time as a sort of internal Party disciplinary executive against rebellious sections of the S.A. under its Berlin Gruppenführer, Kurt Daluege. The Personal Headquarters Guard which Hitler had formed in 1922/3 from reliable and aggressive bodyguards, and which a little later was expanded to the fifty-man strong 'Hitler Assault Squad', was the forerunner of the S.S. Even at that time this Führer-Garde came into being because Hitler was not one hundred per cent sure about the S.A., whose supervision he had to share with officers who were not of Nazi provenance. Hitler operated at the head of his 'Assault Squad' in the crucial days of 8/9 November 1923, and old members of the 'Assault Squad' made up the core of the Headquarters Guard which was again set up in Munich in the spring of 1925. Following this pattern, teams of ten were also created in other local branch groups to protect Party leaders and Party meetings, which from the late summer of 1925 were designated 'Guard Detachments' (*Schutzstaffeln* – S.S.) and furnished with the same insignia which the 'Assault Squad' once had (black ski-caps with a skull and black-bordered swastika arm-bands).

After the re-founding of the S.A., however, the build-up of the S.S. was not continued at first. It stagnated under changing leadership (Schreck, Berchtold, Heiden) with only a few hundred members before 1928. OSAF von Pfeffer even managed to get the Reich S.S. Leader subordinated to the Supreme S.A. Leader.

Numbering about 10,000 at the end of 1929, the S.S. only assumed rapidly growing importance with the appointment of Heinrich Himmler as the new Reich S.S. Leader (6 January 1929). Servile, but exceptionally industrious and eager, Himmler, who had been particularly devoted to the *völkisch* agrarian ideology of the race, blood and soil theory, methodically went about transforming the bodyguard's old code of honour to a specifically S.S. order and élitist ideal and issued strict conditions of enlistment and service for the S.S. The more rapidly the S.A. became a brown mass army with a marked proletarian strain after the flood of new members from 1929/30, the more the 'black' S.S. filled the role of the Party élite, which now attracted former officers, failed academics or the nobility.

Hitler's watchword after the suppression of the Berlin S.A.'s rebellion in April 1931 – 'S.S. man, thy loyalty is thine honour' – became the basic code of the S.S. and of its future task as a sort of security police force within the Party. True, the Reich S.S. Leader remained nominally subordinate to the S.A. Chief of Staff (until 1934). The former could, however, from then on appoint S.S. leaders on his own initiative. More significant, however, was the fact that the S.S., to which the special protection of higher Party leaders as well as Hitler's meetings had already been entrusted (from this arose later the S.S. 'Adolf Hitler Bodyguard Regiment') began in August 1931 to build up its own intelligence service (*Sicherheitsdienst* – SD – security service) under Reinhard Heydrich, the intelligence officer discharged from the Navy. At first this competed with similar confidential information and intelligence services, which had been built up before by various NSDAP Gau directorates, as well as with those inside the S.A. to spy out hostile forces, and in the Reichswehr. However, after the activity of the S.A. intelligence network was largely uncovered and thus much devalued by various indiscretions and finally by the police seizures after the ban on the S.A., the monopoly of intelligence services passed to the S.S. in the summer of 1932. In January 1932 the latter had also been assigned to give security cover for the Brown House in Munich.

Himmler's effort to make the S.S. into a Party élite had achieved an important success with this monopoly of the intelligence services. The same basic idea was served by setting up a race office (later, the Race and Settlement Office) within the Reich S.S.

leadership in January 1932. The agricultural expert, Darré, who was installed in the NSDAP's headquarters from June 1930, became leader of this office. He had recommended himself to the Reich S.S. Leader as a soul mate though his *völkisch*-racist blood-and-soil theories. From this personal union there later developed the S.S. monopoly of National Socialist race and settlement policy.

But the development into a mass movement also had lasting consequences for the Party Organization. The NSDAP was hardly left untouched by its dependence on electoral success after 1930. The opportunistic virtuosity of its propaganda, which skilfully buttered up heterogeneous interests, resulted in the NSDAP itself expanding to become a multi-interest concern.

The 'Hitler Youth' also belonged to the old associations. It emerged in 1926 from a branch of the 'Pan German Youth' and, like the S.S., was under the S.A. Chief of Staff (founder and for many years leader of the Hitler Youth, Kurt Gruber; from 1931 the former leader of the National Socialist Student League, Baldur von Schirach). Then there were the many new auxiliary formations of the NSDAP from 1929/30, which in each case became the focal point and expression of specific vocational and socio-economic groups and their respective ideologies. The first of such formations, the 'League of National Socialist German Lawyers', had been formed in October 1928 by the young Munich lawyer Dr Hans Frank, the defender of Hitler in his political trials (from May 1936, the National Socialist Law Officers' League). This organization also published its own journal, the monthly *Deutsches Recht*, to propagate the *völkisch*-National Socialist 'renewal of law'. Three further foundations followed in 1929: the 'Combat League for German Culture', under Alfred Rosenberg, the 'National Socialist German Physicians League', from 1932 under Dr Gerhard Wagner's leadership, and the National Socialist's 'League of Teachers' under the Gauleiter of the Bavarian East March, Hans Schemm, who from August 1929 also brought out the journal *'Nationalsozialistische Lehrerzeitung'*. However, the special National Socialist organizations which arose within agriculture and the working classes in 1930 achieved far greater importance.

In view of the special hopes which the NSDAP attached to the farmers and agriculturalists, it was typical that instead of creating a special National Socialist farmers' organization they adopted a different but ultimately successful course. The NSDAP's 'Agrarian Policy Apparatus', built up by Darré, was not a separate auxiliary Party formation but rather an integral part of the Party Organization, with its system of Gau, Kreis and local branch technical advisers and rural agents. With the aid of the Agrarian Policy Apparatus, which was solidly built up in the rural areas, the NSDAP took on the appearance of a farmers' party. Apart from the weekly published by Darré from September 1931, the *National-*

sozialistische Landpost, agricultural supplements of the NSDAP's Gau papers served to conduct a carefully orchestrated agrarian propaganda. From the outset this was geared not only to winning National Socialist votes in the countryside, but just as much to the infiltration by NSDAP members of the existing agricultural associations, above all the Reich Land League and the Chambers of Agriculture.

The watchword of Hitler and Darré in 1931, 'Into the Reich Land League', brought astonishingly rapid success, after bitter quarrels with the Christian National Farmers' and Country People's Party and with the German National People's Party. At the end of 1931 the Reich Land League, led by Count Kalckreuth, appointed Darré's deputy Werner Willikens as its president. At the elections to the Chambers of Agriculture at the end of 1931, National Socialist candidates got on average over a third of the new members' seats. And from the spring of 1932, the Reich Land League was already openly siding politically with the National Socialists. During the second round of the Reich presidential elections it supported Hitler, not Hindenburg. Finally it headed the agrarian *fronde* which in the winter of 1932/3 pressured Hindenburg to drop Schleicher and appoint Hitler as Reich Chancellor. National Socialist infiltration of the agricultural organizations and self-governing bodies before 30 January 1933 had already gone further than in any other sector of society.

It is all the more astonishing then that at the same time the NSDAP also managed to gain a foothold on the left among the working class and created a workers' section of the Party in the form of the National Socialist Factory Cells Organization (NSBO). The setting up of trade unions was approved in itself after 1925/6, in the context of discussions on the interpretation of National Socialism, particularly by the left wing of the NSDAP in the North-West, and was included in the conception of a future anti-capitalist, corporatist social order under National Socialism, although the Marxist orientation of trade unions was denounced.

Admittedly, Hitler refused to agree to the idea of setting up distinct National Socialist unions, which had been repeatedly discussed at Party congresses since 1926, but the notion stayed in being as a result of the Party's growth, which also increased the number of workers in the NSDAP.

Cells set up by Party members in various large factories in Berlin in 1927/8, first in the Knorr-Bremse A.G., at Siemens, Borsig, the AEG and the Berlin Transport Company, were the starting point of a National Socialist employees' organization. These early National Socialist factory cells, which were soon copied in the Ruhr area, Saxony and elsewhere, were at first largely made up of foremen, skilled workmen and other white-collar workers opposed to the proletarian Marxist unions. The anti-Marxist stance was integral to the origins of National Socialist factory cells. However, as a result of the economic crisis and mass unemployment, which sharpened social conflicts generally, the National Socialist factory cells also increasingly came under anti-capitalist and Socialist influences.

Events in Berlin pioneered later developments. Here, on the key initiative of the talented young organization manager of the Berlin Gau, Reinhold Muchow, a 'Secretariat for Workers' Affairs' was established within the Gau directorate and at the same time Muchow was appointed by Goebbels as head of the proposed National Socialist factory organization. As with his model for the Berlin Party organization, later adopted by the NSDAP generally (setting up street cells and footholds), Muchow also based his National Socialist activity in the factories on the principle that characterized Red Trade Union organization, that of building cells on a political and propagandist basis, by which means the dominance of the Social Democratic Free Trade Unions was to be ended. The great success of the Berlin experiment, which was strongly supported by the Party's Reichsorganisationsleiter, Gregor Strasser, eventually also persuaded Hitler to sanction the new employees' organization. The fact that in the spring of 1931 numerous factory council elections were imminent, in which the National Socialist factory groups obviously wanted to take part, made matters more urgent and resulted in a 'Reich Factory Cell Division' (RBA) based on the Berlin model being set up within the Party's Munich headquarters under Gregor Strasser, and the 'National Socialist Factory Cell Organization' (NSBO) was recognized as the Party's employees' organization. Its fortnightly journal, *Arbeitertum: Blätter für Theorie und Praxis der NSBO*, published by Muchow appeared from March 1931 onwards.

By the end of 1931 the number of NSBO members rose to 39,000 and by mid-1932 to 100,000. The way was shown by Berlin, where in 1932 under the slogan 'No work place without a Nazi place' (*'Keine Arbeitstelle ohne Nazizelle'*) Goebbels had proclaimed a large-scale action ('Into the factories') and the resolute struggle against 'factory Marxism'.[12] The most convinced exponent of the new wave of National Socialism remained, however, Gregor Strasser, who in his Reichstag speech of 10 May 1932 effectively expressed the 'anti-capitalist' longing of the masses affected and hurt by the économic crisis.

Although the NSBO, which saw itself as the 'S.A. of the factories' was of only marginal importance in the factories until 1933, when compared with the millions of members of the Free Trade Unions, it represented a very strong and active force within the NSDAP. The right to strike recognized in principle by the NSBO, National Socialist participation under its influence in various local and regional strikes in 1932 – during which the NSBO made common cause with the Communists, for example during the strike against the Berlin Transport Company (3–8 Nov. 1932) – also the fact that individual Communists had already gone over to the activist NSBO and that in the NSBO itself and in the 'work force' there was some very pronounced and aggressive talk about 'reaction' and 'capitalism', all these things re-awakened the worries of the middle class and German Nationalist fears about the 'Socialist' tendencies of the NSDAP in 1931/2.

Shortly before Hitler's take-over of power a 'National Socialist Combat League for the Commercial Middle Classes' was set up on the pattern of the NSBO under Adrian von Renteln, which increased still more the multiplicity of socio-political auxiliary Party organizations.

The special position of the S.A., the S.S. and the Hitler Youth, and the proliferation of Party auxiliary organizations show that Hitler's personal leadership of the over-all movement, which was hardly ever seriously questioned politically, did not guarantee the institutional and administrative unity of the Party apparatus. On the contrary, it was evident from early on that with the sort of leadership based on Hitler's *person* and not on his *office* as Party Chairman, the resulting structures (the clientele, the clique or the Führer guard) often violated the principles of a rational, bureaucratic administration and organization.

The structure of leadership, the personnel and the offices of the NSDAP's Reich Directorate

After the chairmanship of the NSDAP passed to Hitler, some of his closer circle took over the business of managing the NSDAP in Munich: his former Sergeant Max Amann as the Party's secretary general (later head of the Party's own Eher-Verlag); Militia Second Lieutenant Franz Xaver Schwarz as treasurer, later Reich treasurer of the NSDAP; Philipp Bouhler at first as business manager of the *Völkischer Beobachter* and later as secretary general of the Party (and from 1934 Head of the 'Führer's Chancellery'), and Rudolf Hess, the student captivated by 'his Führer', as personal secretary. Here Hitler was dealing with a circle of people who willingly subordinated themselves to him and more or less confined themselves to the business of administration but whose importance continually increased with the Party's growth. This goes a long way towards explaining the loyalty of the original management clique, which proved to be more durable than Hitler's relationship with many politically influential and ambitious Gauführer and S.A. leaders.

Hitler was all the more dependent on the loyalty and conscientiousness of the Party secretariat because he personally bothered little with regular office administration, but alongside the NSDAP's real place of business he developed a way of holding personal court, displaying a remarkable mixture of the bohemian and mercenary leader. Hitler's need to go about with artist friends and acquaintances like 'Putzi' Hanfstaengel or the photographer Heinrich Hoffman, or with dubious, often spurious contacts with the 'great world' at home and abroad, like Kurt Luedecke; or to be pampered by the ladies in the salons of leading social circles; to drive about the countryside in fast cars or to withdraw to the holiday bliss of the Haus Wachenfeld near Berchtesgaden – all this stemmed from his old habit of loafing about. This side of him – Austrian, southerner, and combat league leader – expressed itself in his desire to have personal attendants, bodyguards and drivers around him (mostly people of a simple disposition, including Julius Schaub, who served as adjutant until 1945, and of Bavarian origin) and in his desire to maintain a personal security force. From early on, Hitler's half private, half political staff clashed with the Party Chairman's official co-workers. But Hitler's personal leadership also markedly affected the organization of the Party directorate.

The NSDAP rules of association which were registered in the Munich District Court on 30 June 1926 confirmed that the sole chairman, Hitler, could lead the Party independently of majority decisions of the managing board and of committees. On the other hand, the responsibility of the chairman to the general meeting of NSDAP members which the rules specified was of purely nominal significance. But even the collegiate principle of the six committees of the Party directorate referred to in the rules (for propaganda, Party organization, finance, youth organization, S.A., investigation and arbitration), each with its respective chairman and members, was in practice illusory. The committees' functions were in fact subsequently taken over by Amtsleiter appointed by Hitler (from 1933: Reichsleiter). Only the Investigation and Arbitration Committee (*Untersuchungs- und Schlichtungsausschuss* – Uschla), forerunner of the later NSDAP Party court (from 1 June 1934), remained collegiate in name and organization.

The appointment of central Amtsleiter for special Party duties practically amounted to a delegation of the leadership principle and meant that the Party was fragmented vertically in terms of personnel and centred on individuals. It was typical that very often Gregor Strasser did not exercise his powers as Amtsleiter for propaganda (1925–8) and for Party organization (1928–32) from Munich, the seat of the Party's Central Office, any more than Goebbels did his office as Chief of Propaganda (from 1929). Liaison between the top Amtsleiter was guaranteed neither by locale nor institution, but in the last resort only through personal contact with Hitler.

The resulting lack of coherence in the top Party leadership, inexperienced as it was in joint meetings and collective decision-making, was a characteristic feature of the NDSAP's leadership structure. An NSDAP 'Reich directorate', in the sense of an authoritative collegiate body, had only ever existed in theory. Apart from the Party's offices, with the central membership roll and the Party treasury, which always remained centralized in Munich and formed the core of the Party leadership's bureaucracy, the individual Amtsleiter simply operated within their own sphere of influence, whether larger or smaller, departmental or personal in origin. Co-ordination between them remained a more or less insoluble problem.

Their subordination to Hitler was the key, not the administration of the office. It was characteristic of the NSDAP (and here the difference is obvious between the National Socialist principle of leadership and the hierarchical principle in the civil service and the military) that the concept of 'duty', which always meant also an acceptance of the rules and laws of the administration, was evidently secondary to the concept of the 'loyalty' of a personal – and in the last resort blind – following. But the 'Führer absolutism' of individual Party big-wigs also first derived from this process. Provided there was no doubt about their loyalty to Hitler, and as long as Hitler himself did not decide otherwise, they had far-reaching opportunities for decision-making and initiative within their own preserves. Compared with this, Party orders and rules often carried little weight. The movement rested primarily on a mesh of inter-personal relations, and therefore at every level of the Party Organization there were forms of clientele and a system of cliques similar to those at the Party summit; and relations between individuals were far more important (including personal patronage, rivalries and feuds) than within any normal, hierarchically structured bureaucratic apparatus. Since the rules of procedure were secondary, the actual selection of personnel and the allocation of personnel in the most important positions of power determined the ultimate constitutional realities both within the Party and later within the governmental structures of the Hitler state.

Naturally, some tightening up of the organization and bureaucracy of the NSDAP was unavoidable as it became a mass party. This was least noticeable in the Gaue, differing considerably in extent and population, where the power and endurance of the old Gauführer was strongest. Here the situation remained much as it was at the time of the provisional distribution of the Gaue in October 1928. On the other hand the intermediary level of the Kreis (and Kreisleiter) was introduced in 1931/2. In contrast to the Gaue the 850 NSDAP Kreise were almost invariably congruent with the lower state administrative areas. A further rearrangement and concentration was carried out in summer 1932. Thereafter the local branches or – in the towns – the local branch sections (maximum limit 500 Party members) were for the time being divided into various 'supports' and these were in turn subdivided into house or street blocks. In addition, closer collaboration and supervision of the Party Organization was intended with the setting up in the summer of 1932 of two Reich Inspectors (subordinate to the Reichsorganisationsleiter), each with 5 Land Inspectors under them for their respective territories. Lieutenant Paul Schulz, who had caused a stir in the early 1920s as the organizer of various political assassinations, operated as Reich Inspector I; Reich Inspector II was Dr Robert Ley, who had exchanged his office as Gauleiter of the Rhineland for more central organizational tasks in the Reich directorate in Munich in 1931.

The fact that especially deserving or experienced Gauleiter were appointed Land Inspectors (Rust, Lohse, Loeper, Goebbels, Brückner, Mutschmann, Sprenger, Haake, and Ley; for Austria, Theodor Habicht) itself reveals the difficulty of this attempt at centralization. These men were inevitably regarded as irksome spies and rivals by the Gauleiter in those areas of their inspectorate which were not also within their own Gaue. Symptomatic also of the weakness of the Reich and Land Inspectors was the ruling that Kreisleiter could only be removed from office with the confirmation of the Reichsorganisationsleiter, and that Gauleiter could only be displaced by Hitler himself. Here it was again obvious that there was basically no powerful central Party authority between the omnipotent Führer and the Gauleiter. The imposing outer façade of the Party headquarters in Munich, which at the beginning of 1931 moved from the office in the Schellingstrasse to the 'Brown House' converted from the Barlow-Palais near the Königsplatz by Hitler's architect Troost, reflected little real power.

For all this, there was a tightening of central control in the particularly crucial area of Party finances and a greater degree of bureaucratic regularity was achieved. A legally attested order of Hitler's of 16 September 1931, which authorized the treasurer Schwarz to assume the complete control and representation of all the Party's financial affairs, gave Schwarz a formal basis at law. This made it easier for him to keep a closer watch over the Party funds of the Gaue and affiliated associations through his auditors, to introduce uniform book-keeping, to press energetically for the prompt payment of membership dues and, by instructing and training the Gau treasurers, to move towards a sounder bureaucratic financial management.

The Reich treasurer's circulars to the leadership of the Gaue from 1930 to 1937 reveal, however, that the goal of achieving a reliable and uniform financial administration for the Party was still very remote. Subjects of standing complaints and admonition were: the misappropriation of Party money by Gauleiter or Gau treasurers, and above all the unauthorized use of the Party headquarters' share of membership dues by local branches; the holding of unauthorized collections through the associations and lower Party organs; and the high-handed transaction of legal business and property deals by the Gauleiter, who often referred to a personal authorization from Hitler. Even in his statement of accounts of 27 January 1933, Schwarz had to report that, of a total of 34 Gau authorities, only eleven of them paid their subscriptions more or less promptly, whereas all the others were 'often three months and more in arrears with their settlement'.

One special area where such conflicts flared up strongly was that of the Party press. The aim of the Party headquarters was to increase the circulation of the NSDAP's central organs, especially the *Völkischer Beobachter*, as well as that of the *Illustrierter Beobachter*, which from 1926 appeared weekly with Hitler's political commentary, and to develop a centrally controlled Party press on a solid financial footing.[13] As against this, numerous new but generally poorly published and very often heavily indebted regional Party newspapers appeared from 1929/30, from Gau publishers or private National Socialist publishers. The total of 59 dailies which appeared in 1932, either as official NSDAP Gau organs or as National Socialist papers recognized by Party headquarters, achieved in all only a total circulation of some 780,000.[14] It is evident from this that National Socialism informed only a very small sector of the German press and the picture was overwhelmingly one of a rather inadequate, hole-in-the-corner press.

Compared with the NSDAP's Munich central publishing house (Eher-Verlag), which began to develop into a modern and viable concern between 1930 and 1933[15] under Max Amann's skilled management, and which began to take pains with the editorial quality and appearance of its publications, the National Socialist press at the Gau level presented a picture of poverty-ridden improvisation. Judging by this local press, the mass Party of the National Socialists gave the impression not of a united and large organization but rather of a collection of small provincial organizations.

The Party headquarters' press office, set up in the spring of 1932 under Otto Dietrich (a former editor of the pan-German Nationalist *Nationalzeitung* in Essen), published a 'National Socialist Party correspondence' which tried to achieve better reporting in the Party press. But at first it could no more change things than could Amann's attempt to use economic means to break the independence of the Gau publishers to benefit the Eher-Verlag. In other respects, the coexistence of both functions (Dietrich, directly responsible to Hitler as Director of the Reich press office of the NSDAP, Amann from 1932 as Amtsleiter for the Press within Party headquarters) was a pattern for ill-defined and overlapping appointments in the Party directorate, from which a still more significant demarcation conflict was to develop in the future.

The same was true for other parts of the Reich 'directorate'. To begin with this consisted of the governing board of the NSDAP, comprising apart from Hitler as the 'chairman of the National Socialist German Workers' Association e.V' (e.V – registered society), only the treasurer (Schwarz) and the secretary (Fiehler). At the same time the Party directorate functioned as a central Party administration, with separate offices, departments and sections as well as a personal staff attached to Hitler. The two functions were never clearly defined. Those exclusively belonging to Hitler's personal staff were his private secretary, Rudolf Hess, the head of the private secretariat, Albert Bormann (a brother of Martin Bormann), and Hitler's adjutant, Wilhelm Brückner. In addition there was Otto Dietrich in his capacity as Hitler's press chief. By contrast, the Amtsleiter worked in the top Party authorities. To the Amtsleiter posts already foreseen in the Party rules of 1926, i.e. that of the treasurer (Schwarz), of the Reichsorganisationsleiter (Strasser), of the Reich chief of propaganda (Goebbels), of the S.A. Chief of Staff (Röhm), of the Reich Youth Leader (von Schirach), of the Chairman of 'Uschla' (Bach) and of the Party secretary general (Bouhler), there were added in 1932: Hans Frank as head of the Legal Policy Division (RPA – *Rechtspolitischen Abteilung*), the Party's financial expert, Fritz Reinhardt, as Propaganda Chief II (for economic, work-creation propaganda among other things), Max Amann as 'Amtsleiter for the Press'.

In so far as the Amtsleiter did not command their own Party formation (like Röhm or Schirach), they could only exercise their actual right of giving orders with the help of the Gauleiter. Like the Gau and Kreis treasurers, the legal advisers, the press and propaganda section leaders in the Gaue and Kreise were all under whomever happened to be top man (Gauleiter or Kreisleiter) and it was only through these that they received their instructions from the Party directorate. In that respect the Amtsleiter for propaganda, legal matters and the press were the only section leaders of the Party central office who happened to be entitled to give orders, without a vertically organized departmental administration and corresponding power of command of their own. As to their actual political power, they were no different from the heads of the specialist sections or divisions which had been set up after 1929/30, partly in the Reich directorate (within the framework of Reich Organizational Division II), partly alongside the NSDAP's parliamentary group, and which had the task of providing centralized information and advice on various political subjects for the Party leadership and National Socialist parliamentary factions, as well as evolving and presenting National Socialist proposals for reform or guidelines for propaganda.

Many of these sections or divisions became far more important after 1930/1 than the departments of individual Amtsleiter. That was particularly true of Darré's Agrarian Policy Section and the Reich Factory Cell Division under Walter Schumann and Reinhold Muchow, which was subordinated to Reichsorganisationsleiter Strasser.

The new arrangement of the Party directorate and Party Organization, which was made at Gregor Strasser's suggestion in the summer of 1932, was detailed in the 'Official Regulations of the Political Organization of the NSDAP' of 15 July 1932, which tried to take into account more the actual importance of the individual offices, divisions and sections and to achieve at least a measure of co-operation between them. On the basis of this reform all the specialist departments of the Party directorate were in practice put under the Reichsorganisationsleiter. The only independent Amtsleiter to remain were the treasurer, the Party secretary general, the chairman of Uschla, the S.A. Chief of Staff, the director of the Eher-Verlag and – characteristically – the Reich Chief of Propaganda (Goebbels). His relations with Strasser after 1927 were extremely tense and he had meanwhile achieved a clear direct relationship to Hitler both as Gauleiter of the Reich capital and because of his skill at propaganda.

On the basis of this reorganization the Reich Inspectorates I and II figured as central divisions I and II of the Party's organization. The Agrarian Policy Apparatus and the NSBO were promoted to independent central divisions V and XI in keeping with their strong positions, and the various economic advisers and their staffs were grouped together to form a special central division (IV). All the other former Amtsleiter departments and sections within the Party directorate were amalgamated as central division III, which henceforth consisted of twelve mixed divisions: internal policy, legal policy, municipal policy, civil service policy, education, care of war victims, women's work, national health, Germans abroad, technical engineering, press, and navigation.

In practice the arrangement of central division III was merely a nominal combination on paper of separate Party posts and activities, which were hardly connected. To some extent the heads and co-workers of the divisions concerned were not even based in Munich. This was particularly true of the division for Germans abroad, a foundation dating from 1931 for regular contacts with the local branch groups which had arisen some years earlier amongst the Reich Germans in South America and elsewhere. Strasser had handed over the leadership of this improvised office to the Hamburg Gauorganisationsleiter and Reichstag deputy Dr Hans Nieland, who was active in the Reichstag as an expert on those of German stock abroad and who managed the new division from Hamburg, from which the NSDAP's Foreign Organization (*Auslandsorganisation*-AO) emerged in 1933 (under Ernst Wilhelm Bohle). Thus Nieland's jurisdiction overlapped throughout with

other positions and personalities in the NSDAP's Reich directorate. Apart from Danzig and Austria, where the NSDAP was
directly attached to the Political Organization's Reich directorate,
with its own Gaue and Inspectorates, contact with Reich German
National Socialists in Switzerland and Italy was also taken care of
directly from Munich, whilst a special 'Group East' existed under
Karl Motz within central division V for relations with Reich Germans and ethnic Germans in East Europe. But Goebbels too had a
sub-section in Berlin for the news service to Germans abroad in his
capacity as Reich Chief of Propaganda.

Similarly, the civil service policy division was organized outside
Munich (based in Frankfurt) by the Gauleiter of Hesse, Jakob
Sprenger. Sprenger, who had himself been a middle-grade post
office official and from 1929 Frankfurt town councillor and was
already recognized as the Party's expert on the civil service after
1930, had managed a loose organization of civil servants within the
NSDAP from Hesse and from 1932 he also brought out from
Frankfurt the *Nationalsozialistische Beamten-Zeitung*. Admittedly,
even in the summer of 1932, it was apparent that Sprenger met
with strong opposition over questions of future National Socialist
civil service policy from other prominent advisers. One of these was
Hans Pfundtner, a confidant of Hugenberg, who in June 1932 had
sent a memorandum on 'The administrative measures of a National
government in the Reich and in Prussia' to leading National Socialists and who, as the new state secretary in the Reich Ministry of
the Interior under Dr Wilhelm Frick in 1933, really influenced the
civil service policy measures of Hitler's government.

Karl Fiehler's position as head of the municipal policy division
was relatively uncontested. As a former government white-collar
worker and for many years town councillor in Munich, who became Oberbürgermeister in 1933, Fiehler provided a particularly
welcome experience of municipal politics and know-how within the
Party managing board.

Hanns Oberlindober, the National Socialist town councillor from
Straubing, who was severely injured in the War, also came from
the 'old guard' of the Bavarian NSDAP. He was active as a platform speaker and a Reichstag deputy (from 1930) before he became the expert for the care of War victims. The National Socialist
paper which he put out from 1932, *Der Dank des Vaterlandes*,
provided the basis of the special organization he founded in 1933,
'National Socialist War Victims', in which the various German War
victim organizations were eventually integrated.

A new foundation of 1932 was the technical engineering division,
under Fritz Todt, the road-building expert and Hitler's later autobahn builder, who had come across the NSDAP in 1931 and belonged from joining the Party to the staff of the top S.A. leadership. Here too in 1933 a new National Socialist auxiliary orga-

nization, the 'National Socialist League of German Technology', was to develop from the Party office.

It was the other way round with the division for national health, which was first set up on account of the earlier 'National Socialist League of Physicians'. Other medical men in the Party were already playing an important role before 1933 alongside its chief, the Munich physician, Dr Gerhard Wagner. Among others were the Wandsbeker public health officer, Dr Arthur Gütt, a member of the S.S. Race and Settlement Office, whom Frick had made section leader for population policy and the protection of inheritance and the race (1934 ministerial director and head of the division for national health) in the Reich Ministry of the Interior.

Similarly, the setting up of a division for women's work stemmed from an existing auxiliary Party organization, 'National Socialist Womanhood' (formerly the 'Order of German Women') founded in October 1931 under Elsbeth Zander.

The position of the man appointed as head of the internal policy division, Dr Hellmuth Nicolai, was more important but also more problematic. Dr Nicolai had already been prominent for some years through a series of writings on the renewal of constitutional law 'according to natural laws'. He had been dismissed from the Prussian civil service (Oppeln government) and from April 1932 had been National Socialist deputy in the Prussian Landtag. With his relatively concrete reform proposals he proved himself – like Frick – to be one of those administration lawyers in the Party who, irrespective of their racial theories of law and their rejection of the existing state form, postulated a future National Socialist state organized on clear constitutional lines, and thus sooner or later conflicted with Hitler's state practice.

The equally important division for education was headed by Dr Rudolf Buttmann, the leader of the National Socialist parliamentary group in the Bavarian Landtag. Yet his nominal leadership cannot disguise the fact that very different spirits were also active as politico-cultural exponents of the Party. Among them were the leader of the National Socialist League of Teachers, Hans Schemm, who became Bavarian Minister of Culture in 1933 (fatally injured in March 1933); the Hannoverian Gauleiter, assistant master Bernhard Rust (1933, Prussian Minister of Culture); the Prussian Landtag deputy Hans Kerrl (1933, Prussian Minister of Justice; 1935, Reich Church Minister) as the representative of those Protestants who believed in the 'positive Christianity' of National Socialism; Alfred Rosenberg, who with his '*Myth of the Twentieth Century*' had made himself the spokesman for the anti-Christian National Socialist mythology, which Kerrl and Buttmann completely rejected; and a completely different type, the young intellectual author and Freikorps fighter, Hans Binckel (Berlin), who prior to 1930 had been a close colleague of Otto Strasser and the leader writer of various National Socialist journals published by the Kampf-Verlag, and from 1930 National Socialist deputy in the Reichstag, Goebbels's press chief in the Berlin Gau and a leading member of the 'Combat League for German Culture'. The later division of National Socialist cultural policy into Rosenberg, Goebbels, Rust and Kerrl factions was already foreshadowed here.

The defence policy division of the NSDAP's Reich directorate, previously taken care of by Colonel Konstantin Hierl and the former Freikorps leader and Major-General Franz von Epp, was incorporated with the S.A. staff in 1932. However, Hierl retained the special task of controlling the voluntary National Socialist Work Service, which admittedly was not a National Socialist invention but was specially promoted by the NSDAP from 1930 on defence policy grounds as well as for tackling unemployment.

The real significance of central division IV, with its various economic and socio-political advisers and 'experts', was no less problematic. Nominal control was exercised by Captain Otto Wagener, a former staff officer of the 'Baltic Legion' with long-standing contacts with the S.A. (in autumn 1930 he was temporarily Chief of Staff of the S.A.), who, as owner of a sewing-machine factory in Karlsruhe, had been active in the twenties as a small employer and who from 1930 was adviser to Hitler on S.A. economic questions and managerial matters. Wagener argued for a decisive anti-trade union standpoint and in favour of an 'organic' corporatist relationship between the economy and the authoritarian state. Wagener was less dogmatic than Gottfried Feder, whose economic theories had lost a great deal of their propaganda appeal for the NSDAP after 1930, but he hardly had more to offer. Fritz Reinhard, for example, proved to be more useful. A tax and financial expert, he headed the Gau of Upper Bavaria for two years (1928–30) and went on to become the leading National Socialist spokesman in the budget committee of the Reichstag, and became prominent as an active economic propagandist for the Party (publisher of the material for speeches and director of the NSDAP's school for public speaking).

From 1931 Bernhard Köhler, Walter Funk and Theodor Adrian von Renteln also belonged to the inner circle of Party economic experts. Köhler, an academically trained political economist, had already been associated in 1919/20 with Dietrich Eckart and Gottfried Feder and in 1920 had briefly taken over as leader writer of the '*Völkische Beobachter*'. But like Walter Funk, the economics editor of the rightist *Berliner Börsenzeitung*, Köhler was not drawn into Hitler's or rather the Party directorate's circle of economic experts until 1930. This was through Wagener's mediation. Köhler specialized above all in the propaganda and theory of work-creation policy; he was evidently the main author of the National Socialist 'Immediate Programme' of work creation during the electoral campaign of July 1932. By contrast, Funk, who took over editing the NSDAP's economic correspondence, steered a clearly rightist economic course, whereas von Renteln, the leader of the 'Combat League for the Industrial Middle Classes', was the exponent of a middle-class economic and social policy. In addition the young Dr Max Frauendorffer was the special adviser on corporatist ideas in the Reich directorate from 1931.

How little Hitler conceived the make-up of personnel and allocation of responsibility within the Party directorate's economic division as binding or as laying claim to later state duties was already revealed, however, by an order of 22 September 1932 to set up an NSDAP 'Reich Economic Council' as the 'supreme organ for all economic questions' in the Party. This diminished the importance of central division IV, which was only formally instituted in early Summer 1932. Feder and Funk were appointed first and second chairmen of the Economic Council, to which were also to belong *ex officio* the Reichsorganisationsleiter, the heads of the NSBO and of the Agrarian Policy Apparatus as well as other 'individuals' to be appointed by Hitler.[16] The economic division continued in being but it was in future to be bound by the directives of the Economic Council. Whatever motives led to this order, which subsequently had no particular significance, the Party experts were none the less held in mutual check by such nominal allocation and reallocation of Party political duties, whilst Hitler could keep all his options open in economic matters.

Actually Hitler had also been relying on other advisers for a long time. Among these were the director of the electro-chemical works in München-Höllriegelskreuth, Albert Pietzsch (from 1933 President of the Munich Chamber of Industry and Commerce), who had also given Hitler and the Party financial support after 1923; the General Director of Alliance Insurance, Dr Kurt Schmidt (1933/4, Hitler's Minister of Economics); and from the end of 1931, Wilhelm Keppler, the owner of a photo-chemical factory in Ebersbach (Bavaria), who helped to forge links to the I.G. Farben concern and who played a considerable part in forming amongst industrialists the 'circle of friends' of the NSDAP. It was to this circle that Hitler spoke on 18 June 1932 in the 'Kaiserhof' Hotel in Berlin, when he promised among other things to get rid of the trade unions in the event of a National Socialist seizure of power. In addition there were the personal contacts with prominent leaders of the economy after 1930, including Fritz Thyssen, Schacht and von Stauss, chiefly fostered by Göring from Berlin.

If these personal contacts and the economic mood created by them, as well as the confidential promises, are compared with the official Party pronouncements, a very different picture emerges. National Socialism and anti-capitalism, which still played an important theoretical and propaganda role in the official Party literature,

were at least considerably watered down, if indeed not secretly disavowed, by means of confidential approaches and contacts. In this
respect the lack of power and responsibility of the economic division of the NSDAP's Reich directorate also tended to frustrate
those socialist and social-reformist efforts within the Party which
particularly worried Hitler's future partners in government.

In general the sorry state of the economic division simply expressed in a particularly crass way the thoroughly provisional and,
from the viewpoint of rational bureaucratic Party organization, in-
effectual character of the entire Party directorate. If personal and
political deficiences also played an important role in this, not least
the fundamental programmatic weakness of National Socialism, all
the same there was method behind it. The Party's Reich directorate only achieved the minimum of centralized power that was
absolutely necessary for the guidance and technical management of
the gigantic Party apparatus. Thus there was little possibility of any
accretion of power at the top of this apparatus and Hitler remained
indispensable as the integrator of the Party.

This method became particularly apparent after Hitler's break
with Gregor Strasser in December 1932. From the summer of that
year Strasser had the chance of using the new arrangement of the
Reich directorate to become a sort of general secretary of the Party with comprehensive powers. After his dismissal Hitler immediately dissolved the link between the technical-organizational
and political direction of the Party apparatus which had developed
under Strasser.

Robert Ley, formerly Strasser's deputy and then the new Reichsorganisationsleiter, was clearly confined to the technical organization. Thereafter his power was based primarily not on his position
as the Party's Organisationsleiter but on his supervision of the
NSBO, which was also taken over from Strasser. Simultaneously,
Hitler made the Agrarian Policy Apparatus independent and
appointed Darré as Amtsleiter (later Reichsleiter) of the Party,
whilst all other political supervisory functions (supervision of the
previous central divisions III and IV) went to the newly created
'Political Central Commission', whose direction Hitler did not entrust to a prominent Party leader like Strasser but to his private
secretary, Rudolf Hess. The appointment of the weak Rudolf
Hess, who had no Party power base whatever and who had always
felt himself to be simply his Führer's secretary, made clearer than
anything else that Hitler did not want to see a power-conscious
Party leader at the head of the Party apparatus, but merely a more
or less competent business manager who was, above all, unconditionally loyal to him personally.

The political power vacuum in the Party central office which was
enlarged as a result of this was bound to strengthen still more the
centrifugal force of the individual Party associations and regional

Party organizations and leaders, whilst on the other hand those special favourites and fortunates of Hitler gained controlling influence.

The career of Hermann Göring was characteristic in this respect, for he profited most from Gregor Strasser's exclusion in so far as he now became the undisputed second man after Hitler. After his brief employment as S.A. Chief of Staff (1923) Göring had spent several years abroad (Sweden) and he did not take over any function again until 1928 when he became an NSDAP Reichstag deputy, though without Party office. After the election success of September 1930 he became the deputy leader of the National Socialist parliamentary party in the Reichstag. Thanks to his social contacts and because of his undogmatic bearing and ways he had, however, simultaneously earned for himself the position of Hitler's personal confidant and representative in Berlin, and that was decisive. After 1930/1, Göring arranged most of Hitler's confidential contacts and talks with statesmen, party leaders and influential personalities of public life at home. As early as May 1931 he travelled on Hitler's behalf to Mussolini and the Vatican and, after the hostile pronouncement of the German Bishops, he helped to pave the way for the Pope to take a more benevolent attitude towards National Socialism. Göring, who had already arranged Hitler's first reception with Hindenburg in October 1931, was elected President of the Reichstag in summer 1932. He was increasingly drawn into the political limelight and there was no question that in the event of a National Socialist seizure of power a key position would fall to this political gambler, a man who was as ambitious as he was vain but who undoubtedly had considerable diplomatic and political skill.

Göring's rise was based almost exclusively on personal patronage through Hitler and through the political and personal services which he provided for him (not the Party). The principle and instrument of personal government and personal delegation of power, by which means Hitler sought to govern after his appointment as Reich Chancellor, was already foreshadowed in Göring's career.

Notes and references

1. Werner Maser, *Die Frühgeschichte der NSDAP. Hitlers Weg bis 1924* (Bonn, 1965), pp. 256f.
2. As far as I can tell we still have no reliable figures today. The 'Roll of honour of the movement's dead' later contained in the 'Dates on the history of the NSDAP' edited by H. Volz contains the following figures: 1929, 11; 1930, 17; 1931, 43; and 1932, 87. As the Prussian Ministry of the Interior recorded on 23 November 1932, in the ten days before the Reichstag election of 31 July 1932 in Prussia alone 24

people were killed and 285 injured as a result of political violence, apart from dozens of incidents involving explosives. Deutsches Zentralarchiv (DZA), Merseburg, Rep. 77, tit. 4043, no. 126.

3. Erich Eyck, *Geschichte der Weimarer Republik* (Zurich, Stuttgart, 1956), Vol. 2. p. 443.

4. *Parteistatistik*, ed. by the Reichsorganisationsleiter of the NSDAP (Munich, 1935), vol. 1, p. 16 and vol. 3, p. 175.

5. On the age distribution of the NSDAP cf. *Parteistatistik*, vol. 1, pp. 155ff; on the age distribution of the Reichstag deputies see *Statistik des Deutschen Reiches*, vol. 382, III, p. 11. On this see also David Schoenbaum, *Die Braune Revolution* (Cologne, Berlin, 1968), pp. 68ff.

6. According to the *Parteistatistik* (1935), vol. 1, p. 70, annuitants and pensioners made up 1.7 per cent, housewives 4 per cent, students and pupils, 1.2 per cent, Party members without regular occupations 5.2 per cent.

7. The following statistics are based on the figures contained in the *Parteistatistik* (1935), vol. 1, p. 70 and for comparison the figures are given from the *Statistisches Jahrbuch des Deutschen Reiches* for employed groups in Germany (on the basis of the census of 1925).

8. This figure arises from the fact that according to the *Parteistatistik* (Munich, 1935), vol. 1, p. 304, on 1 January 1933, 60,000 of those Party comrades who had joined before 30 January 1933 were still unemployed. If one takes into account that in that period unemployment in the Reich had fallen from 6 million (end of 1932) to 2.6 million, as well as the fact that after 1933 Party members were often favoured for new jobs, this means that the figure is from two to three times greater for 1932.

9. This arises from the comparison of the numbers of workers in the separate German Länder (*Statistisches Jahrbuch des Deutschen Reiches*) with the numbers of workers among the Party members in the NSDAP Gaue prior to 30 January 1933 (*Parteistatistik*, vol. 1, p. 84).

10. Rudolf Heberle has demonstrated for Schleswig-Holstein that in the areas with mainly small- and medium-farming concerns the proportion of NSDAP votes in 1932 went above 80 per cent in some cases. Cf. Rudolf Heberle, *Landbevölkerung und Nationalsozialismus* (Stuttgart, 1963).

11. Cf. Erwin Reitmann, *Horst Wessel. Leben und Sterben* (Berlin, 1933); or Julius Karl von Engelbrechten, *Eine braune Armee entsteht. Die Geschichte der Berlin-Brandenburger SA* (Munich, Berlin, 1937).

12. Cf. Hans-Gerd Schumann, *Nationalsozialismus und Gewerkschaftsbewegung* (Hannover, Frankfurt-on-Main, 1958), pp. 38ff.

13. The overall circulation of the *VB* rose between 1929 and 1932 from 18,000 to about 120,000. After 1930, when as a result of Otto Strasser's removal the NSDAP's Berlin *Kampfverlag* and the North and Central German National Socialist newspapers (*Der Nationale Sozialist*) edited by Otto Strasser were closed down, a Berlin edition of the *VB* appeared as well as the Munich one.

14. Oron J. Hale, *Presse in der Zwangsjacke 1933–1945* (Düsseldorf, 1965), p. 66.

15. Apart from the official party gazettes the Eher-Verlag also published

most of the National Socialist journals as well as the special editions of the associations and auxiliary organizations affiliated to the Party, thus for example the anti-Semitic journal *Die Brennessel*, the *Nationalsozialistische Landpost*, the *Nationalsozialistischen Monatshefte* (jointly from 1930), the monthly edited by the NSDAP's Reich Chief of Propaganda *Unser Wille und Weg* (from 1931), *Der SA-Mann*, *Arbeitertum* and *Deutsches Recht* (both from 1932).

16. Cf. the text of Hitler's order of 22 September 1932 in *NS-Jahrbuch 1933*, p. 350.

Chapter Three

The monopoly of political power (1933)

Without the shift of power towards the conservative and reactionary groups of the right, long prepared in the Weimar era and also achieved in Prussia through a *coup d'état* by Papen in 1932, and without the simultaneous devaluation of the parliamentary system and the political parties, it would have been barely possible for Hitler to bring about the demise of the multi-party state and to make the National Socialist mass movement into the only political force in Germany.

As far as the disposal of the parliamentary system and the establishment of a durable authoritarian government were concerned, Hitler and his conservative and Nationalist partners in the cabinet were just as much at one as in their determination to dismiss completely from Germany's political life the Communist left and as far as possible Social Democracy too, if need be with force. The policy declaration of the cabinet of 'National Recovery' which was broadcast on the radio on 1 February 1933, left no doubt of this intention. It made the 'Marxist parties' responsible for the shambles in Germany and appealed to the German people to give the new men 'four years'.

How far it would be possible in turn to exploit the weight of the National Socialist mass movement against Hitler's coalition partners depended, of course, on whether the new government remained an emergency and authoritarian cabinet, or whether Hitler, as he wished, would have the opportunity of strengthening the initially limited power of the National Socialist movement in the government by means of another election giving him popular backing.

Events in February 1933

Hitler's partners failed to appreciate that the suppression of the left was bound to make the numerical superiority and power of the National Socialist movement count for still more in comparison with the remaining parties of the middle and right, and thus would also prepare their own capitulation. Whilst the aggressive declaration of political war against the left and the methodical expulsion of the Social Democratic mass party from political power and responsibility had already created the essential pre-condition for the fascist infiltration of public life before 1933, the 'National Government's' use of the state's resources to enforce the suppression of the left-wing parties created the crucial political power institutions and the emergency lever which then lent itself for use against the other parties in order to create a monopoly of political power for the NSDAP. This development came about in two consecutive stages. First in February, March and April 1933, the exclusion of the left, an approach still very much endorsed by the coalition partners; then, in late spring 1933 action by the NSDAP through key executive positions which the Party had occupied meanwhile to compel the middle-class and Nationalist parties to renounce their political independence.

Like its forerunners from autumn 1930, Hitler's government was an emergency cabinet which owed its existence not to a parliamentary majority but to the Reich President's right to pass emergency decrees. The Reich President, who according to the working of the government's declaration had given 'the members of the National Government' the job of taking decisive new measures,[1] had tried as far as possible to ensure continuity with previous cabinets by retaining conservative and pro-Nationalist ministerial experts in foreign policy (von Neurath), finance (Schwerin von Krosigk), and justice (Dr Gürtner) as well as in post and transport (von Eltz-Rübenach), in addition to bringing in the Stahlhelm leader Seldte (Reich Ministry of Labour). At the same time strong counterweights to Hitler were created by giving greater responsibilities to Papen and Hugenberg. Hitler had expressed his satisfaction with the fact that apart from himself only two National Socialists belonged to the new government: Goring as Reich Commissioner for the Prussian Ministry of the Interior as well as Reich Commissioner for Air Transport and Dr Frick as Reich Minister of the Interior. Such 'modesty' had made a favourable impression on Papen and Hindenburg, yet it enabled Hitler to have the responsibility for the Prussian police transferred to Göring in spite of strong reservations by the German Nationalists. Hugenberg finally gave up his well-founded resistance to this arrangement when the position of a virtual 'economic dictator' was given to him in the new government by his control of the Reich Ministries of Economics and Agriculture (including the powers of Reich Commissioner for Osthilfe). This was very much in keeping with his ambitions and, in addition, his power was augmented on 4 February when he was given the provisional direction of the Prussian departments for Economics, Agriculture and Labour. Comfort was also drawn from the fact that Papen was allocated the duties of Reich Commissioner for

Prussia in addition to his post as Vice-Chancellor, and he was thus nominally placed above Göring. Moreover, the stipulation that the Vice-Chancellor had to take part in any discussions between the Reich Chancellor and Reich President seemed to ensure the taming and restraint of any purely National Socialist initiatives. Finally, it was expected that the Reichswehr, which according to the constitution was under the supreme command of the Reich President, would not permit the new government to degenerate into a National Socialist monopoly. It is true that the new Minister of Defence, General von Blomberg, and his new Chief at the Ministeramt, Colonel von Reichenau, who replaced von Schleicher and von Bredow, were better disposed towards National Socialism than most of the other generals. But Blomberg made it clear in his appeal to the Armed Forces on 1 February that, like his predecessors, he too was 'resolutely determined' to maintain the Reichswehr as 'an above-party source of state power'.

Moreover, in terms of personnel, National Socialist influence below the ministerial level in the departments of the Reich government was at first kept within strict limits. The State Secretaries appointed in the Reich Chancellery and the Reich Minister of the Interior were Heinrich Lammers (until then Ministerialrat in the Reich Ministry of the Interior) and Hans Pfundtner, experienced experts who admittedly had sympathized with the National Socialist movement for some time, but who were not Party functionaries. Only the new Press Chief of the Reich government, Walter Funk, belonged to the small circle of Hitler's Party counsellors. For the time being the desire to install National Socialist State Secretaries in other departments was kept in check because of the government's partners and was not achieved until March/April 1933, when the situation had considerably improved (appointment of Fritz Reinhardt and Konstantin Hierl as State Secretaries in the Ministries of Finance and Labour). Nor was there at first any marked infiltration by National Socialist personnel in the other big departments of the Reich government. Bernhard Wilhelm von Bülow remained State Secretary in the Foreign Office, Schlegelberger, in office since 1924, continued in the Reich Ministry of Justice, and in the Reich Ministries for Economics and Agriculture Hugenberg appointed two prominent Nationalists as State Secretaries, the pan-German Oberfinanzrat Bang and a member of the managing board of the Reich Land League, von Rohr-Demmin.

Thus the 'containment' of the National Socialists seemed to have been largely successful. Franz von Papen, the busy government maker, was the most certain and irresponsible in this belief. By contrast, opposition was voiced from the outset against participating in any Hitler cabinet by the Stahlhelm (Duesterberg) and the DNVP (Kleist-Schmenzin and Oberfohren among others), who had already had many unhappy experiences with the trustworthiness and partnership of the NSDAP. On the other hand, it is remarkable that at that time Hitler was regarded by the KPD as well as by large sectors of the SPD and Centre Party as the 'prisoner' of the Nationalists' reaction and the latter were seen as the true victors of 30 January. This initial error was attributable in the Communist and Social Democratic camps chiefly to the ideological dogma of the monopoly-capitalist manipulation of fascism, which also to some extent subsequently determined the fatalistic *attentisme* of both parties and in the early years repeatedly prompted members of these parties to emigrate, where they continued to prophesy the imminent collapse of the contradictory capitalist-fascist system.

The leadership of the Centre Party was particularly upset by the fact that it had not participated at all in the preliminary negotiations to form a government, even though a National Government with a broad majority, as Hindenburg had wished, was impossible without the Centre Party, given the existing strength of the parties. The question of including the Centre Party in the government was in fact left open at first, out of consideration for the Reich President. Hitler quickly agreed with Hugenberg, however, that such a step would only 'endanger uniformity of purpose'.[2] Hitler's subsequent negotiations with the Centre Party leaders Kaas and Perlitius on 31 January were merely for the sake of appearances. Since the two men made toleration of the government and their eventual agreement to an Enabling Law conditional upon satisfactory answers from Hitler to a series of written questions primarily concerned with basic constitutional issues, Hitler was able to tell the cabinet and the Reich President that 'unreasonable' conditions made further negotiations to broaden the government impossible, and therefore the government would have to look elsewhere for a parliamentary majority.

Even before the cabinet had been sworn in, Hitler had already demanded the dissolution of the Reichstag and fresh elections on 30 January, but he had encountered strong resistance from Hugenberg and so this decision had been left to Hindenburg. Hitler regarded further new elections as vital to the extension of National Socialist power and as a way of adjusting the still relatively meagre share accorded to National Socialists in the government after the formation of the cabinet and the allocation of the departments. Correctly, he expected a considerable strengthening of the NSDAP if it could conduct its electoral campaign from the platform of government and with the support of the executive, particularly since it now had the goodwill of the Reich President behind it, which was still highly effective in electoral terms. Above all, however, the outcome of such elections would show where the real power lay within the ruling coalition and if more than 50 per cent of the votes were successfully gained for the Hitler coalition, this would also make the government more independent of the Reich President.

Hitler's partners in the government were guilty of the first fateful blow against the concept of 'containing' Hitler when at the cabinet meeting of 31 January 1933 they failed to oppose his pressure for dissolving the Reichstag and for new elections. On the contrary they finally gave way after some squabbling so that Hitler was also able to win over Hindenburg on the very same day. Hugenberg would rather have got the necessary majority for the government in the Reichstag by an immediate ban on the KPD. But in his role as the Chancellor zealous for legality, Hitler warned against such a hasty step, which could possibly provoke a Communist uprising and thereby also create a difficult situation for the Reichswehr. But even Papen's specific suggestion of trying to go ahead with an Enabling Law first, which would only have had any prospect of success in the prevailing situation in the Reichstag if the government had been prepared to give constitutional guarantees to the Centre Party, was not followed up with any conviction by the non-National Socialist Ministers.

After Hitler had solemnly sworn to his partners that there would be no change in the composition of the cabinet after the new elections, Papen involuntarily came to the Chancellor's aid by declaring categorically that this had to be the last election. Thus – in a complete reversal of the constitutional relationship between an election and the formation of a government – Hitler's partners themselves reduced the pending new election to a mere acclamation of the existing government, which, in the nature of things, was bound to mean above all an acclamation of Hitler's Chancellorship.

With the dissolution of the Reichstag on 1 February by an emergency decree of the Reich President and the fixing of new elections for 5 March, Hitler successfully took the first step towards National Socialist domination.

Some difficulties were admittedly caused by the Reichstag Committee for the Protection of Parliamentary Rights (the so-called Supervisory Committee), which was not affected by the dissolution and which was convened on 7 February by its Chairman, the Social Democrat, Paul Löbe – who for many years had been the President of the Reichstag – to debate an SPD motion about ensuring electoral freedom. Such a debate could have been all the more embarrassing since the Supervisory Committee had the right to call on the Chancellor himself or the Reich Ministers. The National Socialists managed to deal with this episode through terror and boycott from below. The task of making debate impossible by prolonged objections and by causing a hubbub against Löbe fell to the National Socialist members on the Committee, led by the National Socialist lawyer Hans Frank. This too was successful and when the

Committee met again a week later, after Löbe had complained to Göring, the President of the Reichstag, the same game was played, only this time more crassly. True, the Centre Party and the SPD as well as the KPD protested most sharply, but they abandoned the attempt to call the Committee together for a third time. The incident was typical of a growing mood of resignation.

In order to exploit the resources of the state to create the best possible prospects for the new government in the election campaign, the cabinet referred to the Communist appeal of 31 January for a general strike, and got the Reich President to issue an emergency decree on 4 February 'For the Protection of the German People'. This so-called 'stand-by decree' had already been drafted by previous governments. In particular, it permitted a ban on the press and on public meetings if 'organs, institutions, authorities or leading state officials were insulted or brought into contempt', or if 'obviously false information' was being disseminated which 'endangered vital interests of state'. These flexible provisions offered wide-reaching opportunities for silencing opposing parties. It is true that there was explicit recognition of the right of appeal to the Reich Supreme Court. The power of police arrest for specific cases of 'suspected subversion' in paragraph 22 of the decree also left open the possibility of judicial appeal and was in any event confined to a maximum time limit of three months.

The key factor in the application of this and other measures turned out to be who controlled the police and administration. It now became clear how important it was not only that there were already National Socialist governments in some of the small Länder, but above all that Prussia had been placed under the provisional control of the Reich Commissioner following Papen's *coup d'état* of 20 July 1932. As a result the new Reich government also acquired provisional control of Prussia where, through Göring's appointment, a particularly favourable opportunity existed for the National Socialists to exploit the power of the state.

The Papen government's attempt to reform the Reich in a more authoritarian direction with the aid of Prussia's co-ordination (*Gleichschaltung*) in summer 1932 had been blocked and to some extent reversed by the interim judgement of the State Supreme Court (25 Oct. 1932). Although prevented from actually controlling the Prussian departments, the Social Democratic Braun–Severing administration therefore continued to count as the duly constituted government in Prussia, which meant above all that it (and not the provisional government appointed by the Reich) represented the Prussian government in the Prussian Privy Council and in the Reichsrat. In addition the provisional government of Prussia (which apart from Papen, Göring, Hugenberg and Professor Popitz (provisional Minister of Finance from 4 Feb. 1933) also included the NSDAP Gauleiter of Hannover, former assistant schoolmaster

Bernhard Rust as the new provisional Minister of Culture) could expect to meet with crossfire and votes of censure from the Prussian Landtag and Privy Council, where the NSDAP and DNVP did not have a majority. In order to change this state of affairs, the provisional government decreed on 5 February the dissolution of all the Prussian provincial diets, district assemblies, parish councils and other local bodies, and new elections were fixed for 12 March 1933.[3] This decree, which among other things was motivated by the urge to simplify and standardize local elections, was intended to bring about a different composition of the Prussian Privy Council. Its originators were perfectly aware of the risk of an appeal to the State Supreme Court, which in fact did happen (among others one was made by the provincial committee of Hannover).[4] However, it could safely be assumed that such a process would take so long that unavoidable *faits accomplis* could be created.

At the same time the dissolution of the Prussian Landtag was set in train. A motion put forward by the National Socialist fraction on 4 February for the Landtag to dissolve itself was rejected by a majority. And the National Socialist President of the Landtag, Kerrl, who put the same proposal to the three-man board which also had powers to dissolve the Landtag, was thwarted by the opposition of the Prussian Minister President Braun, and the State President, Konrad Adenauer.

After discussions in the Reich Cabinet Papen contrived an emergency decree of the President on 6 February 'For the restoration of orderly government in Prussia', which abruptly transferred to the provisional government what powers were still left to the Braun administration (including its representation in the Privy Council). This annulment of the State Supreme Court's judgement was an open breach of the law and another *coup d'état*. The Braun government again appealed to the State Supreme Court, but the Reich government's deliberate delaying tactics in replying to the appeal continually postponed the proceedings and ultimately made them irrelevant when a rather different constitutional arrangement came into force after the new elections of 5 March.[5]) On the strength of the Presidential decree Papen and Kerrl had decided, against Adenauer's opposition in the three-man board, on the dissolution of the Prussian Landtag and to hold new elections on 5 March.

Prussian developments show that even after 30 January 1933, the German President's right of issuing emergency decrees remained for the time being the most important instrument of Hitler's government on its way to concentrating power. Most of all, it cleared the road for Göring, under whose control the Prussian administration – by far the most important Land executive in Germany – developed into an effective arm of the new masters and became, even in February, a new area of direct National Socialist influence.

Papen's 'Prussian coup' of 20 July 1932 had already led to the dismissal of numerous pro-Republican civil servants, most of them Social Democrats, by Göring's predecessor, Franz Bracht.[6] Now there was another extensive re-shuffle of officials which affected those higher civil servants who belonged to the Centre Party and State Party, as well as the Social Democrats who were still left in key administrative posts.

Fourteen police chiefs alone in large Prussian cities were forced to retire by the new Prussian provisional government, as well as a whole string of Regierungspräsidenten or Regierungsvizepräsidenten and district counsellors (Landräte), and in Münster the Oberpräsident (Gronowski) who belonged to the Centre Party. True, Göring could only partially satisfy the wishes of the National Socialist claimants to the posts left vacant; for example, in Dortmund and Hannover, where the S.A. Gruppenführer Schepmann and Lutze were installed as police presidents, initially on a provisional basis because of civil service rights and the continuing need to take account of the Nationalist partners in the Reich government. By contrast, the February re-shuffle, like the change round under Bracht, mostly favoured conservative and Nationalist government experts, and to some extent conservatively inclined landowners from the nobility, former officers and industrial managers. As a result barriers were erected against the later National Socialist infiltration of important offices in the Prussian internal administration which could not easily be removed. Thus, the post of Oberpräsident of Westphalia fell to Baron Ferdinand von Lüninck, a Nationalist champion of the Westphalian Stahlhelm and Green Front. Moreover, the candidacy of the young S.A. Gruppenführer Count Helldorf in Berlin was unsuccessful at first (he became police president of Potsdam in March 1933 and only got the coveted Berlin post in July 1935). Instead, the choice fell on Rear Admiral von Levetzow, who had become prominent as the reactionary leader of patriotic groups and who admittedly had belonged to the NSDAP as a Reichstag deputy from 1932, but who seemed more acceptable than Helldorf to the Nationalists. Department IA especially (Political Police) of the Berlin police headquarters was soon purged of Republican officials under Reventlow's command. Control of the division which later became the independent Secret State Police Office was won by Oberregierungsrat Diels at the end of February 1935. He had already 'proved' himself in the Prussian Ministry of the Interior during the preparations for the 'Prussian coup' as an informant for the Nationalists and National Socialists against his then superiors, Severing and Abegg.

The process of rearrangement was kept within limits in the Prussian Ministry of the Interior itself. Most important was the fact

that the head of the police division, Erich Klausener, who was particularly critical of the National Socialists (and known too as the
leader of Catholic Action), was shunted into the Reich Ministry of
Transport and replaced by Ludwig Grauert, former head of the
employers' associations of the North-West iron and steel industry,
who had belonged for some time to Göring's circle of intimates in
industry and who was also acceptable to the Nationalists. By contrast the Berlin S.S. Gruppenführer Kurt Daluege had to be content for the time being with the honorary post of 'Commissioner
for Special Duty' in the Prussian Ministry of the Interior. In fact,
however, Daluege was already exercising an important function in
the political purging of the Prussian police in this capacity in
February and March 1933, before he could officially take over the
command of the Police Division as the successor to Grauert (who
was appointed State Secretary). The practice of infiltrating Commissioners for Special Duty to get round the obstacles posed by
state and civil service laws was followed elsewhere. The *Frankfurter Zeitung* rightly commented on 9 February 1933, in respect of
Daluege, that 'by means of such honorary commissioners' the executive 'was handing over power to men who were in truth private
individuals' and who 'certainly did not have the civil servant's
obligations' to the state they were supposed to be serving.

By interfering with the personnel of the Prussian Ministry of the
Interior and police administration in February 1933, effective conditions were created favouring the governing coalition and dis-
advantaging the other political forces, particularly those of the left.
Moreover, Göring took care to leave no doubts about what attitude
the new government expected of the executive (in Prussia) in the
election campaign by means of exceptionally pointed verbal instructions to the Oberpräsidenten and Regierungspräsidenten and
through various directives. The order to police authorities of 17
February 1933 was particularly drastic. They were directed to 'ensure the best possible understanding with the National groups'
(S.A., S.S., Stahlhelm) 'whose circles represented the most important forces supporting the state'. Moreover, 'government propaganda was to be supported to the utmost', whereas 'the activity of
organizations hostile to the state was to be opposed with the most
stringent measures' and 'if necessary by the ruthless use of arms'.
And it was tantamount to giving the order to 'open fire' when the
provisional Prussian Minister of the Interior added: 'Police officers
who use weapons in carrying out their duties will be covered by me
without regard to the consequences of resorting to arms. Whoever
misguidedly fails in this duty can expect disciplinary action.'[7]

As a result of this and earlier directives from Göring a strict ban
became the order of the day in Prussia against election rallies and
press appeals by the parties of the left in particular, just as Communist meetings and public demonstrations were generally forbid-

den at the beginning of February in the National Socialist controlled Lands of Thuringia, Braunschweig and Oldenburg. The Berlin
police chief allowed the first seizure of the Communist *Rote Fahne*
and an initial three-day ban on the Social Democratic *Vorwärts*
even before the emergency decree came into force on 4 February.
There were numerous bans on newspapers in Prussia, particularly
after 10/11 February when the election campaign really got underway with the parties' election appeals. The Communist press was
most severely affected and widely suppressed, and to some extent
this was the case outside Prussia as well. Police raids, with seizures
of material, on the Karl Liebknecht House in Berlin (on 2 and 23
February) and on local party offices partially forced the KPD underground even at that time. In Prussia police bans were also directed
against the SPD press in particular. In mid-February *Vorwärts* was
again banned for a week, along with dozens of regional and local
SPD newspapers for varying periods of time. So too were the
organs of the Reichsbanner, of the Free Trade Unions, Otto Strasser's *Schwarze Front*, and even isolated journals of the Centre
Party, for example in Neisse (Silesia). For all that it was still possible to have a ban which had been imposed on the Centre Party's
main paper, *Germania*, rescinded after the personal intervention of
former Chancellor Marx with Göring. On 19 February the Berlin
police also banned a conference of the Socialist League of Culture.
And the congress of 'The Free Word', which took place on the
same day in the banqueting hall of the Kroll Opera House on the
initiative of leftist intellectuals and artists (it was here that the former Prussian Minister of Culture, Grimme, read out Thomas
Mann's impressive anti-National Socialist declaration of humanism,
democracy and Socialism) was broken up by the police before the
discussion began, on account of suspected atheistic (!) pronouncements.

However, Göring overreached himself to some extent with the
draconian bans in Prussia. Most of the bans directed against the
Social Democratic press for alleged defamation of the government
or for 'treasonable' appeals were lifted again by the Reich Supreme Court after the appropriate appeals had been made. The fact
that court reversals frequently followed the many bans in the
second half of February was the worst possible testimony to the
legality of the Prussian executive's actions. Nor was this wholly
acceptable in political terms for the NSDAP. On the other hand
the bans already threatening the left-wing parties because of their
pointed declaration of political war against the NSDAP, tended to
intimidate their newspapers and publishing houses. And the fact
that to defame the government and to bring it into contempt was
already specifically forbidden made even leading Liberal and Republican newspapers, like the *Frankfurter Zeitung* and the *Deutsche
Allgemeine Zeitung*, take pains to express their criticism of the

government in cautious terms. This in turn indirectly lent respectability to the National Socialist leaders.

In addition care was taken through Göring's instructions to the police that S.A. or S.S. terrorists who broke up opposition meetings during the election campaign or who attempted to use force, as in Eisleben on 12 February, against the Communist headquarters, were not named in official police reports, or their cases were hushed up or fixed.[8] One other result, finally, of the 'Directive on shooting' was that the Prussian police often stood by and watched the S.A. terror, as for example in Krefeld on 22 February when the former Reich Minister Stegerwald was knocked down by S.A. men during a Centre Party meeting. Urgent appeals from the Centre Party leadership to the Reich President and Vice-Chancellor 'to end this incredible state of affairs' (in *Germania* on 22 February 1933) finally moved Hitler and Göring to admonish discipline to the NSDAP and to warn against 'provocations'.

A then relatively unnoticed and unpublished police decree of Göring's on 22 February 1933 which had particularly far-reaching political and institutional consequences, ordered a reinforcement of the police by the enlistment of voluntary 'auxiliary police' to combat the 'growing excesses of the radical left, especially in the Communist camp'. Almost exclusively, members of the 'National associations' (S.A., S.S., Stahlhelm) were enlisted for service in the auxiliary police, and they appeared in their uniforms simply wearing a white arm-band bearing the words 'Auxiliary Police'. The decree admittedly specified that setting up the auxiliary police required the approval of the Regierungspräsidenten and that they were to be under police officers,[9] but the practice was very soon different.

The aversion of Papen and Hugenberg to new Reichstag elections had been founded mainly on their fear of the superiority of the NSDAP's mass organization. In an attempt to hold their own to some degree with their National Socialist partners, Papen tried to extend the right bloc of Nationalists and the Stahlhelm towards the middle, to form a Christian–Nationalist united front. But this attempt was shattered chiefly because of Hugenberg's intransigence. The 'Battle Front Black-White-Red' which was subsequently formed and which was nominally led by Hugenberg, Seldte and Papen, could basically rely only on the DNVP's organization during the election campaign and was rather backward in demonstrating how its proposals differed from those of the National Socialists, so that the majority of voters regarded these not as an alternative but merely as a watered-down version of National Socialist propaganda.

Papen, Hugenberg and the other cabinet ministers continued, however, to deceive themselves about the prospects of co-operating with Hitler. Hitler contributed significantly to this deception during these weeks by being generally reticent in his use of the Chancellor's powers of direction, by avoiding confrontation and even occasionally by ignoring suggestions from Frick or Göring if opposition to these was manifestly obvious. One example was the cabinet meeting of 16 February, when Frick – doubtless in agreement with Hitler – suggested that in view of the Supreme Court's reversal of numerous press bans, the appellate court should be kept out by extending the emergency decree of 4 February, but this met with opposition from Hugenberg. Hugenberg surely also registered with satisfaction the fact that Hitler hardly objected to his early economic measures and bills – (protection against debt enforcement in agriculture, grain subsidies, etc.) – which were particularly favourable to agriculture.

During these weeks Hitler deliberately subordinated the urgent questions of economic, financial, social policy and work creation to electoral requirements. Hugenberg's pro-agriculture policy fitted in here, not least in as much as it improved the mood of the farming population at large, where the NSDAP expected more in the elections than from the working class. Unlike Hugenberg, however, Hitler wanted to avoid any binding economic commitment. It was utterly typical that he recommended the cabinet meeting of 8 February, 'to avoid all specific references to the government's economic programme'. He added: 'The Reich government has to capture 18 to 19 million votes. There is no economic programme in the whole wide world which could satisfy such a huge mass of voters.' Nor did Hitler make any concrete economic proposals during his address to leading industrialists on 20 February; instead he diverted his guests by relating the biological 'law' of the survival of the fittest to the 'entrepreneurial mentality', which would be valued in an authoritarian state, whereas democracy protected the weak and the resourceless masses. With all its dogma, this was a skilful wooing! This was confirmed when Göring and Schacht appealed to those present (including Krupp von Bohlen und Halbach, General Director Vögler from the Vereinigte Stahlwerke, and von Schnitzler from the I.G. Farben concern) for support and collected an election fund of several million Reichsmark for the NSDAP.[10]

This generous contribution was an obvious example of how much the material and technical conditions of National Socialist election propaganda had improved since Hitler had become Chancellor. Admittedly, in agreement with Finance Minister Schwerin-Krosigk, Hitler rejected Frick's suggestion to the cabinet that government funds be used for the election propaganda of the Hitler coalition. However, in other respects he exploited the advantage of government for the Party's propaganda all the more indiscriminately. Thus, for example, Frick contrived to have the text of Hitler's radio broadcast of 1 February, his 'Appeal to the German People', distributed through official channels, including the schools,[11] and so it became a draw in the election campaign. After fourteen years of deepest disgrace and humiliation – this was the keynote – the great hour of national awakening had come. The appeal painted the previous 'system' in the blackest of colours and in so doing made all the more of the 'historic turning point' of 30 January. The decision of the 'Field Marshall' (not so long ago a man under heavy attack from the Goebbels press) to form the new government was warmly praised, and the appeal finished with a prayer to the Almighty. The vagueness and lack of detail in the programme, which the opposition parties also attacked, hardly lessened the effect of the appeal, any more than they had Hitler's other big election speeches. The National Socialists knew better than ever how to whip up a frenzy of blind faith. Millions accepted with joy and enthusiasm what seemed to be to the politically mature just empty phrases, as, for example, when Frick explained in an election speech in Dresden on 19 February: 'If people say that we have no policy, then the name of Hitler is policy enough. The crucial thing is the will and the strength to act.'[12]

For the first time the National Socialists also now had the control of a medium which was especially suitable for such politics of the emotions and which magnified their impact: the radio network. The constitution of the German broadcasting system at that time, and the dominant position of the government in the Reich Broadcasting Corporation, which in turn controlled the broadcasting corporations of the individual Länder, proved to be a particularly suitable state of affairs for co-ordinating from above. Weimar governments had also availed themselves in various ways of the broadcasting monopoly, but Hitler and Goebbels were the first to make masterly use of the technical possibilities of this instrument. The radio network was also helpful to Hugenberg, Papen and Seldte, but Hitler profited more from it in that he contrived to have his big election speeches transmitted to all German stations. Goebbels thereby discovered a particular talent which emphatically underlined his claim to the future post of Reich Minister of Propaganda. As a radio broadcaster he personally introduced Hitler's speeches, for the first time on the occasion of the opening election address in the Berlin Sportpalast on 10 February, and he 'set' the right mood in every living room. On 12 February the *Frankfurter Zeitung* reported Goebbels's first performance as his Führer's reporter. 'Herr Goebbels showed himself to be a natural master of the superlative beforehand: enraptured – unparalleled – feverish excitement – tension mounting furiously – the mass audience clusters – all a mass of mankind in which the individual can no longer be recognized.'

The order from Berlin to circulate the Appeal of 1 February and the compulsory broadcasting of Hitler's speeches naturally encountered opposition from non-National Socialist governments, especially in the Länder. In Stuttgart, where Hitler was speaking in the town hall on the evening of 15 February, the transmission cable which the postal service had connected between the hall and the telegraph office was severed, so that the broadcast of the speech was broken off. Hitler reacted furiously to this incident. He got the Reich Minister of Posts to take strict action against the post office officials who had failed to carry out the necessary supervision and declared in the cabinet on 16 February 1933 'that he was not going to stand for a repeat of the Stuttgart goings on'.

The beginning of forceful measures against the Communists and the Social Democrats and the importance of the Reichstag fire decree

The burning of the Reichstag by the former Dutch Communist Marinus van der Lubbe on the evening of 27 February 1933 caused the National Socialist leaders to abandon their original tactics, which merely envisaged a cautious, gradual escalation in the process of intimidating political opponents but no sensational action. Under the direct impact of the Reichstag fire, Hitler, Göring, Goebbels and Frick apparently believed this to be a signal for a general Communist uprising. National Socialist ideology and propaganda, which had always painted a fantastically distorted picture of Communist conspiracy, encouraged this assumption through self-induction, although the overwhelmingly defensive behaviour of the Communists since 30 January as well as the material already seized from them hardly supported such an interpretation, and in any case a Communist attempt at revolution would obviously have been futile. Inevitably, there was a tendency to see the burning as an organized political action in view of the size of the fire and the psychological and political situation during those days, whereas the sole initiative of van der Lubbe, who was caught red-handed, seemed quite improbable to most observers and commentators.

However, the possibility of planned Communist action, which could not be automatically ruled out at the beginning, was already treated as a fact in the first statements by Göring and Goebbels on the night of the fire and in the official explanations and announcements during the following days, whereby suspicion of complicity or connivance was also cast without any proof whatever against the Social Democrats. Thus there was deliberate distortion from the outset. This version, which as the *Frankfurter Zeitung* rightly asserted on 1 March 'failed to consider the possibility of an individual act of terror', was rigidly maintained during the days that followed, when the probability of a carefully planned Communist organized plot became increasingly remote according to the findings and interrogations. In this way the National Socialists actually gave weight to anti-fascist arguments and propaganda which, effectively organized through Willi Münzenberg's underground Comintern headquarters in Paris, now in turn asserted and tried to prove arson by the Nazis, with such telling success that for a long time after 1945 historians largely assumed this to be true. Van der Lubbe's sole guilt was only recently re-established as almost certainly an irrefutable fact.[13].

But the thesis of KPD guilt and instigation, and the shared responsibility of the SPD, could hardly be abandoned by the National Socialist leaders, chiefly because they had argued not only with words but with emergency decrees and with violent measures which were to have momentous consequences.

During the night of 27/28 February, Göring had already ordered the arrest of KPD deputies and leading officials, the closure of all Communist Party offices and premises and an indefinite ban on the entire KPD press, as well as a fourteen-day ban on Social Democratic publications in Prussia. Above all, on the day following the Reichstag fire Hitler's government procured a hasty enactment of a new emergency decree of the Reich President, 'For the Protection of People and State', which introduced a far-reaching state of emergency 'in order to guard against Communist acts of violence endangering the state'. This was quickly to assume fundamental importance over and above the occasion of the Reichstag fire and the defence against a suspected Communist threat for the control of power by National Socialism.

The decree was hastily improvised after preliminary talks on 28 February in the Prussian Ministry of the Interior under the auspices of the Reich Minister of the Interior and was signed by the Reich President on the same day after a short discussion in the Reich cabinet. The Reichstag fire decree was the earliest and perhaps over-all the most important example in the National Socialist era of exactly how far such an improvisation could become an opening to the despotism of the police state, by forgoing any clear legal definition of changes in the law and in the powers of authority, and by making do instead with the general displacement of existing basic and constitutional rights.

Hitler described the purpose of the decree very clearly in the cabinet meeting of 28 February. It was now a matter of a 'ruthless confrontation of the KPD', which had originally been planned for after the elections. In principle it was also welcomed by the non-National Socialist partners in the government, particularly since the Reichstag fire had provided such an ideal excuse. To this end a stroke of the pen (Article 1 of the decree) ended all the basic rights of the Weimar constitution which had been suspended under Article 48 (freedom of persons, the right to freedom of expression, freedom of the press, the freedom of association and public gathering, the inviolability of secrecy of posts and telephones, and the constitutional protection of property and homes). In addition the decree (Article 2) empowered the Reich government 'temporarily to exercise the powers of the supreme Land authorities' if 'the measures necessary for the restoration of public security and order are not implemented in a particular Land'.[14]

The decree, which also (Articles 4 and 6) contained draconian punitive measures (including the death penalty or penal servitude) in the event of any violation of the decree, or attempted assassination of members of the government, arson in public buildings or serious unrest, had one particular omission. It was not followed up by any written guidelines from the Reich Minister of the Interior. Instead the enactment of more specific provisions was left to the Länder, which placed Göring in a position in Prussia to give an extraordinarily wide interpretation to the decree from the outset.

Whereas the Länder not governed by National Socialists confined themselves largely to banning the Communist press, Communist meetings and demonstrations, the closure of Communist Party offices and the detention of prominent KPD officials and deputies, in Prussia there were summary arrests of KPD officials. Here, thousands of KPD officials were imprisoned in the first days following the Reichstag fire. Partial information from the Police Chiefs of twenty-four Prussian administrative districts (of a total of thirty-four, excluding Berlin!) shows a total of 7,784 (95 per cent Communists) arrested before 15 March on the basis of the decree of 28 February 1933.[15] The total arrested in Prussia at this time may well have exceeded 10,000.

The KPD had for a long time expected to be declared illegal and had prepared for it, but the party was none the less surprised by the action taken after the Reichstag fire. The arrests chiefly affected the greater part of the middle range of the cadre of functionaries who were used to waiting for instructions from headquarters in keeping with the bureaucratic and centralized structure of the KPD. Since the Prussian police knew the secret bolt-holes of the Communists they also succeeded in arresting some prominent leaders; for example, on 3 March in Berlin the KPD chairman Ernst Thälmann with a number of his agents. During these days and in the following weeks other KPD leaders and central committee members emigrated, among others Willi Mönzenberg, Alexander Abusch, and Wilhelm Pieck; others, including Walter Ulbricht, stayed in hiding in Germany until the summer or autumn of 1933. The main organizer of the underground KPD, John Schehr, fell into police hands in autumn 1933 and was murdered on 2 February 1934. Prominent members of the intellectual and literary left among those arrested in the first days included Erich Mühsam, Ludwig Renn, Egon Erwin Kisch, Karl von Ossietzky, Bernhard Rubenstein, Professor Felix Halle, the pacifist Lehmann-Russbüldt and many others.

In the cabinet meeting of 2 March 1933, Foreign Minister von Neurath suggested that the hostile foreign press criticism of the measures in Germany should be disarmed at least by a relaxation or lifting of the 'measures against the SPD', but Göring resolutely opposed this. On the contrary, severe action against the SPD could be expected to 'lose it a great deal of support' and this would be 'to the NSDAP's advantage'.

Hitler and Göring well knew that apart from the emotional appeal to the longing for leadership and the faith of the unpolitical, nationalist sectors of the electorate (which Goebbels unerringly provided for by immediately proclaiming 5 March to be the 'Day of the Awakening Nation'), the intimidation of and methodical discrimination against the political left would also have its effect on many anxious and unsure voters. It was therefore characteristic of the particular mentality of the National Socialist leadership that it reacted to foreign press criticism with greater aggression. Göring, for example, publicly declared on 2 March:

My main task will be to stamp out the Communist pestilence. I am going over to the offensive all down the line. . . . The Communists never expected 2,000 of their top-swindlers to be sitting under lock and key just 48 hours later . . . I don't need the fire in the Reichstag to take action against Communism, and its no secret either that if it had been up to Hitler and me the culprits would already be swinging from the gallows.[16]

Göring's directive to the police authorities of 3 March, on the implementation of the decree for the Protection of People and State, showed the same intention to step up the struggle.[17] Thus it affirmed that, apart from basic constitutional rights, 'all other restraints on police action imposed by Reich and Land law' – particularly the regulations of the Prussian Police Administration Law of 1 June 1931[18] – were 'abolished', that is 'in so far as this is necessary and appropriate to achieve the purpose of the decree'. The order also considerably extended 'the defence against Communist acts of violence injurious to the state'. That is to say:

In keeping with the purpose and aim of the decree the additional measures authorized by it will be directed against the Communists in the first instance, but then also against those who co-operate with the Communists and who support or encourage their criminal aims, if only indirectly. To avoid errors, I would point out that any necessary measures against members or establishments of other than Communist, anarchist or Social Democratic parties can only be justified by the decree for the Protection of People and State of 28 February 1933 if they serve to help the defence against such Communist activities in the widest sense.

Here then, 'Communists, anarchists and Social Democrats' were all basically tarred with the same brush and likewise proscribed, whereas special proof of direct or indirect encouragement of Communist efforts still had to be provided if the decree were to be applied to any 'bourgeois' political opponents. A few months later, however, even this qualification no longer applied. In an order to the Prussian police authorities of 22 June 1933 'For the combat of so-called alarmism', Göring himself went so far as to describe even comments 'which are likely to arouse discontent with the measures taken by the National Government' as a 'continuation of the Marxist campaign' and urged the authorities to deal accordingly with the said 'alarmists'.[19]

In spite of such early visible proofs of how far the interpretation and operation of the Reichstag fire decree might be extended, most contemporaries, above all Hitler's Nationalist partners, were apparently unaware of the implications of the state of emergency which had been so carelessly agreed on. The arrests, initially largely directed against the Communists, might suggest the comparison with earlier states of emergency to which Ebert and constitutionally loyal Weimar governments also had had to resort in the early phase of the Republic when the device of detaining Spartacists and Communists had also been used (admittedly under Army rather than police control). Hitler's placatory announcements also reinforced the impression of a purely temporary suspension of rights. Thus, in answer to the question of a correspondent of the *Daily Express* on 2 March as to whether the present suspension of personal freedom was to be a permanent state of affairs, Hitler expressly said: 'No! When the Communist danger is eliminated things will get back to normal.'[20]

When the S.A. and S.S. auxiliary police were disbanded in the second part of 1933 and in Bavaria at the beginning of 1934, the control and administration of the concentration camps for political prisoners continued to be an S.A. and S.S. domain (after 30 June 1934 of the S.S. alone), which in this respect continued to occupy a sector of state power without being controlled by the regular organs of state government and justice. Thus the coercive powers of the so-called penalty of arrest originating in the Reichstag fire decree resulted not only in the deprivation of freedom (alongside judicial investigation or criminal arrest) and in the sovereign police state authority removed from every court and constitutional control but above and beyond in a permanent instrument of (private) Party authority outside the state, more precisely, in the S.S.

These far-reaching consequences of the Reichstag fire decree were admittedly neither foreseeable nor inevitable in the early days of March 1933. Typically, unrestrained revolutionary and terrorist use was only made of the state of emergency created by the Reichstag fire decree after the elections of 5 March had, as it were, given popular sanction to the use of terror.

The election of 5 March 1933

The election which took place under the conditions of a wide-ranging state of emergency, but which none the less offered the last chance of a democratic election to the German people, only just achieved the aim of achieving an absolute majority for the forces behind the Hitler government. The NSDAP and 'Battle Front Black-White-Red' received together 51.8 per cent, and the NSDAP itself 43.9 per cent of the votes. In spite of the great propaganda advantage and the forceful restraint or suppression of opposing parties the NSDAP still remained as far from a majority as ever. Yet the result of the election fulfilled the crucial function assigned to it. It brought the government popular backing which was all the more important in terms of moral support, because with the help of this mandate parliamentary democracy was finally to be buried in favour of an authoritarian leadership.

A particularly striking aspect of the election and in itself a clear sign of its referendum-like character was the record turn-out of over 88 per cent. This was 5 per cent higher than even that of the July election of 1932, which in its turn had already surpassed all the other election turn-outs in the Weimar era. It had been possible to mobilize three and a half million voters who had ignored the last Reichstag election of November 1932 (poll of 80 per cent). And obviously at least half of the five and a half million new Hitler voters (17.2 million on 15 March 1933 compared with 11.7 million on 6 November 1932) consisted of those former non-voters. The attraction of Hitler's personality as Führer and Chancellor rather than that of the NSDAP had tipped the balance. On this point most observers were unanimous. The performance of the other parties explains where the extra votes came from. The DNVP ('Battle Front Black-White-Red') and the Centre Party each gained some 200,000 votes, the SPD and the State Party held on with only small losses (70,000). By comparison the DVP as well as the small Middle Class Party and Farmers' Party forfeited a total of about 850,000 votes and the KPD (5.9 million votes at the election of 6 November 1932) more than 1.1 million votes. The latter apparently benefited the NSDAP. This was renewed confirmation of the considerable subliminal affinity between the radicalism of left and right, although most of those KPD voters who went over to the NSDAP may have been the less convinced or less committed KPD followers who had first become involved with the KPD during the course of the economic crisis but who had again defected and opted for the more successful radical party after the KPD had been virtually suppressed. The NSDAP probably had to thank the coercive measures after the Reichstag fire for at least a proportion of these votes. The local elections which took place in Prussia a week later (on 12 March) fully confirmed that terror and outlawing from above could determine voting behaviour in this way. The momentous events of this one week, when the SPD, the Centre Party, the State Party, and the DVP were excluded from the Land governments outside Prussia, resulted in further drastic voting losses for the KPD, although the SPD, Centre Party and State Party who had held their own remarkably well on 5 March, now also suffered heavy losses.

The Reichstag elections of 5 March, which in Prussia were coupled with the re-election of the Landtag and produced similar results there (NSDAP 44.1 per cent; Combat Front Black-White-Red 8.8 per cent), were an important gain for the NSDAP, not least because in the South German Länder of Württemberg and Bavaria where they were hitherto under-represented, they also succeeded for the first time in capturing a share of the votes similar to the average for the Reich (Bavaria, 43.1 per cent; Württemberg, 42.0 per cent).

The increase in the NSDAP's share of the poll was especially high here when compared with the elections of November 1932 (an average of 11 per cent plus in the Reich), and particularly in the constituencies of Lower Bavaria (20.7 per cent plus) and Upper Bavaria-Swabia (16.3 per cent plus), which had previously been the domain of the Bavarian People's Party, and even in the constituency of Württemberg (13.8 per cent plus). On this occasion the high election turn-out had its effect, especially in the rural constituencies where in some cases (for example, in the Hesse rural districts) it reached 95 per cent.

Table 3.1. The regional strength of the NSDAP according to the Reichstag elections of 5 March 1933 (Electoral districts of the Reich arranged in order of the National Socialist share of the vote)[21]

East Prussia	56.5	Potsdam I	44.4
Pomerania	56.3	Dresden-Bautzen	43.6
Frankfurt/Oder	55.2	Oppeln	43.2
Hanover East	54.3	Württemberg	42.0
Liegnitz	54.0	Weser-Ems	41.4
Schleswig-Holstein	53.2	Upper Bavaria-Swabia	40.9
Breslau	50.2	Leipzig	40.0
Chemnitz-Zwickau	50.0	Lower Bavaria	39.2
Hesse-Nassau	49.4	Hamburg	38.9
Braunschweig	48.7	Coblenz-Trier	38.4
Mecklenburg	48.0	Potsdam II	38.2
Hesse-Darmstadt	47.4	Düsseldorf-East	37.4
Magdeburg	47.3	Düsseldorf West	35.2
Thuringia	47.2	Düsseldorf North	34.9
Rhineland-Palatinate	47.2	Westphalia South	33.8
Merseburg	46.4	Berlin	31.3
Franconia	45.7	Cologne-Aachen	30.1
Baden	45.4		
		In the Reich as a whole	43.9

The NSDAP had now succeeded to a considerable extent in becoming the reservoir for the formerly disparate forces which had turned against the domination of political Catholicism in the countryside. At the same time, however, the policy conceived by the Bavarian and Württemberg Land governments of maintaining Land sovereignty against the Hitler government in Berlin was considerably weakened, if not abandoned.

The table shows that the NSDAP could again achieve big electoral gains chiefly in the agrarian provinces of North and East Germany – even an absolute majority in seven constituencies – but that in eleven constituencies, particularly in the urban-industrial centres of Central Germany and in the Catholic West, the NSDAP proportion of votes was only between 30 and 40 per cent. At any rate the electorate had not opted solely for a National Socialist government. None the less all the efforts of the National Socialist leadership were directed precisely towards this end and the strength of the NSDAP as revealed by the election results facilitated the process of National Socialist revolution, which only now began in earnest and which although it was directed and legalized from above, was first made possible through pressure and terror from below.

The period in which Hitler had been careful to talk about the 'National Government' was now over. In the National Socialist press the election result was at once unanimously interpreted as a victory of the NSDAP alone and as a revolutionary decision. Hitler himself declared in the Reich cabinet on 7 March that he regarded the election as a 'revolution'. The previous regard shown for the Nationalists dwindled visibly and gave way to a new arrogant and dictatorial tone. As all the Communist seats in the Reichstag and Prussian Landtag were vacant after the earlier arrests, the NSDAP had in fact an absolute majority in both parliaments even without the Nationalists. The tactic of arresting the KPD deputies whilst still refraining from a formal ban on the KPD and even permitting a KPD list in the elections had paid off, not least in view of the planned Enabling Law.

The Party revolution from below and the Enabling Law

The election results of 5 March were the starting point for the coordination of the Länder which were not already under National Socialist control and this was completed within the week. The elimination of the federal counter weight to the Hitler government established in Berlin would however, have been difficult to accomplish in a short time by decree alone, even by resorting to the Reichstag fire decree. It was now for the first time that the pressure of the National Socialist movement from below was needed. As a result a terrorist, revolutionary movement rapidly got underway in March which soon completely swept away the restraints still imposed on the NSDAP's power through the formation of the government of 30 January 1933 and everywhere forced the development of a National Socialist monopoly of power, at first in the streets and in public before the process was then formally legalized.

Supported by the auxiliary police powers which were now given to them outside Prussia, the S.A. and S.S. detachments occupied town halls, newspaper offices, trade union offices, and consumer associations as well as finance offices, banks, courts and the like, seized fixtures and fittings and enforced the dismissal or detention of 'unreliable' or Jewish officials. Under the pressure of public reaction, of the terror in the streets and of the demands of the National Socialist associations, a wave of enforced vacations and provisional new appointments began in virtually all the authorities. Whilst the state of emergency created by the Reichstag fire decree had been chiefly felt at first in Prussia, where S.A. and S.S. auxiliary police had often hunted down Communists and other opponents on their own initiative, and where numerous additional personnel changes had been enforced, particularly in top police posts, such manifestations now became widespread. The personal union between the leadership of the local NSDAP combat leagues and the leadership of the state police increasingly perverted the latter's 'duty to keep order' into an instrument of terror for the Party. The picture was similar throughout the Reich. Whereas the rural constabulary and municipal police still tried to some extent to keep to the tenor of the Reichstag fire decree and to the corresponding directives on its implementation when arresting Marxist officials, and valued the orderly carrying out and official notification of all individual measures in keeping with their legal training, the S.A. and S.S. auxiliary police associations which were set up everywhere used the Reichstag fire decree as a warrant for every form of political 'counter-attack' and terrorism. As a result the formal subordination of the auxiliary police to the regular police, and thus to the control of the state, became largely illusory. Known local opponents of National Socialism, no matter what their political provenance, were publicly humiliated, ill-treated or arrested. In Berlin and in other big cities the S.A. boycotted departmental stores and Jewish businesses; in Breslau they enforced the immediate dismissal of Jewish Judges and public prosecutors; in Königsberg they freed National Socialist prisoners. Given the now considerably heightened danger of a ban or boycott, even the large politically independent German newspapers, which until 28 February and even until 5 March had reported extensively and critically on the National Socialist activities, were daily less inclined to risk any accurate reporting and their commentary became increasingly reticent.

Rudolf Diels, Chief of the Political Police department in Berlin at the time has extensively and graphically described this 'seizure of power' by the S.A. and S.S. in March 1933 in his memoirs.[22] As well as police detention of political opponents (so-called detainees – *Schutzhäftlinge*), whose numbers can often be discovered as a result of their official registration by the police authorities (in Prussia the total number of detainees arrested in March and April 1933 came to about 25,000),[23] there were countless arbitrary arrests made by the S.A. and S.S. and subsequently these can no longer be adequately reconstructed. Those arrested were often carried off to S.S. houses, to some cellar or other, or to some 'wild' camp.

During these days Hitler indignantly and brusquely rejected complaints voiced by his Nationalist partners about the uncertainty over the law of the land and the mounting S.A. terror. Hitler's special displeasure was aroused by a letter of 10 March from the Vice-Chairman of the DNVP, von Winterfeld, which was later published in the Nationalist press, in which the Reich Chancellor was urgently requested 'to uphold the inviolable character of the state of law, as the old Prussia of Frederick the Great had once done'.[24] When Papen, too, spoke about S.A. infringements against foreign citizens during a telephone conversation on 19 March, Hitler reacted the next day with a withering reply to the Vice-Chancellor. He had the impression, Hitler argued in his written response, 'that at the moment there is a systematic barrage aimed at stopping the National Socialist uprising'. Then he enlarged on the fact that the 'regrettable' infringements bore no comparison to the 'high treason' of the November criminals and the suppression of the NSDAP in the Weimar period. Rather he 'marvelled at the tremendous discipline' of his S.A. and S.S. men and believed instead 'that history will never forgive us if in this historic hour we allow ourselves to be infected by the weakness and cowardice of our bourgeois world and use the kid glove instead of the iron fist'. He would permit nobody 'to deflect him from his mission' of 'destroying and exterminating Marxism' and he would therefore urgently request him (von Papen) 'not to make these complaints any more in future. You are not entitled to.' This letter, which Hitler deliberately had copied for the Reich President and the Minister of Defence,[25] was an open and an almost threatening rebuff. It illustrated how the 'destruction of Marxism' was to become the standard justification for the subversion of the constitutional and legal order.

Hitler well knew, however, that political terror alone would not suffice and that there had to be positive enthusiasm for the regime too. In the very first cabinet meeting after the Reichstag election of 5 March he informed the cabinet of the decision to set up a 'Reich Ministry of Information and Propaganda'. We cannot tolerate, said Hitler, 'any political apathy'. The danger that the former non-voters won over to the NSDAP on 5 March would sink back into passivity had to be countered and the voters of the Centre Party and of the Bavarian People's Party had yet to be 'conquered'. Besides, it would pay in future to make the appropriate propaganda preparations for any necessary government measures. On 11 March, in spite of the worries of Hugenberg and a few other non-National Socialist Ministers, the cabinet agreed to setting up the new Ministry, whose chief, Joseph Goebbels, also increased the number of National Socialists in the government. On 15 March Hitler explained to the cabinet that it was 'necessary at this stage to channel all the energies of the people towards the purely political, because economic decisions would have to wait for now'.[26]

What was meant by this became clear on 21 March, on the occasion of the convening of the Reichstag elected on 5 March in the garrison church at Potsdam, when the new government arranged the first of those national celebrations which Hitler and Goebbels knew so very well how to stage for public effect. In contrast to and apparently unrelated to the S.A. and S.S. terror, or to the thousands of detainees and the earliest concentration camps which sprang up during these March days in Dachau, Oranienburg, in the Columbiahaus in Berlin, in Sachsenberg, in the Vulcan shipyard near Stettin, in Dürrgoy near Breslau, near Papenburg in Emsland and elsewhere, the National Socialist leadership presented itself at the celebration as a young, devout and idealistic team, seemingly completely in harmony with the great tradition of Prussian and German history. The Chancellor bowed deferentially to the Field Marshall, the S.A. and S.S. were lined up in disciplined order alongside the Reichswehr, and the Church blessed the reconciliation between old and young and the return of German politics from Weimar to Potsdam. The 'brilliance' of 'Potsdam Day', assiduously propagated by film, radio and the press, was the other side of National Socialist policy – alongside the concentration camps and the boycott of Jews – and its impact can hardly be exaggerated. However, it was not opposed to that darker side, and part of the nation failed to grasp this even much later on, but stemmed from that same tendency to build up a dream world decked out with clichés about the past, that same rejection of reality which also generated the unscrupulous hatred of the 'debasing' and 'subversive' Marxist, Jewish and intellectual influences. Potsdam Day was the great display of moderation prior to the passing of the Enabling Law of 23 March.

The National Socialist leaders made no secret of the fact that the Reichstag which was opened in Potsdam on 21 March was to have only *one* task – the passing of a law of four years' duration which would empower the government to take legal measures, including constitutional changes, to 'relieve the distress of the people of the

Reich' on its own authority (not as hitherto only supported by the Reich President's right to issue decrees). After the outcome of the election had already considerably reduced the political importance of the non-National Socialist parties, these had also been substantially restricted in their freedom of movement and action as a result of the National Socialist terror launched from below with the Reichstag fire decree and the co-ordination of the Länder. The KPD had already been made wholly illegal in mid-March. The new wave of bans based on the decree (against which the Supreme Court no longer had any chance of appeal) had, however, also virtually paralysed the SPD press and severely curtailed the operational capacity of the Social Democratic Party apparatus. Most of the SPD civil servants in the state and municipal authorities had already lost their jobs in the second half of March. Officials belonging to the Centre Party or to the liberal parties were, at the least, pushed out of prominent positions.

Those parties outside the government had already played out their political power before the Enabling Law. An organized power struggle against the National Socialist movement which neither the SPD (like the Reichsbanner) nor the unions had risked in February, in order not to provoke the government itself to violate the constitution, had become utterly futile by March. Moreover, the will to resist and the ability of these parties to assert themselves now crumbled visibly. Dazzled by the suggestivity and vitality of the National Socialist movement and cowed by its terrorist revolutionary policies, many members and former supporters of the liberal parties sought to attach themselves to the triumphant NSDAP, which at first accepted the 'March converts' without restriction.

Nor was the Social Democratic unionist left spared from the wave of opportunist adjustments. Many members of the Reichsbanner sought shelter with the Stahlhelm. And the leaders of the General German Trade Union Association (*Allgemeiner Deutscher Gewerkschaftsbund* – ADGB) made it known in a statement of 20 March that, in order to safeguard the trade union organization and establishments in the new state, they were prepared to dissolve their previous tie with the SPD and to co-operate 'loyally' with the Hitler government.

This rapidly spreading demoralization and organizational collapse in March produced various dissolutions, chiefly amongst the small liberal parties but also to a certain extent in the Centre Party, and this was of enormous benefit to Hitler when the Enabling Law was introduced, which confirms that even then there was no longer any question of a free decision. What, for example, was the point of the small German People's Party fraction making a firm stand if it knew that the party members at large no longer supported such an attitude but on the contrary were chiefly concerned with finding a *modus vivendi* with the National Socialist movement.

What is more, it was known that in the event of being refused the necessary two-thirds majority, the National Socialist leaders were determined to wring out the dictatorial powers they desired by force. The fact that the Kroll Opera House, in which the crucial Reichstag sitting of 23 March took place, was cordoned off by the S.A. and S.S., showed clearly enough what the alternative would be if the two-thirds majority were not attained. In these circumstances the result of the ballot was no longer of crucial political importance but rather of purely formal significance, although it was essential in view of the National Socialist leadership's attempt to have their actions legalized. Although none of the eighty-one Communists elected on 5 March – now either arrested or underground – took part in the session and some SPD deputies were also already in custody, the government parties were still nearly 40 votes short of the two-thirds majority. The attitude of the Centre Party (74 seats) and the Bavarian People's Party (18 seats) was therefore crucial. By contrast, the DVP and the State Party with 7 votes all told could not really influence the vote one way or the other.

The National Socialist leaders made no perceptible efforts to get the SPD to agree and indeed were obviously not interested in support from this quarter, but it succeeded in getting the majority of the parliamentary Centre Party to vote for the general authorization it demanded. The National Socialist leadership benefited here from the fact that after the NSDAP's victory at the election a considerable sector of the Catholic population represented by the Centre Party, including several Bishops, among these Cardinal Faulhaber (Munich), wanted to establish a better relationship with the Hitler Party and to revise the previous pastoral attitudes to the National Socialist 'errors' by taking a more positive stance.[27] Hitler had already told the cabinet on 7 March, that the electors of the Centre Party and the Bavarian People's Party were 'only to be won over to the National parties if the Curia drops both parties'.[28] Later Hitler's government deliberately encouraged this tendency by appropriate pressure (Papen's visit to Cardinal Bertram on 18 March) and by displaying its good will towards the Catholic Church. And issues of Church policy, which interested the Centre Party chairman, Kaas, no less than Hitler's constitutional pronouncements, played a considerable part in the talks which Hitler and Frick had with the party's leaders Kaas, Stegerwald and Hackelsberger on 20 and 22 March on the subject of the Enabling Law. Hitler promised to preserve the Confessional schools and the existing Concordat between the Vatican and the Länder of Bavaria, Baden and Prussia. Although he avoided exact promises of this sort in his public speeches on the establishment of the Enabling

Law, his speeches nevertheless stressed in strong terms the new government's regard both for the Church and for Christianity ('The National Government regards both Christian confessions as among the most important factors of our nationality') and underlined the will for good relations with the Vatican. This was deliberately aimed at courting the Catholic Church.

A few days after the passing of the law the changed attitude of the Catholic Church was clearly shown in a statement from the Episcopal Conference at Fulda on 28 March. This officially retracted earlier bans and warnings to the faithful concerning the National Socialist movement and instead proclaimed the readiness of the Catholic population to co-operate positively in the new Reich.[29]

Hitler had, however, also tried to dispel the Centre Party's doubts concerning the Enabling Law on state and constitutional policy. He agreed that in future the government would inform a Centre Party committee which laws were to be passed according to the Enabling Law and it would listen to the committee's opinions.[30] He also promised that there was no plan for the wholesale dismissal of civil servants belonging to the Centre Party and that the government would maintain the independence of the judiciary as well as the principle of the professional civil service and the existence of the Länder.

Certainly, in the text of the Enabling Law itself a reservation was included that the Reich government's legislative measures would not impair the President's rights nor affect the institutional existence of the Reichstag and Reichsrat. In his speech justifying the Enabling Law Hitler repeated the other promises, only in a more general way, without giving them the precise definition or even written confirmation which the Centre Party had apparently been led to expect in the meeting of 22 March.

Yet under the sway of the exceptionally skilful speech which Hitler made to the plenary sitting of the Reichstag on 23 March, the Centre Party agreed to the Enabling Law. A small but important minority of the parliamentary party (with Brüning, Bolz and Stegerwald) who felt that the global law constituted a dangerous precedent which was hardly secure against abuse by any precise provisions, had not been successful. There was similar behaviour among the Democrats (State Party), where Theodor Heuss and the former Minister of Finance Dietrich tried to get a rejection, but were forced to submit to the opposing opinion of the majority of the parliamentary party.

At the close of his speech justifying the law, Hitler declared unmistakably that the government offered the parties the 'chance of a peaceful development and a future understanding built on this' but that he would react 'just as resolutely' to any 'attempt at resistance'.

'Gentlemen, you yourselves can now decide on peace and war!' The Centre Party and bourgeois parties chose 'peace'. Only the Social Democratic parliamentary party, which was still gloomily resigned to the fact that such an unreliable offer of peace and good-will would not in any case apply to them, rejected the bill and they erected a memorial to fearlessness on this most depressing day of German parliamentary democracy with the statement of their spokesman Otto Wels.

The duration set for the Enabling Law proved to be utterly illu-sory. When the date (1 April 1937) arrived for repealing it, the law was promptly renewed for another four years[31] without the public even noticing it. So much had constitutional reality changed in the meantime.

The end of the Parties and the first plebiscitary Reichstag

The emasculation of the Reichstag, which was followed by the au-thorization of the Land governments under the first co-ordination law to pass unlimited legislation without the participation of the Landtage,[32] inevitably meant that the political parties in Germany became superfluous. And in fact the 'end of the parties' was not long in coming either.

The chronological staging as well as the varying degree of com-pulsion was characteristic of the process. The 'Marxist' parties were finished off most rapidly and most harshly. The bourgeois parties were handled with much more care and more by way of helping them to dissolve themselves. Nor were the DNVP and the Stahlhelm spared, although most concessions were made to these NSDAP 'partners'.

The Communist Party and its related organizations were already proscribed by the emergency decree of 28 February 1933 and after that by the global police measures extended against the party's officials, its press and official establishments. The provision in the first co-ordination law of 31 March, according to which all Com-munist seats were to be forfeited at the reconvening of the Land, provincial and municipal assemblies, also meant that the KPD was no longer admitted as a political party. It is true that the Hitler government refrained from issuing a formal ban on the KPD. Hit-ler explained to the cabinet that such a ban was senseless, as not all Communists could be deported. Moreover, there was probably a desire to spare the effort of legalizing a permanent ban, which was not exactly easy to justify on the basis of the Weimar constitu-tion and the existing state of the law, especially since it would have been particularly awkward to prove the Communists' 'enmity to the state' by means of a constitution which the Hitler government itself had subverted. The only measure for liquidating the KPD to be given legal form followed later on 26 May, in the form of the 'Law for the Seizure of Communist Assets' (*RGBl*, I, p. 293), which retrospectively legalized the seizures of the property of the KPD and its related organizations which had being going on for a long time and designated the Länder as the recipients of their assets.

Similar treatment was handed out to the Reichsbanner, which had incurred the particular hatred of the National Socialists as a militant Social Democratic–Republican combat organization. Reichsbanner offices, establishments and associations in Prussia had already been largely paralysed in February and particularly in the early days of March by police coercion, without the need for a ban. The Reichsbanner was formally banned in the week following 5 March in Thuringia, Bavaria and Saxony. And in this same period there were severe police persecutions of the Reichsbanner in Braunschweig, Anhalt and other Länder where the regional organizations and leaders had already taken steps to dissolve themselves during April. The chairman of the Reichsbanner Karl Höltermann, emigrated to London on 2 May to escape the threat of arrest and for a while tried to keep in contact with isolated groups of his party which continued to operate illegally. There was no complete ban on the Reichsbanner throughout the Reich by the Hitler government. In some areas, for example in Pomerania, Reichsbanner offices were only closed at the beginning of May.[33]

The rest of the SPD managing board and party organization were able to operate legally for somewhat longer. But the process of disintegration and decay which had already set in in March (resignation of members and the closure of local branch groups) continued in earnest in April. And after the buildings of the Free Trade Unions had suddenly been occupied by the S.A. and NSBO on 2 May, in spite of the ADGB's readiness to compromise, the SPD in turn daily expected to be suppressed completely, particularly as, following the Social Democratic rejection of the Enabling Law, the National Socialist press waged a running and bitter campaign against the Socialist Party and against its alleged foreign backers and 'treacherous intriguers', and also because after the wave of Communist arrests in March SPD officials and trade unionists were taken into preventive custody in greater numbers.

As a result some members of the managing board, among them the chief editor of *Vorwärts*, Friedrich Stampfer, went to Prague at the beginning of May to prepare for the emigration of the board, which was becoming necessary. The question of whether the Party leadership should emigrate in its entirety to exercise freedom of speech from abroad and to organize underground Social Democratic action in Germany, or whether they should continue to make

use of what legal possibilities remained in spite of increasingly cir-
cumscribed freedom of movement, thus limiting the process of
National Socialist co-ordination by their existence alone, split the
Party management during the final weeks. The trigger was the
Reichstag sitting of 17 May, which Hitler called in order to get a
bigger sounding board in the shape of a Reichstag resolution for
his propagandist peace speech and for his demand for equality
which was chiefly aimed at appeasing the outside world and improving Germany's standing – which was considerably weakened as a
result of the National Socialist terror at home – at the disarmament
talks in Geneva and at other international meetings. After Frick
had warned the SPD against opposing the Reichstag resolution in a
preliminary meeting in the Reichstag Council of Elders, the majority of the SPD parliamentary party were prepared to take part in
the Reichstag sitting and to forgo a negative vote. The main representative of this group was Paul Löbe. However, most of the managing board, led by Otto Wels, opposed this attitude and decided
on emigration. The ensuing split between the Prague and the Berlin SPD management simply gave the regime still more pretexts for
proceeding against the legal SPD organization within the Reich.
After the first number of the *Neue Vorwärts* had appeared in Prague on 18 June, the activity of the Prague managing board in exile
provided the excuse on 22 June to prohibit any SPD activity in the
Reich. Göring's directive from Prussia on 23 June stated *inter alia*:

The Social Democratic Party of Germany is to be regarded as an organization hostile to the state and people, particularly after its action in recent days and weeks. I therefore order the following: all members of the
Social Democratic Party of Germany who still belong to the assemblies
and local councils are forthwith to be prevented from any further exercise
of their votes.

Workers who belong to the Social Democratic Party of Germany are to
be regarded as hostile to the state in the sense of Art. II of the Law on
Factory Councils and Economic Associations of 4 April 1933 . . .

Assets of the Social Democratic Party of Germany and of its auxiliary
or substitute organizations are . . . to be seized by the police according to
the terms of the decree for the Protection of People and State of 28
February 1933.[34]

The ban on SPD activity also had indirect effects on the small
middle-class parties. Because the State Party (formerly the German
Democratic Party – *Deutsche Demokratische Partei, or DDP*) had
been on joint lists with the SPD in the election of 5 March, their
seats in the Prussian Landtag were also vacated after 28 June. As a
result the party decided to dissolve itself on that day. A day later
this also moved the chairman of the German People's Party,
Eduard Dingley, to dissolve the DVP as the majority of his parliamentary colleagues had been urging for weeks. As both these
middle-class parties had ceased to be important before this, the

main problem for the NSDAP in May and June 1933 was the conflict with their Nationalist 'allies'.

After the NSDAP's electoral success on 5 March, Hitler's previous regard for Hugenberg gave way to treating him with arrogance – as the cabinet protocols show – whilst in the DNVP and Stahlhelm those voices increased who in view of the superior strength of the NSDAP and its associations favoured giving up their organizational and party political independence and joining the Hitler movement. This tendency was also apparent within the DNVP's parliamentary party, including those who had thwarted Hugenberg's plan to put forward his own proposal to limit the effects of the Enabling Law with Centre Party backing. After the passage of the law the DNVP's efforts to assert their claim to organizational equality with the NSDAP, by forming German Nationalist combat circles and other special bodies and by pressing for the restoration of the proper legal order, were all the more forcefully opposed by the National Socialists. A major charge here was that the DNVP and Stahlhelm had been infiltrated by members of other parties, including Marxists, whose purpose they served. The house search by the Berlin police of the offices of the chairman of the DNVP's parliamentary party, Ernst Oberfohren, on 29 March, which brought to light various materials on Oberfohren's anti-National Socialist activity and made his resignation inevitable,[35] was a first clear sign of strained relations.

At about the same time there were particularly severe conflicts between the Stahlhelm and the NSDAP in Braunschweig, which subsequently deepened the rift within the Stahlhelm between the pro-National Socialist Seldte wing and the opposing Duesterberg faction and led Seldte to join the NSDAP on 26 April and to offer the leadership of the Stahlhelm to Hitler. This severely damaged the position of the Nationalist Party because many of the Stahlhelm members belonged to the DNVP.

By re-naming itself the 'German Nationalist Front' (*Deutschnationale Front* – DNF) at the beginning of May, the DNVP leaders tried to demonstrate that they had abandoned the parliamentary system more consistently than the NSDAP and were an equally important part of the 'National movement'. But they could not stop the flow of defectors to the NSDAP and soon prominent members of the parliamentary party (Martin Spahn, Eduard Stadtler and others) also took this step. At the same time the National Socialist attacks on the German Nationalists increased in severity and in May there were also many arrests, especially of members of the Nationalist combat circles. In the middle of June individual police chiefs began formally banning the Nationalist Assault Squads on the basis of the Reichstag fire decree(!) and on 21 June Hitler himself launched the general offensive against the DNF by requesting the Land governments through the Reich Governors to dissolve the Nationalist Assault Squads at once. Coercion against the militant organs of the DNF was made possible and carried out by the simultaneous isolation of Hugenberg in the Reich cabinet. After concerted attacks had been made as early as April/May on Hugenberg's position as Minister of Economics and Agriculture by the National Socialist Middle Class Organization and especially by the agrarian organizations, which had meanwhile been co-ordinated by the National Socialist agriculture expert Darré, Hugenberg's independent and diplomatically inept tactics at the World Economic Conference in London[36] in turn provided a weak spot in the cabinet which Hitler was able to exploit skilfully.

At the cabinet meeting of 23 June when Hugenberg again handled things rather clumsily, the Nationalist Party leader had not only Hitler against him but all of the other Ministers, including Foreign Minister von Neurath in particular. Although Hugenberg had still believed in May that his departure from the cabinet would subsequently shake the foundations on which the government had been built and on which the Enabling Law had been founded, and would therefore not be acceptable to Hindenburg either, he now waited in vain for the backing of the President. His offer of resignation on 26 June also meant the end of his party.

Impressed by the measures against the Nationalist assault squads, Stahlhelm leader Seldte had already reached an agreement with Hitler on 21 June, whereby Stahlhelm members were forbidden to belong to any party other than the NSDAP and in addition it provided for the future transfer of the Stahlhelm to the S.A. Afterwards, on 27 June, the Nationalists' executive also signed a 'friendship treaty' with Hitler on the dissolution of the German Nationalist Front.[37] The agreement specified that the members of the party would 'in future be recognized as full and equal co-fighters of National Germany and protected from any offence and discrimination'. Hitler promised the immediate release of the arrested members of the DNF as well as the inclusion of Nationalist deputies in the NSDAP's parliamentary groups and executives in the Reichstag, the Landtage and the municipal assemblies. Although this promise was not always kept, it was a not insignificant concession to members of the Stahlhelm and the German Nationalist Front to sweeten the end of their organizational independence. The Centre Party, the only party apart from the NSDAP still existing at the end of June, had less success in getting this sort of concession.

Just as the Centre Party's agreement to the Enabling Law had been to a great extent 'bought' by the highly conciliatory remarks and promises which Hitler had directed towards the Catholic Church, so the inglorious end of the Centre Party was intimately linked with the negotiations taking place in Rome for a Reich Concordat, which was concluded with the Holy See on 20 June

(*RGBl*, II, p. 79). After the Episcopal Conference at Fulda had called on 28 March for loyal support for the regime, the high-ups of the Catholic Church increasingly supplanted the leaders of the Centre Party both in matters concerning the relationship with the new state and as the chief spokesmen of German Catholicism, as well as becoming Hitler's chief negotiating partners. This was particularly true of Cardinal Faulhaber (Freiburg) and Bishop Berning (Osnabrück). For these men, however, and equally for Pope Pius XI and Cardinal Secretary Pacelli, the question of the Catholic Church's position in Germany, of Catholic influence in school and society, took absolute precedence over the party organization of political Catholicism. The fact that the spiritual leader of the Centre Party, Prelat Kaas, himself left Germany at the beginning of April, gave up his party and co-operated extensively with Papen, who was leading the negotiations for a Concordat in Rome, symbolized the desperate position of the Centre Party. A last attempt to 'board the ship of National Socialism', thereby retaining some residual organizational and political independence, if under the direction of the new 'Reich leader' Heinrich Brüning, encountered strong distrust from the National Socialists and got no backing from the Vatican or from the German clergy. In these circumstances the 'bastion of the Centre Party', which had apparently been so well secured and which had held up so astonishingly in the election of 5 March, broke down surprisingly quickly in the following months. Mass defections from the Centre Party, ideological and doctrinal accommodations with the new regime, all hastened the fall of a Centre Party which at the beginning of 1933 had numbered some 200,000 members.

After Hitler had offered an official government post to the Party chairman Brüning in May and early June, probably to form a counterweight to the tiresome Hugenberg and further to compromise the Centre Party, to which Brüning, however, responded distrustfully and evasively, National Socialist demands for the dissolution of the Centre Party became more and more open after mid-June. Pressure was intensified at the same time by the arrest of members of the Party and the Bavarian People's Party, by governmental obstruction of the still relatively intact Centre Party youth movement ('Windhorst League'), and through the more or less enforced self-dissolution of the Christian trade unions and through other measures. The Centre Party's position finally became hopeless when in article 32 of the Reich Concordat the Vatican itself agreed to Hitler's demand that in future the Catholic clergy in Germany were to be banned from any political activity. Apart from the clergy, therefore, political Catholicism was also generally disavowed, if indirectly. During the last stage of the negotiations for the Concordat from the end of June, the clergy's tendency to sacrifice the Centre Party to the interests of the Concordat was manifest elsewhere.[38] It was not least because of this that on 5 July the Centre Party, by now resigned and disappointed and the last of the political parties, decided to dissolve itself still some three days before the Reich Concordat was provisionally signed. The Bavarian People's Party had already dissolved itself the day before, after Himmler's Bavarian political police had launched a big drive in the last days of June to arrest some 2,000 leading BVP officials and to deliver the *coup de grâce* to the party.[39]

The Reich Concordat, which was the new regime's first international agreement, not only helped to make the Hitler state respectable abroad but also earned Hitler the enthusiastic praise of the Catholic Church at home and, at least in the precarious early phase of the regime, it neutralized the potentially strong counter-force to National Socialism represented by a Catholicism which was strongly rooted in broad sectors of the population. But as Hitler himself told the cabinet, one of the consequences of concluding the Concordat was above all the 'dissolution of the Centre Party', a process which could 'only be described as finished with the conclusion of the Concordat', that is 'after the Vatican ordered priests to keep away from party politics'.[40]

In the final phase of the negotiations to liquidate the Centre Party, which were chiefly conducted by Frick and Gauleiter Kube, the Party tried to get an agreement similar to that secured by the German Nationalist People's Party. However, the National Socialist leadership was only prepared to give an informal undertaking. According to this, former members of the Centre Party would not be humiliated after its dissolution. (In fact most of the Centre Party and BVP officials detained during the previous period were also released again in July.) Some effort was also made to go along as far as possible with the desire of many Centre Party deputies to join the National Socialist parliamentary parties in the Reich, Länder and municipalities as followers. However, unlike the case of the DNVP, Hitler and Frick did not commit themselves to any general influx of Centre Party deputies to the NSDAP, particularly since there was strong resistance to this unwelcome addition within the NSDAP itself. Thus many Centre party deputies did not exploit this possibility either, declaring themselves to be 'without party' or giving up their seats altogether. Brüning himself, bitterly disappointed, not least over Kaas and the attitude of the Vatican, soon escaped the threat of arrest by emigrating, whilst Bishop Berning was appointed Prussian Privy Councillor (Staatsrat) on 11 July in recognition of his services during the Concordat negotiations.

Nine days after the dissolution of the Centre Party on 14 July 1933, the Reich government enacted the 'Law against the Establishment of Parties' (*RGBl*, I, p. 479), which declared the NSDAP to be Germany's only legal political party and threatened punishment (prison or penal servitude for up to three years) for any attempt 'to maintain the organization' of any other political party or 'to form a new political party'. Through a simultaneous law 'On the Confiscation of Property detrimental to the Interests of People and State' (*RGBl*, I, p. 479), the SPD and KPD were threatened in addition with the confiscation of any assets which might 'be used for the promotion of Marxist ends or other ends hostile to people and state', and it was up to the Reich Minister of the Interior to decide on the application of this extremely vague legal definition to specific cases. A further law of that date created the pre-conditions for expatriating political and Jewish emigrants and for confiscating their property.

The single-party state was now a reality. The NSDAP's absolute monopoly as a political party meant that legal political activity was only possible within the NSDAP and Hitler's position of absolute leadership in the Party was also transferred to the government and the state. The National Socialist single-party state meant, at the same time, the Führer state. It was a logical step, therefore, when the Reich Minister of the Interior, Frick, informed civil servants on 20 July that the Hitler salute was 'to be used generally as the German greeting . . . now that the party system has finished and the entire government of the German Reich is under the control of Reich Chancellor Adolf Hitler'.[41]

The tendency to replace parliamentary democracy by referendums and acclamatory resolutions, which was first apparent on the occasion of the Reichstag session of 17 May, was also evident in a law enacted on 14 July, ('The Law on Plebiscites'). The practice of enacting specific laws by the co-ordinated Reichstag or of having certain government measures approved by a referendum, instead of using legislative channels on the basis of the Enabling Law, later became a frequent device to display at home and abroad the popular agreement between the dictatorial government and the majority of the people.

The first need to resort to such a procedure arose after Germany's departure from the League of Nations, a step which Hitler had again announced in an 'Appeal to the German People' on 14 October. It seemed particularly desirable to cover what was a risky action in the prevailing circumstances by a domestic vote of confidence. Besides, this same occasion could be represented by the regime as a matter of national protest against the refusal to give Germany equality of treatment, and it provided the most ideal conditions for getting those broad sectors of the nation outside the existing Hitler supporters to give a vote of confidence in the new government.

The plebiscite held under these circumstances on 12 November 1933 was coupled with the election of a new Reichstag and it was the first popular vote, akin to a confession of faith, of the Third Reich.[42] Urged by the mass demands of National Socialist propaganda to declare their loyalty, the citizens had no alternative other than to choose this or that deputy. Only one prearranged list was put before them and, characteristically this was not an NSDAP list but 'The Führer's list'. The related fears that the secrecy of the ballot box would not be respected and that non-participation in the election could have unpleasant consequences[43] did the rest. So 95 per cent supported the new combined Reichstag list. Hitler had his first 'overwhelming' referendum success and could now claim 'legitimately' to be the leader of the 'entire nation'. The decision to hold not only a referendum but to choose a new Reichstag at the same time also signified the intention of getting rid of the unwelcome followers from the former DNVP and Centre Party. Only the truly worthy representatives of the regime were to sit in the new 'acclamatory Reichstag'. Of course the circle could now be generously enlarged beyond the 'old fighters' and newly emergent forces in state and society could be taken into account. The NSDAP had meanwhile developed into a party of 3 million in which the old Party comrades of the pre-1933 era were only a minority.

Although the new Reichstag was a mere farce by all the rules of democracy, serving merely as a forum for Hitler to make speeches and important announcements, it also acted from time to time as the law-making body of the Third Reich. In particular it was a useful instrument for enacting constitutional changes under a pseudo-legal guise which were not actually provided for under the Enabling Law, or for rushing through (by order) isolated legislation where Hitler believed that this could not be entrusted solely to the still pronouncedly conservative ministerial bureaucracy or to their normal procedures for drafting laws. The new Reichstag acted in the first capacity when on 30 January 1934 it passed the law on the 'Reform of the Reich' at the suggestion of the Minister of the Interior. This decreed the transfer of Land sovereign rights to the Reich and thus constituted an 'improved Enabling Law' on the basis of which the Reich Government was able to order the abolition of the Reichsrat fourteen days later by a simple government statute. An important example of the second-named function was the passing of the 1935 anti-semitic 'Nuremberg Law for the Protection of German Blood', which was brought before the Reichstag (meeting in Nuremberg) because Hitler did not want to wait for the longer process of governmental legislation through ministerial channels.

Notes and references

1. Full text among other things in *Ministerialblatt für die Preussische innere Verwaltung*, (*MBliV*) 1933, I, pp. 160–4.
2. Protocol of the cabinet meeting of 30 January 1933 (IfZ: Fa 203/1).
3. Decree concerning the 'Dissolution of the municipal representative bodies and the municipal associations' and concerning the 'Fixing of the election date for the coming local elections' of 4 February 1933, *Preussische Gesetzsammlung*, 1933, pp. 21f. On this the implementing decree of the Prussian Minister of the Interior of 7 July 1933 (*MBliV*, 1933, I, pp. 127ff).
4. Cf. protocol of the Prussian cabinet meeting of 4 February 1933 (IfZ: MA 156/2), and *Frankfurter Zeitung* of 9 February 1933. According to the report in this paper of 24 February 1933 the Prussian State Council also decided on 23 February to complain against the decree.
5. We can only guess how far the reception of the President of the Supreme Court Dr Bumke by Hitler on 11 February 1933 played a part here. It is, however, striking that the Supreme Court granted the request of the Hitler government to extend the period for answering the appeal of the Braun government, whilst Braun's attempt to have proceedings started before the new elections were met with the answer that in view of 'the complexity of the dispute' no decision was possible before 5 March. Cf. *Frankfurter Zeitung* on 12 January, 18. and 25 February 1933.
6. Cf. on this point Wolfgang Runge, *Politik und Beamtentum im Parteienstaat* (Stuttgart 1965), pp. 237ff. According to this, among those already dismissed by Bracht by the end of 1932 were: 5 Oberpräsidenten, 8 Regierungspräsidenten, 3 Regierungsvizepräsidenten and – through the merging of Landkreise – about 70 Landräte, as well as 11 police chiefs in the bigger towns and, again by means of mergers and economies (which for all that still chiefly affected pro-Republican officials), 69 departmental officials in the Prussian Ministries.
7. *MBliV*, 1933, I, p. 169.
8. On this cf. also the circular of the Prussian Minister of the Interior of 17 February 1933 concerning 'Official statements in the press on political riots' (*MBliV*, 1933, p. 170).
9. Text among other things in *Frankfurter Zeitung*, 25 February 1933.
10. Cf. Bracher, Sauer and Schulz, *Die nationalsozialistische Machtergreifung. Studien zur Errichtung des totalitären Herrschatssystems in Deutschland, 1933–34* (Cologne, Opladen, 1960), pp. 69ff.
11. Cf. protocol of the meeting of the Reich cabinet on 3 February 1933. A circular of the Prussian Minister of the Interior (Göring), which charged the Reich central office of the home civil service to display the Appeal 'as widely as possible throughout the Reich' and above all in government buildings, went out as early as 1 February 1933 (*MBliV*, 1933, I, p. 218).
12. Report of the *Frankfurter Zeitung*, 21 February 1933.
13. Fritz Tobias, *Der Reichstagsbrand. Legende und Wirklichkeit.* (Rastatt, 1962). See also especially, Hans Mommsen, 'Der Reichstagsbrand und seine politische Folgen', in *VJHZ*, 12, 1964, Heft 4.
14. *Reichsgesetzblatt*, 1933, I, p. 83.

15. *Akten des Preussischen Ministeriums des Innern, Politische Polizei,* IfZ: MA 198/2, Bl. 83f.
16. Cited from *Frankfurter Zeitung,* 4 March 1933.
17. *MBliV,* 1933, I, p. 233.
18. Above all Art. 41 of the Prussian Police Administration Law was expressly set aside, which specified that police measures for dealing with public disturbances were only admissible where 'there was a specific threat' and which generally required that in the event of such action 'measures least damaging to those concerned and to the general public' were to be chosen.
19. *MBliV,* 1933, I, p. 731.
20. *Daily Express,* London, 3 March 1933; also quoted in *Frankfurter Zeitung* on 4 March.
21. According to *Statistisches Jahrbuch des Deutschen Reiches,* 1933, p. 540.
22. Rudolf Diels, *Lucifer ante portas* (Stuttgart, 1950).
23. On this cf. Martin Broszat, 'Nationalsozialistische Konzentrationslager 1933–1935', in *Anatomie des SS-Staates* (Olten, Freiburg, 1965), vol. 2, pp. 19f.
24. *Akten der Reichskanzlei,* Bundesarchiv (BA) Koblenz, R43 II/1263. On this see also Hitler von Gaertringen, 'Die Deutschnationale Volkspartei', in *Das Ende der Parteien 1933,* ed. E. Matthias and R. Morsey (Düsseldorf, 1960), p. 590.
25. A copy is in IfZ.
26. Quote according to the protocols of the cabinet meeting (IfZ: Fa 203/1).
27. Cf. Guenther Lewy, *Die katholische Kirche und das Dritte Reich* (Munich, 1965), pp. 44ff.
28. Protocol of the Cabinet meeting (IfZ: Fa 203/1).
29. Lewy, op. cit., p. 53ff and Rudolf Morsey, 'Die deutsche Zentrumspartei', in *Das Ende der Parteien,* p. 652.
30. In fact this committee, which apparently met only once at the beginning of April, was to be powerless. Already on 24 March, on the day the Enabling Law came into force, Hitler told the Cabinet that he was not prepared to allow the committee to have any influence on the government's decision-making and that the Cabinet alone would decide when it should be convened.
31. Law extending the Law for ending the Suffering of People and Reich of 30 January 1937 (*Reichsgesetzblatt* (*RGBl*), I, p. 105). Further extensions of the Enabling Law followed through the law passed by the Reichstag on 30 January 1939 (*RGBl*, I, p. 95) and – indefinitely – through the Führer decree of 10 May 1943 (*RGBl*, I, p. 295).
32. On this basis most of the National Socialist Land governments also introduced enabling laws, which were accepted against the sole opposition of the SPD fractions: on 29 April in Bavaria, on 18 May in Prussia, on 23 May in Saxony and on 8/9 June in Württemberg and Baden.
33. Karl Rohe, *Das Reichsbanner Schwarz-Rot-Gold* (Düsseldorf, 1966), pp. 461ff.
34. *MBliV,* 1933, I, p. 749.
35. How far this was connected with Oberfohren's mysterious suicide on

27 May is not clear. Against the thesis of suicide is the version that the bullet wound found on him was not self-inflicted.

36. Hugenberg had submitted a memorandum to the Economic Committee of the Conference on 16 June, on overcoming the crisis which *inter alia* demanded for Germany's recovery the restoration of a German colonial empire in Africa and the acquisition of new areas for settlement. The submission of these pan-German demands had not been agreed with the Cabinet and Hitler and were rightly regarded as a clumsy move which went beyond Hugenberg's authority.

37. Text in *Das Ende der Parteien*, p. 652.

38. Cf. among others Rudolf Morsey, 'Die deutsche Zentrumspartei', loc. cit., especially pp. 395ff. In addition see K.D. Bracher, *Nationalsozialistische Machtergreifung und Reichskonkordat* (Wiesbaden, 1956).

39. Cf. Karl Schwend, 'Die Bayerische Volkspartei', in *Das Ende der Parteien*, especially p. 507.

40. Protocol of the cabinet meeting of 14 July 1933 (IfZ: Fa 203/3, Bl. 477).

41. *MBliV*, 1933, I, p. 859.

42. The basic question posed by the plebiscite was typical: 'German men and women, do you approve the policy of your national government and are you prepared to proclaim it in keeping with your own opinion and desire and solemnly to acknowledge it?'

43. In fact the Party took reprisals against individual non-voters.

Chapter Four

The coordination of the Länder outside Prussia and the new problem of centralism and particularism

The takeover of power in the Länder outside Prussia in March 1933

In purely theoretical terms the independence of the German Länder according to the constitution, and the Reichsrat as the second constituent organ alongside the Reichstag, were the strongest obstacles against setting up a dictatorship in Germany. But in reality the most important cornerstone of federalism had already been damaged before 1933 as a result of the Reich government's provisional assumption of the Prussian government's authority (20 July 1932) and by the fact that, following the constitution of the German Empire, a renewed link was forged between the government of the Reich and the Prussian Land government and thus in conjunction with this the Bismarckian-Wilhelmine tradition of Conservative–Protestant Prussian hegemony was revived.

The violation of Prussia's independence delivered the Prussian executive to Göring's supreme command after 30 January 1933 and at the same time created (with the authority of the Reich Commissioner) a pattern for other future co-ordinating measures towards the Länder outside Prussia. The National Socialist command over the Prussian executive was naturally far more important than the National Socialist governments which had already existed for a time in a few smaller Länder, as in Thuringia under Gauleiter Fritz Sauckel as Minister President, in Braunschweig under Dietrich Klagges, in Oldenburg under Gauleiter Carl Röver, and in Anhalt under the control of the National Socialist lawyer Alfred Freyberg.

Accordingly the second coup launched against Prussia with the emergency decree of 6 February 1933 also caused extreme disquiet in the other big Länder, particularly since the provisional government (of Prussia) then sent a new deputation of the Prussian state government to the Reichsrat, although the State Supreme Court had categorically ruled in its judgement of 25 October 1932 that 'Reich Commissioners are Reich institutions and are dependent on the authority of the Reich. They cannot therefore represent the Land in the Reichsrat.'

On 16 February the Reichsrat turned its own attention to the situation which had arisen. The majority of its members declared in accordance with a motion from the South German Länder that the Reichsrat took note of the arbitrarily installed representatives of the Prussian provisional government, but referred the question of their legitimacy to the decision of the Supreme Court. Also most of the delegations from the Prussian provinces, above all from the Western provinces, supported this declaration and thereby made themselves the spokesmen for the illegally deposed Braun government. The Reichsrat vote was a painful loss of prestige for the Reich government but it simply made Hitler, Göring and Frick all the more aggressive towards the former Prussian government, which had especially needled the new masters by complaining to the State Supreme Court. The National Socialist smear campaign against Braun and Severing, who were accused among other things of misusing public funds, went too far even for Papen, and as a result he felt obliged to make a public declaration on 'the personal integrity' of Braun and Severing on 18 February.

It was all the more regrettable that the opposition of the Reichsrat and of the Länder lacked the necessary energy and determination. Reichsrat pressure on the government could have been considerably stronger and could have led to a formal defeat for the Reich government if the majority of the Reichsrat had been able to decide as some Reichsrat members suggested that the legitimacy of the representatives of the Prussian provisional government be examined and rejected in the Reichsrat itself, instead of referring the decision to the Supreme Court. But the Reichsrat decision – namely to adjourn further meetings for the time being as far as possible because of the questionable legitimacy of some of its members – was a retreat behind legal formulae which in political terms led to self-exclusion, and was so commented on in the cabinet by the Reich Minister of the Interior, Frick. The weak spots in this unharmonious concert of those Länder not ruled by National Socialist governments were Saxony and Baden, where representatives of the People's Party held the key governmental posts. Thus the acting Minister President of Saxony, Schieck (DVP), himself helped to undermine the independence of the Länder by denying the Reichsrat's right to examine the credentials of its members.

In keeping with the election propaganda before 5 March, the campaign of regional National Socialist Party organizations was strengthened against those Länder governed by or in conjunction with the Centre, the SPD, DVP and State Party. As in Prussia, the National Socialist parliamentary groups in the South German Länder, in Hesse, Saxony and the Hanseatic towns, Hamburg, Bremen and Lübeck, had proposed Landtag dissolutions and new elections at the beginning of February, but these had been refused. The fact that the majority of the Land governments, – Bavaria,

Württemberg, Hesse, Saxony and Hamburg – were only acting minority governments facilitated the attacks of the regional National Socialist organizations and their leaders, who sometimes frankly called for the appointment of Reich Commissioners outside Prussia too, as well as for the dismissal of certain top-ranking officials or the banning of specified newspapers, and such requests were also directed at the Reich Chancellor or the Reich Minister of the Interior.

In Hesse, the National Socialists generated a particularly fierce campaign which was chiefly directed against the Social Democratic Minister of the Interior, Leuschner, who was charged among other things with contravening the intentions of the emergency decrees of 4 February 1933.

Frick and Hitler had admittedly stressed their 'understanding of the federal structure of the Reich' and had promised that they would not damage the rights of the Länder or the Reichsrat. In fact tensions quickly developed under the pressure of the National Socialist campaign. During the election campaign, apart from the SPD Ministers in Hesse, the Württemberg State President, Bolz, who belonged to the Centre Party and the Bavarian Minister President, Held (Bavarian People's Party), all energetically opposed the activities of the National Socialists (who had performed relatively poorly in Bavaria and Württemberg in previous elections) and they warned of permanent damage to the sovereignty of the Länder. It was also typical that most of the Länder which were not run by National Socialists made much less use than Prussia of the possibilities of imposing bans which were offered by the emergency decree of 4 February, and they occasionally even refused direct requests from the government to ban certain newspapers or organizations.[1]

At the same time, however, there were also examples of complaisance which at times already looked like attempts at reinsurance, for example when the government in Baden, which was also notably zealous in banning newspapers, used its own initiative to dismiss the head of the police section of the Baden Ministry of the Interior (Dr. Barck) who had been the target of especially fierce attacks by the NSDAP.[2]

Such feeble submissions naturally reinforced the impression held by Hitler and Frick that they could risk the formal co-ordination of the Länder. During the latter days of February the threat of the Reich Commissioners increasingly hung over the heads of the Land governments. In Stuttgart the National Socialist President of the Landtag, Mergenthaler, openly spoke of steps being taken 'against stubborn State Presidents'. Frick said of Bavaria on 23 February that he would act ruthlessly against any separatist movements.[3] (Bavarian monarchists were then working with the support of wide circles of the Bavarian People's Party for a restoration of the Wittelsbachs under the popular Crown Prince Rupprecht.) And in the Reich cabinet on 27 February Göring announced that by 6 March at the latest 'he would have to ask for the authority to put the Hamburg police under the Reich Minister of the Interior' since – apparently – 'the KPD has a completely free hand in Hamburg'.[4]

Even at this time there was obviously a definite plan to move against the Länder directly following the election of 5 March, particularly since the Reichstag fire decree provided the Reich government with the opportunity to appoint Reich police commissioners. However, since the non-National Socialist Land governments were all the more careful to avoid giving the Reich an excuse to do this, it needed the pressure of the Party from below to provide the necessary pretexts. On this occasion Hitler the Party leader worked skilfully in conjunction with Hitler the Chancellor, or rather with his Reich Minister of the Interior, who was able to refer to the 'spontaneous' action of the Party. Within a few days, by means of revolutionary pressure from below and action from above which this in turn made possible, National Socialist Reich Commissioners were successively entrusted with the exercise of police powers in Hamburg, Bremen, Lübeck, Schaumburg-Lippe, Hessen, Baden Württemberg, Saxony and Bavaria, and within a short time the formation of National Socialist controlled Land governments was enforced.

Following the pattern of events in Prussia, the move against the police, which was the pivot of the executive, was generally the crucial step. The events in Hamburg exemplify this, where the process of co-ordination began earliest. The liberal Senate majority had not dared to refuse an express request by Reich Minister of the Interior Frick for a fourteen-day ban on the SPD newspaper, the *Hamburger Echo*. After that the three SPD senators, including the Police Senator Schönfelder, resigned on 3 March and a day later the Senate President, Dr Carl Petersen (State Party) handed in his resignation, a man greatly concerned with the democratic continuity of the Senate government but now seriously ill. The NSDAP administration then immediately put still stronger demands to the now considerably weakened liberal rump Senate. In particular it was demanded that the control of the police be handed over to a National Socialist and on 4 March Frick also made a corresponding 'recommendation' to the representative of Hamburg in Berlin. The rump Senate suspended the commanding officer of the Hamburg Security Police Colonel Danner, who belonged to the SPD, but opposed the more sweeping demands. Thereupon the National Socialist members of the Hamburg police went into action themselves and on 5 March they hoisted swastika flags on police barracks and buildings. At first this was a purely symbolic gesture of seizing power but it developed into a crucial question of prestige since the rump Senate could not bring itself to give the necessary and unequivocal orders to the majority of thoroughly loyal police officers and men to pull down the unauthorized flags. Frick, who was kept constantly informed by the National Socialist Gau management in Hamburg, immediately exploited the hours of indecision and uncertainty during the evening of 5 March. Referring to the emergency decree of 28 February 1933 and to the alleged inability of the Hamburg Senate to maintain public order, he telegraphed the order that very evening for the appointment of the Hamburg S.A. Standartenführer, Police First Lieutenant Alfred Richter, as the provisional police deputy of the Reich.[5]

On the following day (6 March) a Reich police commissioner was appointed in similar circumstances in Bremen where, in the absence of other sufficiently worthy and qualified Party colleagues, the choice fell not on an 'old fighter' but, at the suggestion of the Bremen Kreisleiter, on the head of the labour exchange, Dr Richard Markert, who had first joined the NSDAP in 1931.[6] Here, too, there had been a public issue of prestige between the NSDAP and the police executive – the spread of National Socialist mass meetings to the precincts of the cathedral close and government buildings (which were barred in principle to political demonstrations). And as in Hamburg the Senate majority's surrender over the matter of hoisting the flags (this caused the SPD senators, among them Wilhelm Kaison, to resign), and their hesitation about using the authority of the executive against the National Socialist provocations, resulted in a crucial loss of power. In Lübeck on the same day the Senate took the initiative in complying with the National Socialist demands and authorized a National Socialist Gau Inspector, Walter Schröder, to take over the police, which none the less did not stop Frick from appointing a Reich Commissioner (the corporation lawyer Dr Friedrich Völtzer).

Whereas in Hamburg the die had already been cast before the Reichstag election, in all the other Länder the background to, and the means of carrying out, the seizure of power were the mass meetings of NSDAP supporters, which were directed and deliberately staged to look like victorious proclamations of revolution, and especially the S.A. and S.S. parades in the centres of the Land capitals and in front of government buildings. Again, the hoisting of flags, black, white and red in colour, and swastikas on town halls and public buildings, which had first occurred in Hamburg and had also become a matter of prestige in Bremen, invariably provided the occasion for threatened or actual conflict with the police executive. The drama of such a 'revolution', which was more theoretical than actual, none the less demonstrated again the National Socialist mastery of psychology. The hoisting of the swastika flags was supposed to be merely a public and symbolic recognition of the movement which had succeeded on 5 March. In practice, however, official complaisance in the face of such public charades meant that the officiating Land governments were putting themselves, as it were, in the wrong and acknowledging that they were out of tune with prevailing public opinion. They gave a 'right' to the organizers of this popular pressure to which they were in no way entitled in the face of the properly constituted Land governments.

The mixture of violent, revolutionary 'seizure' of power and bloodless, mute resignation was also a feature of the co-ordination carried out in Hesse on 6 March. On that day S.A. and S.S. columns, reinforced from the surrounding area, usurped the disposition of armed auxiliary police units, apparently with the connivance of the regular police, and then controlled the streets of the Land capital, Darmstadt, where they were accompanied by detachments of Security Police. Thus the public was given the impression that the National Socialist combat leagues were already accepted and recognized as a new 'force of order'. Isolated clashes broke out when S.A. and S.S. troops enforced the raising of flags on government buildings and the Party headquarters tried to compel the police to hand over control whilst an appropriate order from Frick was already on its way. A Security Police squad was forcibly disarmed, and armed S.A. posts prevented Minister President Adelung and the Minister of the Interior Leuschner from leaving their houses and from any telephonic contact with the outside world. Meanwhile the Reich Commissioner, Oberregierungsrat Dr Heinrich Müller, a close colleague of Gauleiter Sprenger, took over the business of the Ministry of the Interior together with Party administrative experts in the Hesse Landtag[7] and appointed the young S.S. member, Landtag deputy and legal adviser to the Party, Dr Werner Best, as special commissioner for the Hesse Police.[8]

It was easiest to arrange the hand-over of the police to the National Socialists in the Hanseatic towns, where the SPD was still part of the government, by exploiting the harassment and persecution of 'Marxism' which the Reichstag fire had intensified. But two days later, on 8 March, Reich Commissioners were also installed in Baden, Württemberg and Saxony. Here the Party's pressure and ultimatums were still more ruthless, and its claims were also made more openly in the wake of the dynamic revolutionary force which had meanwhile been unleashed by the Party. At this stage the leading local Party or S.A. personalities were installed as Reich Commissioners, rather than some governmental or police expert or other from the National Socialist parliamentary parties: Gauleiter Robert Wagner in Baden, S.A. Gruppenführer Dietrich von Jagow in Württemberg and S.A. Gruppenführer Manfred von Killinger in Saxony.

The coup disposing of the officiating Land government in Bavaria was the most dramatic. Although Minister President Held had received the Reich President's assurance that there was no intention of installing a Reich Commissioner in Munich, here too the ball was set rolling according to the well-tried format with S.A. parades and the enforced hoisting of flags on the town hall and various government buildings. The Bavarian government, which was not disposed simply to give way to public intimidation, pointedly mobilized the Land police but then heard from the Ministry of Defence that the armed forces were not available for 'internal disputes'. None the less, the Bavarian government rejected the ultimatum, delivered by Gauleiter Adolf Wagner, Ernst Röhm and Heinrich Himmler under the threat of an S.A. uprising, to appoint the former Freikorps General and Reichsleiter of the NSDAP, Franz Xaver von Epp as General State Commissioner. This blow to the sovereignty of the Land, occasioned solely by the National Socialist leadership's urge to power, was accepted under protest only when an order from the Reich Minister of the Interior arrived on the evening of 9 March naming Epp as Reich Commissioner.

The installation of Reich Commissioners in itself violated the constitution and nor was there any justification for this in the emergency decree of 28 February 1933. The 'threat of disorder' which the Reich Minister of the Interior gave as the pretext had nothing to do with the 'defence against Communist acts of violence injurious to the state', but, on the contrary, was caused by the mass demonstrations, attacks and intimidation engineered by the exponents and formations of the NSDAP. This first violation of law was not the last however. After the installation of National Socialist police commissioners practically all of the Länder concerned were prepared to facilitate the formation of new rightist governments by constitutional means, through quickly summoning the Land parliaments or dissolving these and holding new elections, and to that extent to accord with the co-ordination required by the political leaders of the Reich. There was no constitutional necessity for this but in any case the new masters in Germany would not by and large agree to what seemed to them likely to be a protracted and uncertain procedure.

Only in Hamburg, Württemberg and Hesse were new National Socialist governments formally and legally elected by the responsible parliaments between 8 and 13 March, after the vacating of Communist seats and the pointed SPD abstentions had made possible a National Socialist–Nationalist voting majority. In this way the merchant and shipper Carl Vinzent Krogmann, who had put himself at the NSDAP's disposal in 1932 and who seemed acceptable to the Hamburg bourgeoisie, became the new President of the Senate for Hamburg and the reigning burgomaster. In Hesse the government was taken over by the National Socialist President of the Landtag, Professer Ferdinand Werner, a veteran of the pre-War *völkisch* movement, who now became State President and

Minister of Culture, whilst Dr Heinrich Müller became Minister of the Interior, of Justice and of Finance. In Württemberg power was shared between Gauleiter Wilhelm Murr, State President and Minister of the Interior and of Economics, and his chief rival in National Socialist Land politics, the former president of the Landtag Christian Mergenthaler as Minister of Culture and of Justice, together with the Nationalist Minister of Finance Dr Alfred Dehlinger, who was taken over from the Bolz government.

In all the other Länder the appointed National Socialist police deputies forestalled the constitutional formation of new governments and instead put in National Socialist special commissioners for the separate governmental departments. In more or less rabid fashion they forced the officiating Land governments to resign, once again by means of transparent and menacing references to the difficulty of otherwise maintaining the public security and order. In Bremen, Baden and Saxony, the Reich Commissioners themselves (Markert, R. Wagner and Killinger) took over the control and formation of provisional National Socialist Land governments. In Bavaria the Reich Commissioner (von Epp) had been accorded not only police powers but more general Reich powers of surveillance from the outset, and the Held government resigned on 16 March as the last of the old Land governments after its authority had been completely undermined by newly appointed commissioners. Reich Commissioner von Epp installed the former chief burgomaster of Lindau and the Landtag deputy, Ludwig Siebert, as provisional Minister President and Minister of Finance. But real influence quickly fell to Hitler's old co-workers and ambitious exponents of the Party, who had their seats in the 'movement's capital' and who were appointed provisional Ministers of State by Epp: the Munich Gauleiter Adolf Wagner (provisional Minister of the Interior), Hans Frank (provisional Minister of Justice) and Hans Schemm (provisional Minister of Education). Two other appointments made in Munich during the night 9–10 March 1933 had, however, far-reaching consequences: the appointment of S.A. Chief of Staff Ernst Röhm as State Commissioner for special duty and of Reich S.S. Leader Heinrich Himmler as head of the Munich police administration, to which the Bavarian police headquarters also belonged (as Division VI) and which was now taken over by S.S. Standartenführer Reinhard Heydrich.

The appointments of Röhm and Himmler as well as the assumption of the positions of the Minister Presidents and Ministerial offices by Gauleiter or S.A. Gruppenführer show that the coordination of the Länder outside Prussia after 5 March was much more favourable to the leading exponents of the National Socialist Party and its combat leagues, or was actually more exploited by them, than had been the case with Göring's policy of appointing civil servants in February. There was barely any trace of fair treatment for the Nationalist partners during the co-ordination of the Land governments in March 1933.

The Party's seizure of power was now complete. Here too, from the second week of March, regional S.A. and S.S. leaders also came in for a large number of the most important posts of police president.[9]

The new Oberpräsidenten in Prussia and the institution of Reich Governors

Neither Papen nor the angry German Nationalists could now prevent mainly NSDAP Gauleiter or S.A. Gruppenführer from also being installed as the new Oberpräsidenten at the head of the Prussian provinces.[10] At the end of March these appointments were: in the province of Brandenburg (Gauleiter Wilhelm Kube; successor in 1936, Emil Stürck), in Schleswig-Holstein (Gauleiter Heinrich Lohse), in Silesia (Gauleiter Joseph Wagner) and in Hannover (S.A. Gruppenführer Viktor Lutze). Additional Oberpräsidenten were appointed in the following months: Gauleiter Erich Koch in East Prussia and S.A. Obergruppenführer Curt von Ulrich in the province of Saxony (Magdeburg) as well as (1934) Gauleiter Franz Schwede in Pomerania (Stettin). Only in the Western provinces of Prussia were Oberpräsidenten chosen from people who had played either no part or an insignificant part in the Party hierarchy, and whose class and career put them closer to the Nationalist establishment: Prince Philipp of Hesse, who had been won over to the NSDAP through the mediation of the pro-Nazi Hohenzollern Crown Prince August William ('Auwi'), as Oberpräsident of the province of Hesse-Nassau (Kassel) and Baron Hermann von Läninck as Oberpräsident of the Rhine province (Koblenz). The latter, like his older brother who had already been appointed Oberpräsident in Westphalia (Munster) in February, had left the state service early in the 1920s because of his anti-Republican stance and he subsequently emerged as the spokesman of the National Opposition and the 'Green Front' in the Rhineland (he was replaced as Oberpräsident in 1935 by Gauleiter Josef Terboven).

With the decree streamlining the Prussian internal administration on 17 March 1933,[11] Göring also took pains to reinforce the Oberpräsident's leading political role as the state government's standing representative in the provinces by freeing him from the business of administration. As a result the Oberpräsident admittedly did not have any actual right to give orders to the intermediate authority of the Regierungspräsidenten, who were directly subordinate to the Prussian Ministry of the Interior. Yet the decree specifically affirmed that the 'opinion of the Oberpräsident' – who in the event of emergency could also issue instructions – 'was of special importance' and could not be ignored by the Regierungspräsident.[12] There was powerful pressure to respect the Oberpräsident's 'wishes' in all cases where the Oberpräsident also happened to be a Gauleiter and who therefore represented the leaders of both the Party and the state in his own person.

Because of the particularly marked discrepancy between province and Gau borders in Prussia (compared with the twelve Prussian provinces there were almost twice as many Party Gaue and Gauleiter), a high proportion of the Prussian Gauleiter held no state office, so that here administrations and Party were often hostile towards one another and the Gauleiter (and higher S.A. and S.S. leaders) believed that they had to be particularly active as 'watch dogs' over the Regierungspräsidenten. To counteract this the Prussian Minister of the Interior (Göring) ruled in an order of 29 May on 'Cooperation between the Oberpräsidenten and Regierungspräsidenten and the Gauleiter of the NSDAP',[13] that the heads of the Land administration had 'to maintain standing contact with the leading personalities of the National Socialist movement, that is, with the appropriate Gauleiter', and further 'to contact them over important measures' and especially to sound out the Gauleiter's opinion on personnel matters. Later, after the dissolution of the other parties, the appointment by order of all the Gauleiter in Prussia as privy councillors (Law on the Prussian Privy Council of 8 July 1933),[14] was also supposed to underline the NSDAP Gauleiter's function in the leadership and representation of the state, without giving them any formal right of command over the executive. The granting of the purely nominal and politically empty title of privy councillor was in that respect simply a sop for those Gauleiter in Prussia who had emerged empty-handed from the share out of the posts of Oberpräsident.[15] At the same time the personal union of the office of Gauleiter and Oberpräsident at the head of the Prussian provinces created a source of authority which acted as a new provincial counterweight and frequently stood in the way of the central Prussian government and prevented uniformity in the Prussian administration.

The co-ordination produced similar results in the Länder outside Prussia.

From the viewpoint of a united state dictatorship and also of the Party programme's call for strengthening the central authority of the Reich it was doubtless problematic that, as a result of the National Socialist seizure of power in the Länder outside Prussia, politically ambitious Party leaders took the helm as State Presidents, Minister Presidents and Ministers and were able to lend new weight to the Land governments under the mantle of 'co-ordination'. But in this early phase, when the Enabling Law was not yet safely through and the Centre Party made its agreement to a four-year suspension of the Reichstag conditional *inter alia* on the maintenance of the Reich's federal structure and the institution of the Reichsrat, Hitler could not simply destroy the independence of the Länder at a stroke of the pen. For this reason the seizure of power in the Länder in March 1933 did not touch the sovereignty and institutional independence of the Länder for the time being. The Enabling Law which came into force on 24 March still expressly recognized the continued existence of the Reichsrat and nourished the illusion that the federal structure of the Reich would be maintained.

Accordingly, the first co-ordination law of 31 March 1933[16] affirmed that the Land governments were empowered to make laws (including constitutional changes) and to reorganize the Land administrations without a resolution of the Landtage, only after some of the new National Socialist Land governments, Württemberg for one, had already got their Landtage to give them the appropriate powers. The continued existence of the Land parliaments, which had mostly been reduced to impotence in this way, was none the less expressly confirmed (and this was quite typical of the purely formal regard for the promise to maintain the independence of the Länder which Hitler had made eight days earlier). At the same time the law directed that the new Landtage should be made up according to the share of the different parties in the Reichstag election of 5 March, whereby the total number of seats was reduced and the seats belonging to the KPD were now also legally abolished. On the basis of this law a similar thing happened to the local self-governing bodies and thus here too representatives of the 'National Government' virtually got an absolute majority from then on.[17]

A few days later, on 7 April, the Reich government passed the Second Law for the Co-ordination of the Länder of the Reich *RGBl*, I, p. 173). which went beyond political co-ordination, decisively changed the constitutional relationship between the Reich and the Länder and further debased Land sovereignty through the new institution of Reich Governor. Hitler himself was responsible for the hasty creation of this new institution and he urged such a solution in the cabinet meeting of 29 March. Thereupon a government commission was quickly appointed, under Papen's chairmanship, consisting of Reich Minister of the Interior Frick, the Prussian Minister of Finance Popitz – a man particularly well versed in Reich matters and administrative reform – and the Cologne expert on state and international law, Carl Schmitt, to 'provide a legal form' for Hitler's 'suggestion'.[18] The fact that this issue was settled within a few days is all the more striking in that future plans for the reform of the Reich were thus considerably prejudiced, even before the process of seizing power could be completed, and consequently before other related central problems of such a reform were fully clarified and solved (i.e., new territorial additions, administrative centralization, Prussia's special position etc.).

Besides, as by this time the non-National Socialist forces in the Land governments had already been practically excluded and in so far as there was no need for a new onslaught against the Land governments, everything points to other considerations being paramount.

The Reich Governors (Hitler had talked at the cabinet meeting of 29 March of setting up 'State Presidents' in the Länder) were supposed to be in future the true representatives of Land sovereignty in place of the impotent Land representative assemblies, and they were to play, as it were, the role of Reich President at Land level (with the right to appoint governments and officials as well as the right to pardon), and at the same time to ensure in the Länder 'compliance with the policies set out by the Reich Chancellor', as Reich 'overseers' appointed by the Reich President at the Chancellor's suggestion. Thus Hitler obviously wanted to prevent a separatist power base which could threaten his leadership in the government and in the Party through a seizure of power in the Länder by the Party and S.A. leaders. In this respect the second law of co-ordination was related to the efforts made by Hitler and the Reich government to curb the S.A. and Party revolution. In fact, during the following months, Hitler and Frick chiefly used the Reich Governors and the fairly regular conferences of Reich Governors (there were conferences in Berlin on 26 May, 26 July and 28 September) to oppose any further advance of the Party revolution. Another pointer to this was the fact that in Munich, where the head of the Party Organization and the S.A. and S.S. had their base and where from 9 March the 'seizure of power' took on the appearance of a revolution confidently steered by the Party, a Reich Governor had already been appointed on 10 April, directly after the enactment of the second coordination law, whereas the appointments of Reich Governors in the other Länder were made in May or indeed even later. Besides, the Reich Governor appointed in Bavaria (von Epp) was the only one who was not a Gauleiter or a higher S.A. leader at the same time. It almost seems as though the law on the Reich Governors was conceived by Hitler primarily with an eye to Bavaria, as a brake against a possible Party revolution there which would be directed at Berlin.

The new provision for Reich Governors was never cancelled and yet the special arrangement for Prussia shows how little this device favoured any comprehensive and standardized reform of the Reich and how much instead it owed to expediency. In Prussia the rights of the Reich Governor devolved upon the Reich Chancellor himself. Papen's previous function of Reich Commissioner for Prussia was thus virtually superseded before the formation of a new Prussian government, which was due as a result of the new elections to the Prussian Landtag, and on 10 April 1933 Göring and not Papen had already been appointed as the Prussian Minister President (and Minister of the Interior), to whom Hitler also handed over the exercise of the Reich Governor's powers in Prussia on 25 April. Thus the second co-ordination law also ultimately helped to strengthen Göring's leading role in Prussia as well as to further weaken Papen's position in the Reich cabinet. By bringing in another National Socialist with the appointment of the former Landtag President Hans Kerrl as the new Prussian Minister of Justice (21 April 1933), the non-National Socialist heads of department in the Prussian government had already been reduced by April to Hugenberg and Popitz.

All the same since Göring was only acting for the Reich Chancellor in his capacity as Reich Governor, the provision of a Reich Governor for Prussia again reinforced what Papen had already done, namely restored the Bismarckian–Wilhelmine fusion between the Reich government and the Prussian state government. In this respect as the later institutional amalgamation of Prussian and Reich Ministries was to show, Göring was following in the footsteps of the old policy, which had based the power and authority of the Reich government essentially on Prussia's supremacy and on its centralized government. But it was precisely this fact which hindered any reform of the Reich that aimed at striking a uniform balance between central government and regional autonomy.

The provisions of the second co-ordination law only corresponded to the aim of territorial standardization, particularly the merger of small Länder to make bigger units, in so far as they envisaged *one* Reich Governor being appointed for several of the Länder with less than 2 million inhabitants. In fact little needed to be done here as long as the problem could be solved by means of the politically desirable device of the Reich Governor, whilst the plans for a territorial re-organization of the Länder were never promoted but indeed were postponed indefinitely, as will become apparent later.

Of the total of ten Reich Governors who were appointed in May/June 1933 (apart from Epp in Bavaria), six were each responsible for one of the bigger Länder (Saxony, Württemberg, Baden, Hesse, Thuringia and Hamburg). Only Lippe-Detmold and Lippe-Schaumberg, Bremen and Oldenburg, Braunschweig and Anhalt, as well as the two Mecklenburgs and Lübeck were each coupled as a Reich Governor's territory. In this way there still remained considerable differences in size outside Prussia too. Whereas Bavaria and Saxony numbered 7 and 5 million inhabitants, the combined Reich Governor territories of Lippe had only 250,000.

The choice of personnel for the new posts of Reich Governor was bound to be of considerable importance in determining the new institution's actual power and political role. In view of the fact that according to the wording of the law of 7 April 1933, the Reich Governor was supposed to carry out the Reich government's policy in the Länder, it is astonishing that Hitler appointed almost exclusively NSDAP Gauleiter as Governors,[19] men whose party political strongholds lay in the Länder and who could therefore be expected to see themselves chiefly as leaders and representatives of their Gaue. In reality, however, Hitler could hardly do anything else. Only the Gauleiter were in a position to get the respect of Land governments which were already staffed by leading members of the Party, since the NSDAP had already shown that it did not have the sort of strong collective Reich directorate above the level of Gaulciter which alone would have enabled it to appoint powerful and acceptable Amtsleiter over the leading organs of Party and state which were amalgamated after the seizure of power. Thus the appointment of Gauleiter as Reich Governors outside Bavaria followed the old principle which the NSDAP had already applied in 1932 when appointing NSDAP Land Inspectors. In short those Gauleiter who were especially powerful and effective because of the size of their Gaue were promoted to Reich Governors above the remaining circle of Gauleiter, although this entailed a risk that such a personal union of Party and state offices not only served to carry out the policies of the Reich as determined by Hitler, but also to create a new particularist centre of gravity in the Länder. Typically, of those appointed as Reich Governors or those Gauleiter who were appointed as Oberpräsidenten in Prussia, about half were identical with the earlier NSDAP Land Inspectors.

Those appointed as Reich Governors were: in Saxony Gauleiter Martin Mutschmann; in Hesse Gauleiter Jakob Sprenger; in Hamburg Gauleiter Karl Laufmann; for the Länder of Braunschweig and Saxony-Anhalt the head of the Gau of Magdeburg-Anhalt, Friedrich Wilhelm Loeper;[20] for the Länder Mecklenburg[21] and Lübeck the Gauleiter of the Mecklenburg Gau Friedrich Hildebrandt; and for the Länder Lippe and Schaumburg-Lippe the head of the Gau of North Westphalia, Dr Alfred Meyer.

In those where the Gauleiter were already Minister Presidents from 1932 or from March 1933, they now took over what seemed, in view of the expected reform of the Reich, the more important office of Reich Governor. Thus, in Württemburg Wilhelm Murr (his successor as Minister President: Christian Mergenthaler), in Baden Robert Wagner (his successor as Minister President: Walther Köhler), in Thuringia Fritz Sauckel (his successor as Minister President Wilhelm Marschler), and for the Länder Oldenburg and Bremen the Oldenburg Gauleiter Carl Röver (successor as Minister President in Oldenburg: Georg Joel).

In these areas supreme Party and state authority had hitherto been combined in one hand but with the arrival of the institution of Reich Governor a new dualism developed in place of this compact authority, which entailed a splintering into conflicting authorities wherever old Party and official rivalries lurked behind the Reich Governor–Minister President set-up, for example like the Gauleiter-deputy Gauleiter relationship (as in the case of Röver and Joel), the relationship between Gauleiter and National Socialist Landtag President (as in the case of Murr and Mergenthaler) or the relationship of Gauleiter to S.A. Gruppenführer (as in the case of Mutschmann and Killinger).

In Bavaria in particular, the rivalry between various long-established positions of power could not be overcome by co-ordination and the provision of a Reich Governor. Of the total of six Gauleiter on Bavarian territory two, Adolf Wagner (Upper Bavaria) and Hans Schemm (Bavarian East March) got Ministerial posts in the Bavarian State Government. The four others, Julius Streicher (Middle Franconia), Otto Hellmuth (Lower Franconia), Karl Wahl (Swabia) and Josef Bürckel (Rhineland-Palatinate), remained without office at first. Hellmuth and Wahl were appointed Regierungspräsidenten in their district in the summer of 1934. Streicher and Bürckel, two particularly forceful Gauleiter, rejected what seemed to them such an inferior office and adopted a highly individual policy line in their Gaue from the beginning, often contemptuous of the state authorities or putting these under pressure. Both regarded the Bavarian Minister of the Interior Wagner, who was also Gauleiter of Upper Bavaria, as just the same as themselves and they were still less impressed by von Epp and the latter's appointee, Bavarian Minister President Siebert, who had no Party power behind him. In Bürckel's case a marked separatist urge soon showed itself mixed up with the Palatinate's efforts to break free from Bavaria, which later found expression in a distinctive 'Westmarch' ideology after Bürckel's simultaneous appointment as Commissioner for the incorporation of the Saar. Similar nationalist ideologies of the border Gaue which heightened the awareness of being different existed in the Gau of the Bavarian East March and in the East Prussian Gau. These manifested themselves in a Gau's own economic or settlement projects, to which end the Gauleiter pressured regional branches of the economy and with whose help they acquired additional private possibilities for influence.

In Bavaria, however, the intransigence (towards the state government as well as towards the Governors) of the S.A. Chief of Staff and of the Reich S.S. Leader was even more evident. Röhm had enjoyed a special position outside the ministerial departments through his appointment as Bavarian State Commissioner for special duty, which he conceived as a general duty of revolutionary control to be exercised by the S.A. As a result a system of S.A. Special Commissioners arose in Bavaria after mid-March 1933 among the Bavarian Kreisregierungen and Bezirksämter, which existed until 30 June 1934 as a private source of authority alongside the state authority and frequently in conflict with it. But the S.S., which occupied the top posts of the Political Police in Bavaria under Himmler's control and for the time being assumed the new role of the Political Police executive in Bavaria, thereby also achieved a special position of power which did not accord with its formal subordination to the Bavarian Minister of the Interior and it certainly escaped the control of the Reich Governor.

On 13 June 1933 Epp affirmed: 'An outright war (of S.A., S.S. and police) is in progress against the state government (and the Reich Governor)', and again in the following spring he complained bitterly about the 'manipulation and undermining via the Party or through Party contacts'. 'Streicher is always off to Berlin and gets sanction [from Hitler] for his own thing. Others let Wagner cover for them, others still go to the S.A. Chief, some to the Chief of Police [Himmler]'.[22] The position of the 56-year-old Epp (like that of Sieberts) suffered chiefly from the lack of a Party power base.[23] His formal higher rank as Reichsleiter of the NSDAP made no difference in regard to Röhm at least, who enjoyed the same rank.

In 1933, however, whenever the office of Reich Governor was exercised in conjunction with the Party office of Gauleiter a considerable position of power was achieved especially since at this time the Reich Governors also had the right to appoint and dismiss civil servants and to supervise the carrying out of the law enacted on 7 April 1933, on the restoration of the civil service in the Länder and municipalities. Hitler himself described the position of the Reich Governor in the Reich Governors' Conference of 22 March 1934 as that of 'viceroy of the Reich' and he added in effect: each must make of his position what he can[24] – a typical device of Hitler's but all the more alarming to the Reich Minister of the Interior because it could not be reconciled with the conduct of an orderly administration.

Actually Hitler was simply expressing what was in any case inherent in this personal union: the tendency towards a selfish assertion and extension of power, whereby the degree to which the individual Reich Governor felt himself to be either the official watchdog of the Reich government or rather Hitler's deputy and the absolute Governor within his area, was chiefly determined by the respective authority or respective Party power base and not least by the respective relationship of these 'old fighters' to Hitler.

As long as Hitler still needed the revolutionary pressure of the S.A., the S.S., the Party, the NSBO and other National Socialist combat organizations and associations for excluding the other parties, he could give only partial and very careful expression of the need to restore the state's authority and the rule of law against the continuing 'revolutionary' tendencies in the Party. When the National Socialist movement had completed its monopoly of political power in July, however, he quickly changed course and proclaimed the end of the National Socialist revolution. All future reorganization of state and society had to be evolutionary, uniform and directed from above. It was no longer the NSDAP's primary duty to fight but to educate.

In conjunction with this change of course Hitler also gave more explicit support from now on to the efforts of the Reich Ministries in Berlin to strengthen and to restore the central government and its authority. This in turn determined the further development of the relationship between Reich and Länder.

The blocked Reich reform

On the initiative of Frick and his adviser Dr Hellmuth Nicolai, who had been brought into the Reich Ministry of the Interior at the end of 1933 as the National Socialist expert on government and the constitution, the new centralized Reichstag which had been elected on 12 November 1933 passed the law changing the constitution (30 January 1934). The Law for the Reconstruction of the Reich stipulated briefly: 'The Land representative assemblies will be abolished. The sovereign rights of the Länder are hereby transferred to the Reich. Land governments are subordinate to the governments of the Reich. The Reich Governors are under the administrative supervision of the Reich Minister of the Interior...' (*RGBl*, I, p. 75).[25]

The extraordinary constitutional significance of the law contrasted strikingly with its brevity (which was none the less typical of Hitler's style of legislation). Basically, this was more a matter of a political declaration of intent than an act of law. In anticipation of the expected outcome of this step Frick emphatically declared on the radio a day later: 'A centuries' old dream has been fulfilled. Germany is no longer a weak federal state but a strong national, centralized country.' This statement was highly premature since all that had really happened was that the old federal constitutional arrangement had been displaced for the time being, whereas very little had yet been done about the form and manner of the new organization and intended 'centralization'.

Some consequences were already implicit at any rate. Thus, along with the ending of Land sovereignty specific sovereign rights passed to the Reich government, like the right to grant amnesty which was not unimportant in this time of political 'purging'. Above all, however, the law expressly subordinated Reich Governors to the Reich Ministry of the Interior's supervision, so that these ceased to be in essence (Hitler's) 'Governors'.

A row immediately flared up about this regulation too. Whereas the constitutional lawyer Carl Schmitt and Nicolai clearly emphasized the Reich government's superiority over the Land governments and the Reich Governors,[26] the latter, for example Reich Governor and Gauleiter Sprenger (Frankfurt), opposed such an interpretation. In this phase, when public and business life was being continually and extensively disrupted by the Party's revolutionary demands and ambitions, Hitler took a positive line on the principle of binding the local Party authorities to the central Reich Government, but in spite of this he shied from saying so openly to his old co-fighters. Thus, in the conference of Reich Governors on 22 March 1934, he again pointed out that the economic situation did not permit unauthorized actions and initiatives by local Party authorities and that the reconstruction of the Reich aimed 'at a centralized Reich with a centralized government', for this was the only way to ensure the required 'enormous development of our strength'.[27] At the same time he appeased the Reich Governors with remarks such as that each of them could 'be as important as his ability made him', and he prevented Frick from making a much sharper statement on this issue.[28] Because of this continuing ambiguity, Reich Governor Loeper (Braunschweig and Anhalt) formally asked the Chief of the Reich Chancellery (State Secretary Lammers) on 7 April, 'If the Reich Governor still has his old position or whether he has become an authority subordinate to the Reich Ministry of the Interior.' If the first were the case, it would not do for the Reich Minister of the Interior or a Ministerialrat acting as his deputy, to treat the Reich Governor as an inferior. He (Loeper) could imagine 'that the professional bureaucrats will happily make use of the opportunity to reduce the Reich Governor's position below that intended by the Führer', especially since he (Loeper) well recalled that the Führer had told the Reich Governors when they were appointed: 'What you make of this position will determine what it will be in the future.'[29] Six weeks later Reich Governor Sauckel made a similar point with the argument that the Reich Minister of the Interior and other Reich Ministers could not simply give orders in matters of Land legislation; rather in the event of a difference of opinion between the Ministers of the Reich government and the Reich Governors or Land governments, the Führer's opinion should be taken. The Reich Minister of the Interior reacted by expressly rejecting this in a written communication to the Reich Chancellor on 4 June 1934:

If we are to preserve the idea of a central, united leadership of the Reich by the Reich Chancellor and his supporting departmental Ministers who together with the Reich Chancellor comprise the government, then it is impossible to refer the decision to the Reich Chancellor . . . in the event of differences of opinion between a Reich departmental Minister on the one hand and a Governor on the other. On the contrary, the decision of the Reich Minister, who represents the Reich government in his area of responsibility, must be recognized by the Reich Governor without the latter being accorded any sort of legal redress against a decision by a Reich Minister in the field of legislation.[30]

Logical and consistent as this attitude was, assuming the existence of state centralism according to constitutional law and the Reichminister's official position according to the rules, it was none the less thoroughly hypothetical in so far as it ignored both the actual power of the Reich Governor/Gauleiter arising from the fusion between Party and state office and Hitler's claim to a position of absolute leadership within the cabinet. What Hitler therefore had Lammers tell the Reich Minister of the Interior was also typical:

The Reich Chancellor also believes that generally speaking[!] it is impossible to refer to his decision differences of opinion between a Reich Minister and a Reich Governor on the legality or expediency of a Land law. It is the opinion of the Reich Chancellor however that an exception must be made in matters of special political importance. It is the Reich Chancellor's view that such a ruling is in accordance with his position as leader.

The proviso was typical too in view of the general constitutional development: in matters of *political importance* the respective Party exponent, or rather Hitler himself, should have the final say, whereby naturally *what* was to be regarded as a matter of political importance could be flexibly interpreted. It is obvious here that Hitler completely threw into doubt the Reich department's clear superiority over the particularist authority in the Land, for which his Minister had asked on the basis of the law for reconstruction. Some of the new 'Gau princes', as Reich Minister of Finance Schwerin-Krosigk put it later, proved to be 'much more stubborn federalists than the former Minister Presidents of the Länder'.[31] Thanks to their old Party ties such men benefited from the fact that they often managed to get an audience with Hitler before a Reich Minister, particularly if the latter was not from the NSDAP. But in the years to come Frick, who was himself an 'old Party comrade', still complained bitterly and frequently about this abuse.

On the whole, however, the Reich Governors and Land governments alike lost weight relative to the Reich government, in that in the course of time legislative and administrative matters increasingly fell to the central departments of the Reich. The earliest and most thoroughgoing 'centralization' occurred in the sphere of justice, after an initial Law for the Transfer of the Administration of Justice to the Reich had already been issued on 16 February 1934.[32] The Reich Ministry of Justice, which had previously been a Ministry for making laws, was merged with the Prussian Ministry of Justice in Berlin and had supreme administrative responsibility for all the courts and officials of justice in Germany. With effect from 1 April 1935, the Land Ministries and authorities for Justice were shut down and transferred to about thirty uniform Higher Central Court authorities which were under the Reich Minister of Justice.

Considering the actual constitutional situation of the Third Reich, the effects of these measures went against the trend. In the prevailing situation they strengthened the weight of the authoritarian centralized state which at that time (1934/5) also entailed weakening the Party's influence, not only because a string of old Party comrades – who had taken over the Ministries of Justice when the Länder were co-ordinated – now lost their jobs, for example Kerrl in Prussia, Hitler's crown lawyer Hans Frank in Bavaria and Otto Georg Thierack in Saxony.. Through their direct subordination to the Reich Ministry of Justice, led by the Nationalist Dr Gürtner until his death in 1941, the chairmen of the Land courts were also further removed from the influence and pressure of local and regional Party authorities. The fact, for example, that the right of amnesty in future belonged to Gürtner's department in so far as Hitler did not exercise this (after 2 August 1934) in his capacity as Head of State,[33] generally ensured fairer treatment than that from Reich Governors. On the other hand, and this certainly counted for more in the long run, the centralization of justice lent itself more readily to authoritarian control and to its increasing self-adjustment, chiefly through dropping (as directed) charges and investigations through the Reich Public Prosecutor's office in cases where the regime or its exponents had themselves committed or instigated political crimes.

There was also deliberate centralization from the outset in the department of the newly created Reich Ministry for Information and Propaganda, whose outposts in the Länder and provinces were generally merged with the personnel and organization of the NSDAP Gau propaganda controls from which they originated and which received the formal status of subordinate Reich authorities in 1937. The importance of the new Ministry as a central controlling authority was all the greater since it not only concerned itself with the management of the radio and the press throughout the country but also, at the expense of the Ministers of Education and of the Interior, attracted to itself the whole area of art and cultural policy through the Reich Chamber of Culture set up in autumn 1933,[34] with its subordinate chambers (for the theatre, music, the visual arts, film, and literature).[35]

Also the creation of additional new Reich Ministries or Supreme Reich Authorities, chiefly at the expense of the 'traditional' departments, helped to shift the weight of the state administration and control to the central Reich departments during these years; for example the installation of a 'General Inspector for the German Highway System' (30 Nov. 1933), the establishment of a special Ministry for the Church on 6 July 1935 (in place of the previous responsibility of the Church policy division of the Ministry of the Interior) and the creation of a Reich office for the planning of living space on 26 June 1935, which were both put under Hans Kerrl; and the removal of forestry and hunting from the Ministry of Agriculture's control and the introduction of a Reich Master of Forestry and Hunting (Hermann Göring) in July 1934.[36]

Such a shift of responsibility was also more and more apparent in the administration of finance, economic matters, labour and education, if at the same time progress was not so rapid and systematic as in the case of the 'centralization' of justice. Instead the development was left to *ad hoc* measures which had the disadvantage of leaving the relationship between the Reich government and the Land governments highly confused.

How much such *ad hoc* or partial solutions could impede a satisfactory redress of the balance between the central government and regional autonomy was shown especially by the amalgamation of the Prussian and Reich Ministries of the Interior, Economics, Agriculture and Labour (only the Prussian Ministry of Finance remained as a Prussian department) which was carried out in 1934. The merger of the departments of the Interior to form 'The Reich and Prussian Ministry of the Interior' under Wilhelm Frick was particularly important. Frick thereby became the first man to head a powerful central government authority. The fusion of the central Prussian and Reich departments undoubtedly marked a further stage in that 'Prussification' of the Reich government which had already been re-started by the provisional government of Prussia, if only because from now on hundreds of Prussian ministerial officials poured into the departments of the Reich, as a result of which the Protestant and specifically Prussian-conservative element in the Reich Ministries was also strengthened, especially in Frick's own Ministry.

The integration of the Reich and Prussian departments which Frick carried out in agreement with Göring was conceived as merely the first step in a comprehensive reform of the Reich, which aimed to combine the intermediate authority of the Reich government, the provincial self-government and the Gau administration on the basis of a subdivision of the Reich into uniform regions (or respectively, Reich Gaue), thus also abolishing the distinction between the Oberpräsidenten (in the Prussian provinces) and the Reich Governors in the Länder outside Prussia, as well as the Land governments still existing alongside the Reich Governors. The law concering the Oberpräsidenten of 27 November 1934 anticipated this aim and at the same time gave these officials the status of representatives of the Reich government in their provinces (similar to that of the Reich Governors).

Much more was expected, however, from a new law drafted by the Reich Ministry of the Interior at the end of 1934 which required effective leadership of the intermediate authority to be transferred to the Reich Governors instead of the Land governments, and to be strictly subordinate to the Reich government. At first Hitler agreed to the basic idea of the draft, but then expressed strong reservations so that the 'Second Law concerning the Reich Governors' (30 January 1935) was a much watered-down version and merely admitted the possibility of joining the offices of the Reich Governers and Land Minister Presidents, without however making this the rule and regulation.

Only in Hesse, where the ruthlessly ambitious Gauleiter and Reich Governor Sprenger had furiously booted out the politically suspect National Socialist Minister President of Hesse, Dr Werner, and replaced him with a more acceptable successor, and in Saxony where the previous Minister President, S.A. Gruppenführer Killinger, a former co-fighter of Röhm's, was forced to capitulate to Gauleiter and Reich Governor Mutschmann after the violent defeat of the S.A., were the offices of Reich Governor and Minister President combined in the hands of the Gauleiter at the beginning of 1935. At Frick's request Hitler had already signed the corresponding orders for the Reich Governors of Württemberg, Baden and Thuringia in May 1935, but their implementation was repeatedly postponed by Hitler and finally abandoned. In March 1935 too, Hitler had already ordered that in future 'All written or spoken public discussion of the reform of the Reich, particularly of questions concerning territorial reorganization, must cease'.[37] That was also especially meant for Frick's colleague Nicolai, who had incurred the special displeasure of the Gauleiter with his draft proposals for reorganizing the Reich. The Gauleiter were bound to be afraid of losing their offices or part of their sovereign territory through such a reform. In 1935 Nicolai left the Reich Ministry of the Interior. His more accomplished successor in the Ministry's constitutional law division was the young National Socialist lawyer Wilhelm Stuckart, who had fallen out with Rust in the Prussian Ministry of Culture in 1933.

By the time further reforms were stopped the Reich Ministry of the Interior had only been able to enforce the enactment of a German Municipal Code on 30 January 1935 (*RGBl* I, p. 49), after a new local government law had already been passed in Prussia on 15 December 1933. Instead of being elected by the local council the new arrangements envisaged the appointment of the burgomaster and local councillors by the state supervisory authority (according to the size of the locality by the Regierungspräsidenten, the Reich Governor or the Reich Ministry of the Interior). The right of nomination lay with the NSDAP's 'authorized representative' (usually the local Kreisleiter). Only in the event of a disagreement for the second time between the supervisory authority and the NSDAP's 'authorized representative' could the former make the nomination. This regulation knocked holes in the principle of local self-government by introducing the Führer principle in the municipalities and was typical of the course followed by Frick. The Party was to be accorded a clearly defined legal say in the appointment of local government leaders but the final decision was to rest with the state supervisory bodies, which meant in the last resort with the Reich Ministry of the Interior.

The only other effective trace of a comprehensive Reich reform was the Law on German Civil Servants which had already been drafted in 1935, but because of Hitler's hesitation it was not passed until 26 January 1937, and will be discussed later. All of the other plans for a comprehensive reform of the Reich – above all the territorial reorganization and in conjunction with this the creation of a united and rationalized regional authority for the administration, with clearly determined rights of self government and subordinate to the Reich government – failed to materialize. Göring's chief adviser in matters of Reich reform, Ministerialdirigent Friedrich Gramsch (Prussian Ministry of State), later declared in restrospect that in 1935 it had become 'pretty well obvious' that Hitler 'just did not want any systematic and clearly regulated reform of the Reich'.[38]

There were obviously a number of reasons which decided Hitler's attitude. It had already been shown in 1933/4 that in the absence of any programmatic preparation and agreement there could be no consensus within the Party owing to the ineffectiveness of the Reich Directorate and the differing interests of the Gauleiter over the various suggestions for a reform of the Reich, which were made among others by the Gauleiter Adolf Wagner, Carl Röver and Fritz Sauckel. Even the smallest changes, like those which were supposed to take effect later between the Land Braunschweig and Prussia,[39] showed how jealously those Gauleiter who had meanwhile been established as Reich Governors, Oberpräsidenten or Land Ministers, were determined to hold on to their offices and influence.[40] Since the Gauleiter kept each other in check on these problems in 1933/4, the far more determined proposals for the reform of the Prussian and Reich Ministerial bureaucracy made the running for the time being. These appealed to Göring and Frick and were aimed at ensuring a clear prerogative for the Reith government and at concentrating the administration (in place of the unco-ordinated Reich administrative departments) at the intermediate level too, for example through the merger between the Prussian and Reich departments. The objections which were raised against this by the Reich Governors and Land Ministers outside

Prussia – among others by the Bavarian Minister of the Interior Wagner in a longer letter to Frick on 23 June 1934,[41] – could not move Hitler, just as long as it suited him in the interests of strengthening his own leadership and authority, to restrain the Party's influence on the state and especially the regional authority of the Gauleiter and S.A. leaders.

But after the blow dealt against the S.A. leadership at the end of June 1934, which had the effect of generally stifling the Party's revolutionary tendencies and ambitions, and after his position as Führer was consolidated through his take over of the Reich President's office following Hindenburg's death (2 August 1934), such reasons lost a great deal of their force. Instead there was a growing tendency for Hitler to oppose any further strengthening and consolidation of the authoritarian and conservative forces in the state administration, especially in the ministerial bureaucracy in Berlin. An early sign of this was his speech before 200,000 political leaders of the NSDAP at the Nuremberg Party Rally on 7 September 1934: 'The state does not command us, we command the state! The state did not create us, we created the state!'[42] Although this formula ('We command . . .') was admittedly not the same as the version which subsequently became current in the NSDAP, 'The Party commands the state' (an interpretation of Hitler's speech which was sharply opposed by Frick, Lammers and other members of the Reich government), yet the drift of the Führer's declaration was still unmistakable. It came out still more clearly in the Conference of Reich Governors on 1 November, in which Hitler spoke of the 'grave fact that even today the state has enemies, some concealed, some lethargic, among the civil servants' who had 'gone over to passive resistance'. Given the difficulty of enlisting qualified recruits from the ranks of the National Socialist movement it would be about ten years 'before we have a bureaucracy which also wants to co-operate'.[43]

As a result of this attitude, which was noticeable from summer 1934, Hitler saw any further strengthening of the central body of civil servants as the main drawback to continuing with the Reich Ministry of the Interior's plans for a reform of the Reich. In addition, as is apparent from Gramsch's remarks cited earlier, there was Hitler's characteristic resistance to any degree of definition and codification of internal constitutional matters which did not seem absolutely vital, because this could obstruct his own arbitrary power of decision making, as well as changes which might seem necessary in future.

Because the reform of the Reich was stopped, the interim situation reached between 1933 and 1935 was in effect frozen: that is to say the expedient of setting up the Reich Governors alongside the old Land Ministries, the frequent overlap between the bounds of the Party Gaue, the provinces, Länder and territories of the Reich

Governor, the different 'types' of Reich Governor (with and without the duties of a Gauleiter, with or without the task of heading the Land government).

In a similar fashion the relationship between the central Reich government and those particularist authorities closely involved with the Party, the Oberpräsidenten, Reich Governors and Land Ministers, remained unresolved during the years 1933–38 and subject to the prevailing struggle for power and to whatever opportunities arose. If important Reich interests were at stake, like the policy of autarky and the armaments industry, then individual and energetic Reich Ministers, Schacht for one, could generally get their way over the Party powerful in the Länder and provinces too. At times the most remarkable combinations arose (like that to support the 'freemason' Schacht by individual Gauleiter to try to put an end to the arbitrariness and independence of Darré's Agrarian and Reich Food Policy Organization). In a number of cases Oberpräsidenten and Reich Governors, who acted like independent Gau kings, finally had to give way; for example in 1938 when Oberpräsident Koch in East Prussia, who had at first refused to recognize a senior Finance President installed in East Prussia by the Reich Minister of Finance, was then persuaded to come round after the Führer's Deputy had also opposed Koch. In this phase the Reich Minister of the Interior could also generally maintain his authority in the realm of internal administration (already long since impossible in the police sector). All the same, the high-handedness of the ambitious Gauleiter and their staffs, based on the personal union of state and Party office – and this also applied to a lesser extent to the Kreisleiter as the party political counterpart and control organ opposite the Land councillors or chief officials – remained a standing force for disruption which continually undermined the effectiveness of the central government.

The end of a uniform administration in The 'Greater German Reich' and the new particularist forces in the annexed territories

In many respects the development during the second half of the Third Reich, especially during the War, rapidly increased the weight of the central departments. One example was the Labour administration. In accordance with the regime's growing need to channel the labour supply to many branches of industry which were already short of workers after 1936, the Labour exchanges throughout the Reich increasingly became part of a centralized system for directing labour from 1938, which became more and more important during the War, and also had to organize the mass influx of so-called foreign workers. A similar situation arose with the state fixing of quotas and the allocation of economic supplies, which was chiefly confined to raw materials before 1939, but was then gradually extended to most foodstuffs and consumer goods. In the course of this process the economic and food offices under the Ministry of Economics or the Four Year Plan grew into a gigantic, centrally controlled bureaucracy. The same development towards a new centralized administration occurred in the armaments sector in the shape of the Military Armaments Inspectorates (under the supreme command of the armed forces) in the Wehrkreise and in the Armaments Commission (set up in 1942) of the Reich Minister for Armaments and War Production (Speer), with their spokesmen in the Gaue. There were further creations necessitated by the War, like the 'Air Defence', an organization under the Reich Minister for Aviation and Commander in Chief of the Air Force (Göring), which emerged in 1935 but which only grew markedly in authority and size after the start of the war and especially as a result of the increase in Allied bombing attacks from 1942.

It is obvious that the growth of special authorities and organizations was occasioned more by the dictates of war rather than being a characteristic of the National Socialist regime, and in every case it was bound to pose a difficult problem for the process of coordination, the over-all supervision and organizational unity of the state administration.

The centralized direction of the administration repeatedly postulated by Frick and other proponents of a National Socialist reform of the Reich and of the administration was never achieved. The Reich Minister of the Interior (after the outbreak of war in his role as Plenipotentiary of the Reich Government) had wanted to claim such a direction for himself over the other Supreme Reich Authorities, and to delegate powers to the Reich Governors or the Oberpräsidenten at the intermediate level (under the supervision of the Reich Ministry of the Interior). However, this plan was finally abandoned in the face of the mushrooming specialist and *ad hoc* authorities. Matters were not helped when the Cabinet Council for the Defence of the Reich appointed commissioners for the defence of the Reich on the day war broke out (1 September 1939) in each of the eighteen Wehrkreise of the Greater German Reich, for which the Reich Governors and Oberpräsidenten (in Munich the original 'strong man', Gauleiter and Minister of the Interior Wagner) were generally chosen. This new measure for the war emergency, which in practice was to give the most powerful Gauleiter the position of supreme commander in the civilian sphere and which enjoined them to co-operate closely with the military commanders of the Wehrkreise, could make only little headway at first because it further overlapped with the already incongruent territorial organizations and offices of the state administration and the Party Organizations and this was bound to cause numerous disputes.

The institution of Commissioner for the Defence of the Reich first became more important in 1942, when with the changeover to total war *ad hoc* combinations of all the forces of the state and the Party became necessary at the intermediate level. The new arrangement through the decree of 16 November 1942, from then on worked on the divisions for defence, generally making the Party Gau areas into Reich defence zones and appointing the Gauleiter as Commissioners for the Defence of the Reich, whether or not they had already previously held state office as a Reich Governor or Oberpräsident. This entailed a considerable promotion and increase of power for the Gauleiter, especially since from then on the newly created economic offices, armaments commissions etc. were also generally adapted to the Reich defence zones. At the same time, however, those departments which were important to the war effort had their discretionary powers strengthened over the Commissioners for the Defence of the Reich too, whereas there was less and less opportunity for the Reich Ministry of the Interior to co-ordinate matters.

The fact that the attempt to reform the Reich had been interrupted made the new improvisation essential; but this only led to one improvisation overlapping another. The actual wartime administration was increasingly dictated by day-to-day needs and deviated more and more from the proper conduct of government until it became increasingly difficult to find a way through the jungle of administrative authorities, among which the new particularist authorities of the Gauleiter and Commissioners for the Defence of the Reich occupied a strong position by the end of the war. And these men had often behaved in a self-willed, self-seeking manner. But the development of the relationship between the Reich central government and the newly installed rulers in the areas annexed by the Reich after 1938, was still more typical of the National Socialist system.

It was already noticeable that the Saar, which had been joined to Germany as a result of the referendum of 13 January 1935, was placed under the administration of the neighbouring Rhineland-Palatinate Gauleiter, Bürckel, who had previously played a leading political role in the area as German Commissioner for the Referendum. However, the setting up of a direct Reich authority under a Reich Commissioner (without the interim stage of a Saar Land government) at that time obviously anticipated a projected reform of the Reich. The law of 30 January mentioned the 'temporary administration of the Saar...until its incorporation in a Reich Gau'![44] This is also confirmed by the similar action taken at the beginning of 1937, when chiefly for economic reasons the city state of Hamburg, enlarged by the territory of the Prussian province of Schleswig-Holstein, was made the Land of 'Greater Hamburg' under a Reich Governor (Gauleiter Karl Kaufmann), who was authorized to head the government there.[45] But Bürckel obviously also felt that his appointment as Commissioner of the Reich in the Saar entailed a greater effort here (in the Western border area) than in the old Reich to ensure that National Socialists led the administration. This subsequently brought him very much into conflict with individual Reich departments but he was supported by Hitler and the Führer's Deputy.[46] And apparently precisely because of his highly forthright policy in the Saar towards the Reich Ministerial bureaucracy, Bürckel also recommended himself to Hitler for other similar jobs, at first (1938–40) as Reich Commissioner for the Reunification with Austria and later (1941–4) as head of the civilan administration in Lorraine.

Bürckel's special task in Austria and the deviation from the pattern of previous duties of a Reich Governor was already apparent from the fact that Bürckel was only active as a Reich Commissioner in Vienna (on the basis of a Führer decree of 23 April 1938) after the referendum on the union with Austria, whereas the Austrian, Arthur Seyss-Inquart and Wilhelm Keppler (previously on a secret mission in Vienna) were appointed earlier because of their services over the Anschluss, the former as first Reich Governor and the latter as Reich Deputy for Austria (especially for economic questions). The special task entrusted to Bürckel by Hitler of assimilating Austria politically to the Reich became the first blatant example proving that by 1938 Hitler no longer wanted to resort to the Berlin ministerial bureaucracy's control to the extent which he had in 1933/4 when co-ordinating the Länder, but preferred instead to rely on the ambitious leaders from the Party's old Guard. At the end of April 1938 Hitler had already refused to grant the Reich Ministry of the Interior's urgent wish to have its power of command confirmed over Bürckel: the Reich Commissioner was 'directly under' him (Hitler).[47] And in mid-May Frick was forced to admit 'that the offices of the Austrian Land do not comply with the Reich Minister's requests because the Reich Commissioner has objected'.[48] Frick's direct written communication to Hitler could not change matters either, and a personal meeting with Hitler (23 May 1938) essentially only confirmed Bürckel's standpoint. The latter was gratefully able to inform the Führer that 'the work of construction can now proceed without hindrance'.[49]

In the following weeks quarrels arose between Bürckel (or between the Reich Governor much patronized by Bürckel, Seyss-Inquart) and the Reich departments, occasioned mainly by the severe purging of the bureaucracy in Austria after the Law for the Restoration of the Professional Civil Service of 7 April 1933, in the course of which Bürckel refused the officials concerned any opportunity of appealing to the departments of the Reich, expressly referring to the agreement of the Führer's Deputy and of Hitler.[50] In the summer of 1938, because Bürckel was also demanding that all traffic between the Reich departments and the Land departments in Austria should pass through his office exclusively, the Reich Minister of the Interior was on the point of handing over any further control of the administrative attachment of Austria, which was his duty as the appropriate central authority, to the Head of the Reich Chancellery, in view of Bürckel's 'direct subordination' to Hitler.[51] Bürckel's attitude was also remarkable in that it was much more arrogant than would have been possible in the years 1934/5; for example in a letter of 18 June 1938 to the Reich Ministry of the Interior:

In so far as agents of Reich Ministries are still active here, they must either be recalled or, if they are urgently needed, they are to be attached to the authorities of the Reich Governor. In any case I categorically forbid them to be given a special position – for example any right of direct reporting over my head. I will not tolerate the setting up of more clearing offices by the Reich Ministries for Austrian Ministries; ... in so far as it concerns those clearing offices already permitted I shall not under any circumstances allow them to have the power to give orders to the Land government, or to make the actions of the Land government dependent on their agreement. Were future officials of the clearing offices to assume such powers, I should have to remove them immediately.[52]

Finally – and this brought the sharpest protests from Frick – Seyss-Inquart and Bürckel did not even hesitate to alter the administrative areas of the former Austrian Federal Länder on their own initiative, by means of an 'interim ruling' without contacting the Reich Ministry of the Interior.[53]

None the less, the fierce jurisdictional conflicts between the Reich Minister of the Interior and Reich Commissioner Bürckel in Vienna were only a foretaste of the still more severe tensions which were to develop after the War began between the central offices of the Reich government and the new particularist authorities active in other areas which were incorporated or annexed. Here it was invariably either 'direct subordination' to Hitler (which in fact meant a far-reaching freedom from control in general) or the 'special authorization' derived from Hitler which provided the lever for breaking out of the legal and administrative framework of the Reich.

Bürckel's term of office in Vienna lasted until April 1940 and during it the Party's influence was firmly anchored in Austria. In 1940 the new administrative arrangement came into force dividing Austria into seven Reich Gaue with seven Gauleiter and Reich Governors (in personal union). Thus for the first time the concept of the Reich Gau signified both the area of the state's administration and of the Party's jurisdiction, and the Reich Governor in Greater Hamburg from 1938 was the administrative head of the area without the parallel organization of a Land government. This new model for the 'Reichgaue' (as the intermediate authority of the Reich government and as a Gau self-governing corporation) was also applied in 1939 to the Sudetenland (under Konrad Henlein as Gauleiter); to West Polish areas incorporated in the Reich on 7 October 1933 (Reichsgau Danzig–West Prussia under Gauleiter Forster and Reichsgau Wartheland under Gauleiter Greiser) in so far as these were not added on as new government districts (Kattowitz, Zichenau) to the Prussian provinces and the Oberpräsidenten or Gauleiter reigning there. However this later practice could no longer be made to work in the 'Old Reich'. Here the anachronistic co-existence of Gauleiter, Reich Governors, Land Minister Presidents and the overlapping territorial areas, remained until the last.

The immediacy of the new Reichsgaue to the Reich was not the same thing as tightening up the administration of the Reich. On the contrary it meant, above all, immediacy to the Führer for the appointed dignitaries, and in that respect the expansion to a Greater German Reich ended the legal and administrative unity of the Hitler state.

Since Hitler had already installed a Reich Commissioner in Austria with special powers to carry out the most effective political purging and Nazification, then such authorized powers were bound to grow immeasurably where it was not simply a matter of the Nazification of a German population but concerned the Germanization of areas which had been conquered by force and which were inhabited by a more or less obstinate non-German population. The rapid annexation to the Reich (as in the case of the formerly Polish 're-incorporated Eastern territories'), or the speedy setting up of a civilian administration (for example, the General Government for the occupied Polish territories, in Alsace-Lorraine, in the Reich Commissionership for the Netherlands, in the former Yugoslav territories of Lower Styria and Krains and finally in the large areas of the Reich Commissionership Ostland [Baltic, White Ruthenia] and the Reich Commissionership for the Ukraine), were not meant to create orderly administrations as quickly as possible after the fighting. In all these instances it was much more a matter of replacing the military authorities which, in keeping with Hitler's political and ideological goals, were as superfluous to him as the bureaucracy of the Old Reich's internal administration, with National Socialist organs of leadership. The latter were less interested in orderly and lawful administration and all the more prepared to start on the political aims of Germanizing and Nazifying in the manner of the old fighting methods of the National Socialist movement.

This was most clearly shown in the case of the Polish Western regions, which in 1939/40 became the first great experimental area for a comprehensive 'racial purification', because here Hitler immediately decided in favour of formal annexation to the Reich and thus the measures which were underway for the enforced purification of Poles and Jews and for Germanization were seriously at variance with the legal and administrative norms which otherwise held true for the civilian administration within the Reich.

The conflict was sparked off much more dramatically than in Austria, typically at first over the question of the proposed appointment of administrative officials (the burgomaster, the privy councillors, Regierungspräsidenten). Inevitably Hitler and his newly authorized heads of the administration of the 'reincorporated' Western Polish territories, especially Gauleiter Koch, Forster and Greiser, could not bring about the ruthless Germanization and suppression of the Poles which they required working with governmental officials of the old school. In this instance, therefore, there were mass appointments of Party leaders (without experience of administration), whilst government officials coming from the Reich Ministry of the Interior were often sent back. In these and other conflicts between the Reich Governors in the new Eastern territories and the Reich Minister of the Interior, it was always the same main issue in the end: how to reconcile Hitler's special authorization with the necessity for (already pressing on economic and other grounds) a uniform administrative and legal system. The practice of installing high-handed Party functionaries in key offices, so Frick complained in December 1939, would mean the 'collapse' of 'internal government in general and not only will the special authorities not be incorporated but they will continually multiply, so that in the last resort the state apparatus will be atomized'.[54]

Frick may have been primarily concerned with the competence and authority of his own department, yet there *was* an extremely close connection between the nature and structure of control, as was certainly shown in the annexed Polish territories. The deliberately created vacuum of lawlessness and disorderliness which existed in the annexed Eastern territories between the end of the military government in October 1939 and the establishment of at least the semblance of an orderly civilian administration in spring 1940, favoured and to some extent first made possible the excesses of the Polish and Jewish massacres, which were carried out by special detachments of the S.S. and of the 'Ethnic German Self-Defence', partly on the initiative of local Party officials. Finally, however, the administrative state of emergency under which these areas continued to suffer in spite of being incorporated in the Reich, generally favoured to a much greater extent than in the Old Reich the development and spread of new forms of special authority alongside the regular state administration and executive. To begin with the S.S. and police, as Himmler's representatives, could establish their own territorial control, as it were, with higher S.S. and police leaders.

Extensive new authorities (like the Security Police abrogated by the S.S.) nominally special organs of the state were in fact subjected by Party exponents to the National Socialist movement's principles of structure, action and leadership. They owed their existence solely to the special 'racial' duties in the Eastern territories and gained an important influence there on the general business of administration, as in the case, for example of the offices which emerged in autumn 1939 of the 'Reich Commissioner for the Strengthening of German Nationhood' (Himmler) who was appointed on 7 October 1939, of which more in due course.

Moreover, it was typical that the office of the Führer's Deputy (from 1941 Party Chancellery), which had been able to exercise only a limited influence on the state administration, civil service policy and legislation in the Old Reich before the beginning of the war, was also first given additional special duties in the Eastern territories, alongside the special rule of the S.S. and the particularist control of the Gauleiter and Reich Governors empowered by Hitler. Thus, in a secret order at the end of 1940 or the beginning of 1941, Hitler arranged that all responsibility would be taken away from the Reich Minister for the Church in the Reichsgau Wartheland; instead the Reich Governor (Gauleiter Greiser) in conjunction with the Party Chancellery (not the Reich government) could make any changes in Church law which differed from the Old Reich. Actually Greiser's special church decree of 13 September 1941, inspired by Bormann, reduced the Churches in the Reichsgau Wartheland to the level of private organizations and established a particularist privilege in an important matter of Reich law. On 1 August 1940, a Reich Chancellery official had already remarked anxiously in a memorandum: 'The question of creating a particular law for the Gau in an area governed by Reich law ... will have to be watched most carefully in view of the very accommodating attitude towards the Reich Governors in the East especially, and in view of its great importance for the unity of the Reich.'[55]

The fact that Greiser and other Reich Governors (or Oberpräsidenten) in the East regarded the special policy in their territories as a more perfect form of National Socialist rule, different from the Old Reich, and that they were proud of their 'model Gaue', simply confirmed that in actual fact changes were taking place in the constitution of the Hitler State. 'The task of building up the Reichsgau Wartheland entrusted to me by the Führer,' Greiser wrote on 29 September 1941 to the Reich Minister of the Interior, 'is not a limited one nor one dependent on the rejection or restriction of departments of the Reich, but an absolute and total political and racial duty.'[56]

But such a total claim to rule also meant that, in keeping with the 'laws of the movement' which had always operated in the NSDAP and in its organizations, the given policy and administration was even more dependent than in the old Reich on the personality of the Gauführer and on his contacts with other power groups in the state and Party, and especially on his relationship to Hitler. But National Socialist satraps in the Eastern Gaue (still more in the Reich Commissionerships in the occupied former Soviet Eastern territories) also reflected the structure of the Hitler movement more than they did that of the authoritarian state, in so far as here irreconcilable contradictions arose and were habitual, even on basic issues of National Socialist policy like the method of Germanization.

Whereas Greiser, who had been Senate President in Danzig until 1939 and who had no Party power base behind him, relied chiefly on Himmler and Bormann and imitated the doctrinaire racial and ideological policy promoted by them, Forster and Koch, who enjoyed long-standing direct ties to Hitler, could not be shaken from their arbitrary policy in their Gaue even by Himmler and the S.S.

The standing conflict between Himmler and the S.S. and both these 'Gau kings' in the East was as typical as their conflict with the Reich departments. Because it was not a matter of the relationship between state and Party but chiefly concerned the opposition between bureaucratic and personal leadership. The claim to total National Socialist dominion, as represented by Greiser, Koch, Forster and others in their territories, could only be achieved at the price of anarchy.

It was all the more important, however, for the 'working' of the Hitler state that the National Socialist conception of the authoritarian state of order, as embodied by Frick, remained in being. This conception, supported by the old conservative bureaucracy, could not indeed curb the individuality of particularist National Socialist despots or prevent the exceptional power of special organizations, but it was nevertheless able to ensure that the administrative structure was in sufficient order round and about such anomalous enclaves to prevent any legal vacuum and irregularity from becoming extensive enough to endanger the regime. But this *coexistence* between state centralization and particularist control (as in general between normal law and emergency law) determined the nature of the Hitler state. And it was typical that top civil servants of the Reich government, especially in the Reich Chancellery, who were right in the middle of these contradictory constitutional tendencies as mediators between Hitler (or between the Gau prince empowered by Hitler) and the central Reich government, finally abandoned any attempt to clarify the relationship between the central government and the particularist authority during the War years. Instead they pleaded for a reasonably tolerable *modus vivendi*. Thus in an observation from the Reich Chancellery on 8 October 1941, on the 'agitated' quarrels between the Reich Minister of the Interior and Reich Governor Greiser (over the special question of their respective right to instruct the Regierungspräsidenten): 'A fundamental settlement of this question can only come about in the course of reforming the Reich. For the moment all that can be done is to find a *modus vivendi*.'[57]

Notes & references

1. Thus for example on 20 February 1933 the Bavarian government refused the request to ban the *Münchener Neuesten Nachrichten*; cf. *Frankfurter Zeitung*, 21 February 1933. There is also some interesting material on this in the files of the Reich Chancellery *Akten der Reichskanzlei*, BA: R43 11/482.
2. On the above see among other things the reports of the *Frankfurter Zeitung*, 18 and 23 February 1933.
3. *Frankfurter Zeitung*, 23 and 25 February 1933.
4. Protocol of the Cabinet meeting of 27 February 1933 (IfZ: Fa 203/1).
5. Details in *Dokumente zur Gleichschaltung des Landes Hamburg*, ed. and commented on by Henning Timpte (Frankfurt-on-Main, 1964).
6. As in the case of Hamburg (see the previous note) the events in Bremen are exceptionally well documented thanks to the work of Herbert Schwarzwälder, *Die Machtergreifung der NSDAP in Bremen 1933* (Bremen, 1966).
7. Müller was Sprenger's right-hand man in his capacity as Party expert on civil service matters. Cf. the publication appearing in the National Socialist Library, Heinrich Müller, *Beamtentum und Nationalsozialismus* (Munich, 1931).
8. The *Frankfurter Zeitung* of March 1933 reported extensively on the events in Hesse. On this see also the morning edition of the WTB of 7 March 1933 and *Akten der Reichskanzlei*, BA: R43 11/1345.
9. Thus for example S.A. Obergruppenführer Edmund Heines in Breslau, S.A. Gruppenführer von Fichte in Erfurt, S.A. Gruppenführer von Helldorf in Potsdam, S.A. Oberführer Wetter in Koblenz, the former Supreme S.A. Leader von Pfeffer in Kassel, S.S. Gruppenführer Weitzel in Düsseldorf, S.S. Oberführer Zech in Essen, S.A. Gruppenführer Schragmüller in Magdeburg among others (cf. the details of personal matters in *MBliV*, 1933).
10. In a party circular of 27 March 1933 the DNVP leadership expressed its regret that 'in spite of the declarations by their leader the National Socialists have certainly not staffed the posts of Oberpräsident with trained officials'. Cited according to Peter Thiele, *NSDAP und allgemeine innere Staatsverwaltung. Untersuchungen zum Verhältnis von Partei und Staat im Dritten Reich*, Phil. Diss., Munich, 1963 (typewritten MS), pp. 145f (based on the *Akten der Preuss. Innenmin*, DZA Merseburg, Rep. 77/2).
11. *Preussische Gesetzsammlung, 1933*, p. 643.
12. Implementing decree of 25 March 1933 (*MBliV*, 1933, I, p. 327).
13. Ibid., p. 649.
14. *Preussische Gesetzsammlung*, 1933, p. 241.
15. Above all the Gauleiter in the Prussian provinces of West and Central Germany: Florian (Düsseldorf), Grohé (Cologne-Aachen), Simon

(Coblenz-Trier), Telschow (Hannover-East), Weinrich (Hesse-Cassel) and Jordan (Halle-Merseburg). Other 'Prussian' Gauleiter, for example Meyer (Westphalia-North) and Loeper (Magdeburg), were appointed as Reich Governors in neighbouring areas outside Prussia.

16. Temporary law for co-ordinating the Länder with the Reich of 31 March 1933. *RGBl, I, p. 153.*

17. The Second Co-ordination Law of 7 March 1933 discussed below flatly stated in addition that 'resolutions of no confidence by the Landtage against chairmen and members of the Land governments' were 'inadmissible' (Art. 4).

18. *Akten der Reichskanzlei*, BA: R43 II/1309. Carl Schmitt also wrote the commentary *Das Reichsstatthaltergesetz* (Berlin, 1933).

19. Material on the appointments of Reich Governors as well as the German Nationalists' counter-suggestions, in BA: R43 II/1376.

20. Died on 23 October 1935; new Reich Governor was then the Gauleiter of the Gau Halle-Merseburg, Rudolf Jordan.

21. Mecklenburg-Strelitz and Mecklenburg-Schwerin were combined to form a Land on 15 December 1933. Cf. *RGBl*, 1933, I, p. 1065.

22. Epp's handwritten comment, in Epp Material, IfZ: MA-1236.

23. It was therefore typical that Epp had already requested (in vain) on 13 June 1933 that if he was to play his role as Reich Governor properly he should also have 'the power of command over the S.A., S.S. and Party organizations in his area' (Epp Material, IfZ: MA-1236).

24. Ibid., protocol.

25. A first implementing statute of 2 February 1934 essentially confined itself to ruling that in future Land laws required the consent of the relevant Reich Minister and that Land officials could be transferred to the service of the Reich.

26. Cf. Nicolai's article in the *Deutsche Juristenzeitung*, 15 February 1934.

27. Protocol in Epp Material, loc. cit.

28. Peter Thiele, op. cit., pp. 92f.

29. *Akten der Reichskanzlei*, BA: R43 II/1376.

30. Letter of 27 June 1934 from the State Secretary in the Reich Chancellery to the Minister of the Interior (answer to the latter's letter of 4 June 1934), both in BA: R43 II/495.

31. IfZ: ZS 145.

32. *RGBl*, I, p. 91. The second and third law for transferring the administration of justice to the Reich followed on 5 December 1934 (*RGBl*, I, p. 1214) and 24 January 1935 (*RGBl*, I, p. 68).

33. Cf. decree of the Führer and Reich Chancellor on the exercise of the right of clemency 1 February 1935 (*RGBl*, I, p. 74).

34. Law on the setting up of the Reich Chamber of Culture, 22 September 1933 (*RGBl*, I, p. 661).

35. Cf. *inter alia* the law on the cinema of 16 February 1934 (*RGBl*, I, p. 95) which authorized the central film censorship office in Berlin under the Ministry of Propaganda with the licensing and supervision of films; in addition the law on the theatre of 15 May 1934 (*RGBl*, I, p. 411) which placed the entire private and public theatre under the leadership and direction of the Reich Propaganda Minister.

36. Cf. the law of 3 July 1934 for transferring forestry and hunting to the Reich (*RGBl*, I, p. 534).

37. Unpublished circular of the Reich and Prussian Minister of the Interior of 14 March 1935 and (with reference to this) the newly published circular of the Reich and Prussian Minister of the Interior of 27 December 1935 (*RMBliV*, I, p. 20). A corresponding order for the Party had already been given by the Deputy of the Führer.
38. Interrogation of Gramsch, 15 July 1947 (IfZ: ZS 717).
39. On this see *inter alia* material in BA: R43 II/1365a.
40. The staff chief of the Führer's Deputy, Martin Bormann, had already tried to prevent any public discussion of the Reich reform on Hitler's behalf at the meeting of the Reich Governors on 28 September 1933 because of these conflicts (IfZ: Fa 600/1, p. 25).
41. Wagner himself criticized the protracted process of the reform of the Reich and complained that because of uncoordinated *ad hoc* measures 'there were more Ministers around now in a Reich ruled by National Socialism than there had ever been in the parliamentary state' and in addition there were also Reich Governors 'who had never existed before'. Therefore he suggested that 'the many Reich Governors, Minister Presidents and Ministers should be speedily got rid of and the former [Land] Ministries' should be turned into 'branch offices of the Reich'. By contrast the merger of Reich Ministries with Prussian Ministries being carried out in Berlin, by which means the former were trying to secure the 'bottom half of the executive which was still missing', and a new 'plague' of the Ministerial bureaucracy was growing in Berlin, generated a great deal of unrest and reawakened the 'spectre of Prussification'. Also worth noting is the criticism of the existing legal position levelled by Wagner directly at Frick: 'According to the present legal position the Reich Governors are under you as Reich Minister of the Interior. Adolf Hitler is Reich Governor in Prussia. He has delegated his authority to the Prussian Minister President. You yourself, however, are also Prussian Minister of the Interior. Thus Adolf Hitler is also legally under you as Reich Minister of the Interior, as is the Prussian Minister President. Since you are synonymous with the Prussian Minister of the Interior, you are subordinate both to the Prussian Minister President and to yourself as Reich Minister of the Interior. Admittedly I am no legal expert and historian but I doubt whether there has ever been a set-up like this before' (BA: R43 II/495).
42. Cf. text of the speech in *Völkischer Beobachter*, 8 September 1934.
43. Protocol of the meeting in BA: R43 II/1392.
44. *RGBl*, I, p. 66.
45. Law on Greater Hamburg and other area settlements, 26 January 1937 (*RGBl*, I, p. 91). In addition, law on the constitution and government of the Hanseatic town Hamburg, 9 December 1937 (*RGBl*, I, p. 1327).
46. Cf. for example the conflict of Bürckel with the Reich Labour Minister Seldte on issues of settlement policy in 1937 (BA: R43 II/208).
47. Note on the files by the Head of the Reich Chancellery, 30 April 1938 after a meeting with the Führer (BA: R43 II/1357c).
48. Letter of the Reich and Prussian Minister of the Interior to the Head of the Reich Chancellery, 17 May 1938 (BA: R43 II/1356).
49. Letter of 30 May 1938 from the Reich Commissioner for the

reunification of Austria with the German Reich to the Head of the Reich Chancellery (BA: R43 II/1357c).

50. Document, ibid.
51. Letter of 13 June 1938 from the Reich and Prussian Minister of the Interior to the Head of the Reich Chancellery and the latter's note of 15 June 1938 (BA: R43 II/1357).
52. Ibid.
53. Letter of 11 August 1938 from the Reich Minister of the Interior to the Head of the Reich Chancellery (BA: R43 II/1310b).
54. Cf. Martin Broszat, *Nationalsozialistische Polenpolitik 1939–45* (Fischer-Bücherei 692, Frankfurt-on-Main M, 1965), p. 59.
55. BA: R43 II/170.
56. BA: R43 II/581.
57. Note by Reichskabinettsrat Ficker, 8 October 1941 (BA: R43 II/1581).

Chapter Five

The foundation and alteration of the social system

The political and economic background

The struggle to control power internally was clearly more important than specific political details for the National Socialist leaders until summer 1933. During these months their entire energy was directed at removing bit by bit any constitutional obstacles and opposing political forces which stood in the way of acquiring comprehensive powers of government and the control of the executive in the Reich, the Länder and the municipalities. The National Socialist movement showed extreme determination and consistency in following this negative aim of removing essential elements of the Weimar Republic's constitutional order, which had already become very fragile before 1933. In this respect the emergency decrees from above and the powers of the National Socialist controlled government of the Reich and of the Länder almost perfectly complemented the terror and the Party's usurpation of power from below. And from the outset a specifically totalitarian tendency resulted from the combination of dictatorial state power and popular ideological mass movement, which immediately spread into the 'pre-political area' of social and public life in order also to encompass the nation's energies as completely as possible, and to eliminate undesirable influences through state regulation or Party political co-ordination and control.

This totalitarian expansion of power began with the Party revolution from below in March 1933. However, most of the basic decisions and laws and the formation of the most important organizations and instances for co-ordinating or regulating economic and professional interest groups, as well as organs of public opinion, education and cultural activity, occurred within the second part of the early revolutionary phase of the government, although this process was not yet completed by summer 1934.

It became clear that the consistency which the National Socialist 'revolution' showed in destroying the existing constitutional order was largely absent when it came to constructive organization and to the centralized exercise of power. On the contrary, the first months of the seizure of power further fragmented the structure of the National Socialist movement, which was in any case ideologically and structurally centrifugal and many sided; if only because in the course of this process individual exponents and organs of the Party could assume positions of power in state and society and could take and exploit such authority for themselves, whilst other forces in the Party strove to win control of state or social power through further revolution. Therefore the NSDAP's political monopoly established on July 1933 did not mean a monopoly in the sense of a uniform operation of power. The alteration of the existing governmental and constitutional conditions and the coordination of individual economic, professional or cultural institutions which was carried out partly from above, partly by being forced through from below and by various regional organizations of the Party under the state of emergency, often took the form of a wild 'proliferation' of National Socialist power. Many different stop-gaps and personal unions of Party, state and (social) autonomous authorities, with unclear boundaries and relations of conflicting discipline and loyalty, arose alongside the power which the Party had more or less usurped together with control over the state executive.

Also the wave of converts to the Party after 30 January 1933, which in the sphere of government chiefly meant an influx from the conservative and Nationalist strongholds but also meant by contrast in the S.A. and NSBO a significant increase in workers or unemployed who were previously pro-Socialist or pro-Communist, intensified the variety of intentions and interests in the camp of the National Socialist regime.

Whereas the lack of friction and formal legality of the most important acts of the seizure of power seemed to a considerable sector of Party members and exponents as a welcome test of the authoritarian state of order for which they strove, other Party groups saw this as a sign that the complete destruction and alteration of the existing 'system' for which they had hoped had not been achieved, but had been hindered by the speedy readjustment of the old forces in state and society. Therefore a second act of revolution was needed.

Thus the process of co-ordination in the pre-political sphere of social life not only brought about a totalitarian enlargement of the state's authority. It also intensified the problem of the duality of power between Party and state, the more so since the regulation of the interest and professional groups stemmed partly from the Party and partly from the state. For this reason, however, it also deserves particular attention because the chronological staging and the given degree of intensity of the rather varied 'co-ordination' of individual social groups reveals the greater or lesser importance and independence accorded to each of these.

Leaving aside the social forces and interests that determined this course of events, then the chief pressure after weeks of internal power struggles was the necessity for Hitler and his leading colleagues to prove the regime's real ability and determination to make changes, chiefly by successfully combating the economic crisis. Hitler was very well aware that his personal prestige could only be confirmed and strengthened by a tangible improvement in the material conditions of the suffering masses. But the more his popular power base grew through such successes, above all in combating unemployment, the more readily he could also put up with the discontent from NSDAP circles over the shortcomings of the National Socialist revolution.

Hitler had already tried in the spring to keep the economy largely out of the struggle for power, even before the general conclusion of the National Socialist revolution was proclaimed in summer 1933. The appointment of Schacht as President of the Reich Bank on 17 March 1933 (in place of former Reich Chancellor Luther, who had been pressed to resign) served among other things to placate the leading forces of the economy, who were accustomed to the model of the authoritarian state of order and economic security. The choice of Schacht for this important post instead of a Party man was calculated to win the trust of domestic and foreign business and to disarm the fear nourished by Gottfried Feder and other National Socialist theorists about possible National Socialist experiments with banking and currency. By contrast, the appointment of the 'high-ranking free-mason' Schacht met the same sort of opposition in the Party as the transfer of the Department of Economics to Hugenberg.[1]

Up to June 1933, as long as Hugenberg officiated as Reich Minister of Economics, no purely National Socialist measures to deal with unemployment were launched in spite of the previously vociferous National Socialist propaganda. The government confined itself at first chiefly to continuing the 'immediate programme' for work creation which the Schleicher cabinet had launched, within which a total of 600 million marks was finally approved for the allocation of public contracts (chiefly for agricultural improvement, and house and street building).[2] Only now did the slight lull in the economic crisis noticeable in the winter of 1932/3 and the measures taken under Papen and Schleicher to stimulate the economy and to create employment have positive effects. But the number of unemployed was still about 4½ million in spite of the seasonal decline in July 1933. After a conspicuously long delay, probably because of the uncertainty of Hitler and the National Socialist leaders on economic matters, a supplementary programme was enacted by the National Socialist leadership on 1 June 1933 after talks with leading industrialists.[3]

The issue of Labour Exchequer Bonds foreseen in the pro-

gramme to a total of one billion Reichmarks to finance public building works (for the construction and repair of autobahns, roads,
waterways, public buildings etc.) and to subsidize certain sectors of
private building (suburban estates and restoration of old buildings)
as well as the tax concessions for home-produced machines and
equipment by industrial, crafts and agrarian concerns, undoubtedly
demonstrated the energetic determination to combat unemployment
actively and as quickly as possible. But many of the provisions in
this programme, which also revealed ideological and Party political
motives (encouragement of women leaving employment through
marriage loans; priority of work for the unemployed from the
ranks of the S.A. and S.S.) tended more towards reducing the
number of unemployed (encouraging short time and favouring
manual labour without the use of machines) than to any rational
stimulation of production, and was therefore at first widely received with pronounced scepticism in industrial circles. That was
principally true also of the creation of employment through public
contracts, behind which state socialist or state capitalist tendencies
were suspected. Even the general director of Alliance Insurance,
who belonged to the NSDAP, Dr Kurt Schmitt, whom Hitler had
appointed Reich Minister of Economics in Hugenberg's place on
29 June 1933 (not least to calm leading economic circles),[4] was critical of many aspects of the Reinhardt programme and of the con-
comitant increased in Party activity to create supplementary jobs.[5]
It was quite the opposite with the project publicly announced by
Hitler as early as 1 May 1933, and again aired before leading representatives of the economy and heavy industry in Berlin on 29
May of undertaking the large-scale building of modern autobahns,
which gradually got underway in autumn 1933 by means of the
Reinhardt programme.[6] Yet apart from work creation (and
strategic-military purposes) this project quite deliberately served to
increase automobile traffic and car production; equally the provi-
dent reduction of motor vehicle tax for newly licensed cars was
supposed to contribute to this too.[7]

Only in the second half of 1933, when the first successes of the
work creation policy were apparent and when (hardly less important) the fear of social and economic experiments which existed in
leading circles of the economy and which was re-awakened by
numerous Party encroachments and announcements, had been
generally appeased by contrary declarations, orders and measures
by Hitler and his Ministers, could the regime count on the support
of the greater part of industry, especially heavy industry. Subsequently it was chiefly the coal, iron and steel, chemical and building industries that profited, especially from forced rearmament and
the military economic policy of autarky, which rapidly increased
in tempo from 1934[8] and, financed through Schacht's ingenious system of Mefo-exchange, then achieved the real breakthrough in sti-

mulating industrial production and bringing down unemployment (fall to an average of only 3 million unemployed in 1934).

The energy which the National Socialist leaders devoted to the ending of unemployment from the summer of 1933 (Hitler described it at the NSDAP Party Congress in Nuremberg on 31 August 1933 as the Party's most important task), the wave of public proclamations, actions, and collections of donations (regarded by many concerns as enforced) to create and finance new jobs which now got underway with much use of National Socialist propaganda and organization, and the official appeals for readiness to make sacrifices to help the unemployed and needy before the winter of 1933/4[9] had a twofold object: It gave the Party a new preoccupation, diverting it, in part at least, from the struggle for political power and directing it towards serving the aims of the state leadership. At the same time, this widespread activity undoubtedly generated in large sectors of the population a heightened awareness of national solidarity and the conviction that the new leaders were making every effort to combat the economic crisis, even if the direct effect of material aid was not unduly significant and although the Party successes in creating new jobs were not at first all that creditable economically speaking (although much exaggerated by propaganda). The fact of this awareness, even if contrived and manipulated, none the less had the effect of stimulating the economy – as Hitler realized very well. And also it concealed and compensated for the fact that at the same time as the regime was energetically improving the material standards of the suffering and the employment prospects for the out of work, the social autonomy of the employees and their free rights were being largely destroyed.

Although the first two years of Hitler's government were chiefly marked by unemployment – progressively relieved it is true but by no means overcome even in summer 1934 – other aspects of the economic crisis at the time were no less depressing. First of all there was the chronic lack of foreign currency. This problem was really exacerbated by the fact that the political upheaval in Germany and the reaction which the dictatorial and terrorist nature of the National Socialist regime aroused abroad, particularly in the West, damaged the export of German goods. This was further magnified by the government's raising of customs duties on agricultural and raw material imports to protect the domestic market and to move towards an intensified policy of autarky. The partial moratorium on the transfer of foreign currency interest payments to foreign creditors[10] which was ordered at the beginning of June on Schact's initiative, and the Reichsmark Credit Account introduced instead, reflected the desperate situation. These unilateral measures, which offended all the more in that they were later supplemented by bilateral credit agreements with individual trading partners (Holland,

Switzerland), and in that respect were bound to give the impression of an unequal treatment of foreign creditors, considerably damaged German credit in the West[11] and had no less adverse effects than the persecution and discrimination against Jews and political opponents of the regime, who sought refuge abroad there. Also, the hope of persuading the outside world to import more German goods through the introduction of blocked credit accounts which could be offset against purchases in Germany, was achieved only to a limited extent. On the contrary, trade relations with once important trading partners dwindled further.

Stricter regulations for the control of currency at home,[12] a renewed unilateral declaration by the government which gave notice of a still stricter reduction of interest transfers to foreign creditors (18 Dec. 1933) and the simultaneous setting-up of a special Reich office for foreign currency control[13] were further steps on the road to autarky by which Germany increasingly shut itself off from the world market. This especially damaged the export-dependent branches of light and heavy industry (the electrical industry and consumer industries, shipbuilding industry, etc.). The regime's policy towards the large social groups in the opening phase of the Hitler state must also be seen against the background of the Reich's general economic situation which has just been sketched in.

The position of the employees: From the destruction of the trade unions to the planned allocation of labour

Various trade union buildings had already been occupied and partially put under NSBO control in the second week of March 1933, by separate S.A. and S.S. actions in different German towns, for example in Dresden, Berlin, Munich. The ADGB, associated with the Social Democrats, had to suffer under these assaults which caused the ADGB Chairman Theodor Leipart to write to the Reich President on 10 March asking for a restoration of legal security.[14] But the NSDAP's attitude towards the unions was still thoroughly disorganized at this time. In general the dominant impression was that only a political-ideological co-ordination should be carried out but that the unions' achievements as such should not be attacked. The Nationalist and Christian workers and white-collar unions[15] also cherished such illusions and these reinforced mistaken assumptions of the ADGB leadership that these would be able to carry their organization over to the new regime by professions of 'positive co-operation' and by abandoning all political pretensions.[16]

In so far as there was any thought on the National Socialist side of a more or less non-violent co-ordination of the existing trade unions through the decisive intervention of the NSBO, an essential difficulty was the fact that in contrast to the social groups the greater majority of workers and employees had kept away from the NSDAP even in March 1933. At the factory council elections beginning that month the NSBO did indeed acquire a significantly higher share of the votes (an average of 25 per cent) than in 1932 (4 per cent) as a result of the changed situation and the fear of many workers and employees that in future left-wing mandates would be wiped out. But the NSBO was as remote as ever from having a majority. For this reason apparently, Hitler and Robert Ley, who had taken over the control of the NSBO as Gregor Strasser's successor, feared that the factory council organs could remain anti-National Socialist organizations. At any rate it was in connection with the disappointing factory council elections that on 4 April the Reich government discontinued all further such elections for six months by means of the Law on Factory Representative Councils and Business Organizations,[17] and in addition empowered the employers(!) to dismiss any factory member in the event of 'suspicion of activity hostile to the state' without the possibility of recourse to industrial law. The law specified in addition that in place of any factory council member affected by such dismissal the supreme Land authority could itself appoint new factory council members without an election. Thus worker participation and the strong position of the Free Trade Unions in the factories was thwarted for the time being.

Shortly afterwards, the crucial blow against the unions affiliated to the ADGB was prepared privately through a secret Action Committee for the Protection of German Labour under the leadership of Ley and Muchow. It began characteristically, however, with large-scale pro-labour propaganda staged in masterly fashion by Goebbels. This reached its climax on 1 May, the day of the international workers' movement which was made an official public holiday for the first time ('Day of National Labour')[18] whereas the 'Day of Potsdam' on 21 March had underlined the supposed harmonization of Prussiandom and National Socialism, the regime now tried to pass itself off as the communal workers' state and staged a mass celebration to honour the 'productive workers of all classes'. In front of about a million people Hitler spoke reprovingly on the Tempelhof Field in Berlin about pride of place, the mistaken underestimation of manual labour and the 'criminal' Marxist device of social 'fratricidal conflict'. In the new Germany the mutual isolation of classes and ranks had to stop. National Socialism wanted to bring the people together and to enable the various 'classes' to achieve better self-understanding and mutual respect for each other. Adopting the familiar style of the national missionary Hitler praised the work power and industry of the people as the greatest asset to the nation, which could no longer be allowed to lie fallow. The new government called on everybody to rid the world of the worries about job security through resolute measures to create work. Hitler's skilfully composed speech typically contained no concrete information about the future social rights of the workers apart from the announcement of the establishment of Labour Service as a social school for the young generation.

The regime undoubtedly succeeded in creating a mood of confidence at the massed events on 1 May with its loud (and for many convincing) declarations of its will for social harmony and the ending of material hardship, and this mood enabled it to carry out on the following day the action which had already been planned for days against the Free Trade Unions, now branded as 'Marxist', without a bigger public outcry and almost without resistance. The National Socialist leadership totally abandoned any legal pretence by taking this step and launched an illegal but precisely prepared Party action. At ten o'clock in the morning, S.A. and S.A. auxiliary police under the command of local Party worthies and NSBO functionaries pulled up in front of the buildings, offices, banks and editorial offices of the Free Trade Unions, occupied and seized their property and all their contents. A succession of leading unionists, including the ADGB Chairman Leipart and Grassmann, were taken into custody but the majority of union employees were given the chance to continue working under newly appointed commissioners.[19] After the demonstration of power most of the other unions, for example the Hirsch-Dunkersche Gewerkschaftsring and the Deutsch Nationale Handlungsgehilfen-Verband (DHV) placed themselves under the Action Committee for the Protection of German Labour, after Robert Ley had proclaimed in an appeal of 2 May the merging of the former unions in a German Labour Front (*Deutsche Arbeitsfront* – DAF). Only the Christian trade unions were given a degree of special treatment, chiefly with an eye to the negotiations for a Concordat and the special situation in the Saar area, but these too were forcibly incorporated in the DAF at the end of June.

An attempt to legalize the coup against the Free Trade Unions was only made subsequently through a distraint order of the Berlin public prosecutor in the course of a judicial enquiry 'against Leipart and colleagues'. It is typical that whilst National Socialist propaganda surpassed itself in the following days and weeks with smears and calumnies about the 'union bosses' and their alleged misuse of 'workers' subs', there was never any trial of Leipart and colleagues. As a result the possession of union property by the newly formed German Labour Front remained illegal until the end of the National Socialist regime, and the problems of property law arising from this fact were to cause the DAF difficulties for a considerable time.

On 10 May 1933 the First Congress of the German Labour Front was staged in Berlin with the participation of all the VIPs of the

NSDAP and government as the formal inauguration of the new united organization under Hitler's 'patronage'. The DAF organizational scheme which was then made known combined the associations which had been co-ordinated and taken over in a 'General Association of German Workers (under the direction of the NSBO leader Walter Schumann) and a General Association of German Employees (under the Danzig Gauleiter Albert Forster, who had emerged from the National Socialist middle-class movement). Both associations were thought of as the first 'pillars' of a corporatist general organization to which it was hoped to add the industrial employers as a third and the craftsmen and commercial middle classes as the fourth pillars at a later date. For the moment, however, the chief emphasis was on the respectively 14 and 9 individual associations subdivided according to profession or trade, of workers and employed each with their individual memberships. The central office of DAF served as the umbrella organization with eleven specialist offices under the direction of Robert Ley. The general organization was arranged territorially in thirteen areas (in each case with DAF area leaders) and these in turn were arranged in Kreis groups and local groups. For the time being the link with the Party was not a legal and institutional one but existed only because Ley was staff leader of the Political Organization of the NSDAP and because nearly all the leading positions of the DAF were occupied by NSBO leaders.

In general this first scheme of organization retained the typical unionist principles of organization with an eye to the union employees taken over in the lower ranks of the DAF, who were hardly indispensable for the time being, and to avoid a mass exodus of former union members, and tried to give the impression that the DAF was the fulfilment of the unrealized dream of the Weimar era, of a large united union. What is more, individual creations like the formation of small and large Labour conventions (for the discussion of important social and labour policy questions), which were chiefly composed of leaders of the separate groups and specialist associations, in effect broke with the strict leadership principle, although at the same time they had only an advisory function and disappeared without any fuss after a while. The new mammoth organization of the DAF could have become a powerful representative of the workers' interests, especially since social revolutionary ideas still played an important part for many NSBO leaders. But it soon became apparent that the most influential forces were those who wanted at all costs to prevent a power factor building up here under the National Socialist flag which might significantly have influenced economic and social policy by taking over traditional union rights.

After NSBO functionaries had already used their newly won power as Commissioners of the co-ordinated trade unions in the first half of May to interfere at various times in the management of business concerns, encouraged in part by Ley himself with remarks on the 'profit-seeking' of the employers[20], there were strict Party orders from Hitler against all such infringements (at the urging of Schacht, leading industrialists and influential representatives of the state economic bureaucracy). Again, in an order of 15 May, in which he prohibited wage negotiations and the conclusion of wage agreements in the individual associations, Ley had announced that such negotiations 'will from now on only be conducted centrally by the Action Committee for the Protection of German Labour'.[21] But the law issued four days later on the setting up of Labour Trustees[22] drastically curtailed these DAF ambitions and destroyed the hope that the DAF or NSBO could continue to exercise what had formerly been union functions in the most important sector of social policy (wage negotiations). The law gave the impression that the Trustees were merely an interim solution 'until the revision of the social constitution' (article 2) and for the time being simply had to make 'binding' conditions for the conclusion of labour contracts instead of the worker and employer organizations. In fact the Trustees were supposed to develop into a permanent institution, although at first it remained unclear and disputed as to whether they should exercise compulsory state arbitration (in the event of conflict) or have the complete and sole power to determine wages.

In any case the way was thus prepared for the ending of independent wage bargaining for worker *and* employer. Enforced governmental regulation of labour conflicts and wage bargaining replaced the free social partnership. It also became apparent that the thirteen Trustees of Labour named by Hitler in mid-June at the suggestion of Land governments or the Reich Minister of Labour (their areas of authority were identical with those of the former optional government arbitrators and thirteen DAF areas), were, as was already implicit to some extent in their origins and previous activity,[23] more sympathetic to the interests of the economy or to the viewpoint of those who most often conformed with these – the public Labour administration and economic bureaucracy – than they were to the workers' interests or to the NSBO's ambitions.

Little is known of discord between employers' unions and the Trustees,[24] though the former welcomed the new authority and the persons chosen for it fairly unanimously, yet in a number of centres, chiefly in Upper Silesia and the Westphalian industrial area where the NSBO was leftish, there were many sharp quarrels between the Trustees and the NSBO officials in the factories and in the co-ordinated workers' associations. In Silesia the director of the DAF's social policy office and the leader of the Stone Worker's Association paid a visit to the Reich Chancellery in Berlin to demand the removal of the Trustee Dr Nagel, who had incurred the displeasure of the NSBO and the workers' association through reducing wages in an unprofitable Silesian metal works. If Nagel were not removed immediately, the NSBO officials urged, there was a real fear 'that the mood aroused in the labour force by the Trustee's behaviour will result in a considerable loss of votes in the coming election'.[25] Although the NSBO officials accused the Trustee among other things of 'not involving the associations' in his decision on wage questions, the Reich Minister of Labour was able to point out that the Trustees were directed precisely not to involve the associations in wage negotiations any more on the pattern of previous arbitration, but as far as possible to make use of individual experts from employer and worker circles. The Party's economic deputy, Keppler, had taken this view at any rate and it could be assumed from various remarks of Ley's that the DAF 'is not authorized' to 'conduct wage negotiations'. The same was true of the NSBO, which had purely political duties.[26] It was also worth noting that the central authority of the Silesian employers' associations had already approached the Reich Ministry of Labour and opposed the NSBO's 'campaign' against Nagel. This was trying 'to wreck the harmonious agreement which Dr Nagel is attempting to achieve with our full support[!] between employers, workers and employees'. If the Silesian economy, wrote the spokesmen of forty-seven Silesian employers' associations 'is to be protected against severe disruptions, which must be avoided in all circumstances in the interests of Germany's over-all policy, it is absolutely essential that the Trustee's authority . . . is firmly established'.[27]

Here as in similar cases it was also customary to impute concealed Marxist tendencies to the NSBO, which the Silesian Trustee also tried to do on this occasion.[28] At the same time, a case like this, where the NSBO did not achieve its desired aim for the time being,[29] also showed that many NSBO spokesmen had made themselves so vulnerable to attacks on their person or on their official conduct that the interests they represented were bound to suffer. During the economic crisis the opinion of leaders of the economy and of the entrepreneurs counted for more than the socio-political demands of the employees. Yet the latter were further discredited precisely because of the prior destruction of the trade unions, which also broke the continuity of the more disciplined and qualified (and in that respect, more convincing) representation of workers' interests through experienced and established trade union leadership, and very often helped highly dubious 'trash' in the NSBO to get to the top. In these circumstances growing criticism of the 'revolutionary' NSBO (as of the S.A.) was already apparent in summer and autumn 1933 among many NSDAP leaders with petit-bourgeois connections, who were anxious to demonstrate their own very often doubtful expert qualifications after they had reached influential positions in the state and the Party and who were bent on accommodating to the old-established society. This in turn contributed directly and indirectly to strengthening the employers' side and to the isolation of the NSBO and the DAF within the framework of the regime.[30]

Fierce conflicts also developed in the Westphalian industrial area between the Trustee of Labour (Dr Klein), or rather his special deputy for worker questions (Hutmacher), and the local DAF and NSBO officials, where the former even dared to threaten police action. The details of this, contained in a long letter from Hutmacher of March 1934,[31] are the more remarkable in that Klein and Hutmacher belonged to the particularly committed advocates of Spann's corporatist state ideas in the NSDAP's economic staff in Düsseldorf and were also in close contact with the Düsseldorf Institute for Corporatist Organization, founded in April 1933 and financed by Fritz Thyssen, which was directed by Spann's pupil Paul Karrenbrock. Hutmacher, who as political director of the NSDAP had the job of a commissioner with the Düsseldorf Chamber of Industry and Commerce, reported on his nine-month spell as the Trustee's special deputy. In numerous dealings with NSBO representatives he had 'discovered the spirit of pure class warfare to a quite shocking degree'. 'More often than not', he had been 'compelled to threaten' NSBO spokesmen and National Socialist factory council chairmen 'with the Secret State Police' and 'to intervene mainly on the employers' part' because the 'spirit of class conflict on the employees' side threatened to choke the economy'. He and his superior Dr Klein had constantly urged that every worker 'must see himself as a soldier in the economy'.

Such reports speak for themselves. They reveal that the Trustees of Labour served the employers' interests in so far as they absorbed a considerable amount of the pressure exerted on the employers by the NSBO, the workers' associations and Factory Councils (in respect of wage rises, engagement of unemployed etc.), whereas massive pressure on the employer seems to have been only rarely exerted by the Trustees.[32] The clash of interests which made the gap between the various exponents of the National Socialist regime tangible also revealed itself at this time in the differing assessments of enforced job creation. The criticism of much 'artificial work creation' repeatedly expressed in late summer 1933 by the employers as well as by the Reich Minister of Economics Schmitt, was sharply rejected by the NSBO, where such purely economic arguments were viewed as a typically capitalist denial of the 'right to work',[33] and on this point at least (notably less on wage matters) Hitler also endorsed the Party or rather NSBO standpoint.

All in all, after the basic decision taken by the appointment of governmental Trustees of Labour an increasing 'de-unionization' of the DAF and NSBO set in by the second half of 1933. In October, apparently at Hitler's direction, Ley launched a DAF propaganda drive in the factories aimed chiefly at the referendum of 12 November, which called for labour peace and propagated the 'idea of the retinue' in the factory.[34] The first draft of a law on the DAF submitted by Ley at the beginning of September, aimed mainly at creating a clear legal basis for the parent organization (as a corporation at public law) and thereby also at promoting it in terms of property law as well as politically as the central organization of the much discussed corporatist social set up, but it was not followed up by the Reich government. On the contrary the initiative for legislation for the so-called social reform was left to the Ministry of Labour.[35]

In contrast to Gregor Strasser, Ley proved himself to be an extremely unreliable and opportunistic advocate of socialist and social reformist aspirations within the NSDAP. A man who chiefly had an eye to pleasing Hitler and himself, he played a considerable part in developing the DAF and NSBO into big propaganda organizations, which lost influence on social policy decisions. And other changes in personnel, for example, the loss of Reinhold Muchow, the real founder and organizer of the NSBO, who was the victim of an accident on 12 September 1933, weakened the NSBO's social revolutionary impulses. The NSBO had grown to 1.1 million members by the beginning of August 1933,[36] and indeed continued to regard itself as the leadership cadre of the National Socialist movement in the factories and in the associations and official posts of the DAF, but it was ever more firmly prevented from controlling the associations and factory councils.

In November 1933 the industrial employers' and entrepreneurial associations also no longer saw any danger in joining the DAF once its socio-political jurisdiction had been so obviously curtailed and the odds on a genuine corporatist self-government by the DAF (whereby the employers would have been short changed by the other general associations) had shortened dramatically.

The reorganization of the DAF initiated after the election of 12 November 1933 was crucial here. It was true that Ley did not yet abandon the aim pursued by the majority of the old NSBO leadership of active DAF participation in the regime's labour and social policy and he declared in the second half of November in the DAF central office that he had 'requested the Führer' to entrust to him 'the treatment of labour law, labour management, factory regulations and wage scales',[37] but in fact he had to pledge himself after the election to public statements and measures which tended towards the complete elimination of the rest of the DAF's unionist, associationist structure and entailed a further commitment to activity which was mainly propagandist in nature. Ley even said at the NSBO Reich Conference in Munich on 21 November: 'The social question is not a matter of wage agreements but a matter of training and educating.'[38] And six days later the leader of the DAF together with the Reich Minister of Labour (Seldte), the Reich Minister of Economics (Schmitt) and Hitler's Party deputy for economic matters (Keppler), had to submit to signing a joint 'appeal to all productive Germans' which proclaimed the future dissolution of the independent General Associations of Employees in favour of an undifferentiated combined membership of employers and employees in the DAF, and which in fact denied the DAF any rights over labour and social policy.

The German Labour Front is the organization for all working men, irrespective of their economic or social standing. In it the worker shall stand alongside the employer, no longer separated into groups and associations which serve to perpetuate special economic or social distinctions or interests. In the German Labour Front a person's worth will be the deciding factor, be he worker or employer...

In accordance with the will of our Führer, Adolf Hitler, the German Labour Front is not the place for deciding material questions of daily working life or for reconciling the natural[!] differences of interest between individual working men.

Methods of procedure will shortly be worked out for the regulation of working conditions which will assign to the leader and retinue of a factory the arrangements prescribed by the National Socialist ideology. The great aim of the Labour Front is the education of all working Germans for the National Socialist State and for the National Socialist way of thought. And in particular it is taking over the schooling of those who will be called on to play an influential role in the factory in the organs of the social constitution, in the labour tribunals and social insurance.[39]

To forestall the impression that the DAF was being watered down, which was particularly obvious in this document, the founding of a DAF leisure project had already been announced with great pathos on 17 November; and both in form and name (*Nach der Arbeit* – After work) it was an unimaginative copy of the fascist Italian model ('Dopo Lavore') which only later received another (hardly more fortunate) name as the National Socialist association of 'Strength through joy' (*Kraft durch Freude* – KdF). This establishment marked out the future path for the development of the DAF as a striking and effective propaganda organization, as a centralized travel company, and the leisure organization with the cheapest tickets.

But the employers' organizations had no objections to that. The Reich Corporation of German Industry which meanwhile had been formed from the combination of separate manufacturers' associations under its 'leader' Krupp von Bohlen und Halbach was already calling on its members in a circular of 28 November 1933 to join the DAF. Specific reference was made to the accompanying text of the previous day's 'Appeal' and it was affirmed with relief that through this the 'German Labour Front's position and sphere of activity... has finally been clarified', and the German employers would now 'freely collaborate' in the 'great aim' of 'restoring a true national community'.[40]

Meanwhile it was not the mooted comprehensive social reform but a Law for the Ordering of National Labour which had been prepared under the direction of the Reich Ministry of Labour,[41] with considerable involvement from the Reich Ministry of Economics.[42] In view of this, Economics Minister Schmitt once again stressed in the cabinet on 1 December: 'The Labour Front is no longer involved in the settlement of wages. Nor is the Labour Front to own economic concerns' since otherwise 'the rest of the economy would be subject to pressure'. In future the regulation of wage rates and labour agreements (this too was a demand obviously directed against the traditions of the Free Trade Unions) were not to be initiated by branches of industry but by the individual plants and the decisions were to be made as before by the Trustees of Labour. In the factory itself, however, 'the director of the concern' must 'also be the leader'. A workers' council of at most ten persons would collaborate 'only in an advisory capacity' and will be formed in agreement between the head of the factory and the NSBO spokesman. 'If agreement cannot be reached [on the composition of the factory council], the Trustee shall decide.'[43]

The draft of the Law for the Ordering of National Labour which was promulgated on 20 January 1934 had been drawn up with considerable speed the previous month and had been dealt with by the Cabinet on 12 January in spite of the reservations of many Ministers about the pace of it all,[44] and it only gave the Labour Front an advisory role in matters of wage and labour agreements (the right to nominate three-quarters of the expert advisory board with the Trustees of Labour). For the rest only a miserable remnant of worker participation remained. The rule that a list of members of factory councils of trust was to be compiled anew each year in agreement between factory leader and NSBO spokesman, and that the factory 'retinue' should be sounded out on this by secret ballot but that in the event of the list being rejected by the retinue the Trustee of Labour could himself appoint a council of trust (Act. 9), shows what a farce had become of the former factory councils. The law made the Trustees of Labour into a permanent fixture and specified that these were Reich officials under the supervision of and subject to the direction of the Minister of Labour. Apart from the Minister of Labour, the Minister of Economics was also empowered 'to delegate additional tasks' to the Trustees of Labour.

The DAF or rather the NSBO had been able to accomplish somewhat more in matters concerning the legal protection of workers. Thus the law contained the provision (Art. 20) that the employer had to have the consent of the Trustee of Labour for the dismissal of more than 10 per cent of those employed. He was also obliged to make factory regulations specifying hours of work, method of payment, terms of piece work, conditions of giving notice etc., so that the worker was at least protected on most important issues against the arbitrariness of the private employer. A typical product of National Socialist ideology, which replaced the legal and material security of workers' interests with the qualified concepts of social conscience and honour, and which could also be used as a form of pressure against the 'members of the retinue', was the introduction of a 'social honour jurisdiction'. This was applicable in cases of maltreatment of workers as well as in the event of any 'provocation' of the retinue against the factory owner and for other offences against the 'factory community', and which was to be exercised by a special Honour Court.[45]

Although the DAF or NSBO had not been able to maintain or to claim for themselves any former trade union gains which were against the employers' interests during the making of the law, they *were* able to do this in a matter which concerned not so much the employer as the prestige of a profession which was particularly distrusted in the Third Reich, namely the legal profession. Thus the statute amending the Law on Industrial Courts proposed (Art. 66) that representation before industrial courts was normally to be undertaken by the DAF legal advisory boards or by lawyers especially authorized by the DAF.[46] It was apparent, moreover, in the relevant labour law provisions of the statute concerning the reconciliation of conflicting interests that the fiction of a community of factory leaders and members of the retinue could not be maintained. The original idea of setting up joint legal advisory boards with the DAF for employer *and* worker had to be dropped and instead the principle of separate advisory boards was recommended after the Reich Minister of Justice had pointed out that otherwise the representation of the parties concerned would be contrary to normal legal practice.[47]

Finally, as well as reflecting the strengthening of the employer's standpoint, the law also confirmed the greater power of the authoritarian state administration: at the insistence of the Minister of the Interior public service workers and employees (including the Reichsbahn and the Reich Autobahn authorities) were excluded for the time being from the provisions of the law (Art. 63).

The real result of the Law on the Ordering of National Labour which was to remain the Third Reich's basic law on social policy, was – to the chagrin of the 'anti-capitalist elements' – the dismantling of workers' rights in favour of state control and of the social partnership in favour of a relationship between leader and retinue in the factories. Logically, therefore, the reorganization of the DAF already initiated earlier had to continue and the course was set for this at the end of January 1934. The main result was that the separate associations for workers and employers were dissolved. The transfer to so-called Reich factory groups (*Reichsbetriebsgruppen* – RGB) was only an interim solution valid until 1938/9 (chiefly to accommodate the previous officials of the associations). They were of little real or political importance whereas for the rest a purely vertical and centralized DAF organization emerged, analogous to the arrangement for the NSDAP (with DAF Bezirk, Gau, Kreis and local group officials and factory, cell and street block look-outs). The crucial responsibilities here went to the specialist sections in the DAF central office or in the respective DAF (Gau, Kreis, branch group) agencies (most important: Organization Office, Personnel Office, Press and Propaganda Office, the Office for Legal Advice, the Social Office, the Office for Professional Training and Factory Leadership).[48]

At the same time the NSBO, once formed as a combat organization and now no longer able to levy special membership dues after summer 1934 gradually lost all political significance and organizational independence. True, out of deference it continued to be entered in the NSDAP Handbook, but as this later commented laconically (in 1938), its functions had been 'transferred to the German Labour Front'.[49] The NSBO only continued to play a nominal leading role as a personnel association of Party comrades within DAF's mass organization, into which practically every German who was active in the industrial commercial sector was forced.[50]

But this process of reorganization met with strong resistance in the NSBO and DAF camp and made only slow and fitful progress in 1934. After much initial euphoria discord clearly grew among workers and employees at the beginning of 1934, when the reaction against other manifestations of more pronounced authoritarian control in state and society (not least too the rise in the cost of foodstuffs as a result of the Reich Food Estate's pro-farmer policy) also played a part.[51] Ley became aware of the disappointment and resistance of the still strong leftist forces among the 'old fighters' in the NSBO. In this connection it transpired among other things that the central office of the DAF, unlike the Reich directorate of the NSDAP, was a strong bureaucratic, collegiate head organization which Ley had been forced to consult as he did the Gau rulers of the DAF, in staff and leader meetings. Ley himself later described the period between spring and autumn 1934 in retrospect as an 'endless internal struggle' whereby he often had to conceal the 'last secrets' and 'dear God, many a one came to grief' whom he had to get rid of because he got in his (Ley's) way.[52] Above all, formerly influential NSBO officials were ousted in the summer after the Röhm affair. The fact that Gregor Strasser, for whose rehabilitation and return (in place of Ley) many old NSBO leaders had hoped, was also murdered in conjunction with the shooting of higher S.A. leaders on 30 June and 1 July was a clear signal that the socialist left within the NSDAP and NSBO was also to be put down. The dismissal of prominent NSBO leaders (Bruckner, Krüger, Hauenstein) who had been old supporters of Strasser and close colleagues of Muchow followed eight weeks later. And on 18 September Karl Busch, the head of the DAF press and propaganda office and an old NSBO propagandist (as well as chief editorial writer of the DAF organ *Der Deutsche*) was also put out in the cold.[53]

Nevertheless, the efforts to involve the DAF more heavily in active social policy again reached a high point in the autumn. What made itself felt in this instance was chiefly the pressure of the DAF apparatus, which was strengthened rather than weakened by the process of centralization and its closer bracketing with the Party Organization and which aspired to greater power. Although Ley (as Strasser's successor) had at the same time become Staff Leader of the NSDAP's Political Organization (from November 1934 with the title of Reichsorganisationsleiter of the NSDAP), this office had only a tenuous existence after the appointment of Hess to the political leadership of the Party and the setting up of the office of the Führer's Deputy. But Ley's new post was able to grow in importance, because he was also able to expand the NSDAP organizational management (with separate offices in Munich and Berlin) into an important central Party office with the help of the gigantic DAF apparatus and the important financial resources of this organization.[54]

Conversely, this connection strengthened the political power of the DAF in the structure of the National Socialist system. For example, the workers saw themselves more or less forced to join the DAF, the local DAF heads became important Party political exponents alongside the local branch groups and Kreisleiter of the NSDAP and (with or without official authority) they could exert a corresponding pressure on small or medium employers. Thus even the numerical growth, the centralization and the bureaucratic consolidation of the DAF as a National Socialist organization gave rise to a new form of influence on the factories, which contradicted the intention of the Law for the Ordering of National Labour.[55]

Although Ley had not hesitated to exclude certain exponents of the DAF's leftish, social revolutionary wing, he permitted a renewed effort by the old leadership forces in the NSBO in autumn 1934 to involve the DAF actively again in social policy. He was obviously less concerned with social policy as such than with enlarging the responsibility of the DAF, which he sought to make into a mass collective of the National Socialist regime through a proverbial flurry of responsibilities.

The former Trustee of Labour in Pomerania, Count Rüdiger von der Goltz, who had been empowered to reorganize and standardize the chambers of commerce and other representative corporations of the industrial economy on the basis of the Law For the Organic Construction of the German Economy (27 February 1934), reported to the Reich Chancellery at the end of October 1934 on the total dismay about this development. In mid-July, Hitler still assured him that the Labour Front was not to concern itself with economic matters and social policy negotiations.[56] The reality had been otherwise:

The Labour Front's Gauleiter complained bitterly in a Berlin conference at the end of September and even in a talk some weeks earlier, that the Labour Front was only allotted the job of training and as a result the worker was losing faith in the Labour Front. Dr Ley declared in a meeting at the end of September that the Labour Front would once again take charge of the social settlement. Whereupon one of the participants welcomed the fact that the social struggle could be renewed once more and, after Dr Ley had interjected with 'Not struggle, settlement', added, 'all right then, settlement'.

Eventually under this sort of pressure Ley had also finally affirmed in a public appeal on 1 October 'that the officials of the Labour Front must not be kept out of the factories as anti-factory elements'. For all this it was now obvious that the basis of the Law for the Ordering of National Labour as well as the prior appeal of 27 November 1933, which Ley had also signed, had been abandoned. Therefore von der Goltz had contacted the DAF Organisationsleiter Claus Selzner at the beginning of October 1934 and had told him 'that Dr Ley had openly flouted the laws' so that he (von der Goltz) was 'put in the painful position' of informing the employers for his part 'that the laws and decrees have not in the least changed and Dr Ley's appeal cannot change anything'.

Then Count von der Goltz reported extensively on the talk which had taken place as a result of this between Selzner and himself on 19 October, when the former was chiefly concerned to find out or rather to clarify 'what the Labour Front now can and cannot do in the factories, since there is total uncertainty over this in the country as well as in the Labour Front and among factory leaders, and in the last resort the Labour Front officials, wearing brown uniforms and with all the trappings of authority, were terrorizing the individual factory leaders – very often small factory leaders'. But Selzner studiously avoided all attempts during the conversation to get a written statement of what should be valid in future and how this might be squared with the existing laws, and instead he declared that sometimes it was necessary 'to create an emergency' by means of political pressure, as indeed Schacht 'is also doing for his part with economic policy etc. by referring to the exigencies of outside world'. Count von der Goltz went on:

I explained that nothing like this could be done against the laws of the Führer which were in force. S. replied that here again he needed only to refer to Dr Schacht, who had virtually crushed Minister Schmitt to the wall so that in the end the Führer realized that Schacht was the stronger, repealed his own law and made Schacht Minister. I replied to this very positively that if these methods had been used at all they would most certainly not be suitable for Ley, Selzner and Goltz as National Socialists, whereupon S. immediately backed down and said naturally that had not been intended, and naturally the Führer should not be deflected from a law through such a situation. One had to bear in mind, however, that the Führer did not make the laws but that his Ministries made them, that there were many non-National Socialists in the Ministries and the Führer could most certainly not foresee all the consequences of the various new articles; the Party was there to demonstrate these results in practice and in this way to ensure that in the end the right thing was always done.[57]

This trend in the DAF's leadership, which Count von der Goltz outlined and which was also remarkable for its tactical calculation, was quite obvious on 24 October, when Ley tried to get Hitler to sign a Decree of the Führer on the German Labour Front prepared by him, in which the DAF was not only described as the organization of all 'those productive of brain and fist' but also considerably extended its authority. Thus article 7 of this decree states that:

The DAF has to ensure labour peace by creating an understanding among factory leaders for the legitimate claims of their retinue, and understanding among the retinue for the predicament and possibilities of their factory. The DAF has the task of finding that compromise between the legitimate interests of all concerned which befits National Socialist ideals and reduces the number of cases which need to be referred to the state agencies solely responsible according to the law of 20 January 1934. The representation of all those concerned which is necessary for this process of conciliation is the exclusive concern of the German Labour Front. The creation of other organizations and any other activity in this field is forbidden.[58]

This decree, published the next day by the German News Bureau, which Ley had procured without involving the Reich departments and the Führer's Deputy[59] immediately elicited an extremely sharp protest from Schacht (who had meanwhile taken over the Ministry of Economics) as well as from Ministers Seldte, Frick and Hess. Hitler was in a quandary since his 'decree' clearly contradicted the Law for the Ordering of National Labour and besides the validity of a 'Führer decree' issued without the countersignature of a Reich Minister and not even published in the *Reichgesetzblatt* (the Reich law gazette) was bound to give rise to considerable doubt.

However, as Hitler was himself reluctant to retract it, the decree stood (despite its questionable legality). At the same time, those Ministers who intervened were directed by Hitler to draft and to submit to him 'more specific legal regulations', by which means it appears that the essential contents of the decree were to be further modified and further public discussion of the decree was to be avoided until then.[60] This was a highly questionable procedure, but for the process of making laws and decrees in the 'Führer State' it was a highly informative one!

Von der Goltz used the above remark of Selzner and the decree of 24 October as an excuse to submit the strongest doubts of the employers to the Reich Chancellery. If the decree and the barely concealed aspirations of the DAF were to remain, then it must 'frankly be said that this development presages the threat of a union of massive force'.[61] In fact the decree of 24 October which Ley had obtained more or less surreptitiously and which was thoroughly disapproved by the responsible Ministers as well as by industry and even by the Party (Hess-Bormann) was the last abortive attempt by the DAF to control the actual labour and wages policy, which in fact had been transferred to the state by the Law for the Ordering of National Labour.

In March 1935 Ley finally had to make a new agreement with the Reich Minister for Economics (Schacht) and the Reich Minister for Labour (the so-called Leipzig Agreement).[62] This did indeed recognize the factory spokesman or local branch spokesman of the DAF as the proper organ of 'social responsibility', but at the same time bound him to the decisions of local labour committees or of the labour economic councils set up in each Trustee's area, in which factory leaders (or chambers of commerce) and DAF district officers (labour councils) were equally represented, so that a purely DAF initiative was forestalled. There was no change in the Labour Trustee's ultimate authority although the projected new committees and councils were to try as far as possible to reach agreement between themselves on current problems of wage regulation and social policy. At the same time (end of March 1935) the DAF acquired the formal status of an 'affiliated association' of the NSDAP,[63] whereby its independence was also limited by the Party.

The organizational extension of the DAF was indeed to go further in future and, dominated by Ley's ambition, it was to assume dimensions[64] which also brought the DAF into many future conflicts with the state and other Party offices. But the period when the NSBO and the DAF saw themselves, and still tried to act as, the organization and mouthpiece for independent workers' interests, was finally over. Instead, the DAF increasingly developed into a great totalitarian organization for the support of the regime's economic (and rearmament) aims. To a considerable extent it combined cultural and social work, specialist professional training and support with ideological schooling, and served to promote increased output and higher worker productivity. No matter how important its efforts were in this area and no matter how much it was able to raise the worker's self-awareness of his status through such undertakings as 'Strength through joy' and other activities, in the last resort this over-all care and control simply further curtailed the independence of employees and increasingly restrained them.

Typically, the yearly ballots for the factory spokesmen (the miserable relic of former worker-participation) which had often produced less acceptable results for the regime in the face of heavy abstentions in 1934/5, and which as a result were not published,[65] took place for the last time in April 1935. On Hitler's express instructions to the Trustee offices were extended by law for a year respectively in 1936 and 1937 and finally indefinitely in 1938.[66]

And in other respects, too, especially in connection with the freedom of choice of employment and place of work, employees' rights were increasingly restricted from 1934/5 in favour of the state-directed allocation of labour. This was achieved first through the Law for the Regulation of Work Allocation of 15 May 1934, which among other things prevented migration to big cities with high unemployment and made it difficult for farm hands to take up employment outside agriculture. Then an additional Law for Meeting Labour Requirements in Agriculture of 26 February 1935 further empowered the authorities to intervene in existing working conditions and 'compulsorily to return to their former agricultural labour' those workers and employees who had previously been engaged in agriculture.[67]

Also on 26 February the 'employment record' or work book was introduced by law for all workers and employees and this created the technical precondition for the comprehensive control and direction of labour supply, which after the ending of unemployment chiefly affected those branches (building and metal workers) where there was a growing shortage of labour after 1935/6 as a result of the regime's emphasis on armaments.[68]

The reintroduction of the work book, which had been largely abandoned in Germany in the second third of the nineteenth century in the train of freedom of movement, clearly showed the reversion once more to a restrictive labour guild system. This course had already been set institutionally in spring 1933, when the previously autonomous Reich Institute for Employment and Unemployment Relief lost its independent character. Instead the Reich Institute and its subordinate labour and Land labour offices later (1938) became direct Reich authorities under the supervision of the Reich Labour Minister (the President of the Institute, Dr Friedrich Syrup, became State Secretary in the Ministry). With the aid of the direct Reich authority for the allocation of labour, which developed into a mushrooming bureaucracy in the following years and ultimately even collaborated in wages policy, the National Socialist regime was in future increasingly able to direct, control and conscript labour.[69]

Another indication of the break which the year 1935 represented in this development was the introduction of the obligatory Labour Service on 26 June 1935, in place of the hitherto voluntary scheme. Through this the Reich Labour Service (*Reichsarbeitsdienst* – RAD), which had initially functioned chiefly as a cushion for unemployed youth, developed into a new state organization in which National Socialist schooling was closely tied up with the state direction of labour and pre-military training.

As in other ways, in the context of the DAF and the National Socialist community KdF, RAD expressed a basic tenet of National Socialist policy: the deliberate ideological, propagandist elevation of manual labour ('Work ennobles'), which on the one hand appealed to and stimulated the workers' self-awareness but chiefly his will to produce and to work and thus fostered social quietism as well as the mobilization of labour energies.

Despite strong reservations by the workers, the National Socialist regime succeeded to a considerable degree in achieving the impression of social harmony and in largely overcoming the active and passive resistance of a labour force which had once been chiefly organized by the Free Trade Unions, even though the regime's restrictive wages policy gave the work force a lesser share than the employers of the economic 'gross national product', which in itself was increasingly enlarged after 1934/5. This, however, was not primarily due to the power of ideological slogans, but rather to the restoration of job security after the years of economic crisis. The fact that Hitler succeeded, with whatever means and for whatever purpose, in virtually ending unemployment as early as 1935, thereby eliminating the risk to their very existence of millions of workers, was the basic precondition for the success of the Third Reich's direction of labour and its social policy, for all the many unreasonable demands and the regimentation involved. Security of employment compensated even for the loss of social freedom and independence. And in general the regimentation of *all* social ranks – if differently arranged – effected a psychological equality which was positively regarded by the lower social classes as a narrowing of the gap between them and those previously in the upper classes. The encouragement of vocational training tended in the same direction too, as did the Hitler Youth's yearly Reich Trades Competition, which improved the promotion prospects for workers and employees, especially of the younger generation. Above all, the role of the Party (and of its many auxiliary organizations, including the DAF) cannot be overestimated. The wide network of National Socialist organizations and auxiliary organizations offered millions of workers and employees as well as the petit bourgeoisie the prospect, through a career in politics, of acquiring prestige, influence and also an imposing material status, equivalent to that of the old upper strata of society and far beyond their vocational, social beginnings, without having to go through the tedious stages of the normal social climb (as Hitler Youth or S.S. leader, or as district leader of the DAF or the NSDAP). In that respect the network of National Socialist auxiliary organizations throughout the country which produced hundreds of thousands of officials who regarded themselves as the new élite, also changed social realities. It broke down (witness the broad, less exclusive class of the new functionaries) old class barriers and increased social mobility.

The co-ordination of trade and craft: National Socialist policy towards the middle classes

The spring months of 1933, when the terrorist, revolutionary activity of the left, Socialist wing of the NSDAP assumed its most violent form with the suppression and co-ordination of the trade unions, were also the high point of the expectations and activity of the middle-class interest groups within the Party. They benefited from the fact that middle-class ideologies and claims formed the original nucleus of the National Socialist movement which before 1933 had to a great extent determined official programme and propaganda and even to some extent practical policy in individual municipalities and Länder. The NSDAP was conditioned and committed to the campaign against the department stores, chain stores, consumer co-operative societies, impersonal business etc., and it expected rapid victories here. This did not alter the fact that the middle-class groups had considerably less economic and sociopolitical weight than heavy industry and the workforce. The discrepancy between the great importance of middle-class ideology in the original Party programme and the relative weakness of the middle-class sector in the social set-up and in the over-all economy was soon manifest. It eventually came about that the middle-class demands of the NSDAP could indeed manage a few quick early victories in 1933, during the course of the Party revolution from below and could endure tenaciously at local Party level in the following years, but on the whole they were even less taken into account by the authoritarian, dictatorial leadership of the regime than the expectations of the left, NSBO wing.

In February 1933 middle-class associations, among them the Reich Corporation of German Handicraft, in whose regional groups NSDAP representatives to some extent already held leading positions,[70] made repeated applications to the new National Government and sought a stronger consideration of their interests, in particular through the appointment of a 'direct representative of the commercial middle class interests' to a leading position in the government. Even before the elections of 5 March, the National Socialist Combat League of Middle-Class Tradespeople under

Theodor Adrian von Renteln figured prominently here, and aimed to bring the claims of the middle-class associations within its sphere with the support of the advisor on craft and commerce in the 'Brown House', Karl Zeleny.[71]

The Combat League, first founded in December 1932 and numerically still relatively weak, which had amongst its members zealous propagandists but only inexperienced and poorly qualified association officials, had little chance, in contrast to Darre's Agrarian Policy Apparatus, of getting a majority and the controlling influence in the corporations, associations and chambers of middle-class business. Hugenberg also forestalled the Combat League's claims by obtaining cabinet authorization on 21 February 1933 to appoint in his Ministry the Nationalist corporation lawyer from the Chamber of Handicrafts in Hannover, Dr Wienbeck, as Reich Commissioner for the commercial middle classes.[72] As a result Zeleny informed the Chancellor at the beginning of March of the reports of National Socialist representatives from middle-class associations which severely criticized Hugenberg's 'manoeuvre' and urgently called for the incorporation of a National Socialist State Secretary for the middle classes in the Reich Ministry of Economics.[73] Wienbeck's appointment as Reich Commissioner for the Middle Classes (with the rank of Ministerialdirektor) was none the less made in March and he took up his office on April.

As a result of the co-ordination of the Land governments and the Party revolution from below after 5 March, however, the position meanwhile basically changed in favour of the National Socialist movement. Within a few weeks the pressure and terror of the National Socialist combat leagues also penetrated the corporations and associations of handicraft and trade, enforced essential personnel and organizational changes there, and to some extent certain legal measures of coercion against department and chain stores through individual National Socialist Land governments.[74] Above all, in the second week of March there began a national boycott of Jewish businesses as well as department stores, chain stores and consumer co-operatives. This was organized by the Party with considerable help from the Combat League and there were many violent measures, extortions etc. The campaign reached its zenith when the boycott of Jewish businesses (including Jewish doctors and lawyers) was officially sanctioned by the state's leaders, which was carried out throughout the Reich on 1 April under the direction of the radical anti-semitic Gauleiter of Nuremberg, Julius Streicher, in reply to the foreign 'atrocity propaganda'. The intended ruin of Jewish business rivals and those large-scale forms of trade which were a thorn in the flesh of craftsmen, small businessmen and the retail trade, went hand in hand with the co-ordination of the middle-class interest groups enforced through intimidation and terror.

After the previous board of the Association of German Department and Commercial Stores had already been forced to resign on 21 March and had had to make way for a new provisional control organized under the direction of a specialist in May as the Reich Association of German Medium-size and Large Retail Trade Concerns, the Combat League succeeded on 25 March in getting the most important key positions in the main associations of German retail trade in the hands of Combat League officials. The new managing director was von Renteln's deputy in the Combat League, Dr Paul Hilland. Subsequently the resignation of all Jewish members of the managing board and the introduction of the leader principle through a change in the statutes was agreed. The co-ordination of the handicraft guilds and associations was completed in a similar fashion. The Berlin spokesman of the Combat League wrote in 1934, looking back:

Outwardly the struggle was over with the seizure of guilds and associations in March of the previous year. As this was also in many cases merely an external co-ordination, it was not always possible on account of the limited membership of the Combat League for the Commercial Middle Classes to get the right person in the right place; none the less, at least those associations which until then had been hermetically sealed against National Socialism were introduced to the idea of Adolf Hitler. Generally, the then leaders voluntarily gave up their offices. In isolated cases, however, a bitter struggle had to be waged against liberal power cliques.[75]

On 3 and 4 May, directly following the action against the trade unions, the official co-ordination of both key organizations was 'solemnly' proclaimed in separate meetings of handicraft and retail trade representatives in Berlin, arranged by von Renteln and Zeleny. From then on the Reich Corporation of German Handicraft and the Reich Corporation of German Trade were to make up a sort of compulsory cartel under authoritarian National Socialist leadership within the context of the projected corporatist restructuring of the economic and social order.

Still more important was the fact that in April/May 1933, with the help of the S.A. and S.S., the Combat League for the Commercial Middle Classes had also brought a large proportion of the local chambers of industry and commerce under its control through the installation of Commissioners and had thus obtained the decisive say for pro-middle-class officials in these public business corporations. When the existing board of the Congress of German Industry and Trade was abruptly displaced in May 1933 and von Renteln and Dr Hilland took over the functions respectively of president and managing director, Hugenberg protested sharply at this interference (19 May 1933), but he could not get his own way, especially since von Renteln had meanwhile arranged for a 'purged' plenary assembly of the Industry and Trade Congress to elect him formally as the new president on 22 June 1933.

None the less, a series of other, weightier obstacles had arisen for the NSDAP spokesmen of middle-class interests, which restrained their ambitions within narrow limits. In the spring of 1933, particularly in the retail trade area in conjunction with the struggle against department stores and consumer co-operatives, and as a result of the momentary ambition of the National Socialist Combat League (in part a result of the concurrently intensified policy of agricultural protection), there was a wave of price increases in the concerns, which produced a sharp reaction from other National Socialist organizations (S.A. and NSBO). The naive idea of a corporatist economy which generally prevailed among the Party's middle-class representatives and which assumed that at this stage each group of producers and shopkeepers could themselves fix the 'proper price', soon had chaotic effects. In Munich the Bavarian Cabinet Council concerned itself with the problem of 'unjustified price increases' on 16 May 1933, and decided to proceed 'if need be with the most severe police measures' against such 'anti-social price rises'.[76] In fact about 200 people were arrested in Munich alone in the following days and their businesses were closed and marked with a sign: 'Business closed by the police because of profiteering – owner in custody at Dachau.'[77]

Even the widespread desire for a comprehensive Reich law for the promotion of middle-class commercial business, which the National Socialist State Secretary in the Reich Ministry of Finance, Fritz Reinhardt, had publicly voiced in mid-April,[78] was only very partially fulfilled. The law finally issued under the auspices of Hugenberg's Ministry of Economics on 12 May 1933, the Law for the Protection of Retail Trade (*RGBl*, I. p. 262) largely confined itself to a temporary ban against setting up new retail businesses and new department stores or chain stores,[79] and also changed isolated provisions of the code of trade practice whereby the state and local authorities acquired stronger powers to withdraw or refuse business concessions (in the event of fraud and unfair competition as well as of 'insufficient demand'). The later law of 23 July 1934 switched over to general state licensing, which determined the future development in trade and handicraft and (in contrast to the idea of corporatist self-government) imposed a state-regulated control of middle-class commerce in place of free enterprise.

It must have been particularly disappointing for the middle-class groups within the Party when the Hitler government also abandoned the struggle against the department stores, which had been preached for years and whose liquidation or 'communalization' the Party programme had specifically urged, because the economic and socio-political absurdity of this campaign against modern and rationalized forms of sales and business soon manifested itself. By continuing the boycott of March/April 1933, which severely damaged the turnover of department stores, it would have been easy to ruin completely this branch of industry. But in view of the simultaneous price rises in retail businesses those Party auxiliary organizations which had to reckon with the mass of unemployed and low-income workers and employees, chiefly the NSBO, had no interest in this either. In any case the threatened bankruptcy of large department stores would have thrown tens of thousands of workers and employees out of work and, not least, would have severely damaged the companies and banks behind them. The labour force and big business alike were interested in avoiding a collapse of this branch of the economy. The plans for introducing a drastic Reich tax on department stores collapsed in the face of this resistance.[80] When at the end of June one of the biggest department-store concerns, the Jewish Hermann-Tietz-Konzern (Hertie), with 14,000 employees, faced the choice of bankruptcy or reorganization, the newly appointed Reich Minister of Economics, Schmitt, made energetic representations to Hitler for reorganization with the help of the Reich. At first Hitler indignantly refused, especially since the Hertie stores had been a special target of the Party boycott in March/April, but in the end he had to bow to the economic arguments. Dr Hilland, the deputy leader of the Combat League, who knew nothing of Hitler's about-turn on this, demanded after the publication in the National Socialist press of the plan for reconstruction at the beginning of July, that 'ruthless' action had to be taken against the 'irresponsible' interest groups behind the plan.[81] A little later on 7 July, Hitler's Deputy, Hess, found himself obliged to bring the Party into line with the changed policy on the department store issue: '... At a time when the National Socialist government believes that its main task is to help as many as possible of our unemployed fellow-men to get work and to make a living, the National Socialist movement must not prevent this by taking jobs away from hundreds of thousands of workers and employees in the department stores and the businesses which are dependent on them. The NSDAP auxiliary organizations are therefore forbidden until further notice to take action against department stores and similar concerns.'[82]

The local Party organizations were frequently perplexed at this directive. When individual stores displayed the Party order in their shop windows to insure against further hardship, the more they drew the Party's fury on themselves. As the toleration edict issued by Hess had stated in order to calm Party comrades that the stand on the department store issue was 'fundamentally' unchanged and that a solution 'in the sense of the National Socialist programme' would follow 'at the right time', the local campaign which the Party comrades proclaimed against buying in department stores went on for years and led to many boycott actions. But in the long run the Reich Economics Minister made his point and he had already pleaded in September 1933 that there should simply be a reduction of the business of the department stores instead of the liquidation which the Party programme envisaged. This added up chiefly to the turnover tax for large concerns introduced in 1935, and the closure by law of refreshment rooms, catering and handicraft services (later also book departments) in the department stores as well as the ban on special sales (apart from the three-day end-of-season sales in summer and winter which were fixed by law) as well as limits on the giving of discounts.[83] After surviving the low point of 1935, when the total turnover of the department stores in Germany fell to 54 per cent of the record turnover of 1928, those stores were able to recover again in the following years in spite of legal restrictions (1936, 59; 1937, 63.9; 1938, 70.1 per cent of 1928 turnover).[84]

After a total of twenty-nine Jewish department stores had been burnt and destroyed and numerous others 'aryanized' in conjunction with the organized pogrom of Jews on the 'Night of broken glass' (9/10 Nov. 1938), the Party's anti-department store campaign also generally subsided. Indeed the aryan department stores, with their rationalized distribution machinery and to some extent strengthened through the enforced exclusion of Jewish rivals, later proved to be an ideal instrument for control under the conditions of quota fixing of the War economy. The discriminatory department-store tax was finally ended with effect from 1 April 1940. It was only as a result of the enforced war-time saving in trade that a succession of department stores closed down as well as retail outlets, when the old hostility towards the big stores of the Party Gauleiter and Kreisleiter again played its part. All in all, however, by this time the purely expedient principles of the state-controlled economy had long since overridden middle-class ideologies.

Long before this and much more unequivocally than in the case of the NSBO and the DAF, the middle-class sector lost its independence and political weight as a separate Party organization. After the activities of the National Socialist Combat League for the Commercial Middle Classes had provoked a growing disquiet in industry and business in the spring of 1933, there were some sharp reactions in June and July. Thus on 2 June, in a letter to von Renteln, Hugenberg and Göring heavily criticized the Combat League whose interference (system of commissioners) in the chambers of industry and commerce had prevented 'medium and larger concerns' 'from participating in the management of the chambers' in favour of small business interests. In June the director of the economic policy division of the NSDAP Otto Wagener, who (together with the Nationalist Möllers) had been appointed as economic commissioner, found himself obliged to forbid the Combat League from appointing any more commissioners or from interfering directly in business life. After Hitler had proclaimed the end of the National Socialist revolution in July 1933, the Combat League was also formally dissolved and transferred to the National Socialist Handicraft, Trade and Commerce Organization, which no longer had the right to enrol new members and was simply a more or less nominal grouping of the old Combat League members within the NSDAP, as much in a state of atrophy as the NSBO.

No more were the original hopes of corporatist self-government fulfilled which had been sponsored in the summer of 1933 with the formation within the DAF òf a General Association of German Craftsmen, Shopkeepers and Traders. The General Association, like similar nominally corporatist forms of reorganization in the realm of the industrial associations, was merely a brief interim solution before the decisive initiative passed to the state authorities. In the trade sector this chiefly happened by means of the authority of the Reich Commissioner for Price Fixing which was revived in 1934, and with the aid of a series of laws imposing stricter standards of training, certificates of qualification and management in the handicraft sector through the official introduction of an obligatory system of guilds under the supervision of the chambers of handicraft and the state economic bureaucracy. The law (of 29 November 1933), on the Provisional Reconstruction of German Handicraft (*RGBl*, I, p. 1015) charged the Reich Ministry of Economics and the Minister of Labour with the creation of a uniform, compulsory organization 'on the basis of corporate duties and the leadership principle'. It was also incumbent on the Minister on the basis of the law to nominate the leader of the Reich Corporation of German Handicraft. The 'first decree' of the Ministries of Economics and Labour which was issued on the strength of this on 15 June 1934, 'On the Provisional Reconstruction of German Handicraft' (*RGBl*, I, p. 493) replaced the free professional associations by a hierarchically arranged system of handicraft guilds under public law with compulsory membership and under the leadership of Grand Masters who were chosen from the chambers of handicraft and who possessed an authoritarian right to direct and to penalize their members in keeping with the leader principle, whereas the resolutions made by the Guild Assembly and the advisory councils and 'observers' chosen from it had subsidiary and advisory functions only. As in the guild specialist groups of the different branches of handicraft, the leader principle was also preserved in the regional combinations of guilds into area handicraft unions (composed of the Grand Masters of the guilds and directed by an area handicraft leader chosen through the chambers of handicraft). At the head of the hierarchical pyramid stood the Reich Master Craftsman, whose simultaneous appointment as leader of the Reich Corporation of German Handicraft could not disguise the fact that this officially ordained guild was chiefly an auxiliary organ of state economic supervision and control.

How little this was a matter of a representation of interests or of a corporate organization for the protection of the middle classes became clear in the following years, when the Reich Corporation of Handicraft itself had to help in the careful weeding out of handicraft concerns according to efficiency and demand. The introduction of the Higher Certificate of Qualification in 1935 and other measures for 'purging the profession' and for the liquidation of 'non-viable' businesses led between 1936 and 1939 to the closure of some 180,000 handicraft concerns (over 10 per cent).[85] Other concerns remained nominally independent, but in practice these were in the industrial sector; to some extent handicraft business communities were also transplanted *en bloc* to industrial works or combined in community workshops.

The measures decreed to 'end overmanning in the retail trade' (decree of 16 March 1939) in conjunction with the simultaneously enforced state control of labour allocation had similar effects. The most notable success of the 'aryan' retail trade and a cheap salve for otherwise unfulfilled economic and social expectations was the forceful elimination of Jewish competition in 1938. Otherwise the retail trade had only a relatively small share in the economic recovery after 1934/5. Sales in 1938 exceeded those of 1928 only in those branches of furniture and household supplies favoured by tax and population policies (marriage loans etc.) In all other branches of retail trade the figures were lower. The cinderella-like role which retail trade played under the National Socialist regime is revealed by the fact that shop assistants declined by 9 per cent between 1933 and 1939 and had to be replaced by family dependents,[86] whereas in the economy as a whole during the same period about 7 million workers were newly employed or re-employed.

All in all it seems that the small commercial middle classes in the Third Reich were by no means so carefully protected as a romantic, nationalist middle-class ideology had imagined. On the contrary they fell behind more quickly and drastically compared with industrial big business than had been the case in previous decades in the context of an increasingly pronounced process of mechanization and industrialization. This expressed very clearly the neglect of consumer business for the benefit of the building, raw materials and armaments economy favoured for reasons of state policy. Although one positive side-result was that the light industrial sector was submitted to a strict viability principle imposed for reasons of state, and was thus forced towards a more rationalized way of business through a considerable reduction in the number of concerns, it was the emphasis on armaments above all which curtailed civilian consumption and on which middle-class ideologies were dashed. This priority also determined the privileged position of at least a part of industry in Hitler's state.

The position of industry in the early years of the National Socialist regime

Whilst the forceful liquidation of the Free Trade Unions and the Nazification of the associations of the commercial middle classes already reflected a differing degree of compulsion and intensity of co-ordination, the representatives of industrial interests were the least affected by the Party political co-ordination, or were in a better position than any other group to deflect the interference and coercive measures threatened by the NSDAP. On 1 April 1933, S.A. men forced their way into the offices of the Reich Association of German Industry, contrived the resignation of the Jewish managing director, Geheimrat Kastl, and enforced the expulsion of other Jewish members of the board. At the same time a Party agent, Dr Hans von Lucke, was assigned to the Association's management on the initiative of the NSDAP's Economic Policy Commissioner, Dr Wagener.

But the leading representatives of the big industrial concerns (Krupp, Thyssen, Siemens etc.) were able to deflect this attempt at direct Party control in industry's leading association relatively quickly, thanks to their standing with Hitler and to the support they had not only from Schacht, Hugenberg or Schmitt, but also from Göring and other influential Party men in view of the secretly agreed policy of increased armaments production. In order to escape the control of National Socialist Commissioners, Gustav Krupp von Bohlen und Halbach, as newly elected leader of the Reich Association, himself undertook a reorganization in agreement with Hitler, which aimed at transforming this loose association into an authoritarian central organization of industry. This was not simply a matter of adapting to the new leader state principle. It was also hoped to create an organ through the strengthened authority of the leading industrial association which could itself exert greater influence on the government's economic policy, in close contact with the economic bureaucracy.

The expectations of industry seemed to be fully confirmed when on 29 May Hitler summoned to the Chancellery for talks on the policy of job creation about fifty leading industrialists and bank directors (among them Krupp, Thyssen, von Siemens, Stinnes, Springorum, Bosch, Vögler and von Stauss), together with the heads of the government's economic policy departments and the Party's economic policy advisors to listen to the advice of the industrialists. On the basis of this first discussion it was agreed in mid-July 1933 to set up a permanent General Council of the Economy in which heavy industry was strongly represented.[87]

It also became apparent that in heavy industry and banking (more than in other branches of the economy) Party encroachments were already being emphatically countered at Hitler's bidding from April/May 1933. Schacht was especially energetic in ensuring that the middle-class National Socialist slogans against 'grasping finance capital' had no basis in revolutionary practice. The National Socialist Economic Commissioner Wagener had already had to issue a statement on 27 April which informed the NSDAP that interference in the industrial economy, especially any 'independent setting up of commissioners of any sort' would not go unpunished in future, now that the 'main head associations have already been adapted' and 'our influence has generally been secured'.[88] When Hitler heard at the beginning of May that an NSDAP member and employee in the Dresden Bank had tried to force himself onto the board of directors with the help of the S.A., he immediately ordered that the man concerned be called to account and expelled from the Party.[89]

Hitler's directive of 31 May to the Reich Governors and the Prussian Minister President was also typical of his concern for the industrial economy, when he tried to stop the wave of Party denunciations and measures against purportedly corrupt leaders of the economy which was widespread in spring 1933, after many years of scandal-mongering by the NSDAP during the time of struggle. To make sure that the vital economic 'reconstruction is not endangered', so the order said, 'the passion noticeable in recent weeks for initiating indiscriminate investigations into offences from an earlier period and for calling the guilty to account, must cease'. The attempt to 'bring leading personalities of the economy to book' often concealed 'not so much a desire for justice' as 'personal feelings, even a thirst for revenge and the pursuit of selfish personal aims'. But this makes 'the leaders of the economy feel like outlaws and brings in its wake nothing short of the paralysis of the responsible management of our economic system'. In many cases too, past 'errors were due less to vulgar self-seeking than to the struggle of business concerns for their very existence. A generous response to such past failings is the proper one for the state organs', and he (Hitler) expected such consideration.[90]

This unusually 'sympathetic' directive for the cares of the industrialist was supplemented two days later by an order from the Reich Minister of Justice to the Land judicial authorities recommending a 'broad-minded treatment' of trial directions with the object of staying proceedings in the event of Party complaints in corruption cases, as well as 'particular care' in dealing with the numerous denunciations among the National associations. There also had to be 'fundamental abstention from the use of police custody in corruption cases'.[91] This initiative for the protection of employers and leaders of the economy against Party attacks was apparently a result of the talk with leading industrialists on 29 May. The general director of Alliance Insurance, Dr Schmitt, who was closely involved with the NSDAP, had then said: Business welcomes the fact that 'today we have a state, thank God, in which there is no need to fear that in six weeks there will be a change of policy'. But the resulting 'security of economic planning' is at the moment still incomplete and will be undermined to some extent by the fact that at the moment 'there is still too much prattle by both qualified and unqualified sources'.[92]

The fact that at the end of June 1933, Schmitt was named Reich Minister of Economics in place of Hugenberg, instead of Wagener or any other exponent of the Party directorate, was also another concession to private big business, especially since Wagener's job as Economic Commissioner also came to an end in mid-July. The simultaneous appointment of Gottfried Feder as State Secretary in the Economic Ministry (a placatory gesture to the Party which Hitler apparently regarded as unavoidable after the NSDAP kicked up a fuss after March 1933 against the Nationalist domination in the economic departments) might indeed have partially offset this effect. It turned out later, however, that Feder remained almost wholly without influence. When Schacht took over the Ministry of Economics a year later he had Feder dismissed without any difficulty. Thereafter the NSDAP's oldest economic theorist dropped completely out of sight politically.

The voluntary co-ordination of the Reich Association of German Industry (as the Reich Estate of German Industry) under Krupp's leadership, like the setting up of the General Council of the Economy, which was only convened once (in September 1933), was a more or less experimental and nominal gesture towards the notion of a 'corporatist reconstruction' of the economy, strongly propagated at that time by sections of the NSDAP (although rather variously interpreted). Within heavy industry this idea was most forcefully represented by Fritz Thyssen, who was in contact with Hitler from 1923 and who had been useful to the NSDAP for many years as a financial supporter and go-between. Even before the take-over of power Thyssen had set up an Institute for Corporatist Organization in Düsseldorf from his own resources in collaboration with the corporatist reformers in the NSDAP Gau staff, which aimed to define the notion of a corporatist economic system and to anchor it more firmly in the Party by holding instructional courses. After the liquidation of the trade unions and the formation of the Labour Front Thyssen, who was then appointed to the Prussian privy council for life by Göring, got Hitler's support for his efforts on 19 May and he was formally authorized to develop further the idea of a 'corporatist organisation' from Düsseldorf. Hitler quite deliberately supported Thyssen on various occasions in the following weeks and months against NSBO and DAF attacks.[93] Thus in the summer of 1933 and particularly in the Rhineland, Thyssen was also regarded by some Party Gauleiter as the special authority on questions about the future economic system.

It was soon obvious that Hitler allowed the proponents of a corporatist economic organization, who wanted to curtail economic liberalism as well as state control, to have their own way only as long as they did not interfere with the more important of the regime's aims, or as long as they were useful in restraining the Socialist aspirations of the NSBO and the left wing of the NSDAP.

New legal provisions like the two cartel laws promulgated on 15 July (*RGBl*, I, pp. 487 and 488), empowering the Minister of Economics (and for the agrarian sector the Minister of Agriculture) to introduce compulsory cartels 'for the purposes of market regulation' (whose legal form and price structure were subject to the supervision and approval of the state economic bureaucracy) already demonstrated in summer 1933 that the authoritarian state leadership was by no means willing to give up the control of the economy. On the other hand the cartel laws, which in many respects were thoroughly favourable to existing cartels and extended their influence over those employees not hitherto subject to cartels, were an early example of the harmony of interest between the National Socialist regime and monopolistic big business, which in itself was a form of 'organized capitalism', especially since state supervision of the structure of cartels and prices was exercised relatively liberally and was often merely a matter of form in the first years of the Third Reich (until the strengthening of the authority of the Reich Commissioner for Prices and the greater bureaucratic efficiency under the Four Year Plan).[94]

The new Minister of Economics, Schmitt, soon had to deal with attempts to extend state control. These were as unwelcome to him as they were to large parts of heavy industry. They came not only from the ranks of the NSDAP, but in particular from the Reichswehr too, where it was felt that the time had come to bring about a stronger military slant to the economy as a whole, under an 'economic dictator' co-operating closely with the Defence Minister.[95] In fact it was not least because of the influence of the Defence Minister that in July 1934 the direction of the Reich Ministry of Economics passed from Schmitt to Schacht, who in his threefold capacity as president of the Reichsbank, Minister of Economics and plenipotentiary for the war economy practically assumed the role of an economic dictator and he was also more successful than Schmitt in getting his own way over the Party.

The armed forces were chiefly concerned with realizing the demand already made by the army ordnance department after 1930 for an intensified development in production of military raw materials (fuel, rubber, ore etc.) This plan met with little response from Schacht but found all the more support from Hitler's new Special Deputy for economic affairs, Wilhelm Keppler, who from August 1933 replaced Wagener as the official Party economic adviser to the Führer (with an office in the Reich Chancellery!).[96] Keppler thereafter had the special task of sounding out new possibilities for the production of German raw materials and stock. On the industrial side I.G. Farben was interested in the production of state subsidized raw materials, especially synthetic fuel production, and had already submitted a corresponding memorandum from their director, Carl Krauch, to the military authorities in September 1933.[97]

The first concrete result of these different efforts, which were really initiated outside the Ministry of Economics, consisted of the so-called 'Benzine Agreement' between I.G. Farben and the Reich government on 14 February 1933. This launched a rapid development of synthetic fuel production largely monopolized by I.G. and with purchase prices guaranteed by the Reich. Further steps in this direction included the founding of the Braunkohle-Benzin A.-G ('Brabag') in autumn 1934 (an association of the lignite industry for the installation of lignite hydrogenation plants, introduced on the express initiative of the Economic Defence Staff) and the construction of a German synthetics industry, likewise mainly in the form of state-subsidized associations of the textiles industry (founding of the Rhineland, South German, Thuringian, Silesian and Saxon synthetics companies).[98]

By contrast, as a result of the opposition of private industry and of the Ministry of Economics, which in the Schacht era objected to the excessive expansion of the production of substitute raw materials which could not be disposed of on world markets, the realization of other projects was delayed until the Four Year Plan (1936). The latter included the production of synthetic rubber (Buna), the erection of new works for mining (low-grade) domestic ores (later taken over by the official Hermann Göring Works in Salzgitter founded in 1937), and for other reasons also the erection of a special factory (financed by the DAF) for the production of the KdF car ('Volkswagen'), whose development had been started in 1934.[99]

Nevertheless the course was already set for increased state control of the economy at the beginning of 1934 when the direct and indirect armaments policy got underway with Schacht's full support. At first the most important instrument for this was the official credits in the form of bills issued by the Reichsbank from 1934 for the Metalurgischen Forschungs-GmbH (Mefo), a Reich company specially formed for this issue and in whose name big firms engaged on armaments contracts (Krupp, Siemens among others) received extensive credits for expanding their production. The total value of Mefo bills issued up to 1938 amounted to some 12 milliard Reich marks. That was no less than 62 per cent of total public expenditure and 16 per cent of total national income at this time. Even in 1934 military expenditure made up 40 per cent of public investment (1933, 23 per cent) and by 1938 this had risen to 74 per cent.[100] Further instruments for directing the economy were the foreign exchange centre and state supervision of the import, consumption and storage of industrial raw materials introduced in March 1934 in view of the precarious currency situation.[101] In addition there was the beginning of the reorganization of imports and exports with bilateral arrangements for the exchange of goods which was introduced into foreign trade with Schacht's 'New Plan' from 1934 onwards. Among other things this resulted in a greater consideration of the demand and production possibilities of the east and south-east European countries for the German economy.

This growing subjection of the industrial economy to state instruments of control and planning was barely compatible even in 1934 with a corporatist administration of the economy on the lines of Thyssen's ideas. Thyssen's fellow spirits, like the Westphalian Labour Trustee Dr Klein and the leading personalities of the Institute of Corporatist Organization (Dr Walter Heinrich, Dr Paul Karrenbrock and Dr Dornow) found themselves exposed from autumn 1933 to increasing attacks from the DAF and other Party authorities, particularly since they were almost without exception followers and pupils of the Viennese sociologist Othmar Spann whose Catholic corporatist teachings Alfred Rosenberg and other Party ideologists had branded as non-National Socialist. Hitler's Economic Deputy, Keppler, bluntly said of the lecturers at the Düsseldorf Institute to the State Secretary of the Reich Chancellery in answer to the latter's enquiry of 21 March 1934 that their pro-Spann 'views on the future corporatist reorganization were incompatible with our Führer's aims'. 'The emergence of those teachers' and the fact 'that too much theory is by no means good for the economy, makes it seem as though the founding of the Institute is not a particularly happy arrangement.'[102] The head of the office for corporatist organization in the Party directorate, Max Frauendorfer, also sided with Keppler and caused the Party to boycott the Institute's courses.[103] Although it was impossible to arrive at a definitive standpoint in the Reich directorate of the NSDAP in June 1934 because of the differing opinions of individual Gauleiter,[104] it was evident that the 'corporatist organization' had been written off. When at the beginning of June 1934 Thyssen himself approached Hitler with a lengthy memorandum sent via Göring in which he repudiated the harsh attacks on his Institute, referring to Hitler's express approval of its work a year earlier, heavily criticized the DAF's course and again defended the principle of corporatist self-government for the economy, he got no answer. Hitler contented himself with the laconic remark to the state secretary of the Reich Chancellery that he 'did not agree' with the drift of Thyssen's report.[105] In 1935 the Institute of Corporatist Organization was dissolved and Hitler banned the Party from any further discussion of 'corporatist organization'. The office for corporatist organization in the Party directorate also ended its activity as a result of a decree of the Führer's Deputy of 18 February 1936. In the same year the Gestapo filed a report on the 'Spann circle' in which the former lecturers at the Düsseldorf Institute figured as disguised opponents of National Socialism. Two years later, after the Anschluss, Spann's followers in Austria and in the Reich were arrested and Thyssen avoided further troubles by emigrating to the USA.[106]

Just as the government of the Third Reich intervened increasingly to direct production, so in the realm of the industrial associations it secured for itself the power to interfere in order to regulate and to control. The Law for the Preparation of the Organic Construction of the German Economy of 27 February 1934 (*RGBl*, I, p. 185), empowered the Reich Minister of Economics to reorganize the whole system of business associations, to set up a centralized compulsory association for individual branches of the economy, to fix their articles of association and 'especially to introduce the leader principle' and 'to appoint and dismiss the leaders of the economic associations'. However, the reorganization undertaken on this basis was sluggish and fitful owing to the differing conceptions of almost all of the participants. It was only at the end of 1934, after Schacht's regulation as the new Minister of Economics on 27 November (*RGBl*, I, p. 1194) that the new organization of the system of industrial associations crystallized: the Reich Group Industry now appeared in place of the Reich Association, with subordinate economic groups and trade associations, whereby the system of associations was tied more closely on a regional basis to the public law authority of the chambers of industry and commerce (in economic areas similar to the Trustee areas). Schacht had also already secured the right to supervise and appoint these in August.[107] Although several new leaders of the Reich and business associations or new presidents of the 'chambers' were appointed (both Krupp as leader of the Reich Association of Industry and von Renteln as president of the Industry and Trade Congress were dismissed), the old industrial associations were still generally able by skilful adaptation to the new set-up to preserve the influence of the concerns and personalities represented in them. This was especially true of the heavy industry sector. It was possible to transfer the former Society of German Iron and Steel Industry to the new Economic Group Iron-producing Industry under the same leadership (Ernst Poengsen) without difficulties, and the old divisional groups (North, West, South-west, Central etc.) remained virtually identical beneath the changed labels.

In so far as plants with similar production were combined in their specialist groups more than hitherto, then 'the plant organization and association organization were roughly the same'.[108] The obligatory character, the stronger authoritarian structure of the associations, their close connection with the chambers of industry and commerce and the state economic bureaucracy made them a peculiar hybrid and made it difficult to determine where self-government by the interest group ceased and the state 'duty to regulate' began.

Conversely, the same was true for many of the new organs of state control. Establishments like the Economic Research Association (Wifo), a subordinate office of the Reich Ministry of Economics, founded in the guise of a private limited company in 1934 and which in particular commissioned the construction of fuel depots in strategically favourable areas, were not only organized along private business lines (as private limited companies), but were often largely free of state bureaucratic restrictions on their business conduct and powers. This meant that the Third Reich, which did not attack the principle of the capitalist private economy but which significantly curtailed the employer's freedom of decision by strongly influencing the direction of production, tried to get by with the minimum of increased state bureaucracy, but in so doing allowed certain experts and interests from industry to exert a strong influence over the regime's control organs, and these were constructed on private business lines. This was an early example of a feature of National Socialist economic planning which also characterized Göring's Four Year Plan and the War Economy Organization of Todt and Speer: alongside the relatively few elements of state bureaucratic supervision, control and planning, the National Socialist regime also used the system of business associations which had been made more dependent on the government, as well as the favoured and widespread form of cartels and big monopolies of the industrial economy, as though these were subsidiary planning authorities. The latter were of course committed to specific guidelines and were in that respect controlled, but within this framework they were able to take far-reaching initiatives for planning and production, to decide on the most suitable action and were also able to get official approval and priority for certain big business interests. Although some large concerns, particularly in the mining and chemical industries profited from this both socio-politically (in terms of power) and materially, the policy increasingly operated as a restrictive command economy of quota fixing and licensing for many small- and medium-sized firms, especially in the consumer goods industry.

Whilst the National Socialist ideology 'tended to stop at the door to the director's room, the stock exchange or bank',[109] there were some changes in the industrial economy which were primarily determined by ideology. They concerned especially 'anonymous finance capital'. Thus changes in share laws in 1934/5 severely restricted the number of limited companies in favour of the personal business company (only companies with at least 500,000 RM capital were permitted as limited companies). Similarly the number of shares was considerably reduced (by raising the minimum value of a share to 1,000 RM) as were the rights of the shareholder (in the board's favour) as well as dividends. Rises in corporation and turn-over tax also limited the growth of business profits but they still left a considerable profit margin for those concerns that thrived under the conditions of National Socialist economic policy.

But the increase in private business profits was certainly not the main outcome of National Socialist economic policy. Nor was it the private businessman who was able to thrive in the Third Reich. In-stead a type of economic leader was thrown up who was half func-tionary of the regime and half private businessman. And even those concerns and branches of industry which particularly flourished in the Third Reich had to pay for this by submitting to increasingly severe conditions of constraint.

The Reich Food Estate and the principles of National Socialist agricultural policy

The NSDAP had secured a firmer foothold in the agrarian in-terest associations and chambers of agriculture than in other sec-tors of the economy even before 30 January 1933.[110] For this reason when the general 'balance' of domestic political forces tip-ped towards the National Socialist leaders after 5 March 1933, the NSDAP's Agrarian Policy Apparatus under Richard Walter Darré quickly secured the leadership of the key agrarian organizations. Here it benefited from the fact that the efforts to unify the system of agrarian associations which had already been going on for years and which had their first success with the creation of the 'Green Front' in 1929 received new impetus as a result of the economic crisis and became more pronounced, both amongst the regional farmers' unions and in the Reich Land League after the formation of the distinctly pro-agriculture government of Hitler and Hugen-berg.

These efforts, strongly influenced by the National Socialists from the outset, received effective 'assistance' from the fact that the President of the Union of Christian Farmers' Societies, Andreas Hermes, who had hitherto resolutely opposed any merger with the big farmers' Reich Land League and who was also highly critical of the NSDAP, was arrested on 20 March 1933 on suspicion of embez-zlement. When the President of the Bonn chamber of agriculture and National Socialist sympathizer Hermann von Lüninck (later Ober-präsident of the Rhineland province) took his place, negotiations opened almost at once in Berlin on 31 March for a merger be-tween the farmers' unions and the Reich Land League. These rapidly went in the NSDAP's favour, particularly since in the per-son of Wilhelm Meinberg another close collaborator of Darré's joined the Reich Land League's managing board alongside Werner Willikens under the acting (without party) President, Kalckreuth. After Darré had publicly demanded in the *Völkische Beobachter* on 2 April that no opponents of National Socialism could be tolerated in the governing board during the formation of a united organization and that the NSDAP's Agrarian Policy Apparatus had to be proportionately represented, he (Darré) was unanimously 'requested' on 4 April to take over the chairmanship of the Reich Leader Community of the agricultural associations which were going to be united.

The arrest of Hermes, however, who had been president of the German Agricultural Co-operatives (Raffeisen), also smoothed Darré's way to the leadership of the system of agricultural co-operatives which the NSDAP had previously been much less successful in penetrating than they had the agricultural interest groups. When the governing board of the Reich Association met on 19 April to consider Hermes's arrest, Darré appeared at the meeting with some of his staff assistants and forced the resignation of the managing board and the election of a new board on which three members of the NSDAP's Agrarian Policy Apparatus were represented. On 20 April, for the Führer's birthday, Darré was able to announce that at this stage he had also assumed the leadership of 40,000 rural co-operatives which were integrated in the Reich Association.

Thereupon the 'third pillar' of agriculture, the German Council of Agriculture (the chief organization of the chambers of agriculture) submitted without resistance to National Socialist control. Its President, Dr Brandes, had already conveyed a resolution of the Council of Agriculture to Hitler on 31 January 1933, warmly welcoming the new government 'whose leadership and composition gave hope that economic policy would develop along national lines' and expressing the desire for a 'strengthening of the domestic market' and a 'lasting restoration of profitability in agriculture'.[111] At the invitation of Brandes Hitler appeared in person at the plenary meeting of the Council of Agriculture in Berlin on 5 April and emphatically declared himself in favour of the policy of 'maintaining the farming sector' as the enduring foundation of the German nationality ('We know from history that our people can exist without towns, it is impossible to exist without the farmers'), but at the same time he also expressly urged the farming sector to 'support the government unconditionally'.[112] Thereupon, as Brandes informed the Reich Chancellor on 6 April, the plenary meeting 'pledged' the government its 'unreserved and united support' in a 'resolution which was accepted unanimously'.[113]

It became clear even during these days however, through the arrest of Nationalist chairmen and leading members of local chambers of agriculture, that the NSDAP aspired to sole leadership in the agricultural organizations and was trying in this way to make up for its failure to control the state's agrarian policy, which Hugenberg refused to relinquish. In these circumstances Kalckreuth and Brandes too were no longer required. At the beginning of May the former was sharply attacked in the National Socialist press; Kalckreuth was charged with personal gain, causing him to resign and to demand an enquiry on 5 May. Darré's staff leader Wilhelm Meinberg became the new President of the Reich Land League and at the same time manager of the Reich Leader Community of the agricultural associations. Brandes drew his own conclusions when on 12 May he recommended the board members of the Council of Agriculture to resign in order to leave the way open for a unification of all the groups involved in agriculture 'under one leader', whereupon Darré, at first provisionally, got the presidency of the Council of Agriculture.

When shortly afterwards Baron von Lüninck was given the post of Rhenish Oberpräsident, Darré had himself granted unlimited powers and the title of Reich Farmers' Leader at a meeting of the Reich Leader Community of the agricultural associations on 28 May. Thus the powers of the director of the NSDAP's Agrarian Policy Apparatus and the leadership of all the self-governing organs and professional organizations of agriculture were united under Darré. Darré, although lacking power because of his relatively short career in the Party even as a member of the NSDAP's Reich directorate, was exceptionally ambitious and had been able to get his own way more obviously than Ley or von Renteln during the co-ordination of the workers' associations. This was a result of the favourable conditions which existed for the National Socialist seizure of power in agriculture because of the absence of any serious rivals and probably the NSDAP's greater ideological and programmatic clarity in its agricultural policy. Darré was to succeed beyond this in also getting the control of the *state's* agrarian policy.

Opportunities for attacking Hugenberg's powerful position as head both of the Reich and Prussian Ministry for Food and Agriculture were at first harder to come by for the NSDAP. Hugenberg's energetically conducted policy of support for agriculture, the heart of his economic policy, which was supported by his state secretary von Rohr, was carried out chiefly through raising the prices of agricultural products and state aid to indebted agricultural concerns ('stay of execution'). It was a policy that could hardly be bettered in a material sense. Darré and his colleagues therefore concentrated all the more on ideological criticism: Hugenberg's agrarian stabilization policy was still too 'capitalistic', it took too much account of the interests of the large landowners and lacked the clear foundation of *völkisch*, racial ideology.

Since nobody could foresee that Hugenberg's ministerial activity would be short-lived, Darré tried to put forward some official expression of the basic ideals of his agrarian programme (introduction of the principle of inalienable entailed farms with 'acreage' sufficient to be worked by a family concern) at the beginning of May through the National Socialist-led Prussian government. With the agreement of the Prussian Minister President Göring, the National Socialist Minister of Justice, Kerl, introduced the 'entailed farm' legislation which had been worked out by the NSDAP's Agrarian Policy Apparatus, and which was passed by the Prussian Ministry of State on 15 May 1933 against Hugenberg's objections.[114] The enactment of this law, which betrayed the hand of the blood-and-soil ideologist Darré even more clearly than the later Reich Entailed Farm Law of 29 September, revealed considerable shortcomings of legal form and ambiguities.[115] It was also an open affront to Hugenberg, who was now obliged to agree to one of the veterans of the National Socialist farm leaders on Darré's staff, Major (retired) Werner Willikens (from 1930 one of the chairmen of the Reich Land League), joining the Prussian Ministry of Agriculture as State Secretary.[116] At the same time public attacks against the Nationalist Minister for Agriculture were intensified in the National Socialist press and by the co-ordinated agricultural associations.

When Hugenberg retired from all offices in the Hitler government at the end of June 1933 Darré's accession as the fourth National Socialist Minister alongside Göring, Frick and Goebbels, was inevitable. Hugenberg's (non-party) State Secretary von Rohr remained in office for another three months but was then displaced by the qualified agriculturalist and former National Socialist deputy in the Prussian Landtag, Herbert Backe. Apart from the new Department of Propaganda (Goebbels), agrarian policy was the one area in which the leading functionary of the Party directorate took over the control of the co-ordinated professional organization as well as the appropriate Ministry. Therefore in the agricultural sector conditions were right for an especially intensive co-ordination, and this was also ensured through the personal union and the accumulation of offices. Only in this sector of the economy was the so-called corporatist reorganization not only mooted but became (admittedly not in Othmar Spann's sense) a legal reality and part of a comprehensive system of public cartelization and planning which replaced the former freedom of trade and the free market economy. The structure of the comprehensive organization of the Reich Food Estate, whose operations staff (with Hermann Reischle as staff leader and Wilhelm Meinberg as head of administration) had emerged from the NSDAP's Agrarian Policy Apparatus,[117] was based on the Laws On the Reich's Responsibility for the Regulation of the Corporatist Reorganization of Agriculture of 15 July 1933 (*RGBl*, I, p. 495) and On the Provisional Organization of the Reich Food Estate and Measures for Market and Price Controls for Agricultural Products of 13 September 1933 (*RGBl*, I, p. 626) and a series of supplementary decrees. The new compulsory organization, also embracing the fishing industry and marketing and processing concerns in the food business, was, on the one hand, a corporatist, centralized organization geared to the Party's leader principle with its own hierarchical arrangement (Reich farm leader, Land farm leader, Kreis farm leader, local farm leader), on the other, as a mammoth syndicate under public law of co-operatives, economic associations and specialist offices, subject to the supervision and intervention of the Reich Minister for Food and Agriculture; it was delegated with numerous powers for regulating distribution, fixing prices and profit margins, for the standardization and planning (reducing or stimulating) of production and selling (including the right of imposing disciplinary penalties). At the same time, like the period before 1933 or even to some extent under Hugenberg, the traffic in certain particularly vital agricultural products (grain, milk, eggs, cattle and fats) was subjected to a greater degree of direct state supervision and price fixing (uniform pricing for bread, grain and butter in 1933 and 1934) and was controlled directly through the official Reich agencies which were subordinate to the Ministry.

The organizers of the Reich Food Estate, who were admittedly continuing the neo-physiocratic 'system of political economy' developed even before the First World War by the theoretician of the League of Farmers, Gustav Ruhland,[118] made no secret of the fact that in the area of agriculture and food production they were clearly breaking with the principles of free trade and the free market economy. However, they managed quite successfully to improvise measures of control, quota fixing and price regulation, staged in each case according to priority and economic importance, although this was due less to the ideologue Darré than to his colleagues. A purely bureaucratic form of planned economy was avoided and instead in many areas the 'market agents' and business cartels of the Reich Food Estate were used as the instrument of a type of indirect, differentiated planned economy, on whose operation the co-ordinated interest groups and the Party (in the shape of the agricultural consultants) could exert influence as well as the state.

Next to the organization of the Reich Food Estate, the Reich Entailed Farm Law of 29 September 1933 was the most important innovation of National Socialist agricultural policy, although the law was of more ideological than economic significance. The right to an entailed farm introduced for about a third of the agricultural concerns (agricultural smallholdings and estates of over 125 hectares were excluded) was to be a privilege reserved for those of German blood active as farmers and owners of the more productive medium concerns capable of farming. In future the honorific designation 'peasant' (*Bauer* as opposed to 'agriculturalist' *Landwirt*) was applied to these alone. Registration as an entailed farm (*Erbhof*), on which the *Erbhof* courts ruled in the last resort, meant that the state guaranteed the inalienable and indivisible family holding, with its liability kept to the minimum and which only a descendant could inherit. The real meaning of the law was to bind the *Erbhof* peasant irrevocably to the soil and arbitrarily curtail the rights of the co-heirs. But the law could only have been really successful in terms of a national stabilization of rural holdings or even in the sense of re-structuring agriculture, if the viable family *Erbhof* had been made the norm for rural tenure and if the great landed estates as well as the smallholdings had been gradually transformed to *Erbhof* property through partitioning and mergers. But the National Socialist leadership never tackled such a land reform. The numerical proportion of entailed farms never rose above the 35 per cent reached in 1933.[119] And the advantages of the guarantee of possession were offset in many respects by the disadvantages of state tutelage and economic restraint. Even during the discussion of the law in the Reich Cabinet on 26 September 1933, Minister of Justice Gürtner, Economics Minister Schmitt and Vice-Chancellor von Papen expressed fears that the *Erbhof* peasant would be completely 'isolated from trade and commerce' by the law and made into a state vassal, which could result in declining production. But Darré and Hitler insisted on the priority of demographic considerations. The criticism which Hugenberg's former State Secretary, von Rohr, made in a memorandum to the Reich Chancellery in August 1934 was far more severe, from a desire 'even without office to be of service to the Fatherland and to the Reich Chancellor': 'A quite new, less acceptable type of satiated peasantry will be created' by the *Erbhof* right. The majority of farmers reject the law 'because it contradicts their view of what is right and violates their feeling of freedom'. The law was evidently dictated more by farming theory than by farming practice. 'If the peasant has to keep his farm even if it doesn't feed him, if the heir to the farm has to take up the peasant's calling even if some other career offers him better prospects, the tie with the farm will become a crushing burden.'[120]

Rohr's views were confirmed by simultaneous reports of the Prussian Oberpräsidenten and Regierungspräsidenten, which showed that the conviction 'that the *Erbhof* legislation was fair had not yet generally been established' in the countryside; that this legislation would be 'severely criticized by many agriculturalists' and doubt would be expressed above all as to 'whether it was necessary to restrict the peasant's right to determine who inherited the land as the law required'.[121]

In fact the commitments resulting from the *Erbhof* right often caused economic stagnation and immobility. The restriction of credit opportunities contributed among other things to the fact that agriculture in the Third Reich was not modernized and mechanized to the extent which was both necessary and otherwise possible. This was probably the main reason why no noteworthy measures were taken to increase the number of entailed farms in the following years, when agricultural production became the most important yardstick and the realization of the ideology of restructuring agriculture became more and more remote because of the inevitably renewed flight from the land sparked off by the attraction of revived industries.

The organization and policy of the Reich Food Estate was no less contested than the *Erbhof* right. The reports of the Prussian Oberpräsidenten and Regierungspräsidenten in summer 1934, which have already been cited, reveal that many farmers disapproved of the Reich Food Estate's Organization and the officialdom of local and district farm leaders which had developed as a result. Nevertheless the policy of stabilizing agriculture enforced by Hugenberg and Darré in 1933/4, when the burden during these years of crisis had been deliberately shuffled onto other sectors of the population because the farmers had ideological priority, undoubtedly made a strong political impression in the countryside. This was only gradually modified in the following years when it became clear in spite of the yearly celebrations honouring the peasants and other ideological and propagandist displays, that even under the National Socialist regime agriculture was not keeping pace with the general growth in national income,[122] but remained a permanently needy part of the economy, although it continued to be cared for by the Hitler Youth's Land Service and by the Labour Service (often with more of an eye to propaganda than to provide real help).

As was the case with the co-ordination of other economic groups and associations, the Reich Food Estate could no more do away with economic laws than social conflicts, but merely gave them a new expression. As a large self-contained organization with its own authority and one particularly closely involved with the NSDAP's Agrarian Policy Apparatus, the Reich Food Estate was regarded both by state and Party authorities as a 'state within a state' or as a 'party within a party'. Even Schacht himself during the years of his greatest influence (1934/5) very often could not get his way against the ideological darling, the Reich Food Estate, and the opposition between Schacht and Darré which became a permanent conflict was a crucial reason in 1935/6 for Göring's rise – first as an intermediary and finally (as Deputy for the Four Year Plan) to the position of economic supremo, when he outmanoeuvred Schacht as well as Darré and made the Reich Food Estate a branch organization of the Four Year Plan.

As an organization outside the Party in theory but in fact closely involved institutionally and in terms of personnel with the

NSDAP's Agrarian Policy Apparatus and built up according to the National Socialist leader principle, the Reich Food Estate repeatedly came into violent conflict with the NSDAP, the S.A. and the DAF, especially in the agricultural provinces of the Reich. Here demarcation disputes and organizational rivalries very often expressed social and economic differences of opinion and conflicts of interest. In East Prussia where Gauleiter and Oberpräsident Erich Koch, who came from the Ruhr area and leaned towards the Socialist wing of the NSDAP, had long seen the main enemy of the Party amongst the rural conservative 'reaction', and where the NSDAP had an especially strong following among small farmers and agricultural labourers, there were already fierce quarrels with the peasant leaders and agricultural consultants installed by Darré in the summer of 1933. The East Prussian Land spokesman of the Reich Food Estate and Vice-President of the East Prussian Chamber of Agriculture, Hans Witt, complained bitterly in a letter to Hitler on 19 July 1933 that Koch had sharply criticized the 'corporatist reorganization' of agriculture in front of the Party's district leaders and had described it as a 'new version of the old interest parties' which merely 'promotes reaction and counter-revolution'. Witt also denounced Koch to Hitler as a proponent of an 'absolute Party dictatorship on the Bolshevik model in every sphere of life' and 'whilst denying any organically developed organization' Koch had openly shown that he had no time for 'free peasants' and that he (Witt) and other peasant leaders were 'not proletarian enough' for Koch. Also Koch had clearly referred to 'the reactionary circles surrounding the Führer', and in general was always talking of counter-revolution.

When Koch found out that Darré's underlings in East Prussia were providing evidence against him in Munich for both Hitler and the Führer's Deputy (Hess), he had a number of agricultural consultants abruptly expelled from the Party and threatened them with the concentration camp. When Darré complained, these measures were reversed through a decision of the supreme Party court (Reich-Uschla) in autumn 1933,[123] but the differences remained for a long time. Darré had similar sharp conflicts with other Gauleiter or S.A. leaders. The Chief of the Command Office (Führungsamt) of Röhm's staff, S.A. Obergruppenführer Krausser, complained in a communication to Darré of 24 May 1934 that the 'treatment of the settlement question by the Reich Food Estate' was contrary to S.A. expectations and warned that he would ask for instructions from the Chief of Staff of the S.A. 'to take steps to counter the anti-S.A. attitude of the Reich Food Estate'.[124]

Gauleiter Karpenstein (Pomerania) declared in a circular of 12 June 1934 to the political leader of his Gau: The attitude of the Land peasant leader shows that 'the Reich Food Estate in Pomerania' had 'isolated itself from the political organization'. In particular 'the functionaries of the Reich Food Estate' had 'launched a momentous struggle against the offices of the Labour Front in the Land, which offends against 'the honest principles of the National Socialist national community'. Obviously the peasant leaders of the Reich Food Estate were made out in this way to be a new vested interest group.[125]

These quarrels were particularly violent during the early phase of the National Socialist regime but they also continued later. In the spring of 1938 a dispute between the Reich Farm Leader and the DAF was again brought before the Reich Chancellery. Ley had suggested to Darré that the Reich Food Estate itself was implicated in the rural labourer's flight from the land. 'The drift to industry where wages and prices were not so rigidly tied is not surprising if the to some extent still disastrous working and living conditions of the agricultural following is taken into account.' The social welfare of rural labour necessary to stem this flight from the land, so Ley ended his letter to Darré, cannot be provided by a 'one-sided representation of interests' but 'simply and solely' by the Party and the DAF. Darré complained about the DAF's criticism which was continued in the following months and which gave the impression that 'the Reich Food Estate has done nothing as yet for the agricultural following', and he irritably hit back on his part by accusing the DAF of constant efforts to extend its authority.[126]

These and similar episodes clearly show that the social and economic conflicts of interest in the wake of the process of co-ordination were in no way ended, but were tangled up with the jurisdictions and power interests of the rival National Socialist organs and their respective 'leaders', and that an open and honest decision was barely possible. It was precisely because the reality of the pluralism of social and economic interests was denied and attention was focused instead on the national community by National Socialist ideology and propaganda that the politics of interest took the least satisfactory and most underhand form. The incompatibility between ideology and reality quickly became apparent in the realm of National Socialist agricultural policy. But David Schoenbaum has correctly pointed out in his study of the Third Reich's 'brown revolution' that in contrast to the corporatist middle-class ideology, the national soil and peasant ideology was a fixed component of Hitler's thought, and in this case the discrepancy between ideology and reality was not due to cynicism but was enforced by harsh economic realities. Hitler held on all the more firmly to the unfulfilled ideal of the blood-and-soil nation and he projected in the distant future an agrarian domain which would be conquered by the sword, and this could not be achieved within Germany's borders before 1939.

The agricultural sector again generally confirmed that in co-ordinating the big economic interest groups the National Socialist rulers went about things in a'thoroughly irregular and opportunist way. A more tolerant or more dictatorial process, a stricter or a looser form of control by the state or the Party or through the corporatist-styled new central organizations was chosen according to the opportunities available, or to the traditional political stance of the associations and according to the domestic importance of different social forces or in respect of the government's primarily military and autarkic aims.

The crucial factors here were economic relevance and the elimination of those personal and political ideological influences which most obstructed the regime. Yet this co-ordination lacked any constructive content in the sense of any comprehensive sociopolitical reform. Instead of a systematic rearrangement of the relationship between social forces, for which the Socialist elements within the NSDAP as well as the corporatist theoreticians hoped in vain, the general dependence of all interest groups on the state and Party was merely intensified. What appeared to be a lessening of conflicts of interest and was passed off as such by propaganda was in reality the result of this political link, which made the co-ordinated interest associations themselves into subsidiary organs of the political regime. The economic and social conflicts of interest were not ended by co-ordination but were conducted along the conveyor belts of the political system.

Within this political system the process of co-ordination caused a further duplication of institutions, authorities, leadership claims and positions of power. The social pluralism transformed itself into a pluralism of new formations of the regime in the shape of additional state, quasi-state and Party political authorities and organizations. And the permanent conflict between rival groups and leaders which was in any case inherent in the structure of the National Socialist movement (an inescapable corollary of the National Socialist leader principle) was additionally beset and heightened by the socio-economic conflicts of interest, which were indeed denied but all the same were not removed.

In addition, the varied nature of the co-ordination, which in the industrial and agricultural sector concealed more than it changed, demonstrated that in the economic sphere clear limits were set to the control of the National Socialist regime. As a movement which had itself sprung from the panic and resentments of liberal society, National Socialism had to stop short of such enforced measures as would not only have affected the private business principle of liberal-political society, but would have changed it in a revolutionary way (like nationalization and a fully planned economy). For the moment the totalitarian restraint of private business initiative was possible only to the extent to which compensation could be provided: at first (in the crisis) through economic security, further through a state-guaranteed rise in production and sales in certain areas, and finally through the systematic encouragement of speculation about the nation's future, which nourished the hopes for a grandiose expansion of the bases of the economy through the successes of National Socialist policy. This expectation of future territorial and political expansion of the Reich's power – which determined the 'atmosphere' of the economy too in the years 1935 to 1938, and promised first of all the expanded Greater German market and ultimately a position of hegemony at the expense of other nations – was in the last resort probably the most important compensation for the partial loss of private business freedom. Imperialism was the essential safety-valve for what was even in peace time an economy increasingly adapted to and ordered for the conditions of war.

Notes and references

1. On Hitler's authority the State Secretary in the Reich Chancellery, Lammers, approached the NSDAP's liaison staff in Berlin on 22 March 1933, and tried to suppress in the Chancellor's name all the attacks being made by the Party against Schacht (BA: R43 II/233).
2. Here, as in the case of the supplementary Reinhardt Programme decided in June 1933 for lowering unemployment, the declaration already made by Hitler in the Cabinet in February 1933 that public work creation had above all to favour rearmament, could not be realized at first. Reichswehr Minister von Blomberg had already stated in spring 1933 that the Reichswehr was in no position during that financial year to give more than 50 million marks for supplementary provisions. Cf. Dieter Petzina, 'Hauptprobleme der deutschen Wirtschaftspolitik 1932–1933', in *VJHZ*, 15, 1967, Heft I.
3. *RGBl*, I, p. 233. And the implementing decree to this of 28 June 1933 (*RGBl*, I, p. 425) and the Second Law for Decreasing Unemployment (*RGBl*, I, p. 651). The initiator of this programme was the National Socialist financial expert Fritz Reinhardt who had been officiating as the State Secretary in the Reich Ministry of Finance since April 1933.
4. On 13 July 1933 Schmitt stated in front of leading business personalities: 'The Führer has repeatedly affirmed that nothing can be done without the business chiefs and that any attempt at socializing the economy was bound to shatter on their resistance.' The National Socialist leadership was thus aware that the 'maximum' security of business planning in our economy had to be achieved 'as quickly as possible' and that without legal security and the chance of forward planning 'the businessman's decisions will be most severely restricted'. Cited after Schulthess, *Europäischer Geschichtskalender*, 1933.
5. On 13 August 1933 Schmitt made the point in a speech in Cologne that the measures for public employment creation could still provide only the spark and stimulus. The great problems of really overcoming unemployment could not be mastered by appeals like 'Germans, place orders' and by corresponding interference in, and pressures against, individual concerns, or with official Party proclamations of success in

overcoming unemployment in individual areas (this referred above all to the behaviour of the Gauleiter and Oberpräsident Erich Koch in East Prussia). Schulthess, op. cit.

6. On 27 June 1933 the law on the setting up of a state concern 'Reich autobahns' was issued through the German Rail Company and Dr Fritz Todt, the originator of this project, was charged with its planning and execution (formal appointment of Todt as General Inspector for German Roads on 30 November 1933 (*RGBl*, I, p. 1016).

7. Cf. the alteration to the motor vehicle tax law of 10 April 1933 (*RGBl*, I, p. 192) and the law on the abolition of motor vehicle tax of 31 May 1933 (*RGBl*, I, p. 315).

8. The share of the armed forces in Germany's public expenditure rose from 25 per cent (1932) and 23 per cent (1933) to 49 per cent in 1934 (and in the following years percentages were: 1935, 56; 1936, 68; 1937, 70; and 1938, 74). The turning point after 1934 for stimulating armaments becomes even clearer by comparing the absolute figures for armed forces expenditure (in millions RM): 1933, 720; 1934, 3,300; 1935, 5,150; 1936, 9,000; 1937, 10,850; 1938, and 15,500. In 1938 these figures made up about 19 per cent of the national income.

9. Opening of the first 'Winter aid action against hunger and cold' in the Reich Ministry of Propaganda on 13 September 1933. (Hitler's opening speech closed with the sentence: 'We have broken the international solidarity of the proletariat so we will build up the living national solidarity of the German people.') Cf. Max Domarus, *Hitler. Reden und Proklamationen 1932–1945* (Munich, 2nd edn, 1965), vol 1, pp. 300f.

10. Cf. the law on payments owed abroad, 9 June 1933 (*RGBl*, I, p. 349). This was supplemented at the same time by the stricter duty to notify any currency and property owned abroad: Law against betraying the German Economy, 12 June 1933, (*RGBl*, I, p. 360).

11. On this cf. the documents on the problem of payments policy in *Documents on German Foreign Policy*, series C (1933–37), vols. 1 and 2 (listed separately in the contents under 'Financial Questions').

12. Law of 7 December 1933 (*RGBl*, I, p. 1045).

13. *RGBl*, I, p. 1079.

14. Contained in *Akten der Reichskanzlei*, BA: R43 II/531. Another communication from the ADGB to Hindenburg, together with numerous documents telling of specific measures of force against ADGB functionaries and buildings, was sent on 5 April 1933 (ibid.). It is clear from this that on 25 March 1933 the official buildings and offices of the ADGB in some forty larger and smaller German towns had been occupied by the S.A., S.S. or the police and there were also further occupations and seizures of union buildings and property during the following days, which effectively paralysed the work of the Free Trade Unions in the places concerned. The union officials had to endure 'monstrous terror'. The number of those arrested rank 'into hundreds'.

15. Various appeals and overtures of these associations to the new Reich government were indicative of this and are contained in *Akten der Reichskanzlei*, BA: R43 II/531; thus the letters of the German Nationalist Shop Assistants Association (DHV) of 1 February, of the

chairman of the main committee of the National Industrial Workers and Trades Association of 15 March and 20 April, and of the General Association of Christian Trade Unions of 21 April 1933.

16. Further evidence of these well-known efforts is provided by a letter of 12 April 1933 to the Reich Chancellery from the newly appointed National Socialist State Commissioner to the chief burgomaster of Berlin, Dr Lippert. In this Lippert said that leading members of the ADGB had shown their readiness for 'positive co-operation' and he recommended that Leipart should be received by the Head of the Reich Chancellery. But the latter refused after conferring with Hitler, who had apparently already decided on excluding the unions by force (BA: R43 II/531).

17. *RGBl*, I, p. 161. The suspension of elections to the factory councils was prolonged until 31 December 1933 by the law of 29 September 1933 (*RGBl*, I, p. 667).

18. Law of 10 April 1933 (*RGBl*, I, p. 191).

19. On the events in individual cities, thus in Berlin, Cologne, Hamburg, Hannover, Frankfurt-on-Main, Munich etc., see WTB detailed reports contained in BA: R43 II/531.

20. In an order published in the NSBO organ *Arbeitertum* on 15 May 1933, Ley had warned 'irresponsible elements in the employers' camp' against using the dissolution of the trade unions 'to curtail wages and thus to satisfy their lust for profit'.

21. Published in *Arbeitertum*, 15 May 1933.

22. *RGBl*, I, p. 285; implementing law on this of 13 June 1933 (*RGBl*, I, p. 368).

23. The WTB announcement of 15 June 1933 (in BA: R43 II/532) gives a survey of the life and career of the Trustees of Labour appointed by Hitler on this date. Most of them were experts in the field of labour law, came from industry, chambers of industry and commerce or from state labour and business authorities, where they had already had some experience as mediators. Only a few were old NSDAP members and most were probably nearer to the Nationalist right in social policy too. Two of them, Dr Klein (Westphalian economic district) and Völtzer (North March area) were followers of Othmar Spann and his corporatist ideas. Cf. documents collected by the Security Police in 1936, 'The Spann circle' (IfZ: Dc 15.15., pp. 7f).

24. To some extent political hostility towards individual Trustees was coupled with the particular interests of different branches of the economy who felt that they had not had sufficient support. In Saxony Gauleiter and Reich Governor Mutschmann (in contrast to Minister President von Killinger) made himself the spokesman of small business organizations. In August 1933 he demanded the recall of the Saxon Trustee of Labour, Ministerialrat Hoppe, and the fact that Mutschmann felt himself put out by Hoppe's appointment played a part here. Thus in a letter to Killinger dated 30 August 1933 he tried to have Hoppe withdrawn from his post 'to which he had been appointed without my agreement'. But Killinger successfully deflected this effort in agreement with the Reich Ministry of Labour. Not until March 1934 was Hoppe, who at his own request resigned on

account of these difficulties, replaced by the new Trustee, the NSBO spokesman for Saxony, Stiehler, who was also acceptable to small business. Cf. the material in BA: R43 II/532.

25. Note of the Reich Chancellery, 7 November 1933 (BA: R43 II/532).
26. Note of the Reich Chancellery, 8 November 1933, ibid.
27. Ibid.
28. Letter of the Trustee Dr Nagel to the Reich Labour Minister on 14 November 1933 (BA: R43 II/532). As early as 5 August 1933 Dr Nagel had been very critical of the NSBO during a personal talk in the Reich Labour Ministry and to amplify this had sent a four-sided written report to the Ministry on 7 August, in which he said that it was possible to show in various ways, in keeping with the undermining of the NSBO through Marxist and class-war tendencies, 'that in wage negotiations the NSBO puts the struggle for wages to the fore and thus the employers were again being pushed in the opposite direction . . . This combativeness also explains the many interferences by the NSBO in the economy.' In his area the following cases had emerged: a mutiny in the main steelworks at Gleiwitz, a strike in the Hohenzollern colliery, interference in the management of the Henriette steelworks in Primkenau, deliberate 'sabotage of management and machines' in the Freiwaldau clay and stone works, and the threat of strike in a brickworks after the announcement of the new wage levels which he (Dr Nagel) had fixed as well as threats of strikes in many plants after the dismissal of individual workers (BA: R43/ II/ 532).
29. But Nagel later resigned of his own accord and was replaced in the spring by Dr Jüngst.
30. In his first report as Reich Governor on 10 June 1933 Gauleiter Sauckel told of greater difficulties being caused for the authority of the political leadership of the NSDAP by NSBO interference in the economy. Many unemployed had attached themselves to the NSBO and were favoured with jobs, whilst unemployed in the S.A. and S.S. often remained without employment. For this reason strong 'resentment within the S.A. and S.S. against the NSBO' had become noticeable (BA: R43 II/1382).
31. Letter from Hutmacher of 23 March 1934 to the Reich Chancellor, containing many interesting enclosures (BA: R43 II/532). The reason for this whole exchange was the projected (and in March 1934 this was carried out) removal of Dr Klein to Bremen, where he replaced the former Trustee Dr Markert.
32. Among these exceptions was the Trustee of Labour for the Rhineland, Wilhelm Börger, who was (from 1930) Land spokesman for the NSBO and who was the one Trustee of Labour who was mentioned positively in the NSBO organ *Arbeitertum*, e.g. his declaration: 'We are not trustees of the money bag but trustees of labour' (*Arbeitertum*, 15 July 1933, p. 9); cf. also Börger's article in *Arbeitertum*, 15 September 1933. Börger recalled after the War that he had already tried with the NSBO leader W. Schumann through Hess in 1933 to prevent the NSBO falling into Ley's hands, and then had quarrelled violently with Ley in 1934 (IfZ: ZS 834).

33. On this cf. the article by Bernhard Köhler in *Arbeitertum*, 1 September 1933, pp. 12f under the heading, 'We will not tolerate any setback to work creation'.
34. Cf. Ley's speech to the labour force at the Siemens works in Berlin which was reported in *Arbeitertum* on 1 November 1933, in which he said: 'We are all soldiers of labour, some of us command and others obey. We must cultivate obedience and responsibility again. Soldiers of labour, the one in this position, the other in that position. We can't all be at the wheel; for then there would be none to hoist the sails and haul on the ropes. No, we can't all do the same thing, this must be obvious.' Naturally, each must have 'his due reward . . . No employer can have any interest in having a poorly paid labour force.' These utterances are particularly typical of Ley's ambivalent, cautious style of expression.
35. Cf. BA: R43 II/531.
36. After the ban introduced on membership of the NSDAP from 1 May 1933 the enrolment of additional members in the NSBO was also stopped from 5 August.
37. Cf. the text of Ley's otherwise unpublished comments in *Arbeitertum*, 1 December 1933, especially p. 14.
38. Cited according to WTB report of 21 November 1933, in BA: R43 KK/531.
39. Text of the appeal, which was not published in the general press, in BA: R43 II/521.
40. Text of the circular letter together with an accompanying letter of 29 November 1933 from the Manager of the Reich Estate of German Industry, Dr Jacob Henle to the State Secretary in the Reich Chancellery, in BA: R43 II/531.
41. The person chiefly responsible here was Ministerialdirektor Dr Werner Mansfeld, who after his earlier work as lawyer to the association for mining interests had first been brought into the Ministry by Hugenberg as an expert on labour law in May 1933.
42. The Reich Minister of Economics and not the Reich Minister of Labour spoke about the draft in the closing Cabinet discussion on 12 January 1934; cf. protocols of the cabinet meetings (IfZ: Fa 203/4, Bl. 631ff).
43. Cf. protocol of the ministerial discussion of 1 December 1933 (IfZ: Fa 203/3, Bl. 601f).
44. *RGBl*, 1934, I, p. 45.
45. The Court of Honour was to be made up of a member of the judiciary appointed by the Minister of Justice in agreement with the Minister of Labour (as chairman) as well as a plant leader and a councillor of trust (as assessors) and could impose the following penalties: Admonition, reprimand, disciplinary fine up to 10,000 RM, deprivation of authority as plant leader or councillor of trust, removal from place of work. The jurisdiction of the Courts of Social Honour seems mainly to have worked out to the disadvantage of the plant leaders. Cf. David Schoenbaum, *Die Braune Revolution* (Cologne, Berlin, 1968), p. 128.
46. The idea originally desired by the DAF envisaged legal representation exclusively through the DAF. But in 1933 both the League of Nation-

al Socialist German Lawyers (among other things in a letter to Ley on 12 December) and the Minister of Justice resolutely opposed the Minister of Labour on the grounds that such a regulation implied defamation of and discrimination against lawyers; on this cf. BA: R43 II/548b. The DAF had already been given the sole right to make suggestions when convening assessors and labour courts through the law of 18 May 1933 (*RGBl*, I, p. 276).

47. Letter of the Reich Minister of Justice to the Reich Labour Minister on 12 December 1933 (BA: R43 II/548b).
48. On this cf. details in the *Organisationsbuch der NSDAP* (Munich, 1938), pp. 185–232.
49. Ibid., p. 185.
50. The agricultural groups combined in the Reich Food Estate were not normally separately members of the DAF (the rural labourers were an exception to some extent); instead, in order to preserve the fiction of a corporate system, it was a corporate member of the DAF.
51. A quote from the report of Reich Governor Sauckel (Thuringia) to Hitler on 13 March 1934 provides one proof among many: '... so I have to report that there has been a turn for the worse at the moment in the mood of the industrial population and work force. I regard the symptoms of this as worthy of note and very serious. They are partially to be sought in the efforts of certain circles to permit price rises of foodstuffs and clothing, as well as of raw materials and building materials, whilst virtually at the same time some firms have propagated and even carried out wage reductions. Here obviously extremely serious criticism is being generated with the NSBO and the Labour Front which is bound to have a disastrous effect on the mass of the labour force unless counter-measures and suitable statements are made immediately ... In view of the change of mood, which has not only been detected by me but was unanimously recognized in a meeting of the Thuringian Kreisleiter yesterday, I would like to emphasize that it is absolutely essential to re-establish the authority of the Gau managements over the other Party organizations, who think of themselves in the first instance and not about the whole...' (BA: R43 II/1382).
52. Speech by Ley at the Leipzig DAF congress in December 1935, cited in Hans-Gerd Schumann, *Nationalsozialismus und Gewerkschaftsbewegung* (Hannover, Frankfurt-on-Main, 1958), p. 101.
53. Cf. ibid., pp. 104f.
54. The influential Amtsleiter in the sphere of the Reichsorganisationsleiter of the NSDAP were at the same time Amtsleiter through personal union of the corresponding management authorities of the DAF. In fact the large majority of the leading personnel of the Reich organizational management came from the leadership of the DAF. The Reichsorganisationsleiter had his office at Barer Strasse 15, Munich. By contrast most of the offices of the DAF central bureau were divided between various agencies; the most important offices being at Potsdamer Strasse 180. The particularly strong and independent organization of the DAF resulting from its own financial resources (DAF membership dues) also aroused the special displeasure of the Reich Ministers for Economics, Finance and Labour, who in a meeting on 13 July 1934

established that the DAF 'was receiving an income of 26 million from its approximately 20 million members', of which no less than 45 per cent was spent on the costs of administration. For this reason the Finance Minister demanded that the DAF should be under his financial control. But this demand apparently went too far for Hitler, who got the State Secretary in the Reich Chancellery to inform the Finance Minister that he (Hitler) wanted the leader of the DAF, Dr Ley, to be involved in any further discussion of the problem (BA: R43 II/ 531). In fact the DAF was not placed under the financial supervision of the Minister of Finance but (from 1935) under that of the Reich Treasurer of the NSDAP.

55. How strongly this pressure was felt is shown, for example, by a letter from the machine factory August Reissmann AG in Saalfeld (Thuringia) on 27 October 1934 which was sent both to the Reich Governor and to the Land government as well as to the chamber of trade and industry, and in which complaints were made among others that the DAF was constantly approaching plants with demands for more donations. 'The predecessor of the German Labour Front, the trade unions, managed with a fraction of the funds which the German Labour Front is now claiming . . . We want a systematic and effective dismantling of all these extra organizations.' The DAF Kreis leader in Saalfeld severely criticized this letter from the firm of Reissmann on 5 November 1934 and attacked the anti-social and anti-National Socialist attitude of the plant leadership. It is indicative of the barely checked pretensions to power of the DAF and NSBO that it is stated in the letter: 'The Party comrades and NSBO spokesman working in the firm feel that this Plant leader . . . must be dealt with' (BA R43 II/ 531).

56. File note by von der Goltz, handed over to the State Secretary of the Reich Chancellery on 26 October 1934 (BA: R43 II/530).

57. Ibid.

58. Printed in the *Organisationsbuch der NSDAP*, ed. Ley (Munich, 1938), pp. 185ff.

59. Three and a half years later, when the draft of a law on the DAF was still being disputed, the staff chief of the Führer's Deputy, Martin Bormann, told the Head of the Reich Chancellery (letter of 5 March 1938) that on 23 October 1934 the Führer's Deputy (Hess) had sent Ley a draft of a law concerning the DAF (in which it was envisaged that the Führer should determine the articles of association). Thereupon Ley 'without informing the Führer's Deputy, had gone to the Führer the next day, 24 October 1934', and had had 'the said decree signed' which 'had not been discussed either with the Party offices concerned nor with the relevant state authorities' (BA: R43 II/530a).

60. Note by the Head of the Reich Chancellery (Lammers) after the Reich Ministers had aired their objections to Hitler on 27 October 1934 (BA: R43 II/530). Hess wrote to Ley on 31 October 1934: 'The Führer's decree of 24 October 1934 must be amplified and – as far as it is necessary – corrected. Therefore I am requesting in agreement with the Führer that until the new decree is issued, there should be no implementing provisions for the decree of 24 October; in addition

discussion of the decree in the press is to be avoided as far as possible' (BA: R43 II/530a).

61. BA: R43 II/530.
62. Cf. *Organisationsbuch der NSDAP*, pp. 473ff.
63. Order on carrying out the law to secure the unity of Party and state of 29 March 1935 (*RGBl*, I, p. 502).
64. With a staff of from 30,000 to 40,000 full-time employees the DAF was by far the most extensive of the NSDAP's branch organizations; cf. David Schoenbaum, op. cit., p. 120.
65. Cf. H.-G. Schumann, op. cit., pp. 128ff.
66. Laws of 31 March 1936 (*RGBl*, I, p. 335), 9 March 1937 (*RGBl*, I, p. 282) and 1 April 1938 (*RGBl*, I, p. 358). There is material on the origin of these laws in BA: R43 II/547b. As is apparent from a letter in these files from the Minister of Labour of 24 May 1938 to the Reich Chancellery, the Deputy to the Führer and the Minister of Economics in particular argued for the end of elections to the councils of trust. The Minister of Labour himself, as well as the Minister of the Interior and the S.S. Leader had doubts about this, feeling that it could give rise to the impression that 'the National Socialist state is no longer sure of getting the support of the labour force' and that 'elections were being avoided for fear of getting an uncertain result'. Reich Minister of the Interior Frick especially had already voiced his doubts in a letter of 20 November 1937: There was a danger that changing the law 'will be widely regarded within the work force as an attack on its social position ... If the spokesmen no longer basically need the confidence of the retinue, then they no longer appear as their spokesmen in the eyes of the retinue but at best as spokesmen of the plant leader or of the DAF, or at any event as organs imposed from outside. The question would then arise as to how far the term "council of trust" could still be justified.'
67. Cf. Friedrich Syrup, *Hundert Jahre staatliche Sozialpolitik* (Stuttgart, 1957), p. 418. On this whole problem also, David Schoenbaum, op. cit., pp. 129ff.
68. Of these later measures the most important are: the laws and decrees for fulfilling the labour requirements in the metal industries of 7 November 1936 and 11 February 1937, the introduction of the need for authorization when employing new building workers through decrees of 6 October 1937 and 30 May 1938; finally the labour conscription decree of 22 June 1938, which on the basis of the decree of 13 February 1939 also envisaged compulsory employment for unlimited periods.
69. Cf. F. Syrup, op. cit., pp. 407ff. After 1 August 1939 the heads of the employment offices also functioned at the same time as agents of the Trustees of Labour. This meant that the pressing concerns of labour allocation for the employment offices (instead of social policy considerations) now also increasingly dominated the whole wages policy.
70. Thus, for example, the Prussian Landtag deputy of the NSDAP Schmidt-Nordstemmen as deputy chairman of the North West German Craft Association, which was the strongest and most influential group within Reich Association; cf. letter of the National Socialist dep-

uties Brusch, Schramm and Heinke of 2 February 1933 to Hitler (BA: R43 II/277).

71. On 17 February 1933 Hitler received the managing board of the Reich Association of German Handicraft in the Chancellery, without involving the Economics Minister (Hugenberg) but in the presence of von Renteln and Zeleny and agreed to the appointment of a spokes-man of middle-class business to 'a key position'. Note on this in BA: R43 II/277.

72. Protocol of the cabinet meeting of 21 March 1933 (IfZ: Fa 203/1).

73. Cf. letters of Zeleny to the Reich Chancellery on 6 and 8 March 1933 (plus enclosures) (BA: R43 II/277).

74. Thus the National Socialist government in Hesse introduced a doubl-ing of the existing departmental store tax on 27 March 1933 and its extension to cut-price and chain stores; cf. Heinrich Uhlig, *Die Warenhäuser im Dritten Reich* (Cologne, Opladen, 1956), p. 96.

75. Cited by H. Uhlig, op. cit., p. 72.

76. *Völkischer Beobachter*, 20 May 1933, Supplement.

77. Cf. H. Uhlig, op. cit., p. 106.

78. *Völkischer Beobachter*, 15 April 1933.

79. The period first envisaged to 1 November 1933 was several times pro-longed through later amending laws.

80. The law promulgated on 15 July 1933 for regulating the departmental store tax and chain store tax for 1933 (*RGBl*, I, p. 492) empowered the Land governments or municipalities who had the right to impose the tax, at the most to double the tax rate. In contrast to most of the other Länder Prussia, under the influence of Göring and the Prussian Minister of Finance Popitz, made no use whatever of this provision. Cf. H. Uhlig, op. cit., p. 100.

81. Cf. H. Uhlig, op. cit., p. 116.

82. Published in· *Völkischer Beobachter*, 10 July 1933.

83. Cf. H. Uhlig, op. cit., pp. 152ff.

84. Cf. the statistics in H. Uhlig, op. cit., p. 224.

85. *Das Dritte Reich im Aufbau*, ed. Paul Meier-Benneckenstein, vol. 6, pt. 5: *Wirtschaft und Arbeit* (Berlin, 1942), pp. 122f. Cf. also the figures given for individual handicrafts branches in D. Schoenbaum, op. cit., pp. 171ff.

86. Cf. D. Schoenbaum, op. cit., p. 185f.

87. Protocol of the discussions with the industrialists on 29 May 1933 and material on the General Council of the Economy and protocol of the first session of the General Council on 20 September 1933, in BA: R43 II/536 and R43 II/320f.

88. Announcement of WTB, 27 April 1933.

89. Note of the Reich Chancellery, 5 May 1933 (BA: R43 II/1195).

90. The text of the unpublished decree in (BA: R43 II/1263).

91. Directive of the Reich Minister of Justice of 2 June 1933 (BA: R43 II/1263). Actually the orders referred to could not, however, wholly prevent employers who were particularly unwelcome to the Party from being subsequently taken into custody. Thus the NSBO organ *Arbeitertum* reported in its issue of 15 October 1933 with barely con-cealed satisfaction on two particular factory owners who had been 'put in the concentration camp of Wuppertal-Beyenburg on the initia-

tive of the responsible offices of the German Labour Front' because they had not kept to the list of prices agreed between the metal workers' association and the employers, and approved by the Trustees of Labour. In general it is possible to show that during the more or less terrorist phase of arrests in spring and summer 1933 jealousy on the part of the Party and its organs against people from higher social classes, rich Jews etc. often played a major role, so that Hitler's order of 31 May 1933 was undoubtedly often ignored. Characteristic of this (and in this context unique in its naive frankness, only possible at this early period) was an announcement of Gauleiter Bürckel in the Rhineland-Palatinate Gau paper the *Rhein Front* of 19 April 1933, which is cited in full below because of its rarity value:

'There are a number of applications here concerned with the release of political detainees. It must be recognized that the petitioners are mainly active on behalf of imprisoned Jews and the better-off detainees. Not least in this connection I should like to draw attention to the available medical reports which document the unsuitability for imprisonment of mainly Jews. *As yet nobody has interceded on behalf of poor workers who are in custody*! Thus I believe it right to state:

"1. That priority be given to freeing those imprisoned workers for whom nobody has yet interceded."

"2. Those political prisoners, for whom most of the petitions have been made, *will be released last.*"

"3. Jews may only be released in future if in each case two petitioners or the doctors who state that the Jews are ill are imprisoned instead of the Jews. Neustadt, 18 April 1933, The Gauleiter."

A newspaper cutting of this announcement is in the files of (probably a state) authority (at the moment BA: *Sammlung Schumacher*, no. 271) with the following very revealing comment of a departmental chief: 'How much longer can this fool [Gauleiter Bürckel] expose the great National Socialist revolution to general ridicule?'

92. Protocol of Hitler's talk with leading representatives of the economy on 29 May 1933, in BA: R43 II/536.
93. Fritz Thyssen, *I paid Hitler* (New York, Toronto, 1941), pp. 119–28.
94. Arthur Schweitzer, 'Organisierter Kapitalismus und Parteidiktatur 1933–1936', in *Schmollers Jahrbuch für Gesetzgebung, Verwaltung und Volkswirtschaft*, 79, 1959, Heft. 1, pp. 57ff.
95. Ibid., p. 41ff.
96. Cf. testimony of Keppler (IfZ: ZS 1091).
97. Cf. Dieter Petzina, *Autarkiepolitik im Dritten Reich. Der nationalsozialistische Vierjahresplan*. Schriftenreihe der *VJHZ*, vol. 16 (Stuttgart 1968), pp. 27ff.
98. Ibid., pp. 37 and 100.
99. On this cf. Paul Kluke, 'Hitler und das Volkswagenprojekt', in *VJHZ*, 8, 1960, Heft 4; also BA: R43 II/753.
100. Cf. René Erbe, *Die nationalsozialistische Wirtschaftspolitik im Lichte der modernen Theorie* (Zurich, 1958), pp. 25 and 34.
101. Law (of 22 March 1934) concerning the Traffic in Industrial Raw Materials and Semi-manufactured Goods (*RGBl*, I, p. 212).
102. Note by Keppler of 21 March 1933 for State Secretary Lammers (BA: R43 II/527b).

103. Letter of Dr Dornow to State Secretary Lammers, 15 May 1934, ibid.
104. The staff chief of the office of the Führer's Deputy, Martin Bormann, informed Lammers on 12 June 1934 that Hess again wanted to discuss fully the matter of the Düsseldorf Institute 'with the Gauleiter concerned (in the Rhineland)'. BA: R43 II/527b.
105. Note by the State Secretary of the Reich Chancellery of 7 July 1934, ibid.
106. On this cf. also the testimony of Walter Heinrich (IfZ: ZS 244).
107. Decree concerning the chambers of industry and commerce, 20 August 1934 (*RGBl*, I, p. 790).
108. G. Schulz, in Bracher, Sauer and Schulz, *Die nationalsozialistische Machtergreifung.* (Cologne, Opladen, 1960), p. 652.
109. D. Schoenbaum, op. cit., p. 155.
110. On this and the following cf. Horst Gies, *R. Walter Darré und die nationalsozialistische Bauernpolitik 1930 bis 1933.* Phil. Diss, University of Frankfurt-on-Main, 1966.
111. BA: R43 II/203.
112. Report of WTB of 5 April 1933 on the plenary session of the Land economic council, ibid.
113. Ibid.
114. GS 1933, p. 165. Cf. also Bracher, Sauer and Schulz, op. cit., pp. 572f.
115. For example the legally unqualified sentence (Art. 1, para. 3): 'The peasant has only one child who may take over the *Erbhof*'.
116. Willikens went on record after 1945 as saying that when appointed by Hitler he had been given the express instructions to push Hugenberg aside as Minister. Because he didn't welcome this idea he was charged with lacking 'guts'. As the later second State Secretary in the combined Reich and Prussian Ministry for Food and Agriculture Willikens, alongside Herbert Backe, no longer played a major part (IfZ: ZS 1622).
117. On the details cf. the writing of the leader of the Staff Office of the Reich Food Estate, Dr Hermann Reischle, who was himself heavily involved in building up the Reich Food Estate, *Aufgaben und Aufbau des Reichsnährstandes* (Berlin, 1934; enlarged 2nd edn, 1936).
118. Cf. Reischle, op. cit., p. 89 and the introduction by Darré, p. 6.
119. D. Schoenbaum, op. cit., p. 201.
120. Extensive résumé of the memorandum, which is not itself in the files, in a five-sided comment by the Reich Chancellery, 22 August 1934 (BA: R43 II/193).
121. Extract from the agricultural policy sections of the reports of the Prussian Oberpräsidenten and Regierungspräsidenten in August 1934, ibid.
122. For details, D. Schoenbaum, op. cit., pp. 208ff.
123. Material on the above in *Akten des Parteigerichts* (Document Centre, Berlin), copies in IfZ: Fa 508.
124. BA: R43 II/207.
125. BA: R43 II/203.
126. Letter from Ley to Darré, 25 May 1938, and note in the files by Reich Chancellery concerning Darré's complaints to the DAF of 30 May and 16 September 1938, in BA: R43 II/194.

Chapter Six

Party and state in the early stages of the Third Reich

Before 1933 the most active cadres of the NSDAP, especially its uniformed groups (S.A., S.S., Hitler Youth), had been engaged in a tough and often illegal struggle not only with political opponents but also with the existing state order and its organs. Terrorist and anarchist tendencies were deeply rooted in the Hitler movement as a result of the twelve year '*Kampfzeit*' ('time of struggle'), and the confederate structural principles of this movement arising from the traditions of the front-line fighter and the Freikorps defied regulation by the state just as in 1919/20 the Freikorps resisted integration in the state's new Reichswehr. But the NSDAP had itself called for a 'strong state' in common with other forces of the National Right and in this connection had fiercely attacked the patronage of officers by the democratic parties from 1929 to 1930, under the slogan of 'restoration of the professional civil service'. Among the motives which prompted millions of Germans to vote for Hitler a crucial role was played by the longing for strong leadership, which stemmed from the authoritarian tradition and was intensified during the economic crisis, and the longing for more uniformity, discipline and efficiency in the organization and government of the state. Most of those who voted for Hitler were certainly more attracted by the ostentatious military discipline of the S.A. than by its revolutionary behaviour. They desired a restoration of the authoritarian state of order on a popular basis, a 'total' state instead of the instability of Weimar governments. Consequently the relationship of National Socialism to the state was itself contradictory. The longing for a new order could not be realized without the destruction by force of the existing constitution. Restoration made use of terrorist revolution. Legal and illegal techniques for the seizure of power were closely interwoven.

The rapid process of seizing power in 1933 disposed in a few months of the different political parties, the division of state power between the Reich and the Länder, the barriers of privilege to the exercise of power, and finally also upset the balance between the legislative and the executive, which had already been profoundly shaken through the previous emergency governments. Co-

ordination had markedly prohibitive effects and categorically excluded certain persons, concepts and organizational forms during
the establishment of the Hitler regime. But this did not automatically bring constructive unity and homogeneity for the regime as
was seen during the co-ordination of the social and economic interest associations. Rather, a new and antagonistic division of pow-
er-roles arose on the basis of a seizure of power which was carried
out partly from above and partly from below. Some exponents and
organs of the Party took over positions of power in the state,
others were hostile and critical of 'the state', still seeking control
and far-reaching revolution. Besides, the NSDAP was not the sole
beneficiary of the collapse of democracy. The conservative forces,
especially in the Reichswehr and bureaucracy, who under the ban-
ner of impartial service to the state nevertheless incorporated the
tendency towards an authoritarian state played a considerable
part in the seizure of power. And from the outset the traditionally
strong cohesion and *esprit de corps* in the armed forces and administration proved itself to be a brake on the dynamism of the
NSDAP.

A basic problem from the outset was the question of how the
relationship between state and Party was to be determined after
the monopoly of political power: whether the Party was to be reduced to the role of a state Party and subordinate auxiliary organization, with the task of complementing the authoritarian state
dictatorship in propaganda terms and organizationally, as in other
European dictatorships during the inter-war period, or whether it
was to have a clear position of power over the government, as in
the Soviet Union. Actually this problem was never settled but instead remained unresolved. The chief reason why there was not a
political or indeed constitutional solution to the dualism of state
and Party was that neither possessed sovereign but only devolved
power, subject to the charismatic leader. The unrestrained will of
the Führer and the personal loyalty (not primarily dependent on
office) demanded by him increasingly caused in the state, as it had
already done in the Party, the collapse of normal codes of conduct
and of the institutional, corporate unity and coherence of the government. Instead and to an ever-growing degree the process of
seizing power and the further dynamic development of the Third
Reich juxtaposed a polyocracy of state departments with the hetero-
geneity of the Party auxiliary organizations, and from this there
developed all forms of amalgamation, coexistence and conflict between Party and state offices and responsibilities.

Thus in so far as it is possible to speak in general terms of a
widespread dualism of Party and state, this was a secondary mani-
festation of the National Socialist regime and was controlled or
modified from time to time in this or that direction through the
Führer's power, equally detached from Party and state but making

use of both reciprocally. However, since the absolute leader could only get his way through the power of the Party or of the state, and in this respect remained dependent on both, it is possible to talk of a 'triangular structure', a Party–state–Führer absolutism as the basis of the National Socialist regime. What was crucial in the development of this triangular pattern was the fact that the process of seizing power was by no means straightforward but instead alternated between revolution and an authoritarian brake on revolution and mixed the two together.

The successes and limits of the Party revolution in spring 1933

Whereas Hitler's take-over of power began on 30 January 1933, the Party's seizure of power only began after the Reichstag election of 5 March. This election was in no small measure a Party victory, and when Hitler made use of the active revolutionary and terrorist collaboration of the Party in the ensuing co-ordination of the Länder, the NSDAP's revolutionary urge, which had been kept in check during the preceding weeks, could no longer be contained. It was this revolution from below which first broke through the limits which were still imposed on the NSDAP during Hitler's appointment as Reich Chancellor in a coalition Cabinet with the Nationalist Right, and it paved the way to complete National Socialist rule. The institutional forms of this Party revolution from below were chiefly the S.A. and S.S. auxiliary police as well as the system of Commissioners which was set up from March 1933.

The appointment of leading exponents of the Party as Reich Commissioners in the Länder provided the impulse for these Commissioners to delegate further special powers of authority, chiefly to reliable National Socialists, to co-ordinate the different central departmental authorities as well as the intermediate and lower authorities of the state administration. After the leadership of the Land governments had come under National Socialist control the regional and local leaders of the NSDAP, the S.A., S.S. and NSBO frequently claimed for themselves, and usurped the powers of, political Commissioners in state and municipal authorities, and even too in public and private concerns. In exercising such delegated or expropriated powers as Commissioners, the S.A., S.S. and NSBO leaders profited above all from the fact that they had their own revolutionary executive to hand with the S.A. or S.S. auxiliary police, whose nominal 'auxiliary' function was in practice generally reversed: not police officers but S.A. and S.S. leaders determined the actions and the police who accompanied them, very often intimidated as a result of the new National Socialist command, had frequently only to provide the semblance of legality. Even on 30 May 1933, the S.A. Chief of Staff arrogantly ruled in an S.A. directive that the Special Commissioners of the S.A. are 'just like the police chiefs etc. (belonging to the S.A.), S.A. leaders in the first instance and organs of the state administration in the second instance'. It also had to be made clear 'that the auxiliary policeman remains above all an S.A. and S.S. man. I expressly urge all S.A. and S.S. leaders and men transferred to the auxiliary police to keep this in mind.'[1]

The spokesmen and confidential agents of the Party in the authorities and concerns had a special function during the process of political purging. To some extent they assumed the functions of National Socialist Commissioners and made their demands, mainly regarding personnel, to the authority chiefs or factory leaders, or acted as informers and agents who called for 'cleansing measures' through the Party or National Socialist departmental Minister from outside. Thus in March/April 1933 Special Commissioners were active in almost all Reich and Land Ministries and their subordinate authorities, arranging trials and enquiries and contriving the dismissal of politically undesirable or Jewish officials and employees. Isolated remaining documents on the activity of Special Commissioners attached to the authorities prove the extent to which the informing which took place was determined by the hunt for jobs and lust for office. It was only thinly veiled by political and ideological motives.[2]

The Special Commissioners were in the main agents who had been installed by the head of the authority concerned – albeit at the urging of the Party and its exponents – and in that respect they were *formally* state Commissioners; but there were also many Commissioners who were sent into public concerns, union buildings, business organizations and local administrations by the Party and its auxiliary organizations, notably the S.A., acting on their own authority. Of doubtful legality, these were increasingly opposed by business leaders, by Hitler's Nationalist partners, as well as by many National Socialists who had meanwhile reached the top in the state authorities and who now claimed the leader principle and power of the state for themselves, and who saw their authority threatened by the flock of Kreisleiter, Gauleiter and S.A. Special Commissioners.

In Bavaria especially – the heart of the National Socialist movement with the seat of the Party's central office – the claim of the NSDAP, S.A. and S.S. to supremacy over the state administration was resolutely pressed after 9 March, if in different ways. Here too the revolutionary power of the S.A. Special Commissioners also became particularly onerous and unwelcome to the official authorities.

On 12 and 14 March Röhm, as Bavarian State Commissioner for Special Duty, had ordered the appointment of S.A. Special Commissioners in the six Bavarian Kreis governments (administrative districts) and in the district offices[3] and he had simultaneously transferred to them the command of the auxiliary police in their area. Whereas the Reich S.S. Leader Heinrich Himmler (then still under the Chief of Staff of the S.A. but soon more successful than the latter) concentrated on consolidating the organization and personnel of the limited but concrete *state* authority over the Political Police in Bavaria with the aid of the S.S., Röhm saw revolutionary pressures on the state authorities from *outside* as the main duty of the S.A., and regarded the unofficial S.A. Commissioners as an essential means of perfecting the National Socialist seizure of power. Although only formally and nominally appointed as State Commissioner in Bavaria, Röhm conceived his function beyond this as the one supreme Reich Commissioner who had to keep the revolution alive and prevent its premature demise with the aid of the S.A.'s combat organization. He underlined this general claim in March 1933 by also appointing S.A. Gruppenführer and Obergruppenführer outside Bavaria as S.A. Commissioners (for example Gruppenführer Ernst in Berlin, or Obergruppenführer Heines in Breslau), although he only succeeded in building up a systematic network of S.A. Commissioners at all the levels of the internal administration in Bavaria.

The S.A.'s revolutionary pretension to power and the hardly less marked arrogance of individual Gauleiter who in part, like Streicher in Nuremberg or Bürckel in the Rhineland-Palatinate, conducted a National Socialist revolution and seizure of power on their own bat, by anti-semitic actions (Streicher) or through experiments in 'people's socialism which were more sympathetic but just as injurious to legal rights (Bürckel), were difficult to control as long as Hitler still used terrorist intimidation from below as a means of seizing power. It was therefore typical that an appeal from Hitler of 10 March 1933, calling for discipline from 'Party comrades, S.A. and S.S. men' and especially prohibiting them from 'disturbing business life', nevertheless at the same time invoked terrorism. Whenever the orders of the National Socialist leaders of state are opposed, said the appeal, 'such resistance must be thoroughly and immediately broken', nor was the Party 'for one second' to be deflected from the watchword 'destruction of Marxism'.[4] A Party order which the Reichsorganisationsleiter of the Party, Robert Ley, directed at 'the Gauleiter'[5] on Hitler's behalf concerning civil service policy, was similarly ambiguous. Stating that it was 'not advisable for local branch leaders, Kreis leaders S.A. Truppenführer' and other subordinate organs of the Party to approach the authorities directly with requests for the dismissal of officials and the filling of posts, it sanctioned at the same time the Party's claim to control the state administration in principle in so far as it affirmed that only the Gauleiter had the right to express such 'wishes', whereby it was admittedly also necessary to nominate suitable experts as replacements.

In fact there was a great danger in March 1933 that the personnel policy of the state would be largely taken over by the Party and that the state administrative apparatus would be progressively undermined. Therefore Göring and Frick, in particular, backed the promulgation on 7 April of the Law, for the Restoration of the Professional Civil Service[6] which partially subjected the purging of the civil service apparatus to clear legal conditions and entrusted the carrying out of the measures concerned to the state offices themselves. Although this law, which was mainly responsible for the dismissal from office of Jewish, Communist and Social Democratic officials, was an essential precondition for the National Socialist seizure of power in the administration, it was at the same time calculated – having regard to the circumstances in which it appeared – as an important means of containing the revolutionary incursions of the Party in the state administration and not least intended to placate the Conservative coalition partners, who were themselves heavily involved (especially the Prussian Minister of Finance, Popitz) in the drafting of the law. There was clearly also a worry 'that a too extreme purging of the civil service would cause a collapse. It was not yet completely certain at the beginning of April 1933 that the civil service would remain unconditionally loyal to the "new state"'.[7] Thus Frick stressed during the ministerial conference of 25 April the need for as short a delay as possible in carrying out the law so that the disruption of established rights was kept within tolerable limits for civil servants, and Göring stated expressly on Hitler's behalf that they should proceed with consideration and generosity out of respect for 'the Reich President's person'.[8]

The tendency to restrain the Party revolution already shown in the spring by policy towards the civil service (similarly by economic policy) was obviously contrary to the more radical ideas on revolution and the seizure of power of many prominent Party leaders in the Länder, provinces and municipalities. Here the Party's 'March revolution' which was most resolutely carried out in Munich because of the concentration there of ambitious Party exponents, was to some extent quite deliberately regarded as the model for the real National Socialist revolution which would follow the Berlin prelude of the arrangement between National Socialists and Conservative-Nationalist forces. This was evident for example when the Bavarian Gauleiter and Minister of the Interior, Adolf Wagner, stated in a memorandum on the relationship between Party and state on 23 March:

Whilst the development in the Reich originally swept Bavaria along with it, we are now in a position working from Bavaria outwards to drag the other Länder forward and not least the Reich, in a National Socialist direction. For this reason the revolution in Bavaria must be kept alive and continued long enough for the National Socialist movement in Bavaria to become the state.[9]

Far more severe, more aggressive and more cynical was the criticism within the S.A. of those manifestations of the national 'uprising' which gave the impression with victory celebrations and declamations that the revolution and struggle were already over after the nominal compromise between the Liberal-Conservative forces and the National Socialist movement. Here the distinction already familiar from the pre-1933 period between the soldierly 'combativeness' of the S.A. and the S.S. and the 'bossdom' of the NSDAP's Political Organization again came into play. An order of the S.A. Chief of Staff Ernst Röhm of 30 May 1933 illustrated this:

There have been enough celebrations. At this stage I want the S.A. and S.S. to disengage themselves conspicuously from the rest of the festivals and to devote themselves exclusively once more to the tasks reserved to them alone. There are those who fight for victories, those are the soldiers, and there are those who celebrate victories and let themselves rest on their laurels, those are the others. The S.A. and S.S. have gained a victory on a barely conceivable scale, of which they may justly be proud. But before them lies the task of completing the National Socialist revolution and creating the Third Reich. It seems to me that there is still some tough work and a hard struggle before us. It is worth preparing and steeling ourselves for this. It is of no consequence that every day a 'co-ordinated' bee-keeping society or skittle club makes declarations of loyalty or that town streets are named after contemporaries . . .[10]

However inadequate Röhm regarded the existing results of the seizure of power because they were too much determined by tactical considerations (for the Reichswehr, the bureaucracy, the economy, the Church), yet the urge towards further revolution was unclear and diffuse in its purpose. Reich Governor von Epp who perceived the S.A.'s ambitions in Munich particularly clearly, remarked in a hand-written note of 13 June: 'The S.A. continues the revolution. Against whom? With what aim? Discontent alone gives no revolutionary right . . . Party without leadership. It doesn't know what to do. The old aim is no longer there. The dissatisfied want more revolution.'[11]

The development of Party membership

The question of what role the NSDAP should play in the Third Reich after the take-over of power, whether it should be a select cadre and élite Party of the regime or a representative and de-politicized mass organization on the broadest base, was bound to be decided not least by the development of its membership and enrolment. A rapid influx of new Party members began after 30 January 1933. The wave of 'March converts' as the new proselytes were cynically named in the Party's jargon, threatened to overwhelm the NSDAP particularly in March 1933 under the impact of the Party revolution from below. In order to check this development the NSDAP Reich Treasurer decreed a bar on NSDAP enrolments (not for the S.A., S.S. and Hitler Youth) with effect from 1 May. This basically applied until 1 May 1939, although it was relaxed for former Stahlhelm members even by the end of 1935 and, in spring 1937, for other 'Party aspirants' in related subsidiary Party organizations. But since some 1,600,000 new members were admitted between 30 January 1933 and the ban on enrolment, the notion of a carefully selected cadre Party was riddled with holes from the beginning. All the same, some attempt was made at first to preserve this principle. Thus on 26 June 1933, the Führer's Deputy decreed the introduction of a two-year probationary period for new members, who only received a membership card in this period but not a Party book and they were not yet allowed to wear the brown shirt. Hitler also underlined the elite function of the Party at this time, for example when he declared at the Nuremberg Party rally on 3 September: 'Out of 45 million grown men, three million fighters have organized themselves as bearers of the nation's political leadership.' This nucleus was to be maintained and in future selection was to be tougher, not easier.[12] In fact it was chiefly Hitler himself who increasingly violated this principle after 1935 by making a series of exceptions and after 1937/8 also worked towards the position where almost all leading exponents of political and public life joined the Party or – without asking for it – were promised honorary membership of the NSDAP or honorary S.A. and S.S. rank. This shows that the Party was still hardly regarded as a hand-picked organization for the formation of a political elite (which it could hardly be, given the quality of its training), but rather more as a broad organization for mobilizing, controlling and disciplining the nation and especially those groups most vital to national policy. This changed conception ultimately won through when in 1939 the bar to membership was lifted completely and Hitler established the maxim that about a tenth of the population should be in the Party organization. Even the regulation operative after 1942, according to which the Party Kreisleiter and Gauleiter had to make the relevant decision on the admission or non-admission of new members, hardly meant an effective selection for the NSDAP, which had grown to some 6 million members by the end of the War.

Actually the mass influx of new members in 1933 had already markedly changed the structure of the NSDAP as a Party of uncompromising 'old fighters'. In some Gaue, where the NSDAP was still relatively poorly organized before 1933, the number of Party members (Parteigenossen-Pg. s) joining after 30 January 1933 made up over 80 per cent of the membership, as for example in Coblenz-Trier, Cologne-Aachen, and Mainfranken. All vocational groups, workers too, shared in the mass influx to the NSDAP in spring 1933 (267,000 workers already belonged to it before 30 January, 488,000 were new to it), so that by and large the sociological composition of the Party shifted only slightly in comparison with the situation in 1932 in the direction of the middle classes. But the particularly high proportion of the new entrants among civil servants and teachers was noteworthy (44,000 civil servants and about 13,000 teachers belonged to the NSDAP before 30 January 1933, 179,000 civil servants and 71,000 teachers joined it during the months of the seizure of power). According to official Party statistics (situation at 1 January 1935) membership among the whole of those who were employed was reckoned at 7.3 per cent (among workers, 5.1 per cent, among farmers, 3.8 per cent). By contrast no less than 20 per cent of all civil servants and 30 per cent of all teachers were already members of the Party in 1933/4 (among employees the share was 12 per cent, among self-employed 15 per cent).[13] In this respect it is clear that entry to the NSDAP seemed particularly advisable to the holders of public offices in spring 1933. The tendency to protect one's office by joining the Party underlined the NSDAP's development into a state party. It carried loyalty to the Party (in competition with the civil servant's code) into the corps of civil servants but conversely also reinforced the Party's tendency to conform to the state, although this did not end the mixture of coexistence and conflict between Party and state.

Hitler's dissociation from the S.A. and the Party leadership

In many respects Hitler himself worked at first towards a separation of Party and state in spring 1933, before stressing more strongly the link with the state in the second phase of the seizure of power (from summer 1933) thereby fostering that unresolved situation of semi-subordination, semi-control function which continued to determine the abnormal position of the Party in the Third Reich.

Another factor which played a part in the separation of state and Party was the decision to keep the seat of the NSDAP's Reich directorate in Munich (which Hitler expressly confirmed at the Nuremberg Party rally at the beginning of September 1938), whilst only a small 'NSDAP liaison staff' was maintained in the Reich Chancellery in Berlin. The argument that it was better to see with two eyes and to concentrate the task of leading the nation through the NSDAP in Munich remote from the seat of the Reich government in Berlin, was certainly not the sole determinant here. It was much more that the decision also corresponded with Hitler's effort to prevent the Party from having any direct influence over the government. The desire for such a dissociation was expressed still more clearly in Hitler's Party directive of 21 April 1933, when he named the head of the Central Political Commission of the NSDAP's Reich directorate, Rudolf Hess, as his Deputy and gave him the power 'to resolve all questions concerning Party leadership on my behalf'.[14]

The appointment of Hess as 'Deputy to the Führer' again showed that Hitler did not intend to promote and strengthen the NSDAP's Reich directorate, but on the contrary sought to prevent any pronounced concentration of power below his own authority as Führer. The best way to do this was by empowering someone who had no power base whatever within the NSDAP, and also who was not a strong personality but who, as former Secretary and proven follower of 'his Führer', offered the best guarantee that he would always act simply as a loyal servant in carrying out Party business. The most urgent need at this time was chiefly to curb the arbitrariness of individual Party big-wigs and organs through Hess and the staff of the Führer's Deputy which was set up in the Brown House in Munich (with Martin Bormann as Staff Chief). Hess, who at Hitler's suggestion also had the right to take part in meetings of the Reich cabinet from the end of June 1933,[15] thereby acted as a buffer between Hitler and individual Party leaders, sparing Hitler many unwelcome direct confrontations. The effort to avoid such confrontations and to keep himself in the background was an essential element of Hitler's leadership technique, enabling him to keep clear of conflicts (at the expense of others) in order as far as possible to play the part of the final and benign arbiter.

The effort to keep the revolution alive through the S.A., which had grown beyond two million members since Hitler's take-over of power, intensified in proportion to the extent to which the Party Organization was already being curbed in its actions and ambitions in spring 1933 and forced to acquiesce in government policy from above because of the link between state and Party offices. In a covering letter to Hitler at the time Röhm expressed his fears still more clearly than in the S.A. directive of 30 May 1933, already quoted, that the revolution could stagnate and the S.A. and S.S. could degenerate to mere propaganda troops. This could only be countered and the 'watchdog of the revolution' with its great tasks ahead could only be kept primed for immediate action by reviving the 'martial spirit':

S.A. leaders! We do not want nor may we ask anything for ourselves. Leave the posts and honorary positions to others. When those few of us who have taken over such offices as well as their S.A. or S.S. leader positions see that their duties as S.A. leaders suffer because of it, they will gladly give up those other offices and be proud to be leaders in the brown army. Because this alone has changed Germany's fate, this alone will also gain and maintain the victory of pure, unadulterated nationalism and socialism.[16]

It was again evident here that in contrast to Goebbels, Himmler, Darré and numerous NSDAP Gauleiter, who were able to attain new and lasting positions of power after spring 1933 precisely because of the link between state and Party office, Röhm tried to take the opposite course by keeping the S.A. mass army distant from the state, whilst simultaneously increasing its power, improving its training and equipment, so creating an independent instrument of power of such weight that, so he assumed, the future course of the Third Reich just could not dispense with the S.A. What contributed to this notion was the expectation that in spite of Hitler's assurances to the contrary to the Reichswehr as a whole, the S.A. leaders (mostly former officers or Freikorps leaders) would in the long run have a decisive influence over the armed forces and he (Röhm) could take over the role of the future Army and Defence Minister. The S.A. Chief of Staff indeed prudently avoided any opposition to Hitler but he inevitably tried to make Hitler more dependent on the S.A. The adoption of the tactic of strengthening the S.A. organization, which was an area where Röhm's particular ability lay as a military organizer, was a reflection of the lack of clear aims in the drive for further revolution. But it was precisely such an emphasis on the military training and growth of the S.A., seemingly devoid of recognizable political aims but motivated only by vague criticism of the existing seizure of power, which was bound to make the Reichswehr feel especially uneasy. In the last resort Röhm was chiefly concerned in one form or another to maintain in the Third Reich the importance which the S.A. had always enjoyed during the *Kampfzeit*, but since the S.A. more than any other part of the Hitler movement defied incorporation in a bureaucratic system of state control, the hostility which inevitably resulted from this increasingly took the form of revolutionary unrest in the S.A. and generated an inherently blind dynamic force for its own sake. In June 1933 Röhm made a public stand in the *Nationalsozialistische Monatshefte* on the theme of the 'S.A. and the German revolution', and sharply criticized the 'philistines and grumblers' who asked what was the point any more of the S.A. and S.S. The 'idea of many "co-ordinated" people and even many dignitaries who today call themselves National Socialists', who desired peace as the first civic duty, was in truth a betrayal of the revolution. 'Whether it suits them or not, we shall continue with our struggle. If they finally grasp what it's all about: with them! If they don't want to: without them! And if need be:

against them!' Obviously this remark by the S.A. Chief of Staff was also bound to upset Hitler, whose criticism of the S.A.'s revolutionary activity was reinforced by Göring, Frick and others.

Even during the ministerial discussion on 25 April 1933 on the subject of carrying out the law on the professional civil service Göring had declared that 'the army of Commissioners is gradually threatening to undermine and shake the authority of the new state',[17] and the first dismantling of the system of Commissioners was ordered for Prussia through his decree of 5 May 1933, on the basis of which the Special Commissioners appointed by the Party and the NSBO had to be withdrawn.[18] But Göring was not yet ready to risk action against the S.A. and S.S. Commissioners. An internal police directive of the Prussian Minister of the Interior of 7 June 1933, on the organization of the auxiliary police in Prussia, complied with the wishes of Röhm and Himmler in so far as it specified that in future in Prussia too (corresponding to the earlier example of Bavaria), auxiliary police agents of the Security Police were only to be recruited from the S.A. and those for the political police exclusively from the S.S. At the same time, however, Göring sought to intervene and to 'nationalize' the power of command over the auxiliary police in Prussia of the S.A. Chief of Staff and the Reich S.S. Leader by appointing both as Prussian 'Ministerial Commissioners' for the auxiliary police.[19]

The ending of the 'revolution from below'

Determined counter-moves against the continuation of the revolution from below began in July 1933 after the S.A. had fulfilled their last important function with their terrorist back-up for the dissolution of the other parties, and even individual S.A. leaders detected a serious threat to the state's authority in continuing to use indiscriminate terror.[20] As the S.A. had experienced an even bigger boost after the order to integrate the approximately 500,000 strong Stahlhelm (3 July), a clear statement now seemed all the more necessary to Hitler. Hitler prepared the way for future directives and measures for 'ending the revolution' in his speech before the Reich Governors in Berlin on 6 July 1933. In clear contrast to Röhm he stressed that 'inward education' was the great task of the Party in future, following the 'achievement of outward power':

> More revolutions have succeeded at the first assault than have been successfully absorbed and brought to a standstill. Revolution is not a permanent condition ... The stream of revolution once released must be guided into the secure bed of evolution. Here the education of the people is most important ... The ideas in our programme do not commit us to behaving like fools and destroying everything, but to realizing our conceptions wisely and carefully ... The Party has now become the state, all power be-

longs to the Reich authority. The emphasis of German life must be prevented from shifting back again towards individual areas or indeed organizations. No longer does authority derive from any one part of the Reich but only from the concept of the German people as a nation.[21]

In the following days Frick and Goebbels endorsed this with circulars and proclamations, and the latter also spoke of 'concealed bolshevist elements', against whom vigilance was the order of the day. Prussia once again led the way with specific measures. Here the auxiliary police were officially disbanded on 15 August.[22] After the Prussian Minister of Justice Kerrl had granted an amnesty on 25 July 'on the occasion of the conclusion of the National Socialist revolution', for criminal acts committed by Party comrades in their zeal for seizing power, the Prussian Ministry of Justice established a 'Central State Prosecutor's Office' on 1 August as a special section of the Ministry with the influential co-operation of the newly named National Socialist State Secretary, Roland Freisler.[23] This was a mobile prosecution office and in future was to investigate all punishable transgressions by S.A. and S.S. men on the spot and if need be to make arrests and to initiate legal proceedings. Already in June, the Prussian Ministry of the Interior in conjunction with the Prussian Ministry of Finance had been trying, chiefly through stopping the funds previously made available to the S.A. and S.S. auxiliary police, to dismantle the multitude of unruly S.A. and S.S. detention camps and to transfer them to a few large state-accredited camps (Oranienburg, Lichtenburg, the moorland camps in Emsland). The over-all total of political detainees which in Prussia (on 31 July 1933) was about 15,000, was in future to be reduced to 10,000 at the most and the Prussian Land police were to be more heavily involved in guard duties.[24] In fact there was a significant reduction in the detention cases and detention penalties in Prussia from summer 1933 as a result of the stricter guidelines of the Prussian Gestapo Chief, Diels, who at this time was working closely with Göring in suppressing the S.A. and S.S. terror. In February 1934 the Prussian Gestapo in agreement with the Central State Prosecutor's Office was able to clear out the concentration camp illegally set up near Stettin, where there had been a great deal of maltreatment of detainees. In April 1934 several major offenders among the S.S. leaders were sentenced to several years' penal servitude and terms of imprisonment.[25]

In this respect the situation in Prussia differed from that of the other Länder, particularly Bavaria, where the Party political authorities were still supreme throughout. The effort made by the Bavarian Minister of Justice, Frank, and his public prosecutors to carry out investigations in the Dachau camp against the S.S. leadership which had condoned and concealed a series of murders of prisoners was jointly hindered by Himmler and Röhm in early summer 1933. And when the excessive and improper application of measures for protective custody in Bavaria in spring 1934 also led to complaints by the Reich Minister of the Interior and the Reich Governor (von Epp) to the Bavarian Minister of the Interior (Gustav Wagner), they were answered with a report (obviously at the instigation of Himmler and Heydrich) which as Epp subsequently affirmed, was 'open to attack and refutation in every sentence' and crammed full of 'errors, distortions, misrepresentations and lies'.[26]

The often-repeated declarations and directives in summer 1933 for ending the revolution completely failed to persuade the S.A. Chief of Staff to give up the over-all supervision and control tasks claimed for the S.A. in building up the state in the Third Reich. After the auxiliary police had gradually become less important and the idea of 'Commissioners' had been discredited, Röhm ordered in Bavaria on 1 September 1933 that former S.A. Special Commissioners were to be renamed 'Special Agents' (with the Kreis governments) and 'Special Deputies' (at the district offices). These still continued to have the task of making sure 'that the entire development of the state is shaped in keeping with the National Socialist movement and revolution'.[27] This directive amounted to a separate control function for the S.A. (alongside that of the Party) and for the Bavarian political police, meanwhile appropriated by Himmler and the S.S. For this reason it met with fierce resistance from Gauleiter Wagner and the conflict of interests between Himmler and Röhm was also bound to be intensified by this development. Röhm could only afford to behave in this manner, however, because Hitler (in a way typical of his scheming, evasive style of leadership) refrained from giving clear orders to the contrary in his capacity as Supreme S.A. Leader, but rather appeared to agree when Röhm (as he reported to the meeting of the Bavarian State government on 20 October 1933) drew Hitler's attention to the fact 'that the bureaucrats' plan is to let everything peacefully go its own way again, as before'.[28] Hitler's double dealing showed itself when in autumn 1933 he set the Reich Governors (in the Reich Governors' conference of 28 September) against the S.A. during confidential meetings and indicated that the advocates of a 'second revolution' were his enemies, whose 'hash we would yet unexpectedly settle',[29] whilst at the same time he allowed Röhm to instal Special Agents of the Supreme S.A. Leader in Prussia in place of the S.A. auxiliary police Commissioners in the Ministry of State, and alongside the Oberpräsidenten, Regierungspräsidenten and regional councillors. Thus Göring was obliged to amend the directive of 7 June on the S.A. and S.S. Commissioners. The text of the new order stated more or less clearly that the duty of the Special Agents of the Supreme S.A. Leader attached to the Prussian authorities was to make 'suggestions' and effect 'improvements' to the administration so that the state administration did not sink into complacency now that 'all opposition' had been 'removed along with the parties'.[30] Judging from the wording this looked like constructive collaboration with the state, but in fact the continued activity of the S.A. Commissioners meant prolonging the conflict between state and Party.

The question of 'constructive' integration of the leading exponents of the S.A. and Party in the state preoccupied people increasingly from the summer of 1933. Hitler had personally told the Reich Governors on 28 September 1933, that he 'intended to integrate the National Socialist Party gradually into the Reich authority. Perhaps it was appropriate to set up an S.A. Ministry.' He was thinking in addition of setting up a Senate of the National Socialist movement.[31] Actually, lucid ideas were lacking and the creation of a supreme Party corporation with clearly regulated rights of consultation and decision-making in the leadership of the state would have been incompatible with Hitler's personal claim to leadership. The idea of a supreme 'Senate of the NSDAP' (along the lines of the Italian Grand Council of Fascism) had been around for years as the pet idea of various Party leaders and a 'Senate Room' had already been providently set up in the Brown House in Munich. In fact although this idea still appeared as a future project in the NSDAP's hand book of 1938,[32] it was never realized. On the contrary, Hitler was already apprehensive about the combined meetings of large numbers of prominent Party, S.A. and S.S. leaders which took place in Berlin at various times during 1933, and he adopted a noticeably hostile attitude towards the efforts supported among others by Walter Buch (the Chairman of the Party-Uschla), to turn the functionaries of the movement into a proper leader corps.[33] In a Party circular of 13 October the Staff Chief of the Führer's Deputy (Bormann) commented in respect of the often expressed wish for a 'special association of old Party members', that 'there were cogent reasons why the Führer regarded such a gathering as impracticable and therefore he forbids it'.[34] Instead, what did emerge from the idea of a closer link between Party and state was the law drafted by the Reich Minister of the Interior, the Law for Ensuring the Unity of Party and State of 1 December 1933 (*RGBl*, I, p. 1016).

The law affirmed that 'After the victory of the National Socialist revolution' the NSDAP which in future was to enjoy the status of a corporation under public law was 'the bearer of the concept of the German state and is inseparably tied to the state'. In order to 'ensure the closest co-operation between the Party and S.A. offices and the public authorities, the Führer's Deputy and the S.A. Chief of Staff will become members of the Reich government'. The law also provided for the establishment of special Party and S.A. courts, in view of the 'greater responsibilities' of Party and S.A. members 'towards the Führer, the people and the state'. These courts were also to have power to demand 'custody and detention' in addition to the usual Party penalties. In fact this never happened. The Party jurisdiction remained an honorary jurisdiction without sovereign powers of punishment over freedom and life. And in other respects, too, the law proved itself to be extremely problematic, to some extent ambiguous and even merely declamatory. Typically, it did not declare the NSDAP to be the 'bearer of the state' but only 'the bearer of the German idea of the state', that is to say that it did not establish an *institutional* and *constitutional* but only a vague *theoretical* supremacy of the Party over the state. The transformation of the NSDAP into a corporation under public law specified by a later decree of 29 March 1935,[35] also proved to be of doubtful value for the Party. It was indeed an improvement when compared with its previous status as a 'registered society', but it was wholly unsatisfactory for the advocates of Party supremacy, especially since corporations under public law were basically under the supervision of the state government, so that the legal outcome of its new status could mean subordination rather than supremacy for the Party. The Party struggled against this 'unreasonableness' but all suggestions for change – for example the idea of declaring the Party to be a corporation subject to *special* (as opposed to *public*) law got nowhere because nobody was in a position to define the Party's status with legal concepts other than those of public law, which was always bound to mean the law of the *state*.

Still, with its classification as a corporation under public law it was formally made legal for the NSDAP from then on to be financed not only from its own income (chiefly membership dues) but in addition and to an increasing degree from the state budget. As a result it became dependent on the Reich Ministry of Finance. The financial bureaucracy of the Reich, led by Schwerin-Krosig, only rarely dared to reject or to cut back on the Party's financial demands, and these were mostly submitted by the Reich Treasurer of the Party as a global, categorical demand and not as a detailed application with itemized statements.[36] Since the Reich Treasurer of the NSDAP rather than the Reich Minister of Finance or the audit office of the German Reich also had the sole power to examine Party expenditure (including those funds provided through the state budget), the NSDAP was actually pretty well autonomous when it came to financial administration. This special authority also accounted for the strong position of the Party Treasurer in the Reich directorate of the NSDAP. He alone had the sole right of command in his sphere and was therefore generally able even after 1935 to prevent individual Gauleiter from acting independently in financial matters.

The *political* implications of the law to ensure the unity of Party and state were much less satisfactory for the NSDAP. The appointment of Hess and Röhm as Ministers (without portfolio!) within the Reich government admittedly gave the NSDAP and the S.A. the right to participate in governmental legislation and the appointment of civil servants, but it gave no executive powers to the two Party Ministers and in that respect was hardly likely to ensure the supremacy of the National Socialist movement over the state. It was much more the case (which was doubtless in accordance with Frick's draft) that this regulation tended to direct Party influence on the state primarily along the ministerial route, and thus channelled it and committed both Party Ministers to the methods of the ministerial bureaucracy.

Far from creating an 'insoluble' link between Party and state the law worked in favour of the authoritarian central apparatus of state, in spite of the illusory elevation and appeasement of the Party, and this together with the intended halting of the Party revolution was its primary function, as indeed circumstances demanded. It was no coincidence that a few days later (8 November) Goebbels declared in the Sportpalast in Berlin that the National Socialist movement has 'always striven for the total state'.[37] What Hitler understood by the 'fusion of Party and state' was the clear subordination of the Party to the state leadership and instead of the Party's dynamism coming from below the Party was to be transformed into an organ of the masses exclusively obedient to the Führer, for extending and expanding the state's power and government policy in terms of propaganda and organization. This was particularly apparent in the address Hitler delivered to the assembled Gauleiter in Berlin on 2 February 1934. An unsigned note (Bormann?) on this discussion stated:[38]

The Führer stresses. Essential tasks of the Party are:
1. To make the people receptive to the projected government measures.
2. To help carry out the measures ordered by the government throughout the nation.
3. To support the government in every possible way.
In addition the Führer stressed that those who maintained that the revolution had not ended were fools ... On the contrary we needed an administrative apparatus in all fields, which would enable us to realize National Socialist ideas at once. Here the rule must be that no more orders and plans can be submitted and discussed than the apparatus can digest ...
The Führer described the main immediate task as the selection of personnel who were able and willing to carry out the government's measures with blind obedience. The Party must bring about the stability necessary for Germany's entire future; it must ensure this stability, and no monarchy could do this. The first Führer had been chosen by fate; the second must have a loyal sworn community behind him from the start. Nobody with his own power base may be chosen ...
We must not fight amongst ourselves; differences must never be re-

vealed to outsiders ... Even the consequences of mistaken decisions must be offset by absolute unity ... Therefore no superfluous discussions either! Problems not yet decided by individual officials must under no circumstances be discussed in public because otherwise the power of decision would be given to the masses in this way. That was the madness of democracy, but through this the value of any leadership was squandered. Whoever has to make the decision must make it and the others must support him ...

Apart from this we must always fight only *one* struggle at a time. One struggle after the other; actually the saying should not be 'Many enemies, much honour', but 'Many enemies, much stupidity'. Besides the nation as a whole cannot wage a dozen battles at the same time and understand the issues. Accordingly we must always instil the nation with but one thought, concentrate it on *one* idea. It is particularly necessary in all matters of foreign policy to have the entire nation behind you, as if hypnotized, the entire nation must be involved in this struggle as if they were passionate participants in a sport's contest; this is vital. If the whole nation takes part in the struggle, they too will be losers. If they are disinterested, only the leadership loses. In the one case the nation's anger will rise against the opponent, in the other, against their leaders.

The Party's future task as a mass organization 'blindly' obedient to the authority of the Führer and magnifying that by propaganda could not have been formulated more clearly (or one-sidedly). Above all too, here was the ruthless expression of the essence of that totalitarian propaganda which (lacking a clear ideology and programme) was deliberately aimed at achieving not political education for the nation but at 'hypnosis', at unleashing the nation's 'passion for taking a chance'. With the tactical order to fight only *one* battle at a time, Hitler forged a maxim which he was to observe not only in foreign policy but in truly Machiavellian fashion in domestic policy too during the following months.

The emasculation of the S.A.

From March 1934 at the latest, Hitler abandoned the efforts noticeable earlier to persuade the S.A. leadership peacefully to relinquish its political ambitions and instead deliberately steered towards violent confrontation. Months before the bloody action on 30 June 1934, the S.A. was isolated and defamed within the Party and the regime and the S.A. provided plentiful opportunities for this through the overbearing and disrespectful behaviour of its leaders. Hitler's principal allies here (apart from Göring and Goebbels in Berlin) were the S.S. and the Reichswehr.

Whereas Hitler allowed S.A. ambitions to be opposed more urgently by the Reich Governors and Gauleiter or by Hess and individual Ministers,[39] whilst he himself remained as before in the background and refrained from giving his own direct commands to the S.A.,[40] in winter and spring 1933/4, S.S. control of the political police, first established by Himmler and Heydrich in Bavaria, was soon extended to the Political Police in the rest of the Länder. The Reich S.S. Leader assumed over-all control of these at this time and finally, in April 1934, in Prussia too, where Göring's former Gestapo chief, Diels, retired and Himmler (although at first also nominally representing Göring and having the official title of 'Inspector') took over the actual direction of the Prussian Secret State Police, whilst Heydrich went into the Prinz-Albrecht Strasse as the new Chief of the Secret State Police Office (*Geheimes Staatspolizeiamt* – Gestapa).[41] This concentration of the Political Police under the Reich S.S. Leader, as the leader of a Party auxiliary organization, was admittedly in keeping with the general integration of administration and executive (after the sovereignty of the Länder was ended). It was, however, typical that the process of integration in this instance (Political Police) was not accomplished through the relevant state central department, the Reich Minister of the Interior, but was bound to militate against and to neutralize the latter's simultaneous efforts to standardize Political Police procedures (use of preventive custody). In constitutional terms Himmler's concentration of the Political Police was not so much a process of centralization as an accumulation of Land responsibilities, which was also revealed by Himmler's accumulation of titles at that time (Political Police Commander of Bavaria, Deputy Chief of the Prussian Gestapo, Commander of the Political Police in Baden, Württemberg, Braunschweig, Hesse, Saxony, Thuringia etc.). Until 1936 (appointment of Himmler as Chief of the German Police) there was legally no Reich organ of Political Police, but merely a joint organ of the Länder in the form of Himmler's personal control exercised institutionally from Prussia, whereby the Prussian term (Gestapo) also came into general use. As to the organization of this command such a concentration of powers did not signify *incorporation* in the Reich's centralized state administration but the *separation* of the Political Police from the structure of the internal administration, which meant institutional independence for the Gestapo on the basis of the revolutionary take-over of the Political Police by the S.S., such as had been achieved in Bavaria in March 1933. This was also connected with the assimilation which was now methodically carried out by Heydrich (by linking the offices in the leadership of the Gestapo and SD) between the (state) Political Police and the Party security service (*Sicherheitsdienst*-SD).

The fact that Hitler did not want to see the Political Police under the ministerial bureaucracy of the Reich Ministry of the Interior and bound by the regulations of the bureaucratic state administration was undoubtedly in line with his basic aim of controlling this indispensable instrument for his regime directly, or through his proven loyal personal follower, Himmler. Here, more clearly than any other sphere of state authority, the relationship perfected in the National Socialist movement between the person of the Führer and the following became the foundation of a power apparatus which has therefore rightly been described as the embodiment of the 'Führer authority' which stood above Party and state.[42] Since at this time (spring 1934) it was in keeping with Hitler's intentions to reinforce the Reich government's authority over the Party's special power, the Political Police would hardly have been so rapidly and deliberately made independent by means of the S.S. if there had not been a specific plan in view: the emasculation of the S.A.

However little of the whole background history of the witch hunt against the S.A. beginning in spring 1934 is as yet clear, it is quite certain that Himmler and Heydrich fanned the flames with the help of the SD and the Political Police and S.S., through spying and making specific denunciations; that armed S.S. detachments were the real agents of Bartholemew night on 30 June, and that the S.S. ultimately profited most from this action. But there was also close collaboration between the S.S. and the Reichswehr, which had a particularly fatal effect on the further development of the Third Reich. The disparity between the Reichswehr's ideas on military policy, which regarded the S.A. as a thoroughly welcome military reinforcement but one to be clearly subordinated to the Reichswehr's structure and supreme command, and the ideas of Röhm, who wanted to see 'the gray rock' of the Reichswehr submerged 'in the brown flood' of the S.A.,[43] had become more and more apparent in the early months of 1934. Hitler was obviously on the side of the Reichswehr in this dispute. Moreover since the claim of the Reichswehr officers to control the armed power was disputed by most of the S.A. leaders, who despised those officers as reactionary and unpolitical, extremely tense relations developed in many places between officers and S.A. leaders and the armed S.A. staff guards. Since the latter's military exercises increasingly worried the Reichswehr, influential Reichswehr leaders (especially the Chief of the Ministeramt, von Reichenau) were by spring 1934 also preparing to use force instead of reconciling their differences with the S.A. When in June Hitler finally engineered the surprise coup against the S.A. leadership where it was assembled in Munich and Bad Wiesee, the Reichswehr played a key role by supplying weapons and transport for the S.S. Adolf Hitler Bodyguard Regiments (under Sepp Dietrich) and other S.S. units ordered to Munich. The Reichswehr also stood by ready to intervene itself in the event of any stronger S.A. resistance against the S.S. detachments. Not only Blomberg and Reichenau but also the Chief of the Army Command, General von Fritsch, and the then head of the Truppenamt, General Ludwig Beck (the later leader of the conspiracy against Hitler of 20 July 1944), as well as the most important officers in the Wehrkreise detachments were kept informed of the action (if admittedly not on the treacherous, murderous style of its execution) and were ready to give active support. The explana tion that the conflict between S.A. and Reichswehr leaderships was resolved by Hitler, Himmler, Göring etc. 'without the Army's help' is no longer tenable on the basis of more recent evidence.[44]

The details of the action in the course of which Röhm and dozens of other higher S.A. leaders were summarily shot by armed S.S. men in Stadelheim prison in Munich or in the camp at Dachau, whilst at the same time similar actions took place in Berlin, Breslau and other places and sometimes took days, need not be described here. The exact number of those shot, which ran into hundreds, is still not known today. Typically, at the same time as Röhm and his closest followers from the S.A. were murdered, not only were former 'traitors' (Gregor Strasser) disposed of and many personal accounts of local S.S. leaders settled, but also Hitler's old opponents (von Kapp, von Schleicher) as well as prominent conservative and liberal critics, who had spoken up in the previous weeks and months (Edgar Jung, Erich Klausener) were treacherously murdered.

This simultaneous brutal silencing of the criticism from the right (Papen too now lost his post as Vice-Chancellor and subsequently served Hitler in a special diplomatic mission in Vienna) already indicated that the triumph of the ('state bearing') conservative forces, now freed of their most dangerous opponents once Röhm's ambitious leadership of the S.A. had been ended, was a pyrrhic victory in the long run. All the same the pre-emptive, bloody suppression of the S.A.'s ambitions and its subsequent reduction to the status of a military sports association under Röhm's successor Victor Lutze, which played no further part worth mentioning as a power factor in the Third Reich in spite of its numerical strength, meant first and foremost the definitive stop to the party revolution from below. Only now, after 30 June 1934, were the S.A. Special Deputies in Prussia, Bavaria and the other Länder abolished, the S.A. (in favour of the S.S.) removed from the management and control of the concentration camps, and the representation of the National Socialist movement in the Reich cabinet confined to the 'Führer's Deputy'. It was only now that the way seemed free for the 'authoritarian state' and in fact there was a marked decline in the oppressiveness of public life in the Third Reich, a noticeable restoration of legal security and a lessening (although not the end of) the state of emergency. During the years 1936/7, the Hitler state seemed to be determined by the conservative bearers of the state and by conservative notions of order at least as much as by the dynamic force of the National Socialist movement, particularly since in this period the bureaucratization of the Party became more pronounced.[45]

In the conflict between the conservative supporters of the regime

and those sections of the National Socialist movement where unrest chiefly originated, Hitler had quite deliberately ranged himself
alongside the former. Consideration for the Reich President played
a part here, in whose circle (as in that of Papen and of the Reichswehr Generals) criticism of the S.A. was particularly severe,[46] –
the more so since the problem of the Reich President's successor
was already being posed in spring and summer 1934 as a result of
Hindenburg's visible senility and illness, and Hitler could hardly be
sure without the support of the Reichswehr whether the Reich
President's office would be transferred to him smoothly (and with
it the supreme command over the Reichswehr according to the constitution). The fact that Hindenburg died just five weeks after the
Röhm affair made this consideration more important. Both events
ideally complemented each other in speeding up the development of Hitler's absolute leadership. The political emasculation of
the S.A., whose leadership had been the only significant political
power not subordinated to Hitler and indeed had been almost his
equal, was followed on 2 August by Hitler's appointment as Reich
President. From then on he had all the insignia of power for himself, as leader of the only Party, head of the government and head
of state. From then on soldiers and civil servants (including the
Ministers of the Reich government) had to swear a personal oath
of loyalty to Adolf Hitler, 'the Führer of the German Reich and
German people', which replaced the oath to the constitution. With
the revival of the personal vow of allegiance a part of the monarchy was restored at the same time. In reality Hitler's power as
Führer exceeded that of any monarch. The notion of 'divine right'
was replaced by the claim that the Führer was the saviour
appointed by Providence and at the same time the embodiment
and medium of the unarticulated will of the people.

Halting the Party revolution from below paved the way for Hitler to perfect the supreme power of the Leader, but it was not just
a matter of finally emasculating or temporarily restraining those
forces within the National Socialist movement which (like the S.A.
or the Gauleiter of the NSDAP) had been relatively speaking most
independent from the outset. It could also be seen in the simultaneous progress towards abandoning many programmatic points
and ideals of the National Socialist movement which had promised
a new world (however utopian) to many Party comrades and had
also involved an idealistic commitment and hope over and above
the belief in the Führer. It was not by chance that at the same time
as the S.A. was dethroned the National Socialists, the corporatist
and middle-class theorists and the proponents of Reich reform were
also disappointed. Among old Party comrades it was felt that by
stopping the revolution Hitler had also betrayed the Party's ideals.
Depending on the quality of those 'ideals', however, this also
meant that the National Socialist movement could become less

dogmatic and that it was possible to restrain those ideologues, fanatics and hotspurs who when it came to the practice, failed as 'technicians of power'. The process of seizing power, as it probably appeared above all to Hitler himself, was also an intensified process of selection for the National Socialist movement. It clarified for Hitler with whom, in which direction and how far it was possible to go in the given circumstances. Here the setbacks and hardships which beset the new government as a result of the Party jostling played a key role. This was apparent in two areas: that of foreign policy and Church policy. For this reason these examples will be more closely illustrated in the following two digressions.

Digression A: The failure of a revolutionary foreign policy

Just as the internal political stability of the new regime was incomplete in many respects until summer 1934, so the situation in regard to foreign policy remained precarious in this period. Apart from various disagreeable decisions made by Hitler's government, such as the stoppage or reduction of debt payments to foreign creditors, at first it was the catastrophic worsening of foreign opinion, particularly in the western democracies in view of political developments within Germany, which also directly and indirectly affected official foreign policy. The terrorist witch-hunt against Jews, Communists, Social Democrats and Democrats, the mass arrests, the cruelties, the concentration camps, the Jewish boycott, the burning of books and the strong refugee movement of political emigrants and Jews (by summer 1933 about 50,000 refugees had left Germany[47]) were all the more shocking because these things were happening in Germany, the civilized land in the heart of Europe, and because the national fanaticism and irrationalism which held sway there also awakened the fear of serious threats to neighbouring countries.

From the beginning Hitler sought to counter this 'atrocity propaganda' abroad, not only by public speeches in which he affirmed the peaceful intentions of the new National Government (this was very noticeable in the Reichstag speech of 17 May 1933), but also through a series of interviews, especially with selected representatives of the more sympathetic foreign press. Characteristic are Hitler's interviews with Ward Price, the chief correspondent of the Conservative London *Daily Mail*, whose owner Lord Rothermere was counted among the few English admirers of Hitler and in 1933/4 himself encouraged a series of interviews with Hitler and to some extent even chose their themes in order to break the ice for Hitler in Great Britain.[48]

But Hitler's rhetorical efforts to allay foreign opinion were repeatedly frustrated by the sort of remarks and actions which exposed the radicalism and aggression behind National Socialism. Moreover, the thoroughly diverse aims and the somewhat self-inflicted dilemma of the early foreign policy of the National Socialist regime frequently expressed the changing and still unresolved domestic struggle within Germany, and in particular the mixture of official and Party policy. It also reflected Hitler's unclear and hesitant attitude in this phase, when he could not control the different forces of Party and state or deliberately manipulate the many levels of foreign policy as confidently as he would be able to later, but was still feeling his way. Here too he could only gradually take the initiative.

When his government was formed Hitler had been compelled to leave the running of the German Foreign Office to the Nationalist career diplomat Baron von Neurath, and to agree not to let the Party interfere with the diplomatic corps. In fact at first the Foreign Office was able (like Hugenberg with his economic policy) to carry on with the old national revisionist policy without any notable changes. At the same time the NSDAP attempted to move in more or less independently of the official Foreign Office line, whereby Hitler also played the role of Party leader rather than head of government.

A typical sign of this was the establishment of a special NSDAP Foreign Policy office (*Aussenpolitisches Amt* – APA) on 1 April 1933 under the leadership of Alfred Rosenberg who had been Hitler's foreign policy adviser for many years. Rosenberg, who had strengthened Hitler in his anti-Bolshevist doctrine and in his effort to collaborate with England and Italy against Communism, regarded himself as a sort of shadow Foreign Minister and tried in particular to inject a specific Party political and ideological note into foreign policy through contacts with fascist or semi-fascist parties and groups abroad and through ties with anti-Communist refugees inside Germany. His first visit to London in May 1933, which he undertook with Hitler's full agreement in the belief that by exploiting contacts with like-minded British individuals he could change the anti-National Socialist mood of British public opinion and of the British government through personal visits and ideological pronouncements, had already turned into a miserable fiasco.[49]

Under Rosenberg the APA continued to exist and later was also able to interfere in foreign policy from time to time. However, it never became a serious counterweight to the Foreign Office. Rosenberg's own diaries from the year 1934[50] testify to the weakness of his position, which of course only spurred him on to reinforce at every opportunity Hitler's aversion to the 'clique of plotters' at the Foreign Office.

By 1934 he was no longer regarded as a candidate for a later National Socialist replacement for von Neurath. This role increasingly fell to the more adroit foreign merchant, Joachim von

Ribbentrop, who only came to the NSDAP in the final years before the take over of power, but who was able to impress Hitler in Berlin through his social and international contacts. From 1933/4 it was Ribbentrop's main concern to persuade England to co-operate with the Third Reich and in 1934 he was able to maintain his own office in Berlin ('Ribbentrop Bureau') which was financed by the Party and attached to the Party central office. He was also given official appointments by Hitler: at first from April 1934 as special envoy for disarmament questions, then (1935) as Ambassador in London.

The damage wrought by the tactless pressure from the Party in the opening phase of the Third Reich was particularly obvious in a sphere of foreign policy which the Party regarded as its own domain and where it counted on rapid successes: in relations with Austria and other groups of neighbouring Germans abroad, among whom there were either formal subsidiary organizations of the NSDAP (in Austria and Danzig for example), or 'movements for renewal' which were strongly influenced by the NSDAP and which also clamoured for power under the impact of the National Socialist victory in the Reich. From the standpoint of the NSDAP and also of Hitler this was not so much a matter of foreign policy in the sense of relations between states, as a matter of policy on the race as a whole in the sense of National Socialist ideology, and in that respect it was a question of attempting to extend the seizure of power or process of co-ordination to those areas beyond the frontiers mainly populated by Germans, where a conquest of power from within seemed both possible and advantageous, above all where independent or autonomous areas were concerned (Austria, the Saar, Danzig, and Memel). Actually these efforts failed in the most important cases. Only in the state of Danzig, where the NSDAP under Gauleiter Albert Förster had the strongest support from the Reich both materially and in terms of propaganda, was it possible to get a bare majority with 51 per cent of the votes in the Volkstag elections of 28 May 1933 (as in East Prussia on 5 March 1933), and thus to form a National Socialist Senate government legally (with Hermann Rauschning and from autumn 1934 with Arther Greiser as Senate President)

The NSDAP was also less strong and had to operate more cautiously in the Saar region so as not to endanger the cohesion of the German parties standing for attachment to Germany at the referendum arranged for February 1935. At the initiative of the NSDAP's plenipotentiary for the Saar, the Rhineland-Palatinate Gauleiter, Josef Bürckel, the Party finally made do with the formation of the 'German Front', a coalition of German liberal parties from the Centre of the NSDAP, in whose control Catholic politicians also played a crucial role besides the National Socialists.

But Austria became a real foreign policy test case in the effort to export the seizure of power.[51] Although there was no doubt on any examination of the objective facts that a take-over of power by the Austrian NSDAP in Vienna would not be tolerated by those powers interested in maintaining Austrian independence, especially the fascist government in Italy, but would be seen as concealed annexation, Hitler fully supported NSDAP efforts in this direction until June 1933. Given the smooth take-over of power by the NSDAP in the Länder outside Prussia, there was obviously a belief in an equally rapid success in Austria too, particularly since the Austrian NSDAP, with its Land Inspector appointed by Hitler in 1931, the Reich German Theo Habicht, was able under the impact of events in Germany significantly to broaden its appeal by merging with the Home Defence and the Pan-Germans and to set in motion a wave of National Socialist campaigning and propaganda. In order to deal more effectively with the mounting unrest and the influence of Germany, the strongly anti-Socialist Austrian government under Chancellor Engelbert Dollfuss, which based itself on the Christian Socialists and the semi-fascist Heimwehr, went over to a presidential system of emergency decrees as a result of the indecision of the Nationalrat. There thus arose for the NSDAP in Austria a situation similar to that of 1932 in the Reich under Papen and Schleicher. Although according to their political complexion the Heimwehr and Dollfuss could have been suitable partners for Hitler, as Mussolini in particular and the rightist Hungarian government of Gömbös pointed out in the expectation of building a common foreign policy bloc, the leaders of the Austrian NSDAP were unmistakably working for the fall of Dollfuss. Typically, they employed the devices tried and tested in Germany since the onset of the economic crisis: the demand for new elections on the grounds that the existing government no longer complied with the prevailing will of the people. Hitler also officially made this his demand in March 1933.

Thus Germany's policy to Austria had been taken in tow by National Socialist party politics. The demand was all the more explosive since the German Reich Chancellor was at the same time also the supreme leader of the Austrian NSDAP and consequently leader of the radical opposition in a neighbouring country. Since Dollfuss in no way fulfilled the requirements of the National Socialist movement, Hitler had the propaganda and terrorist activity of the Austrian NSDAP and S.A. supported from the Reich through appropriate measures of boycott (ban on travel into Austria by introducing a 1,000 Mark charge). The German Foreign Office, which merely counselled caution in view of the severe foreign policy dangers in the tactics of pressure and subversion, was largely excluded from all this. Theo Habicht alone was Hitler's agent in policy towards Austria until summer 1933.

Hitler's attitude changed only when the conflict took a sharp turn for the worse in June/July and unleased highly serious international repercussions for Germany. Thanks to cover from Italy, the Doll-fuss government did not hesitate to counter NSDAP coercion, riots and outrages, which were dangerously increased in early July, with the expulsion of Habicht, the arrest of other National Socialist functionaries and finally (19 June 1933) with a ban on the NSDAP's activity and the dissolution of the S.A. in Austria. The counter-measures taken by the Reich in response to this (arrest of the head of the press department of the Austrian Embassy, the formation of the Austrian Legion from refugee S.A. and S.S. men on the Bavarian–Austrian border, massive propaganda by the Land Inspectorate of the Austrian NSDAP, which was moved to Munich, through the radio and illegal propaganda flights over Austrian territory) soon alarmed the outside world, and gave rise to the danger of a formal intervention by Italy and the Western Powers, as the Italian Ambassador duly warned at the end of July.

Since von Neurath too now overcame his initial reticence and gave definite warnings, Hitler drew back willy nilly. Habicht was compelled to be more cautious and the German Foreign Office's influence on policy towards Austria became stronger. The failure of the attempt to achieve a quick seizure of power in Austria like the National Socialist revolution in Germany could no longer be ignored, even if nobody wanted to admit this in the NSDAP.

In addition there were similar experiences in other countries at the same time. In the Sudeten areas, the political prospects of the National Socialist Movement (DNSAP), which had experienced a strong upturn in the German population in spring 1933, were blocked by the outcome of the actions for treason brought by the Czech authorities and the banning of the DNSAP which was subse-quently decreed at the beginning of October. National Socialist propaganda and activity also extended to the Germans beyond the border and had already caused a particularly sharp reaction from the Polish government. Indeed in this case it had even reinforced the notion of forestalling Hitler by a Franco-Polish preventive war while this was still militarily possible.

But on the international stage too, the National Socialist regime had to suffer a series of painful rebuffs at this time: at the World Economic Conference in London in June, in the League Council in May/June 1933 during the debate about the violation of the con-vention on Upper Silesia through the persecution of Jewish citizens (Bernheim Petition) and at the International Labour Conference in Geneva, which Robert Ley abruptly left in the end after serious charges were made by the delegations of other countries.

Germany's foreign policy isolation could hardly have been great-er than it was in the middle of 1933. Hitler was also aware of this and from then on he tried to restrain the more or less uncontrolled pressure on all sides at once for influence abroad and instead tried to determine specific priorities in foreign policy. Thus the immediate Party political and *völkisch* aims which were pursued at first but which were not yet attainable owing to the present impotence of the National Socialist regime, including the Austrian question, receded into the background, whereas questions crucial to consolidating the regime's international position and to its long-term objectives took priority. To these belonged the negotiations for a settlement with Poland, which had been underway since early summer and which resulted in the signature of a German–Polish Non-Aggression Treaty on 26 January 1934. At the same time the efforts to achieve good relations with the Soviet Union which had been continued in the traditional way until summer 1933, died away and co-operation between the Reichswehr and the Red Army was terminated. Above all an effort was again made to improve relations with Italy and Göring's visit to Mussolini at the beginning of November served this aim.

In some respects the break-off of the Geneva negotiations on disarmament and the departure of Germany from the League (14 October 1933) worked against Party ambitions in foreign policy. This decision, which Hitler had still wanted to avoid at the end of September but which he reached after talking with the Reichswehr leaders, because he was bound to fear that further discussion of the revised English proposal for a staged achievement of equality of armaments under international control would expose the National Socialist regime's determination to speed up rearmament, was without doubt fairly risky in view of the then foreign policy situation of the Reich. Once the step was taken, and had again aroused lively mistrust abroad, it forced the National Socialist regime to be all the more careful and reasonable in other areas of foreign policy.

This revealed itself in policy towards Austria. When Habicht, who had tried in vain in autumn and winter to get a personal meeting with Dollfuss to secure the Austrian NSDAP's participation in the government by amicable means, again directed a massive declaration of hostility at the Dollfuss government in conjunction with the leader of the Austrian S.A., he came to realize that this no longer corresponded with Hitler's intentions. However, Hitler failed (chiefly because of the strongly critical mood which also existed for other reasons within the Party and S.A. against his policy line) to rebuff Habicht clearly and tried for a while to keep various options open. This duplicity severely strained the relationship with Mussolini, who countered the new National Socialist pressure on Vienna, which Hitler had failed to disavow energetically enough, with the conclusion on 17 March 1934 of an economic and consultative agreement with Austria and Hungary (Rome Protocols). In addition Mussolini threatened closer co-operation with France and this soon forced Berlin to be reasonable. At the same time

Hitler's indecision reinforced the growing mood of hopelessness within the Austrian NSDAP (as well as in Habicht) and an attempt was made to escape from this by a 'leap in the dark'.

Although relations with Italy seemed passably restored by June 1934 after Hitler's first personal meeting with Mussolini in Venice, this very meeting was wrongly interpreted by the plotters within the illegal Austrian NSDAP as signifying the end of Italian support for Dollfuss and was taken as the signal for preparing a putsch in anticipation of a new Austrian Chancellor, as well as NSDAP participation in the government together with the usual personal benefits. This desperate act led to the murder of Dollfuss on 25 July 1934 but was unsuccessful in other respects and was the biggest fiasco of early National Socialist foreign policy. Habicht's immediate dismissal and Hitler's public dissociation from the putsch could not prevent the Third Reich from sinking to a new low in its international standing, particularly in relations with Italy which clearly demonstrated its determination to defend Austrian independence by immediately sending troops to the Brenner.

The fact that Italy's friendship was again forfeited also provided indirect support for French policy. Under Foreign Minister Barthou's lead, France was making vigorous efforts after Germany's departure from the League and the devaluation of the Franco–Polish alliance (as a result of the German–Polish pact) to strengthen the East European Little Entente (especially the alliance with Prague), and above all to include the Soviet Union in a security system directed against National Socialist Germany. The entry of the USSR into the League of Nations on 16 September 1934 was a first, and for Hitler a very painful, success for this policy.

Within Germany the overwhelmingly negative foreign policy balance of the first year and a half of the National Socialist government helped to check those Party ambitions which had done so much damage to foreign policy. But the abortive putsch in Vienna, preceded by the ban of 13 July 1933 on the two rival National Socialist parties in the Memel area on account of violent assassination attempts, marked above all the end of the attempt to export the seizure of power with the aid of the Party to German-populated areas beyond the borders. The freedom of movement of various Party sections in the sphere of policy towards ethnic Germans (including the NSDAP's Auslandsorganisation) was more strictly curtailed, partly by the German Foreign Office, partly through the setting up of *ad hoc* co-ordinating bodies (*Volksdeutscher Mittelstelle*–Vomi), which consisted to a greater degree of experienced 'experts' in work on ethnic Germans and less of Party men. The domestic consequences arising from the failures of the revolutionary foreign policy showed themselves particularly clearly here, as in the case of Habicht's removal and Papen's despatch to Vienna.

Digression B: The conflict with the Evangelical Church

Although one of Hitler's most important achievements in 1933 was his success, chiefly through the Concordat, in persuading the Catholic Church to adopt a more positive attitude and to be loyal towards the regime, relations rapidly cooled when it became clear that the National Socialist regime systematically set out to obstruct and subsequently to co-ordinate or suppress all activities of the Catholic Church apart from pastoral care (especially its youth organization, and unions, the Catholic press, the lay movement of Catholic Action among others). The fundamental nature of this opposition showed itself to a more marked degree than it did against the Protestant Church. 'Roman' Catholicism, according to the concepts of the *völkisch* ideology, counted next to Jewry and Marxism as the special enemy of a 'North Germanic' ideology. It was typical that throughout the entire period of the Third Reich there always existed in the Gestapo and SD in the departments for counter-surveillance and counteraction a section (in addition to one for Jewry and Marxism) for 'political Catholicism', whereas the Protestant Church was not classified as a fundamental ideological enemy. Moreover, the scale of political persecution was on the whole different. As against the hundreds of Catholic clerics who often spent years in the concentration camps, there were relatively few Protestant clergy imprisoned for long periods. Although it was impossible to reconcile Christianity and National Socialism in the last resort, National Socialism was far more affronted by the Catholic Church because of its universal, supra-national character, its stronger institutional independence and spiritual authority. It was also obvious here that the growing suppression and persecution of the Catholic Church, the criminal actions against the Catholic clergy, the closure of Catholic public schools, the confiscation of Catholic monasteries etc., met with relatively scant criticism and objection among the conservative bearers of the Hitler state (in the administration, judicature, armed forces). Thus to a certain extent the NSDAP and the Nationalists and conservatives (quite overwhelmingly Protestant) shared hostile attitudes towards the Catholic Church and its strong public influence.

From the outset things were very different for the Protestant Churches. Because of its tradition as the state church it already enjoyed strong support from the Prussian-conservative elite in the civil service and the military, as well as from the Reich President too. Conversely, the NSDAP could also count not only on the goodwill and loyalty of the Protestant camp but above and beyond this on a substantial active following. This came chiefly from various groups among the Protestant laity and pastors who in 1932 had combined as the 'Confessional Movement of German Christians' and in the Church elections in the area of the Old Prussian

Union in November 1932 had gained about a third of all seats in the Church parish and synodal assemblies. The 'German Christians' under their 'leader' the pastor and Party member Joachim Hossenfelder were the equivalent to a National Socialist group in the Evangelical Church. Through the take-over of power by the NSDAP they expected (as did other auxiliary organizations and groups within the National Socialist movement) the fulfilment of their particular wishes and ideas: the renewal of the Protestant faith in the sense of a 'true' people's Church and the end of the provincial fragmentation of the Church and of the Protestant Church's authoritarian-patriarchal constitution based on Bishops and Superintendents by means of a united national Reich Church strongly influenced by the laity and the pastors.

Within the NSDAP (as in the German *völkisch* movement in general) there existed from the outset a group of old Hitler partisans who in contrast to the 'atheists' Alfred Rosenberg, Martin Bormann and others, believed in a union of National Socialism and Protestant Christianity. Prominent representatives of this strand were among others the Gauleiter Wilhelm Kube and the one-time leader of the NSDAP group in the Prussian Landtag, Hans Kerrl (from spring 1933 Prussian Minister of Justice). This trend appeared to be confirmed and reinforced during the crucial years of the struggle for power before 1933 when the NSDAP displayed its positive attitude towards Christianity through sharp attacks on 'atheistic' Marxism and through its advocacy of *völkisch*-Christian schooling. Hitler also knew how to give the impression of the pious, humble leader through frequent public invocations of 'the Almighty' and 'Providence', and in the Protestant districts of the Reich S.A. and S.S. men were often ordered to turn out *en masse* for services in order to reinforce this impression. The pseudo-religious posturing of National Socialism, which was regarded from the beginning by a minority of Protestant Christians as sacrilege, did not however fail to have its effect among large sectors of Protestant believers and it explains the rapturous veneration which was given to Hitler from those same Christian Protestant circles.

As to the Protestant Church there were virtually no ideologically motivated departures of National Socialists from the fold until 1933. The revolution of 1933 had rather the effect of virtually stopping the move away from the Church, which had long been a feature of the Socialist workforce especially during the economic crisis, so that the year of the seizure of power could even seem to be the 'year of the Church'.[52] It was not only the struggle against 'godless Marxism' and 'Jewish materialism' but other features of National Socialist propaganda which very often found willing listeners among the believers of both Christian Confessions in Germany. Thus the condemnation of 'degenerate art', modern 'free thinking' and 'moral decay', of the 'subversive intellectuals', or the call for new authority in leadership, for the 'organic bonding' and moral 'regeneration of the national community'. A considerable part of this ideological rhetoric which the NSDAP had sucked up from all available sources was indeed itself derived from Christian convictions, and was part of the resentment and ideologies which had been formed in Christian community life in the process of confrontation with a form of society and modern development which were neither understood nor wanted.

The sensational conflicts which began in late spring in and with the Protestant Church were (unlike the relationship to the Catholic Church) not just primarily the expression of a deliberate and more or less uniformly aggressive policy by the regime, but rather the result of thoroughly disparate trends within the National Socialist camp on this issue, which at the same time cut across the general conflict between revolutionary and conservative-authoritarian forces in this phase of the seizure of power. The basic idea of the new constitution for the Evangelical Church (creation of a Reich Church with a Reich Bishop), the realization of which was the main reason for the quarrels in 1933, was generally approved in principle in spring 1933 not only by the German Christians but also by the leading representatives of the regional Churches and the German Evangelical Church League. The question was how far the constitution and new direction of the proposed Reich Church would be determined by the Church itself or would be imposed under pressure from the German Christians or on the state's behalf, that sparked off the conflict between the traditional and overwhelmingly conservative Church authorities and the German Christians, who enjoyed the support of the Party. Hitler himself initially tried to avoid an open conflict between these wings, particularly since he hardly expected any more of the radical forces of the German Christians than he did from the *völkisch* enthusiasts who tried to revive a pagan Germanic mythology.

Individual Party efforts from below in March/April 1933 to extend the seizure of power to the Evangelical Church were quickly stopped. Thus the Reich Minister of the Interior, Frick, had had the appointment of a National Socialist Church Commissioner in Mecklenburg-Schwerin cancelled, which moved the Mecklenburg Land Bishop Rendtorff to register his gratitude by demonstratively joining the NSDAP and publicly acknowledging 'our God-given leader Adolf Hitler'.[53] (Soon he too was of a different view.) Also the fact that in conjunction with this incident Hitler appointed on 25 April Ludwig Müller, a man known to him for years, as his Deputy in Evangelical Church affairs (he was a relatively moderate supporter of the state Church and the conservative Königsberg army chaplain) and not one of the radical German Christians (Hossenfelder got a job as the Church expert in the Prussian Ministry of Culture) showed his readiness to compromise.

As the new protector of the 'Confessional movement' Müller was at first able to persuade the German Christians to formulate a very moderate programme and to take a rather restrained line on the draft of a constitution for the new Reich Church, which was worked out at the time in agreement with Hitler under the chairmanship of the president of the German Evangelical Church League, Hermann Kapler.

Conflict only became unavoidable when Müller, pressed by the German Christians, expressed the desire to be appointed as Reich Bishop and the German Christians subsequently (23 May) publicly proclaimed his candidature. But the representatives of the regional Churches voted on 27 May with a bare majority against Müller for Pastor Friedrich von Bodelschwingh. Without the promptings of Müller and the German Christians Hitler would probably have been agreeable to Bodelschwingh's candidature but he could hardly accept this solution once the Party had launched a vigorous campaign against him and so he too expressed his displeasure. As Kapler consequently resigned from his offices as President of the Ecclesiastical Chancellery and of the Evangelical Church Council of the Old Prussian Union, there was an opportunity for state intervention in Prussia. On 25 June Education Minister Rust appointed a Church Commissioner (August Jäger) who then allocated to the German Christians the leading positions of the Church administration by abolishing ecclesiastical assemblies and appointing state plenipotentiaries (the new President of the Supreme Church Council was the German Christian lawyer, Dr Friedrich Werner). These and other simultaneous acts of force (occupation of the buildings of the Evangelical Church League by the S.A.) proved to be, however, both less skillful and successful. There was a wave of public protest which even the Reich President joined with unwonted resolution at the end of June 1933, by telling Hitler that he wanted the conflict settled. This above all was the reason why the new constitution for the Evangelical Church, worked out basically by the Kapler committee, came into force on 14 July with the signature of the leaders of all twenty-eight Land Churches (*RGBl*, I, p. 471). At the same time Church elections were arranged throughout Germany for 23 July. These were expected to sanction Jäger's measures and to provide a majority for Müller's election. Hitler had to avoid another defeat for the Party for the sake of his own reputation. For this reason he personally interceded for the German Christian Party in the run up to the election and they eventually got some two-thirds of the votes.

The election (in which former non-voters who were normally indifferent to the Church but who were mobilized by the Party played a key rôle) and the meeting of the newly elected Old Prussian General Synod (4 May 1933), as well as Müller's election as Reich Bishop at the National Synod convened at Wittenberg (27 Sept.

1933), marked the high point of power and prestige for the German Christians, who to the horror of foreign observers dominated these Evangelical Church assemblies with their brown shirts and radical demands.

But the danger which had become apparent to the Evangelical Church after the Church elections, of Protestantism being submerged and infiltrated by National Socialist 'concepts' also generated resistance. On 21 September an organized opposition of the pastors was formed in the shape of the Pastors' Emergency League (Confessional Church), whose initiators were three prominent pastors in West Berlin: Martin Niemöller (pastor in Berlin-Dahlem quarter), Gerhard Jacobi (pastor at the Kaiser Wilhelm Memorial Church) and Eitel Friedrich von Rabenau (Church of the Apostle Paul, Berlin-Schöneberg). One week later 2,000 Evangelical pastors signed a protest against the new leadership and organization of the new Church which had been created at the National Synod in Wittenberg, and by January 1934 over 7,000 pastors had joined the Emergency League, whose 'Brethrens's Council'[54] was led by the general secretary, Martin Niemöller. The opposition of the Confessional pastors against the use of the Aryan paragraph within the Church could not grow all that rapidly and could not appear too openly, not least because it was not based on a fundamental rejection of the National Socialist regime, but as a rule combined opposition to certain radical manifestations and ambitions of that regime with a fundamental approval of the revolution of 1933. The attitude of the former Imperial U-boat Captain Martin Niemöller was typical in this respect. He called the Emergency League into being in September 1933 but at the same time in a greetings telegram to Hitler in November 1933 welcomed Hitler's decision to leave the League of Nations because it was in the national interest.[55]

The new Reich Bishop tried to overcome the split in the Evangelical Church which had become apparent with the formation of the Emergency League, by taking a relatively moderate course (the Aryan paragraph was not incorporated into Church law). On 17 October the Führer's Deputy instructed the Party to maintain neutrality over Church matters. In effect this was a dissociation from the German Christians. When at a big rally in the Berlin Sportspalast on 13 November the German Christians again publicly put forward radical proposals which in practice tended towards a complete Nazification of the Evangelical Church and its Confessions (introduction of the leader principle, the National Socialist Aryan paragraph, elimination of Jewish elements in the Bible etc.), and when the pastors in the Emergency League reacted with sharp denunciations from the pulpit, Müller felt himself obliged to withdraw his patronage of the German Christians. Deprived of the support of Party and state the German Christians subsequently broke up into rival groups and rapidly lost significance.

The attempt to bridge differences through a middle course, to isolate the intransigent originators of the Pastors' Emergency League and to ensure the government of the Church under the Reich Bishop, had some success in 1934 in Prussia and with the smaller provincial Churches but it ultimately failed. Hitler dared not take extreme measures in this conflict and so it came about that under a regime which was otherwise so strict, pastors who were dismissed from office, like Niemöller, were confirmed in office by their parishes, continued to carry out their duties and in May 1934 even set up a formal rival organization to Müller's Church rule with the Barmen Confessional Synod. Strongly influenced by the theology of Karl Barth, it also provided theoretical justification for disobedience in the face of state interference with the Church, which ran counter to the tradition of German Protestantism as the state Church. It was chiefly the Bishops of the largest of the old Prussian Evangelical Churches, Bishop Wurm in Württemberg and Bishop Meiser in Bavaria, in whose Churches even in 1933 the German Christians (as in Hannover too) had remained a minority, who opposed the resolutions at the new National Synod convened by Reich Bishop Müller in August 1934. These envisaged among other things the introduction of an official oath for pastors and Church officials (analogous to the oath of loyalty to Hitler demanded of state officials after Hindenburg's death). The Gestapo imposed house arrest on both Bishops, but this use of state means only strengthened the resistance of the pastors in the Emergency League. On 19 October 1934 they gathered in the Dahlem town hall for the second Reich Confessional Synod, thus openly declaring war on the Reich Bishop and his Church Deputy Jäger, and called the Council of the German Evangelical Church into being as a formal opposition organ. The attempt to impose a new authoritarian constitution for the Reich Church had failed. Müller's Church Deputy Jäger was dismissed and in November 1934 the Reich Bishop felt obliged partially to restore former Church rights. His complete loss of authority was revealed by the fact that in agreement between the Brethren's Council and the Lutheran Land Bishops, a Provisional Church Directorate was set up (headed by Bishop Marahrens of Hannover) at the end of 1934, which effectively governed the Church although the Reich Bishop termed the new organ illegal and ordered all pastors and Church officials to ignore it.

Although Müller never formally relinquished his office, nobody took any notice of his existence after 1935. However, through his laws on the Trusteeship of the Regional Evangelical Church (11 March 1935), on the Legal Competence of the German Evangelical Church (26 June 1935) and above all through the appointment of a Reich Church Minister (Hans Kerrl) in place of the Church policy division of the Ministry of the Interior and the Ministry of Culture, the attempt was launched to bind the Evangelical Church more closely to the regime through the extension of direct state supervision and tutelage. Kerrl's aim to bridge differences through the creation of Church committees in the separate Land Churches, in which the Confessional pastors as well as moderate German Christians were represented, seemed at first wholly successful, particularly since General Superintendent Zoellner, who was highly esteemed by the Confessional Church, made himself available as chairman of the Reich Church Committee. Yet as at the beginning of 1935 the Provisional Church Government had already through all too conciliatory gestures towards the regime (order to hold services of thanksgiving for the Führer on the occasion of the 'return home' of the Saar) aroused the hostility of the Niemöller wing, which was equally intransigent on these issues, so too a pro-Nazi appeal of the Reich Church Committee ('We approve the formation of the National Socialist nation on the basis of race, blood and soil'[56]) became the occasion for a new protest from the Confessional Church.

Although the previous unity of the Confessional Church on the issue of the relationship to the Reich Church Committee broke up (the Brethren's Council categorically rejected the idea of collaboration, the Council of the Evangelical-Lutheran Churches reserved the right to refuse or to collaborate on specific issues), Kerrl's new Church authority faced a similar situation in 1936 to that facing the Reich Bishop in 1934, particularly since the simultaneous effort by the Party and the Hitler Youth to end the Confessional Church's influence on public life and education gave greater cause for complaint. In a letter of 4 June 1936 to the Reich Chancellery, the Provisional Church Government applied their complaints directly to Hitler and among other things also expressed concern that 'very often devotion given in a way due to God alone' was accorded to the Führer.[57] The fact that the communication not only bypassed the Reich Church Minister but also became known abroad and led to the arrest of the suspected perpetrators of the indiscretion (the Justitiar of the Provisional Church Government Dr Weissler) again sharpened the conflict. In February 1937 Dr Zoellner also gave up his office in protest against the interference of the Gestapo. Hitler, who was increasingly vexed by this turn of events, believed he could control the problem by the same means as those used in summer 1933, and on 15 February 1937 he ordered the holding of new Church elections, whereby apparently there was also some idea of encouraging the German Christians. But when a united front of the Evangelical Churches quickly formed at this indication and many public declarations of prominent Church leaders started to circulate (a letter from the Brandenburg Superintendent Otto Dibelius to Hitler which was distributed in thousands of copies was particularly effective), Hitler drew back. On 25 June all Church policy pronouncements for preparing for the election were banned and the election did not take place.

Hitler had again suffered a rebuff. The Reich Church Minister had been no more successful at co-ordinating the Evangelical Church than the Reich Bishop. The National Socialist regime abandoned the effort at institutional co-ordination. Instead a more pronounced attack was made on individual efforts directed against the regime from the ranks of the Evangelical Church. In this context Niemöller too was arrested by the Gestapo in 1938 (after his release from detention pending investigation) and put in the concentration camp at Sachsenhausen. It made no difference to Niemöller's case when Hitler proclaimed a 'civil truce' in Church policy quarrels for the duration of the War. The valiant pastor became widely known at home and abroad through the regular intercessions of the Evangelical Church parish congregations and he remained in the concentration camp until the end of the War, although carefully protected from S.S. measures in special quarters.

Even in this exceptional case, where the Gestapo directly intervened, it is obvious that the National Socialist regime felt obliged to an astonishing degree to behave within acceptable limits towards the Evangelical Church, which it had long ceased to do in the case of other opponents. For present purposes the conflict with the Evangelical Church thus serves as an example of how narrow were the limits imposed on the National Socialist leadership's freedom of movement when from the outset it was not just a matter of the opposition of smaller or larger groups of pastors, Bishops and parish congregations, but also of the widespread, united disapproval and obstruction of influential Protestant-conservative forces in leading offices of the state (administration, judicature, armed forces), who in these matters stood up relatively courageously behind those Church leaders and their followers who were under public attack, and frequently knew how to cover for them and protect them. In no other sphere of the National Socialist efforts at co-ordination were the Reich President, leading officers of the armed forces, Ministers and prominent government officials, lawyers and judges so forceful in rejecting the alien influences and indoctrination of National Socialism. And the knowledge of this direct and indirect (active and moral) support made possible in the first place the public appearance of both Niemöller, whose services in Dahlem were demonstratively attended by the leading conservative circles of Berlin, and of other Church leaders. The administration of justice in particular, which in numerous other political trials tended to be more biassed towards the government, helped to thwart the proposed coercive measures against the Evangelical Church through a series of judgements between 1934 and 1936, upholding the complaints of the Church and its spokesman against the Reich Bishop and the Reich Church Minister. Exactly how forthright even otherwise quite diffident conservative Ministers under Hitler could be at this stage, when it came to defending the Church and religious education, was shown for example on 1 December 1936 on the occasion of the passing of the Hitler Youth law. This made the Hitler Youth obligatory and gave the Reich Youth Leader von Shirach the status of a Supreme Reich Authority. The Reich Minister for Posts and Transport, von Eltz-Rübenach, remarked on this occasion in Hitler's presence (according to the protocol): He approved the draft law 'on condition that the Hitler Youth, in keeping with the Führer's promise, would not in any way undermine the religious values which parents had instilled in their young'.[58] When some weeks later the Minister, like other Ministers, was to be accorded the golden Party emblem, he objected that he could not accept the honour if in so doing he sanctioned the Party's anti-Church stance. After this repeated snub Hitler accepted Eltz-Rübenach's resignation in February 1937 (successor: Dr Ohnesorge Reich Ministry of Posts and Dorpmüller for the Reich Ministry of Transport).

The relative goodwill shown by the Berlin ministerial bureaucracy was also typical when it came to applications for compulsory retirement by officials who in keeping with their Christian convictions openly rejected parts of the National Socialist ideology, and in that respect conflicted with the Law on German Civil Servants (*Deutsches Beamtengesetz* – DBG) of 1937, which (in Art. 71) required that the civil servant must 'at all times give unqualified support to the National Socialist state'. Since such compulsory retirements required Hitler's decision in the last resort, the applications concerned often came to the Reich Chancellery for the final ruling. And the Head of the Reich Chancellery, who apparently felt particularly uncertain and uncomfortable with such matters, occasionally permitted several advisers and divisional heads in the Reich Chancellery to give their opinions. *One* such case, which concerned the assistant master from Halberstadt, Dr Walter Hobohm, seems typical of this process both in type and treatment and has been chosen from the documents as an example.

Dr Hobohm, a fifty-year-old teacher of history, French and English at the I Secondary School in Halberstadt, had made a written request in June 1937 to cancel his membership of the National Socialist League of Teachers (NSLB) because he could not accept the ideological-religious aspect of the Party which frequently tried to suppress 'confessing Christianity' in public life. The Gau official in the education office in the Gau of Magdeburg-Anhalt and the NSDAP Kreisleiter in the Kreis Halberstadt-Wernigerode (the latter pointed out that H. was 'a confessing Christian through and through' and that a 'precedent might be set' by his departure from the NSLB) refused the request on the grounds of Hobohm's political reliability. Duly informed, the division for secondary schools attached to the Oberpräsident in Magdeburg endorsed this in a report to the Reich and Prussian Ministry for Science, Education and National Culture, which subsequently began on enquiry against Hobohm with a view to enforced retirement according to Art. 71 of the DBG. During his hearing Hobohm declared that he did not reject National Socialist ideology as such, but rather could not approve 'the direction taken by Reichsleiter Rosenberg ... because it conflicted with Christian principles'. From a 'Christian point of view [he] was obliged to acknowledge the working of a higher order as well as blood and race, since otherwise one would arrive at a sort of racial materialism'. After the Führer's Deputy had also declared to the Reich Education Minister on 26 January 1938 that Hobohm had 'made it quite clear that he rejected rather important programmatic points of the National Socialist movement and thereby the state', State Secretary Zschintzsch in the Education Ministry subsequently reached this conclusion:

Although it is true that assistant master Hobohm is regarded in his official capacity by his colleagues as a man of strong duty and in character as a man of honourable sentiments and firm convictions, yet according to the finding of this enquiry he belongs to those circles who are so committed to the Church faith that they cannot adopt a National Socialist stance ... In agreement with the judgement of the head of the education office (S.A. Obersturmbannführer Knipfer)[59] it is impossible to feel that Hobohm will ever be so deeply committed to National Socialism that as a teacher he can win over the pupils entrusted to him for the National Socialist cause ... Also his view on the Jewish question cannot be reconciled with the demands made of a National Socialist official. Unreserved support for the National Socialist state and National Socialist ideology cannot be expected in view of the reservations expressed by H. ... the conditions for retirement according to Art. 7 of the DBG are therefore fulfilled.

This communication together with the entire 'Hobohm file' went to the Reich Chancellery on 13 December 1938, where Ministerialrat Ehrich (division A) recommended on 2 January 1939 without any dissenting view of his own a decision from Hitler corresponding to the request of the Reich Minister of Education. Lammers, however, also sounded out the division responsible for constitutional issues, division B. Reichskabinettsrat Dr Killy then arrived at the following dissenting judgement on 15 March 1939:

The facts have been thoroughly examined and discussed in several meetings. There are in our opinion considerable objections to agreeing with the Reich Education Minister's proposal in this instance ... The sole fact to date to come out of the enquiry which might support the conclusion that the official can no longer be guaranteed to support the National Socialist state at all times would be the fact that the official in question rejects Rosenberg's conceptions in so far as these conflict with the Christian faith.

It does not seem feasible to retire officials according to Art. 71 of the DBG solely on this ground. Quite apart from the fact that Rosenberg himself describes his work as a purely personal statement of belief, which does not automatically carry the Party seal of approval, such a decision would not be without considerable objections in view of Art. 24 of the Party programme and the guarantee of freedom of worship so often publicly proclaimed. Even in his last speech to the Reichstag on 30 January 1939, the Führer made the following 'solemn pronouncement'. 'Nobody has yet been persecuted in Germany because of his religious convictions, nor will anybody be so persecuted! ... Given this state of affairs, our opinion must be that the condition for retiring according to Art. 71 of the DBG has not been fulfilled and in view of the declaration of the Führer quoted above it seems impracticable to recommend him to decide in favour of enforced retirement.

The head of division B, Lammers's deputy, Ministerialdirektor Kritzinger, endorsed this view. Since the opinion of divisions A and B were divergent Lammers also asked for the view of his personal adviser, Reichskabinettsrat von Stutterheim. The latter arrived at the following conclusion five months later on 4 August 1939:

The idea that failing to agree with Rosenberg's viewpoint fulfils the requirement for using Art. 71 of the DBG must be emphatically rejected. The mere fact of an official belonging to the Confessional Church is also in my opinion no reason for imposing retirement according to Art. 71 of the DBG ... In my view, Hobohm's compulsory retirement could only be justified if in his case ... the following conviction was assumed: Hobohm does indeed recognize the Party programme and the main propositions of National Socialism. None the less he has strong doubts as to whether in practice the policy of the Party and of the state will keep to this programme and confine itself to the said proposals. He is inwardly convinced that this policy will in the last resort bring about a decline in the Christian faith amongst the German people. He regards this development as so disastrous that in critical times he will not be able to bring himself to support the state unreservedly, which according to his conviction will be the agent and executor of this development. For my part I am not convinced that this assumption is the correct one in Hobohm's case. There are merely certain probable grounds to be found in Hobohm's written and spoken remarks, and the fact that apparently both the Party authorities and the Education Minister and the Reich Minister of the Interior are persuaded that Hobohm holds such a view cannot be overlooked in the last resort either. If one reflects, moreover, that disavowal by state and Party offices who have been active in this case is politically undesirable, I also think that it is impossible to recommend to the Führer that Art. 71 be applied in this instance.

Lammers inclined, as Kitzinger remarked on 14 August 1939, towards Stutterheim's view but he was unable, in spite of the pressure from the Reich Minister of Education for a rapid settlement of this case (Hobohm was put on leave with pay for the duration of the investigation), to bring the matter to Hitler's attention by November 1939 as a result of the outbreak of war. To bypass this unpleasant state of affairs Lammers therefore proposed to the Reich Education Minister on 14 November 1939, that he examine whether because of the changed situation caused by the outbreak of war (shortage of personnel), compulsory retirement could be forgotten, or whether on the contrary 'the situation created by the War' made 'compulsory retirement more urgent'. In view of the apparent dampening down of the struggle with the Church which was desired during the War, the Reich Minister of Education came to a decision a year later (autumn 1940), 'after listening to the Oberpräsident and in agreement with the Führer's Deputy', to discontinue the action against Dr Hobohm. The latter was reinstated but was no longer allowed to teach the 'discipline' of history.[60]

This case has been deliberately set out at length although it certainly does not bear witness to heroic deeds on the part of the ministerial bureaucracy. It demonstrates rather how in the last resort that bureaucracy in spite of its better judgement (Stutterheim decision) looked at political realities and was prepared to make voluntary adjustments. For all that, the duration and expense of the process and the acceptance of the beliefs of confessing Christians which was expressed by representatives of the Party, show how difficult it was to impose strict repression in such cases. The ambiguity of National Socialist ideology, which in turn expressed the fact that National Socialism could not dispense with at least partial agreement with the traditional conservative values and their spokesmen (the civil servants, Officer Corps and in the broader sense, the National Conservative inclined middle classes), precluded the most severe totalitarian measures in the struggle against the Church and Christian opposition. This was also due to the fact that right into the War prominent National Socialists were continually to be found who themselves opposed the hostile intentions of Rosenberg, Himmler or Bormann by appealing to 'positive Christianity'.

An example of this is Rosenberg's abortive attempt in autumn 1939 to elevate his position as 'Deputy of the Führer for the supervision of spiritual and ideological schooling and training of the NSDAP' (from 24 Feb. 1934) to a right of direction extending over and beyond the Party even to state authorities. Rosenberg was chiefly concerned to build up his position vis-à-vis his rival, Goebbels, whose flexible propaganda technique always seemed irresponsibly 'free' to the Party ideologue Rosenberg. And the moment seemed propitious because the Minister for Propaganda had fallen foul of Hitler at this time through a fresh love affair (Lida Baarova). Rosenberg's intention was categorically opposed by virtually all the other Party and state authorities who were in any way also responsible or partly responsible for ideological matters (Reich

Education Minister Rust, Reichsorganisationsleiter Ley, the Führer's Deputy, the Reich S.S. Leader, Hitler's head of the Chancellery Philipp Bouhler, who was responsible from 1934 for examining the NSDAP's official publications). In the present context, however, the fierce resistance which the Church Minister Kerrl offered to any promotion for Rosenberg is of particular interest. Kerrl attached a great deal of the blame to the author of the *Myth* for the failure of his (Kerrl's) own efforts to reach a compromise between the Church and National Socialism. Thus Kerrl wrote to the Head of the Reich Chancellery on 23 December 1939: 'Over the past years the name of Rosenberg has in a way become for broad sectors of the people – rightly or wrongly – a symbol for hostility towards the Church and Christianity.'

And in a departmental meeting on 10 February 1940 in which Rosenberg also took part, Kerrl underlined his objection:

He saw a danger in Rosenberg's appointment because in view of the prevailing uncertainty about the concept of 'ideology' in relation to religion the appointment of Reichsleiter Rosenberg must be seen as a move against Christianity and the Church. But the Third Reich needs Christianity and the Churches because it has nothing to replace the Christian religion and Christian morality. The fact that it is essential to reject the present form of the Church, which stems from a politically outmoded era, does not alter this fact. Among the people, Rosenberg counts as the exponent of the anti-Church, anti-Christian trend.

His appointment will result in marked unrest among the people, which is precisely what we must avoid under all circumstances during the war.[61]

On 21 February Lammers noted that he had 'spoken with the Führer today': 'The Führer reluctantly agreed with the objection raised by the Reich Church Minister. Therefore the Führer has been unable to sign any of the submitted drafts.'[62]

Although Kerrl's position in the structure of the National Socialist regime was itself conceivably weak and was to be still further weakened, this evidence is none the less quite typical. Later, too, when Heydrich and individual Gauleiter tried to use the War precisely for intensifying the struggle against the Church, when Bormann roundly declared in an internal circular of June 1941, that 'National Socialism and Christianity are irreconcilable', and when the clerical opposition was at the time quite openly proclaiming the criminal nature of the S.S. (Bishop Graf Galen), still Hitler continually shunned taking comprehensive steps to persecute the Churches. More than anything else, the charismatic Führer feared the unpredictability of a broad, oppositional movement of the faithful. And he probably felt instinctively that the Third Reich, as Kerrl had argued, still needed the Churches: the sound of their bells when victories were celebrated, the Church prayers for 'Führer, people and Fatherland', the piety of large sections of the population, as long as this generated political quietism.

Notes and references

1. Order of the Supreme S.A. Leader of 30 May 1933 (Epp Material IfZ: MA-1236).
2. A revealing example of this is provided by the documents contained in the files of the Reich Chancellery (BA: R43 II/1157e) on the activity of the Special Commissioner of the Reich Economics Minister for Personnel and organizational matters of the Reich Statistical Office, who was appointed under pressure from the National Socialist agents and had already brought about the suspension of the President of the Reich Office, Professor Wagemann on 17 March, as well as other leading officials.
3. Material (photocopies) on this, in IfZ: Fa 115.
4. Text of the appeal published inter alia in *Frankfurter Zeitung*, 12 March 1933.
5. *MBliV*, 1933, p. 282.
6. *Gesetz zur Wiederherstellung des Berufsbeamtentums vom 7.4.1933 in der Fassung der Änderungsgesetze vom 23.6., 20.7. und 22.9.1933 und verwandte Gesetze nebst den neuesten Durchführungsverordnungen.* Commentary by Hans Seel (Berlin, 1933).
7. Hans Mommsen, *Beamtentum in Dritten Reich. Mit ausgewählten Quellen zur nationalsozialistische Beamtenpolitik* (Stuttgart, 1966), p.'45.
8. Cf. sources in Mommsen, op. cit., pp. 159f and 163.
9. Cited according to Peter Thiele, *NSDAP und allgemeine innere Staatsverwaltung*, Phil. Diss., Munich, 1967, p. 105.
10. Epp Material, IfZ: MA-1236. There is a remarkable similarity in tone between this instruction and Oswald Spengler's roughly contemporary criticism of the National Socialist seizure of power contained in his publication *Jahre der Entscheidung* (1933): 'This is no time and occasion for celebration and feelings of triumph. Woe to those who confuse mobilization with victory! The seizure of power has been carried out amidst a maelstrom of strengths and weaknesses. I am very worried by the way it is being so noisily celebrated each day.'
11. Handwritten notes of Epp of 13 June 1933 (Epp Material, IfZ: MA-1236).
12. On this as on the related development of NSDAP membership: Ulf Lükemann, *Der Reichsschatzmeister der NSDAP. Ein Beitrag zur inneren Parteistruktur*, Phil. Diss, Free University, Berlin, 1964, pp. 30ff.
13. Cf. *Parteistatistik*, vol. 1, ed by the Reichsorganisations leiter of the NSDAP, Munich. On the basis of this estimate it states in the *Parteistatistik*, vol. 1, p. 75: 'There is no doubt here that most of the officials and teachers are opportunists ... It is advisable for the Party high-ups to keep a special eye on and to examine the officials and teaching profession...'
14. Text of the order in the *Akten des Parteiarchivs der NSDAP* (Hoover Institution, Stanford, USA), reel 50, folder 1182.
15. Protocol of the cabinet meeting of 30 June 1933, (IfZ: Fa 203/2).
16. Cf. Andreas Werner, *S.A. and NSDAP. S.A.: 'Wehrverband', 'Parteitruppe' oder 'Revolutionsarmee'. Studien zur Geschichte der S.A. und der NSDAP 1920–1933*, Phil. Diss., Erlangen, 1964, pp. 593f.
17. Cf. Mommsen, op. cit., p. 162.

18. *MBliV*, 1933, p. 553.
19. Printed in Shlomo Aronson, *Heydrich und die Anfänge des SD und der Gestapo* (1931–35), Phil. Diss., Free University, Berlin, 1967, p. 100 (there without date, but this comes from taking into account the decree of 30 October 1933 (*MBliV*, 1933, p. 1304).
20. Thus the Special Commissioner of the Supreme S.A. Leadership with the government of Upper Bavaria, S.A. Gruppenführer Schmid, wrote to the Bavarian Minister President Siebert on 1 July 1933: 'The authority of the state is being endangered by the universal and unjustified interference of political functionaries in the machinery of normal government. Every NSBO official, NSBO local branch leader, NSBO Kreisleiter ... the leader of every political base, local branch leader, political Kreisleiter is issuing orders, which impinge on the lower command structures of the Ministries, that is to say in the authority of the Kreis governments, district offices, right down to the smallest outpost of the rural constabulary. Everybody is arresting someone ... everybody is threatening somebody with Dachau. Businesses are being forced to dismiss any number of employees, without any knowledge of the facts, businesses are forced to take on employees ... Uncertainty about authority has set in right down to the smallest rural police station, which is most certainly bound to have a disastrous and disruptive affect on the state' (Epp Material, IfZ: MA-1236).
21. *Völkischer Beobachter*, 7 July 1933.
22. Circular of the Prussian Minister of the Interior of 2 August 1933 (*MBliV*, p. 932a).
23. Cf. *JMBl*, 1933, pp. 235 and 249. Also on this Rudolf Diels, *Lucifer ante portas* (Stuttgart, 1950), p. 311 and the Nuremberg 'Juristenprozess' (III), Prot. (d), p. 4437. The central public prosecutor's office, which was transferred to the Reich Ministry of Justice in 1934, was dismantled in 1937 at the Party's urging.
24. On the foregoing, Martin Broszat; 'Nationalsozialistische Konzentrationslager 1933–1945', in *Anatomie des SS-Staates* (Olten, Freiburg, 1965), vol. 2 pp. 24ff.
25. Diels, op. cit., pp. 394ff.
26. Cf. Broszat, 'Nationalsozialistische Konzentrationslager', p. 34.
27. Cited in P. Thiele, op. cit., p. 316.
28. Ibid., p. 118.
29. Protocol of the meeting in BA: R43 II/1392, where it says of Hitler's remarks: '... it was urgently necessary to dispose immediately of revolutionary manifestations. There was no longer any sort of revolutionary National Socialist aim in Germany. Behind those forces who vainly pursued those sorts of aims there lurked in reality the old political order. Those elements were the stooges of the Reich Chancellor's political enemies. This was particularly obvious if one remembered that the Reich government and all the Land governments were now in fact National Socialist. He knew well enough that there were many unhappy creatures whose ambition had not been satisfied. Obviously, no attention would be paid to these. He would not tolerate the conduct of such individuals for much longer, but would suddenly interfere.'

30. Circular of the Prussian Minister präsident of 30 October 1933 (*MBliV*, p. 1304).
31. BA: R43 II/1392.
32. The *Organisationsbuch der NSDAP*, ed. by Reichsorganisationsleiter of the NSDAP (Ley), (Munich, 1938), says (p. 487): 'The great Senate envisaged for later will constitute a further link between Party and state. The great Senate is a purely Party institution, which will at the same time be the supreme state authority.'
33. Testimony of Walter Buch in the statement of 16 May 1947 (IfZ: ZS 855).
34. *Zusammenstellung der bis zum 31.3.1937 erlassenen und noch gültigen Anordnungen des Stellvertreters des Führers* (intended only for official reference) (Munich, 1937), p. 20.
35. Also known as the Second Law for Securing the Unity of State and Party (*RGBl*; 1935, I, p. 502). This law ordered the formal dissolution of the NSDAP as a registered society in the register of societies and at the same time drew a more exact distinction between 'auxiliary formations' (*Gliederungen*) and 'affiliated associations' of the NSDAP. To the former, which had no separate legal identity and no assets of their own, belonged the S.A., S.S., NSKK, the Hitler Youth, the National Socialist League of German Students and National Socialist Womanhood; to the latter, with their own legal identity and assets (admittedly under the supervision of the Reich Treasurer of the NSDAP) belonged, the National Socialist League of German Physicians, the League of National Socialist German Lawyers, the National Socialist League of Teachers, the National Socialist Public Welfare, the National Socialist Care of War Victims, the Reich League of German Civil Servants – all registered associations – and the National Socialist League of German Technicians and the German Labour Front.
36. Thus the former Ministerialrat in the Reich Ministry of Finance, Paul Schmidt-Schwarzenburg, reported in an affidavit of 10 June 1948 that during the years of 1933/4 it was not only the top S.A. leadership which 'was always coming with new demands for money to the Reich Finance Ministry', which made for 'lasting conflicts' because the representatives of the S.A. 'were not prepared to justify adequately their claims for finance nor to give the required information on the use of the funds in question'. The Reich Treasurer too, who had also finally (1934/5) 'intervened rigorously against the mismanagement of the NSDAP' and no longer put up with the fact 'that as well as his own representatives, representatives of the auxiliary formations were negotiating with the Reich Minister of Finance', had not normally 'been prepared ... to give the required information on the strength, composition, business needs, equipment etc. of the auxiliary formations. Instead the Reich Treasurer of the NSDAP contented himself with the repeated justification that the Party and its auxiliary formations were carrying out sovereign state duties and the examination of the regularity and efficiency of any measures needing to be taken was the sole responsibility of the Reich Treasurer.' Thus Schwarz's representative Damson often preferred to deal with the State Secretary (Reinhardt), who as an old fighter and occupant of

high Party rank perhaps had access to more detailed confidential information. In this context Schmidt-Schwarzenberg affirmed that for
the financial years 1934 and 1935 the yearly Reich contribution for the
auxiliary formations of the NSDAP (excluding the concentration
camps, troop detachments, funds for pre-military training through the
S.A., Austrian Legion and other special funds) came to about 50 million RM, that in 1936 this rose to 70 million, by 1937 to 100 million
and subsequently (largely due to Party buildings, the development of
the Party organizations, the setting-up of many new offices for the
Party's economic, legal, labour and cultural advisers etc.) still more
steeply (1938, 145 million; 1939, 245 million; 1940, 270 million; 1941,
320 million; 1942, 400 million; 1943, 450 million; and 1944, 500 million). IfZ: ZS 511.

37. Cf. *Völkischer Beobachter*, 9 November 1933.
38. Contained in *Akten des Hauptarchives der NSDAP* (Hoover Institution, Stanford, USA), reel 54, folder 12901.
39. Thus it was doubtless on Hitler's urging that Hess wrote in the *Völkischer Beobachter* on 22 January 1934: 'Today and indeed in the future there is not the slightest need for the S.A. and other such organizations to go their own way ... On the contrary, it would endanger
the whole if they put their own interests above those of the Party as a
whole. And they would never meet with the Führer's approval.'
Schwerin-Krosigk stated later (7 Aug. 1952) that from the beginning
of 1934 Hitler had repeatedly urged him (Schwerin-Krosigk) to refuse
Röhm's demands, which Hitler himself did not want to do directly,
for money (30 million RM per month) for military equipment and
the development of the S.A., on the grounds of the financial situation
of the Reich. Cf. IfZ: ZS 145.
40. In an undated memorandum of Reich Governor von Epp of April or
May 1934, in which Epp described 'the security of the authoritarian
legal order' as the 'precondition of our internal well-being', he specifically commented that the directive of 10 July 1933 to the Reich Governors for ending the revolution had 'not had the expected success',
largely 'because the relevant instructions had not yet been given to
the S.A.' (Epp Material, IfZ: MA-1236).
41. Cf. on detail Hans Buchheim, 'Die organisatorische Entwicklung der
politischen Polizei in Deutschland in den Jahren 1933 und 1934', in
Gutachten des Instituts für Zeitgeschichte (Munich, 1958), pp. 294ff.
42. Hans Buchheim, 'Die SS- das Herrenschaftsinstrument', in *Anatomie
des SS-Staates* (Olten, Freiburg, 1965), vol. 1, pp. 13ff.
43. Cf. Helmut Krausnick, 'Der 30 Juni 1934. Bedeutung-Hintergründe-
Verlauf', in *Aus Politik und Zeitgeschichte*, *Beilage zur Wochen-
zeitung 'Das Parlament'*, 30 June 1954.
44. Cf. Klaus-Jürgen Müller, 'Reichswehr und "Röhm-Affäre". Aus den
Akten des Wehrkreiskommandos VII', in *Militärgeschichtliche Mit-
teilungen*, ed. Militärgeschichtlichen Forschungsamt (Freiburg), no. 1/
1968, p. 117.
45. Among other things a letter of Göring's of 31 August 1934 to Hess is
symptomatic in this context, when the former declared on the basis of
the situation reports of the Prussian Oberpräsidenten and Regierungspräsidenten, that a further purging was needed not only of the S.A.

but of the whole Party apparatus, of 'elements against which the people rightly take offence', in order to 'improve the mood' in what was still a bleak economic situation (BA: R43 II/1263).

46. An example of this were the extracts sent to the Reich Chancellery at the beginning of 1934 from a letter from an unidentified but highly placed person to the Reich President dated 13 January, which said that the unity of the nation could only be preserved 'if the top leaders were strong enough to make a timely intervention and dispose of those leaders lower down who are not suitable and thus not worthy to be called leader' (BA: R43 II/193).

47 Thus according to estimates of the German Foreign Office; cf. *Documents on German Foreign Policy* (hereafter cited as *DGFP*), series C, vol. 1, no. 456.

48. Concerning the setting up and content of three interviews which Hitler gave to Ward Price in mid-October 1933, mid-February 1934, and the beginning of June 1934, see *Akten der Reichskanzlei*, BA: R43 II/474. An extract is given below from Price's piece on the interview of 16 February 1934, three weeks after the surprising conclusion of the German–Polish non-aggression pact of 26 January 1934, as an example of this disarming interview technique. Price wrote: 'I told the Chancellor that his Peace Pact with Poland has come as a great surprise to the outside world, and that some people explained it as being intended to form the basis of an ultimate joint attack by Germany and Poland upon Russia with a view to acquiring territory.' As to Hitler's reply, Price reported: 'He laughed incredulously; "What? We take territory from Russia? Ridiculous".' Typically, however, Price did not put the obvious question to Hitler about what importance was to be attached to remarks to the contrary in *Mein Kampf* and instead tried to reassure his English readers with his own explanation. 'I would add here on my own account that although Herr Hitler, in his book *Mein Kampf*, written ten years ago, recommends to Germany the aim of acquiring territory in Russia as a home for future settlers, the fall in the German birth rate which has taken place since then has stopped the expansion of the country's population, so that the need for increased territory is less urgent.'

49. Rosenberg's debut in London caused a storm of indignation in the British press and in the House of Commons and Prime Minister MacDonald also refused to receive Rosenberg. The German Ambassador von Hoesch wrote with barely concealed satisfaction to the German Foreign Office on 15 May 1933 that the visit was going extremely badly and had not produced 'any improvement whatever in the atmosphere here'. Cf. *DGFP*, series C, vol. I, no. 237. Similarly blunt criticism of clumsy and undiplomatic behaviour by leading National Socialists was made at the same time on the occasion of the visit of the Reichsleiter of the NSDAP and Bavarian Minister of Justice Dr Hans Frank in Austria. Cf. memorandum of 19 May 1933 of the Head of Political Division II in the German Foreign Office, Ministerialdirektor Köpke (*DGFP*, series C, vol. 1, no. 249).

50. *Das politische Tagebuch Alfred Rosenbergs 1934/5 und 1939/40*, ed. by Hans-Günther Seraphim (Göttingen, Frankfurt-on-Main, Berlin, 1956).

51. On the following see especially, Dieter Ross, *Hitler und Dollfuss. Die deutsche Österreich-Politik 1933–34* (Hamburg, 1966). Here the heterogeneous aims and forces are especially emphasized which produced this policy and its fluctuations.

52. Figures for Berlin in Friedrich Zipfel, *Kirchenkampf in Deutschland 1933–45* (Berlin, 1965), p. 18f.

53. Cf. Hans Buchheim, *Glaubenkrise im Dritten Reich* (Stuttgart, 1953), pp. 89f.

54. Friedrich Zipfel, op. cit., p. 40.

55. Cf. the documentation, 'Ein NS-Funktionär zum Niemöller-Prozess', in *VJHZ*, 4, 1956, p. 313.

56. Zipfel, op. cit., p. 91.

57. Zipfel, op. cit., p. 94.

58. BA: R43 II/525.

59. As is apparent from a written remark of 2 January 1939 in the files of the Reich Chancellery, Knipfer had stated during the hearing on 12 November 1938 that 'Hobohm was known to him as a decent and honourable character of strong convictions. He had a very good teaching record and enjoyed the confidence of the pupils to a considerable degree. But it was precisely because of this influence over the young that he felt that [Hobohm] was dangerous as an educator and especially as a teacher of history.'

60. The whole process in BA: R43 II/447.

61. BA: R43 II/1200a. Here too other events leading up to comprehensive authorization desired by Rosenberg to 'protect the National Socialist ideology'.

62. BA: R43 II/1200a.

Chapter Seven

The civil service and the administration

The attitude and policy of the new rulers towards the civil service and the bureaucratic corporations of the state administration was bound to be of particular importance for the development of National Socialist control. From the beginning two conflicting tendencies were evident.

The one, represented particularly by Reich Minister of the Interior Frick, by the National Socialist League of Civil Servants and also by the youthful elements in the state apparatus who were sympathetic to the National Socialist movement, started from a basically positive appraisal of the professional civil service and tried to encourage the trend towards an authoritarian state run by civil servants which had been launched during the period of emergency government, and to take this further in conjunction with the National Socialist leader principle in the direction of providing an elite leadership role for the civil service in the National Socialist state. It was believed that with National Socialism a united common will had again come into being, as in old Prussian times. In contrast to the changing governments and political aims of the Weimar Republic this offered the chance for a new state bureaucracy, educated in the spirit of National Socialism, to escape from the role of the subordinate executive and instead to take over responsible and 'creative' leadership duties, thus becoming a 'genuine pillar of the National Socialist state'.[1] In the National Socialist call for abandoning the caste privileges which still pertained to some extent in the recruitment of the civil service, and for giving up its one-sided legal training in favour of an unconditional application of the principle of ability and a more pragmatic and political schooling, hope was seen for creating a new type of 'administration leader', such as the National Socialist Minister for Justice, Kerrl, tried to create in Prussia in 1933 (for the rising generation of justice officials), among other things by setting up training centres for junior barristers. Closely linked with these ideas was the call for rationalizing the administration and for a greater concentration of specialist departments under the heads of the internal administration at the different levels of the state (Reich,

Länder, provinces, Regierungsbezirke, Stadtkreise and Landkreise).

The other strand of civil service policy, most noticeable among the majority of the 'old fighters' and NSDAP functionaries, started from a basic distrust of the civil service. Instead a 'state within a state' opposed to the National Socialist claim to leadership was seen in the special rights of the civil service and in its traditionally strong cohesion, in the homogeneity of the bureaucracy on the basis of similar education and origin, in the usual selection procedures for filling the posts in the higher service and also in the overwhelmingly conservative attitude of the civil servants. As a result the main effort here was to exert permanent pressure by infiltrating the bureaucracy with reliable National Socialists, by Party consultation in the matter of civil service appointments as well as by other means, and to set up a system of control for the civil servants.

The two trends need not have been diametrically opposed since Frick, for example, also strove for a bureaucracy sympathetic to National Socialism and he approved the co-operation of the Party in the appointment of top civil servants, as was provided in the Municipal Code of 1935. The fact that in spite of this the inclination towards schooling and controlling the bureaucracy increasingly came into conflict with the ideas of an authoritarian 'Leader-state' was ultimately due above all to the fact that the National Socialist ideal of the politically united state, which was the premise of the advocates of the more elitist conception of a National Socialist civil service, was a thoroughly inappropriate fiction. National Socialist schooling could never result in a training for the compact corps of state leaders because of the irrational, voluntaristic character of the National Socialist leader principle, but was bound to have an irritating and disruptive effect in view of the administration's traditional code of duty and its bureaucratic and legalistic *modus operandi*. Also the notion of a decentralized, independent administrative leadership and administrative concentration was opposed to the inevitable departmental centralization and the polyocracy of government departments, which was encouraged and reinforced precisely because Hitler identified the activity of the state almost exclusively with the effectiveness of the executive measures having priority at any given moment, and he was uninterested to an extreme degree in questions concerning the administrative order and the long-term internal organization of the state. These two conflicting tendencies clearly came into play even in the early stages of the Third Reich over the question of political purging and civil service personnel policy.

The attempt to get control of the key positions in the state administration which Göring was already making in February 1933 and which then assumed massive and revolutionary proportions, was in this respect the least difficult problem, since here it was mainly a matter of 'dispensable' political officials (State Secretaries, Oberprä-

sidenten, Regierungs-präsidenten, police chiefs, regional councillors) who could be displaced legally or prematurely pensioned off.
But no doubt it was already apparent here that the NSDAP hardly
had a sufficiently trained reserve to man these leading positions
with anything like as well qualified experts. The most radical and
sweeping change over to National Socialist personnel occurred
among the Prussian Oberpräsidenten and the police chiefs.[2] When
it came to the burgomasters of the towns and above all the local
authorities, where equally drastic changes were enforced, the
NSDAP was already obliged to a considerable extent to resort to
people who had first joined the Party after 30 January 1933.
According to the official Party figures for 1935, of the total 2,228
town chief burgomasters and burgomasters, 1,049 (47 per cent)
were old Party members, 694 (31 per cent) new Party members
and 485 (22 per cent) non-Party members. As to the 49,443 municipal burgomasters the situation was still less favourable to the
NSDAP: 9,517 (19.3 per cent) old Party members, 20,114 (40.6
per cent) new Party members, 19,812 (40.1 per cent) non-Party
members. Also, as matters stood in 1935, among the total of 689
regional councillors the situation was similar: 198 (28.8 per cent)
old Party members, 235 (34 per cent) new Party members, 256
(37.2 per cent) non-Party members.[3] A later report of the Reich
Minister of the Interior of May 1941 concerning the staffing of the
regional councillors' offices in the Reich[4] contains further information on this point. From these it is evident that at that time (1941)
in Prussia only 66 of the total 365 regional councillors' offices, that
is barely a fifth, were staffed with personnel who had occupied this
office before 1933. In between, however, the majority of these had
likewise joined the Party (in 1941 in Prussia there were only 11 regional councillors who did not belong to the NSDAP; 152 Prussian
regional councillors had joined the Party after 30 January 1933).
About half of the total (365) consisted of administration specialists,
the other half of people without any training in government. In the
Länder outside Prussia, with a total of 304 regional councillors, in
1941 the number of non-Party members had also fallen to 11, but
the number of old Party members (42) and especially that of the
inexperienced administrators (9) was significantly smaller, because in
the Länder outside Prussia even the Reich Governors and the
National Socialist Ministers of the Interior mostly dared not disturb
the particularly well-developed tradition (above all in South Germany) of having legally trained top government officials.

In view of the non-National Socialist Ministers in the Reich
cabinet or because of the preference for expertise rather than
loyalty, the old Party members were also relatively thinly spread in
the highest posts in the ministerial bureaucracy. Even among the
state secretaries to the Reich Ministers the only ones who could
count as old Party functionaries were really Reinhardt (Ministry of

Finance), Freisler,[5] (Ministry of Justice), Darré's state secretaries Willikens and Backe, the state secretary for the voluntary Labour Service, responsible to the Reich Minister for Labour, Hierl, and the state secretary in the Ministry of Propaganda, Funk. State secretaries Zschintzsch (Ministry of Education), Pfundtner and Stuckart (Minister of the Interior) and Lammers (Reich Chancellery) were trained lawyers or government officials and only joined the NSDAP later; the state secretaries in the German Foreign Office (von Bülow, 1937: von Mackensen, from 1938; von Weizsäcker), in the Ministry for Economics (Posse), in the Ministry for Labour (Krohn), in the Ministry for Transport (Koenigs) in the Ministry of Post (Ohnesorge) and in the Air Ministry (Milch) were like the first state secretary in the Ministry of Justice (Schlegelberger), impartial professionals.

The number of Party members was far smaller among the ministerial officials who were absolutely essential. In a critical memorandum on 'National Socialist personnel policy in the central authorities', S.A. Obersturmbannführer von Helms complained in May 1934 that the positions of personnel heads in the Ministries were most certainly not filled (as had been foreseen in a circular of Frick's of 14 July 1933)[6] by 'reliable National Socialists', and that old Party members only played a dwindling role in the ministerial bureaucracy; 'there is a great danger that in the foreseeable future even National Socialist heads of authorities will only have a bureaucratic apparatus behind them whose members will be devoid of any true National Socialist values.'[7] As an example Helms cited the Prussian Ministry of the Interior, in which there were only 18 old Party members, 29 new Party members and about 20 Party applicants among a total of 270 ministerial officials of the upper, middle and lower range, whilst most of the 200 officials have 'not even deemed it necessary . . . to become a member of the Party'.[8] Even at the beginning of 1938 the Führer's Deputy complained in a critical communication on the personnel policy of the Ministry of Labour that among the 38 ministerial councillors in his Ministry there were only five Party members, who had all joined the NSDAP after 1933.[9] Conditions were similar in most of the other Ministries and also in the subordinate specialist departments.

Thus the fact that the execution of the Law on the Professional Civil Service of 7 April 1933 was entrusted to the heads of the state authorities and that the Party could only recommend dismissals from the service through their reports, was an essential precedent for civil service policy. Because National Socialist departmental heads like Frick accepted the principle of the professionally trained civil servant and numerous adverse experiences with National Socialist functionaries who were installed in the administration at the beginning strengthened the conviction that the National Socialist state also had to preserve the principle of the professional civil service with a settled career structure, including the retention of the system of grades, standardized conditions of promotion and the absolute validity of the supervisory and disciplinary powers of the authorities, the opportunities for Party political influence were limited from the outset once the Law for the Restoration of the Professional Civil Service had diverted the process of political purging into legal channels. Dismissal from the service on political grounds, which was made possible by this law, was strictly enforced chiefly in regard to Communist and also mainly against Social Democratic officials. In addition there was a general dismissal of Jewish civil servants (until 1935 with the exception of those First World War participants who had been at the front). But since both categories played only a small role numerically in most departments (especially in the specialist departments) the effects of this law undoubtedly fell below Party expectations.

Although hardly more than 1 to 2 per cent of the total of 1,500,000 civil servants were retired or dismissed without pension from the service on political or racial grounds (the law also provided for early retirement and displacement to a lower office to rationalize the administration or because of insufficient qualifications) this is not all that significant in view of the fact that the higher civil servants in what were the most politically important inner circles of the administration were in general much more heavily 'purged'[10] than those in the middle and lower ranks of the service or in the specialist departments. For all that, this low figure confirms that it is impossible to speak of a revolutionary restructuring of the civil service; instead the projected overhaul was 'largely forestalled by the internal cohesion of the civil service apparatus'.[11]

Besides, the application of the law restoring the professional civil service became more liberal and flexible after the period originally envisaged for its completion (up to 31 Dec. 1933) was extended several times as a result of the complexity of the process ('proof of Aryan status' among other things), and in between the basic political tendency had set in towards ending the National Socialist revolution. The former S.A. Deputy for Police Department Personnel matters in the Prussian Ministry of the Interior (von Helms) was not far wrong when he wrote at the end of May 1934:

Already people again dare to defame those old, tried fighters of the movement who were taken into the administration on political grounds to form a counterweight to outdated, outmoded and less reliable, dead old stock, by accusing them of having insufficient knowledge and recommending them to get some experience in administration.[12]

Typically, by spring and summer 1933, even the new National Socialist heads of departments, for example Frick and Göring, were already categorically refusing any right of consultation of the Party's civil service organization when appointing officials. And in the most National Socialist department, the Reich Ministry for People's Enlightenment and Propaganda, the Minister (Goebbels) insisted on the observance of official channels in an internal circular of 11 April 1934:

The Reich Ministry for People's Enlightenment and Propaganda is a National Socialist Ministry. It will be conducted in practice and in terms of personnel along strictly National Socialist lines. The important posts of the Ministry are almost exclusively staffed by long-standing and reliable National Socialists. Under these circumstances it is inadmissable for subordinate officers in the Ministry, when having differences of opinion with superiors, who have been appointed by the Minister himself . . . to involve themselves with civil service or Party offices outside this Ministry . . . And the Minister himself is Gauleiter of Berlin and a member of the NSDAP's Reich directorate. Thus the Party is anchored in the Ministry even in its highest office. For all these reasons I absolutely forbid any going outside official channels with those recurrent difficulties which inevitably arise daily within the department. In future such attempts will be punished by immediate dismissal or disciplinary action.[13]

The circular quoted above shows not only that even in the Ministries which were strongly National Socialist in terms of personnel, the internal solidarity and the official hierarchy of the authority was emphasized against external Party political influences. In addition the self-confident language of the circular makes it clear that in the structure of the Hitler state the highest degree of power and authority could be claimed precisely where Party and state offices were as closely enmeshed in personnel terms or institutionally as they were in Goebbels's Ministry.

The opposite example of a National Socialist head of department who lacked the Party political powers corresponding to his authority in the state was the Minister for Education, Bernhard Rust, who not least for this reason was forced to assign some duties to Goebbels and obliged to watch whilst cultural policy was increasingly transferred to other state and Party offices. One of the intermittent co-workers of Rust, the provisional Director of the Office for Science in the Reich Ministry of Educaton, Dr Otto Wacker (also S.S. Oberführer and National Socialist Education Minister in Baden) recognized the Rust Ministry's weakness very clearly. In a long letter which Wacker sent to Rust on 3 November 1938 (a copy went to the Reich S.S. Leader at the same time), he attributed the fact 'that in the field of cultural policy . . . a range of larger and powerful forces was active whose work . . . ran parallel', chiefly to the 'lack of any constructive relationship between the head of the Ministry and the Party', 'in contrast to other Reich authorities' where there was a closer link between Party and state in the form of a personal union. Since the 'political position of the Reich Ministry of Education was actually very weak', the settlement of important questions through the Ministry was made vastly more difficult. As soon as 'larger issues of more far-reaching importance come up, especially matters concerning fundamentally new creations in a National Socialist spirit, the weakness of the Reich Ministry of Education as a purely state body confined to the state sector is mercilessly exposed'. Wacker pleaded that at least in the area of scientific policy an 'organizational link should be set up between the head of the Office for Science in the Reich Education Ministry and a corresponding post in the NSDAP', and it can hardly be doubted that here he was thinking of a link with the Reich S.S. Leader, who (through Heydrich) also informed Hitler of Wacker's idea.[14]

It was apparent, however, precisely in the sector of education and cultural policy, that a *Party political* task, such as that of Rosenberg as the 'Führer's Deputy for the supervision of the overall spiritual and ideological schooling and education of the NSDAP' or of Ley, with the Education Office of the Reichsorganisationsleiter of the NSDAP, was no more of an aid to top political power and importance than the authority derived from the *state* alone.

The foregoing digression showed sufficiently clearly that the relative stability of the old civil service corps was not particularly informative on the greater or lesser political importance of the individual ministerial and administrative departments in the Third Reich, but that in the last resort these issues were decided much more by factors other than that of civil service policy. However, although it was increasingly, and ultimately to an extreme degree, the case that the actual authority of individual departments in the Hitler state could only be consolidated if it was rooted in Party political power (or in some authority granted personally and directly from Hitler), then such a penetration of the normal divisions of authority within the state by the changing and uncertain power structures of the National Socialist movement and Führer clientele, was only possible in the first place because the idea (nourished by Frick and others) of a possible marriage between the authoritarian administration and the National Socialist leadership principle to make up the 'total state' did not have the desired result. Instead the relatively successful defence of their autonomy by the administration and the civil service brought with it, or rather strengthened, the tendency to disavow these politically or to reduce their importance.

Admittedly in the years 1933/4 this development was not yet inevitable. It was still possible to believe that the concept of the authoritarian and centrally governed state was also being realized through the monopoly of the state's civil service policy. In this sense it could also be seen as a victory when after the burdensome S.A. Special Commissioners were disposed of in summer 1934, Party collaboration in the Reich government's policy and legisla-

tion affecting personnel was confined solely to the position of
the Führer's Deputy.

By means of a circular to the Reich Ministers Hitler had at first
'decreed' on 27 July 1934 that 'the Führer's Deputy, Reich Minister Hess, has the position of a participating Reich Minister in the
working out of draft laws in all the Reich departments.'[15] When as
a consequence of taking over the Reich President's office the right
to appoint civil servants also fell to the Führer, and on 1 February
1935 the relevant Führer decrees had ordered that Hitler personally reserved to himself the right to appoint the Reich and Land civil
servants in the higher ranks (from salary groups A2c),[16] the
Führer's Deputy promptly claimed a share in these civil service
appointments on 7 February: The political opinion to be given by
the Party (alongside the opinion on professional qualifications by
the respective head of department) must 'be brought to the
Führer's attention without fail' in order to facilitate any decision
and to 'guarantee the creation of a sound National Socialist higher
civil service corps'.[17] On 24 September, after more negotiations in
which the Munich Gauleiter Wagner was also involved on the Party's behalf, there was a 'Decree of the Führer and Reich Chancellor' which envisaged the participation of the Führer's Deputy in all
civil service appointments to be made by Hitler personally.[18] But
unlike the sphere of municipal administration the Party was given
no right to make recommendations. Instead the practice recommended by the Reich Minister of the Interior was established,
whereby the appointments proposed by the departments could be
regarded as approved by the Führer's Deputy if the latter had
raised no objection to the recommended appointment within three
or four weeks.[19] Because of this regulation the normal process of
civil service appointments remained in practice an internal matter
of the authority concerned and Party intervention occurred only in
exceptional cases. The fact that the Führer's Deputy agreed to this
practice was probably chiefly due to the structure and weakness of
the apparatus available to Hess's staff for this purpose.

When the Führer's Deputy was given the right to participate in
legislation in July 1934, Hess and his Staff Chief Bormann set up a
special division alongside the political division responsible for Party
affairs (Division II)[20] for so called 'constitutional' issues (Division
III). This served as it were as the ministerial office of the Führer's
Deputy and since it dealt exclusively with bills and civil service
questions it seemed to Hess absolutely essential to transfer the
work of this division to experienced administrative officials familiar
with the law. Its director (with the rank of Ministerialrat) was (until 1941) Walther Sommer, an administration lawyer and NSDAP
member from Thuringia, who had been president of the Land
administrative court and of the Thuringian disciplinary court. At
first Sommer had only a small staff of officials to hand, who were

all, like him, civil servants and who were loaned to the Brown
House in Munich at the request of the Führer's Deputy by the respective Reich or Land departments in the normal way of transferring civil servants. Division III of the Führer's Deputy which was
responsible for 'supervising' the government's legislation and personnel policy and which like the separate Ministries was divided into respective sections for internal, legal and economic policy, was
thus in both civil service and budgetary terms itself a part of the
state administration. Inevitably, therefore, the officials who were
attached to this division for a few years by different Ministries or
other state departments – who were admittedly as a rule Party
members but by and large not old members and functionaries of
the NSDAP[21] – did not adopt a radical Party line on legislative and
civil service issues but instead exercised a mediating role between
the Party offices and the state Ministries, particularly since the latter continued to be their parent authorities and certainly very often
expected support from them.[22] At any rate, it is certain that the
constitutional division of the Office of the Führer's Deputy (from
1941 Party Chancellery under the direction of Bormann) was little
suited to translate into practice the words so readily cited in Party
circles: 'The Party commands the state.' It was more the case that
here a 'nationalization' of the responsible sector of the Party Chancellery took place. This did not have to mean inevitably a weakening of Party collaboration in the legislation and civil service policy
of the government if a strong, tightly organized NSDAP Reich
directorate had stood behind Hess's staff. As this was not the
case, and neither was the Party's will effectively co-ordinated and
concentrated elsewhere, the staff of the Führer's Deputy under the
command of the weak Hess could never be a particularly strong
counterweight to the will of the government as long as the Reich
Ministers voted to some extent unanimously on basic issues.

All the same, the judgement on political reliability required of
the high-ups of the NSDAP in matters of civil service appointments and promotions for which the Führer's Deputy was responsible at the government level, had far-reaching effects on the state
civil service. The need of many officials to be in the Party's 'good
books', as well as in those of their superiors in the service, greatly
affected the traditional civil service conception of duty, created
standing conflicts between duty to the service and career ambitions
and put into question one of the most important principles of the
professional civil service – the right to promotion according to
length of service. For this reason the civil service Minister, Frick,
and other departmental heads also opposed the view of the
Führer's Deputy that a negative political judgement by the Party
on a civil servant or civil service candidate irrevocably bound the
authority head and thus became a sort of Party right of veto. Later
in 1937/8 a compromise was reached whereby the Ministers could

air their views to Hitler against such a use of the veto so that in specific cases appointments and promotions according to a Minister's suggestion were possible (in spite of a hostile opinion of the Party).[23]

Only the armed forces were able to continue to escape such Party influences and to prevent military duty from coming into conflict with considerations of Party political reliability. The Defence Ministry had already forbidden Reichswehr personnel to be simultaneously S.A. members after the Röhm affair. And after the reintroduction of conscription (16 March 1935) the Defence Ministry secured the provision in paragraph 26 of the new National Service Law of 25 January 1935 (*RGBl*, I, p. 609), that servicemen should forgo any political activity and suspend their membership of the NSDAP and any of its ancillary organizations 'for the duration of active military service'. In the unpublished explanation of the National Service law it said on this point that servicemen 'were subject to a special structure of command and discipline and a clear separation of conflicting authorities (armed forces and Party) is essential'.[24]

The officials, employees and workers of the armed forces were, however, allowed, on the basis of a directive of the Defence Minister on 10 September 1935 to the Supreme Commander of the three armed forces, membership of the NSDAP and its ancillary organizations and associations, but the assumption of any Party offices was forbidden. The directive in general also stressed for the civil servants of the armed forces the absolute binding force of the military offficial channels: 'Only the official channels of the armed forces are responsible for settling service matters. The duty to maintain confidentiality on official matters also applies towards the Party.'[25] Hitler accepted this without protest[26] and faced with the resolute desire of the armed forces, he also decided on 25 October 1935 that the participation of the Führer's Deputy in civil service appointments 'shall not be applicable in the case of the armed forces'.[27] After tensions between the Party and armed forces and especially between the armed forces and the S.S. had generated a good deal of misgiving among the conservative Officer Corps of the Army in the second half of 1934, which among other things was inflamed by the conflicts over the Evangelical Church, Hitler felt obliged to adopt a course of deliberate appeasement towards the leadership of the armed forces. The efforts of the S.S. (in place of the S.A.) to maintain their own armed units, the S.S. militarized formations and the S.S. Death's Head formations in the concentration camps, were limited at the request of the Army High Command to infantry-trained forces (minus artillery) to a total strength of three regiments. Thus Hitler's promise to the leaders of the armed services of 20 August 1934, that he would regard it as 'his most sacred duty to intercede for the continuance and inviolability of the armed forces' and 'to ensure that they were the sole bearer of the nation's arms', seemed to have been kept if not strictly according to the letter, then at least in keeping with the general sense of it. And beyond this the Führer on various occasions – most notably during an address to officers and Party leaders at the Berlin State Opera on 3 January 1935 – expressed his unbounded confidence in the armed forces and was thereby able skilfully to create the impression that he, the Führer, far removed from the Party squabbles, was sincerely concerned with the partnership of the 'two pillars' of the National Socialist state (armed forces and Party). It was for this reason that not only Blomberg and Reichenau but also the Chief of the Army High Command, General von Fristsch, whom many officers regarded as the guarantor of a conservative Nationalist order against the despotism of the Party, largely exempted Hitler from their criticism of the Party and they personally and their subordinates tried to adopt an attitude of loyal co-operation in the National Socialist state. Of course a deep gulf continued to exist between the conservative-authoritarian concept of the state peculiar to the armed forces, and the National Socialist movement's urge to dominate. But as the readiness of the armed forces to swear a personal oath to Hitler (in place of the oath to the constitution, people and Fatherland) had already shown, the conservative outlook of the higher Officer Corps lent itself all the more easily to the acceptance of Hitler the absolute Leader, since this idea was itself rooted in the monarchical tradition of the personal command and obedience to the person of the monarch.[28]

In contrast to the armed forces Hitler needed to take much less account of the civilian state bureaucracy after the emasculation of the S.A. How quickly the pendulum of change swung here is shown by comparing Hitler's remarks to the Gauleiter in February 1934, which demanded the strict subordination of the Party to the state, with his pronouncements in autumn 1934 at the Party rally in Nuremberg, when he proclaimed the watchword: 'The state does not command us, but we command the state.' And to the Reich Governors in November 1934 he expressed strong criticism of the political reliability of a large proportion of the civil service.[29] For this reason Hitler apparently had little interest in the early restoration by law of the 'well-earned privileges' of the professional civil service after the conclusion of the purges initiated through the Law on the Professional Civil Service of 7 April 1933. From 1934, however, the Minister of the Interior was pressing for clarification of civil service rights, especially since the ending of Land sovereignty made particularly urgent a uniform system of rights for Reich and Land civil servants. A draft of a new civil service code worked out by the Reich Minister of the Interior in agreement with the Minister of Finance was already available in 1934. Its passage was delayed, however, for over two years largely due to objections by Hitler and the Führer's Deputy until January 1937. The mere fact that in the draft a list of the special 'rights of civil servants' was drawn up alongside their 'duties' seemed to the Party to smack too much of the conception of the *Beamtenstaat*. In the end the compromise title 'Protecting the legal position of civil servants'[30] was agreed. The option also remained open (Art. 71) in the law to retire prematurely a civil servant if he 'can no longer be relied on to support the National Socialist state at all times'. Although, as we have already seen, any arbitrary application of this provision was restricted by the fact that in such cases a regular service enquiry was prescribed and dismissal could only be effected on the suggestion of the state service authorities,[31] the principle of an *impartial* professional civil service was once more expressly abandoned with these paragraphs. Hitler and Hess's staff also opposed the regulation of civil servants' pension claims envisaged in the draft law. There was not enough confidence to attack this basic pillar of the professional civil service, but for all that an express confirmation by a National Socialist law was considered to be 'politically unacceptable', because this would signify that the full-time 'dignitaries' of the NSDAP had a lesser legal standing.

In the discussion (and postponement) of the Law on the German Civil Service during these years the struggle chiefly centred on the possible conflicts between the civil servant's duties and the requirements of a functioning administration on the one hand, and the Party political claims over Party members within the bureaucracy on the other. So it was settled that civil servants who at the same time also held higher offices in the Party or in its affiliated associations (from Kreisleiter and Standartenführer upwards) should only be displaced in agreement with the Führer's Deputy. On the other hand, the completion of a National Socialist training which the Party wanted as a precondition of civil service appointments was not accepted by the departments of the Reich, since clearly defined and specific conditions of this sort could not be formulated. Also the principle of absolute obedience of civil servants to their service superiors (Art. 7) was successfully preserved. The regulation of 29 June 1937 said on this point: 'If a civil servant who is a member of the NSDAP appeals against an order of his superiors by referring to contrary orders from Party offices, the superior must examine with particular care how the interests of the state can be squared with those of the Party. In doubtful cases he has to try to resolve difficulties through discussion with the Party office... For the civil servant his superior's order is binding until a decision has been reached.' Similarly, the departments of state resolutely opposed civil servants being called to account by a Party court for anything to do with their official duties.[32] The most prolonged dispute was over a regulation requested by the Führer's Deputy, whereby the NSDAP members among the civil servants should be permitted to report on official procedures liable to damage the Party not only to their service superiors but also to the Führer's Deputy. All the departmental Ministers, including Göring and Goebbels, fiercely opposed this claim. Dr Schacht, President of the Reichsbank and Minister of Economics, declared on 7 January 1937 that such a provision was not only irrelevant since 'in the National Socialist state . . . every Minister' is bound to 'enjoy the trust of the Führer and thus of the Party', and was also 'dangerous for service discipline because it would be the official and the departmental Minister who decided in the first instance on whether the service procedures in question were injurious to the NSDAP'. In that respect the proposal did not foster unity but 'rather hostility between state and Party'.[33] Although the Führer's Deputy stuck to his proposal, Hitler finally gave in to the united resistance of the departments and decided instead that any report on procedures injurious to the Party should in addition to the service superior, go directly to the Führer, and for this purpose was to be addressed to the Head of the Reich Chancellery. This regulation (Art. 42) undoubtedly conflicted with Bormann's intentions and in the last resort was a success for the state departments over the Party. It was also due to the largely united pressure of the Ministers over this question and above all to a talk between Frick and Hitler that on 26 January 1937, Hitler declared himself in the Reich cabinet to be 'finally in agreement' with the passage of the law, even though on the very same day he had ordered a further delay on account of the disputed Article 42.[34]

The Law on the German Civil Service (*Deutsches Beamtengesetz* – DBG) of 26 January 1937 and the Reich Disciplinary Code for Civil Servants issued on the same day were, alongside the German Municipal Code of 30 January 1935, the only comprehensive body of law which the Reich Minister of the Interior could achieve in the context of the desired reform of the Reich and the projected consolidation of the authoritarian state government. For all that the legislation was a rare example of what a united cabinet could achieve under Hitler. It was soon apparent, however, that there was no hope of further advance in this direction, and instead the situation began to deteriorate.

After the passage of the DBG not only was criticism of the civil service policy of the departments intensified by the Führer's Deputy, whose spokesman was increasingly Hess's Staff Chief Reichsleiter Martin Bormann,[35] but there were also stronger public attacks by the Party against the 'reactionary' bureaucracy.

This was not simply a matter of the favourite charge of inflexibility due to 'antiquated' attitudes. On the occasion of the discussion in the Reich cabinet about altering the civil service salary structure Hitler also criticized the 'rigid salary scheme' for civil servants.

This had to be shaken up by special provisions for exceptions in favour of 'the really able', in order to give greater emphasis to the principle of ability in the administration too. Otherwise the mere 'honour of being a civil servant' could not prevent the 'brain drain' to the private business sector. Hitler, who in this context compared the parity principle of civil service pay, which in his opinion was restrictive of ability, directly with Communism,[36] touched here on a general problem of the professional civil service in our modern, mobile industrial society. It was not exactly misguided for him to want a keener proficiency drive such as prevailed in the business sector for the civil service too. The fixing of equal and more general salary rights probably irritated Hitler not least because it underlined the special position of the civil service and its status as a caste remote from the general conditions of competition, not indeed better placed in material terms but much better protected. Of course the proficiency drive was more or less ideologically and politically inherent in the National Socialist regime, for which reasons the demand to end the special rights of civil servants, which was not in itself unreasonable, was thoroughly in keeping with the National Socialist movement, for it could manipulate the individual more surely the more he was detached from the special conditions of his station.

When in 1938/9 it was a matter of setting up a new civilian administration in the newly annexed areas (Austria, the Sudeten areas, the Memel area, the reincorporated Eastern territories), Hitler took care in this way as already described in another context, to impose strict limits on the influence of the Reich Minister of the Interior and of the other departments on civil service appointments. By contrast Party influence was strengthened from the outset. A circular of 12 July 1938 from the Head of the Reich Chancellery to the Reich Ministers was typical of Hitler's more pronounced about-turn over civil service policy:

A number of separate events have led the Führer and Reich Chancellor to express himself on the implications of Article 71 of the Law on German civil servants. The Führer believes that the application of Article 71 of the DBG is not only justified in those cases in which a civil servant consciously rejects the National Socialist ideology. Article 71 of the DBG must also be applied where an official although he does not consciously or deliberately reject the National Socialist ideology reveals through the nature of the work of his office, in particular through his official or unofficial leadership, that he is emotionally or intellectually unsympathetic to the National Socialist ideology.[37]

The DBG had expressly affirmed in Article 171, paragraph 1 that in the case of officials of justice compulsory retirement according to Article 71 may 'not be based on the actual content of a decision taken in the exercise of judicial authority';[38] yet Lammers stated in the circular of 12 July 1938 already cited, that 'in the

Führer's view' this did not preclude even 'a judicial decision from being used as the excuse to initiate proceedings according to Article 71 of the DBG' if particular circumstances favoured such a course. Finally the circular stated:

The Führer wishes to remind the top service authorities responsible for the application of Art. 71 of the DBG that with regard to the interpretation given in this order they should take greater care and use stricter criteria than hitherto to ensure that those civil servants whose activitiy is no longer welcome to the Third Reich, are removed.

The more impatient, more aggressive tone of the last sentences could not be ignored. Only there was little to be done with such general 'declarations of will' by the Führer in the face of an administration dependent on clear, ascertainable facts. Which went to show that it was not without reason that for a long time Hitler had basically wanted to prevent the enactment of the DBG. Now this could no longer be so easily rescinded. The following incident was typical among others: Seven months after the order quoted above the personnel chief of the Reich Ministry of Justice, Ministerialdirektor Nadler, asked his colleague in the Chancellery, Ministerialdirektor Kritzinger, whether it was advisable to get a decision of the Führer in the many cases where the Führer's Deputy requested an application for compulsory retirement of officials of justice according to Article 71 of the DBG, but where the Minister of Justice himself could find no grounds for such action. Kritizinger, who prepared a memorandum on this on 9 February 1939, concluded after studying the text of the DBG that 'the service superior of the official . . . 'must judge for himself whether the due condition for compulsory retirement had been met'; otherwise 'I can see no reason for the responsible departmental Minister to get a 'ruling' from the Führer', considering that the latter can also order an enquiry according to Article 71 on his own authority, at any time.[39] Actually, according to the prevailing civil service law even the Führer could not simply order the dismissal of a civil servant but could only institute proceedings for compulsory retirement.

A more blatant example of the collision between the dictatorial will of the Führer and prevailing civil service law arose in spring 1940, when Hitler had learned that the officials of the German civilian government in the occupied Czech and Polish areas had had sexual relations with Polish or Czech women. He thereupon abruptly instructed Bormann to tell the Reich Minister of the Interior that he (Hitler) wanted such officials 'to be dismissed immediately from the state service and without pension'.[40] Frick, who in any case was thoroughly browbeaten by this time, was prepared in principle as a good National Socialist to go along with this order and after some delay suggested to the Reich Chancellery on 31 July 1940 that both civil servants and the civil service disiciplinary tribunals should take note of the Führer's view. As the chief representative of the Reich government, however, he wondered whether 'for reasons of equity' such a ban on sexual relations with Polish and Czech women should not be extended to all those people closely linked with the state or the Party (public service employees, servicemen, Party members), and in addition he requested from the Reich Chancellor the view of the Reichsprotektor in Prague (von Neurath) and the General Governor in Cracow (H. Frank) on the possible political consequences. In the Reich Chancellery opinion from the outset was that the action suggested by the Reich Ministry of the Interior was 'not practicable' since the legal situation simply required that formal service proceedings be taken, which would be indispensable in any case 'to establish the facts correctly'. Whereas the General Governor declared that in occupied Poland matters would be handled in accordance with the Führer's ban and 'for severe infringements . . . immediate dismissal' was foreseen, the Reichsprotektor advised against any statement to the officials 'until the will of the Führer has been fully clarified'. He had to point out in addition 'that a ban on extra-marital intercourse will be difficult to effect', especially since transgressions 'normally come to light through malicious gossip' and it was hardly desirable to encourage this. And since the ban was probably chiefly concerned to prevent mixing between races it is worth bearing in mind finally that the Czechs are 'already strongly infused with German blood' and therefore the basic issue to be clarified first is, 'to what extent Czechs can be Germanized'. Since Hitler explained to the Reichsprotektor a few days later (23 Sept. 1940) 'that the racially desirable and non anti-German elements of the Czech people can be germanized', this further complicated the problem of a sensible and legally binding definition and specification of the Führer's will. In the end the standpoint of the Head of the Reich Chancellery was accepted and on 13 December 1940 he informed the Ministry of the Interior:

There is no basis for the assumption that when expressing his will through Reichsleiter Bormann, the Führer wanted to set aside the law which he passed on 26 January 1937, for the cases coming under consideration here. The Führer's wish is rather to be understood as meaning that when the relevant facts of the case are presented, the formal service disciplinary procedure is to be initiated and carried out with all haste with the aim of dismissal from the service without pension.

At the same time, so that matters *were* accordingly interpreted (thus as it were channelling the Führer's will into legal paths), Lammers urged in a decree that all Reich authorities were generally to encourage civil servants 'to behave with dignity, on or off duty' and to draw attention to the fact that dereliction of duty could be punished as a serious offence against the service. This was especially true 'if civil servants have sexual relations with persons of Polish origin' (the Czech problem was tacitly excluded). In such a case a civil servant would have to expect prompt disciplinary action which 'according to the Führer's will ... should end in principle in dismissal from the service without a pension'. Frick followed this suggestion in a circular directive of 12 February 1941 to all the relevant Reich authorities. Thereby the 'black Peter' was finally passed on to the disciplinary courts. How these reacted in such cases as were pending is not known.

The foregoing example shows how at the hands of the state administration, which despite its political compliance was bound to cling to legally ordered procedures if it did not want to go under in turn, many arbitrary commands of the Führer were 'transformed' or else petered out. Equally, it illustrates the fact that the departments of the Reich government themselves, which ultimately were increasingly reduced to carrying out subsidiary administrative and legal work, still distilled what there was of legal formality from the most unreasonable of the Führer's pronouncements (Bormann's communication took up a full four sides!). In this way the administration conducted by the professional civil service worked like a filter of the Führer's authority. It excluded anything which could not be clothed in legal form but it zealously transformed anything which was amenable to legal dress to binding directives and decrees and in so doing first made them generally practicable.

From 1937/8 the loss of prestige and importance of the state civil service rapidly increased in tempo in spite of the relatively successful defence of its position against attempts at directly undermining it. The collapse of Frick's conception of the authoritarian National Socialist state with an elite Führer civil service as its most important pillar could be disguised neither by the introduction of civil service uniforms nor by the assumption of Party and S.S. honorary ranks by higher civil servants. The general bar on promotion for non-Party members from Ministerialrat upwards, which the Führer's Deputy desired (Bormann) in spring 1939 and which could only be fended off with effort,[41] Bormann's pressure in March 1940 to consider more the political aspects of civil service promotion instead of 'considerations related to length of service' (the fact that a civil servant had not violated the political principles of National Socialism was not sufficient proof of reliability)[42] and other examples of criticism which Hitler made of the Reich Minister of the Interior's civil service policy, chiefly through Bormann, and which were increasingly sharp in the early years of the War – all show the failure of Frick's ideas. In a letter from Frick to Hitler at this time,[43] the Reich Minister of the Interior stated resignedly:

I have, my Führer, always seen it as my duty as your civil service Minister since 1933, to make available to you for the great tasks of state policy a highly qualified professional civil service and to develop in it the old Prussian conception of duty as well as the National Socialist character, as is the case with the German armed forces. The course of the last years makes me doubt, however, whether my efforts can in any way be regarded as successful. To an ever growing degree, according to the agreed observations of my department and all other departments, bitter feelings are spreading in the professional civil service about the lack of appreciation of their abilities and services as well as of unjustified neglect. The feeling of being left defenceless is beginning to cripple the best creative forces ... There can no longer be any talk whatever of the professional civil service being preferred as a body enjoying the special trust of the state leadership ... Above and beyond this the civil service is subjected in public, indeed even in the Party press, to every possible charge. In part this is due to false information but also in part to ignorance or even malicious distortion, and occasional mistakes of the sort which arise in any large organization become the starting-point for irresponsible generalizations reminiscent of the worst periods of the class war ... The civil service is also suffering badly from the fact that new tasks are not being entrusted to it, but to the Party organizations, although this often concerns genuine administrative duties ...

The last of Frick's complaints quoted here shows how the checkmating of the civil service in the traditional administration chiefly succeeded. However little headway was made in remodelling the inner structures of the conservative state bureaucracy in order to create a blind following of the Führer (even if Party infiltration, control and disavowal severely undermined the former homogeneity and the former self-confidence of the civil service), the emasculation of the bureaucracy made all the more certain that the structures of the Reich government itself were increasingly disrupted through direct special powers from Hitler, through the accumulation of authority in the hands of individual powerful Party satraps as well as through new central organs which were fused with the Party or the private economic sector. The old government departments and the administration subordinate to them remained outwardly undisturbed. But the real decisions were made without them; the old ministerial bureaucracy was increasingly bypassed and politically neutralized.

Notes and references

1. Cf. the memorandum of Fritz Dietlof von der Schulenberg of September 1937, in Hans Mommsen, *Beamtentum im Dritten Reich*, p. 149. See here also (pp. 137ff) the memorandum of Schulenburg of April 1933 which argued along similar lines.
2. As is apparent from a report of September compiled for the office of the Führer's Deputy by S.A. Obersturmbannführer and Oberreigierungsrat Dr Hans von Helms (until autumn 1934 personnel chief

for the higher service of the police administration in the Prussian Ministry of the Interior), up to June 1934, 31 of the total of 40 Prussian police chiefs were old Party comrades, including 22 higher S.A. leaders and three S.S. leaders. But this was not true of the higher officials of the police presidencies, where the old Party comrades made up 10 per cent at the most (IfZ: Fa 113). The term 'old Party comrades' used here applies (in accordance with the *Parteistatistik* of 1935) to those members who joined the NSDAP before 30 January 1933. A different ruling was introduced on the basis of an order from the Führer's Deputy of 8 May 1934 according to which all NSDAP members registered up to 1 April 1933 counted as 'old Party comrades'.

3. This is according to the figures from the *Parteistatistik* of the NSDAP (as of 1 January 1935), vol. 1, pp. 244, 260, 264. The important regional variations can be seen from these too. Thus it appears that of the local burgomasters in the North and East German NSDAP Gaue (strongholds of the German Nationalists) the percentage of non-Party members sometimes exceeded 50 per cent (thus in Pomerania, East Prussia, Hannover East, Weser-Ems), as was also the case in the rural Catholic Gau of Coblenz-Trier; whereas the share of non-Party members among the regional counsellors was very high, particularly in South Germany (Swabia, 90.5 per cent; Bavarian East March, 84.7 per cent; Munich-Upper Bavaria, 65.4 per cent; Baden, 62 per cent; and Franconia, 52.9 per cent).

4. BA: 43 II/1136b.

5. Brought in by Kerrl as State Secretary in the Prussian Ministry of Justice; after this had been merged with the Reich Ministry of Justice, Freisler became second State Secretary there alongside the partisan legal expert Schlegelberger.

6. Printed in H. Mommsen, op. cit., p. 166.

7. Ibid., p. 173.

8. IfZ: Fa 113 (the unpublished section of the memorandum in Mommsen, op. cit., pp. 171ff).

9. BA: R43 II/1138b.

10. By far the highest figure for dismissals on political and racial grounds, some 12 per cent, was that for higher officialdom in the Prussian internal administration, which had contained a relatively large number of SPD and DDP members; cf. Hans Mommsen, op. cit., p. 56.

11. H. Mommsen, op. cit., p. 59.

12. Ibid., p. 172.

13. BA: R 55/19. In the original draft by Goebbels the end of the last sentence had merely mentioned 'immediate dismissal'. But the Minister obviously felt obliged to make an amendment after talking with his advisers because of considerations of civil service rights, since the dismissal of civil servants was impossible without a formal disciplinary procedure, which in the last resort was outside the Minister's power. This is an interesting episode throwing light on the fact that the arrogant leadership practice of the NSDAP could not automatically be transferred to an administration subject to legal regulations.

14. For this whole episode see BA: R43 II/1154a. Lammers informed Heydrich on 23 December 1938 that Hitler had been told about

Wacker's memorandum, but had argued by contrast 'that the Reich Minister for Science, Education and Culture had to be allowed to deal with the organizational questions in his own sphere'.

15. BA: R43 II/694. The decree opened with the revealing formula (in the context of Hitler's new tone towards the Reich Ministers) 'I decree...' and had been drawn up in Bayreuth, where Hitler was staying for the Richard Wagner festival. It had obviously been preceded by a talk with Hess, Bormann and other Party leaders in Bayreuth. These were all the more concerned to ensure the Party's influence over the government in other ways after the emasculation of the S.A. (and the ending of the S.A. staff chief's participation in the government). On the other hand the fact that such participation was confined to 'the staff of Hess' was to prevent the arbitrary interference of the Party in state policy, such as had become quite evident at this time over policy towards Austria (murder of Dollfuss). It is therefore probably not wholly by chance that the decree was issued at the same time that Hitler resolved (again from Bayreuth) to exclude Habicht from policy towards Austria and to send Papen to Vienna.

16. *RGBl*, I, p. 73–4.

17. Letter of the Führer's Deputy, 7 February 1935, to the Head of the Reich Chancellery (BA: R43 II/421).

18. *RGBl*, I, p. 1203.

19. Circular of the Reich and Prussian Minister of the Interior, 9 October 1935, to the Supreme Reich Authorities, the Prussian Ministerpräsidenten and the Reich Governors (BA: R43 II/421).

20. Under Helmuth Friedrichs from March 1934, formerly general secretary of the NSDAP in the Gau Hesse-Cassel.

21. One of the later officials of Division III of the Party Chancellery, Dr Karl Lang, stated after the end of the War that many leading officials (including Sommers's successor, Dr Gerhard Klopfer) had been active in the Division who had first joined the Party in 1933 or later. It even transpired that non-Party members were transferred to the Division and remained there. (IfZ: ZS 1220). Cf. also the information on this point of other former officials of Division III of the Party Chancellery (ZS 812; ZS 352; ZS 683).

22. Willi Gölz, a former official of Division III of the Party Chancellery, even maintained that the 'ambiguous position' of these officials between Party and state had 'in most cases worked out in favour of the state authorities, particularly since very many experts had come to the Party Chancellery with clear instructions from their Ministries' (IfZ: ZS 683, Bl 15).

23. Correspondence on this between the Reich Ministry of the Interior, the Deputy of the Führer and the Reich Chancellery at the end of 1937, beginning of 1938, in BA: R43 II/421.

24. Text *inter alia* in the *Akten der Reichskanzlei*, BA: R43 II/426.

25. Ibid.

26. Note by the Head of the Reich Chancellery, 24 September 1935, Ibid.

27. Copy of the letter concerning this matter from the Reich Minister of Defence to Hitler, 24 October 1935, and note of the Armed Forces Adjutant attached to Hitler, Colonel Hossbach, 25 October 1935, Ibid.

28. On the foregoing see above all Helmut Krausnick, 'Vorgeschichte und

Beginn des militärischen Widerstandes gegen Hitler', in *Vollmacht des Gewissens* (Munich, 1956).

29. Also typical in this respect were Hitler's deliberate remarks in the Cabinet meeting of 24 January 1935 on the occasion of the discussion of the draft of the German Municipal Code: 'The central and local authorities' were 'still too heavily staffed by adherents of the former, now disbanded political parties.' 'I shall have fundamentally changed this state of affairs in 20–30 years. The armed forces had always remained aloof from the earlier commotion made by the political parties. In that respect the relationship between the armed forces and the new state had been by far the clearest from the very beginning.'

30. Cf. H. Mommsen, op. cit., p. 93.

31. Justification of Art. 71 affirmed: 'The National Socialist state must have the possibility of terminating the official position of those civil servants who have shown by their words, deeds or omissions that the National Socialist state can no longer rely on them absolutely. In order to protect civil servants from groundless and spiteful charges such measures can only follow on the basis of an enquiry with the chance of interrogation under oath, concerning actual statements. The decision rests with the Führer and Reich Chancellor; only the supreme service authority in agreement with the Reich Minister of the Interior can make the necessary application to the Führer and Reich Chancellor.' Cf. BA: R43 II/419a. The Deputy of the Führer only had the right to apply for an enquiry according to Art. 71 in the case of officials leaving or being excluded from the NSDAP. This regulation, which later resulted in actual discord (cf. BA: R43 II/447) could mean in individual cases that non-Party members among the civil servants were better protected against politically motivated demands for dismissal than Party members.

32. It was expressly stated in the implementing decree of 29 June 1937 (to Art. 8) that official approval of testimony before the Court also held good for the Party Courts.

33. Letter of 7 January 1937 from the Reich and Prussian Minister of Economics to the Reich Minister of the Interior (BA: R43 II/4209). Also cited by Mommsen, op. cit., pp. 215f.

34. Both notes on the files concerning this made by the Head of the Reich Chancellery are in BA: R43 II/420A.

35. On this cf. the different cases in BA: R43 II/447, 1138b, 421a, 423a, 425.

36. Protocol of the cabinet meeting of 9 December 1937. (IfZ: Fa 203/5).

37. BA: R43 II/447.

38. This passage had been included to protect judicial independence at the desire of the Reich Minister of Justice.

39. BA: R43 II/447.

40. Letter from Reichsleiter Martin Bormann to Reich Minister of the Interior, Frick, 4 April 1940, with the opening address: 'Dear Party comrade Dr Frick' (BA: R43 II/423a). Here too are the references cited below.

41. See the references to this in BA: R43 II/421a.

42. Letter from Bormann to the Head of the Reich Chancellery, 6 March 1940, ibid.

43. Undated copy in BA: R43 II/424.

Chapter Eight

The Reich government and the Führer's authority in the first years after 1933

In the first year and a half of the Third Reich, with its disruptive changes in state, society and public life, three centres of power had formed among which a tense unstable balance existed: the single Party monopoly, the centralized governmental dictatorship and the personal absolutism of the Führer had all been realized at the same time. The 'containment' of Hitler by the conservative forces of the government with the help of the Reich President had failed. But the seizure of power by those forces in the Party pressing for the complete overthrow of the political and social order had nevertheless been arrested half way by the conservative bearers of the state and by those followers of Hitler who had been given governmental powers, and during the second half of the process of seizing power had been defeated in virtually every sphere. In that respect the concept of containment was by no means completely shattered. Only Hitler, whose leadership claim went far beyond his powers of office and had a popular and charismatic basis independent of his official powers, emerged as the real victor from the conflicting pressures of the revolution and the process of stopping that revolution.

The years following the seizure of power (until about 1937/8) were determined internally less by marked changes in the constitutional state of affairs, such as had been threatened in 1934, but more by a stabilization of this state of affairs. In effect this simply meant stagnation in so far as the currents and cross-currents of rival claims to control and of power organizations were not brought within a unified system of government. Instead the dynamic force inherent in these conflicting claims was only temporarily contained or restrained. The failure to achieve a formal establishment and codification of the system of control in various areas (Reich and administrative reform, the elaboration of a new civil and criminal law, the determination of the relationship of Party to state, of the Führer's authority to the Reich government etc.) was the really crucial factor in this phase of relative normalization. But the absence of such a definition threatened to allow the flood-gates to open at any time and to release a dynamic energy which had merely been dammed up. And in fact after a few years the interim phase of relative stability was brought to an end by a surge of new changes in the power and organizational structures of the National Socialist regime, and a process followed of increasing duplication and overlapping through fresh improvisation.

The weak point of the National Socialist seizure of power seemed at the beginning to be chiefly in the Reich cabinet, where after 30 January 1933 Hitler could only rely unreservedly at first on his old followers Göring and Frick. Relatively little changed here in the first years of the Third Reich. Admittedly four additional National Socialist Ministers joined the cabinet by 1935, Goebbels, Darré, Hess and Kerrl, whilst Hugenberg and Papen left. But among the (1935) total of twelve departmental chiefs of the Reich government, the seven conservative Ministers (Neurath, Blomberg, Schacht, Schwerin-Krosigk, Seldte, Gürtner and Eltz-Rübenach) had until 1937/8 a considerable weight in relation to the five National Socialists (Göring, Frick, Goebbels, Darré, Kerrl)[1] not only numerically but also because of the importance of their departments.[2] The position of the Ministers and State Secretaries as independent and solely responsible heads in their departmental realm also remained untouched under Hitler, particularly since the 'Joint standing orders of the Reich cabinet' passed in 1924/6 were not formally repealed after 1933. On the contrary, the authority of the individual departmental Ministers to give orders (above all in the sphere of internal administration, of justice, of education and finance, the economy, employment) grew considerably with the ending of the sovereignty of the Länder. In addition the Enabling Law created for them an independent legislative initiative within their departments.

To be sure certain shifts of authority between the individual Ministers became apparent early on. Thus the special position of the Minister of Finance as the one responsible for the over-all Reich budget was restricted not only vis-à-vis the armed forces (aggregate budget) and Göring's Air Ministry in conjunction with the forced armaments policy, but also vis-à-vis the Party, which had its own treasurer. For all that the Minister of Finance still exercised a strong influence especially in the early, financially insecure years of the Third Reich, and he was also able among other things to check the build up of the Goebbels Ministry and to stunt the growth of the apparatus of the 'S.S. and police'.[3] It was more significant, however, that already in 1933/4, as a result of the co-ordination of public life and partly too as a result of the initiation of certain measures felt by Hitler to be urgent, Special Deputies and 'Leaders' of special Reich organizations began to appear alongside the Ministers, or only formally under them, and who secure in Hitler's personal confidence, could pursue their respective special policies independently of the Reich government and with the aid of their own leadership apparatus. In that respect they could undermine the unity of the government and the monopoly of government by the Reich cabinet.

Special Powers for Fritz Todt

The first comprehensive special authority of this sort was given to Hitler's road-building expert Dr Fritz Todt, who on 30 June 1933, was appointed by Hitler as General Inspector for German Roads in conjunction with the crucial new programme of autobahn building. Hitler acted largely independently here. The appointment had not as far as can be seen from the protocols of the cabinet meetings been formally decided in the cabinet. On the contrary Hitler had assured Todt on his own authority at the beginning of July 1933 that he (Todt) would not be 'attached to any Ministry' but would be directly 'subordinate to' the Reich Chancellery. And here Hitler had obviously decided without consulting the Reich Ministry of Transport that Todt's task was in effect to be responsible 'for the over-all supervision of German roads with the object of building a large-scale network of autobahns'.[4] Todt, who had been especially patronized by Hitler from the outset, confidently demanded later in September 1933 that the responsibilities of the Minister of Transport which fell within his (Todt's) new sphere of duty, be taken away from the Minister.[5] The latter was more or less presented with a *fait accompli* and in a talk in the Reich Chancellery on 6 October he had to agree to give up the previous division K (*Kraftfahr- und Landstrassenwesen*) of his department to Todt, who received the rank of a 'Higher Reich Authority' and was to be budgeted for through the Reich Chancellery.[6] A little later Todt convinced himself that this was not enough and that he also required legislative powers (in respect of new road legislation etc.) and thus needed the status of 'Supreme Reich Authority'.[7] But on 9 November, the Reich Minister of the Interior expressed grave doubts about a corresponding draft decree presented to the Reich Chancellor on 1 November, since the envisaged ruling was diametrically opposed to his efforts to bring about the 'amalgamation of similar and related areas of the administration' and to 'end the special authorities'. In a subsequent discussion between heads of departments which took place on 24 November, Frick enlarged on his objections in Hitler's presence to the effect that it was already impossible for the Reich Chancellery in view of its current personnel situation, 'to exercise the required control over the General Inspector'. Thus he felt it was essential for the budgeting to be done in the Ministry of Transport.[8] In addition State Secretary Reinhardt (Reich Minister of Finance) raised 'doubts on constitutional law': 'A Supreme

Reich Authority presupposes the existence of a Reich Minister' and for this reason he argued for the incorporation of the General Inspector in a Reich Ministry.

But Hitler, who was particularly taken by Todt's autobahn programme and wanted his favourite to be able to work free of restrictions, stuck to his guns: An already existing authority would 'only incidentally and thus inconclusively tackle' the new task. 'The sort of new task foreseen in the building of Reich autobahns also requires a new institution.' There 'is no question of setting up a new Ministry. The proposed authority only needs to be ministerial in character' (which meant apparently: in respect of powers of decision), but it should 'be freed of any routine work to preserve the vitality essential to carrying out the allotted task'. The authority had above all 'to provide inspiration' and should 'have nothing to do . . . with administration as such'. The General Inspector should 'simply be the organizer who stands above the whole outfit'. For this reason his position 'must not be measured by the standards of other governmental posts', which was also to be 'taken into account' with the most generous possible 'payment of the General Inspector'.[9] Even at that time Hitler stated: 'In the course of further economic measures the need will probably arise' to create 'still more of this type of establishment', 'for example in the sphere of substitute fuels'. At Hitler's special request the 'objection raised' by the other departmental heads were 'set aside' and on 30 November 1933 the decree of the Reich President was issued 'On the General Inspector for the German Road System' (*RGBl*, I, p. 1057) which accorded the latter the position of Supreme Reich Authority directly subordinate to the Reich Chancellor.

This unusual construction was a typical pattern for the emergence of central organs directly subordinate to the Führer and outside the Reich government. Todt had indeed been given authority to initiate legislation and to make administrative decrees corresponding to ministerial powers, but not the job of administration typical of other Ministries. Instead he had a quite special task of planning and organization. In carrying this out he appeared to the existing road and building authorities, as a Supreme Reich Authority empowered to issue extraordinary decrees;[10] and to the private building firms, as the allocator of state contracts and the organizer of groups and firms set up for specific circumstances, and of large masses of building labourers who were appropriately allocated. The greater importance of the duties of the General Inspector as opposed to the normal departmental duties of the Reich Ministries was underlined by the fact that he was directly responsible to Hitler and by his authority to take extraordinary measures (for example in the realm of traffic law, wage regulations etc.). The position of the 'General Inspector for the German Road System' was, so to speak, an element of direct Führer authority (for particularly urgent *ad hoc* measures) alongside the normal state government and administration. The leadership apparatus which developed from Todt's commission was a peculiar mixture of authoritarian and economic management. The numerous building sites, contractors and autobahn labour camps under him made up a gigantic state building concern, but which at the same time, because of the authority of its head to legislate and issue decrees, could secure for itself the administrative arrangements necessary for the most effective completion of its job. This became the foundation for Todt's later appointment as the 'Chief Special Deputy for the Regulation of the Building Sector' in the context of the organization for the Four Year Plan (December 1938). And when in 1937/8 the new military emphasis was on building the Western defences, the combination of building management and official allocation of labour which had already developed for building the autobahn, was again applied more extensively under Todt's direction. The decrees issued primarily for the purposes of building the West wall for 'ensuring the necessary Labour for tasks of special political importance' (22 and 30 June 1938), which made possible a great deal of compulsory labour conscription of building workers and firms, were another essential step towards the development of the united ensemble under Todt's command of building authorities, private firms and conscripted employees and workers, into an independent organization, the 'Organization Todt' (OT). The real originator and director of the OT was the construction engineer Xaver Dorsch, whom Todt had brought into the Berlin headquarters from a Munich construction firm at the end of 1933, and had made the director of the division for constructional engineering. During the War when Todt, who had already received an endowment of 100,000 RM from Hitler for his special services, was also appointed as Reich Minister for Armaments and Munitions (1940), the OT, whose headquarters was a group of offices of the new Ministry, developed into a construction force. It increasingly undertook military tasks, with special OT task forces and OT building inspectorates attached to the individual Army Groups, under whom the armed forces' construction units were also ultimately placed. The uniformed OT members in the front commands were subject to a quasi-military compulsory service. But the OT also employed on their construction sites in the Reich and the occupied areas hundreds of thousands of foreign civilian labourers and prisoners-of-war, including Jews and concentration camp prisoners conscripted for labour. Todt's three official posts (General Inspector for the German Road System, Chief Special Deputy for the Regulation of the Construction Industry, Minister of Armaments and Munitions) created an extraordinarily strong position for the OT and made it into one of the most important of the special organizations of the Hitler state. The peculiarity of the OT's legal position and its authority lay in the fact that it combined the organization of many branches and firms from the private construction industry, with the powers of the state building authority and with the state control of labour service and conscription in the building sector. This *ad hoc* combination freed the OT from many legal and administrative obstacles, gave it a great degree of flexibility, mobility and effectiveness but also made it (like the armed forces, the S.S. and police) into a 'state within a state', which often escaped the control of the general state administration and also made it into a typical organ of the extraordinary executive – directly under the Führer and alongside the Reich government proper and its administrative departments.

The Leader of the Reich Labour Service

Another early example of the appearance of such special authorities within the National Socialist state was the Labour Service. After a Reich Commissioner for the Voluntary Labour Service had already been appointed in conjunction with the work creation programme of the last Weimar governments, Reich Minister of Labour Seldte at first took over this task in the Hitler government. Already on 31 March 1933, he had to agree to appoint the National Socialist Deputy for the Labour Service, Konstantin Hierl, as Director of the Labour Service (with the rank of State Secretary). Within a few months Hierl had disposed of the various Party political, clerical and other supporters of the different Labour camps and made the voluntary Labour Service into a National Socialist association, which in February 1934 was named the 'National Socialist Labour Service'. The thirty Gau Labour directorates newly set up under Hierl's command were state offices of the central authority but were freed from the previous connection with the Land employment offices and had become an employment authority in its own right, which recruited its personnel primarily from the auxiliary organizations and groups of the Party (Hitler Youth, S.A. etc.) and in its internal structures was more like a Party association than a state authority. After countless quarrels with Hierl, Seldte, who had practically no control over this development, gave in to Hierl's pressure and suggested to Hitler that the Labour Service should be removed from his department and made independent as a separate Supreme Reich Authority under Hierl's direction. Here, too, there was opposition from the Reich Minister of the Interior who feared a 'splintering of the Reich administration' through such an arrangement and did not think it was feasible 'continually to place new authorities under the Reich Chancellor'. In this case, however, Frick got his way. After the first suggestion he made of putting the Labour Service under the proposed S.A. Ministry (after the overthrow of Röhm) had failed, Hierl was given the powers of a Reich Commissioner for the Labour Service in place of Seldte on 3 July 1934, but in this capacity he was under the Minister of the Interior. Admittedly in this way the creation of yet another Supreme Reich Authority was avoided. In practice Hierl's independence in the administration of his Labour Service was hardly affected. On the contrary, when labour conscription was eventually introduced by law on 26 June 1935 (*RGBl*, I, p. 769), the Reich Labour Service (*Reichsarbeitsdienst* – RAD) grew alongside the armed forces to an ever bigger special organization, which also had its own jurisdiction during the War (1940).[11] The 'Leader of the Labour Service', who remained according to his state office a State Secretary subordinate to the Reich Minister of the Interior and did not become a member of the cabinet, was in practice an independent director of a special Reich organization. Moreover the ambiguous position of the RAD as an official state organization for Labour conscription and for pre-military training, in which however – unlike the armed forces – National Socialist principles of leadership and National Socialist schooling played a major role, made it into a model for the merger of state and Party which was always to be the precondition for real independence in the Hitler state. Eventually in August 1943, when Himmler took over the Ministry of the Interior, the Labour Service also formally left the Ministry of the Interior's jurisdiction and the Reich Labour Leader Hierl became the head of an independent Supreme Reich Authority directly responsible to Hitler.[12]

The Reich Youth Leader

The Leader of the Hitler Youth had reached this goal still earlier. The Hitler Youth had at first taken over the Reich Committee of German Youth Associations during the Party revolution in spring 1933. Then, Schirach had already been named as 'Youth Leader of the German Reich' by Hitler on 17 June 1933, after the expulsion from the Committee of Jewish, Socialist and other party political youth associations and the majority of the other youth associations had been persuaded to join the Hitler Youth, which among other things also took over the Youth Hostel Service and the youth employment work of the National League for Germandom Abroad (*Volksbund für das Deutschtum in Ausland* – VDA). This was not simply a matter of a state office but much more of an almost revolutionary (or even 'corporatist') supervisory function for the whole area of the youth movement. By virtue of this the Leader of the Hitler Youth decided on the recognition of the separate youth organizations and their leaders and with their help he was able to promote the further expansion of the Hitler Youth to an all-embracing Reich Youth Movement (end of 1934: 3,500,000 members). Yet it was not enough for the leadership of the Hitler Youth merely to be anchored to the Party. After the resumption of general conscription and the introduction of labour conscription in 1935, it seemed essential to have a direct state duty, particularly in respect of pre-military training, if it was not to fall behind the Labour Service on the one hand and the state education policy of Rust's Ministry on the other. Hitler had already approved in principle this effort to convert the Hitler Youth movement to a state youth movement at the end of 1935. But the strong resistance of Rust against such a new rival central office of state in the education sector, and the Minister of Finance's critical objections to the plans proposed by Schirach for a future state youth leadership, delayed this particular project until the end of 1936.[13] The draft presented by von Schirach, of a law concerning the leadership of the Reich Youth, once again aroused the fundamental disquiet of the Ministers of Finance and the Interior at the repeated 'creation of an independent Reich special authority apart from the general administration'.[14] Frick also argued in this instance in favour of attachment to the general administration in order to preserve the connection with the other administrative authorities at least at the provincial and Regierungsbezirk levels. Hitler insisted, however, on the setting up of a Supreme Reich Authority which would be 'directly' responsible to him (Hitler) and he urged the Education Minister through Lammers 'to withdraw his' basic 'objection and not to voice this in the cabinet meeting on 1 December'.[15] It is of particular interest too that Hitler also denied the wish of the Supreme Commander of the Armed Forces (Blomberg) for a share at least in the implementing statutes of the law (as these also 'concern the question of recruitment to the armed forces').[16] Thus Hitler regarded the Hitler Youth, like the Labour Service, as a National Socialist counterweight in education and military training to the unpolitical armed forces.

On 1 December 1936 the cabinet passed the Law on the Hitler Youth, whereby the Hitler Youth became a compulsory youth organization for all male and female German youth (between ten and eighteen years old) and the Youth Leader of the German Reich received 'the position of a Supreme Reich Authority', who was 'directly subordinate to the Führer and Reich Chancellor'. But the Finance Minister was able to thwart Schirach's original idea that in this way he could budget for and staff a large proportion of the Hitler Youth leadership within the Supreme Reich Authority at the Reich's expense, because the Reich Treasurer of the NSDAP also resolutely opposed such an independent budgeting for the leadership of the Hitler Youth. Thus only a State Secretary's position was approved for Schirach himself, and for three of his head office colleagues a Ministerialrat post each. But these were to be financed from the over-all sum approved by the Reich Minister of Finance for the Reich Treasurer of the NSDAP.[17] In terms of financial control the Supreme Reich Authority led by Schirach therefore remained subordinate to the Party. The announcement of this Supreme Reich Authority, which was not given any right to make its own state decrees either,[18] was apparently aimed simply at promoting the Reich Youth Leader politically against other central authorities of the state (Education Minister) and also at involving him in any state laws which concerned the youth of Germany.[19]

The Reich S.S. Leader and the Chief of German Police

By far the most fateful example of this process in the early years of the Third Reich – of making a part of the Reich's authority independent through simultaneously combining Party and state duties to set up a special organization directly responsible to the Führer – concerned the S.S. and police. The crucial precondition was the concentration of the Political Police of the Länder under Himmler and Heydrich, which had already been completed in spring 1934, as has been outlined earlier. This was tied up with the infiltration of top positions in the Political Police by S.S. leaders, and the simultaneous fusion of the S.S. intelligence apparatus (SD) with the machinery of the state Political Police. Complementing this was the fact that after the emasculation of the S.A. (and as it were tacitly continuing its former auxiliary police powers), the S.S. completely took over the control and guarding of the state concentration camps. S.A. concentration camps which still existed, for example Oranienburg near Berlin, were taken over by the S.S. or dismantled after 30 June 1934. But the Land police installed in Dachau and elsewhere for guard duties, were also replaced by S.S. guard units appointed from head office and paid for from Land funds, from which the S.S. Death's Head formations developed (total strength at the end of 1934: about 2,000). At the same time (summer 1934) as Heydrich united the departments of the Political Police in the Länder under his control on Himmler's instructions, another higher S.S. leader, the former Commandant of the Dachau camp, Theodor Eicke, was appointed by Himmler as Inspector of Concentration Camps and leader of the S.S. Guard units (4 July 1934), and placed directly under Himmler. Just as the Political Police in the Länder had been taken over from Munich as the starting point of the Reich S.S. Leader (Commander of the Bavarian Political Police), so Eicke struggled after 1934, using the Dachau model as a starting point, to unify the concentration camps (introduction of general guard and punishment provisions, training of the guard units, arrangement of the camp hierarchy according to Commandant's office, political department, adjutant's office, administration, detention camp, liaison and block leaders etc.). Up to and including 1936 the concentration camps, whose number was greatly reduced after 1934, and the S.S. Death's Head formations as well as the Political Police were under the Länder for budgetary purposes.[20] They were transferred to the Reich Budget in 1937, as was the Gestapo and three big Reich concentration camps arose in place of the former small camps, Dachau (near Munich), Sachsenhausen (near Berlin), Buchenwald (near Weimar) with a total (1937) of just 10,000 prisoners and about 4,000 members of the S.S. Death's Head formations.

The armed S.S. squads, which were formed at various places in 1933 as a sort of revolutionary strike force (alongside the S.A. Field Police serving similar purposes in 1933/4), made up the third crucial starting-point and power base of Himmler and the S.S., besides the Political Police and the concentration camps. The most important and the biggest of these armed S.S. units was the Adolf Hitler Bodyguard Regiment put together under Sepp Dietrich in Berlin in summer 1933 from 120 hand-picked S.S. men, which had already sworn a personal oath of loyalty to Hitler on 9 November 1933. This procedure thus took place long before Hitler took over the Reich President's office and has rightly been described as 'one of the first acts constituting the authority of the Führer in Germany's public life'.[21] The 'Bodyguard' was also Hitler's key agent in the strike against Röhm on 30 June 1934, and as a result of this 'test' Hitler had promised that the Bodyguard Regiment would be developed into a modern armed regiment. Moreover in 1934/5, two further formations of armed S.S. (in Munich and Hamburg) were set up as well as two S.S. Junker Schools (in Bad Tölz and Braunschweig). At the wish of the armed forces the S.S. militarized formations were basically limited to these three regiments until 1938. Service in the Reich-financed S.S. militarized formations counted as a substitute for military service, although the armed forces reserved the right to examine the budget. It was impossible to break the long-standing and stubborn resistance of the armed forces on one crucial point until after the resignations of Blomberg and Fritsch. Through Hitler's decree of 17 August 1938 (on the occasion of the Sudeten crisis), the Reich S.S. Leader was empowered to recruit members from the general S.S. for service in the armed S.S. units, above the previous permitted strength of the militarized formations and Death's Head formations,[22] when apart from voluntary enlistment the emergency enlistment of members of the general S.S. became possible on the basis of the decree on emergency service of 15 October 1938 (by the end of 1938 the militarized formations and the Death's Head formations came to a rough total of 20,000).

These armed S.S. units were the typical example of a special authority which rested on the Party *and* the state but which had detached itself from both and had become independent. They were no longer subject to the administrative and financial control of the Party (the Reich Treasurer), nor were they part of the state police. They were not subject to the Ministries of the Interior of the Reich or of the Länder but were exclusively answerable to the Reich S.S. Leader, who in this respect was an exponent of the direct authority of the Führer. As to Himmler's special capacity as the Head of the Reich Security Service, in the Reich Chancellery and in other public buildings in Berlin (which apart from SD sentries and members of the Bodyguard Regiment were looked after by a group of specially hand-picked detectives under the direction of the Munich S.S. Leader and Police Captain Rattenhuber) the direct responsibility of the Reich S.S. Leader to the Führer and Reich Chancellor was also formally regulated in 1935.[23]

The gradual detachment of the police from the internal administration, which began in the Political Police sector, was much more contentious and complicated. The concentration of the Political Police of the Länder under Himmler was already tending towards the creation of a separate Ministry of State Security in 1934/5, and was opposed from the outset to the central authority, including the police administration, of the Reich Minister of the Interior. The latter also wanted to put an end to the uncoordinated action of the Political Police in the Länder and to subject it to binding regulations through the process of 'centralization' (thus among other things by means of his decrees on custody of 12 and 26 April 1934).[24] However since in the meantime the Political Police authorities in the Länder had been made almost everywhere into Supreme Land Authorities, directly responsible to the government and occupied by Himmler and Heydrich in the wake of the National Socialist seizure of power, the practical administration of the Political Police had also become independent in such a way that the Reich Minister of the Interior was no longer even kept sufficiently informed, let alone his right of direction respected. As a result the question became more and more urgent as to whether the responsibility for the Political Police should lie with the Reich Minister of the Interior or with the Reich S.S. Leader in his capacity as Commandant of the various Political Police forces in the Länder.[25] Documented conflicts from this period show that Himmler was already getting Hitler's support when he disobeyed clear instructions from the Reich Minister of the Interior,[26] and Frick on his part complained that the Commandant of the Land political police was 'submitting' police matters directly to the Führer and

Reich Chancellor 'without informing him' (Frick).[27] The S.S. Obergruppenführer Daluege, who was taken over by Frick from the Prussian Ministry of the Interior and who ran the police department in the combined Reich and Prussian Ministry of the Interior also felt that the separation of the Political Police from the general police was dangerous and in an extensive memorandum submitted to Hitler in November 1935 he recommended that the Political Police should again be combined with the general police force in conjunction with the essential unification of the whole Reich police force.[28] Of course Daluege also argued for police recruitment in future to be chiefly from the S.S. and in favour of joining 'the S.S. in closer or looser form to the police'. But he was after a 'centralization' of the police through the ministerial authority of the Reich and Prussian Ministry of the Interior, which in practice would have created the central police command for himself, whereas it was bound to benefit Heydrich's position if the Gestapo remained an independent authority assigned to the Prussian Ministry of State. It also proved to be to Heydrich's advantage that building up a united Reich police force was only conceivable in conjunction with a reform of the Reich involving reorganizing the entire internal administration, whereas the centralization of the separate Political Police forces was easier to carry out. The Head of the secret state police also received unexpected support here from the armed forces, which had already called in summer 1935 for 'the creation of a centralized organization and direction of the Political Police in the Reich', because this was thought necessary in the interests of more rational and effective collaboration with the military counter-espionage (from 1934 under the direction of Captain Canaris).[29] On the other hand some of the Prussian Oberpräsidenten, for example, Erich Koch in East Prussia, objected to the fact that the state police offices active in the provinces were not under them, but on the contrary took their orders exclusively from Himmler and Heydrich, and so they supported Koch's criticism of the Gestapo's autonomy which was 'injurious in the highest degree to the authority of the state'.[30]

The tug of war over legally defining the Gestapo's position lasted from 1934 until February 1936. The Prussian law on the Gestapo finally enacted on 10 February 1936,[31] bore the clear marks of an unresolved compromise. Through the provision contained in the law that the Secret Police Office (Gestapa) in Berlin was the 'Supreme Land Authority' of the Gestapo, whose functions at the intermediate level were to be carried out by separate state police offices in the regions, the autonomy of the Gestapo organization was acknowledged. The law also specified that the regional offices were to be 'simultaneously placed under the competent Regierungspräsidenten' and had 'to comply with the directives of the later and keep them informed in all matters concerning the Political

Police'. In fact opposition to the general internal administration counted for much more since at the same time the Gestapo's organizational independence entailed a fusion of S.S. and SD personnel and institutions with the Political Police, and thus the particularly pronounced structure of Leader and following in the S.S., as well as the S.S.'s specific ideological concept of the political enemy also became crucial for the Gestapo. And provisions to prevent this in the law on the Gestapo remained largely illusory, particularly since in their attempt to achieve autonomy for the Gestapo Himmler and Heydrich had Hitler's full support. It was more or less simply as a face-saver that the Gestapo law specified: 'The responsibilities of the constituted legal authorities remain untouched.' Indeed this same law confirmed that dispositions in the affairs of the secret state police were 'not subject to checks by the administrative courts'. Thus the Gestapo's special position was clearly expressed. Heydrich's collaborator Werner Best finally illustrated this too with the words: 'Thus the acknowledged need has been met for the separation of the state police, which acts *according to special principles and needs*, from the administration working *according to general and uniform legal rules*.'[32]

A little later Himmler also had his first key success in his simultaneous efforts to control the entire police and bring about its amalgamation with the S.S. True, he did not get his own Police Ministry, but he was empowered by a decree of Hitler's of 17 June 1936 (*RGBl*, I, p. 487), to 'unify the control of police duties in the Reich' and was given the title 'Reich S.S. Leader and Chief of German Police within the Reich Ministry of the Interior'. Like the law on the Gestapo, this hotly disputed definition of Himmler's official role contained two conflicting elements. This title, which was achieved against Frick's opposition, signified over and above the personal union the *institutional* joining of the S.S. leadership to the control of the police. The addition of the words 'within the Reich Ministry of the Interior' and the further stipulation contained in the decree that the Chief of German Police was 'personally and directly subordinate to the Reich and Prussian Minister of the Interior', was by contrast a concession to the Reich Minister of the Interior, who wanted to preserve the connection between the police and the internal administration. Another sign of compromise was the fact that as Chief of German Police Himmler did not get ministerial rank but was merely given the position of State Secretary, and he was only authorized to attend meetings of the Reich cabinet 'in so far as matters within his sphere of authority are concerned'. The fact later confirmed by supplementary decrees, that the Reich S.S. Leader and Chief of German Police was to be 'within his own sphere of office the standing representative of the Minister',[33] made it clear that his subordination to Frick was more or less purely nominal.[34] It was above all because Himmler was directly responsible to the Führer in his capacity as Reich S.S. Leader (his subordination to the Chief of Staff of the S.A. was formally ended after 30 June 1934) that he could easily escape from the simultaneous responsibility to the Reich Minister of the Interior, or even indeed reverse this relationship. In pratice Himmler soon interpreted the task of representing the Minister which the decree of 17 June 1933 afforded him in such a way that he (Himmler) also had an acting joint responsibility in matters of general internal administration. Later (1939) this claim found formal recognition when Himmler became Frick's deputy in his capacity as Chief Plenipotentiary for the Reich Administration. But the relationship between the internal administration and the police was very often reversed as Frick's standing progressively deteriorated in the early years of the War and, as has already been explained, the respective heads of the civilian administrations, especially in the newly annexed and occupied areas, acquired a position and independence through their more or less direct relationship to the Führer. The Reich S.S. Leader and Chief of German Police, who regarded the administration of these areas in principle as primarily a matter for the Political Police, now sought on his part (as it were in place of the Minister of the Interior) a central authority to give orders to the heads of the civilian governments.[35] At the end of 1942 Hitler was resolved to change the existing set-up in the Ministry of the Interior and Lammers and Hitler agreed in private in March 1943, 'to work out how at some later date the police could be detached from the Reich Ministry and put under a Police (security) Minister in the person of the Reich S.S. Leader'.[36] Finally, in August 1943, the issue resolved itself when Himmler the Police Chief took over the Reich Ministry of the Interior and Frick was fobbed off with the job of Reichsprotektor in Bohemia and Moravia.

This reversal of the relationship between the Minister of the Interior and the Chief of Police of the Hitler state was the most extreme result of the development launched in 1936. However, at that time this was neither foreseeable nor inevitable. The 'centralization' of the police and its fusion with the S.S. was only achieved at the top at first, with the institutionalization of the link between the Reich S.S. Leader and Chief of German Police, and the setting-up in the Reich Ministry of the Interior of a 'Head Office Security Police' (Gestapo and Criminal Police) under the direction of S.S. Gruppenführer Heydrich, and a 'Head Office Order Police' (Rural Constabulary and Municipal Police) under the direction of S.S. Obergruppenführer Daluege. Apart from the Gestapo the process of centralization and amalgamation with the S.S. was pursued most deliberately in the case of the Criminal Police (changing of the Prussian Land Criminal Police Office to the Reich Criminal Police Office on 16 July 1937). At the intermediate level, however, the Criminal Police remained, in contrast to the Gestapo with its own system of regional directorates and offices, part of the general police administration, although an additional vertical chain of command was created through the appointment of Inspectors of the Security Police and of the SD. This also made the Criminal Police at the province, Land and Regierungsbezirk level, more dependent on the central authority. It is true that the setting up of the Reich Security Office (*Reichssicherheitsamt* – RSHA) on 27 September 1939 could not overcome the independence of the separate state authorities or Party offices who were now supposedly integrated (state police, Criminal Police, SD), but it did strengthen the process of institutional fusion under the direction of the Chief of Security Police and of the SD (Heydrich), as well as the coordination of the Criminal Police by the S.S. By contrast, in the case of the Order Police and police administration it was more difficult to dissolve the disciplinary, organizational and legal ties with the Land and local administrations, so that in this instance the tie with the S.S. (granting of S.S. service ranks to police officials etc.) often remained of a more nominal character and was less able to affect the nature of the state authority.

A circular directive of Heydrich to the state police directorates of 17 December 1936, in which there was a warning against 'excessive arrests' as otherwise the Gestapo's 'keenest weapon' would be 'discredited and the widespread attempts to end protective custody would be encouraged',[37] shows even at the end of 1936 how contentious were the special executive of the Gestapo, already attained in principle, and its monopoly of the power to make arrests free from any control by the law. In addition it is significant that at the same time the Chief of the Security Police Office in the Reich Ministry of the Interior (Werner Best) was trying to end the direct subordination of the concentration camp inspectors to Himmler and to put the camps under the Gestapo for the purposes of administration, in order to control them more strictly and to curb their often extraordinarily arbitrary conduct.[38] But these efforts met with as little success as Frick's earlier attempts to curb the Gestapo through the general internal administration.

A fundamental point emerges from all this. The institutions of the Führer's authority, with their specific Leader-retinue structures, stemming from the inherent traits of the National Socialist movement, tended repeatedly to generate new positions having a 'direct' relationship with the Führer and to encourage these in turn to strive for a separate existence, like some permanent process of cell-division. This was particularly true of the continually inflated area of authority of the Reich S.S. Leader. Although this 'state within a state' increasingly undermined the unity of the entire state administration, it lacked the characteristics of a solid corporative, bureaucratic compactness and unity. Like the National Socialist system as a whole, the Reich S.S. Leader's area of command presented in miniature the picture of a progressive growth of subsidiary offices, ancillary organizations and leader authorities, which could only be held together with difficulty at the top. As the control of key areas of the state police, especially in the Security Police, was fully in the hands of fanatical S.S. leaders (which was not normally the case in the relationship between Party and state administration), the National Socialist fighting organization's principle of 'movement' originating in the period before 1933, was preserved intact in this S.S. co-ordinated executive. Whilst the revolutionary S.A. had been emasculated and tamed, the special position of the S.S. continued to rest on the revolutionary emergency power which had been assumed in 1933. The continuation of the struggle against real or suspected enemies which was institutionalized in this way, coupled with the S.S. commitment to the absolute Führer ('Your honour is your loyalty'), and the special elite idea injected into the S.S. 'Order' by Himmler, generated a particular zeal among higher and lower S.S. leaders. Each sought in his own way to serve 'his Reich Leader' and the Hitler state with 'toughness', 'resolution' and 'energy' in the pursuit of enemies and long-term utopian aims. Himmler repeatedly encouraged such initiative by allowing considerable independence and these men were proud and 'expert' enough to carry out unquestioningly tasks which were felt to be difficult if not impossible. Moreover as the ruling organ of the Third Reich the S.S. remained largely outside the law and habitually behaved as an extraordinary 'task force' with the knowledge of being a special elite. Behind this, there lurked the old, potentially criminal 'morality' of the volunteer and Combat Leagues. On the other hand it was the state police apparatus which first provided the S.S. with the instrument for translating National Socialism's propaganda picture of the enemy, as stereotyped as it was vague, into the bloody reality of a bureaucratically planned and organized campaign against opponents. Only after the fusion with the police were slogans like the 'Jewish question', the 'freemason problem' and other hostile figures in the National Socialists' ideological rhetoric 'taken literally' as it were, bureaucratically systematized, allotted to departments and made the basis of a branch of zealously refined Criminal Police science and technique. Before 1933 the notion that the 'Jewish question' would have to have some sort of final 'solution' was common to the radical anti-semites of all the regions, as bombastic as it was imprecise. The fact, however, that this slogan (final solution of the Jewish problem) could become the ultimate goal of a secret operation of the Security Police, planned as if by the General Staff and perfectly organized, was the result of the bureaucratization of the National Socialist ideology in the context of the merger between the S.S. and the police.

Göring's power base

An accumulation and proliferation of responsibilities, offices and staffs similar to that in the Reich S.S. Leader's realm was characteristic of the National Socialist system at the top in the early years of the Third Reich, above all of Göring's area of authority. Although in this case it was not so much a matter of having power outside the government and state organization, yet Göring's abundance of offices soon upset the balance of the collegiate Reich cabinet. As well as his position as Prussian Minister President and Minister of the Interior, Göring had effected the creation of the Reich Aviation Ministry as a new Supreme Reich Authority in May 1933, by extending the scope of his office as Reich Commissioner for Aviation.[39] The transfer of the Prussian Ministry of the Interior to Frick (1934) was offset by the fact that in July 1934 Göring acquired control of another Supreme Reich Authority, as Reich Forestry Commissioner and Controller of the Hunt, but then in 1935 he was given the supreme command of the Luftwaffe and the rank of colonel-general during the process of reconstructing the armed forces. Since the Luftwaffe had to be completely reconstructed and was given special priority in Hitler's armaments programme, Göring also gained increasing influence from this position over the entire policy of rearmament and autarky in 1935/6. Already in autumn 1935, Göring had intervened on Hitler's behalf in the violent conflict between Darré and Schacht, where the problem was to reconcile the armaments sector's claim for foreign exchange with the growing demands of the foodstuffs sector, owing to poor cereal yields.[40] And when in 1935/6, as well as the 'bread crisis' the question (especially important for the Luftwaffe) of fuel production caused quarrels between Schacht and Blomberg over the degree and methods of state planning and stimulation of production, Göring was also charged by Hitler in April 1935 with re-examining the existing foreign exchange and raw materials policy. Finally in September 1936, he was put in charge of carrying out the Four Year Plan to achieve autarky.

And in other areas too, Göring's position as Hitler's special confidant meant that his actual powers exceeded his nominal authority. This was particularly true of the sphere of foreign policy. As had already been the case before 1933, Göring conducted important negotiations on Hitler's behalf without the Foreign Minister and wove the threads of the National Socialist policy of alliances through his various state visits abroad (in Italy, Yugoslavia, and Poland). Even during the years 1933 to 1936, Hitler's inclination was obviously to entrust important contacts with leading foreign statesmen to Göring (or the Special Envoy, Ribbentrop) rather than to the diplomats at the Foreign Office.[41] It was typical too of the style of leadership of Hitler's foreign policy that repeatedly the

Foreign Office was only very inadequately informed about such missions or the agreements which were reached in this way and there was a great deal of ambiguity as a result.

Göring's position as a 'second leader' was also shown among other things from the fact that he built up his own extensive news service independently of the official Reich government sources with his so-called 'Research Bureau' at the Aviation Ministry, formed in spring 1933. In reality the Research Bureau had nothing to do with either the Aviation Ministry or 'research', but was a concealed centre for collecting information under the official supervision of the Prussian State Ministry (state secretary Koerner), with hundreds of technicians, decoding specialists and translators, which specialized particularly in tapping phone conversations inside the Reich and monitoring foreign radio transmitters as well as diplomatic and secret military transmitters. The most important items gleaned in this way were compiled into secret reports each day and distributed to a small circle among the top leaders of the National Socialist regime ('Brown sheets'). In some cases, for example during the Czech crisis in autumn 1938, knowledge of the news transmissions of foreign powers as monitored and deciphered through the Research Bureau played an important part in the decision making of the National Socialist leadership. Although later the Bureau, which was eventually to have a staff of 3,000,[42] declined in importance and its information often proved irrelevant, the control of this special news service was a particular attribute of the power which early on separated Göring from his ministerial colleagues. Control over the Research Bureau also compensated to some extent for the control of the Gestapo being given to Himmler. It also supported Göring's foreign policy activities and facilitated his access to Hitler, who attached particular value to information from news services.

Göring reached the peak of his power with the task of directing the Four Year Plan, which brought him the position of a Minister supremo with his own right to issue decrees in the field of economic policy and labour allocation policy. This commission, one of the consequences of which was the setting up of the General Council of the Four Year Plan (as an inner economic cabinet), not only brought about the resignation of Schacht as Minister for Economics in November 1937, and as President of the Reichsbank in January 1939 (the former Press Chief of the Reich Government and state secretary in the Propaganda Ministry, Walter Funk, took over both jobs in succession). It also caused, as will be seen, a serious shift in decision-making at the expense of several departments and Ministers of the Reich government. These efforts coincided with important personnel and organizational changes at the top of other departments (armed forces and Foreign Office) and with the final end of the collegiate cabinet meetings of the Reich government. Before we come back to these changes, which mark a

break in the internal constitutional development comparable to the
ending of the National Socialist revolution of 1933/4, we must consider the earlier position of the cabinet and the forms of government legislation.

The end of collective cabinet decisions

According to the provisions of the Weimar constitution – still formally operative – the Reich government was (Arts. 52 to 58) a collegiate authority which, under the chairmanship of the Reich
Chancellor, had jointly to debate and decide by a majority on the
legislative proposals of individual Reich Ministers, as well as on
questions 'which concern the area of authority of several Reich
Ministers'. The casting vote went to the Chancellor only in the
event of deadlock. But Hitler only observed the regular procedures
of cabinet meetings in the first few months of his chancellorship,
when the Reich government was still a coalition cabinet in character. In the months of February and March 1933 there were meetings of the Reich government on average every two days (31 in
all), in April/May 1933 the frequency of meetings had halved (16
meetings in all), and thereafter the period between Cabinet meetings was considerably longer (in the period June 1933 to March
1934 only 29 and between April and December 1934 only 13 meetings). From 1935 the routine meetings of the government, which
were still held with some regularity until then at the rate of once
or twice a month, also ceased. The cabinet was only called at intervals of many months when it was necessary to pass quickly
whole series of laws which had been meanwhile prepared elsewhere (1935, 12; 1936, 4; 1937, 6 meetings). The very last meeting
of the Reich cabinet took place on 5 February 1938.[43]

From the outset no formal votes were taken in the cabinet
under Hitler's chairmanship, particularly since Hitler's Nationalist
coalition partners could hardly press for such a democratic procedure. The protocols of the cabinet sessions of spring 1933 reveal
that at this time Hitler took care not to come into conflict with the
majority of Ministers and for this reason he often deferred his own
suggestions or those of his National Socialist Ministers. At this
time also, the cabinet was still very much a place for the technical
discussion of individual decisions and of material for laws. But this
was already beginning to change in April 1933, when the monopoly
of political power passed to the National Socialist movement, because the Enabling Law made the right of the Reich President to
issue decrees largely dispensable. As a result the support of the
non-National Socialist Ministers from the President was weakened.
In order to prevent such a development, Hugenberg among others
had suggested in the cabinet meeting of 15 March 1933 that for

the purposes of the new authoritarian Reich constitution the President should also take part in any legislation concerning the constitution after the passage of the Enabling Law. But this idea was rejected by Hugenburg's State Secretary Meissner himself, with the argument that such 'participation by the Reich President' was 'unnecessary' and nor would Hindenburg 'want this'.

The fact that the Enabling Law passed on 24 March 1933 stated that 'the national laws enacted by the Reich cabinet shall be prepared by the Chancellor', showed how greatly strengthened the Chancellor's position was as a result of the law. Whereas according to the Reich constitution the Chancellor formerly had to countersign the Reich laws prepared by the President (Art. 70 of the Weimar constitution) and in so doing to assume the political responsibility (towards the President as well as parliament), now the Chancellor in person had the right to make laws, to accept political responsibility and the right to execute the laws. By definition of his authority he had the decisive influence on law making, now solely the prerogative of the Reich government. And he alone decided on the execution of national laws.

But this robbed the concept of 'law' of its essential meaning. Because it was precisely the legislative *procedure* prescribed by the constitution (reading and passage by parliament) which comprised the essence of a *law*, and distinguished it from *decrees* (including those of the Reich President). But, again, it was precisely these provisions in the constitution concerning legislation (Arts. 68 to 77 of the Reich constitution) which were struck out by the Enabling Law. In future the laws passed by the Reich government on the basis of the Enabling Law were only *laws* in *name*, but in form were hardly distinguishable from decrees and ordinances. And the constitutional requirement according to which the Reich government had to reach a collective decision (on legislation etc.) was by and large untenable, because the leader principle also operated in the cabinet. Even on 22 April 1933, Goebbels observed that: 'The Führer's authority in the cabinet is absolute. The Führer decides.'[44] Thus the only part of the formal legislative process which was not attacked by the Enabling Law was the stipulation that all national law had to be 'announced in the *Reichgesetzblatt*', that is to say, published. This meant that only the regime's published laws (and decrees and ordinances) could count as valid.

Proof of Hitler's changed status in the cabinet was the fact that after the referendum of 12 November 1933, Vice-Chancellor von Papen offered Hitler the formal homage of the cabinet, which praised him as the genial Führer of people and government and reduced the Ministers to plain 'staff' of the Führer.[45] And Hitler's own work style as head of government also began to change at this time. Otto Dietrich, Hitler's Press Chief, described this later:

When Hitler first moved into the Wilhelmstrasse in 1933, he went about his unaccustomed tasks with diligence and punctuality. As long as Hindenburg was virtually his neighbour – their offices were separated only by those of the Foreign Office – Hitler appeared at his desk every morning at ten o'clock. He regularly, though reluctantly, conducted cabinet meetings; at that time he did not yet have a majority in the cabinet and had to accept compromises, infuriating though these were to him. For that reason he later on called cabinet meetings more and more rarely, and after 1937 not at all . . . At the end of 1933, Hindenburg, whose health was failing, retired to East Prussia. That was the end of Hitler's hard-working schedule. He once more reverted to his habit of rising at noon and during the day entered his offices only for important receptions. All other work was taken care of in his apartment as he stalked about his rooms, dropping a word here and there and settling important matters in the most casual fashion.[46]

The Führer's separation from the government and its consequences for the legislative process

The crucial break in the development of the relationship between the Reich government and the Führer's authority finally resulted from Hitler's assumption of the office of Reich President. The Law (of 1 August 1934) concerning the Head of State of the German Reich (*RGBl*, I, p. 747), which was confirmed on 19 August by a referendum, also made the notion of the 'Führer' official, with its new description of Hitler's office (Führer and Reich Chancellor', or 'Führer and Supreme Commander of the Armed Forces').[47]

Whereas the law passed on 17 October 1933 concerning the oath of the Reich Ministers (*RGBl*, I, p. 741) had still kept close to the Weimar Republic's law on Reich Ministers of 27 March 1930, and had retained the oath to the 'constitution and to the law', the Ministers were now legally obliged to swear an oath of loyalty and obedience to the 'Führer of the German Nation and People', and there was no more mention of the constitution.[48] The constitutional lawyers of the Third Reich were in agreement thereafter that all power lay with the Führer alone. It was stated in a memorandum from the Reich Ministry of the Interior of November 1935: that 'the Führer state had replaced' the state as an entity at law and no longer recognized the existence of 'many wills' but 'just the single will'.[49] The division leader and deputy of the Head of the Reich Chancellery, Ministerialdirektor Wienstein, used a similar formula in a lecture to the Academy of Administration in Bonn on 15 December 1936: 'Today the Reich government is no longer a cabinet in the former sense, in which all decisions were made on a majority basis, but a Führer Council, which advises on and supports the decision made by the Führer and Reich Chancellor.'[50]

Although the personal will of the Führer had replaced the power of the state, this did not mean with regard to the administrative practice that the Führer from then on played a greater personal role in the conduct of the government. Indeed the opposite was the case. The downgrading of the cabinet to an 'apparatus' for carrying out the Führer's will was coupled with Hitler's growing dissociation from the daily routine of government. The Führer's 'absolutism' expressed itself, in accordance with the original meaning of the word, in the 'separation' of the Führer's authority from the Reich cabinet. This was shown among other things by the fact that Hitler now made the former Bureau of the Reich President, which was available to him as head of state, into an independent Supreme Reich Authority, as the Presidential Chancellery. State Secretary Lammers became the Head of the Reich Chancellery (with the rank of Reich Minister from 26 November 1937) in place of Hitler, and thus became the real manager of the Reich government.[51] As the position of Minister lost its political character, so the bestowal of ministerial rank (for example in 1936 on the Supreme Commander of the German Army, Colonel-General von Fritsch, and the Supreme Commander of the German Navy, Admiral Raeder)[52] became as common as the creation of new Supreme Reich Authorities. One example of such unnecessary promotion of a new authority was the Reich Office for the Disposition of Living Space under the direction of Hans Kerrl, which was set up by the Law on the Regulation of Land Requirements for Public Authorities of 25 March 1935 (*RGBl*, I, p. 468). It was consistent with this that the normal distinction between the powers of the political Minister and those of the professional State Secretaries was abolished through a change in the Reich government's procedural rules on 20 March 1935, to the extent that from then on State Secretaries were also empowered to sign laws on behalf of their respective Ministers (whereas before in the event of being unable to sign laws a Minister had had to be represented by another Minister).[53]

This in itself shows that the Führer state structure tended towards an increasingly far-reaching delegation of the right to legislate and to issue decrees. In that respect Minister Lammers was correct when he observed in a leading article on the 'State Leadership in the Third Reich' in the *Völkischer Beobachter* at the beginning of September 1938: 'It is by no means the case that the basically total concentration of supreme authority in the person of the Führer entails an excessively pronounced and unnecessary centralization of government in the hands of the Führer.' According to National Socialist concepts, Lammers continued, regard for 'the authority of the subordinate leader down below' precludes interfering in every single one of his acts and measures. 'This basic principle is applied in such a way by the Führer in his leadership of the government that the Reich Minister's position is actually more independent than it used to be, although the Reich Ministers are now subject... in their sphere of office to the Führer's unconditional right of command.'[54]

In accordance with the constitutional theory of the Führer state, the greater part of a Minister's exercise of the power to legislate and issue decrees merely comprised carrying out what were basically already indicated and fixed expressions of the Führer's will. But since the Führer failed to exercise a timely, orderly and scrupulous control and direction of Ministerial legislation and decree-making – and here the discrepancy between theory and practice became more marked as time passed – there was no guarantee at all that what the Führer allowed to go on unopposed was in fact legally and politically unimportant, or merely the 'administration' of the Führer's will. The very fact that Hitler increasingly avoided regular discussion with his Ministers and that, not least because of his personal style of work and leadership, he only tended to exert his influence to map out the basic direction of any important reorganization and ignored quite vital specific problems and disputes, leaving these to be resolved by means of ministerial regulations,[55] meant increasingly that important legal decisions were being taken within the individual departments. But from the point of view of the Führer system this was bound to cause problems, since the routine participation of the Führer's Deputy was also confined to the *government's* legislation and did not involve him in the making of decrees by the Ministries and by the other offices directly responsible to the Führer.

In that respect the practice of state very often failed to accord with the idea of the Führer state. The separation of the Führer from the government, his 'absence' and the growing difficulty for Ministers to get access to Hitler (particularly noticeable in the summer months which Hitler largely spent at Obersalzberg near Berchtesgaden), frequently resulted in an uncoordinated juxtaposition of the Reich government and the Führer's authority. The authoritative Führer's will was expressed only irregularly, unsystematically and incoherently. In some instances, for example, with the promulgation of the Law Preventing the Transmission of Hereditary Disease of 14 July 1933 (*RGBl*, I, p. 529), and in the case of the Nuremberg Laws of 15 September 1935,[56] the legislative initiative was very much with Hitler and his Party advisers. The enactment of the laws was more or less imposed on the Reich cabinet and forced through in the face of considerable opposition.[57] In other cases Hitler obstructed laws considered necessary by the Reich government or by individual Ministers by delaying or indefinitely postponing them, for example, the draft of a new penal code which was basically ready even in 1935. But it also happened that drafts of laws by National Socialist Ministers, which Hitler had to let through in the face of strong resistance from the 'conservative' departments, still failed because there was also obstruction from more important National Socialist circles, as in the case of the draft of a new law on the press which Goebbels submitted in autumn 1936.[58] On the other hand the example of the German Civil Service Law (DBG) of 1937 shows that occasionally Hitler permitted the passage of important drafts of laws when the case for a simple rejection had been made difficult by the fact that he had already allowed protracted preparations and departmental talks. And besides, Hitler's subsequent criticisms of specific provisions of the DBG, thus concerning Article 171, reveal that the Führer had not grasped the legal and political implications of many of the articles contrived by the Ministerial bureaucracy in this comprehensive package of legislation before its passage and signature, just as conversely in other instances he was forced to admit that his 'will as the Führer' could not be given legal form or even subsequently had to be revised.[59]

At any rate the examples briefly indicated here show that governmental legislation in the Third Reich was not simply a logical carrying out of the Führer's will, but that it very often involved a troublesome confusion and conflict. Although National Socialist theoreticians never tired of describing the Führer's will as the supreme law of the Third Reich, the Führer's will was by definition not a law but simply *volition*, which if it was to be publicly defined and made generally binding invariably needed interpreting by governmental lawyers.

For this reason too it was impossible to dispense completely with the collegiate process of legislation. Admittedly Hitler wanted to avoid cabinet debates where possible. These forced him to take up a position during the general exchange of views and to intercede on behalf of this or that Minister in front of the whole cabinet. For this reason Hitler often urged individual Ministers beforehand not to bring up their doubts and objections again. After a few painful episodes when at the wish of some Minister or Party high-up he had given orders which conflicted with already existing decrees or laws, Hitler himself directed that drafts were only to be submitted to him for passing and signature when agreement had been reached between all the departments concerned. The responsibility for observing these procedures lay with the Head of the Reich Chancellery, who therefore as a rule also had to sign the Führer decrees creating or reorganizing governmental duties and setting up new authorities etc. By this time since voting had not only ceased in the cabinet but Hitler had also virtually stifled any general discussions with his Ministers, the cabinet meetings had lost any real purpose. It was thus only logical that the process of passing laws in the cabinet without discussion, as was increasingly the case after 1935/6, was gradually replaced by circulating written material and the clarification of disputed issues between the departments was shifted to the inter-ministerial section talks or discussions between heads of departments.

From Hitler's point of view this had the advantage that he was no longer bothered by run-of-the-mill legislative drafts which had little political relevance, and he could stand back in the case of contentious and more important issues until he was finally ready to make his opinion felt more effectively from outside (through Lammers, Hess, Bormann or other intermediaries, or even sometimes through individual Ministers during preliminary exchanges) than he could during group discussion. In this way the initiative for making and preparing laws passed largely to the ministerial bureaucracy. The latter, unchecked by directives from the cabinet or the Führer, were themselves able to produce laws and implementing statutes in many matters of lesser political importance and, as the growing size of the Reich statute book shows, they could operate the legislative machinery at full blast.

On the other hand, the end of regular political discussions in the cabinet, the absence of any reliable and regular information on the Führer's will for cabinet members and the increasingly sporadic and abrupt transmission of directives from the Führer, which were often obscure in their meaning and effects and arrived through different and often unreliable middle men, generated a crippling uncertainty even over politically unimportant legislative projects. The cabinet divided more and more into Ministers who were well or ill informed, through frequent or infrequent talks with the Führer. As a result the disintegration of the government into a polyocracy of separate departments was accelerated. Departmental policies and decrees increasingly replaced the collegiate government. And the spread of departmental decree-making, which in any event was encouraged by Hitler's preference for short-term basic laws, became still more significant through the growing number of central authorities directly subordinate to the Führer, or so subordinate in practice.

The abortive proposal for a law on government legislation (1936/7)

This state of affairs caused a considerable headache for the Reich Minister of the Interior, who also regarded himself as the Minister responsible for the constitution of the Third Reich. At that time Frick and his State Secretaries Pfundtner and Stuckart believed that the ominous irregularity of the legislative and decree system could be 'contained' and bound by new rules. To this end a draft sent to the Reich departments in November 1935 of a law on the promulgation of legal regulations of the Reich at first tried to maintain the basic principle that even those legal provisions which are 'not issued in the form of a law' needed to be publicly proclaimed in the requisite official organ of publication to be so effective. This was after it had repeatedly happened 'that authorities of the Reich had not published directives undoubtedly containing legal provisions in the approved official organs of publication, but somewhere else'. The 'regrettable legal confusion' resulting from this was due to 'the abnormal excess of official organs of publication', and as a result there was no longer any regard for an orderly promulgation of legal provisions. In the last resort this could only be ended by redefining the distinction in legal form between laws, official decrees and administrative regulations, which had been hitherto blurred as a result of the changed constitutional system. The authors of the draft expressly referred to the confusion arising from the fact that the old legal formulae, which had in fact become obsolete, continued to survive as apparently operative in the legal terminology, whereas on the other hand it was very common for a Minister himself to make legal provisions. Thus by means of a decree 'a formal right of law, which was published in the *Reichsgesetzblatt*, might be altered or destroyed'. All the same, in order to preserve the special status of governmental laws (which were still subject to some extent to a formal process of decision-making in accordance with the Reich government's standing rules), the Reich Ministry of the Interior worked on the assumption that apart from the Führer decrees only those decrees made with the participation of the 'Führer Council' (Reich cabinet) were valid in the Third Reich as the direct act of will of the political leadership and needed to be proclaimed in a prominent place (*Reichsgesetzblatt*). According to the concepts of order in the new Führer state, all other enactments and decrees could no longer be regarded as the direct expression of the leadership's will, but only as giving concrete forms to that will (and thus were to be announced elsewhere).

These suggestions,[60] which would have given the cabinet a share in the 'Führer's authority' as a 'Führer Council', and accordingly promoted the government's legislation in keeping with the theory behind the Führer state as well as fixed the procedures more precisely, were self-contradictory in many respects. They were more artfully constructed than convincing. After objections were raised against the draft by several departments in the first half of 1936, the Minister of the Interior stated on 7 September 1936 that he would 'not pursue the matter further' for the time being.[61] But in the following months Frick conceived the plan which was to serve the same end, a 'Law concerning governmental legislation' in place of the Enabling Law, which expired on 31 March 1937. A corresponding draft whose contents are not known was submitted by Frick on 26 January 1937 (on the same day as the Law on German Civil Servants was passed and the cabinet met for its final session under Hitler's chairmanship). But Hitler, who had apparently given Frick the green light beforehand, no longer wanted anything to do with the matter: 'He [Hitler] had had doubts about whether it was right to pass such a law at this particular time.' He was more inclined to favour an 'extension of the Enabling Law ... It would not be practicable to reorganize the whole process of Reich legislation until a new basic law had been created, which would have to be brief in form and learnt by the children whilst they were still at school.'[62]

That was as much an empty promise to a distant future as the idea of appointing a Senate of the NSDAP to become the Supreme Leadership council. It was obvious that Hitler did not want to be committed to any new legal procedures and constitutional law whatever, and the attempts by Frick or the ministerial bureaucracy of the Reich Ministry of the Interior to secure such a commitment wrongly assumed as ever that the Führer's authority could be subordinated to or reconciled with an authoritarian principle of government.

Notes and references

1. Hess was Reich Minister without portfolio, like Hans Frank (from 1934).
2. This strength was increased through the Prussian Finance Minister Popitz, who also belonged to the Reich cabinet.
3. Concerning the difficulties caused to the Minister for Propaganda by the rejection of official posts by the Reich Minister of Finance, cf. the sworn testimony of Leopold Gutterer of 6 July 1948 (IfZ: ZS 490). There is a remarkable example of the resistance by the bureaucracy of the Ministry of Finance to the expansion of the apparatus of the S.S. and police, namely the negotiations of 1938/9 on setting up S.S. and police jurisdiction; cf. *Akten des Reichsfinanzministerium*, BA: R 2/12 196.
4. Cf. letter from Todt to the Reich Chancellor on 6 July 1933 with the report of the agreement made between Hitler and Todt (BA: R43 II/508). It also appears from this letter that Hitler had authorized Todt to have an official car and to select it himself.
5. Material for Todt's discussion of this with the Head of the Reich Chancellery on 20 September 1933 (BA: R43 II/508).
6. Memorandum of the Reich Chancellery of October 1933, ibid.
7. Undated note by the Reich Chancellery of October 1933, ibid.
8. Summary of the departmental heads talk in the Reich Chancellery on 24 November 1933, ibid.
9. As is clear from the files (BA: R43 II/508), Hitler had left Todt to name his own salary when appointing him. Subsequently a salary on a par with salary group B (State Secretary) was agreed in the region of 22,000 RM yearly. As well as this Todt was put on the board of directors of the German Rail Company from January 1934. On 29 March 1934 he asked Hitler if he could draw the directorial fee of 6,000 RM

annually to offset the increased expenditure occasioned by his numerous official journeys, which Hitler approved. On 18 April 1935 the Reich Ministry of Finance informed Todt that he could not draw this salary according to the rules, whereupon Hitler agreed that he (Todt) could receive an equivalent sum from a fund personally available to Hitler, which Todt also used.

10. As Head of a Supreme Reich Authority Todt also appointed officials to the building authority. But this gave rise to difficulties after 1937 after the right of appointing civil servants had been restricted apart from the Führer to Reich Ministers according to the law on the German civil service. But the appointments which Todt made illegally in ignorance of this provision were only subsequently legalized by a special authorization for these exceptions (Führer decree of 21 September 1940).

11. Details in Wolfgang Benz, 'Vom Freiwilligen Arbeitsdienst zum Arbeitsdienstpflichtgesetz', in *VJHZ*, 16, 1968, Heft 4.

12. References on this in BA: R43 II/516 and 517.

13. References on this in BA: R43 II/525.

14. Circular letters of the Minister of Finance, 28 November 1936 and of the Minister of the Interior, 8 June 1936, ibid.

15. Letter of 28 November 1936 from the Head of the Reich Chancellery to the Reich and Prussian Minister for Science, Education and Culture, ibid.

16. Handwritten comment by Lammers of 30 November 1936 (on Blomberg's letter of the same date): 'The Führer does not want this.'

17. This unusual arrangement had an interesting repercussion for administrative law when the former financial manager of the Hitler Youth, Georg Berger, refused to continue to manage the financial affairs of the Hitler Youth after his appointment as Ministerialrat and went into private business in 1939, but at first refused to relinquish his official capacity voluntarily. Since his appointment had been for life, the Reich Treasurer, who was not a civil servant himself but who regarded the financial manager of the Hitler Youth as his subordinate, had no possibility of terminating Berger's official standing. Only in 1941 was it possible to persuade Berger voluntarily to give up his rights as a civil servant.

18. When the title of the already existing 'Official Gazette of the Reich Youth Leadership of the NSDAP' had been changed after 1 December 1936 to 'The Official Gazette of the Supreme Reich Authority of the Youth Leader of the German Reich and the Reich Youth Leadership of the NSDAP', Schirach had to change this arbitrary title from summer 1937, whereby the Reich Youth Leadership pretended to a right of making state decrees, at the instigation of the Reich Chancellery and the Reich Minister of the Interior, to the 'Official News Bulletin of the Youth Leader of the German Reich and the Reich Youth Leadership of the NSDAP'. Cf. the previous references on this matter in BA: R43 II/468.

19. At the particular prompting of Schirach, Lammers requested the Reich Ministers on 4 October 1939 'to go along as far as possible with the wish of the Youth Leader to be heard before the passing of any laws which affect German youth' (BA: R43 II/515).

20. Of course the Reich made a grant per head for the detainees in the concentration camps.

21. Hans Buchheim, 'Die SS–das Herrschaftsinstrument', *in Anatomie des SS-Staates*, vol. 1, p. 191.

22. Cf. H. Buchheim, op. cit., pp. 208ff.

23. Communication of the Head of the Reich Chancellery of 22 October 1933 to the Reich S.S. Leader: 'On behalf of the Führer and Reich Chancellor I have the honour to inform you that the Reich Security Service envisaged in Section V of the Budget, part 14 will be under you. You are in full command of the members of the Reich Security Service and in this capacity you will be directly responsible to the Führer and Reich Chancellor. This power of command gives you sole responsibility for the Reich Security Service' (BA: R43 II/1103). There are also many other references concerning the Reich Security Service here.

24. Cf. M. Broszat, *Nationalsozialistische Konzentrationslager*, pp. 35ff.

25. Cf. memorandum of the Reich and Prussian Minister of the Interior of spring 1935, cited ibid., pp. 39f.

26. Thus on 30 January 1935 in a directive to the Bavarian State Chancellery, the Reich Minister of the Interior had ordered an examination of the disproportionately (in comparison with Prussia) high number of detainees in Dachau, with a view to the release of some of these. Himmler, who was responsible here in his capacity as Commander of the Bavarian Political Police, sent a copy of this document to Hitler and commented laconically on this: 'Submitted to the Führer 20 February 1935. The prisoners stay where they are' (*Akten Persönlicher Stab Reichsführer-SS*, IfZ: MA 302, B 7001/02).

27. Letter from the Reich and Prussian Minister of the Interior of 10 January 1935 to the Prussian Minister President as the Chief of the Secret State Police (IfZ: MA 302, Bl. 7699f).

28. Daluege's memorandum on the German police covering some twenty-two sides is in BA: R43 II/391.

29. Letter from the Reich Defence Minister and Commander-in-Chief of the Armed Forces to the Führer and Supreme Commander of the Armed Forces, 1 July 1935 (BA: R43 II/391).

30. Cf. the letters of Frick and Himmlerin autumn 1935, cited in H. Buchheim, op. cit., pp. 49f.

31. GS. 1936,. p. 21.

32. Werner Best, 'Die Geheime Staatspolizei', in *Deutsches Recht*, 1936, pp. 125ff.

33. Cf. H. Buchheim, op. cit., p. 59.

34. At first Frick tried to forestall any infringements of this subordinate relationship, for example, in a directive of 25 January 1937 to the division heads and section leaders and the offices of the RFSS in the Ministry of the Interior, when Frick stated that against his instruction a draft of a law (of the Chief of the German Police) had been sent for consideration to offices outside the Ministry. 'This is an impossible state of affairs. It not only undermines the unity of the Ministry, which must at all costs be preserved to the outside world, but the offices who behave in this way run the risk that I shall not approve the draft in part or in whole' (IfZ: MA 435).

35. On this cf. the events sparked off by the letter from the Chief of the Security Police (Heydrich) to the Head of the Reich Chancellery, 18 September 1941 (BA: R43 II/396).
36. Note by Lammers of 11 March 42 (BA R43 II/393a).
37. *Allg. Erlass-Sammlung* (edited by Reich Security Head Office), SF VIIIa, p. 2.
38. Cf. Martin Broszat, op. cit., pp. 75f.
39. Decree concerning the Reich Aviation Ministry, 5 May 1933 (*RGBl*, I, p. 241).
40. Cf. Dieter Petzina, *Autarkiepolitik im Dritten Reich*, pp. 32f.
41. The former Vice-Chancellor von Papen, who was active as Ambassador in Vienna from summer 1934, was also directly subordinate to Hitler.
42. On this cf. the testimony of Schellenburg (the later head of the Foreign News Service of Reich Security Main Office) and the former Amtsleiter of the Research Office, Ministerialdirektor Schappers (IfZ: ZS 291 and ZS 1409. Also here (ZS 1734) a memorandum of eighty-three sides by Ulrich Titel on the Research Office).
43. The figures emerge from the available protocols of the sittings of the Reich cabinet, and 'Ministerial discussions' (confined to Reich Ministers) and 'Meetings of the Reich Ministry' (involving State Secretaries and other cabinet members) are treated alike as 'cabinet meetings' (IfZ: Fa 203).
44. Joseph Goebbels, *Vom Kaiserhof zur Reichskanzlei. Eine historische Darstellung in Tagebuchblättern* (Munich, 1942), p. 302.
45. Protocol of the cabinet meeting of 14 November 1933 (IfZ: Fa 203/3).
46. Otto Dietrich, *12 Jahre mit Hitler* (Munich, 1955), pp. 249–51.
47. From spring 1939 at Hitler's express wish the term 'The Führer' became largely customary in communications between the authorities; cf. the Reich Chancellery's note of 5 August 1939 and further material on this point from the year 1942 in BA: R43 II/583a.
48. Law concerning the oath of Reich Ministers and members of the Land governments, 16 October 1934 (*RGBl*, I, p. 973).
49. Commentary on the draft of a law on the announcement of legal regulations of the Reich sent by the Reich Minister of the Interior to the departments (BA: R43 II/694).
50. Text in BA: R43 II/1036.
51. On this cf. the letter of Ministerialrat Wienstein (Reich Chancellery) to Ministerialrat Medicus (Reich Ministry of the Interior), in BA: R43 II/1036. Lammers's dual role was expressed in the joint term 'State Secretary of the Reich Chancellery' and 'State Secretary of the Reich government'; cf. the *Handbuch für das Deutsche Reich 1936*, ed. by the Reich and Prussian Ministry of the Interior, p. 12.
52. Decree of the Führer and Reich Chancellor of 20 April 1936; cf. on this the remarks of Ministerialdirektor Wienstein (Reich Chancellery) of 15 December 1936 (see also note 50).
53. Decree of the Führer and Reich Chancellor on changing the standing rules of conduct of the Reich Government of 20 March 1935; *Reichsministerialblatt 1935*, p. 433.
54. *Völkischer Beobachter*, Munich ed., 3 September 1938.
56. Law on German Citizens, and Law for the Protection of German

Blood and Honour, 15 September 1935 (*RGBl*, I, p. 1146).

55. A particularly drastic example of this was provided by the Law for the Consolidation of the German Reich (*RGBl*, 1934, I, p. 75), whose extremely important basic aims were merely set out in a few generally formulated sentences but which, probably for symbolic reasons (anniversary of the take-over of government), were announced in the form of a law, although virtually all of the concrete legal questions connected with it were still unresolved. Under these circumstances the provision contained in Art. 5 of this law ('The Reich Minister of the Interior is to issue the necessary legal regulations and administrative instructions for carrying out the law') meant in practice delegating constitutional legislation and the head of state's right to determine the laws for the reorganization of the state to the Minister of the Interior.

56. Law on German Citizens and Law for the Protection of German Blood and Honour, 15 September 1935 (*RGBl*, I, p. 1146).

57. The law preventing the transmission of hereditary disease which had been drafted in the Ministry of the Interior was passed by the cabinet meeting of 14 July 1933 in the face of the determined resistance of von Papen, who referred to the Catholic Church's opposition in principle to sterilization. Hitler replied to this (according to the protocol): 'that any measures which served to preserve the nation were justified'. The steps to be taken were 'morally irreproachable when one proceeded on the assumption that people with hereditary illness continued to propagate without restraint whilst on the other hand millions of healthy children remained unborn'. The 'logic' of taking into account the unborn to justify active measures to prevent births is typical of Hitler's *völkisch*-ideological thought pattern. Statistics that the Reich Minister of the Interior sent to the Führer via the Reich Chancellery on 4 July 1935 provide information on the extent to which the law took effect. According to these, in 1934 a total of 84,525 applications were made for sterilization (by those with hereditary illness, their legal representatives, doctors or sanitorium heads). Of the total 31,000 sterilizations carried out in 1934 (through surgery) there were 89 cases of death. When the amending law of 26 June 1935 was being enacted Hitler's interference was still more evident. The Reich Physicians' Leader of the NSDAP, Dr Wagner, had already asked Frick on 8 January 1934 for the law of 14 July 1933 to be supplemented so that in cases where one of the parents suffered from hereditary illness pregnancies could also be terminated. But this application had been rejected because of the influential doubts of the head of the Health Department in the Reich Ministry of the Interior and NSDAP member, Ministerial Direktor Dr Gütt. Wagner later discussed this matter with Hitler during the Nuremberg rally at the beginning of September 1934 and informed him of his intention as leader of the National Socialist League of Physicians to circulate a confidential letter to the Gauleiter of the Office for Public Welfare and the Amtsleiter of the Land and provincial offices of the KVD (*Krankenversicherung*? [sic] – health insurance), in which doctors were to be asked to terminate pregnancy 'for reasons of eugenics' in spite of the fact that there were no legal provisions for this. Hitler

told Wagner (as the latter informed the Ministry of the Interior on 13 September 1934): 'he would be the supreme judge and would therefore ensure that no doctor would be punished who terminated a pregnancy on the grounds of eugenics, for the health of the German nation was more important than the letter of the law.' In the circular which Wagner subsequently sent out on 13 September 1934 it stated: 'Although in such cases . . . there was still no legal justification, no doctor would be punished who terminated pregnancy . . . for reasons of eugenics.' The Minister of the Interior felt himself obliged to draft a corresponding law to this effect, but Ministerialdirektor Dr Gütt had continued to have serious doubts (*inter alia* because of the impossibility of fairly establishing the charge of hereditary illness in the case of extramarital pregnancies); he told Ministerialrat Wienstein (Reich Chancellery) on 5 October 1934 'he had the impression that the Führer had only been given biassed information about the problem' and therefore would like to speak to the Führer together with Minister Frick. None the less Hitler gave unqualified approval to Wagner's action on 11 October 1934, and informed the Head of the Reich Chancellery that he did not wish to discuss the matter with Dr Gütt and Minister Frick. All the same, the law passed on 26 June 1935 took account of the doubts of Dr Gütt in so far as it merely envisaged terminations of pregnancies where the mothers suffered from hereditary illness. The references cited in BA: R43 II/720. On the genesis of the Nuremberg Laws of 1935 and Hitler's initiative over this, cf. the illuminating account of Bernhard Lösener, 'Das Reichsinnenministerium und die Jugendgesetzgebung', in *VJHZ*, 9. Jg. 1961, H. 3.

58. After the draft of the press law had at first met with objections from the Ministry of the Interior in November 1936, Reichsleiter Amann informed the Reich Chancellery that the Führer had already agreed to the draft in its existing form and 'had decided that the objections of the departments would not be taken into account' (Note by the Reich Chancellery of 24 November 1936). Also when the Defence Minister criticized the draft in the following days Hitler maintained (according to the note made by Lammers on 28 November 1936) 'that the objections of the Reich Ministers . . . were to be ignored'. It was only when the Gestapo also took a stand against the draft (feeling its authority to ban newspapers threatened by the draft) that Hitler allowed the law to be removed from the agenda at the end of November 1936, and finally to be postponed indefinitely in February 1937 (BA: R43 II/467).

59. The example of the Führer decree of 15 October 1934 concerning the DAF, cited above on pp. 151–3, which had to be revised later, is a particularly clear example of this.

60. BA: R43 II/694.

61. Ibid.

62. Protocol of the cabinet meeting of 26 January 1937 (IfZ: Fa 203/5).

Chapter Nine

Departmental polyocracy and the forms of Führer absolutism

Another wave of personnel and organizational changes in the Reich in 1938/9 had the effect of more rapidly undermining the cohesion of the Reich government and the previously still partially intact authority of influential Reich departments. It seems all the more justifiable to regard the year 1938 as a break in the constitutional development of the Hitler state, since these changes coincided with the end of National Socialism's conservative guise and of moderation at home (Reich Crystal Night on 8/9 November 1938 was typical of the revival of terrorism) and the beginning of more active expansionist policies abroad. Three episodes occurring roughly at the same time were symptomatic of the nature of this change. The resignation, or dismissal, of the former Command of the armed forces and Army (Blomberg, Fritsch, Beck) in January/February 1938, the simultaneous replacement of Reich Foreign Minister von Neurath by Ribbentrop and the displacement of Schacht from his responsibility for economic and fiscal policy through the construction of the Organization for the Four Year Plan. In all three instances leading personalities were expelled who enjoyed the authority of conservative experts in their own sphere, who had hitherto been a strong bulwark against Party influences (this was true at least of Schacht and Fritsch) and who had been regarded as pillars of political moderation and the rule of law in the Third Reich. The discharge of these men not only altered the composition of the personnel of Hitler's closest circle of advisers (besides Göring, chiefly Himmler Heydrich and Bormann came to the fore at the same time). It also resulted in a serious break-up of the relatively compact leadership apparatuses and departments which had been managed by those who had been overthrown.

The reorganization of the Armed Forces Command

The independence of the armed forces and Army Command, previously respected by Hitler, ended with the Blomberg–Fritsch crisis, after Hitler had already registered great displeasure at the opposition of the Chief of the Army Command and Chief of the General Staff (Beck) both against his foreign policy gamble at the time of the reoccupation of the Rhineland in March 1936, and the revelation of his (Hitler's) foreign policy goals in the meeting of 5 November 1937 (Hossbach Memorandum). The fact that the pliable and complaisant Blomberg had compromised himself in the eyes of the officer corps and had brought about his own resignation through his marriage to a prostitute, and in doing so had indirectly involved Hitler (who had attended the wedding celebrations) in the scandal, was simply the trigger for Hitler's decision to submit the armed forces to his own will more strongly than had been the case so far. In order to take revenge for 'his Blomberg' Hitler now had no scruples in making use of the evidence assembled and presented by Göring and Heydrich, insinuating that Fritsch had homosexual relations, and thus he engineered the resignation of the awkward Chief of the Army High Command by means of an infamous intrigue. The fact that Fritsch and Beck reacted to the sordid and untenable insinuations by resigning instead of making public denials, admittedly shows that for a long time the 'independence' of the Army had only applied to the military apparatus and not to its influence on policy. And the animosity of the officers towards the Party, S.S. and Gestapo did not seriously affect their submission to the Führer. Moreover Hitler's success in carrying out the union with Austria against the military objections of the Army High Command and the ensuing national enthusiasm, generally compensated most officers – as was often so later – for their 'misgivings' about internal developments and for the humiliation they had suffered. The re-shuffle at the top of the armed forces, which Hitler ordered on 4 February 1938, in conjunction with the Blomberg–Fritsch crisis,[1] disposed of the previously strong post which Blomberg had enjoyed of 'Defence Minister' and 'Commander in Chief of the Armed Forces'. In place of the purely honorary function assumed by Hindenburg as Commander in Chief of the Armed Forces, Hitler himself took over the command of the armed forces (previously left to the Defence Minister). The Defence Ministry ceased to exist as an independent part of the government. And from the old Armed Forces Office of the Defence Ministry arose the High Command of the Armed Forces (*Oberkommando der Wehrmacht*-OKW) headed by General Keitel and directly subordinate to Hitler. Like the replacement for Fritsch, the much less stable Commander in Chief of the Army General von Brauchitsch (with General Halder as the new Chief of Staff), Keitel had the 'equivalent status to a Reich Minister' as Head of OKW. The equal standing of the offices of Chief of the OKW and of the Commander in Chief of the Army achieved in this way ended the former hierarchy of ranks at the top of the armed forces. It also encouraged permanent rivalry between the OKW and OKH (Commander in Chief of the Army – *Oberkommando des Heeres* – OKH) and increased Göring's influence as the most influential, together with Hitler, and from then on also the highest ranking (with his appointment as Field Marshal on 4 February 1938) among the Chiefs of the three divisions of the armed forces.

Next to Göring Himmler was the real victor of this episode. For a long time he had intrigued with Hitler against Fritsch and other high-ranking Army officers and he above all had launched the Fritsch crisis with Heydrich's support. The new leadership of the armed forces and of the Army could no more prevent the considerable increase of armed S.S. units ordered by Hitler in summer 1938, than the introduction at the same time (and actually realized in October) of a separate S.S. and police jurisdiction. Although the Fritsch crisis marked the real birth of resistance for *individual* officers to Hitler, this was chiefly because the Army and the armed forces as a *whole* had not functioned in this same crisis as a stable political factor internally, or as an effective counterweight to the dynamic threat to law and order posed by the absolute rule of the Führer.

The German Foreign Office under Ribbentrop

The change of personnel at the head of the Foreign Office was no less momentous. Foreign Minister von Neurath seemed as 'unsuitable' as Fritsch and Beck for the transition to an offensive and risky foreign policy which Hitler had secretly announced in November 1937. The fact that Hitler brought about Neurath's departure (in the guise of a transparent appointment to a 'Secret Cabinet Council' which never actually functioned)[2] and Ribbentrop's appointment as the new Foreign Minister at the same time as the reorganization at the top of the armed forces, underlines the programmatic character of and the connection between both measures. Under Neurath's direction the Foreign Office had largely escaped Party influences but had also been increasingly confined to carrying out the routine tasks of the foreign policy service. In the case of various exceptionally important foreign policy decisions (introduction of general conscription, reoccupation of the Rhineland etc.) Hitler had presented his Foreign Minister with *faits accomplis*. Other important initiatives of National Socialist foreign policy were conducted through special emissaries of Hitler. Joachim von Ribbentrop had become prominent among these as Hitler's 'Deputy for Foreign Policy Questions' (from 1934); for example on the occasion of the Naval Agreement with Great Britain (1935), of the Anti-Comintern Pact with Japan (1936) and as the Ambassador in London appointed by Hitler personally. Unlike Rosenberg, his chief rival among the NSDAP's foreign policy 'experts', Ribbentrop could not point to any noteworthy career as an 'old fighter' or Party functionary. His political position was derived exclusively from the personal services which Ribbentrop, the wine and spirits importer, had been able to render the Führer before the take-over of power in Berlin, as a contact man and as the much-travelled expert adviser on things foreign and on languages. For this reason and in spite of all his efforts he had not yet been able to make it as Reichsleiter of the NSDAP, although the Ribbentrop Bureau, which was attached to the staff of the Führer's Deputy and had a staff of some sixty (in 1936),[3] increasingly overshadowed Rosenberg's Foreign Policy Office (*Aussenpolitisches Amt* – APA). The 'Bureau's' staff was arranged in territorial sections consisting of German foreign languages experts and journalists from abroad, young graduates and lecturers from the *völkisch*-geopolitically inclined Berlin Hochschule für Politik (including Albrecht Haushofer, Eberhard von Thadden, Peter Kleist), a number of personal friends of Ribbentrop (Martin Luther, Rudolf Likus, Horst Wagner) and occasionally prominent collaborators (including Prince Philipp of Hesse, the son-in-law of the Italian King Victor Emmanual III, as the contact with the Italian government). Ribbentrop made particular efforts to strengthen his relations with influential Party leaders and had especially good contacts with Himmler, who gave him the rank of S.S. Gruppenführer in 1936. Ribbentrop was apparently after an important official post in the field of foreign policy and was pressing Hitler to this end when, in 1937, he had already drafted a scheme for reorganizing the Foreign Office.[4] This aimed at transforming it into an instrument of offensive National Socialist foreign policy modelled on the lines of the operational division of the General Staff.

Although Hitler had previously often overlooked Ribbentrop's demands it now apparently seemed advisable to him, in the context of the change of leadership in the armed forces and the Army, to use Ribbentrop's appointment as the new Foreign Minister to break up the conservative, aristocratic 'isolating layer' at the Foreign Office, represented by diplomats of the old school like von Neurath, von Bülow, von Hassell, von Dirksen etc. From the outset there was marked animosity between most of these experienced diplomats and civil servants and the new Minister, as self-satisfied and parvenu as he was superficial and pathologically ambitious. At the same time Ribbentrop knew well enough how to make a few important officials at the Foreign Office into his personal confidants and aides, including the indispensable Head of the Legal Division, the man acknowledged as the 'grey eminence', Friedrich Gaus,[5] whereas relations with the new State Secretary (Ernst von Weizsäcker) became very cool even after a few months. But there was no general resistance to Ribbentrop especially since his appointment as Foreign Minister also signified promotion and increased responsibility for the Foreign Office, whose loss of prestige in the old National Socialist system of leadership had inflicted hardship on the younger officials in particular. Actually Ribbentrop, who vigorously activated relations to the official Party offices and – in bitter conflict with Goebbels – revived the foreign news and propaganda operations at the Foreign Office, was able to restore many of the responsibilities which had formerly been lost to this office. But this was achieved only at the cost of a lasting change in the structure of the office. This meant that at the least Ribbentrop strove to give a Nazi look to the Foreign Office through the introduction of uniforms for diplomats, through bestowing honorary S.S. ranks on leading officials or through compulsory membership of the NSDAP for officials under him. More important were the personnel changes, particularly at the top of the office and in the newly created divisions. Ribbentrop not only slipped a substantial clique of personnel from his old 'Bureau' into the Foreign Office (Luther, Likens, Hewel, von Thadden, Sonnleitner, Gottfriedsen, Abetz among many), he also deliberately appointed to central posts officials who were personally known to him, thus the former adviser from the London Embassy, Ernst Woermann, or diplomats who had been shoved out to politically unimportant posts because of their support for National Socialism, like Karl Ritter. Furthermore, he attached to the office a series of amateur researchers from the Party (Keppler, Veesenmeyer among others), who came into action almost everywhere during the months to come as agents and 'shock troop leaders' of aggressive National Socialist 'diplomacy', when it was necessary to overthrow governments or to prepare for a forced German entry or a German protectorate (thus in 1938/9, the Anschluss and the proclamation of the 'independent' Slovakia; in 1941, the erection of the Croatian Ustasi State; and in 1944 the occupation of Hungary). Above all the new 'Bureau of the Reich Foreign Minister' and the new Germany Division led by Ribbentrop's friend and State Secretary, Luther, were imposed on the Foreign Office as a more or less inexperienced new leadership apparatus and as a continuation of the 'Ribbentrop Bureau'. The Germany Division, which was also physically separated from the rest of the Foreign Office, was responsible for any contact with the Party offices which Ribbentrop required, especially with the S.S. Through this ran the cross ties which later involved the Foreign Office in the S.S. policy of deporting Jews or recruiting ethnic Germans and Germanic S.S. troops in the occupied or allied countries. This collaboration between Himmler and Ribbentrop through the Germany Division also found organizational expression in the institution of the 'police attachés' who were posted to a number of German Embassies in South-east Europe after 1941.

The separation and discrepancy between the old office which the State Secretary managed as the head of the authority and the new plenipotentiaries, special divisions and leadership staffs attached to Ribbentrop's person, was illustrated all the more graphically after the outbreak of the War, when Ribbentrop and his staff of closest collaborators were often no longer in Berlin but near the Führer's headquarters, and finally when, after the opening of the Russian campaign, he set up his own mobile Field HQ (at first in Himmler's special train 'Heinrich' and later in his own special train 'Westphalia'). From then on the real conduct of foreign policy increasingly passed from the Office to these leadership staffs. Ribbentrop's directives to German Ambassadors and envoys abroad frequently went direct from his Field HQ and there too he received the most important news from abroad. Those in his closest circle (his Bureau Chief Hewel, his personal advisers von Rinteln and Sonnleitner) were often better informed than the State Secretary at the Foreign Office, so that the rivalry between the career diplomats and Ribbentrop's new men grew increasingly acute.

One growing practice during the War was typical. Instead of a diplomat of the old school being appointed as Ambassador to the small and dependent allies of Germany, Party exponents were installed almost like Governors of the Greater German Reich. Since at this time Ribbentrop also had to resist S.S. encroachments on foreign policy, former higher S.A. leaders were also brought into play again. In 1940/1 four of these (Ludlin, von Jagow, von Killinger, Kasche) were installed as Ambassadors one after the other in Pressburg, Budapest, Bukharest and Zagreb, but former collaborators from the Ribbentrop Bureau were also similarly employed (Otto Abelz as Envoy to the Vichy Government in France). Finally in 1941 Ribbentrop also set up a special Information Service of the Foreign Office alongside the normal foreign missions, in order to compete with the SD in the area of news services. Towards the end of the War other well-known and energetic National Socialist outsiders (Neubacher, Veesenmeyer, Rahn) were despatched with extraordinary special powers when it was necessary to give a helping hand to an ally. These emissaries were frequently personally instructed by Hitler and like the leading officials of the Germany Division only nominally functioned as representatives of the German Foreign Office but were in reality personal confidants and agents of Ribbentrop and Hitler. Their confidential tasks and extensive special powers increasingly overlapped and cut across the normal procedures, official representatives and responsibilities of the foreign service. After the onset of the War there was a progressive disorderliness about normal duties. The rational organization of the German Foreign Office was increasingly stifled by new authorizations, special organizations and leadership apparatuses for pushing through *ad hoc* measures.[6]

The organization of the Four Year Plan

The authorities directing the economic policy of the Third Reich presented a similar picture after Göring was entrusted with carrying out the Four Year Plan. After full employment had been restored Schacht put up much stronger resistance against any further forcing of the pace of rearmament and against helping to finance any new undertakings for autarkic raw materials production which were not economically viable. Schacht's stubborn efforts to maintain the stability of the currency and the export capacity of the German economy under world market conditions, could no longer be reconciled after 1937/8 with Hitler's determination to step up still more the production of new materials which were vital for armaments and defence.[7] The exclusion of Schacht, who in 1935 had also been given the secret task of general plenipotentiary for the war economy, brought to a close the period when National Socialist economic policy had still been strongly geared to the market economy. The change signified, over and above the change of personnel, a far-reaching shift of economic policy responsibilities and decisions to new leadership apparatuses. The new Minister for Economics and President of the Reichsbank, Walter Funk, who had much less influence in this position than Schacht had enjoyed, was no less affected by this shift than his predecessor.

The more intensive form of state planning and control which was required to achieve the armaments and autarkic economic policy goals of the Four Year Plan involved the fusion of already existing leadership authorities and the creation of new ones. However, since the Four Year Plan did not entail switching to a fully planned economy, but merely set out state production programmes which were to have absolute priority in certain key areas, whilst maintaining the basic structure of the private and market economy, there was no systematic construction of any comprehensive state economic administration. Instead new central 'business groups' (above all for price controls, the allocation of raw materials and foreign currency and for the supply of labour), as well as 'general plenipotentiaries' for the individual key areas of production under the Four Year Plan (iron and steel, chemical industries, building, motor vehicles etc.) were organized alongside and above the existing economic bureaucracy of private authorities. In appointing business group leaders and general plenipotentiaries of the Four Year Plan Göring was primarily influenced by principles of expediency. Thus Party functionaries (like the Silesian Gauleiter Josef Wagner as new Price Commissioner) were given central planning and leadership tasks alongside official State Secretaries, officers from the economic staffs of the Airforce and Army as well as leading industrialists. The supreme co-ordinating body was the General Council for the Four Year Plan, headed by Göring or by State Secretary Koerner (Prussian State Ministry) on Göring's behalf.

In order to make use of the departments of the Reich government for the purposes of the Four Year Plan, Göring had made the State Secretaries of the Ministries for Economics, Agriculture, Labour and Transport, business group leaders or members of the General Council. In this way the Commissioner for the Four Year Plan could interfere almost at will in the Ministries concerned and the authority of the departmental Ministers involved suffered considerably. As a result Darré's influence rapidly dwindled after 1938, whereas his ambitious State Secretary Backe became the strong man of the Agriculture and Food Ministry as Göring's agent. Similarly Seldte, the Minister for Labour, became increasingly less important compared with his State Secretary Syrup. Given the dual subordination of these State Secretaries, the duty to Göring was invariably the decisive factor, whose prestige chiefly rested on his special relationship of trust to Hitler. The Reich Ministry of Economics, which Göring himself had taken over at first after Schacht's departure, was also reorganized in 1938 to fit in with the aims of the Four Year Plan. In practice it was downgraded to the 'Executive organ of the Commissioner for the Four Year Plan'.[8] The Organization for the Four Year Plan largely deprived the economic departments of the Reich government of the substance of economic policy decision-making and transferred this to individual special agents. The personalized structure of the Organization for the Four Year Plan resulting from this lacked the clearly ordered division of responsibilities characteristic of a state economic administration but it had the advantage of being more flexible. This was shown both in Göring's management[9] and in the structure and appointments to the offices of the business group leaders and general plenipotentiaries. A good example of this above all was the appointment of Carl Krauch as general plenipotentiary for chemicals (1938) and as Director of the Reich Office for Economic Consolidation (subordinate to the Reich Ministry of Economics).

Krauch, a member of the board of I.G. Farben from 1926, had taken a leading part in the development of synthetic fuel production in the Leuna Works of that company. (Fischer–Tropsch process). He had played a considerable role after 1933 as adviser to Göring's Aviation Ministry and to the Central German *Braunkohle-Benzin-AG* (BRABAG), which had been founded and given Reich guarantees in Schact's time for the production of synthetic fuel. When the Organization for the Four Year Plan was set up Krauch was at first given control of the division for research and development in the Office for Raw Materials and Stock, which was headed by Colonel Löb (Aviation Ministry). In this capacity the I.G. Manager Krauch soon proved himself superior to Colonel

Löb's more ponderous military planning bureaucracy. He had the full support of the board of I.G. Farben (Bosch), could make use of the I.G. planning staffs and also took over some I.G. employees as co-workers in the Office of the Four Year Plan. After Krauch had convinced Göring of Löb's mistaken calculations in 1938, Krauch was given all the key powers as general plenipotentiary for chemicals to step up production in this by far the most important sector of production of home-produced raw materials. Although the Reich Ministries of Aviation and Economics pressed for Krauch to leave I.G. Farben and join the state service when he took over this influential office, and Göring was also prepared to offer him the post of State Secretary, Krauch turned the chance down after consulting Bosch.[10] Not only did he retain his membership of the board of I.G. Farben but in 1940 he was appointed as chairman of the supervisory board of I.G. Farben, and thus until 1945 combined the management of the most important planning authority for chemical production with the leading position in I.G. Farben, by far the most important monopolist concern in the German chemicals industry.

Without doubt Krauch was eminently well qualified as a scientist and as a business organizer to ensure a skilful development of synthetic petrol, Buna and other chemical products. And because of his ties with I.G. Farben and other branches of the chemicals industry, which furnished the authorities for the Four Year Plan with free industrial management and expertise, he was probably the most suitable person for the job from the point of view of effectiveness of planning and production. The fact that Krauch's influential state post was an honorary one, that he was not formally employed by the state and did not even exist as far as the budget of the Reich administration was concerned, was an arrangement which met with considerable suspicion both among industrial firms other than I.G. and among the state economic bureaucracy, which was used to a strict separation of public and private commissions. Although Krauch also refuted any suggestion of unfair advantage being given to I.G. Farben, by employing independent consultants, none the less the personal union of private and state leadership of the economy created in his job and in his staff was essentially problematic, for the running of the Third Reich's economy, although increasingly typical. Krauch himself described this type of control as an assumption of state duties by the independent sector of the economy; other theoreticians spoke of a new form of 'commission management'. There is no disputing the efficiency of this principle. It was extended in a similar way during the War for the whole area of weapons and armaments production under the direction of the new Minister for Armaments, Todt, and above all under Todt's successor Albert Speer (from 1942).[11] But it is equally evident that in this way the whole area of economic planning and state subsidies escaped any reliable administrative control by the state. Admittedly the ultimate power of decision (establishing priorities, setting up production programmes, allocating raw materials and labour etc.) rested with Göring and the General Council of the Four Year Plan or – later under Speer – with the leadership staff of 'Central Planning'. All the same their decisions were very strongly influenced by the suggestions or demands of the general plenipotentiaries or (under Speer) the 'committees' and 'rings' from the private sector of the armaments economy, which as a rule were staffed by managers from the corresponding branches of industry and subordinate to the Armaments Ministry, and whose technical and expert arguments the small central leadership authorities hardly ever resisted. In these semi-official, semi-private co-ordination and planning staffs the principles of the Führer state already imposed on the traditional state apparatus blended with the apparatus of leadership and co-ordination of industry in a virtually indistinguishable whole. Just as the National Socialist leaders increasingly used special organizations from the Party, with their distinctive leader structure and way of working, or special agents from the NSDAP for public tasks, especially when it was essential to force through measures which seemed urgent without being restricted by the general administration and its regulations, so the industrial leadership apparatus of private business was unhesitatingly exploited at the expense of a uniform state administration in the interests of short-term productivity.

The further development of the economic planning authorities during the War

As in other areas of the organization of the Führer state, it happened in the loose structures of the economic administration of the Four Year Plan, that the allocation of duties originally planned was changed constantly, according to whatever new urgent tasks and aims there were and according to the energy and ambition of individual agents. Some subordinates, like Krauch, became independent whilst other offices lost their importance and new commissions arose. Thus matters did not rest either when Paul Pleiger, a National Socialist industrialist from Westphalia who was friendly with Göring, took over the management of the Hermann Göring Works, which had been founded largely with state capital in Salzgitter bei Braunschweig in 1937 to exploit domestic iron ore. On the contrary the Hermann Göring Works developed under Pleiger's management (chiefly through the construction of new works in Austria as well as through partnerships and amalgamations with other undertakings) into a gigantic concern. It extended beyond the mining and machine industries to shipping and had hardly anything to do with the original purpose of the Four Year Plan. A completely new construction of the Four Year Plan arose after the Polish campaign in October 1939 in the form of the 'Main Trustee Office East', which was charged with the trust administration of all the Jewish and Polish industrial wealth seized in Poland, and in this capacity (under the direction of the trustee Max Winkler, who had already been commissioned earlier with the job of turning the Jewish press ventures in the Third Reich into 'aryan' concerns) it acquired the status of a new central Reich authority as well as its own right to make regulations.

Moreover Todt prepared the way for his appointment as Armaments Minister (1940) from his Office of the Four Year Plan for the regulation of the building industry. And the finished combination of offices, which had been enlarged under Todt and later inherited by Speer, developed into the real controlling force behind the war economy after 1941/2; it also restrained Göring and in practice replaced the Organization of the Four Year Plan which continued to exist in name. Just as Göring had once frustrated the economic Ministries of the Reich government by appointing their State Secretaries to be his business group leaders, so after 1942 Speer incorporated Göring's State Secretary in the Aviation Ministry, General Milch, as well as the Defence Economic Staff of OKW (General Thomas), in his system of 'Central Planning', and in this way he more or less excluded Göring. But the same tendency of individuals and offices to make themselves independent also spread within Speer's organization towards the end of the War and undermined his own leadership. Thus in 1944, the chief of the technical bureau of Central Planning in Speer's Ministry, Karl Otto Sauer, Todt's former friend and collaborator, was appointed by Hitler as Special Deputy for the so-called 'Hunter Programme' (for the urgent production of fighter planes), and in this capacity he was given commissions and authorizations directly from Hitler, whereas Speer began to lose the Führer's confidence at the same time.

It is practically impossible to define the structure of the economic planning authorities which developed after the Four Year Plan according to the categories of any bureaucratic state administration. Nominal functions and ancillary organizations signified little. The actual process of decision-making changed and depended on the fluctuating development of personal relations and groupings, on the changing authority (derived from Hitler in the last resort) of key figures like Göring, Todt and Speer, and on the personal loyalites and ambitions of their agents. And here the business interests of the organs and managers from the private economic sector who were involved in the process must not be underestimated.[12]

Within the Third Reich's organization for a war economy, the overwhelming drive present under the conditions of war for the greatest possible economic efficiency (most strongly exemplified in the knowledge and practice of private heavy industry), was intensified as it were by the basically anti-bureaucratic passion of the National Socialist principle of leadership. Since the Party had nothing to offer on economic issues and since neither the state-owned Hermann Göring concern nor the S.S. enterprises developed from the concentration camps[13] (especially in the building materials sector) were particularly viable, the private business structure of heavy industry best corresponded with the National Socialist principle of leadership. The absolute priority for realizing a given project with the greatest possible flexibility of organization; allowing of considerable personal freedom of movement for the leading representatives entrusted by the board (or leadership); action according to the principle of procuration and not according to strictly applied rules of conduct – the Party had all these things very much in common with private enterprise. Therefore under the conditions of total mobilization for war, both could ideally complement each other, especially since the special organs of the Führer state – the Reich Defence Commissioners, Reich Governor Sauckel as General Plenipotentiary for the Allocation of Labour (from 1943), the Gestapo and the Inspector of Concentration Camps etc. – could respectively employ their extraordinary powers and means of coercion to ensure the maximum productivity for a war economy which was managed in the spirit of private enterprise. For this reason the success of the Four Year Plan, or the extraordinary achievements of Speer as Armaments Minister, which in 1943/4 made it possible for German armaments production to be increased threefold in spite of Allied supremacy in the air, was inseparable from these other factors and aspects.

Thus Speer's successful utilization of the dynamic force of private enterprise for armaments production was closely related to the introduction of a similar 'entrepreneurial' approach in the sphere of 'work creation', under the direction of the new General Plenipotentiary for the Allocation of Labour (*Generalbevollmächtigten für den Arbeitseinsatz* – GBA), which was instituted with Speer. 'Central Planning' under Speer established the raw materials and labour force requirements according to the extremely urgent demands of the separate industrial production committees. The GBA (Sauckel) then received the appropriate order from the head of the division for the allocation of labour in 'Central Planning', whereas the state authorities formerly responsible for establishing labour force requirements were largely excluded from this matter. Instead, to a considerable extent Sauckel recruited employees of the labour offices into mobile employment detachments, which with the aid of the police brought together millions of 'foreign workers' in the occupied territories and pumped them in to the Reich armaments industry as forced labour. This type of labour 'creation' through deliberate police actions and the use of 'flying' detachments etc. increasingly replaced the supply of war labour before 1942, which had generally been regulated by means of state emergency decrees. The practice of *ad hoc* measures and of concentrated actions instead of regular and orderly administrative activity reflected an economic policy wholly geared to results.

The massive extension of forced labour with the help of foreign workers, whilst by no means complete use was made of domestic resources (the employment of German women in the Second World War lagged far behind that of women in England), also considerably affected the concentration camps. The overall total of prisoners in these camps had already risen to some 100,000 by 1942 and was forced up to about half a million by the end of the War (some 95 per cent of non-German prisoners, with Russians, Poles and Jews comprising the largest share). Yet, according to Himmler's way of thinking, the 'less valuable' concentration camp prisoners offered a labour supply which was available and transferable at all times and especially for 'assignments' (and if need be 'worked to death') when it was necessary to set about crucial new tasks or to make basic changes in armaments production 'without regard to any losses'. Thus, for example, the construction, setting-up and operation of the underground V-bomb production in the South Harz fell in the first instance on the 30,000 concentration camp prisoners who were hurriedly transported there for this purpose after the Royal Air Force attack on Peenemünde, and who were kept in the most desperate conditions and put to work in the underground tunnels with considerable 'wastage of manpower'. Here the guarantee of secrecy through the S.S. supervision of the prisoners and the additional S.S. and police measures in this 'prohibited area' (seizure of land among other things) 'facilitated' the carrying out of a 'crash programme' of armaments production, which Hitler wrongly expected to have a decisive effect on the War.

It is clear from all this that under Hitler the particular form and development of economic and labour allocation planning increasingly helped to undermine the unity of the state administration and Reich government through special organizations and separate leadership apparatuses. Although this process of disintegration had definite limits, initially the National Socialist leadership provided more and more opportunities, alongside the public and ostensibly legal exercise of power and government, for carrying out further aims by means of secret directives and with the aid of separate leadership authorities and special organizations. The latter had been trained by then and the general state administration was either kept in ignorance or only partially involved in a subordinate role.

The outbreak of War as the break in the policy and constitutional structure of the National Socialist regime

The crucial turning point in all this was the beginning of the Second World War. But not in the sense that the regime's progressive use of force and its extension at home had been primarily determined by the external factor of the War itself. On the contrary, the hard core of the National Socialist movement was fixed on war for internal reasons. Just as the National Socialist dogma advocated the 'iron rule' and the struggle between races and a spirit of war was extolled as permanent in the teaching methods practised in the Hitler Youth and Hitler Schools, so too the domestic policy of the Hitler regime after 1933 was directed primarily towards preparing the nation to fight. By arousing the national fighting spirit and by transforming first the Party, then the state and society, into a complete fighting community, National Socialism had deployed its real strength and skill. The First World War had already shown what feats of energy such a total spirit of war could generate, and what social, spiritual and moral illusions of renewal could be fostered in this way as additional motivating factors. Hitler built on to this 'experience'. The determination to 'lift' Germany above the 'shame' of 1918, the fanatical resolution to renew the struggle for Germany's world power and regeneration more decisively than in the First World War – here was Hitler's true gospel. And this was a matter of getting 'more living space', as the Reich Chancellor had secretly informed leading officers immediately after his appointment at the beginning of February 1933, and as he then repeated with greater attention to the immediate future in his memorandum on setting up the Four Year Plan as well as in the talk with his Generals on 5 November 1937. Hitler's impatience in foreign policy after 1937/8, the frequently attested worry he had from that time that he might not be at the height of his faculties when the 'Great War' had to be fought, all show how much this struggle preoccupied him. And war was more than just a means to an end. Through war National Socialism came into its own, as it were, and returned to its true element.

However rationally Hitler the foreign policy maker and strategist could pursue short-term goals, the aim of waging the great battle for living space for the race became all the more irrational. Typically there was no logical and rational foreign policy planning for this and Hitler steered towards this goal all the more surely through instinct. This was the case in 1939, when he risked full-scale war although he believed he could prevent it, and in 1940/1, when he discontinued the offensive in the West in order at last to wage 'his war' in the East against the Soviet Union.

We have already described, or at least indicated, that the transition to an offensive and aggressive foreign policy in 1937/8 went together with stepping-up the domestic struggle against the Church and the Jews, against the hitherto largely respected conservative forces in the Army, bureaucracy and judicature. Hitler's speech to the Reichstag on 30 January 1939 on the occasion of the sixth anniversary of the take-over of power is worth noting. Not since 1933 had Hitler attacked so fanatically in public the 'spiritual weaklings', the decaying 'social castes'. He argued for the *völkisch* 'laws' and predicted of the Jews that in the event of another world war then 'the result will not be ... a victory for Jewry but the destruction of the Jewish race in Europe'.[14]

The internal policy measures initiated immediately after the beginning of the War at Hitler's personal command, for stricter police action against and the summary execution of criminal and anti-social 'parasites', for the killing of 'incurable lunatics' and above all the thorough 'consolidation' for 'strengthening German nationhood' which was undertaken in the 'incorporated' Polish areas (deportation of Poles and Jews, settlement of ethnic Germans), reveal that for Hitler the War had a much wider purpose than a mere military one. It was a matter of 'racial' war, which also had to be waged at home almost like a second stage of the National Socialist revolution.[15] At the same time there was a rapid expansion of those already existing channels of command, special authorizations and extraordinary executive authorities which were directly under the Führer. In short the *substance* of this more extreme policy was inextricably bound up with the progressive dissolution of the normal *type* of centralized civil government.

The Ministerial Council for the Defence of the Reich: The disintegration of the system of decrees

After Hitler's decision during the War to don the 'field grey' and with his at first intermittent but from 1941 almost permanent transfer to the changing locations of the 'Führer Headquarters', remote from Berlin, the Führer was also physically 'distant' from the Reich government. When the War began Hitler basically ceased to be Reich Chancellor, that is the actually controlling head of the Reich government. The decree of 30 August 1939 setting up a Ministerial Council for the Defence of the Reich (*RGBl*, I, p. 1539) with the heir designate Göring as chairman, underlined Hitler's determination to delegate the business of government more than ever before.

This Ministerial Council had only six standing members, in accordance with a war contingency plan of 1938: Göring (chairman), Frick in his new capacity as 'General Plenipotentiary for the Reich Government' (*Generalbevollmächtigter für die Reichsverwal-*

tung – GBV), Funk as 'General Plenipotentiary for the Economy' (*Generalbevollmächtigter für die Wirtschaft* – GBW), besides Keitel as Chief of OKW as well as Lammers and Hess. In theory this War Cabinet could have become a new collegiate organ of the Reich government with Göring as head of the cabinet. In practice, however, Göring did not make use of such possibilities. Instead, like Hitler, he soon urged that any extensive legislative schemes should be shelved during the war. On 5 June 1940 a Führer decree was also issued which ordered 'that all laws and regulations which are not directly relevant to the defence of the Reich must be postponed indefinitely'.[16]

The fact that the Ministerial Council (whose decrees, unlike the laws of the Reich government, were not executed by Hitler but only by Göring – chiefly through the countersignature of the GBV and the Chief of the Reich Chancellery – and were normally prepared between the departments) could generally operate without Hitler and only needed his consent in doubtful cases, basically meant strengthening the legislative initiative of the departmental heads of the Reich government. The decrees of the so-called 'Board of Three' (GBV, GBW, Chief of OKW) made up a still shorter procedure, Frick having over-all direction and the authority to sign, and for non-economic legal ordinances it had practically the same power to issue decrees as Göring in his capacity as the agent for the Four Year Plan.

The GBV tried to define clearly the numerous existing ways of passing laws and decrees in a circular of 1 March 1940. In the event he had to admit that 'any clear demarcation between... the different legislative procedures was impossible',[17] and that instead action had to be taken in specific cases according to urgency and expediency. In fact the irregularity of the process increased all the time, especially since the nominal responsibilities and the relations between the political leaders and authorities rapidly and progressively degenerated during the War. Complaints piled up from individual departments about their not being informed about drafts of regulations in accordance with the rules of procedure. Thus Bormann, as head of the Party Chancellery, who after Hess's flight to England in May 1941 formally succeeded the Führer's Deputy (with the position of a participating Reich Minister), complained on 29 October 1941 in a letter to Lammers that a decree signed by Frick and Ley (in his capacity as Reich Commissioner for Housing), and published in the *Reichgesetzblatt* (1941, I, p. 534), concerning the building of dwelling houses and settlement offices, had not been shown to him (Bormann) or the responsible Reich Labour Minister and was 'against the Führer's express will'. Bormann remarked in this connection:

Whereas the legislation of the Reich was originally too cumbersome and subject to too many formal requirements, in recent years it has undergone a loosening up and the likely consequences of this must be recognized in good time if serious threats to the state leadership are to be avoided.[18]

It was emphatically confirmed within the Reich Chancellery that the composition of the law stemmed 'to an ever-growing degree from decrees by the individual departments' and that ministerial implementing decrees no longer merely comprised more technical and related provisions, as had formerly been the case, but an essential part of the new regulation itself. Since 'there is no superior office which rules on differences of opinion', the tendency was growing in particular for the specially authorized heads of departments not to involve other departments, chiefly 'when no particularly strong *political* resistance was expected from these'. Besides there was also a tendency for various heads to eliminate the possible objection of other departments by seeking 'a ruling from the Führer' beforehand. This was 'all the more disturbing because as a result the authority of not only individual departments but also of the Führer will be undermined if it subsequently transpires that a projected regulation cannot be carried out'.[19]

Already in May 1941 the deputy of the Chief of the Reich Chancellery had stated after a departmental discussion on the right of association in the Reichsgau Wartheland:

The following was typical of the shifts of responsibility between the Reich Ministers and other central offices: The theme of the discussion was the question of how the matter of Reich law should be ordered in a new province. The following offices had a say in the matter: Agent for the Four Year Plan, Central Trustee Office East, Reich Commissioner for the Consolidation of German Nationhood, Deputy of the Führer, Reich Security Office. Ministers of the Interior and Finance kept right out of it, the representative from the Reich Ministry of Justice merely made suggestions for wording.[20]

A further complication arose from the fact that the Ministerial Council's power to make law for the defence of the Reich was limited 'to the territory of the German Reich' (including the General Government) on the express decision of Hitler in October 1942, and was not extended to the various heads of the civilian administrations in the other areas under German control. Therefore the 'intolerable situation' arose (which Lammers had tried to prevent through a letter to Göring), that 'in the event of a matter being regulated for the entire area of control of the Greater German Reich' the Ministerial Council had to discuss separately 'with the Reich Minister for the occupied Eastern territories, with two Reich Commissioners (Norway and Netherlands), six heads of the civilian administrations (Lower Styria, South Carinthia, Alsace, Lorraine, Luxemburg, Eupen-Malmedy) and the competent Military Commanders' to determine 'whether or not the said persons were willing to issue the relevant decree for the areas under their control'.[21]

Just as in this case Göring (whose influence had meanwhile dwindled markedly) made no special efforts to enforce the Ministerial Council's general power to make laws in the face of opposition from Reich Commissioners and civilian administration heads who were directly responsible to the Führer, so Lammers also after 1941/2 increasingly ceased to be an impartial manager and co-ordinator of the Reich government. Instead the Head of the Reich Chancellery increasingly felt himself obliged to secure political allies and to make political deals before he brought any dispute before Hitler or moved one way or the other. A serious quarrel had already arisen between the GBV (Frick) and Lammers at the beginning of 1942, on the question of the independence of the civilian administration in the West (Alsace–Lorraine). Frick categorically rejected the claim of the head of the civilian administration to budgetary independence and had rightly requested the Head of the Reich Chancellery to submit this question to the Führer for his decision. Lammers, who was only too familiar with Hitler's tendency to favour those Gauleiter acting as heads of civilian administration, clearly did not want to incur Hitler's displeasure with such a submission and in so doing to exhaust further his already dwindling opportunities for discussion with the Führer. Therefore he rejected a submission to the Führer on the grounds that Hitler did not want to be bothered with questions about technical organization, whereupon Frick reacted with a sharp letter of protest on 27 February 1942. He reminded the Head of the Reich Chancellery that this was by no means a minor technical problem but, 'by its nature', the form the budget took concerned the 'foundation of the constitutional order of the Third Reich', and therefore the Führer's decision was vital. In the event of his refusing to get a decision from the Führer he (Lammers) would have 'sole responsibility' for the 'possibly disastrous consequences'.[22]

This highly unusual tone for an exchange between Reich Ministers shows how far the internal dissolution of the Reich government had gone under the impact of the power structures of the Führer state. Another conflict concerned the Reich S.S. Leader's arrogant policy of civil service appointments. He often got approval directly from Hitler for appointing and promoting S.S. leaders as high-ranking police officers without the prior consent of the Reich Minister of Finance. Schwerin-Krosigk had protested bitterly about these methods to Himmler in February 1942 ('Talks between heads are pointless when without regard to the outcome of these the number of leading officials is simply increased, and when recommendations for appointments over and above the current budget proposals are made to the Führer and then the necessary means are later demanded of the Finance Minister.') And although Himmler assured Lammers in July 1942 that the matter was 'closed', there were many other similar cases which prompted Schwerin-

Krosigk to approach the Head of the Reich Chancellery yet again in January 1943. As a result a meeting took place between Lammers and Himmler in March 1943. But Lammers did not play the part demanded of him. After Himmler had explained that in his line of work there were frequently occasions when a quick appointment was needed and when there was no time to contact the Minister of Finance beforehand, both came to a friendly agreement that in future in such cases, the Reich S.S. Leader should get the Führer's agreement not only for the appointment but also expressly for the necessary finance.[23]

Lammers had to put up with some strong criticism from his own officials in the Reich Chancellery because of this 'understanding'. Thus Reich cabinet counsellor Killy observed in a notice of 20 March 1943 that he could 'not accept that this was an improvement', particularly since he had the impression that 'within the sphere of the Reich S.S. Leader and Chief of the German Police permanent organizational effects could very easily result from a state of affairs conditioned by the War'. The Reich S.S. Leader was obviously trying to secure a general authorization for himself (like that of the armed forces) which would make him independent of the Reich Minister of Finance's approval in each case. Therefore Killy recommended his chief to have another meeting with the Reich S.S. Leader but Lammers decided on 22 March, that he could not imagine the 'slightest prospect of success' from that.[24] Direct authorization from the Führer on the one hand, and the inaccessibility of the Führer on the other hand, increasingly proved to be the decisive factors in the exercise of power, and not the nominal responsibility and organization of the Reich government.

Direct access to Hitler: Speer and Goebbels

Whereas the majority of Ministers in the Reich government hardly ever had access to Hitler, a few heads of department were all the more able to secure a 'place in the sun', especially Himmler and Ribbentrop, with their own Field Headquarters near the Führer's Main Headquarters. In addition the strength derived from their personal position of trust and the importance of their offices enabled Göring in the early years of the War and Speer in the second half of the War to get relatively easy access to Hitler. Speer benefited from the fact that he enjoyed Hitler's personal goodwill as the former 'Architect of the Führer Building' and architectural organizer of the Nuremberg Party rallies, and he was able to consolidate this through his skilful management as Armaments Minister. Even Bormann was envious of Speer's virtuosity in getting Führer decrees. This is clearly shown by the quarrels with Bormann on the occasion of the decree of 2 September 1943 'Concerning the

Concentration of the War Economy' (*RGBl*, I, p. 529), which Speer had got through with great speed and which was extremely far-reaching in its consequences. But the quarrel was resolved by Hitler basically in Speer's favour.[25]

In the second half of the War, however, Goebbels's influence again increased. Alongside Himmler, Bormann and Speer, Goebbels finally became Hitler's most important Minister. Since Hitler more and more shunned public speeches and meetings after 1942, when the War was clearly turning against Germany and he only seldom came out of the 'Wolf's Lair' bunker in East Prussia, the responsibility for the whole area of propaganda increasingly devolved on Goebbels. The Minister of Propaganda, instinctively sure in his trade, recognized that the change which set in after the first euphoric phase of national victory offered new and even greater opportunities for propaganda. Goebbels knew that amidst the grave emergency the appeal for grim readiness for sacrifice and fighting and the defiant national solidarity generated in this way could be even more effective than the rapture of enthusiasm. Thus in the notorious meeting at the Sportspalast in Berlin on 18 February 1943 (shortly after Stalingrad) the Reich Minister of Propaganda was able to drive the audience to that fanatical endorsement of his own total willingness to make sacrifices, which was later bound to appear as an expression of mass hysteria. In fact without a knowledge of the psychological make-up of broad sectors of the German people, which was successfully manipulated by Goebbels's propaganda, it is difficult to understand their attitude in this phase of the War. Admittedly doubt and criticism was then also spreading throughout Germany and heavy suffering was exacted by the War, which by 1945 had destroyed the lives of some two million German soldiers and much German housing and property. But the more readily people had turned to Hitler for years and acclaimed him, the more difficult it was to understand the real difficulty now. Nobody wanted to give the lie to himself; there was talk about it being a pledge of faith to hold out in the hour of need. True, most no longer believed in a 'final victory' but there was all the less inclination to think about defeat because in the nature of things this had to mean victory for and the supremacy of the Soviet Union. Goebbels knew how to exploit brilliantly this psychological mixture of panic, faith, self-pity and self-deception, which also induced moral blindness to the growing excesses of the regime against Jews, Poles, Eastern workers etc. Goebbels was indispensable as the propagandist of commitment to total war and thus his responsibilities grew and this considerably strengthened his standing with Hitler. The fact that Hitler designated Goebbels as Reich Chancellor at the end of his Political Testament shows the special appreciation which the Minister for Propaganda had earned from his Führer during these years.

Chancelleries and adjutants

Given the increasing seclusion and 'withdrawal' of the Führer at the same time as there were mounting rivalries and overlapping of responsibilities etc. all requiring a decision from the Führer, the transmission of the Führer's pronouncements, enactments and commands became ever more important, as did the function of the established go-betweens in Hitler's vicinity. The coexistence of different more or less official chancelleries, secretaries and adjutants, already familiar from the '*Kampfzeit*', was typical of Hitler's style of leadership and of his tendency to keep several options open at the same time.

Apart from the Reich Chancellery as the 'regular' channel of communication between the Ministers of the Reich and Hitler, the Presidential Chancellery was of only minimal political importance from the outset (responsible among other things for some of the clemency cases, the granting of titles and orders, greetings, awarding prizes, various tasks of representation, the carrying out of the Head of State's prerogative for appointing and dismissing civil servants). What political importance it did have was still further diminished when after taking up the office of Reich President Hitler set up a separate Chancellery of the Führer of the NSDAP by means of a decree of 17 November 1934, under the direction of the former secretary general of the NSDAP's Reich directorate, Reichsleiter Philipp Bouhler. The creation of this staff, generally thereafter referred to as the 'Führer's Chancellery',[26] underlined Hitler's separate role as national leader as well as that of Reich Chancellor, Head of State, and Head of the Party. At any rate it transpired that the 'Bouhler Bureau' was primarily preoccupied with personal petitions from the people to the Führer. Like Bouhler, the leading employees of the 'Führer's Chancellery' were almost all functionaries from the Party apparatus. One of its divisions under Albert Bormann, Martin Bormann's brother, acted as Hitler's 'Private Chancellery' (Albert Bormann therefore officiated as a sort of personal adjutant at the same time). From the outset the ambiguous official nomenclature (Chancellery of the Führer or of the Führer of the NSDAP), the staffing of the office with Party men and the fact that many petitions to the Führer from the Party were handled by Bouhler's office, made ambiguous not only the demarcation with the Presidential Chancellery (for example in clemency cases), but above all with the staff of the Führer's Deputy. The more Martin Bormann emerged as the key figure on this staff and finally as the successor to Hess and as the self-confident leader of the Party Chancellery, the more the power of the Führer's Chancellery was curtailed as a result. In a key discussion with Bouhler in 1942, Bormann stressed above all that the 'Führer's Chancellery' should, in contrast to the Party Chancellery, concern itself only with 'specific cases' and 'not with matters of principle'.[27]

Apart from these more or less extensive Chancelleries the 'Führer's adjutancy' was the innermost command apparatus. The adjutancy which was staffed by a small circle of Hitler's personal followers from the S.A., S.S. and the Party (Brücker, Schaub, Wiedemann, Albrecht, Schultze etc.[28] and from 1938 apparently exclusively from S.S. leaders), was chiefly responsible before the outbreak of the War for organizing Hitler's agenda and for his supervision. The more Hitler retreated after 1935/6 from the regular conduct of government business, the more important the role of the adjutancy became in transmitting the Führer's pronouncements. Documents from the period of summer 1939 reveal that the Head of the Reich Chancellery even then occasionally had to send polite if not servile notes to the Führer's adjutancy to get an audience with Hitler.[29] It also became customary at this time for Hitler to authorize individual adjutants, above all S.S. Gruppenführer Julius Schaub, to inform the departmental heads by telephone of certain instructions and views of the Führer. The use of adjutants as intermediaries for directions from the Führer to the individual heads of departments clearly showed Hitler's low opinion of the Ministers concerned, and was apparently so intended. Thus especially Schaub, for example, frequently went into action when Hitler needed to criticize specific decisions of the Courts or even to order the amendment of such judgements.[30]

The leadership of the armed forces had special access to Hitler as the Supreme Commander of the Armed Forces, through the armed forces adjutancy set up in 1934. But in practice this was more a matter of representatives from the Reich Defence Minister (or from OKH, OKL, OKM) assigned to Hitler, who in the event of disputes placed their loyalty to their military superiors above that to Hitler. The attitude of the armed forces adjutant, Hossbach, during the Fritsch crisis was an example of this.

Although it was still fairly typical until 1938/9 to have a competing assortment of different heads of chancelleries and adjutants under Hitler, this subsequently changed. Then Martin Bormann became more and more obviously the master of the Führer's antechamber.

Martin Bormann and the Party Chancellery

Bormann, who had run into the NSDAP at the beginning of the 1920s as the organizer of an illegal Freikorps formation, had already gained access to the management group of the NSDAP's Reich directorate before 1933 as the director of the NSDAP Relief Fund. His contact with Hitler and other Party heads was underpinned by more intimate ties, through his marriage to the daughter of the director of the Party Court (Walter Buch) and through his brother, Albert Bormann. As is apparent from a letter to Hess of October 1932, Bormann was at that time already playing the part of a pedantic but energetic spokesman for the Party, who tried to press Hitler to part company with the 'swine' surrounding Röhm.[31] But as Staff Chief of the Führer's Deputy Bormann was also active as expert and adviser to Hitler in managing the funds which were made available to Hitler personally from various sources (donations of industry etc.), a role for which his previous office in the financial administration of the NSDAP qualified him. Having advanced to the position of NSDAP Reichsleiter from 1934, he organized and directed the acquisition of the House Wachenfeld and other premises at the Obersalzberg near Berchtesgaden, as well as the transformation and development of the 'Berghof' with the nearby complex of buildings which finally went to make up Hitler's summer residence. This activity involved Hitler directly and was already throwing the Staff Chief to the Führer's Deputy into continuous close personal contact with Hitler from 1934/5. From about 1938, when Hitler was driving the Party along at a faster pace on various internal policy fronts and when Hess's well-meaning attempts at compromise hardly seemed opportune to him, Bormann increasingly acted as the independent director of the Hess Bureau and conducted his business largely from the Berlin branch of the 'staff', which now acquired a new importance in place of the old 'Liaison Staff of the NSDAP'. When at the outset of the War Hitler finally ordered the setting-up of a Führer Central HQ ('Special Train of the Führer'), Bormann followed him there as his 'permanent attendant'.[32]

The coupling of both these functions, the control of the Party's political co-ordinating central office (staff of the Führer's Deputy) and the permanent attendance on Hitler and his advising of Hitler on personal matters too, comprised the basis of Bormann's special position of power. This did not, however, automatically entail any corresponding strengthening of the Party directorate as such.

There was very little structural change in the forlorn set-up of the NSDAP's Reich directorate. Although Bormann conducted the business of the staff of the Führer's Deputy towards the state and the Party much more energetically than Hess, he was no more able to end the 'direct responsibility to the Führer' of individual Gauleiter or Reichsleiter than he was to end the serious conflicts between them and the weakening of power engendered by this. True, Bormann tried to ensure the unity of the Party, through the 'confidential news and information from the Reich Chancellery', through a more dogmatic interpretation of National Socialist ideology and in other ways. He also planned to break up the special authorities within the Party and to give more effect to the Party

Chancellery's claim to leadership by disentangling the personal union between Party and state offices, by dividing up the Party Gaue, and appointing younger Gauleiter etc. But he was able to achieve little in this direction until the end of the War. It was with good reason that the Oldenburg Gauleiter, Röver, concluded in a long memorandum from 1942, that 'it is impossible to speak any longer of a united and centrally governed higher Party leader corps'. Each has 'made himself more or less independent'. The 'authority of the Reich directorate' of the NSDAP has 'suffered considerably' from the conflicts between the different Reichsleiter.[33] Even under Bormann the NSDAP Party Chancellery was a long way from the position of the Communist Politburo. The personalized National Socialist leadership principle, with its built-in tendency to make powerful office-holders independent, prevented the emergence of an omnipotent bureaucratic central leadership. But it was precisely to another effect of this leadership principle, personal (i.e. independent of any) power office, that Bormann owed his special position.

This was already clearly shown by Bormann's official status. After Hess's flight to England Hitler at first decreed on 12 May 1941 that 'from now on the office of Führer's Deputy' would be 'designated the "Party Chancellery"', and that its leader was 'as before' Martin Bormann, who was 'personally responsible' to him (Hitler).[34] A special decree of the Führer of 29 May, 'concerning the position of the Chief of the Party Chancellery', expressly confirmed his special rank (equivalent to ministerial) and his participation in the government's over-all legislation. On 12 April 1943, however, Hitler also institutionalized Bormann's position as his 'personal aid in charge', by granting him the additional official title of 'Secretary to the Führer'.[35] Thus the outside world became aware of what the initiated had known for a long time, namely that the Chief of the Party Chancellery had meanwhile become the powerful man in the Führer's HQ, whom in practice all had to acknowledge, without whose consultation there was no longer any decree of the Führer, and who could finally operate against other offices by reference to 'the Führer's opinions' in a way which remains almost inconceivable.

It was from this dominant position in the Führer's HQ (not really as Chief of the Party Chancellery) that in the final years of the War Bormann became the Minister supremo, the controlling Minister of the Reich government, whereas the Head of the Reich Chancellery, Lammers, sank as it were to the level of Bormann's messenger. After Hitler had already ordered on 12 August 1942 that all communications on Party matters 'from Reichsleiter, Gauleiter, Association leaders and independent offices of the Reich directorate', so far as these could not be passed directly to him, were 'to be sent exclusively through the Chief of the Party

Chancellery', Bormann requested the Head of the Reich Chancellery in June 1943 to send through him (Bormann) in his capacity as secretary to the Führer(!), all urgent government matters which Lammers could not himself submit to the Führer 'because of his absence', and 'not to direct these to the armed forces adjutancy or to the personal adjutancy'.[36] Without Bormann's goodwill Lammers would have been completely checkmated in the exercise of his duties as acting head of the Reich government. For this reason he believed that he largely had to comply with the request of the secretary to the Führer, with whom he formed close friendship at this time. As a result there was a formal pact between Lammers and Bormann on 17 June 1943, in which both agreed, almost in the manner of two court servants, how future audiences with the Führer would be arranged. Bormann promised Lammers to take him along with him when discussing affairs of government with the Führer and only exceptionally to have an audience by himself with Hitler, unless both agreed that a 'meeting (desired by a Minister for example) with the Führer was superfluous'.[37] Subsequently this arrangement worked out in Bormann's favour. Lammers barely had a single further talk with Hitler. By contrast, Bormann, with Lammers's submissive acceptance, exercised the co-ordinating functions of the Head of the Reich Chancellery during the final two years of the regime. The secretary to the Führer had taken over the government.

The secret Führer decree. Example: Reich Commissioner for the Consolidation of German Nationhood

The changed form and quality of numerous Führer decrees and Führer commands during the War corresponded to the deterioration of the government's process of decision-making. The device of the Führer decree (alongside the laws and decrees of the Reich government) had grown from the right of the Reich President to determine and to change the organization of the Reich government or of the Supreme Reich Authorities.

Until 1939 the application of Führer decrees was largely confined to such 'decrees on organization'. But when War began this was increasingly combined with actually composing or changing the substance of the law, or else with the delegation of powers to make law. This was bound to cause difficulties as these decrees were indeed signed and formally issued by Hitler but instead of being published were only made known to the Supreme Reich Authority through official channels.

An example of this was the Führer decree entrusting the Reich S.S. Leader and Chief of German Police with the tasks of a 'Reich Commissioner for consolidating German Nationhood' (*Reichskom-*

missar für die Festigung Deutschen Volkstums – RKF) on 7 October 1939.[38] The decree empowered Himmler to 'eliminate the harmful influences of such alien parts of the population as constitute a danger to the Reich and the German community'. Even in this confidential text, however, this was only a veiled and watered-down version of the powers verbally given to Himmler forcefully to remove Jews and Poles from the annexed areas of Poland and to settle Germans there. In fact there arose on the doubtful legal basis of this secret decree a new Central Reich Authority belonging to Himmler (at the top of the Staff Central Office of the RKF under the direction of S.S. Brigadeführer Ulrich Greifelt), with numerous subordinate offices and S.S. staffs, constituting a separate administrative authority alongside the normal organs of the civilian administration in the 'incorporated Eastern territories' (later also in other occupied areas). To this belonged the RKF's 'Land Offices' which exercised the right in principle belonging to the Main Trustee Office East (*Haupttreuhandstelle Ost*–HTO), of seizing and administering in trust Jewish and Polish property.[39] Thus in these new areas Himmler could considerably increase the influence of the Security Police without more ado. Here he installed 'Higher S.S. and Police Leaders' as though they were territorial commanders of the S.S. and police, and thus at the same time he had available in these areas his own extraordinary administrative authorities under his command, or he could give direct orders to the civilian administration in his capacity as RKF.[40] As a result it was much easier in these new areas than it was in the Old Reich to erect independently of the normal state administration an organizational network of the RFSS' Command in its various capacities, and thus to introduce a correspondingly greater degree of martial law.

This was shown, for example, by the construction of new concentration camps. The installation of such camps and the transfer of the required land to the S.S. had always been subject to tedious negotiations in the Old Reich, in which all had been involved and especially the financial departments.[41] By contrast Himmler basically found things easier in the 'incorporated Eastern territories'. Thus the building of by far the largest of all the concentration camps, Auschwitz, could be started here, in the formerly Polish district of Kattowitz. The Land Office in Kattowitz high handedly proceeded to seize an area of land of some 40 square kilometres on Himmler's behalf and at the request of the Inspector of Concentration Camps, who was subordinate to Himmler. Then the Security Police under Himmler enforced the evacuation of seven (Polish and Jewish) villages in this area. The Reich S.S. Leader was almost self-sufficient here and thus it was not by chance that Auschwitz was selected along with other centres in Poland (Chelmno, Belzec, Treblinka, Majdanek, Sobibor) as the main place for the mass extermination of the Jews. For this responsibility, the planning and carrying out of the 'Final solution to the Jewish problem', also fell on Himmler in 1941.[42]

When later the Reich Governor and Gauleiter in the Tyrol and Carinthia also made use of the RKF's right of seizure in their capacity as agents of the RKF, in order to acquire Church lands for the settlement of ethnic Germans, there was a sequel which was typical of the effect of secret Führer decrees. The Church offices had complained about the seizure to the Reich Administrative Court in Vienna because they were unaware of the Führer decree of 7 October 1939, and for this reason the action of the Reich Governors was bound to seem illegal. The administrative officials were thus put in a position where they had to rule on complaints which (as the Senate President of the Vienna Administrative Court subsequently informed the Reich Minister of the Interior) 'quite rightly charge the authorities concerned ... with breaking the law', although those authorities were in fact covered through the secret decree. The President of the Administrative Court emphatically pointed out that 'quite intolerable consequences for an orderly administration' would arise if decrees changing the law (like the Führer decree of 7 October 1939)[43] were 'not published' and were issued 'only as internal regulations' but 'which were still supposed to be legally binding outside too'. The Court, the Senate Presidents concluded, had temporarily set aside the normal procedure in order to give the Reich authority concerned the opportunity to 'regularize the application of ... Führer's decree' through a 'supplementary announcement'.[44] Other secret Führer decrees which had been issued meanwhile and which had the effect of changing the law – for example the decree of 15 January 1943 concerning the general mobilization of labour, which contained the provision that in taking the measures concerned the Supreme Reich Authorities could 'get round any obstructive legal provisions',[45] caused similar problems.[46]

The Euthanasia order and the 'Final Solution of the Jewish problem'. The legal and organizational preconditions

The confidential Führer decree which authorized the RKF to 'eliminate' alien population groups without actually spelling out the details was in essence already no longer a decree on organization but a command to fight and to destroy, delivered to an apparatus suited to this end.

This was still more true of those other infamous secret orders which Hitler gave after the start of the War for the liquidation of large groups of people, the so-called 'Euthanasia Order', the 'Commissioner Order' and the 'Order for the Final Solution of the

Jewish Problem'. It could be shown from the example of the RKF decree that this sort of command, in so far as the content was kept secret from the regular organs of administration or could be disguised, was likely to be most easily carried out when an extraordinary apparatus directly subordinate to the Führer was available, and which was tightly organized enough (like the area of operations of the RFSS in the 'incorporated Eastern territories') for the execution of the secret measures to take place without any particular attempt to inform and to involve the normal state organs. This had no longer been the case for a considerable time within the Old Reich. Certainly not to the extent that it was true of occupied Poland, especially since in Germany there was much less guarantee of maintaining secrecy or suppressing news about local measures of coercion than there was among the police-controlled population of Poland. For this reason it is worth noting that Hitler involved the RFSS only secondarily in the measures which were set in motion at about the same time as the RKF decree, for putting to death the mentally ill in Reich mental homes. But in this instance all the main levers for carrying out the policy were operated by persons and offices directly subordinate to the Führer. Thus Hitler's personal physician, Karl Brandt, and Philipp Bouhler, the Chief of the Führer's Chancellery, were appointed as the main agents for this action, to whom the Führer also gave a secret written 'authorization' backdated to 1 September 1939.[47] The real moving spirit from Bouhler's staff was the latter's deputy, Oberdienstleiter Victor Brack, to whose 'Central Office' also went requests to grant 'euthanasia' for the incurably ill. The killing in such a case of an incurably sick child in a Leipzig hospital even before the War, occasioned by Hitler's order through Brandt, Brack and his colleague Dr Hefelmann as well as other doctors positively inclined towards euthanasia, subsequently turned out to have been Hitler's starting-point for the general action initiated after the outbreak of the War, when the extent of the process had little to do with the original meaning of euthanasia. Brandt and the colleagues of Bouhler sought out a small group of doctors in favour of euthanasia, who were appointed in the Führer's Chancellery and 'licensed' with specific promises of immunity from punishment on the basis of the secret paper originating from Hitler. They were enjoined to strict secrecy and authorized as 'experts' under the cover name of the 'Reich Working Group for Asylums and Hospitals'[48] to select the sick people who were to be killed. The head of the section for Asylums and Nursing Homes in the Reich Ministry of the Interior's health division (Dr Linden) directed by the former S.S. doctor and Reich Health Leader, Dr Leonhard Conti, took over the 'registration' of the sick in the various asylums through the despatch of innocent-looking questionnaires. A cover organization recruited from the S.S. transport fleet, the 'Welfare Transport Company for Invalids Ltd' carried out the 'transfer' of those selected to be put to death to institutions specifically allocated for the process of elimination (above all Hadamar in Hesse, Hartheim near Linz, Grafeneck in Württemberg, Sonnestein in Saxony). Chemists from the Institute of Criminal Technology of the Reich Criminal Police Office tried out gassing techniques with carbon monoxide,[49] and a further cover company organized by the Führer's Chancellery (Welfare Foundation for the Benefit of Asylums) was responsible for the over-all financing. Only a small circle of about fifty people (doctors and technicians) were kept fully informed of the extent and scope of this action in the course of which some 70,000 people (by no means all of them incurably ill) were put to death. The directors of the asylums were merely informed of a 'transfer' of those selected for the purpose of special observation and treatment. Of the Ministers of the Reich government apparently only Lammers had been informed directly by Hitler about the secret authorization of the doctors, but also apparently in a way which could encourage the belief that it concerned clear 'cases of euthanasia'.

There is a manifest politico-ideological connection between the euthanasia action and the laws on sound marriage already issued in 1933 and 1935, which introduced legal sterilization and the termination of pregnancy in cases of hereditary illness. Equally evident, however, is the difference between the procedures. Whereas in the one case special administrative and court authorities were authorized with the legally prescribed process of submitting proposals and making decisions, the cover organizations and secret authorizations concerned with the euthanasia action were deliberately constructed as instruments outside the law, which indeed functioned through bypassing the state authorities set up by the National Socialist government itself. It must not be forgotten that even the legally regulated process of sterilization and termination of pregnancy afforded a great deal of latitude of judgement for official doctors and the courts concerned with healthy stock, and in view of the grave consequences here had removed these 'laws' a long way from the principle of law and the protection of the law. In this respect the form of National Socialist legislation itself paved the way for the later state of lawlessness. The collapse of administrative and departmental cohesion (in this case making the health administration independent, already undertaken in 1934,[50] and the increased subordination of the health division of the Reich Ministry of the Interior), the use of plenipotentiaries and offices directly subordinate to the Führer (Dr Brandt, the Führer's Chancellery, the Criminal Police Office from the RFSS' authority) and the earlier general devaluation of the legislative process through the practice of authorizations from the Führer, constituted the essential preconditions of the euthanasia action. The fact that this had to be abandoned in 1941 because complaints from the public, the judiciary and the administration multiplied, and individual Ministers (Gürtner, Lammers) insisted to Hitler on a legal ruling, can also be viewed as evidence for the fact that constitutional developments in the Führer state had not yet gone far enough within the Old Reich for such actions to take place 'without friction'. The extraordinary apparatus of the Führer's authority was bound to clash sooner or later, and thus to generate conflict, with the administration and judicature within what were still bound to be close legal restraints in the Old Reich.

This experience undoubtedly contributed to the fact that the latter mass murder of the Jews was shifted to remote Polish and Soviet Russian areas and to the especially enlarged 'jurisdiction of the Reich S.S. Leader' which existed there. Thus the staff of 'gas technicians' set up for the euthanasia action under the guiding influence of Victor Brack were employed once more. Otherwise the procedure was much the same; a small circle of S.S. leaders who were fully informed, were sworn to secrecy and 'authorized' with specific reference to the 'effect of law' of the Führer's will;[51] and apart from this only partial information and involvement for other offices. The preceding dissolution of governmental and administrative unity (for example in the form of the Germany Division of the German Foreign Office) was also 'maintained' in this instance. The emergency apparatus directly responsible to the Führer represented by the Security Police and the S.S. had become big enough and sufficiently independent itself to take charge of carrying out the mass crimes. And the offices of the state administration which were still bound by the law were sufficiently split up and largely bereft of their security and self-confidence through the lasting effects of competition with authorities directly subordinate to the Führer, through the infiltration of Party personnel, ideological training etc., and accordingly had become susceptible to manipulation. Thus they could be saddled with what were often partly technical, legislative and executive motions (without being fully informed of the ultimate aims of the leadership) necessary to the development of the over-all process of 'the final solution of the Jewish question'.

This criminal mass destruction of the Jews must not be seen simply as the continuation of the legal discrimination against Jews after 1933. Procedurally this was in fact a break with former practice and in that respect had a different quality. All the same, the previous laws and decrees which step by step had further discriminated against the Jews in Germany, had subjected them to emergency laws and had condemned them to a social ghetto, paved the way for the 'final solution'. The progressive undermining of the principle of law through measures cast in legal form finally resulted in an utterly crude, lawless, criminal action.

Notes and references

1. Decree on the leadership of the armed forces, 4 February 1938, (*RGBl*, I, p. 111).
2. Decree on the setting up of a secret cabinet council, 4 February 1938, (*RGBl*, I, p. 412).
3. Cf. the testimony of Eberhard von Thadden (IfZ: ZS 359).
4. Cf. Hans-Adolf Jacobsen, *Nationalsozialistische Aussenpolitik 1933– 38* (Frankfurt-on-Main, Berlin, 1968), pp. 313ff.
5. On Ribbentrop's close relationship to Gaus, whom the later foreign Security Service Chief Walter Schellenberg called the 'whore of the Foreign Office' in his affidavit of 30 April 1947 (IfZ: ZS 291/IV), Gaus himself stated: Ribbentrop had needed him (Gaus) not only because of his experience but 'for 90 per cent, one might say 98 per cent of the time' as 'his letter-writer in his personal affairs', and especially in the conflicts over competence with other National Socialist bigwigs, which had been Ribbentrop's main preoccupation (IfZ: ZS 705).
6. Cf. Paul Seabury, '*Die Wilhelmstrasse. Die Geschichte der deutschen Diplomatie 1930 bis 1945*. (Frankfurt-on-Main, 1956), pp. 167f.
7. The memorandum of the managing board of the Reichsbank which was sent to Hitler on 7 January 1939 shortly before Schacht's resignation, with its sharp criticism of unrestrained inflationary government spending, clearly testifies to Schacht's viewpoint (BA: R43 II/234).
8. Dieter Petzina, *Autarkiepolitik im Dritten Reich*, p. 67.
9. The apparatus and leading civil servants of the Prussian State Ministry were available to Göring as management authorities of the Four Year Plan. As one of those officials (Ministerialdirigent Friedrich Gramsch) said later, to the regret of the civil servants Göring 'could not be persuaded to adopt normal ministerial procedures'. Thus State Secretary Koerner, who in practice had the position of a manager of the Four Year Plan, had often not been informed by Göring when the latter gave orders in his 'impulsive way'. 'When Göring was away travelling, it often happened that he gave direct orders and that then somebody or other appeared in Koerner's office and told him that he had seen Göring and that the latter had given this or that instruction.' Also 'many orders were given which were transmitted through the adjutancy or the Staff Office [of Göring]', particularly during the War when Göring was absent from Berlin and staying in his Headquarters (IfZ: ZS 717).
10. Cf. Krauch's own testimony on this (IfZ: ZS 981); in addition the testimony of the former State Secretary of the Prussian Ministry of Finance, Friedrich Landfried, who was attached to the new organization in the Ministry of Economics (IfZ: ZS 1122).
11. On this cf. A.S. Milward, *Die deutsche Kriegswirtschaft 1939–45* (Stuttgart, 1966) and Gregor Jansen, *Das Ministerium Speer. Deutschlands Rüstung in Krieg* (Berlin, 1968).
12. Worth noting in this context are the remarks made by Sauckel to the American interrogating officers after 1945, when he stated: 'The Speer Ministry . . . was, as we used to say, a shop which you could never get to the bottom of, but which had no standard administrative

practice in the sense of a bureaucracy . . . It was a gigantic complex in which, although it was exceptionally fragmented, the so-called self-government of private business was involved in the form of [company] committees and trusts. What was free or autonomous and what was official in all this we could no longer work out' (IfZ: ZS 434).

13. Cf. Enno Georg, *Die wirtschaftliche Unternehmungen der SS.* (Stuttgart, 1963).
14. Max Domarus, *Hitler. Reden und Proklamationen 1932–45* (Munich, 1965), vol. 2, p. 1058.
15. Hitler's physician Karl Brandt testified after the end of the War that in conjunction with the plans for legally regulating euthanasia which had already been considered during the years 1933–35, and then postponed because of resistance from the Churches, Hitler had told the National Socialist Physicians' leader Wagner in 1935 that such measures could 'be carried out more smoothly and easily' during a war'. Cf. *Medizin ohne Menschlichkeit. Dokumente des Nürnberger Arzteprozesses*, ed. and annotated by A. Mitscherlich and F. Mielke. (Fischer Bücherei, Frankfurt-on-Main, 1960), p. 184.
16. Cf. on this the references in BA: R43 II/694a.
17. BA: R43 II/695.
18. BA: R43 II/694a.
19. Noted comment of Ministerialdirektor Kritzinger of 10 November 1941 on Bormann's letter of 29 October (BA: R43 II/694a). After consulting with Bormann, Lammers sent out a circular from the Führer's headquarters to the Reich government departments, in which he requested the strict compliance with regulations (participation of the departments) in the drafting of decrees; ibid.
20. Note on the files by Kritzinger, 2 May 1941 (BA: R43 II/170).
21. Letter from the Head of the Reich Chancellery to the Chairman of the Ministerial Council for the Defence of the Reich, 10 September 1942 and a note on the files concerning Hitler's decision of 23 October 1942 (BA: R43 II/695).
22. Details in Hauptarchiv Berlin-Dahlem: Rep. 320/132.
23. Comment of the Head of the Reich Chancellery of 11 March 1943, (BA: R43 II 393a and here too can be found the events mentioned earlier).
24. Ibid.
25. What was unusual here (and which is not to be found elsewhere at this time in the face of Bormann's opposition) was the frank and determined tone with which Speer reacted to Bormann's objections; for example, when Speer had Bormann informed on 18 August 1943: 'I fear that because of your letter the passage of the decree could be postponed for a long time and perhaps also should be postponed.' In view of the War situation he (Speer) could 'not agree to any further delaying of the decree'. He therefore begged 'to suggest that on Friday the 20th of August [1943] the content of the decree can finally be agreed between us' (BA: R43 II/610). Speer also managed, in contrast to the other Reich Ministers, to acquire the right to give orders to the heads of civilian administration outside the Reich in spite of their protest, in Hitler's supplementary order of 5 September to the decree of 2 September 1943 (BA: R43 II/610a). But the following ex-

tract from the telegram to Bormann already cited is indicative of Speer's management style: 'I must not be restricted by considerations of administrative law.'

26. Thus also in the lecture by Wienstein of 1936 already quoted, on the organization of the leadership and management in the Third Reich, see above p. 282.

27. Bormann's letter to Bouhler, 8 March 1942 (BA: R43 II/1213a). Because his authority was repudiated by the staff of Hess, Bouhler had requested alternative employment from Hitler in spring 1940 ('a greater task in the colonies'), but in vain. Cf. letter of Bormann to Lammers, 24 June 1940 (BA: R43 II(694).

28. On this cf. *inter alia* the testimony of Julius Schaub (IfZ: ZS 137) and the account by Fritz Wiedemann, *Der Mann der Feldherr werden wollte* (Kettwig, 1964).

29. Letter from the Head of the Reich Chancellery to the Führer's adjutancy, 16 August 1939. Lammers referred here to urgent matters 'which must be dealt with' and wrote *inter alia*: 'I should like respectfully to draw the Führer's attention to this and and to ask when he can receive me' (BA: R43 II/587a).

30. Cf. also M. Broszat, 'Zur Perversion der Strafjustiz im Dritten Reich', in *VJHZ*, 6, 1958, Heft 4.

31. This five-page letter of 5 October 1932 is in the *Akten des Parteiarchivs*, (Hoover Institution Stanford, USA), reel 17, folder 319.

32. Bormann informed the Head of the Reich Chancellery on 1 September 1939 that: 'From now on I will be in permanent attendance on the Führer, and therefore will no longer be able to represent the Deputy of the Führer during the discussions of the Ministerial Council for the Defence of the Reich after the Führer has left Berlin' (BA: R43 II/605).

33. Photo copy of the undated memorandum in IfZ: Fa 204, pp. 72f.

34. Text of the decree in BA: R43 II/1213 and 1213a.

35. On this cf. the letter from Bormann to Lammers, 1 May 1943, in which the former referred to the 'special duties' for the Führer which had been his preserve 'for years' (BA: R43 II/1154).

36. Telegram from Bormann, 15 June 1943, to the Head of the Reich Chancellery (BA: R43 II/583):

37. Note on the files by Lammers, 18 June 1943 (BA: R43 II/583).

38. Text in BA: R49/1 and in Nuremberg Documents NG-962; on the origins of the decree cf. M. Broszat, *Nationalsozialistische Polenpolitik 1919–1945* (Stuttgart, 1961), pp. 18f.

39. Cf. Himmler's decree on this, 10 November 1939, on the 'Collaboration of the authorities of the Reich S.S. Leader with the Main Trustee Office East', in *Haupttreuhandstelle Ost. Materialsammlung zum internen Dienstgebrauch*, pp. 8ff (Nuremberg Documents 2207–PS).

40. Usually either the Reich Governors or Oberpräsidenten of these new territories (thus Gauleiter and Reich Governor Greiser in the Warthegau) or the respective 'Senior S.S. and Police Chief' in personal union were appointed as territorial deputies of the RKF.

41. The files of the Reich Ministry of Finance concerning Emsland are an example of this (BA: R2 Zg 1955ff./24 006).

42. Cf. Raoul Hilberg, *The Destruction of European Jews*. (Chicago, 1961).

43. In the case of the RKF's right of seizure it was a matter of extending to the Reich Commissioner for the Consolidation of German Nationhood the authority of the Law concerning Land Provision for the purposes of the armed forces of 29 March 1935 (*RGBl*, I, p. 467).

44. Copy of the letter of the leading Senate President of the Vienna Senate of the Reich Administrative Court, 19 February 1943, to the Minister of the Interior (BA: R43 II/695).

45. Cf. Letter from the Ministry of the Interior to the Head of the Reich Chancellery, 2 April 1943 (BA: R43 II/695).

46. To give legal effect to the Führer decree authorizing the RKF, the Reich Ministry of the Interior suggested issuing an order of the General Plenipotentiary of the Reich Government, to be published without further informing Hitler. Thereby the corresponding power to 'secure Land provision . . . for the settlement of Reich and ethnic German settlers' would be transferred to the RKF and would have retrospective effect. The Reich Chancellery and the RKF were in agreement; Bormann however appears to have raised objections (cf. note on the files by Lammers of 18 June 1943 (BA: R43 II/695). At any rate no such order is to be found in the *RGBl*.

47. Text *inter alia* in *Medizin ohne Menschlichkeit*, p. 184.

48. With its office in Berlin, Tiergartenstrasse 4 (thus the designation 'T 4').

49. On this cf. also Bert Honolka, *Die Kreuzelschreiber. Ärzte ohne Gewissen. Euthanasie im Dritten Reich*. (Hamburg, 1961), pp. 15f.

50. The basis of this was the law of 3 July 1935 on the unification of the health system (*RGBl*, I, p. 531); and the implementing decrees on this of 6 February 1935 (*RGBl*, I, p. 177) and 22 February (*RGBl*, I, p. 215).

51. On this cf. *Kommandant in Auschwitz. Autobiographische Aufzeichnungen von Rudolf Höss* (Stuttgart, 1958), p. 153. Höss tells here of the crucial orders given by Himmler: 'In the summer of 1941 . . . I was suddenly summoned to the Reich S.S. Leader in Berlin, and indeed directly through his adjutancy. Contrary to his normal practice he talked to me without his adjutant being present, in the following sense: The Führer had ordered the Final Solution to the Jewish problem; we – the S.S. – had to carry out this command . . . You must preserve absolute secrecy about this order, even against your superiors.'

Chapter Ten

Law and justice

The foregoing illustration of the connection between the ending of formal legislative procedures and of the administrative unity of the Reich on the one hand and the criminal actions of the National Socialist regime on the other, suggests that it is particularly necessary to supplement our account of the internal constitution of the Third Reich with at least a brief description of the position and organization of justice and of the change in the substance and procedures of law in the National Socialist era.

Hitler's take-over of power occurred in a country which admittedly had only a weak history of democracy but which possessed a solid constitutional tradition. The legality of the administration and judicial independence had been recognized in principle from the end of the eighteenth century in Prussia and the other German Länder and this had been firmly consolidated in the course of the nineteenth century. However much National Socialism was opposed in principle to the liberal conception of constitutional government subject to the rule of law, it could not simply destroy all the liberal-constitutional elements of public and private law and revert to the police state of the seventeenth or early eighteenth centuries. Without a certain degree of legal security, which after all first guaranteed the functioning and viability of the complex structure of the modern economy, society and administration, the National Socialist regime itself could never have existed and could not have achieved anything.

But in contrast to Soviet Communism, National Socialism was unwilling or rather unable to effect a radical and systematic transformation of liberal legal principles and the accompanying judicial procedure and standing; this would have been difficult to actually carry out without a corresponding revolutionary change of the social structure. The National Socialist attitude to inherited liberal law and to the traditional independence of the judicature was as negative as it was opportunistic. Apart from isolated attempts at reform and renewal, a compromise was reached with the existing judicial system as it was with the existing bureaucracy and the armed forces. But at the same time the most varied effort was made to alter law and justice in case after case and to limit its application or to correct this whenever it particularly threatened to frustrate the Führer's aims and desires or those of the Third Reich's state executive or special authority. The forms and effects of this partial destruction, undermining and perversion of the law, a few important landmarks of which will be discussed shortly, least affected civil law. More particularly, the principle of private property and its attendant legal provisions were only slightly affected. And it was typical that in civil law disputes the NSDAP and its organs hardly enjoyed any special status in the Courts after 1933 either.[1] The main field of conflict was public law and particularly criminal law. Here in the first weeks after Hitler's assumption of power that 'dualism of state measures and standards' (Ernst Fraenkel) was already in evidence and was to remain typical of the Third Reich. The events of March 1933 offered an example of this.

It was during these weeks as a result of the Reichstag Fire decree (28 Feb. 1933) that the basic state of emergency had been created which permitted the police, or rather the S.A. and S.A. auxiliary police, to launch a counter-offensive (protective custody) uncontrolled by the judiciary, and the National Socialist leadership was ready to exploit thoroughly the possibilities of this situation to achieve a monopoly of power for the NSDAP with terror and violence. In these circumstances Hitler and Göring were bound to be particularly displeased that the criminal act of arson in the Reichstag, which had been the reason for proclaiming the state of emergency, was to become the occasion for proceedings before the Reich Supreme Court. Hitler was rightly concerned that the Supreme Court's findings would not fully endorse earlier government declarations about the fire being a signal for a Communist uprising and that foreign press criticism would be given fresh impetus. He urged in the cabinet meeting of 2 March 1933 that: 'The outcry in the foreign press would be forestalled if the culprit were hanged immediately.' In the cabinet meeting of 7 March, Hitler and Frick again emphatically demanded that the action of the Supreme Court against the arsonist van der Lubbe be prevented and that he should be hanged at once after a summary trial. Since the prevailing law for arson provided only for penal servitude and the corresponding threat of execution contained in the Reichstag Fire decree of 28 February was only passed after the deed in question, Frick called for a 'Lex van der Lubbe', which would retrospectively sanction the carrying out of the death sentence through hanging. State Secretary Schlegelberger, the representative of the Reich Ministry of Justice, expressed strong misgivings about such a blatant violation of the legal principle of *nulla poena sine lege* which was accepted in all civilized states. Nevertheless he promised to try to do what he could. In fact, three weeks later on 29 March, a retrospective 'Lex van der Lubbe' (*RGBl*, I, p. 151) was illicitly passed on the basis of which the accused was later condemned and executed. As a result, however, of the resistance of the Reich President and the Reich Minister of Justice, Hitler had to let the Supreme Court proceedings run their course. The representatives of justice had consented to a typical compromise. A *principle* of law had been waived but the *authority* of the judicature had been successfully defended. Many similar 'adjustments' by the judicature were to follow this example.

Three new decrees were issued on 21 March ('Potsdam Day'!) with the help of the Reich President's power to pass emergency laws, which also made lasting changes in Germany's legal system and were of particular importance: an amnesty for quashing all punishable offences which were committed 'in the struggle for the national renewal of the German people',[2] the law against malicious gossip,[3] and the decree on the setting-up of Special Courts *RGBl*, I, p. 136). Whereas the decree on amnesty quashed all punishments which had been imposed on National Socialists for political offences and crimes (the Potempa murderer was also freed as a result), the decree on malicious gossip ensured that even spoken criticism of the new regime was punishable (by imprisonment and in severe cases by penal servitude).

On 28 February 1933 an emergency decree had already been issued along with the Reichstag Fire decree, 'against treason to the German nation and against treasonable activities' (*RGBl*, I, p. 85), which enlarged the concept of treason and high treason beyond the provisions of the penal code, introduced an increase in the penalty and provided greater influence for the Reich government over the procedure of criminal prosecution through the judicature. Individual articles in the decree were extraordinarily far reaching. Thus Article 3 specified as 'treasonable' and punishable (not less than three months' imprisonment) even the dissemination of information already known to the outside world, in so far as 'if it had not already been brought to the attention of a foreign government or publicly transmitted' it had 'endangered the well-being of the Reich'. This meant nothing less than the suppression of any unwelcome news *at home* whose circulation could not have been prevented abroad, and thus stood the notion of treason on its head. And apart from this the law against malicious gossip of 21 March created an instrument for stifling criticism which was harmless in itself but which was intolerable to the National Socialist leadership.

At the same time with the increase in the actual political punishments an apparatus of justice specially run and organized for prosecuting political crimes was called into being in the form of the

Special Courts. The decree specified that a Special Court was to be set up alongside every Higher Land Court and that it was to be responsible for trying all infringements against the Reichstag Fire decree and the new law against malicious gossip. The procedures of the Special Courts, whose number and responsibilities grew considerably in later years – like those of the People's Courts of Law set up in 1934 for high treason and treason – were very much 'simplified' and streamlined when compared with the normal criminal processes. Instead of the judicial collegiate principle, the position of the President who had to reach decisions with two associate Judges was considerably reinforced and with it his influence on the opening and conduct of the proceedings. Also the judicial authorities could influence the hearing of evidence and a 'summary trial' was possible through the lapse of the judicial preliminary examination and the curtailment of appeal rights.

The law against malicious gossip and the decree setting up Special Courts were obviously submitted to the cabinet by the Reich Ministry of Justice under pressure from the National Socialist leaders in order to counter the pointed attacks which Hitler, Göring and Frick above all had levelled against the judicature in conjunction with the affair of the Reichstag Fire.[4] But the foundation of a harsh criminal justice was obviously also related to the spread of a highly summary prosecution of political crimes by the S.A. and S.S. auxiliary police and the instrument of preventive custody. The Reich Ministry of Justice was trying to document the reliability of the judicature in keeping with the new government, as in the case of the 'Lex van der Lubbe', by means of an extraordinary new law for political crime and criminal procedure. It was believed possible to influence the National Socialist leadership to return to legality and the state of law and at least to restrain the revolutionary and arbitrary use of force which was underway during these weeks through substantial legal concessions, indeed even through partially abrogating the law and the constitution. This calculation was not wholly wrong but again it played into Hitler's hands, especially in so far as it enabled him to capture all the key positions whilst preserving that appearance of legality which was then particularly necessary on domestic and foreign policy grounds, and perhaps it even made the seizure of power possible in the first place.

The statistics on political crime still published in the statistical yearbook for 1933 but later kept secret illustrate the practical effect of the new law on political crime. Whereas within the German Reich in 1932, a total of 268 people had been tried for high treason, of which 250 had been legally sentenced (the numbers were still lower for the preceding years), Table 10.1 presents the picture for 1933:[5]

Table 10.1. Statistics on political crimes for 1933

Nature of the offence	No. of those tried (including acquittals)	No. sentenced
High treason (according to Arts. 83–86 of the penal code)	2 000	1 698
Contravention of the Reich Presidential Decree of (28 Feb. 1933) For the Protection of People and State	3 584	3 133
Contravention of the Reich Presidential Decree (of 28 Feb. 1933) against Betrayal of the German People and Treasonable Activity	1 106	954
Contravention of the Reich Presidential Decree (of 21 March. 1933) for Defence against Defamation of the Government of National Recovery	4 466	3 744
Total	11 156	9 529

There was some progress under the influence of efforts to end the National Socialist revolution in reducing *quantitively* the use of terrorist force in the state of emergency from summer 1933. The common cause against the S.A. which Hitler, Göring, Frick and other National Socialist exponents of the state authority made with the Reichswehr, the Reich President, the economy and the bureaucracy, tended as much in this direction as did the 'centralization' of justice. The latter process not only removed the administration of justice from the influence of the Land National Socialist governments and Party authorities, but also annulled many of the provincial penal laws which had been arrogantly introduced in the Länder during the process of seizing power, with all the attendant diversity of the legal system.[6] In this period, 1934/5, during which various proceedings were also taking place against S.A. and S.S. personnel for maltreating political prisoners, it was believed in the Reich Ministry of Justice that the legal state of emergency in the concentration camps and the custody penalties could be dispensed with through a policy adapted to National Socialist ideas of severe sentencing for political crimes, as well as through a *völkisch*-authoritarian reform of criminal law and justice. In fact there is every reason to believe that between 1934 and 1937, the political cases sentenced by the judicature (Special Courts and People's Court of Justice), and as a result the number of political prisoners sitting in the judicature's prisons, was numerically greater than those detained for political reasons in the concentration camps during this same period (on average from 5,000 to 8,000). The People's Court alone 'settled' in the years 1934–7, about 450 cases of high treason and some 575 cases of treason.[7] But still the lawless state of emergency was not completely ended. The Gestapo law of 10 February 1936 and the firm institutionalization of the concentration camps (although admittedly these were greatly reduced in number at this time) under the control of the S.S. made the state of emergency at law a lasting feature of the Third Reich. With the establishment of the principle that the Gestapo's action could not in any way be controlled by the administrative courts either, the Gestapo was given the crucial responsibility, namely the chance to decide for itself what acts were to count as 'political' and which of these should come under the control of the Political Police (rather than under the administration of justice for political crimes). Admittedly efforts made by the Reich Ministry of Justice to confine the application of preventive custody by the police to those cases which did not come under the criminal law provisions of the penal code for political crimes which had been introduced meanwhile, had some success in practice during these years (1934–7)[8] but they never led to a clear and binding demarcation.[9]

As a result, from 1934/5, prosecution by the Gestapo (and commitment to the concentration camps) was already assuming the character of supplementing or correcting judicial criminal prosecution. In order to preserve the authority of the judicature 'as a rule' local public prosecutors, especially in cases of prosecution for political National Socialist and was unwilling to allow a judicial system the most doubtful ways, were themselves making agreements with the relevant Gestapo local offices, so that the latter had the chance to arrest political prisoners when they were released from the criminal institutions of the judicature.[10] In other instances there were serious quarrels as a result of such 'correction of justice', particularly since the State Secretary responsible for criminal law matters in the Reich Ministry of Justice (Roland Freiser) was himself a fanatical National Socialist and was unwilling to allow a judical system remodelled in the spirit of National Socialism to be trimmed by the police. These quarrels took on the appearance of conflicts over jurisdictions between different organs of the National Socialist regime as each sought in its fashion to put National Socialist principles into effect and in so doing likewise referred to the will of the Führer. This was especially so whenever the Gestapo presumed to correct even decisions of the People's Court, which (under the direction of the former National Socialist Minister of Justice from Saxony, Thierack) had been expressly assigned by Hitler in 1934 (in place of the Reich Supreme Court) as the supreme authority in matters of political crime and had been staffed by reliable National Socialists. The following case, which took place in March 1937, was typical.

A former Communist arrested by the police and charged on

suspicion of high treason, because she had alledgedly taken part in illegal gatherings of former KPD and SPD members, had been released by the Second Senate of the People's Court because of lack of evidence. Two Gestapo officials who had been sent to the trial by the Secret State Police Office wanted to arrest the released woman immediately after judgement was delivered, whereupon there was a violent quarrel with a Judge and the President in charge of the hearing. The latter declared in the course of this 'that it was inadmissable to arrest people who had been released by the Court'. The People's Court had been set up 'by the Führer and Reich Chancellor and hence, as the highest Court in the German Reich, was completely sovereign', and it was 'an intolerable state of affairs' for its judgements to be set aside by the 'criticism of an administrative authority'.[11] This protest prevented the arrest of the released woman in the court-room but not from being taken into custody by the Gestapo two days later at her home.

Until 1938/9 in general the main trend was for 'collaboration' between the Administration of Justice and the Political Police, whereby the latter also still exercised some restraint in employing its illegal measures. In isolated cases, however, the 'correction of justice' by the police openly took the form of aggressive criticism deliberately calculated to put pressure on the judicature.[12] On 23/24 January 1939 the Reich Minister of Justice made this matter the occassion of a special talk with public prosecutors and higher Land Court Presidents. It then became clear that even the highest officials of justice had no objection against a large proportion of police 'preventive measures', and individually the public prosecutors had themselves requested the Gestapo to make arrests if the legal evidence was insufficient to convict, whereas only a small proportion of 'correction' cases were regarded as injurious to the authority of the judicature.[13]

The People's Court also went along with Gestapo practice in the end. On 21 January 1939, President Thierack had still declared in a letter to the Reich Ministry of Justice that according to the 'combined members of the Senate including the officiating Judge', preventive custody was 'intolerable once there had been an acquittal'.[14] A year and a half later on 29 July 1940, the senior public prosecutor at the People's Court informed the Reich Minister of Justice:

I have discussed with the President of the People's Court, in so far as it concerns cancellation of warrants for arrest by the People's Court, the question whether and how far it is advisable to hand over to the Secret State Police those persons detained on suspicion of anti-state activities after the warrant for their arrest has been cancelled... Pending alternative instructions I shall act as follows in future: in agreement with the President of the People's Court I shall basically hand over the persons concerned to the Secret State Police if an acquittal or a stay of proceedings is ordered, or if the sentence is declared to have been served through the detention itself, unless the Secret State Police give express orders to the contrary. If there is an acquittal because innocence has been proved, I shall inform the Secret State Police before the transfer takes place and ask them whether this is then really necessary. On the other hand, should the Secret State Police declare the penalty of arrest to be necessary, I shall arrange for the transfer.[15]

This was, at any rate in the realm of the People's Court, a complete surrender to the Gestapo in all matters concerning political crime. The original attempt of the judicature to exert some influence over and to regularize police measures of detention, for example by involving lawyers, had been stood on its head. And so too had the romantic ideas propagated especially by Hans Frank, the leader of the League of National Socialist German Lawyers and President of the Academy of German Law, that the *völkisch* Führer state would restore Germanic principles of law and the independent German judiciary. With 'grave concern about the state of legal security in Germany' Frank's deputy in the National Socialist League of Lawyers had still declared for his part (22 Aug. 1935) 'that overriding the law whenever arrests were made by the Gestapo' was 'completely incompatible with the National Socialist conception of security at law . . . in conflict with the natural regard for law of the northern races' and encouraged the calumny 'that the activity of the Secret State Police – like the Russian Czecha – was outside the law and purely despotic.'[16]

Such dreams of a *völkisch* authoritarian state of law along National Socialist lines, which then (1935) lay behind the abortive draft of a new Penal Code, had long been dashed by the time the War began. The judicature in assuming that this was the only way to preserve its standing had increasingly made compromises and had helped to bury the law itself. Already accustomed from Weimar times to excuse injustice in political matters because of so-called 'national emergencies', as long as the proper national ends were served, the German Nationalist Reich Minister of Justice (Dr Gürtner) had himself signed the law on 3 July 1934 after the bloody action caused by the Röhm affair, and subsequently declared this action to have been 'justified' as a measure to overcome a national emergency (*RGBl*, I, p. 529). This signature was not easy for a Reich Minister of Justice who was naturally well disposed towards the law and the constitutional order. But he believed himself capable of acting so because (like the conservative forces in the Reichswehr and bureaucracy) he expected a return to greater legal security to follow the emasculation of the S.A. But soon more such 'compromises' became necessary. Public terror had been reduced but too often unlicensed brutality still reigned in the Gestapo prisons and the concentration camps. The internal guard regulations of the S.S. in the concentration camps even made it a matter of duty for the S.S. posts to shoot prisoners in cases of the slightest insubordination or threat of escape. The information given to the public prosecutor's offices about such cases of men being 'shot whilst escaping' also ceased after 1934.[17]

In one case of the shooting of two prisoners in the Columbia House concentration camp in Berlin in spring 1935, the Berlin public prosecutor reported that: 'Regulations cannot excuse those accused. Since they do not constitute laws they cannot redress . . . the illegality of this action. This is a case of a regrettable discrepancy between service orders and what is legally permissible.'[18] But since the heads of the Administration of Justice did not want to conflict openly with the action of the Gestapo and the S.S., which was obviously sanctioned 'from above' (Hitler), the judicature took refuge in such politically sensitive cases (where it was credible at all for the Gestapo or S.S. personnel concerned to have acted 'according to the regulations') in the fateful practice of 'suspending' charges placed by the appropriate public prosecutor's office and submitting a report only to the superior authorities of justice (the Ministry in the last resort). In this way the legal principle was suspended whereby the public prosecutors' offices were obliged to prosecute all offences impartially within their sphere of activity. This was a remarkable example of the way in which the authoritarian state by forcing the public prosecutors to submit much more to such direction prepared the way for the state without law.

A formal 'gentleman's agreement' was reached between the Ministry of Justice and the Gestapo in 1937 concerning the criminal prosecution of police officials who were guilty of maltreating prisoners undergoing police investigation (which the judicature occasionally heard of through the examining Judges or during Court proceedings). The Ministry of Justice undertook in such cases to abstain from any criminal prosecution if the Gestapo could confirm that the police officials concerned had not acted arbitrarily but in accordance with regulations of the so-called 'intensive interrogation' (which according to the Gestapo was necessary from time to time).[19] Nevertheless the confessions extorted in such police 'interrogations' provided some courageous Judges or lawyers with the opportunity during the Court hearing to demonstrate the emptiness of the charges brought by the Gestapo.[20] Certain procedural techniques of the judicature, as for example hearings *in camera* (which also meant without Gestapo observers), could then help to reinstate the law. And because 'outright' acquittals generally entailed subsequent arrest by the Gestapo, Judges and lawyers occasionally 'agreed' to sentences of imprisonment which were basically unlawful, simply to preserve the accused from the attentions of the Gestapo for a while. The unlawful deprivation of freedom in the prisons of the judicature served in this instance as protection from imprisonment in the concentration camps. Such perversions were also the result of the dualism between the state of actions and the state of rules. Generally, however, this dualism produced the opposite effect: the self-adaptation of the judicature and of statute law to the dictatorial will of the Führer.

Personnel policies and organizational measures encouraged this development too. The 'purging' as a result of the Law for the Restoration of the Civil Service also affected the officials of justice and a law issued on the same day on the admission to the office of lawyer (*RGBl*, I, p. 188) was the basis for the exclusion of the considerable number of Jewish lawyers. Even though the figures for Judges and public prosectors forcibly retired on political grounds in 1933 was relatively small in view of the almost exclusively 'middle class' structure of justice and because the percentage of 'non-Aryans' among the officials of justice was much less than that among lawyers,[21] the principle of the irremovability of Judges was violated. In spite of many Judges and officials of justice joining the Party and the co-ordination and enforced incorporation of the 'German League of Judges' in the centralized organization of the League of National Socialist German Lawyers,[22] there was hardly any success in staffing even the leading positions in the Administration of Justice with 'old fighters' of the NSDAP. None the less, the attitude adopted by individual Judges towards the Party and its ideals, watched closely as this was by the local dignitaries of the NSDAP, was in the long-run to the advantage or disadvantage of their career, just as it was in the civil service. This was all the more so for the previous pattern of autonomous allocation of business between the Courts was increasingly curtailed by independent judicial authorities after 1933 and was transferred to the Administration of Justice.[23] It is true that the collegiate principle of the Courts and their judgements was preserved (President and Associate Judge) even in the Special Courts (although also generally reduced through the 'measures for simplification' after the outbreak of the War).[24] This was an element inherently opposed to the Führer principle but it could not be eliminated without a total transformation of the judicature, and this helped to make the judicial process a standing thorn in Hitler's side. In addition the greater dependence of the public prosecutors on the centralized political control in the Reich Ministry of Justice had important consequences for the co-ordination of justice. This was encouraged by the fact that the Law on Civil Servants of 1937 also made public prosecutors (not as previously only chief state counsels) political civil servants, who could be retired at any time and recalled. Moreover, the powers and rights of the public prosecutors' offices (and therefore the influence of the Administration of Justice) were increased over the accused during the trials, chiefly at first in the proceedings of the Special Courts and, in the context of streamlining criminal law proceedings after the beginning of the War, in normal jurisdiction too.[25]

The National Socialist influence on the personnel and organizational structures of justice, on the composition and the procedures of the Courts, was not achieved by a complete upheaval but through the penetration and infiltration of those structures at every conceivable point. The same was true of the connection between the judgements which were delivered and the written body of law. Here, too, the plans for a comprehensive reform of criminal law were suspended. Instead, in the non-political area, more severe penalties were introduced for individual crimes, through, for example, the Law against the Violent Habitual Criminal issued on 24 November 1933 (*RGBl*, I, p. 995), which envisaged a fixed term of imprisonment as well as an indefinite period of 'safekeeping for security' for repeated offences and crimes. Here too the judicature tried to make the illegal S.S. and police measures 'superfluous' through its own draconian changes in the law. The Bavarian Political Police for example at that time had already started sending the so-called anti-social elements (layabouts, drunks, homosexuals) to the concentration camps. But even these measures could not stop the Criminal Police, who had meanwhile been co-ordinated by Himmler and staffed by S.S. men, from introducing 'preventive arrest' as another means of coercion outside the law (as well as political custody) in 1937. This was subsequently regularized by a decree of the Reich Minister of the Interior concerning the prevention of crime (14 Dec. 1937).[26]

Generally speaking – and this was also partly true of the area of civil law – legal decisions were supposed to be free of any rigid adherance to statute law and the door opened to National Socialist ideals and to 'popular instinct' through a greater freedom in interpreting the law. This came about by means of the law of 28 June 1935 changing the Penal Code, which anticipated the proposed comprehensive criminal law reform by requiring 'analogy' to be made the basis of legal decisions. The new provision specified that in future the Judge not only had to examine whether a punishable offence had been committed according to the written interpretation of the law, but also whether an act 'deserved punishment according to the *principles* of a Penal Code or according to popular feeling' (*RGBl*, I, p. 839). Pro-National Socialist Judges had thereby been given a great deal of latitude to interpret the law and the general watering down of the principle of *nulla poena sine lege* had commenced. But this analogy paragraph, which was vigorously promoted by leading National Socialist lawyers (Frank, Freisler, Rothenberger) had much less influence on the judgements of lawyers versed in statute law than those propagandists would have liked. Another reason for this was that neither the 'popular instinct', nor the 'National Socialist ideology', nor the 'will of the

Führer', which according to these appeals should be the basis of the interpretation of the law, was really clear and thus applicable in the judicial process. For the same reason the attempts at providing a National Socialist training for law students and lawyers did not help matters much either. It was possible to denounce the process of 'thinking in terms of precedents' but very difficult to put a judicially applicable doctrine in its place. Thus there was a partial dismantling of old law but no creation of a new National Socialist law.

Even before the War began Hitler was taking part in this process of dismantling by occasionally disputing personally Court verdicts which seemed inadequate to him. When a series of hold-ups occurred in 1938 in some instances through the use of road blocks, which caused alarm for a period, the unusual step was taken on 22 June 1938 of Hitler personally issuing a law comprising only one sentence: 'Whoever sets up a road block with intent to commit a crime will be punished by death' (*RGBl*, I, p. 651). Besides this a decree of 20 November 1938 (*RGBl*, I, p. 1632) also extended the jurisdiction of the Special Courts, hitherto confined to political crimes, to criminal cases. Nor did Hitler hesitate to interfere in legal decisions on behalf of his personal followers, thus at the end of 1938 in the divorce proceedings of his old fellow fighter Hermann Esser, when the head of the Reich Chancellory (Lammers) and the Reich Minister of Justice (Gürtner) themselves were roped in to bring the Führer's interpretation of the law to the attention of the officiating Berlin Land Court.[27]

Already in 1938/9 there were numerous attacks against the judicial system and a systematic disparagement of individual Court verdicts by certain National Socialist press organs, especially *Das Schwarze Korps* (an S.S. weekly),[28] and after this the opening of the War marked the real period of progressive radicalization for law and justice too. At first this took place through a continuation of the course embarked on in 1938 with the road block law. After the War began a whole series of laws on war crimes were passed, containing a far greater number of threats of execution than had previously been the case, amidst reference to the special conditions of war and to the loss of the lives of German soldiers. The most notable were the decree on the emergency broadcast measures of 1 September 1939 (*RGBl*, I, p. 1683), the decree on the War economy of 4 September (*RGBl*, I, p. 1609) and the decree on subversive elements of 5 September (*RGBl*, I, p. 1679). In addition on 25 November came the extension of punitive measures in cases of subverting the military power (*RGBl*, I, p. 2319) and on 5 December the decree against violent criminals (*RGBl*, I, p. 2378). Thus the number of crimes punishable by the death penalty multiplied within a short period. This trend continued in the years that followed and according to the calculations of the American prosecution at the

Nuremberg Trials produced a situation where compared with three acts already subject to the death penalty before 1933, the threat of execution at law applied to no less than forty-six categories in the years 1943/4.[29] The draconian increase in severity of the criminal law provisions was considerably stimulated by the corresponding changes in criminal procedure which came into force on the day war broke out with the 'Simplification Decree'.[30] These extended still further the jurisdiction of the Special Courts, allowed the setting-up of new Special Courts, and the curtailment of defence and sentencing in summary trials. In addition, the arrangement of the so-called 'extraordinary appeal' was created through the law of 16 September 1939 which changed the provisions of the general criminal procedure, of the military power's procedures and of the Penal Code (*RGBl*, I, p. 1841). Here the Administration of Justice was given the possibility of setting aside legal judgements which seemed insufficiently severe through the senior public prosecutor at the Supreme Court and of ordering a retrial before a special Criminal Senate of the Supreme Court.

It is obvious that such a robust toughening up of criminal law went far beyond what could be regarded as a legitimate increase in precautions against crime during time of war. Although the Nationalist Reich Minister of Justice Gürtner was also in favour of harsh criminal justice, he was not primarily moved to issue this decree through his concern for the security of the Reich and the protection of the public in wartime. Once again, through more intensive ways of fighting crime, as desired by Hitler and practised by Himmler, the attempt was being made to take the wind out of the sails of criticism coming from those quarters. It was believed that the cause of justice could be served by proving that it too could be 'harsh'.

Later special criminal decrees, for example the infamous Decree concerning the Criminal Law Protection against Poles and Jews in the Incorporated Eastern Territories of 4 December 1941 (*RGBl*, I, p. 759) took this increase of penalties further and made the system of justice into an instrument for the struggle against undesired racial groups which went hand in hand with the military cam-

Table 10.2.

1938	23
1939	220
1940	926
1941	1,109
1942	3,002
1943	4,438
1944 (Jan.–Aug.)	2,015
Total	11,733

paigns. As a result, the number of death sentences imposed by the civil Courts rose steeply. The figures for 1938 to August 1944 from the files of the Reich Ministry of Justice provide the following balance sheet (Table 10.2) of death sentences confirmed for the Reich (excluding the Protectorate).[31]

The genesis of the Special Criminal Decree for Poles and Jews which perverted the law to an extreme degree[32] reveals clearly enough the familiar mechanism of this development. The security police were able under wartime conditions first to extend considerably what had been until 1938/9 the still relatively limited area covered by the state of emergency under its control in the Old Reich, and then in the newly annexed areas.[33] After this the judicial authorities had the greatest difficulty even in being allowed to conduct criminal prosecutions in these new areas, alongside the security police and the ruling organs (largely staffed by National Socialist functionaries) of those civilian government heads who were directly responsible to the Führer. When the principle of judicial authority was successfully established in those provinces governed according to the methods of the 'Master Race', it was at the cost of an almost total erosion of legal procedure and legal protection. As before, the judicature was only barely able to slow down the course of events and certainly could not stop it.

During the War Hitler sharply criticized the lawyers in his 'Table Talk', and had even on occasion called them 'parasites' and 'criminals'.[34] After the death of Gürtner (29 Jan. 1941) he felt that the time had come for a public humiliation of the legal authorities. Thus he had it formally confirmed through a proclamation in the Reichstag session of 26 April 1942 that he had 'the legal right' to dismiss from office 'Judges who clearly fail to recognize the mood of the hour' and this 'without regard to so-called vested rights and without going through the usual procedures'.[35] German Judges felt this act to be a 'brutal attack' and so did the acting Minister of Justice, Schlegelberger. This was followed on 20 August, with the involvement of Bormann and the Party Chancellery, by the appointment of the 'old Party comrade' and former President of the People's Court Thierack as the new Minister of Justice. Thierack's assumption of office and the simultaneous transfer of Freisler to the People's Court introduced the final and most extreme phase of the sell-out of the judicature.

Under Freisler's direction the People's Court became, especially with the trial of the plotters of 20 July 1944, the prime example of Party justice along the lines of the Stalinist show trials. And Thierack deliberately tried to get Hitler to regard the judicature in a more favourable light by voluntarily giving up some of the responsibilities of justice which had until then been successfully defended against the attacks of the S.S. and the police. Thus he came to an agreement with Himmler whereby several thousand criminals in the judicature's prisons were transferred to concentration camps (chiefly Mauthausen) where they were 'worked to death' within a short while. In addition the new Minister thereafter allowed criminal prosecution of Polish and Soviet Russian civilian workers in the Reich to be carried out solely by the police without involving the judicature. 'Criminal trial in court', so the subordinate police officers were informed on 30 June 1943 by Kaltenbrunner, the Chief of the RSHA newly appointed after the attempted assassination of Heydrich, would only take place 'if the police authorities require the holding of such a criminal trial', if it seems appropriate 'for reasons of public opinion' and 'if it has been established beforehand that the Court will in fact impose the death penalty'.[36] This complete reversal of the relationship between police and judicature corresponded to a roughly contemporary suggestion made by Himmler to Bormann,[37] when the Reich S.S. Leader criticized the 'mistaken attitude of the forces of justice who were active in the Eastern territories', who did not see their duty 'to ensure the interests of the German people in this area but felt that they were there to make "law"'. He (Himmler) therefore suggested that a 'clear line of demarcation' should be drawn and care should be taken 'that criminal law protection against Poles and members of other races in the East is exclusively the concern of the police'.

The link between the progressive expansion of the authority of the S.S. and the police apparatus unrestricted by the law, and the simultaneous radicalization of the racial policy of the National Socialist leadership during the War, can be seen here time and time again. But along with the other special powers and special agencies directly subordinate to the Führer (which increased rapidly in the second half of the War), the disruptive arbitrariness engendered as a result inevitably had its effect on the over-all policy and constitutional order of the National Socialist system. The rule of the state of emergency spread from the edges of the Reich towards the centre and here too it contributed towards further undermining legal security. The excessive and irrational rise in the use of force during the last stages of the War finally threatened the control of the National Socialist system itself. But this merely reflected the agony of a regime seeking to prolong its existence through the desperate 'energy' of such a resort to force.

Notes and references

1. On this cf. Ernst Fraenkel, *The Dual State. A Contribution to the Theory* of *Dictatorship* (New York, London, Toronto, 1940).
2. Decree of the Reich President for ensuring immunity from criminal prosecution, 21 March 1933 (*RGBl*, I, p. 134).

3.   Decree of the Reich President to prevent malicious attacks against the government of National Recovery, 21 March 1933 (*RGBl*, I, p. 135).

4.   When the draft of the law against malicious gossip was presented in the Reich cabinet, State Secretary Schlegelberger said on 21 March 1933, according to the protocol of the meeting, 'that the Reich Ministry of Justice, particularly himself who was head of the office at the time [Minister Gürtner was ill], felt that the attacks against the judicature coming from the cabinet were very harsh. It was self-evident that the judicature would give the utmost support to any government, but particularly the present government of national recovery, in any efforts aiming to protect the state against high treason and treason and such similar tasks.'

5.   According to the *Statistisches Jahrbuch für das Deutsche Reich* (54. Jg., Berlin, 1935), pp. 530f. From this source it is also apparent (p. 329) that a total of 5,365 actions were brought in the Special Courts in 1933 (4,794 of these for misdemeanours and 571 for crimes) and that the Special Courts passed 3,853 sentences. In 1934 there were 4,021 actions brought before the Special Courts (2,944 for misdemeanours and 1,077 for crimes). Overall 2,767 sentences were passed. The *Statistisches Jahrbuch für das Deutsche Reich* contains no figures on the jurisdiction of the Special Courts in later years.

6.   Thus, for example, the National Socialist state government in Bavaria issued a law 26 April 1933 for combating corruption and informing (Bavarian *Gesetz- und Verordnungsblatt*, p. 123) which clearly infringed on the criminal law rights of the Reich and had to be revoked on 24 May 1933.

7.   Figures according to the information from Walter Wagner, who will shortly be bringing out the results of his work on the findings of the People's Court.

8.   One basis for judging this is provided by the complete reports of the Bavarian Political Police (BPP) for the period 30 March to 2 November 1936. During this period 1,791 people were arrested by the BPP, an unusually high proportion for petty offences which were generally not serious enough to prosecute ('behaviour injurious to the state', 'insulting the Führer', 'bringing the swastika into contempt', etc.). On this cf. M. Broszat, 'Nationalsozialistische Konzentrationslager 1934–1945', in *Anatomie des SS-Staates*, Bd 2, p. 46 ff.

9.   Reich Minister of Justice Gürtner requested such a demarcation in his letter of 22 August 1936 to the Reich S.S. Leader and Chief of the German Police. In his reply (via S.S. Gruppenführer Best) of 7 October 1936 the S.S. Leader maintained on this point that in specific cases 'the penalty of preventive custody was also applicable for punishable offences'. Cf. *Akten des Reichsjustizministeriums*, BA: R22/1467.

10.   There is various material on this in *Akten des Reichsjustizministeriums*, BA: R22/1467. Of particular interest is the report of the public prosecutor at the Higher Land Court in Dresden to the Reich Minister of Justice, drafted 26 June 1936, concerning his agreements with the president of the State Police Office of Saxony regarding a 'close' and 'profitable collaboration' between the public prosecution and the Political Police in political crimes. Also characteristic was the request

of Ministerialdirektor Dr Crohne, the responsible division leader for political crimes in the Ministry of Justice, to the Gestapo on 13 April 1938, for the latter 'to examine closely whether the action of preventive custody in matters of high treason . . . which was felt by the convicted person and his supporters to be an additional punishment, was absolutely necessary as a preventive measure'.

11. According to the report of the Gestapo to the Reich Minister of Justice 7 March 1937 (BA: R22/1467).

12. On this cf. also the later testimony of the then President of the Hanseatic Supreme Land Court in Hamburg, Curt Rothenberger, who stated that in Hamburg after the Röhm affair there had hardly been any more interference in justice by the Party and Gestapo. It was only when war began that judgements were increasingly changed by the police (BA: 7 S 477).

13. Cf. the protocol on the talk (BA: R22/1467).

14. Ibid.

15. Ibid.

16. Letter of the deputy of the Leader of Reich Lawyers to the Minister of Justice, ibid.

17. Cf. the official diary of the Minister of Justice Dr Gürtner (Nuremberg Documents PS-3751).

18. Ibid., entry of 29 May 1935.

19. Details on this in *Justiz im Dritten Reich. Eine Dokumentation*, ed. Ilse Staff (Fischer-Bucherei 559, Frankfurt-on-Main, 1964), pp. 118ff.

20. Ibid., pp. 122ff.

21. Thus in the area of the Higher Land Court of Hamburg in 1933 a total of 31 (mainly Jewish) judges and public prosecutors were dismissed and 44 Jewish lawyers were excluded from the Bar Association. Cf. Werner Johe, *Die gleichgeschaltete Justiz. Organisation des Rechtswesens und Politisierung der Rechtsprechung 1933–1945, dargestellt am Beispiel des Oberlandesgerichtsbezirks Hamburg* (Frankfurt-on-Main, 1967), pp. 66ff. In the district of the Higher Land Court at Hamm in 1933, 18 and, on the basis of the Nuremberg Laws, a further 13 Jewish Judges were dismissed; in addition 13 Judges were disciplined for political reasons (enforced retirement or demotion to a lower office). Cf. Hermann Weinkauff, 'Die deutsche Justiz und der Nationalsozialismus', in *Die Deutsche Justiz und der Nationalsozialismus*, Pt I (Stuttgart, 1968), p. 102.

22. Details of this development in H. Weinkauff, loc. cit., pp. 102ff.

23. Cf. Albrecht Wagner, 'Die Umgestaltung der Gerichtsverfassung und des Verfahrens und Richterrechts im nationalsozialistischen Staat' in *Die deutsche Justiz und der Nationalsozialismus*, Pt I, pp. 207f.

24. Ibid., pp. 228ff.

25. Text in the collection of decrees for official reference issued by the Reich Criminal Police Office, *Vorbeugende Verbrechensbekampfung*, December 1941, Bl. 41.

26. Albrecht Wagner, loc. cit., p. 281.

27. This case is fully documented in *Akten der Reichskanzlei*, BA: R43 II/11506. Especially typical in this connection is a letter sent by Lammers to Gürtner dated 23 November 1938, in which the former explained that he wanted to draw attention to the Führer's opinion,

'since the interpretation which the Führer and Reich Chancellor gives, as ultimately the sole law-maker of the Third Reich, to a law which he has issued seems of particular importance to me'.

28. The Reich Ministry of Justice was still at pains at this time to rebut this criticism. Cf., for example, the reply appearing in *Deutsche Justiz* on 27 January 1939, p. 1750 to thirteen attacks by *Das Schwarze Korps* in the years 1937/8. In February 1939 Gürtner also made an effort to get Himmler personally to stop these attacks (IfZ: Himmler-files, folder 47).

29. *Nürnberger Juristenprozess*, III, Protokoll(d), p. 4460.

30. Decree concerning measures relating to the constitution of the Courts and the administration of justice (*RGBl*, I, p. 1758). An exact de-marcation of jurisdiction in criminal procedures and especially of the jurisdiction of special Courts came later through the so-called 'Juris-diction decree' of 21 February 1940 (*RGBl*, I, p. 405).

31. IfZ: Fa 103.

32. Cf. on this M. Broszat, *Nationalsozialistische Polenpolitik*, pp. 137ff.

33. In the Old Reich too, Himmler and the Chief of the Security Police (Heydrich) were empowered to take extraordinary measures at the outbreak of the War. On these grounds the Chief of the Security Police issued a circular which was sent to the organs of the Security Police which called for ruthless action against offences against the people and the state and which stated that 'on orders from above if need be' there would be 'brutal liquidation of such elements' (BA: Slg Schumacher, no. 271). As a result even in autumn 1939 isolated sum-mary executions were already being carried out by the S.S. in the concentration camps of the Old Reich of criminals, war saboteurs and the like. Alarmed by these episodes, Minister of Justice Gürtner urgently requested Hitler at the end of September to clarify 'whether crimes within non-occupied territory [Reich territory] are to be punished according to the rules of war, or by the police without trial and sentence'. Hitler let it be known obliquely via Lammers on 14 October 1939 that 'in isolated instances' he could not forgo giving the Security Police orders of this sort 'because the Courts (military and civilian) had not shown themselves able to adapt to the special needs of war' (Nuremberg Documents NG-190).

34. Cf. the conversation of 22 July 1942. Henry Picker, *Hitlers Tisch-gespräche im Führerhauptquartier 1941–2* (Bonn, 1951), pp. 259f.

35. Text of the Hitler speech and the Reichstag resolution moved by Gör-ing after it in *Volkischer Beobachter*, 27 April 1942.

36. Contained in *Allgemeine Erlass-Sammlung des Reichssicherheits-hauptamt*, 2 A IIIf, p. 131.

37. Letter of 8 July 1943 (Nuremberg Documents, NG-2718).

Chapter Eleven

Conclusion

The complex structure of the National Socialist regime, its short-lived but revolutionary existence, the demagogic nature of its ideology, and the lasting processes of social and socio-psychological deformation which it touched off, the contradiction between this regime's shapelessness and the extraordinary development of its power – all this defies any simple explanation. Nor can the present account provide such an explanation. But at least a few of the insights which have been picked up and illustrated can now finally be summarized and formulated in more general terms. The main purpose in doing this will be to examine the effectiveness and development of National Socialist policy in conjunction with the regime's structural features and its change, and to illustrate their interaction.

Success in overthrowing the Weimar Republic and in establishing the Hitler regime was primarily due to the collaboration between the conservative opposition to democracy and the National Socialist mass movement. The prelude to 30 January 1933 confirms that in view of the distribution of power then pertaining in Germany and the severe crisis afflicting the political and social system under the Weimar Republic, it was impossible either to revert to an authoritarian state on the old model (without the element of social integration afforded by a popular movement), or for National Socialism to seize power on its own (without the conservative supports in state and society). In that respect the alliance of 30 January was in line with contemporary anti-democratic ideologies which ever since the First World War had already been proclaiming and predicting in more or less vague terms ('conservative revolution', 'revolution of the right' etc.) the restoration of élitist and authoritarian principles of order by means of a total national revolution. This contradiction between modern techniques of action and restorative ideological elements, the half-revolutionary, half-reactionary relationship to the traditional state and social order, had appeared in the National Socialist movement from the outset.

The fusion of authoritarian and totalitarian trends had intensified as a result of the expansion of the NSDAP to a national mass Party after 1930. The alliance between the Swastika and the Black–White–Red had already been anticipated within the Party through the mass influx of middle-class protest voters before it became the foundation of the Hitler government on 30 January 1933. Of course subsequent developments quickly exposed the antagonism between these dissimilar elements and partners. Thus far at least the distinction of type between authoritarian and totalitarian governments is well-founded. But the attempt to bring about this uneasy alliance in spite of this, and the equilibrium which lasted in practice until about 1937/8 between the stabilizing factors of an authoritarian and regulated state and the totalitarian forces of the National Socialist movement, had for all that a constitutive importance for the Third Reich and made the consolidation of the Hitler state possible in the first place. It was only on the basis of this stability in the first instance that the later expansion of power and process of radicalization took place, which was determined by the growing superiority of the totalitarian forces of the regime.

The first years of the Third Reich, when the question of how the dualism between the 'movement' and the governmental dictatorship would develop had not yet been finally resolved, show the working of this dualism particularly clearly. The essential features of the thoroughly contradictory organizational, legal and power structure of the Hitler regime can only be properly understood with this antagonism in mind.

It was of crucial significance that the so-called seizure of power in the years 1933/4 oscillated between making revolution and halting the revolution. The structure of power and the allocation of authority which developed in this stormy first phase were not the outcome of any clear concepts or united action, but rather of numerous separate, sometimes overlapping but seldom co-ordinated and frequently opposing processes, which stemmed from the Party revolution from below, the expansion of the central state dictatorship from above and the often more or less spontaneous co-ordination and adjustment in social and public life outside politics. The fact that this stormy early phase was brought to a close with the establishment of the absolute power of the Führer in the summer of 1934 meant that the arrangement for the internal shaping of the Reich, which was still a long way from being clarified and resolved, was interrupted and both the revolutionary tendencies within the Party and those forces of the state of order which had grown stronger from the middle of 1933, were blocked. The share-out of power reached at this point was more or less 'frozen' for the time being with its contradictions and contrary tendencies. Examples of this were the tangled arrangements for the relationship between the Party and the state which had arisen in various areas of public and political life in 1933/4, as evidenced by the hostile or mutual coexistence of separate state and Party offices at the local and

Kreis level and in certain political departments; the personal union of state and Party office at the Land and province level or else with individual Ministers and Reichsleiter of the Party; the institutional interlocking of Party and state, for example in the sphere of the S.S. and the police or the propaganda offices; the Party's legal right to be consulted over civil service policy and governmental legislation etc. But these different patterns of the relationship between Party and state, which could also entail the enlargement and increase of the state's authority, did not determine by themselves the nature of the structure of government which emerged from the 'seizure of power'. The current organization of the government and administration had already been significantly altered in other ways in 1933/4. That is to say by means of new central Reich Authorities, in part directly responsible to the Führer, in accordance with the special political intentions of Hitler's government (Propaganda and Aviation Ministries, Inspector for Road Building, Leader of the Reich Labour Service); by means of new branches of the executive and of the judicature (Trustees of Labour, Special Criminal Courts, Courts for the entailed farms and for ensuring sound heredity); by separating previously subordinate branches of the administration (Political Police, Health Offices) and through new types of public law organs with combined planning, co-ordinating and self-governing functions (Reich Food Estate, Reich Chamber of Culture among others).

This mingling of official, semi-official and Party political institutions and responsibilities, which also tended to mix the state bureaucratic organization and the structures of the associations of private business with the Führer principle derived from the National Socialist movement, made the boundaries between the state, society and the Party fluid, and created, as it were, a totalitarian partnership between them. The complex institutional traits of the regime which arose in 1933/4 reflected the pluralism of forces and centres of action which were trying during this phase to establish their own spheres of influence and power, their own particular interests and their own views on the nature and direction of the new regime. Just as the NSDAP's mass movement had already begun to infiltrate broad sectors of society and public life by setting up numerous auxiliary organizations, offices and associations and through its entry to the parliaments, Land and municipal governments, so the process of co-ordination in 1933 constituted a new, still more intensive form of fusion and confrontation between the National Socialist movement and the old leadership forces in state and society. The speed and smoothness with which this co-ordination generally took place, provided certain 'essentials' of National Socialism were acknowledged and the corresponding conclusions were drawn (the elimination of democratic procedures, and of Jewish, Marxist, and left-liberal forces of leadership), show that very often it was more a matter of readjustment than a revolutionary upheaval. But this also resulted in a significant proportion of the National Socialist movement being incorporated in the nominally co-ordinated, new centralized associations. Co-ordination signified that the social forces were contained but very often at the price of a simultaneous dilution and a further softening and splitting up of the National Socialist movement.

There was both necessity and method in this development in so far as only confrontation and collaboration with the powerful specialists and experienced established forces of leadership could bring about the transformation from propaganda movement to a governing organization. There was pressure on both sides for collaboration and this was also decisive not least in the Ministries and the state administrations. Collaboration offered those nominally co-ordinated and established leadership forces and specialists who were prepared to 'co-operate loyally' the possibility of recommending themselves to their new masters through their particular ability and activity, of contributing their own ideas in order to fill the vacuum left by the National Socialist programme, or else of carrying out their proposals for reform with the help of National Socialism. At the same time this collaboration provoked an expert screening and replacement of National Socialist functionaries and filtered from the vague aims of the National Socialist ideology those elements which were attainable and practicable in the given circumstances. The tactic of allowing individual scope and experiment, which Hitler had already successfully adopted towards the Party before 1933 in order to encourage initiative, spontaneity and activity, was now applied over and over again but chiefly in the realm of practical government measures, of technical and economic management and organization. The relatively generous nature of the process of co-ordination for the liberal middle class and conservative groups in state and society was a precondition for a successful National Socialist take-over of power. Because it was only with the aid of those 'co-ordinated forces' that demagogic activity could successfully be transformed to practical control. Terrorist intimidation on the one hand, to demonstrate unmistakably the new masters' claim to leadership, and halting the revolution on the other hand to prove the determination to govern effectively even at the cost of the 'old fighters' – the seizure of power swung between these two interdependent poles and in so doing helped the Hitler regime to succeed.

The marriage of an authoritarian system of government with the mass movement of National Socialism seemed to be successful in spite of considerable friction over key points, and also to have overcome the shortcomings of the authoritarian system. With the aid of different auxiliary organizations of the Party and the subsidiary organs which emerged from the process of co-ordination, the regime considerably extended its influence over the public and society in general without requiring wholesale standardization and bureaucratization. In this way it proved possible for the power of political and social forces to be magnified and this could then be concentrated on certain politically desirable focal points. The stimulus to the national economy and the reduction of unemployment which was achieved in this way even in 1934, created a reservoir of popular faith which was crucial in the early phase. At the same time the intensity of the national self-image and propaganda, however vague its positive 'contents' might have been, increasingly drew the individual towards the forum of national events and helped to loosen his social, familial and confessional ties. This propaganda, as well as the proficiency drive which the regime stimulated, and the greater mobility between the social classes already guaranteed through the network of auxiliary Party organizations, caused the *individual member of the race* to identify himself with the whole in a way which he had been urged in vain by reasoned arguments as a *citizen* of the Weimar Republic. But it was precisely this willingness to identify and to make 'self-sacrifices' that was deliberately aroused by the National Socialist regime with a mastery of psychology (political education through intensive national appeals and compensation for lack of social status through the wholesale provision of *völkisch*, national status symbols), which increased the regime's power to integrate and its suggestivity, and created the psychological climate which enabled the National Socialist leadership to demand a far greater national commitment.

The transfer of Hitler's absolute control as leader over the Party to the government, the state and the nation was another extraordinarily important integrating factor. As Hitler ceased to be merely the leader of the Party (the installation of the 'Führer's Deputy' underlined this aspect) the charismatic 'belief in the Führer' appeared to many civil servants as well as to Reichswehr officers as an element for associating the old authoritarian state (with the personal rule of the monarch) with the National Socialist Führer state.

By the end of the period of the seizure of power, in summer 1934, the Party had largely been converted to its new role of giving practical encouragement to increased productivity. Its most able functionaries had taken over state departments and from then on these defended the state's authority. The Party summit, as before politically and organizationally weak (separate Reichsleiter, Führer's Deputy, Reichsorganisationsleiter) had secured only a very limited right of say in the government. The revolutionary system of Commissioners had been dismantled, the political pressure of the S.A. mass organization had been brutally eliminated and the revolutionary NSBO had also been largely shunted away from real social policy towards making propaganda and giving advice. Even the Gauleiter, who had been considerably strengthened in 1933 at the Land and province level, through their personal union with leading state offices (Reich Governor, Oberpräsidenten, Land Ministers, Land Minister Presidents) lost for the time being something of their customary independence when the sovereignty of the Länder was ended and with the 'centralization' of important departments. In foreign policy and economic policy attempts at direct revolutionary Party policy had been thwarted not least on account of the dilettantism of the protagonists concerned. Those rival Party offices which nevertheless survived (in foreign policy: Rosenberg's Foreign Policy Office, the Auslandsorganisation of the NSDAP under Wilhelm Bohle, the Ribbentrop Bureau, the Volksdeutsche Mittelstelle, Göring's Research Bureau etc.) neutralized each other to some extent and had only slight political importance. The quantitative extent of the illegal use of force (preventive custody, concentration camps) had been limited and even in the Jewish question a reversion to legal processes could be detected (the heavy Jewish emigration progressively declined between 1934 and 1937).[1]

Conflicts between the Party and the state and between the regime's forces of leadership and institutions admittedly assumed a considerable importance, but the positive benefits to the regime of this rivalry at least balanced the negative results of it. Because the struggle for responsibility and power often left conflicts unresolved (whether deliberately or through diffidence) it could just as easily increase efficiency and power as be destructive. The coexistence and conflict of uncoordinated authorities very often undermined solidarity and uniformity in the exercise of power, but it also led to conflicting personalities, organs and controversial ideas keeping each other in check. Moreover this rivalry produced compromises and mutual arrangements which stabilized the system of government as a whole and the absolute control of the Führer at the top. The dualism between the state of rules and the state of actions in the realm of criminal prosecution was one example of this. The lawless use of terror and the state of emergency for fighting political opponents was considerably reduced from the middle of 1933, although not ended, under the influence of the conservative, authoritarian forces of the regime. The abortive attempts to do away completely with preventive custody and the concentration camps merely led to a 'disciplining of terror' (stricter subjection of the S.S. and the Gestapo to internal regulations), and caused a significant increase in severity of criminal justice. The characteristic attempts between 1934 and 1938 to reach some 'tolerable' arrangement in the conflict between a criminal justice bound by law and uncontrolled criminal prosecution through the Gestapo were in the interests of both sides and for this reason were not wholly fanciful. Here as in other areas efforts until 1938 to resolve the antagonism between the state of rules and the state of actions outweighed the manifestations of a partially regulated exercise of power. The Party Organization – its structures altered and regulated mainly by means of controls emanating from the Reich Treasurer of the Party – had lost its political impact and seemed well on the way to becoming an auxiliary organ of the state leadership. And the conservative forces of the regime, the armed forces in particular (thanks to rearmament and the reintroduction of general conscription), as well as the ministerial bureaucracy still occupied a strong position purely by virtue of their institutional authority.

The various attempts made in the years between 1934 and 1937 to determine important functions of the new 'authoritarian and total Führer state' (as Lammers put it in a lecture in October 1934)[2] legally and constitutionally (criminal law, Reich reform, governmental legislation, law on the civil servants etc.) suggest that in this phase even many of the old Hitler partisans thought it was possible to harmonize the authoritarian and totalitarian elements and they tried to do this. And until 1938 the actual substance of National Socialist domestic and foreign policy kept largely within the bounds of traditional German Nationalist and national conservative ideas and aims. And where this was not the case, as in Church policy, the National Socialist extremists and even the Reich Church Minister had to suffer considerable loss of face.

Hitler himself took account of these considerations by generally acting as the 'honest broker' between the authoritarian and totalitarian elements of the regime until 1937/8, and refrained from setting out radical ideological aims both at home and abroad. In contrast to the unambiguous comments made by Hitler before 1933, which criticized the programme of a national policy of revision as utterly inadequate and wrong, Hitler's actual foreign policy until 1938 followed traditional aims and indeed after this, with the agreement with Stalin, the campaign against Poland and war against the Western Powers.

The fact that these were merely 'stages' towards an ultimate goal of quite different proportions was admittedly difficult to detect until 1937 and even later was still concealed from the general public. If one merely assumes that the ideological determining factor, the motive force of the National Socialist regime and personified above all in Hitler, remained basically unchanged and identical from the very beginning and that *only* the tactics and outward appearance changed it is easy to overlook the fact that this 'only' was still of crucial importance for the prevailing condition of the state. This was still determined for the time being chiefly by the current actual and concrete affairs of policy, of government and of legislation and not, or only secondarily, by the long-term aims and secret plans for the future. That was also true even of Hitler, who as a rule subordinated his utopian and ultimate goals to a highly realistic, often cynical political expediency in following immediate aims. It was

precisely because Hitler viewed matters concerning the state system almost solely in terms of present usefulness that government
and state under the Third Reich. was constantly being reorganized
according to what were the most pressing aims of the moment. But
this meant that the institutional realities of the structure of government arising from merely tactical and fleeting changes of policy
automatically continued. Hitler might make concessions to the
Reichswehr and bureaucracy or conversely to the S.S., to Bormann
and individual special agents simply to attain certain specific ends,
but these concessions could not simply be revoked by a stroke of
the pen. The organizational and legal consequences of even tactical
directives from the Führer tended to persist.

Here it must also not be forgotten that propagandist concealments are not merely untruthful and unreal. As long as the foreign
policy propaganda of the Third Reich stressed peaceful national revisionism and in so doing energetically stressed respect for neighbouring countries and their interests, this affected the consciousness and the constitution of the nation and of the regime. Any
propaganda creates reality to the extent to which it is believed and
determines the thoughts and actions of the faithful. In November
1938 Hitler himself was displeased with the undesired outcome of
his own propaganda. For years he had been forced to talk of peace
and as a result a public mood had arisen which no longer reckoned
with war. Thus it then became necessary 'to gradually adjust the
psychology of the German people' and to make it clear to them
'that some things . . . can only be accomplished by force'.[3]

As the transition took place to an expansionist foreign and war
policy the relative moderation and the conservative and authoritarian restraint and stability of the Hitler regime also came to an end
at home. From then on Hitler finally abandoned the attempt to
reach a compromise between traditional nationalist and National
Socialist aims and methods.

An accelerating process of political aggressiveness and extremism
set in, which was closely related to the more rapid regroupings of
internal power relationships and jurisdictions and, above all, to the
progressive emasculation of the state. The almost panic-ridden
anxiety evidenced by Hitler in the years 1937/8 that – after the preceding period of relative moderation – it might not be possible to
take off for the great final aims, was not confined solely to foreign
policy. Parallel to this was the notion that the internal system of
government had to be changed too and orientated more positively
towards fighting ends instead of towards governmental and organizational tasks if the 'movement' was not to become bogged down
and if the absolute control of the Führer was not to be restricted
by bureaucratic governmental apparatuses and rules. Hitler's
address to the leaders of the armed forces and of the German
Foreign Office attested in the Hossbach Memorandum (5 Nov.

1937) revealed the Führer's will to war and his radical aims, and must have enabled him to see at the same time how much agreement he could expect from his hitherto relatively cautiously treated conservative partners. This was just one of the deliberate provocations and tests of strength which ushered in the new, more aggressive policy course. The ensuing change of leadership in the armed forces and German Foreign Office, the reorganization and intensification of economic planning already initiated through the Four Year Plan (Schacht's resignation), the final ending of collegiate cabinet meetings (February 1938), the rapid growth of concentration camps and armed S.S. units, the simultaneous massive onslaught against the judicature and the bureaucracy, the disavowal and pruning of the authority of the central Ministries in favour of the Governor in annexed Austria who was directly responsible to the Führer, the planned pogrom against the Jews of November 1938 and other roughly contemporary events, show quite clearly that the structure of the regime which had emerged from the process of seizing power and which remained relatively stable in the years following, was now broken in numerous places. The fact that Hitler even reactivated the long dormant terrorist power of the S.A. for the Reich Crystal Night was anachronistic when viewed from the perspective of the stage then actually reached in the reorganization of power, but it was symptomatic of the determination to remove the crust of bureaucratic and lawful consolidation by force. Only then, after the preceding stabilization and extension of power, did the way seem clear for the second phase of the National Socialist revolution.

Here the most extreme consequences of certain mechanisms arising from the earlier amalgamation of totalitarian and authoritarian elements revealed themselves for the first time. Such a 'mechanism' had managed to restrain the utopian National Socialist ideas of a new order and in that respect had facilitated the process of 'coordination' and adjustment. But at the same time it led to the selection of the purely negative elements of National Socialist ideology and to their systematization. It was always a hallmark of National Socialist ideology that only its negations were concretely and clearly specified (the struggle propagated against Jewry, against Marxism, pacifism, and the democratic 'system' among others), whereas the proposals for a new order were highly ambiguous and contradictory. Nourished primarily on resentments, anxieties, uncertainties and feelings of hatred, the National Socialist movement had always shown its strength before 1933 chiefly in the fanaticism of the struggle against its enemies and prevailing circumstances. At that time this basically destructive tendency could still be perceived and presented positively as a passionate determination to change the existing and unsuccessful state of affairs, and could be linked with any likely ideas on reform and reorganization in political and social life. To that extent the National Socialist movement before 1933 still shared the 'innocence' and 'openness' of all revolutionary causes. This changed when the organization for government was established. Then the impracticality was revealed of almost all the ideas aimed at reorganizing the structure of state and society. Whenever National Socialist splinter groups or auxiliary organizations tried to realize what were partially conceived aims in 1933/4, they were thwarted by opposing forces. The more or less corporatist ideals of National Socialism, the pursuit of a comprehensive new order for agriculture and for restructuring agriculture, the ideas for reforming the Reich and the proposals for a revolutionary recasting of the army, civil service and judicature – none of these could be achieved. The strength and ability of the National Socialist movement was only sufficient to endanger the existing state of affairs and partially to undermine it. On the other hand, it became apparent with every effort made to realize reforms in specific areas of the political and social system that National Socialist ideas themselves were controversial and impracticable, and for this reason any concrete proposal for change met with massive resistance both within the Party and from those forces in state and society whose partnership and support was vital to the 'Government of National Recovery'. But the less chance there was of converting National Socialism's ideological dogma to the tasks of constructive reorganization, the more exclusively that ideological policy focussed on the negative aspects and aims which primarily affected only legal, humanitarian and moral principles, but which appeared to be socially or politically unimportant.

Since a policy of national regeneration through restructuring agriculture and land reform was not so easily attainable, and since even the state-controlled programmes for increasing the population and for racial hygene could only operate within narrow limits, then if the basic civil liberties and the bases of civil society were to remain untouched, the population policy and racial policy were bound to be concentrated all the more on the negative measures directed against groups who were socially despised in any case, those with hereditary illness and the Jews. The laws on healthy stock passed in 1933/4, in which Hitler and the Party were heavily involved, enforced the sterilization of the mentally ill and those with hereditary illness, whilst the Nuremberg laws (of 1935) for the protection of the blood – which made marriage and intercourse between Germans and Jews punishable – were almost a substitute for the absence of other revolutionary successes by the Party. They were also cheap concessions which were granted relatively lightly to the fanaticism of National Socialism by the conservative forces of the regime and of middle-class nationalist society. This was repeated on a larger scale later with the National Socialist population policy in the incorporated Eastern territories. The attempts at a 'positive' Germanization of these large areas through the 'addition' of ethnic German stock or through the selection of 'worthwhile nordic stock' were relatively limited both in extent and significance because harsh realities, claims, opposing interests and practical difficulties repeatedly prevented progress and the ideology itself was often a barrier. By contrast the negative side of this 'consolidation of German nationhood' could be widely implemented and with relative ease, e.g. deportation, dispossession and discrimination against the 'inferior' Polish nationality. It was the same in 1934 when the revolutionary power of the S.A. was brutally emasculated but the S.S., which had specialized in terrorizing those already debased 'enemies of the state and people', maintained and consolidated the standing which it had gained in the Political Police in 1933. In the S.S. concentration camps it was not, at that time at least, so much a question – as it was in the case of the S.A.'s comprehensive claim to power under Röhm – of an ideological policy which was bound to upset the appointed bearers of political and social power in the Third Reich, but more a matter of dealing with those who were already divorced from the social and political structures: Marxists, Jews, Bible students, anti-social elements, homosexuals, and criminals.

Although it was chiefly Hitler who on the one hand peremptorily halted the further revolutionary ambitions of the S.A. and of other elements in the movement, and who on the other hand repeatedly diverted the legislation and other measures of the regime towards these negative aims of ideological policy, it would be very superficial to view this development primarily as a consequence of Hitler's personal influence. Hitler simply embodied the 'logic' of the National Socialist movement, whose propagandist and political *raison d'être* had always been to preach revolutionary renewal whilst at the same time as far as possible pleasing all the groups and elements of middle-class society. The stereotyped negations of this ideology had always been the one thing on which the 'extremism of the middle' could agree, and which allowed it the illusion of a community of purpose: the inflation of its own worth, the rejection and defamation of all that was foreign and 'abnormal', of everything which was out of tune with the dictates of petit-bourgeois values of order and attainment.

However, the selection of the negative elements of the ideology (these alone were realized and the other aspects remained the subject of propaganda and wishful thinking) which occurred during the process of seizing power and in the course of the Third Reich's subsequent development, meant that the hitherto purely demagogic anti-feelings and ideologies were then institutionalized and thus systematized and perfected. And this was one outcome of the fusion of the ideological movement of National Socialism with the structural principles of an authoritarian, absolutist, bureaucratic

organization. The link between the S.S. and SD and the Political
Police is the prime example of this. Hostile groups and complexes
(from Jewry to Freemasonry) which had become stereotyped in-
gredients of the ideology, not least because condemnation of these
was necessary for psychological reasons, now became a matter for
the administration. The addiction to pogroms and the activism and
spontaneity which had largely characterized the S.A. terror in 1933
was progressively eliminated. The spectre of the 'Jewish question'
and other matters concerning enemies and parasites were now
tackled rationally, technically and bureaucratically. But since the
practical (rather than the propagandist) activity of the ideological
movement was almost exclusively geared to these negative aims,
the only conceivable further development had to be by way of a
continued intensification of the measures directed against Jews, the
mentally ill and anti-social elements etc. But discrimination could
not be stepped up *ad infinitum*. As a result the 'movement' was
bound to end up by wreaking physical destruction. The mass murder of the Jews was no more planned from the outset than the preceding and progressive use of legal discrimination against Jews.
Here, as in the prosecution of the irrational foreign policy goal of
Lebensraum, the National Socialist leadership was unable to deflect the consequences of their dynamic force. On the contrary it
was typical that the ideological figment of the 'Jewish question' was
resorted to again and again and was tackled by repeated partial
'solutions' until the only step left was the 'final solution'. But to
carry out this ultimate perversion of the ideological movement required the institutionalized dogmatism for combating the enemy –
such as had been bred in the S.S. and Security Police. Here was an
apparatus which 'under cover of darkness' finally exterminated a foe
which had once been necessary on grounds of propaganda by
means of a technically versed 'pest control' which was as efficient
as it was cold-blooded. This was the lethal and at the same time
paradoxical outcome of an anti-Semitism which had once served as
a popular propaganda device.

The obsession of foreign policy with the arch enemy Bolshevism
corresponded to the focussing of the National Socialist combat
movement at home on the Jews and other 'national parasites'.
Here again the real ideological opponent was one who did not belong to the established family of nations. Just as the Jews had been
an easy target for aggression at home and the stimulus for a far-
reaching incitement and mobilization of forces, so the Soviet
Union, standing outside the concert of European powers and ostra-
cized as an alien body, was believed to provide the best target for
pursuing an imperialistic expansion of living-space unpunished and
without risk.

The loss of momentum which the National Socialist leadership
had to endure as the unavoidable consequence of the seizure of

power and the consolidation of the regime drove them to return time and time again to this handful of hostile aims. As in the case of the anti-Jewish measures, however, the constant harping on the concept of living-space was bound to lead to a progressive escalation of an aggressive foreign and war policy, which was more and more remote from the earlier rationality of foreign policy decisions and increasingly subject to an irrational ideological fanaticism. But even here the actual institutional and structural development of the regime played its part.

As long as the organizational coherence of the various branches of the National Socialist regime was to some extent preserved, as long as the Führer's will was not completely remote from the state and the government and there was a minimum of all-round readiness to co-operate and compromise between the rival authorities, leadership groups and apparatuses, a certain degree of rationality, control and self-regulation was guaranteed. But the growing decline of the regime's centralized character and its progressive splintering into new centres of activity that tended to devour neighbouring authorities and make themselves indispensable according to the law of motion underlying the leadership principle, increasingly disrupted any rational over-all organization of government and reinforced the particularist egocentricity of the respective departmental values and ideologies.

The prevailing tendency to resort to expediency constantly extended the regime's institutional jungle after 1938. As time passed the Third Reich was more and more burdened with the elements and relics of *ad hoc* authorities and with their offices and organizations, which owed their existence to considerations of expediency that no longer applied. Improvisation led to Nemesis. Because of the multiplicity of conflicting forces the Führer's will (even when Hitler had something different in mind) was ultimately only able to influence events in this or that direction in an uncoordinated and abrupt fashion, and it was certainly not in a position to watch over and to curb the new organizations, authorities and ambitions which developed as a result. The institutional and legal results of the intermittent orders and decrees of the Führer became increasingly unfathomable and clashed with later authorizations granted by him. Even as organizational shells devoid of political importance they threatened the uniformity and orderliness of the exercise of power and the organization of government. This is why it would also be impossible and illusory to provide a diagrammatic sketch of the organization of the National Socialist regime in the form of a chart for the period after 1938. Unless, that is, it were possible to discover a means of showing how on a chart of such nominal institutions the real source of power and the actual decision-making changed from case to case.

But the more the organizational jungle of the National Socialist regime spread out the less chance there was of restoring any rationally organized and consistent policy-making and governmental process. The mushrooming of institutions, special powers and specific legal arrangements, which caused an increasingly bitter struggle for protection and favour as well as a steeper decline in rational policy-making and allocation of responsibilities, led to the establishment in each case of different techniques of organization and this, in turn, contributed to a speeding up of the 'movement' and a radicalization of measures. To suggest that the development of National Socialist policy only consisted in steering towards and carrying out prefabricated long-term ideological aims in small doses is an over simplification. Like the mass terror in spring and early summer 1933, the growing anarchy and resort to violence backed up by secret orders and special authorizations during the War was not based on a regime where power was totally controlled either. On the contrary it took place amidst a progressive division of power, an increasingly fragmentary process whereby particularist power apparatuses made themselves independent and where any over-all co-ordination and regularity was missing. The disruption of the unified bureaucratic state order, the growing formlessness and arbitrariness of legislation and of decision-making, and of transmitting decisions, played a part in speeding up the process of radicalization which was every bit as important as any ideological fixity of purpose.

Admittedly Hitler's obsessive preoccupation with specific ideological and political principles proved to be a decisive driving force behind National Socialist policy. But the Führer was not in the least able to decide entirely for himself on the whether, when and how of specific measures. His 'spontaneous' decisions were invariably the reflection and expression of the internal constitutional order and the external position of the regime. The practicability of carrying out, as well as the actual significance of, ideological aims which had been hitherto of a very general nature was only decided once certain patterns of power and responsibility had changed.

The fact that the Hitler state embarked on a course of progressive radicalization and, as it were, reverted to the combat movement whose miserable end seems so strangely akin to the wretched origins of the National Socialist movement was not inevitable. An alternative to this ongoing radicalization, which was bound to mean self-destruction, had offered itself in 1937/8 in the form of regressing simply to a more or less conservative-authoritarian system along traditional lines. A longer duration of the relative stability reached in constitutional developments by 1937 would have been tantamount to a further consolidation, bureaucratization and normalization of the regime and this – as Hitler realized instinctively – would have threatened the National Socialist movement (and the position of the charismatic Führer). Such a reversion to the authoritarian state of order, or, rather, the maintenance of the *status quo* of 1937/8, was what the overwhelming majority of the conservative opposition of officers and diplomats vaguely had in mind, and this got underway as a result of the break in 1938. They might have prevented the gruesome perversion of the irrational use of force, restored the state of law and the value of humanitarian principles and thus have saved the German nation from the worst. But it is probable that such a regime could not have been all that able or long lasting. *Morally* the conservative resistance to Hitler deserves all honour. *Politically* it was no less helpless than Hitler's conservative partners in 1933. For it was precisely because it was felt both necessary and long overdue to overcome the despotic and authoritarian structure of German society, and because the democratic attempt to bring about change had not had enough support or success, that gave the Hitler movement its blind and dynamic social driving force. The fact that the resolute and fanatical determination of National Socialism to bring about change found such mass acclaim was also a clear sign that large social forces were clamouring to be released from traditional ties and for greater social mobility and equality. National Socialism really owed its sociopsychological suggestivity and its technically modern methods of wielding power in the first place to this pressure to break down those traditional social structures which had been consolidated in Imperial Germany in the face of industrialization and which had hardly been touched in the Weimar Republic.

And finally here lay one of the most significant, if at first negatively defined, consequences of National Socialist control. The conservative, authoritarian forces, institutions and standards of state which had initially comprised the element of stability in the Third Reich were in the end more and more undermined by the National Socialist regime and partly liquidated by brutal force, as after 20 July 1944. Admittedly the National Socialist regime was unable to realize the idealized social set-up which lured it on but the dynamism of the movement left hardly one of the old structures untouched. That was as true of the armed forces and bureaucracy as it was of the Churches and even of the old type of authoritarian teacher and entrepreneur. The basis of the traditional resistance to modernity and liberality was damaged by Hitler every bit as much as were the structures of the state of law and of democracy. For this reason the second attempt, made after Hitler, to bring about democratic self-determination in the political and social life of Germany had less opposition to overcome. But the social revolution brought about by National Socialism was incomplete. The old authoritarian forces of resistance had been grievously weakened but no new political and social structure had been developed for the social forces released to hold on to after the demise of the Hitler state. This lack of continuity and orientation left only recourse to the Weimar era or to foreign precepts and it is one of the heavy burdens bequeathed by National Socialism. Daily this can still be seen in our own times in the numerous manifestations of a damaged national and political self-confidence.

Notes and references

1. Yearly figures for Jewish emigration from German areas follows: 1933, 63,400; 1934, 45,000; 1935, 35,500; 1936, 34,000; 1937, 25,000; 1938, 49,000; and 1939, 68,000 (according to the documents of the Reich Association of Jews in Germany, *Deutsches Zentralarchiv Potsdam*, Rep. 97).
2. Published in *Deutsche Justiz*, 1934, pp. 1290ff under the heading 'The State Leadership in the Third Reich'.
3. Hitler's secret speech on 10 November 1938 to representatives of the German press (*VJHZ*, 6, 1958, Heft 2, p. 182).

Bibliography

(revised for the English edition)

General accounts

Hannah Arendt, *The Origins of Totalitarianism*. New York 1951.
Heinz Boberach, *Meldungen aus dem Reich*. Neuwied, Berlin 1965.
Karl Dietrich Bracher, *Die deutsche Diktatur. Entstehung, Struktur, Folgen des Nationalsozialismus*. Köln, Berlin 1969. (English trans. *German Dictatorship*: origins, structure and consequences of *National Socialism*. Harmondsworth 1973.)
Karl Dietrich Bracher, Wolfgang Sauer, Gerhard Schulz, *Die national-sozialistische Machtergreifung. Studien zur Errichtung des totalitären Herrschaftssystems in Deutschland 1933/34*. Köln, Opladen 1960.
Martin Broszat, *German National Socialism 1919–1945*, Santa Barbara, Calif. 1966.
Alan Bullock, *Hitler: A study in tyranny*. London 1952.
Ralf Dahrendorf, *Gesellschaft und Demokratie in Deutschland*. München 1965. (English trans. *Society and Democracy in Germany*. London 1968.)
Max Domarus, *Hitler. Reden und Proklamationen 1932–1945* (2 vols). München 1965.
Joachim C. Fest, *Das Gesicht des Dritten Reiches. Profile einer totalitaren Herrschaft*. Munchen 1964. (English trans. *The Face of the Third Reich*. Harmondsworth 1972.)
Joachim C. Fest, *Hitler. Eine Biographie*. Frankfurt, Berlin, München 1973. (English trans. *Hitler*. Harmondsworth 1977.)
Helga Grebing, *Der Nationalsozialismus*. München 1959.
Sebastian Haffner, *Anmerkungen zu Hitler*. München 1978. (English trans. *The Meaning of Hitler*. London 1979.)
Franz Josef Heyen, *Nationalsozialismus im Alltag. Quellen zur Geschichte des Nationalsozialismus vornehmlich im Raum Mainz–Koblenz–Trier*. Boppard 1967.
Walter Hofer, *Die Diktatur Hitlers bis zum Beginn des Zweiten Weltkrieges*. Konstanz 1959.
Hajo Holborn (ed.), *Republik to Reich: The making of the Nazi revolution* (Ten essays). New York 1972.

Friedrich Meinecke, *Die Deutsche Katastrophe*. Wiesbaden 1946. (English trans. *The German Catastrophe*. London 1950.)

Franz Neumann, *Behemoth, The Structure and Practise of National Socialism 1933–1944*. Toronto, New York, London 1944.

Ernst Nolte, *Der Faschismus in seiner Epoche*. München 1963. (English trans. *Three Faces of Fascism*. London 1965.)

Wolfgang Schieder (ed.), *Faschismus als soziale Bewegung. Deutschland und Italien im Vergleich*. Hamburg 1976.

Gerhard Schulz, *Deutschland seit dem Ersten Weltkrieg 1918–1945*. Göttingen 1976.

Peter D. Stachra (ed.), *The Shaping of the Nazi State*. London, New York 1978.

John Toland, *Adolf Hitler*. New York 1976.

Hugh Trevor-Roper (ed.), *Hitler's Table Talk*. London 1953.

Robert G. Waite, *The Psychopathic God Adolf Hitler*. New York 1977.

The NSDAP before 1933

William Sheridan Allen, *The Nazi Seizure of Power: The experience of a single German town 1930–1935*. Chicago 1965.

Heinrich Bennecke, *Hitler und die SA*. München, Wien 1962.

Volker R. Berghahn, *Der Stahlhelm*. Düsseldorf 1966.

Wilfried Böhnke, *Die NSDAP im Ruhrgebiet 1920–1933*. Bonn, Bad Godesberg 1974.

Karl Dietrich Bracher, *Die Auflösung der Weimarer Republik*. Villingen 1964.

Peter Bucher, *Der Reichswehrprozeß. Der Hochverrat der Ulmer Reichswehroffiziere 1920/30*. Boppard 1967.

Francis L. Carsten, *Reichswehr und Politik 1918–1933*. Köln, Berlin 1964. (English trans. *Reichswehr and Politics, 1918–1933*. London 1966.)

Werner Conze/Hans Raupach, *Die Staats- und Wirtschaftskrise des Deutschen Reiches 1929/33*. Stuttgart 1967.

Eugene Davidson, *The Making of Hitler*. New York 1977.

Ernst Deuerlein (ed.), *Der Hitler-Putsch. Bayerische Dokumente zum 8. und 9. November 1923*. Stuttgart 1962.

Andreas Dorpalen, *Hindenburg in der Geschichte der Weimarer Republik*. Berlin 1966. (English trans. *Hindenburg and the Weimar Republic*. Princeton, N.J. 1966.)

Theodor Geiger, *Die soziale Schichtung des deutschen Volkes*. Stuttgart 1932.

Joseph Goebbels, *Vom Kaiserhof zur Reichskanzlei. Eine historische Darstellung in Tagebuchblättern* (38th edition). München 1934.

Rainer Hambrecht, *Der Aufstieg der NSDAP in Mittel- und Oberfranken (1925–1933)*. Nürnberg 1976.

Rudolf Heberle, *Landbevölkerung und Nationalsozialismus*. Stuttgart 1963.

Helmut Heiber, *Das Tagebuch von Joseph Goebbels 1925/26 mit weiteren Dokumenten*. Stuttgart 1961.

Volker Hentschel, *Weimars letzte Monate. Hitler und der Untergang der Republik*. Düsseldorf 1978.

Wolfgang Horn, *Führerideologie und Parteiorganisation in der NSDAP (1919–1933)*. Düsseldorf 1972.

Peter Hüttenberger, *Die Gauleiter. Studie zum Wandel des Machtgefüges in der NSDAP*. Stuttgart 1969.

Eberhard Jäckel (ed.), *Hitler. Sämtliche Aufzeichnungen 1905– 1924*. Stuttgart 1980.

Gotthard Jasper (ed.), *Von Weimar zu Hitler 1930–1933*. Köln, Berlin 1968.

Michael H. Kater, *Studentenschaft und Rechtsradikalismus in Deutschland 1918–1933. Eine sozialgeschichtliche Studie zur Bildungskrise in der Weimarer Republik*. Hamburg 1975.

Udo Kissenkoetter, *Gregor Straßer und die NSDAP*. Stuttgart 1978.

Albert Krebs, *Tendenzen und Gestalten der NSDAP. Erinnerungen an die Frühzeit der Partei*. Stuttgart 1959.

Reinhard Kühnl, *Die nationalsozialistische Linke 1925 bis 1930*. Meisenheim 1966.

Peter H. Merkl, *Political Violence Under the Swastika: 581 early Nazis*. Princeton, N.J. 1975.

Peter H. Merkl, *The Making of a Stormtrooper*. Princeton, N.J. 1980.

Alfred Milatz, *Wähler und Wahlen in der Weimarer Republik*. Bonn 1965.

Jeremy Noakes, *The Nazi Party in Lower Saxony, 1921–1933*. Oxford 1971.

Joseph L. Nyomarkay, *Charisma and Factionalism in the Nazi Party*. Minneapolis 1967.

Dietrich Orlow, *A History of the Nazi Party 1919–1933*. Pittsburg 1969.

Günter Plum, *Gesellschaftsstruktur und politisches Bewußtsein in einer katholischen Region 1928–1933. Untersuchungen am Beispiel des Regierungsbezirks Aachen*. Stuttgart 1972.

Geoffrey Pridham, *Hitler's Rise to Power: The Nazi movement in Bavaria*. London 1973.

Karl Rohe, *Das Reichsbanner Schwarz-Rot-Gold*. Düsseldorf 1966.

Paul Sauer, *Württemberg in der Zeit des Nationalsozialismus*. Ulm 1975.

Eberhard Schön, *Die Entstehung des Nationalsozialismus in Hessen*. Meisenheim a. Glan 1972.

Gerhard Schulz, *Aufstieg des Nationalsozialismus. Krise und Revolution in Deutschland*. Frankfurt, Berlin 1975.

Dirk Stegemann, 'Zum Verhältnis von Großindustrie und Nationalsozialismus 1930–1933. Ein Beitrag zur Geschichte der sog.

Machtergreifung'. In: *Archiv für Sozialgeschichte*. Hannover 1973.

Gerhard Stoltenberg, *Politische Strömungen im schleswig-holsteinischen Landvolk*. Düsseldorf 1962.

Albrecht Tyrell, *Führer befiehl . . . Selbstzeugnisse aus der Kampfzeit der NSDAP. Dokumentation und Anlyse*. Düsseldorf 1969.

Albrecht Tyrell, *Vom 'Trommler' zum 'Führer'. Der Wandel von Hitlers Selbstverständnis zwischen 1919 und 1924 und die Entwicklung der NSDAP*. München 1975.

Thilo Vogelsang, *Reichswehr, Statt und NSDAP*. Stuttgart 1962.

Ludwig Volk, *Das Bayerische Episkopat und der Nationalsozialismus 1930–1934*. Mainz 1965.

Andreas Werner, *SA und NSDAP (1920–1933)*. Phil.Diss. Erlangen 1964.

Georg Franz Willing, *Die Hitlerbewegung*. Hamburg, Berlin 1962.

Zdenek Zofka, *Die Ausbreitung des Nationalsozialismus auf dem Lande. Eine regionale Fallstudie*. München 1979.

Party, State and the Armed Forces

Hans Günter Adler, *Der verwaltete Mensch. Studien zur Deportation der Juden aus Deutschland*. Tübingen 1974.

Shlomo Aronson, *Reinhard Heydrich und die Frühgeschichte von Gestapo und SD*. Stuttgart 1971.

Waldemar Besson, *Württemberg und die deutsche Staatskrise 1928–1933*. Stuttgart 1959.

Willi A. Boelcke, *Kriegspropaganda 1939–1941. Geheime Ministerkonferenzen im Reichspropagandaministerium*. Stuttgart 1966.

Hans Buchheim, Martin Broszat, Helmut Krausnick, Hans Adolf Jacobsen, *Anatomie des SS-Staates* (2 vols). Freiburg 1965. (English trans. *Anatomy of the S.S. State*. London 1968.)

Harold C. Deutsch, *Das Komplott oder die Entmachtung der Generale. Blomberg- und Fritsch-Krise*. Konstanz 1974.

Peter Diehl-Thiele, *Partei und Staat im Dritten Reich* (2nd edn). München 1971.

Rudolf Diels, *Lucifer ante portas*. Stuttgart 1950.

Otto Dietrich, *12 Jahre mit Hitler*. München 1955.

Ortwin Domröse, *Der NS-Staat in Bayern von der Machtergreifung bis zum Röhm-Putsch*. München 1974.

Ernst Fraenkel, *The Dual State: A contribution to the theory of dictatorship*. New York, London, Toronto 1940.

Norbert Frei, *Nationalsozialistische Eroberung der Provinzpresse. Gleichschaltung, Selbstanpassung und Resistenz in Bayern*. Stuttgart 1980.

Helmut Groscurth, *Tagebücher eines Abwehroffiziers 1938–1940*. Ed. by Helmut Krausnick and Harold C. Deutsch. Stuttgart 1969.

Lothar Gruchmann, 'Die "Reichsregierung" im Führerstaat. Stellung und Funktion des Kabinetts im nationalsozialistischen Herrschaftssystem. In: *Klassenjustizz und Pluralismus*. Festschrift for Erich Fraenkel. Hamburg 1973.

Walter Hagemann, *Publizistik im Dritten Reich*. Hamburg 1948.

Oron J. Hale, *Captive Press in the Third Reich*. Princeton, N.J. 1964.

Helmut Heiber, *Goebbels: A biography*. New York 1972.

Klaus Hildebrand, *Deutsche Außenpolitik 1933–1945. Kalkul oder Dogma*. Stuttgart, Berlin, Koln, Mainz 1971. (English trans. *The Foreign Policy of the Third Reich*. London 1973.)

Andreas Hillgruber, *Hitler, Strategie, Politik und Kriegsführung 1940–1941* Frankfurt 1965.

Heinz Höhne, *Der Orden unter dem Totenkopf. Die Geschichte der SS*. Gütersloh 1967.

Hans Adolf Jacobsen, *Die nationalsozialistische Außenpolitik 1933–1938*. Frankfurt/M., Berlin 1968.

Gregor Janssen, *Das Ministerium Speer. Deutschlands Rüstung im Krieg*. Berlin 1968.

Werner Jochmann, *Nationalsozialismus und Revolution*. Frankfurt/M. 1963.

Werner Johe, *Die gleichgeschaltete Justiz*. Frankfurt/M. 1967.

Ian Kershaw, *Der Hitler-Mythos 1920–1945*. Stuttgart 1980.

Louis P. Lochner, *Joseph Goebbels. Die Goebbels-Tagebücher aus den Jahren 1942–43*. Zürich 1948.

Horst Matzerath, *Nationalsozialismus und kommunale Selbstverwaltung*. Stuttgart, Berlin, Köln, Mainz 1970.

Klaus-Jürgen Möller, *Das Heer und Hitler. Armee und nationalsozialistisches Regime 1933–1940*. Stuttgart 1969.

Hans Mommsen, *Beamtentum im Dritten Reich*. Stuttgart 1966.

Horst Rehberger, *Die Gleichschaltung des Landes Baden 1932/33*. Heidelberg 1966.

Ernst-August Roloff, *Bürgertum und Nationalsozialismus. Braunschweigs Weg ins Dritte Reich* Hannover 1961.

Dieter Ross, *Hitler und Dollfuß, Die deutsche Osterreich-Politik 1933–1934*. Hamburg 1966.

Wolfgang Runge, *Politik und Beamtentum im Parteienstaat*. Stuttgart 1965.

Klaus Scholder, *Die Kirchen und das Dritte Reich*. Frankfurt, Berlin, Wien 1977.

Herbert Schwarzwälder, *Die Machtergreifung der NSDAP in Bremen 1933*. Bremen 1966.

Paul Seabury, *The Wilhelmstrasse: A study of German Diplomacy under the Nazi regime*. Los Angeles 1954.

Albert Speer, *Erinnerungen*. Berlin 1969. (English trans. *Inside the Third Reich*. London 1970.)

Christian Streit, *Keine Kameraden. Die Wehrmacht und die sowjetis-*

chen Kriegsgefangenen 1941–1945. Stuttgart 1978.
Henning Timpke, *Dokumente zur Gleichschaltung des Landes Hamburg*. Frankfurt/M. 1964.
Fritz Tobias, *Der Reichstagbrand. Legende und Wirklichkeit*. Rastatt 1962. (English trans. *The Reichstag Fire*. London 1963.)
Hugh R. Trevor-Roper, *The Last Days of Hitler*. London 1947.
Walter Wagner, *Der Volksgerichtshof im nationalsozialistischen Staat*. Stuttgart 1974.
John W. Wheeler-Bennett. *The Nemesis of Power: The German army in politics 1918–45*. London 1953.

Economy and society

Stefan Bajohr, *Die Hälfte der Fabrik. Geschichte der Frauenarbeit in Deutschland 1914–1945*. Marburg 1979.
Martin Broszat, Elke Fröhlich, Falk Wiesemann (eds), *Bayern in der NS-Zeit. Soziale Lage und politisches Verhalten der Bevölkerung im Spiegel vertraulicher Berichte*. München 1977.
Horst Gies, *R. Walther Darré und die nationalsozialistische Bauernpolitik 1930 bis 1933*. Phil. Diss. Frankfurt/M. 1966.
Richard Grunberger, *A Social History of the Third Reich*. London 1971.
Timothy Mason, *Arbeiterklasse und Volksgemeinschaft. Dokumente und Materialien zur deutschen Arbeiterpolitik 1936–1939*. Opladen 1975.
Alan S. Milward, *The German Economy at War*. London 1965.
Dietmar Petzina, *Autarkiepolitik im Dritten Reich. Der nationalsozialistische Vierjahresplan*. Schriftenreihe der *VJHZ*, vol. 16. Stuttgart 1968.
Hans Pfahlmann, *Fremdarbeiter und Kriegsgefangene in der deutschen Kriegswirtschaft 1939–1945*. Darmstadt 1968.
David Schoenbaum, *Hitler's Social Revolution: Class and status in Nazi Germany 1933–1939*. New York 1966.
Hans Gerd Schumann, *Nationalsozialismus und Gewerkschaftsbewegung*. Hannover, Frankfurt/M. 1958.
Arthur Schweitzer, *Big Business in the Third Reich*. Bloomington 1964.
Friedrich Syrup, *Hundert Jahre staatliche Sozialpolitik*. Stuttgart 1957.
Henry Ashby Turner, *Faschismus und Kapitalismus in Deutschland. Studien zum Verhältnis zwischen Nationalsozialismus und Wirtschaft*. Göttingen 1972.
Heinrich Uhlig, *Die Warenhäuser im Dritten Reich*. Köln, Opladen 1956.
Heinrich August Winkler, *Mittelstand, Demokratie und Nationalsozialismus. Die politische Entwicklung von Handwerk und Kleinhandel in der Weimarer Republik*. Köln 1972.

Other specialist studies

Reinhard Bollmus, *Das Amt Rosenberg und seine Gegner. Studien zum Machtkampf im nationalsozialistischen Herrschaftssystem.* Stuttgart 1970.

Hildegard Brenner, *Die Kunstpolitik im Dritten Reich.* Hamburg 1963.

Martin Broszat, *Nationalsozialistische Polenpolitik 1939–1945.* Frankfurt/M. 1965.

Hans Buchheim, *Glaubenskrise im Dritten Reich.* Stuttgart 1953.

John S. Conway, *The Nazi Persecution of the Churches 1933–45.* London 1968.

Alexander Dallin, *German Rule in Russia 1941–1945: A study of occupation policies.* London, New York 1957.

Enno Georg, *Die wirtschaftlichen Unternehmungen der SS.* Stuttgart 1963.

Ulrich von Hassel, *Vom anderen Deutschland* (new edition). Frankfurt/M. 1964.

Helmut Heiber, *Walter Frank und sein Reichsinstitut für Geschicht des Neuen Deutschland.* Stuttgart 1966.

Roul Hilberg, *The Destruction of the European Jews.* Chicago 1961.

Peter Hoffmann, *Widerstand, Staatsstreich, Attentat. Der Kampf der Opposition gegen Hitler.* München 1979.

Michael H. Kater, *Das 'Ahnenerbe' der SS. Ein Beitrag zur Kulturpolitik des Dritten Reiches.* Stuttgart 1974.

Lothar Kettenacker, *Nationalsozialistische Volkstumspolitik im Elsaß.* Stuttgart 1973.

Arno Klönne, *Hitlerjugend. Die Jugend und ihre Organisation im Dritten Reich.* Hannover 1955.

Robert L. Koehl, *RKFDV, German Resettlement and Population Policy 1939–1945.* Cambridge, Mass. 1957.

Kommandant in Auschwitz. Autobiographische Aufzeichnungen von Rudolf Höß. Stuttgart 1958.

Helmut Krausnick, Hans-Heinrich Wilhelm, *Die Truppe des Weltanschauungskrieges. Die Einsatzgruppen der Sicherheitspolizei und des SD.* Stuttgart 1980.

Konrad Kwiet, *Reichskommissariat Niederlande.* Stuttgart 1968.

Jochen von Lang, *Der Sekretär. Martin Bormann: Der Mann, der Hitler beherrschte.* Stuttgart 1977.

Gunter Lewy, *Die katholische Kirche und das Dritte Reich.* München 1965. (English trans. *The Catholic Church and Nazi Germany.* London, 1968.)

Hans-Dietrich Loock, *Quisling, Rosenberg und Terboven. Zur Vorgeschichte und Geschichte der nationalsozialistischen Revolution in Norwegen.* Stuttgart 1970.

Otto Meißner, *Staatssekretär unter Ebert–Hindenburg–Hitler.* Hamburg 1950.

Alexander Mitscherlich, Fred Mielke, *Medizin ohne Menschlichkeit. Dokumente des Nürnberger Ärzteprozesses.* Frankfurt/M. 1960.

Christian Petry, *Studenten aufs Schafott. Die Weiße Rose und ihr Scheitern.* München 1968.

Werner Präg, Wolfgang Jacobmeyer (eds), *Das Diensttagebuch des deutschen Generalgouverneurs in Polen 1939–1945.*

Rudolf Rahn, *Ruheloses Leben.* Düsseldorf 1949.

Eva G. Reichmann, *Die Flucht in den Haß.* Frankfurt/M. 1956.

Konrad Repgen, *Hitlers Machtergreifung und der deutsche Katholizismus.* Saarbrücken 1967.

Gerhard Ritter, *Carl Goerdeler und die deutsche Widerstandsbewegung.* Stuttgart 1954. (English trans. *The German Resistance.* London 1958.)

Hans Rothfels, *Die deutsche Opposition gegen Hitler.* Frankfurt/M. 1958. (English trans. *German Opposition to Hitler.* London 1970.)

Wolfgang Scheffler, *Judenverfolgung im Dritten Reich.* Berlin 1964.

Hans-Guenther Seraphim, *Das politische Tagebuch Alfred Rosenbergs 1934/35 und 1939/40.* Göttingen, Frankfurt/M., Berlin 1956.

Friedrich Thyssen, *I Paid Hitler.* New York, Toronto 1941.

Horst Ueberhost, *Elite für die Diktatur. Die Nationalpolitischen Erziehungsanstalten 1933–1945.* Düsseldorf 1969.

Fritz Wiedemann, *Der Mann, der Feldherr werden sollte.* Velbert, Kettwig 1964.

Friedrich Zipfel, *Kirchenkampf in Deutschland 1933–1945.* Berlin 1965.

Index

ADGB, *see* General Association of German Trade Unions
Adolf Hitler Bodyguard Regiment, 38, 271, 272
AEG, 40
Agrarian Policy Apparatus, 39, 48, 52, 53, 120, 157, 172–3, 174, 178–9
Agriculture, Chambers of, 40
Agriculture, Council of, 173, 174
Agriculture, Ministry of: Hugenberg at, 58, 59, 88, 174–5; State Secretary, 59; and cartels, 167; and Four Year Plan, 301
Air Defence, 121
Air Transport, Göring as Reich Commissioner for, 58
Allocation of Labour, General Plenipotentiary for (GBA), 305
Amtsleiter (official for special duties), 43, 46; limited powers, 47; reorganization, 48
'Appeal to the German People': (Feb. 1933) 68, 93; (Oct. 1933) 91
Area Handicraft Unions, 162
Armaments Commission, 121
Armaments and Munitions, Ministry of: Todt at, 266, 302, 304; Speer at, 304, 305, 312
Armed Forces: share of public expenditure, 183; and Party reliability, 250–1; Hitler as Supreme Commander, 282, 295, 315; Command reorganization, 294–6; Adjutancy, 315
Association of German Department and Commercial Stores, 158
Asylums and Hospitals, Working Group for, 321
August Reissmann AG, 188
Austrian Legion, 219
Aviation Ministry, 301, 302; as Supreme Reich Authority, 278; 'Research Bureau', 279

Barmen Confessional Synod, 227
'Battle Front Black-White-Red', 67; in March 1933 election, 75, 76
Bavarian People's Party, 80, 98; and Enabling Law, 82; dissolution, 89, 90
'Benzine Agreement' (1933), 168
Berlin Transport Company, 40, 42
Borsig, 40
Braunkohle-Benzin AG ('Brahag'), 168, 301
Business Group Leaders, 300, 301, 304

Catholic Action, 222
Catholic Church: Hitler's courting of, 82–3, 88–9, 90; Concordat with Reich, 88–9, 90, 222; growing suppression and persecution of, 222
'Central Planning', Speer system of, 303, 304, 305
Central State Prosecutor's Office, 205
Centre Party, 6, 8, 62; movement to right, 7; omitted from Hitler's first government, 60, 61; ban on press of, 66; violence against, 67; in 1933 election, 75, 76, 80; and Enabling Law, 81, 82–4, 87, 88, 105; fall of, 88–90
Chemicals, General Plenipotentiary for, 301, 302
Christian Farmers' Societies, Union of, 172
Christian Trade Unions, General Association of, 184
Church, Ministry for, 50, 116, 227, 229
Cinema, Law on (1934), 130
Civil Servants, Disciplinary Code for (1937), 253
Co-ordination of the Länder of the Reich, Second Law for (1933), 106, 107, 108, 130
Combat League for the Commercial Middle Classes, 42, 52, 156–9, 161–2

Combat League for German Culture, 39, 51

Communist Assets, Law for Seizure of (1933), 85

Communists, *see* German Communist Party

Concentration of the War Economy, decree on (1943), 313

Confessional Movement of German Christians, 222–7, 228

Confiscation of Property detrimental to the Interests of People and State, Law. on (1933), 91

Congress of German Industry and Trade, 158, 170

Consolidation of German Nationhood, Reich Commissioner for (RKF), 318–20, 327

Consolidation of the German Reich, Law for (1934), 294

Construction Industry, Todt as Chief Special Deputy for Regulation of, 266

Corporatist Organization, Institute for, 166, 169–70

Corporatist Reorganization of Agriculture, Law on the Reich's Responsibility for the Regulation of (1933), 175

Country People's Party, 27, 40

Criminal Police, 275–6; and 'preventive arrest', 338

Culture, Reich Chamber of, 115, 130

DAF, *see* German Labour Front

Dank des Vaterlandes, *Der*, 49

'Day of the Awakening Nation' (5 March 1933), 73

Defence, Ministry of: military control of, in last years of Republic, 9–11; directive on political activity, 250; loses command of armed forces, 295

Defence Leagues, 19, 20

Defence of the Reich, Commissioners for, 121–2

Defence of the Reich, Ministerial Council for, 308–12

Defence of the Republic, Law for (1922), 5

Deutsch Nationale Handlungsgehilfen-Verband (DHV), 140

Deutsche Allgemeine Zeitung, 66

Disciplinary Code for Civil Servants (1937), 253

DNVP, *see* German National People's Party

DVP, *see* German People's Party

Economic Consolidation, Reich Office for, 301

Economic Council, 52–3

Economic Defence Staff, 168

Economic Research Association, 171

Economics, Ministry of, 135–6, 152, 157, 159, 162, 166, 167–8, 171; Hugenberg at, 58, 59, 88, 135; State Secretary, 59, 166; Schmitt at, 136, 144, 147, 166; cartel laws, 167; Schacht at, 167, 168; impartial state secretaries in, 244; and Four Year Plan, 301

Economy, General Council of the, 164, 166, 190

Education, Ministry of: Party members in, 244; weak political position, 246–7

Eher-Verlag, 42, 46, 48, 55–6

Employment and Unemployment Relief, Reich Institute for, 154

Enabling Law (1933), 77, 91, 105, 263, 280, 281; passing of, 80–4, 87, 88; extensions of, 84, 94, 287–8

Ensuring the Unity of Party and State, Law for (1933), 207–9, 237

Entailed Farm Law (1933), 175, 176–8

Erbhof right, 177

Establishment of Parties, Law against (1933), 90

Ethnic German Self-Defence, 126

Euthanasia Order, 320–3, 325

Evangelical Church: conflict with, 222–34, 250; new constitution, 224–5; elections, 225–6; split in, 226–9; attempt to bind more closely to regime, 228–9; Gestapo intervention, 228, 229; coercive measures against, 229–34

Factory Councils and Economic Associations, Law on (1933), 86, 139

Farmers' Party, 75

'Final Solution', 320, 323, 327

Finance, Ministry of, 58, 288; State Secretary, 59; Party dependence on, 208; Party members in, 244; and new civil service code, 251; authority of Minister, 263, 311–12

Foreign Office, 216–21; von Neurath at, 58; State Secretary, 59; Party pressure on, 216–18, 221, 299; impartial state secretaries in, 244; bypassing of, 278–9, 299; under Ribbentrop, 296–9; Germany Division, 298, 323; Information Service, 299

Foreign Organization, 48

Foreign Policy office (APA), 216, 297

Forestry and Hunting, Göring as Reich

Minister of, 116, 278
Four Year Plan, 121, 167, 168, 171, 178, 266, 278, 279; Organization for, 300–3, 304, 324; new construction of (1939), 304
Frankfurter Zeitung, 65, 66, 69, 70
Free Trade Unions, 41, 66, 85, 155; action against, 139–40, 165, 166, 183–4
'Free Word' congress (1933), 66
Freikorps, 2, 19, 20, 193, 315
'Führer's Adjutancy', 315
'Führer's Chancellery', 42, 314
Führer's Deputy: office of, 127, 150; later designated Party Chancellery, 127, 249, 317; Hess as, 202; status of, 207, 213; right to participate in legislation, 248–9, 284; and civil service appointments, 248, 249–50, 252–3, 261; Division III of, 248–9, 260; Bormann as, 309, 316

Gaue (main regional administrative units), 44, 47, 124; press of, 46; as defence zones, 122
Gauführer, *see* Gauleiter
Gauleiter, 47; types before 1933, 33; 'old fighters' as, 34–5; rivalry with Land Inspectors, 45; and finance, 45–6; as Oberpräsidenten in Prussia, 104–6, 118; as Reich Governors, 109–10, 111, 118; differing interests in Reich reform, 118; as Defence Commissioners, 122; opposition to S.A., 210
General Association of Christian Trade Unions, 184
General Association of German Crafts-men, Shopkeepers and Traders, 162
General Association of German Employees, 141
General Association of German Trade Unions (ADGB), 8, 81, 85; assault on, 138, 139–40, 183–4
General Association of German Workers, 141
General Plenipotentiaries (of Four Year Plan), 300, 301, 302, 303, 305, 308–9
German Agricultural Co-operatives, 173
German Blood, Nuremberg Law for Protection of (1935), 92, 292
German Civil Service, Law on (1937), 118, 230, 252, 253, 254–5, 285, 287, 335
German Communist Party (KPD), 5–6, 28, 62, 99; share of young, 30; aim of suppression against, 57, 65–6, 70–4,

77; initial error over Hitler, 60; Hitler's warning against ban on, 61; ban on press of, 66, 71; alleged complicity in Reichstag fire, 70–4; losses in 1933 election, 75–6, 77; made illegal, 81, 82, 84–5
German Craftsmen, Shopkeepers and Traders, General Association of, 162
'German Day' (1922), 19
German Democratic Party (later State Party, q.v.), 86
German Department and Commercial Stores, Association of, 158
German Economy, Law against betraying (1933), 183
German Economy, Law for Organic Construction of the (1934), 151, 170
German Employers, General Association of, 141
German Evangelical Church, Law on Legal Competence of (1935), 227
German Evangelical Church League, 224, 225
German Handicraft, Law for Provisional Reconstruction of (1933), 162
German Handicraft, Reich Corporation of, 156, 158, 162–3
German Highway System, General Inspector for, 116
German Industry and Trade, Congress of, 158, 170
German Labour, Action Committee for Protection of, 139, 140, 142
German Labour Front (DAF), 168, 169, 237; formation of, 140, 166; First Congress (1933), 140; organizational scheme, 141; restrictions on, 142, 143; conflict with Labour Trustees, 144; de-unionization and reorganization, 144–6, 149–55, 186–9; strengthened political power, 150–3; conflict with Reich Food Estate, 179, 180
German League of Judges, 337
German Municipal Code (1935), 117–18, 242, 253, 261
German National People's Party (DNVP), 6, 7, 8, 12, 40; effect of agricultural crisis, 27; opposed to participation in Hitler cabinet (1931), 59; in 1933 election, 75; and Enabling Law, 82, 87; defections from, 87, 90; end of, 87–8
German Nationhood, Reich Commissioner for Strengthening of, Himmler as, 127
German Nationalist Front (DNF), 87–8 ·
German Nationalist Shop Assistants'

Association, 183
German People, Decree for Protection of (1933), 62
German People's Freedom Party, 20
German People's Party (DVP), 6, 7; losses in 1933 election, 75; and Enabling Law, 82; dissolution, 86
German Police, Chief of, 274–7
German-Polish Non-Aggression Treaty (1934), 220, 221, 239
German Rail Company, 183, 288
German Road System, Todt as General Inspector of, 264–7, 288–9
German Trade, Reich Corporation of, 158
German Trade Unions, General Association of (ADGB), 8, 81, 85, 138–40, 183–4
German Workers, General Association of, 141
German Youth Associations, Reich Committee of, 268
Germania, 66, 67
Gestapo, 211, 222; interference in church affairs, 228, 229; dispute over legal definition of, 273–4; Himmler's control of, 274–5, 279; and prosecution of political prisoners, 333–4; and criminal prosecution of police officials, 336. *See also* Political Police
Governmental Legislation, proposed Law on (1937), 287–8
'Green Front', 7, 14, 104, 172
Gruppenführer, 36–7, 104; as Special Commissioners, 197
Guard Detachments, 37

Handicraft, Chambers of, 162
Harzburg Front, 3, 20
Head of State of the German Reich, Law concerning the (1934), 282
Hermann Göring Works, 168, 303
Hermann-Tiet-Konzern (Hertie), 160
Higher Certificate of Qualification, 163
Hirsch-Dunkersche Gewerkschaftsring, 140
Hitler, Adolf: denial of revolutionary aims, 10; constant demand for rearming, 10; support from industry and banks, 14; *völkisch* ideology and programme, 17–19; aggressive style, 18–19; foreign policy programme, 22; charismatic leadership, 23–6; first Party chairman, 25, 42–4; as Supreme S.A. Leader, 36; his earlier 'Assault Squad', 37; as Reich Chancellor, 40,

54, 61, 68, 280; his personal Party leadership style, 42–3; Amtsleiter subordination to, 58–60; presses for new elections, 60–1; election propaganda, 68–9, 73; use of broadcasting, 69–70; and Reichstag fire decree, 71–2, 74, 329; regards 1933 election as 'revolution', 77; defence of political terror, 79; decision to set up Ministry of Propaganda, 79–80; courting of Catholic Church, 82–3, 88–9, 90, 222; justification of Enabling Law, 83–4; offensive against German Nationalist Front, 87–8; dissolution of Centre Party, 90; as absolute leader of single-party state, 91–2, 214; move against Länder, 98–104, 106, 123–7; and institution of Reich Governors, 106–12, 117; and blocked Reich reform, 113–19; and economic and industrial problem, 135, 137, 164–5, 166–7, 169; pro-labour propaganda, 139; decree on German Labour Front, 152; use of terrorist intimidation, 197, 215; dissociation from S.A. and Party leadership, 201–4; and ending of revolution, 204, 206–15; aim to make Party subservient, 209–10, 251; violent confrontation with S.A., 210–15; appointed Reich President, 214, 282; efforts to allay foreign opinion, 215–16; foreign policy, 215–21, 278; religious policy, 222–34; creation of special authorities, 263–5, 267, 269–70, 278, 283; changed status in Cabinet, 281–2; as Führer and Supreme Commander of Armed Forces, 282, 295; absolutism and growing dissociation from government, 283–6, 306; re-shuffle at top of armed forces, 295–6; preparation for war, 307–8; inaccessibility and delegation of government, 308, 312, 313, 315–18; secret Führer decrees, 318–23; attack on judicature, 341
Hitler Assault Squad, 37
Hitler Movement, *see* National Socialist German Workers' Party
Hitler Youth, 8, 155, 156, 178, 193; origin of, 39; and undermining of religious values, 228, 230; as auxiliary formation, 237, 269; position of Leader, 268–70, 289
Honour, Courts of, 148, 186
Hunter Programme, 304

I.G. Farben, 52, 168, 301–2
Illustrierte Beobachter, 46
Industrial Courts, Law on (1934), 148
Information and Propaganda, Ministry
    of: setting up of, 79–80; Goebbels as
    Chief of, 80, 246, 313; centralization,
    115; Party members in, 244, 246;
    insistence on observance of official
    channels, 246
Institute for Corporatist Organization,
    166, 169–70
Interior, Ministry of, 49, 50, 58, 116, 117;
    personnel, 59; Frick at, 91, 97, 99,
    112–14, 123–4; Reich Governors
    sub-ordinate to, 112–14; and reforms,
    117–18, 119–20, 131; conflicts with
    Reich Commissioners and Governors,
    123–4, 125–8; Party members in,
    244; and new civil service code, 251,
    257; and control of police, 274–5,
    290; reversal of relationship with
    police, 275; memorandum on power
    of Führer state, 282; abortive
    proposals for law on government
    legislation, 286–9
International Labour Conference (1933),
    219
Investigation and Arbitration Committee
    (Uschla), 43, 47, 48
'Iron Front', 8

Judges, German League of, 337
Justice, Reich Ministry of, 58, 236;
    merger with Prussian Ministry,
    114–15, 259; Party members in, 244;
    and political crimes, 331, 332–3; and
    Political Police, 334; and criminal
    prosecution of police officials, 336

Kampfzeit (time of struggle), 29, 34, 35,
    193, 203, 314
Knorr-Bremse A.G., 40
KPD, *see* German Communist Party
Kreis (administrative unit), 44, 47
Kreisleiter, 44, 45, 120, 150

Labour, General Plenipotentiary for
    Allocation of (GBA), 305
Labour, Ministry of, 58, 143, 145, 147,
    162; State Secretary, 59; impartial
    state secretaries in, 244; Party
    members in, 244; and Four Year Plan,
    301
Labour Exchequer Bonds, 135
Labour Requirements in Agriculture,
    Law for meeting (1935), 154

Labour Service, 140, 155, 244; position of
    Leader of, 267–8
Labour Trustees, 142–4, 147, 184, 191
Land Inspectors, 45, 109
Land Offices, 319
Land Requirements for Public
    Authorities, Law on Regulation of
    (1935), 283
League of National Socialist German
    Lawyers (later National Socialist Law
    Officers' League), 39, 187, 237, 335,
    337
League of Nations, 219; Germany's
    departure from, 91, 220, 226; Russian
    entry to, 221
Leipzig Agreement (1935), 153
'Lex van der Lubbe' (1933), 329, 330, 331
Living Space, Reich Office for
    Disposition of, 116, 283
Luftwaffe, 278

Main Trustee Office East, 304, 319
Malicious Gossip, Law against (1933),
    330, 331, 343
Metalurgischen Forschungs-GmbH
    (Mefo), 168
Military Armaments Inspectorate, 121
Myth of the Twentieth Century, The
    (Rosenberg), 27, 50

National Industrial Workers and Trades
    Association, 184
'National Labour, Day of', 139
National Labour, Law for Ordering of
    (1934), 147, 148–9, 150, 151, 152–3
National League for Germandom
    Abroad, 268
National Service Law (1935), 250
National Socialist Automobile Corps, 37
National Socialist Factory Cells
    Organization (NSBO), 40–2, 48, 52,
    186; control of trade union buildings,
    138, 140; and factory council
    elections, 139; and German Labour
    Front, 141–51; clashes with Trustees,
    142–4, 185; alleged Marxist
    tendencies, 143, 185; increasing
    de-unionization, 144–5; and legal
    protection of workers, 147–8, 185;
    loss of political significance, 149, 187
National Socialist German Physicians'
    League, 39, 50, 237, 292
National Socialist German Workers'
    Association, 47
National Socialist German Workers'
    Party (NSDAP): first political
    successes, 1–4; fluctuating

membership, 1; disruptive agitation, 4; hardship from 1924–8, 5; coalition with national conservative right, 8–9; in last years of Weimar Republic, 9–15, 20; ideology, 17–19, 21–2, 26–7, 29, 70; as *völkisch* movement, 17–19; anti-Semitism, 17, 18, 26, 27, 78, 157, 161, 163, 323, 337; combative style, 19, 20, 34; use of political terror, 19, 25, 78–9; propaganda and demonstrations, 19, 21, 23, 26–9, 79–80; support of other right-wing groups, 20; social revolutionary tendencies, 20–1; leftish 1920 Programme, 20–1, 27; romantic phraseology, 21–2, 23; charismatic leadership, 23–5, 29; development into mass movement, 25–9; electoral tactics, 25–6; spread of agitation to countryside, 27, 39–40; membership, 29–30; sociological structure, 30–2, 200–1; personnel and organization, 32–5, 44–54; leadership stock of 'old fighters', 34–5; auxiliary organizations and associations, 35–42; foothold among working class, 40–2; leadership structure, 42–6; personnel and office of Reich Directorate, 44–54; finances, 45–6; press, 46; civil service policy, 49, 119, 198, 241–58; achievement of monopoly of political power, 57–92; apparent 'containment' of, in cabinet of 'National Recovery', 59–61, 78; exploitation of Prussian developments, 62–5, 104–6; 1933 election propaganda, 68–70; use of broadcasting, 69–70; measures against Communists and Social Democrats, 70–4, 77, 84–6; and Reichstag fire decree, 71–2, 73, 74, 78, 99, 329; success in 1933 election, 74–7, 195; regional strength, 76; co-ordination of Länder, 77, 84; revolution from below, 77–84, 195–9, 204–10; emasculation of Reichstag, 80–4; liquidation of other parties, 84–92; Concordat with Catholic Church, 88–9, 90, 222; as Germany's only political party, 91; seizure of power in Länder outside Prussia, 96–112; and control of police, 99–100, 101–2, 103; and new Oberpräsidenten in Prussia, 104–5; leaders as State Presidents, 105; institution of Reich Governors, 106–12; interrupted Reich reforms, 112–20, 122; attempted centralized direction of administration, 120–1, 133; growth of special authorities, 121; and annexed territories, 122–9; concept of authoritarian state of order, 128; economic situation, 135–8, 300; work creation policy, 135–7, 305–6; currency problem, 137–8; destruction of trade unions, 138–56, 164; and allocation of labour, 147–9, 155, 305; virtual ending of unemployment, 155; policy towards middle classes, 156–62; measures against department and chain stores, 157, 159–61; and industry, 164–72; agricultural policy, 172–82; Party-state-Führer absolutism, 195; system of Commissioners, 195–7, 204; development of membership, 199–201; ending of revolution, 204–10; blind obedience to authority of Führer, 210; June 1934 purge, 212–13; foreign policy, 215–21, 296–9; Church policy, 222–34; rise of special authorities, 263–5, 267, 269–70, 278, 283, 318, 320; and forced labour, 306; chancelleries and adjutants, 314–18; and Führer decrees, 318–20; and 'Final Solution', 323; attitude to law and justice, 328–42; and political crimes, 330–6; use of terrorist force, 332, 335–6; and war crimes, 339–40

National Socialist Handicraft, Trade and Commerce Organization, 162
National Socialist League of Civil Servants, 241
National Socialist League of German Students, 39, 237
National Socialist League of German Technology, 50, 237
National Socialist League of Teachers, 39, 50, 230, 237
National Socialist Middle Class Organization, 88
National Socialist Motor Transport Corps, 37
National Socialist Public Welfare, 237
National Socialist War Victims, 49, 237
National Socialist Womanhood, 50, 237
National Socialist Work Service, 51
Nationalist Assault Squads, 87–8
Nazi Party, *see* National Socialist German Workers' Party
Neue Vorwarts, 86
NSBO, *see* National Socialist Factory Cells Organization

NSDAP, *see* National Socialist German Workers' Party
Nuremberg Laws (1935), 92, 284

Oath of the Reich Ministers, Law concerning (1933), 282
Obergruppenführer, 197
Oberpräsidenten, 104–6, 109, 118, 120, 121, 243
Order Police, 275–6
Organization Todt (OT), 266–7

Pan German Youth, 39
Party Chancellery, 127; Bormann as head of, 249, 309, 314, 315–18
Pastors' Emergency League, 226–7
Penal Code, changes in, 335, 338, 340
People's Courts of Law, 331, 332–5, 341, 343
People and State, Decree for Protection of (1933), 71–2, 73, 86
Plebiscites, Law on (1933), 91
Poles and Jews, Special Criminal Decree for (1941), 340–1
Political Central Commission, 53
Political (Party) Organization: leadership selection process, 31–4; tension with S.A., 35–6; regional structure, 36; effect of mass movement development, 39; closer supervision of, 45; rearrangement of, 48–52; curbing of, 202
Political Police, 211–12; S.S. control of, 211–12, 270–2; as Supreme Reich Authority, 272–7; Himmler as Chief, 274–5; centralization of, 275; fusion with S.S., 275–7; arrests by, 333, 343; collaboration with Administration of Justice, 334
'Potsdam Day' (March 1933), 80, 139, 330
Presidential Chancellery, 314
Professional Civil Service, Law for Restoration of (1933), 123, 198, 244–5, 251, 337
Protection of German Blood, Nuremberg Law for (1935), 92, 292
Protection of German Labour, Action Committee for, 139, 140, 142
Protection of the German People, Decree for (1933), 62
Protection of People and State, Decree for (1933), 71–2, 73, 86
Protection of Retail Trade, Law for (1933), 159
Protection squads, *see* S.A.
Protestant Church: early good relations

with, 222–4; conflict with, 224–34. *See also* Evangelical Church
Provisional Reconstruction of German Handicraft, Law on (1933), 162
Provisional Organization of the Reich Food Estate and Measures for Market and Price Controls for Agricultural Products, Law on (1933), 175
Prussian Police Administration Law (1931), 73, 94
Prussian Privy Council, Law on (1933), 105

Race and Settlement Office, 38, 50
Reconstruction of the Reich, Law for (1934), 112–14
Red Front Combat League, 9
Reform of the Reich, Law on (1933), 92
Regulation of the Building Sector, Todt as Chief Special Deputy for, 266
Regulation of Land Requirements for Public Authorities, Law on (1935), 283
Regulation of Work Allocation, Law for (1934), 154
Reich Association of German Handicraft, 156
Reich Association of German Industry, 14, 28, 146, 164, 166, 174
Reich Association of German Medium-size and Large Retail Trade Concerns, 158
Reich Broadcasting Corporation, 69
Reich Cabinet, 202, 243; early Party weakness in, 263; end of collective decisions, 280–2; separation of Führer's authority from, 283, 308–12; wartime, 308–12; 'Board of Three', 309
Reich Chancellery, 128, 314–15; State Secretary in, 59; small 'liaison staff' in, 201; Supreme Reich Authorities directly subordinate to, 264, 265; Head as real manager of government, 282, 308; Hitler's remoteness from, 308–12; subordinate to Party Chancellery, 317–18
Reich Church, creation of, 224–6
Reich Church Committee, 228
Reich Commissioners, 58, 59, 98, 267, 268; installed in Länder outside Prussia, 99, 100, 101–3, 122–3, 125, 127, 195; for Consolidation of German Nationhood, 318–20, 327
Reich Corporation of German Handicraft, 156, 158, 162–3
Reich Defence Commissioners, 305

Reich Directorate, 201, 316
Reich Directorate personnel and offices, 44–54; division for Germans abroad, 48–9; civil service policy division, 49; municipal policy division, 49; technical engineering division, 49; national health division, 50; internal policy division, 50; defence policy division, 51; economic division, 51–3
Reich Estate of German Industry, 166
Reich Factory Cell Division, 41, 48
Reich factory groups (RGB), 149
Reich Food Estate, 149, 175–80
Reich Governors: institution of, 106–12; Gauleiter as, 109–10, 111, 118; subordinate to Ministry of Interior, 112–14; Second Law concerning (1935), 117; Conference of (1934), 119; as Defence Commissioners, 121–2; conflicts with Ministry of Interior, 125–8; opposition to S.A., 206, 210
Reich Group Industry, 170
Reich Inspectors, 45
Reich Labour Service, 155
Reich Land League, 28, 40, 172–3, 174, 175
Reich League of German Civil Servants, 237
Reich President: Hindenburg as, 6, 13, 14, 61; right to pass emergency decrees, 7, 58, 61, 62, 81, 83, 330; Reichswehr under supreme command of, 9, 59; and Enabling Law, 83, 280–1; Hitler's take-over as, 119, 214, 282–6
Reich Security Office, 276
Reich Trades Competition, 155
Reichgaue, 124–5
Reichsbank, 135, 168
Reichsbanner, 8, 15, 81; banning of, 85
Reichsmark Credit Account, 137
Reichsorganisationsleiter (National Organization Leader), 45, 48
Reichsrat, 106; abolition of, 92; and legitimacy of representatives of Prussian provisional government, 97
Reichstag: 1928 elections, 1; 1932 elections, 25, 75; dissolution of (1933), 60–61; burning of building, 70–1, 78; 1933 elections, 74–7, 195; emasculated by Enabling Law, 80–4, 106; first plebiscitary, 91–2; and Reich reform, 112
Reichswehr, 61, 193, 220; and lifting of ban on S.A., 4, 10–11; strong position in last years of Republic, 9–11, 59; and 1934 coup against S.A.,

212–13; and Party influence and loyalty, 250–1
Reinhardt Programme, 135, 136, 182
Relief Fund, 37, 315
Research Bureau, 279
Retail Trade, Law for Protection of (1933), 159
Rome Protocols (1934), 220
Rote Fahne, 66

S.A. (Storm troopers), 8, 223, 237, 250; lifting of ban on (1932), 4, 10–11; earlier Reichswehr suspicion of, 10; formation, 19; early link with Hitler movement, 19–20, 34, 35, 193, 195–9; growth of, 25; sociological analysis of leadership, 32–3; tension between Political Organization and, 35–6, 199; autonomous organization, 36–7; special units, 37; rebellions and re-founding, 37–8; in auxiliary police, 65, 67, 74, 78–9, 80; control of concentration camps, 74; seizure of power, 78–9, 104, 105, 107, 110–11, 138, 183, 195–9; Stahlhelm's transfer to, 88, 204; in Länder outside Prussia, 101, 102, 103, 104, 110–11, 117; and Special Commissioners, 111, 196–7; blow against leadership, 119; unemployment in, 136; and middle classes, 158, 159; conflict with Reich Food Estate, 179; Hitler's dissociation from, 200–4, 206–9; and ending of 'revolution from below', 204–8, 214; moves against, 205, 206–7, 210–15, 238–9; June 1934 coup against, 212–13; in Austria, 218, 219, 220; occupation of church buildings, 225; maltreatment of political prisoners, 332
Schwarze Front, 66
SD (Security Service), 38, 212, 222, 270, 276, 290
Security Police, 275–6, 277
Siemens, 40
Simplification Decree (1939), 340
Social Democrats (SPD), 27, 62; control of Prussian government, 4, 62; coup against, 4, 8, 64; loss of power in Weimar Republic, 5, 6–7, 8–9, 58; share of young, 30; suppression, 57, 66, 70, 73, 81, 82, 85–6, 98, 99; initial error over Hitler, 60; ban on press of, 66, 81; alleged complicity in Reichstag fire, 70, 71; in 1933 election, 75, 76; rejection of bill for Enabling Law, 84, 85; final dissolution, 85–6; dismissed from civil service, 245

Socialist League of Culture, 66
SPD, *see* Social Democrats
Special Agents, 206
Special Commissioners, 111, 196–7;
    dismantling of, 204, 206, 247;
    renaming of, 206; continued activity,
    207
Special Courts, 330, 331, 332, 337, 340,
    343
Special Deputies, 206, 213
Special Duty, Commissioners for, 65
S.S. (Protection squads), 35, 156, 203,
    223, 237; origin, 37–8; growth of,
    38–9; intelligence service, 38; race
    and settlement policy, 38–9, 50; in
    auxiliary police, 65, 67, 74, 78–9, 80;
    control of concentration camps, 74,
    205, 270–1, 306, 319, 335–6; seizure
    of power, 78–9, 104, 105, 107,
    110–11, 138, 183, 195–9; in Länder
    outside Prussia, 101, 102, 103, 104,
    110–11; and Polish and Jewish
    massacres, 126; unemployment in,
    136; and middle classes, 158; moves
    against, 205, 207; control of Political
    Police, 211–12, 270–2; and June 1934
    coup against S.A., 212–13; in
    Austrian Legion, 219; clerical
    denunciation of, 234; tension between
    armed forces and, 250; Death's Head
    formations, 250, 270, 271–2; as
    Supreme Reich Authority, 270–7;
    Bodyguard Regiment, 271, 272;
    fusion with police, 275–7; increase of
    armed units, 296; maltreatment of
    political prisoners, 332
Stahlhelm, 8, 19, 20, 81, 200; refusal to
    join Hitler cabinet, 59; in auxiliary
    police, 65, 67; rift in, 87; Hitler's
    concession to, 88; transfer to S.A.,
    88, 204
State Party: in 1933 election, 75, 76; and
    Enabling Law, 83; dissolution, 86
State Secretaries, 59, 243–4, 283, 301
State Security, Ministry of, 272
Storm troopers, *see* S.A.
'Strength through joy', 146, 154
Study Group North-West, 20
Suffering of People and Reich, Law for
    ending the (1937), 94
Supervisory Committee (Committee for
    the Protection of Parliamentary
    Rights), 61–2

Supreme Court, 93, 97, 333; judgments
    on Prussia, 62, 63; reversal of press
    bans, 66, 68; judgment on Reich
    Commissionaries' dependence on
    Reich authority, 96; and Reichstag
    fire, 329–30
Supreme Reich Authorities, 115, 121,
    230, 264–5, 267, 269–70, 278, 283,
    318, 320

Transfer of the Administration of Justice
    to the Reich, Laws for (1934–5), 114,
    130
Transmission of Hereditary Disease, Law
    preventing the (1933), 284, 294
Transport, Ministry of, 65; impartial state
    secretaries in, 244; and Four Year
    Plan, 301
Trust, Councils of, 147
Trusteeship of the Regional Evangelical
    Church, Law on (1935), 227

Unity of Party and State, Law for
    ensuring the (1933), 207–9, 237
Unity of State and Party, Second Law
    for securing the (1935), 237

Violent Habitual Criminal, Law against
    the (1933), 338
Völkischer Beobachter, 26, 46, 51, 55
Voluntary Labour Service, 267
Vorwarts, 66, 85

War Economy, Decree on Concentration
    of (1942), 313
War Economy Organization, 171, 300
Wehrkreise, 121
Welfare Foundation for the Benefit of
    Asylums, 322
Welfare Transport Company for Invalids
    Ltd, 321
Windhorst League, 89
Work Allocation, Law on Regulation of
    (1934), 154
Workers' Affairs, Secretariat for, 41
World Economic Conference (1933), 88,
    95, 219

Young Plan, 3, 4, 27
Youth Hostel Service, 268